INDIAN AFFAIRS ANNUAL 2008

INDIAN AFFAIRS ANNUAL 2008
(In 9 Vols.)

Vol. 9

Chronology of Events
(29-02-2008 to 31-03-2008)

Shailendra Sengar

KALPAZ PUBLICATIONS
KALPAZ PUBLICATIONS
DELHI - 110052

Indian Affairs Annual 2008

Rs. 6300 (Set)

ISBN: 81-7835-693-7 (Set)
ISBN: 81-7835-702-X (Vol. 9)

Published in 2008 in India by
Kalpaz Publications
C-30, Satyawati Nagar,
Delhi-110052
E-mail: kalpaz@hotmail.com
Phone : 9212729499

Laser Type Setting by: Quick Media, Delhi
Printed at : Singhal Print Media, Delhi

INDIAN AFFAIRS ANNUAL 2008

Chronology of Events

(29-02-2008 to 31-03-2008)

6228. (29-2-2008) NEW DELHI : The Finance Minister, Shri P Chidambaram, while presenting the Budget proposals in the Lok Sabha today, informed the House that the final report of the Committee on Financial Inclusion has been received. The Government has proposed to accept the following two recommendations: (a) To advise commercial banks, including RRBs, to add at least 250 rural household accounts every year at each of their rural and semi urban branches; and (b) To allow individuals such as retired bank officers, ex-servicemen etc. to be appointed as business facilitator or business correspondent or credit counselor. Shri Chidambaram said "Government's policy of a careful and calibrated opening of the financial sector has proved successful. We shall continue to take measured steps". He further stated that banks will be encouraged to embrace the concept of Total Financial Inclusion. Government will request all the scheduled commercial banks to follow the examples set by some public sector banks and meet the entire credit requirements of Self-Help Groups (SHG) members, namely income generation activities, social needs like housing, education, marriage etc. and debt swapping, he added.

6229. (29-2-2008) NEW DELHI : Government is investing heavily in the Accelerated Irrigation Benefit Programme (AIBP) and the Rainfed Area Development Programme and in the management and augmentation of water resources. Presenting the Union Budget 2008-09 in Lok Sabha today the Finance Minister, Shri P. Chidambaram said under AIBP, 24 major and medium irrigation projects and 753 minor irrigation schemes will be completed in this financial year. In 2008-09 the estimated outlay for the above scheme is Rs. 20,000 crores with a grant component of Rs. 5,550 crores. Shri Chidambaram said Rainfed Area Development Programme has been finalized with an allocation of Rs. 348 crores. He said that priority will be given to those areas that have not been the beneficiaries of watershed development scheme. The Minister announced allocation of Rs. 500 crores for the centrally sponsored scheme on micro irrigation. He said the scheme will cover 400,000 hectares under drip and sprinkler irrigation.

6230. (29-2-2008) NEW DELHI : General Budget 2008-2009 Finance Minister Shri P. Chidambaram announced Rs. 644 crores for the National Agriculture Insurance Scheme (NAIS). Presenting the Union Budget 2008-09 in Lok Sabha today he said the scheme will continue in its present form for Kharif and Rabi. The Minister announced that 50 crores will be allocated to Weather Based Crop Insurance Scheme that is being implemented as a pilot scheme in selected areas of five States. He said Government will continue to provide fertilizers to farmers at subsidized prices. Government is examining proposals to move to a nutrient based subsidy regime and alternative methods of delivering the subsidy. The Special Purpose Tea Fund set up last year for re-plantation ad rejuvenation will be provided Rs. 40 crore. Similar funds will be provided to support other plantation crops such as cardamom with an outlay of Rs. 10.68 crores, rubber with Rs. 19.41 crores and coffee with Rs. 18 crores.

6231. (29-2-2008) NEW DELHI : The Rural Infrastructure Development Fund (RIDF) is the main instrument to channelize bank funds for financing rural infrastructure, and it is quite popular among State Governments. It has been proposed to raise the corpus of RIDF-XIV in 2008-09 to Rs. 14,000 crore. It has also been proposed to operate a separate window under RIDF-XIV for rural roads with a corpus of Rs. 4,000 crore. All phases of the National Highway Development Programme continue to make progress. The completion ratio in the Golden Quadrilateral is 96.48 per cent and in the North South, East West Corridor project is 23.36 per cent. Special attention is being paid to SARDP-NE, a programme devised for the North Eastern region. 180 kms of roads were completed in 2007-08 and the target for 2008-09 is 300 kms. It has been proposed to enhance the allocation for the NHDP from Rs. 10,867 crore in 2007-08 to Rs. 12,966 crore.

6232. (29-2-2008) NEW DELHI : Government's forward looking policy is driving the growth of Information Technology and Information Technology Enabled Services. It has been proposed to enhance the allocation to the Department of Information Technology from Rs. 1,500 crore in 2007-08 to Rs. 1,680 crore in 2008-09. A scheme for establishing 100,000 broadband internet-enabled Common Service Centres in rural areas and a scheme for establishing State Wide Area Networks (SWAN) with Central assistance are under implementation. A new scheme for State Data Centres has also been approved. It has been proposed to provide Rs. 75 crore for the common service centres, Rs. 450 crore for SWAN and Rs. 275 crore for the State Data Centres.

6233. (29-2-2008) NEW DELHI : In order to give a fillip to the micro, small and medium enterprises, it has been proposed to create a risk capital fund in the Small Industries and Development Bank of India (SIDBI). As on January 31, 2008, the Credit Guarantee Trust with SIDBI had extended guarantees to 89,129 units for an amount of Rs. 2,479 crore. SIDBI will reduce the guarantee fee from

1.5 per cent to 1 per cent and the annual service fee from 0.75 per cent to 0.5 per cent for loans up to Rs. 5 lakh.

6234. (29-2-2008) NEW DELHI : The two principle schemes for Textiles-the Scheme for Integrated Textile Parks (SITP) and the Technology Upgradation Fund (TUF)-will be continued in the Eleventh Plan period. All 30 integrated textile parks have been approved and 20 units in four parks have commenced production. It has been proposed to maintain the provision for SITP at Rs. 450 crore in 2008-09. The provision for TUF is proposed to be increased from Rs. 911 crore in the current year to Rs. 1,090 crrore in 2008-09. The cluster approach to the development of the handloom sector has made rapid progress. 250 clusters are being developed. 443 yarn banks have been established. By March 2008, over 17 lakh families of weavers will be covered under the health insurance scheme. It has been proposed to increase the allocation to Rs. 340 crore in 2008-09. In order to scale up both infrastructure and production, it is proposed to take up six centres for development as mega-clusters. Varanasi and Sibsagar will be taken up for handlooms, Bhiwandi and Erode for powerlooms, and Narsapur and Moradabad for handicrafts. Each mega-cluster will require about Rs. 70 crore. It has been proposed to start the process with an initial provision of Rs. 100 crore in 2008-09.

6235. (29-2-2008) NEW DELHI : The Government has approved the continuation of the Rajiv Gandhi Grameen Vidyutikaran Yojana during the Eleventh Plan period with a capital subsidy of Rs. 28,000 crore. An allocation of Rs. 5,500 crore is proposed for the Yojana (including NER) in 2008-09. An allocation of Rs. 800 crore has been provided for the Accelerated Power Development and Reforms Project. The poor state of transmission and distribution (T&D) so far has been a drag on the sector. Huge investments are required to be made in T&D, but linked to fundamental reforms. Hence, it has been proposed to create a national fund for transmission and distribution reform. The details of the scheme will be worked out and announced very soon.

6236. (29-2-2008) NEW DELHI : The saving rate and investment rate by the end of 2007-08 is estimated to be 35.6 per cent and 36.3 per cent respectively. The trend is reflected on the foreign investment side also. During the period April-December 2007-08, foreign direct investment amounted to US$ 12.7 billion and foreign institutional investment to US$ 18 billion. The Government policy is to encourage all sources of investment, domestic and foreign, private and public. The Government proposes to provide Rs. 16,436 crore as equity support and Rs. 3,003 crore as loans to Central Public Sector Enterprises (CPSEs). As of now 44 CPSEs are listed. It is the policy of the Government to list more CPSEs in order to unlock their true value and improve corporate governance.

6237. (29-2-2008) NEW DELHI : The Flagship Programmes-National Rural Employment Guarantee Scheme (NREGS), Jawaharlal Nehru National Urban

Renewal Mission (JNNURM), Rajiv Gandhi Drinking Water Mission (RGDWM) and Total Sanitation Campaign (TSC) got enhanced allocation in the General Budget 2008-09. Presenting the Budget in Lok Sabha today, the Finance Minister, Shri P. Chidambaram asserted that more money would be provided to meet the legal guarantee of employment under NREGS. Shri Chidambaram said in NREGS would be rolled out to all 596 rural districts in India. Initially an amount of Rs. 16,000 crore will be provided for this purpose. The allocation for JNNURM will be increased from Rs. 5,482 crore in 2007-08 to Rs. 6,866 crore in 2008-09. Similarly, the allocation for RGDWM has been enhanced from Rs. 6,500 crore in 2007-08 to Rs. 7,300 crore in 2008-09. An amount of Rs. 1,200 crore has been provided for the TSC in 2008-09.

6238. (29-2-2008) NEW DELHI : The Government has proposed to increase the allocation for National Rural Health Mission (NRHM) to Rs. 12,050 crore. Presenting the General Budget 2008-09 in Lok Sabha today, Finance Minister Shri P. Chidambaram stated that NRHM is the key instrument of intervention by the Central Government. He said, the goal is to establish a fully functional community owned, decentralized health delivery system. 462,000 Associated Social Health Activists (ASHAs) and link workers have been trained and are in place. 177,924 Village Health and Sanitation Committees are functional. 323 district hospitals have been taken up for upgradation. Shri Chidambaram further stated that the National Aids Control Programme would be provided Rs. 993 crore. On the other hand an amount of Rs. 1,042 crore will be provided for polio eradication programme in 2008-09.

6239. (29-2-2008) NEW DELHI : Good news for Anganwadi workers! Their remuneration will be increased from 1,000 per month to Rs. 1,500 per month. This was announced by the Finance Minister, Shri P. Chidambaram while presenting the General Budget 2008-09 in Lok Sabha today. Likewise, the remuneration of Anganwadi Helpers will be increased from Rs. 500 per month to Rs. 750 per month. Over 18 lakh Anganwadi workers and helpers will benefit from the increase.

6240. (29-2-2008) NEW DELHI : The Government will establish 16 Central Universities in each of the hitherto uncovered States. This was stated by the Finance Minister Shri P. Chidambaram while presenting the General Budget 2008-09 in Lok Sabha today. Shri Chidambaram said the Government also proposed to set up three IITs in Andhra Pradesh, Bihar and Rajasthan; two IISERs at Bhopal and Tiruvananthapuram; and two Schools of Planning and Architecture at Bhopal and Vijaywada. More institutes of higher education, as promised by the Prime Minister, would be established during the Eleventh Plan period, he added. A grant of Rs. 5 crore has been proposed for the Deccan College Post-Graduate and Research Institute, Pune which is one of the oldest institutions of modern learning in India.

6241. (29-2-2008) NEW DELHI : The North Eastern Region (NER) continued to receive special attention and enhanced allocations. In the General Budget 2008-09 presented in Lok Sabha today by the Finance Minister, Shri Chidambaram an amount of Rs. 1,445 crore has been provided to the Ministry of Development of North Eastern Region(DONER). The total Budget allocation for NER, spared over different ministries/departments, will increase from Rs. 14,365 crore in 2007-08 to Rs. 16,447 crore in 2008-09. Shri Chidambaram further stated that the North Eastern Region especially, the border areas face special problems that cannot be tackled in the usual course or through normal schemes. Hence, the Government proposed to identify the urgent needs of these areas and addressed them through a special mechanism. A sum of Rs. 500 crore in a fund dedicated for this purpose has been set aside in the Budget.

6242. (1-3-2008) NEW DELHI : Indian Civil Account Organisation Day was celebrated here today. On this occasion, Controller General of Accounts (CGA), Government of India, Shri V.N. Kaila delivered the keynote address at a function held here to celebrate the day. He also released the training calendar and brochure of the Institute of Government Accounts and Finance (INGAF), which is the training arm of CGA and has over the years emerged as a premier training institute in India and aboard in core sectors of public sector financial management, budgeting and internal auditing. It was on this day in 1976 that the Departmentalization of Union Accounts (Transfer of Personnel) Act, came into force. This momentous legislation led to the creation of the Indian Civil Accounts Service, which mans the Departmentalized Accounting units of the Civil Ministries in Government of India. This path-breaking move ensured decentralisation of Government Accounting, better transparency, more user friendly system and smooth functioning in this core activity of the Government Financial Management. Chief Controller of Accounts (CCAs), Controller of Accounts (CAs) and Pay and Account Officers (PAOs) etc. all are part of this system. CGA has been mandated to administer all the matters related to Accounts and Controllership functions of funds of the Union Government. CGA has been entrusted with the responsibilities of formulating general principles of accounting relating to Union or State Governments, overseeing the maintenance of adequate accounting standards of Central Civil Accounts Offices, preparation of Annual Appropriation Accounts (Civil) and Finance Account of the Union Government and its presentation to the Parliament.

6243. (1-3-2008) NEW DELHI : Hazardous industrial wastes are of three types namely, recyclable, landfillable and incinerable. As per the Hazardous Wastes (Management & Handling) Rules, 1989 amended in 2003, the recyclers of non-ferrous metal wastes, used oil and waste oil are required to obtain registration from the Central Pollution Control Board (CPCB) for the purpose of recycling such wastes. Registration is accorded by CPCB only to the recyclers having environmentally sound recycling facilities. Solid wastes which are of high calorific value and hazardous liquid wastes are disposed of in incinerators equipped with appropriate air pollution control devices. Those hazardous wastes which are unfit for recycling and incineration are disposed of in secured landfill sites. Certain categories of these hazardous wastes require stabilization before they are sent for landfilling.

6244. (1-3-2008) NEW DELHI : All State Governments have been provided with high-tech nurseries and research input for production of high yielding quality seeds. Increasing forest productivity through quality seeds holds a very high priority in the National Forestry Research Plan, though there is no separate scheme being operated at present by the Central Government in this regard. A comprehensive plan for planting stock improvement was launched under the World Bank aided Forestry Research and Education Project through Indian Council of Forestry Research and Education by the Central Government. Under this programme. No specific criteria for making the quality seeds available to user agencies have been adopted so far.

6245. (1-3-2008) NEW DELHI : There are 514 Wildlife Sanctuaries in the country. Some of the important Protected Areas in the country are having dedicated veterinary staff posted (mainly on deputation) by the concerned State Governments. In some States, veterinary staff is deployed in Zoos and also with the Forest Departments at the State level for looking after the necessities of wildlife sector in the State. Similarly, the assistance of the veterinary staff of the State Animal Husbandry Departments / Veterinary Colleges is also utilized as and when required. As per the information available, 4 tigers and 21 elephants have reportedly been killed due to train/road accidents during the last three years. However all these cannot be attributed to the lack of timely and proper medical care, as most of the deaths are instantaneous. Government of India is providing financial and technical assistance to the State/UT Governments under the various Centrally Sponsored Schemes-'Development of National Parks and Sanctuaries', 'Project Tiger' and 'Project Elephant', for activities aimed at developing wildlife veterinary care-infrastructure, training vets etc.

6246. (1-3-2008) NEW DELHI : Illegal felling and smuggling of rare and costly trees like Sandalwood and Teak has been reported from various parts of the country during three years from 2004 to 2006. The worth of these trees is approximately Rs 10205 lakhs. No large scale illegal felling and smuggling of rare and costly trees like sandalwood and teak has been reported from different parts of the country. However incidents of illicit felling and smuggling do take place and details in this regard as furnished by the State/UT Governments and the Directorate of Revenue Intelligence are given in annexure. The protection and management of forests is primarily the responsibility of the State/UT Governments. The steps taken by the Government of India and State/UT Governments are as follows: Legal measures like Indian Forest Act, 1927, Wildlife (Protection) Act,

1972, Forest Conservation Act, 1980 and Environment Protection Act, 1986 and the rules, guidelines thereof various State Acts and Rules thereof. Management measures, like working of forests according to approved Working Plans, involvement of local communities in protection and management of forests. Financial measures, like providing assistance to the States / Union Territories under Centrally Sponsored Schemes. Under the Centrally Sponsored Integrated Forest Protection Scheme, funds are provided to States and Union territories primarily for strengthening of Infrastructure for protection of forests from illicit fellings, fires, encroachments etc.

6247. (1-3-2008) NEW DELHI : A total of 168 power projects have been accorded environmental clearance during the last three years. This includes 128 thermal power projects, 39 hydroelectric projects and 1 nuclear power project. The State-wise break-up of these projects and their capacity is given in Annexure. As on 15th February, 2008, 43 power projects are pending for environmental clearance, which include 37 thermal power projects, 5 hydroelectric projects and 1 nuclear power project. To facilitate early decision on these projects, their status is monitored continuously. Environment Impact Assessment (EIA) Notification, 2006 provides for appraisal of the impact that a project will have on the environment. This is done through EIA reports submitted by the project proponents and assessed by the multi-disciplinary Expert Appraisal Committees constituted by the Ministry of Environment & Forests for the purpose.

6248. (1-3-2008) NEW DELHI : The Union Finance Minister Shri P. Chidambaram was congratulated for presenting a budget with increased outlays for social and agriculture sectors without imposing any additional burden. In a letter addressed to the Minister, Shri Ravi Kant President of Society of Indian Automobiles Manufacturers (SIAM) commended that increased spending on social sector, infrastructure and agricultural sector including a loan waiver programme have been achieved without imposing any additional taxes on the corporate sector and the manufactured product is truly remarkable. Writing on behalf of automotive industry, the SIAM conveyed their appreciation to Shri P. Chidambaram and the officials of the Finance Ministry for unveiling a special package for the industry. The letter said that the union budget has recognized the automobile industry a driver of growth in the manufacturing sector, the economy at large and its ability to further increase employment. Shri Ravi also offered the society's cooperation to address issues relating to availability of finance and ensuring a stable interest rate regime.

6249. (3-3-2008) NEW DELHI : The Union Cabinet today gave its approval to the following proposals on the basis of the recommendations made by Empowered Committee of Secretaries (EFS): i) San Cristobal Project, Venezuela : To authorize OVL for formation of a Joint Venture Company with CVP/Petroleos De Venezuela S.A.(PDVSA), Venezuela for development of San Cristobal field located in Orinoco

Oil belt, directly or through OVL's existing/new wholly owned subsidiary. ii) Najwat Najem Appraisal, Development and Production Sharing Agreement (NNADPSA) Qatar Project : To authorize OVL to invest upto USD 102.21 million in the project directly through its own resources. iii) To authorize ONGC to provide funding and guarantee support to OVL, if required in both the projects above without seeking budgetary support from the Government of India. The project provides OVL the opportunity to obtain significant equity ownership (40%) in one of the largest Oil producing countries in partnership with the host National Oil Company in a Joint Venture. It will be first OVL property in oil rich Venezuela and may open up other business opportunities, especially in the Orinoco Heavy Oil belt where development opportunities are coming up. The projects will provide Hydro-carbon reserve accretion to OVL through implementation of exploration work programme.

6250. (3-3-2008) NEW DELHI : The Pre-matric scholarship scheme is for eligible students of class I to X belonging to the Minority communities. It is to be implemented through State Governments/Union Territory Administrations with funding being shared between the Centre and States in the ratio of 75:25. 100% financial assistance will be provided to Union Territories. Students with not less than 50% marks in the previous final examination, whose parent's/ guardians annual gross income, from all sources, des not exceed Rs. One lakh are eligible for award of scholarship. It is proposed to award 25 lakh scholarships during the 11th Five Year Plan. Thirty percent of the scholarships are earmarked for girl students. This information was given by the Union Minister of Minority Affairs Shri A.R. Antulay in reply to a written question in the Lok Sabha today.

6251. (3-3-2008) NEW DELHI : The size of the annual plan for 2008-09 for the State of Orissa was finalized here today at a meeting between the Deputy Chairman Planning Commission, Shri Montek Singh Ahluwalia and the Chief Minister, Shri Naveen Patnaik. The State will have a plan size of Rs.7500 crores. This would include additional Central Assistance of Rs. 100 crores (of which Rs.30 crores is grant) for projects of special interest to the State. Another Rs.100 crores of special grant was given for improving the stretch of highway between Vijaywada and Ranchi within the State. In his remarks, Mr. Ahluwalia said the State has been improving in plan performance. He said investment climate continues to be positive but efforts should be made to engineer early execution of commitments. Investments in agriculture infrastructure and human development sector needs to be stepped up. Suitable policy measures should be taken to create a conducive environment that fosters growth of entrepreneurship and encourages private sector investments. The State Government should diversify economy with a view to insulate it from natural calamities and to divert under-employed labour force from farm sector to non-farm sector. Attention was drawn to high incidence of poverty, unemployment and low per capita income. It was also pointed out that State's education and health indicators were still less than the national average. Efforts should be further intensified to reduce this gap during Eleventh Plan period. Attention was also drawn to high transmission & distribution losses and low rural electrification. The State Government was advised to give priority to skill development and rural connectivity. Briefing the Commission on development strategy for the Eleventh Plan, the Chief Minister said the State would aim at a growth rate of over 9 per cent during the Plan to reduce poverty by 15 percentage points. For inclusive, broad-based & sustainable growth, agriculture and allied sector would be given priority. He said the State has achieved an annual growth rate of 8.59 per cent during the Tenth Plan period against the target of 6.2 per cent.

6252. (3-3-2008) NEW DELHI : Shri Kamal Nath, Union Minister of Commerce and Industry, has called for a review of negative lists to expand trade in goods and enlarging the scope for further trade cooperation among SAARC countries. India has unilaterally decided to reduce its negative list with reference to the Least developed Countries (LDCs) of SAARC from seven hundred and forty four to around five hundred and the necessary notification to this effect would be revised within a few months. This was stated by Shri Kamal Nath while addressing the Third SAFTA Ministerial Council meeting here today. He said: "in keeping with our commitments, we have already notified the advancement of the trade liberalisation programme in respect to LDCs by one year and with effect from 1st January 2008, the import duty on all items other than those in the negative list has been reduced to zero". The Meeting was attended by Dr. Sheel Kant Sharma, Secretary General of SAARC; Shri G.K. Pillai, Commerce Secretary; and representatives from the SAARC region. Speaking on the occasion, Shri Kamal Nath emphasised that the SAARC region is broadly characterised by more or less similar developmental levels of member countries and the biggest challenge before us is the pursuit of economic development with inclusive growth. He said that SAFTA is the first major step towards economic cooperation and integration within the region. "We all appreciate that the agreement is only the initial step and requires a continuous effort by all of us to improve and smoothen its implementation", he added. While drawing the attention of the participants, Shri Kamal Nath said that the regional study on Trade in Services has been completed, which would give government an opportunity for an effective services agreement amongst SAARC countries. As regards for upgradation of global supply chain, he said that it would be natural for us to adopt technical standards in accordance with global benchmarks. "In India, we are trying to see that this transformation is least painful both for the producers within the country and those connected with our supply chain outside the country'. "Various SAARC mechanisms have focused on developing specific short, medium and long term cooperation projects to deliver direct benefits to the people. Operationalisation of the SAARC Development Fund and full implementation of SAFTA would pave the way for this development.

The South Asian University and the SAARC Food Bank can also bring benefits to South Asia", the Minister said.

6253. (3-3-2008) NEW DELHI : As per CEA report, out of 5,93,732 inhabited villages as per 2001 Census, 4,87,351 villages have been electrified as on 31st December 2007 in the country. As on December 2007, there were 106381 villages yet to be electrified, as per the progress report published by CEA. The continuation of Rajiv Gandhi Grameen Vidyutikaran Yojana (RGGVY) in the XIth Plan period has been approved for attaining the goal of providing access to electricity to all households, electrification of about 1.15 lakh un-electrified villages and electricity connection to 2.34 crore BPL households by 2009. The capital subsidy of Rs. 28000 crores during the Eleventh Plan period, at this stage has been provided.

6254. (3-3-2008) NEW DELHI : During the period April, 2007 to January, 2008, the consumption (availability) of electricity in Maharashtra was 78,277 MU. According to the projections in the 17th Electric Power Survey Report prepared by the Central Electricity Authority (CEA), an electrical energy requirement of Maharashtra has been assessed at 113,878 MU for the next year. The availability of power for Maharashtra, based on the proposed generation target for the year 2008-09 is expected to be 62194 MU from its own generation and 25218 MU from the Central generating stations. According the 2001 Census of India, there are 41,095 inhabited villages in the State of Maharashtra, out of which 36077 (87.8%) have been electrified by the end of December, 2007. For the purpose of power generation, the leading power equipment manufacturer Bharat Heavy Electricals Ltd. (BHEL) has intimated that it envisages to fabricate power house structures, parts of boiler structures and ducts at MAHAGENCO sites where projects are being executed by BHEL.

6255. (3-3-2008) NEW DELHI : During the period April, 2007 to January, 2008, the energy shortage in Maharashtra was 16,289 MU (17.2%) and the peak shortage was 4844 MW (26.4%). According to the anticipated power supply position worked out by the Central Electricity Authority on the basis of demand forecast made in the 17th Electric Power Survey and the capacity addition programmed during the 11th Five Year Plan, the energy requirement in Maharashtra is likely to be met in full but the State is likely to face peaking shortage of 3532 MW (16.1%) at the end of 11th Plan (2011-12). Review meetings are convened by the Central Electricity Authority, Ministry of Power as well as at the level of Minister of Power from time to time to discuss the prevailing power supply position and the measures required to expedite completion of on-going power projects. The energy and peaking shortage in Maharashtra during the current year (April, 2007 to January, 2008) have marginally reduced to 17.2% and 26.4% respectively as compared to 17.4% and 26.7% during the corresponding period of last year (April, 2006 to January, 2007). This information was given by Union Minister for Power, Shri Sushilkumar Shinde in the Rajya Sabha today.

6256. (3-3-2008) NEW DELHI : Some of the prevalent clean coal technologies and steps being taken to adopt these technologies in India are as follows: (i) Supercritical Technology In India supercritical units of 660 MW are under installation at Sipat and Barh Thermal Power Stations (TPS) of NTPC Ltd. Apart from these, a number of supercritical units with unit size of 660/800 MW have been planned to be set up by NTPC Ltd. and State utilities. Ultra Mega Power Projects are also envisaged to be with supercritical parameters. (ii) Circulating Fluidised Bed Combustion (CFBC) Technology Four CFBC units of 125 MW each are operating at Surat lignite TPS and Akrimota TPS in Gujarat. Six CFBC units of 125 MW each are under execution at Surat Lignite, Giral TPS and Barsingsar TPS. CFBC units of 250 MW are being installed at Neyvelli by Neyvelli Lignite Corporation. (iii) Integrated Gasification Combined Cycle (IGCC) So far the world over, IGCC technology has been adopted for low ash coal which is not suitable for Indian high ash coal. In India, efforts are underway to develop this technology through indigenous efforts. Supercritical generating units are being manufactured by a number of countries viz, USA, Japan, Germany, Korea, Russia, China etc. BHEL has also on-going collaboration for manufacture of supercritical boilers and turbine generators with M/s Alstom and M/s Siemens respectively. M/s Larsen & Toubro Limited (L&T) has also formed a joint venture company for manufacture of supercritical boilers and turbine generators with M/s Mitsubishi Heavy Industries (MHI), Japan. CFBC boilers are already being manufactured in India and BHEL has been supplying boilers and turbine generators for 125 MW and 250 MW supercritical units installed by power utilities. This information was given by Union Minister for Power, Shri Sushilkumar Shinde in the Rajya Sabha today.

6257. (3-3-2008) NEW DELHI : According to the information available with the Central Electricity Authority (CEA), the generation capacity of Captive Power Plants (CPP) of capacity more than 1 MW was 21468 MW as on 31.3.2006 and 22335 MW as on 31.3.2007. During the year 2005-06, 5364.74 Million Units of electricity have been exported by these CPPs to the utilities. No sanction is required under the provisions of the Electricity Act, 2003 for setting up captive power plants. Government has taken various legislative, policy and administrative measures to facilitate captive generation and utilization of surplus capacity. Under the Electricity Act, 2003, captive power plants, including group captive, have been freely permitted. The Act provides that any person may construct, maintain or operate a captive generating plant and dedicated transmission lines. Under the provisions of the Act, every person, who has constructed a captive generating plant and maintains and operates such plant, shall have the right to open access for the purposes of carrying electricity from his captive generating plant to the destination of his use subject to the availability of transmission capacity. National Electricity Policy, notified in February, 2005, emphasizes the need for bringing surplus capacity available with a large number of captive and standby generating stations in India to the grid continuously or during certain time periods. Tariff Policy, notified in January, 2006, recognizes that captive generation is an important means to make competitive power available and urges the Electricity Regulatory Commissions to create an enabling environment that encourages captive plants to be connected to the grid. The conference of Chief Ministers, on power sector, held in May, 2007, under the chairmanship of the Prime Minister, has resolved to facilitate captive power plants to provide the spare generating capacity to the grid and strive to do away with restrictive levies, duties and regulations in a time bound manner. This information was given by Union Minister for Power, Shri Sushilkumar Shinde in the Rajya Sabha today.

6258. (3-3-2008) NEW DELHI : The Minister of State for Textiles, Shri E.V.K.S. Elangovan, informed the Lok Sabha today, in a written reply to a question by Dr. Dhirendra Agarwal & Shri Harikewal Prasad that the government is aware of the need for increasing investment in the textile sector so as to modernize the textile industry and to make it internationally competitive. The investment required to modernize the textile industry is estimated at about Rs. 1,50,600 crore during the 11th Plan period, bulk of which has to come from the private sector. Major plan schemes such as Technology Upgradation Fund Scheme (TUFS), Scheme for Integrated Textile Parks (SITP) etc. are accordingly designed in such a way as to encourage private investment in the textile sector. Under TUFS, the total project cost sanctioned as on 31.03.2007 is Rs. 86020 crore. The Minister further informed that the financial targets in terms of plan expenditure during the last three years have been, by and large, achieved. However, no specific targets for employment generation have been fixed. It is expected that enhanced investment in the textile sector would lead to creation of additional employment.

6259. (3-3-2008) NEW DELHI : For promotion of handloom textile exports, the Government of India has announced a Scheme under the name of Marketing & Export Promotion Scheme for implementation in the country during the 11th Plan. The Scheme provides financial assistance to the handloom agencies for development of exportable handloom textile products and domestic as well as international marketing thereof. Apart from the above scheme, the Government of India has also been implementing the following schemes for the overall development of handloom textile industry:-(a) Integrated Handloom Development Scheme (b) Diversified Handloom Development Scheme (c) Handloom Weavers Comprehensive Welfare Scheme (d) Mill Gate Price Scheme This information was given by the Minister of State for Textiles, Shri E.V.K.S. Elangovan, in the Lok Sabha today, in a written reply to a question by Shri Navjot Singh Sidhu.

6260. (3-3-2008) NEW DELHI : The potential of small hydropower projects (up to 25 MW) and wind power together are estimated at 60,000 MW. Out of this small hydro power is estimated at 15,000 MW and that of wind power is 45,000 MW in the country. The Ministry of New and Renewable Energy (MNRE) is responsible for the subject of small hydro up to 25 MW. As per the Central Electricity Authority (CEA), the total hydroelectric power potential in the country is assessed at about 150,000 MW equivalent to 84,000 MW at 60 per cent load factor. The Ministry is encouraging development of both small hydro power (SHP) and wind power in the country through various fiscal and financial incentives. So far, SHP projects of 2061 MW and wind power projects of 7940 MW (as on 31.1.2008) have been set up in the country. The Ministry is providing central financial assistance (CFA) for the setting up of small / mini hydropower projects both in public and private sector. The CFA is also given to community / individual watermill owners for development and upgradation of watermills for mechanical as well as electricity generation (3-5 KW). The CFA is to meet 75 per cent of the project cost limited to Rs. 30,000/- per water mill for mechanical application and Rs. 1.0 lakh per water mill for mechanical and electrical applications.

6261. (3-3-2008) NEW DELHI : The Puga Valley in Ladakh in Jammu and Kashmir and Tatapani in Sarguja District of Chhattisgarh have been identified as potential sites for tapping the geo-thermal energy for power generation and thermal applications by the Ministry of New and Renewable Energy. A study was carried out by NGRI. Such studies are also in progress through NGRI in Surajkund in Jharkhand, Badrinath-Tapovan in Uttarakhand and Satluj-Beas and Parvati Valleys in Himachal Pradesh. The Ministry is encouraging participation of private sector in all forms of renewable energy, including geo-thermal energy. The Ministry has encouraged the private sector participation in geo-thermal energy by allowing access to the data collected on geo-thermal resource in India by the National Geophysical Research Institute (NGRI), Hyderabad through the Ministry's support. The Ministry also facilitates the private sector to undertake their own investigations / assessment studies for geo-thermal energy and submission of Detailed Project Report (DPR) to the concerned State Government for exploitation of this resource. None has approached the Ministry for financial support during the last three years for harnessing the geo-thermal energy.

6262. (3-3-2008) NEW DELHI : In rural regions of the country power is being generated from non-conventional Energy Sources like wind, biomass, solar and small hydro projects. The grid interactive power generation installed capacity from the renewable sources has reached 11273.62 MW till last December. State wise details are given at Annexure-I. It has been estimated that around 84776 MW energy/power can be generated.

6263. (3-3-2008) NEW DELHI : The Minister of Petroleum and Natural Gas Shri Murli Deora has called for enhanced bilateral cooperation between India and Romania. Addressing the inaugural session of Indo-Romanian Joint Working Group on oil and natural gas, here today Shri Deora emphasized the need for identifying new opportunities, tapping and utilizing potential for mutual benefit in oil & gas sector. He suggested that companies of two countries should collaborate in exploration not only in India but also in third countries. Shri Deora offered to share Indian expertise and experience in revamping and modernizing refineries. Shri Deora also informed that a research project is on the anvil which will facilitate combined work by two sides for geological studies of the Himalayan belt. This he said will open a new vista for cooperation in the Indian sub-continent. Referring to the rich history of long standing friendly relations between India and Romania, Shri Deora acknowledged valuable contribution of Romania in the development of oil and gas sector. Romania supplied first oil rig to India in March, 1956 along with many other drilling rigs and work-over rigs in our early days of oil and gas development, some of which are still operational. Besides Romanian side trained many engineers of ONGC and helped our India flag ship E&P company in its oil field technology and equipment. The first public sector refinery at Guwahati was also built with Romanian collaboration which was inaugurated by the first Prime Minister Pt. Jawaharlal Nehru on 1st January, 1962. Bilateral cooperation has also covered petrochemicals, power and metallurgy projects in India. Romania has been involved in major Indian projects such as the thermal power plant at Singareni, the Mangalore pelletizing plant, the Durgapur agglomeration plant and the Hyderabad tractor plant. Speaking on the occasion Dr. Varujan Vosganian, Minister of Economy and Finance, who led Romanian delegation, stressed the need for boosting bilateral cooperation between India and Romania particularly in the energy sector. He added that Romania regards India as one of the most attractive investment destination. Dr. Varujan said that the deep cultural ties can contribute to further growth of economic relations. He offered participation of the Romanian companies in building oil and gas storages, pipelines and other infrastructure in which Romania has expertise and specialization. Referring to the contribution of Romania in the development of Indian oil and gas sector, the visiting Minister said that the high GDP growth rate and vast natural resources of India makes it a priority country for Romania in Asia. Presentations were made by ONGC on exploration production and by GAIL on gas sector from the Indian side and by Romgaz and AEM Timisoara from Romanian side.

6264. (3-3-2008) NEW DELHI : Dr. Satyanarayana Dash, a 1973 Batch IAS Officer of Kerala Cadre has taken over as the Secretary, Ministry of Heavy Industries & Public Enterprises. Earlier he was Secretary, Department of Ex-Servicemen Welfare, Ministry of Defence. Shri Dash replaced Dr. R.C. Panda who retired on superannuation. A post-graduate in Physics and Economics and a Doctorate in Economics, Dr. Dash held many responsible positions before joining the Ministry of Heavy Industries & Public Enterprises.

6265. (3-3-2008) NEW DELHI : Under Craftsmen Training Scheme being implemented through ITIs, a trade of two year duration namely "Information Technology & Electronics System Maintenance" (IT&ESM) has been included where mobile phone repairing and maintenance is part of the courses curriculum.

Similarly a short term course on "Repair and Maintenance of Cellular Phones" has been included under the scheme "Skill Development Initiatives" being implemented through Vocational Training Providers including ITIs. This information was given by the Minister of State for Labour and Employment Shri Oscar Fernandes (Independent Charge) in a written reply in the Lok Sabha today.

6266. (3-3-2008) NEW DELHI : Proposals for financial assistance have been received from two States to set up new Industrial Training Institutes (ITIs) under the proposed National Skill Development Mission. This includes setting up of 40 new ITIs in the State of Kerala at a cost of Rs 214 crore and 105 ITIs in the State of Bihar. However, the setting up of the proposed National Skill Development Mission is still under consideration of the Planning Commission. This information was given by the Minister of State for Labour and Employment Shri Oscar Fernandes (Independent Charge) in a written reply in the Lok Sabha today.

6267. (3-3-2008) NEW DELHI : Congress spokesman Shri Singhvi said we are happy at the significant and notable progress that India has made at the IAEA talks. We are particularly happy that a vast area, a diverse area of differences have been covered and ironed out in this fifth round of talks. We are very optimistic and we are very positive of the outcome of talks in the IAEA specially in view of the great momentum and the great convergence in the last few days in the fifth round of talks. The government remains committed to the desirability of the deal and we are equally optimistic and positive about the deliberations and the conclusions of the joint mechanism which shall necessarily follow after the IAEA talks. We are sure that with the broad agreement on so many issues at the IAEA, importantly with the virtual acceptance of all or most of India's points in respect of the India specific safeguards, we are sure and confident that with the virtual acceptance of most, if not all, of India's points in respect of the India-specific safeguards at Vienna, with respect to India's version of the India-specific safeguards, we are confident of a reasonable and constructive approach by all sections of the joint mechanism. We have absolutely no reason to be pessimistic or negative either about the IAEA talks or about the joint mechanism or about the deal. To a question that you say you are sure that IAEA has accepted all your concerns and the deal will come through, Shri Singhvi said I am not saying they have accepted our concerns. What I am saying is that in the last few days we have moved to a very significant area of convergence. We have not given any details because those details are matters for the appropriate interlocutors to announce. But it is a matter of happiness and satisfaction that a significant area of the India-specific safeguards and in particular several areas of differences have been ironed out. You will know about the details when it comes back to India, when it comes back to the joint mechanism and we are only expressing satisfaction a) at that stage and b) expressing our hope and confidence that since reasonable people are involved at all levels we will get a positive, sympathetic understanding of the whole thing in the joint mechanism. To a question that some sections of the media have reported that they will withdraw support if the government goes ahead with the deal, Shri Singhvi said it is absolutely speculative and hypothetical to worry about these events in the womb of the future which to us are not even probabilities or possibilities today. We have no reason to comment on them. So I reject all such doomsday scenarios. To a question that a TRS leader has made allegations against Smt. Sonia Gandhi on the Telengana issue, Shri Singhvi said I have not seen or heard this statement. If what you are saying, in terms of words used, is correct, then we reject this allegation and condemn it. It is not factually or politically true. Let me remind you that it was the TDP and the BJP which campaigned from before 1998 on the slogan of "one vote two states". That slogan, the same TDP and the BJP are trying to fish in troubled waters, was conveniently forgotten by them. It is the Congress President, the Congress Party and the UPA which put it in its CMP. We didn't campaign and forget about it, we put it in our manifestos. It requires consensus and we are totally involved in generating that consensus. And naturally it is in the light of that need to generate that consensus that Smt. Gandhi has been authorised by the PCC to take a decision. To a question on the farmers issue Shri Singhvi said it is wrong to judge great achievements and great leap forward by reference to what is not done. This is being non-generous in your acknowledgement of the great thing done. The fact that we have done this in one particular measure and policy does not mean that we are not concerned about other segments of the population. The size of the problem is always large, the resources available are always limited. The irrigation allocation given along with loan waiver has been increased from eleven thousand to twenty thousand crores, almost hundred per cent. There is always scope for improvement and we are open to concrete suggestions but it takes time. But let us not belittle or look down upon a historic, unprecedented, unique and unparalleled initiative.

6268. (3-3-2008) NEW DELHI : Estimates of employment and unemployment are obtained through quinquennial labour force surveys conducted by National Sample Survey Organisation. Last such survey was conducted during 2004-05. As per last two quinquennial rounds of National Sample Survey Organisation (NSSO) on employment and unemployment, employment opportunities on usual status basis have increased from 397 million in 1999-2000 to 459.1 million in 2004-05. No study has been conducted by the Ministry of Labour & Employment to assess the impact of appreciation of rupee against dollar. This information was given by the Minister of State for Labour and Employment Shri Oscar Fernandes (Independent Charge) in a written reply in the Lok Sabha today.

6269. (3-3-2008) NEW DELHI : Central Water Commission (CWC) under Ministry of Water Resources is monitoring storage position of 81 important reservoirs spread all over the country, of which as many as 36 reservoirs have significant hydro-power benefits with installed capacity of more than 60 MW each.

The combined live storage in these 81 reservoirs at the beginning of monsoon *i.e.* 1st June, 2007 was 25 per cent of their designed capacity and stood at 41 per cent of the designed capacity as on 28th February 2008. The present storage is 89 per cent of the last year's storage and 117 per cent of last 10 years average storage during the same period. Out of these 81 reservoirs there are presently 14 reservoirs where this year's storage is 80 per cent or less than the average of previous 10 years and in the remaining 67 reservoirs the storage is more than 80 per cent of the average of previous 10 years. In order to derive the best possible benefits from the available water, Central Water Commission is keeping in touch with the Department of Agriculture and Cooperation and providing information of the weekly storage position to the Crop Weather Watch Group for evolving suitable crop strategies and also apprising the situation to various Departments and Ministries involved in Water Resources Planning.

6270. (3-3-2008) NEW DELHI : The Central Government has declared 14 water resources projects as National Projects subject to working out the mode of financing in consultation with the Ministry of Finance and Planning Commission. For these projects it is proposed to provide 90% project cost of irrigation and drinking water component of the project as Central Grant after techno-economic appraisal of the Detailed Project Report and Investment clearance by the Planning Commission. The details of the 14 National Projects are given below. The irrigation benefits from these projects is estimated to be about 21 lakh ha apart from additional indirect irrigation benefits and availability of drinking water.

6271. (3-3-2008) NEW DELHI : Ministry of Water Resources has sanctioned implementation of 5,000 programmes in 2 to 3 crop seasons through 63 identified institutes at the cost of Rs.24.4685 crore with the objective of demonstrating the technologies available to the farmers for increasing productivity and profitability of agriculture through generating synergy among water, crops and their varieties, agronomic practices, soil nutrients and implements in 26 States/UTs. The Eleventh Plan document has identified the Acceleration Irrigation Benefits Programme; Repair, Renovation and Restoration of Water Bodies; Command Area Development and Water Management and Flood management as important core programme for which appropriate outlays have been made. This information was given by the Minister of State for Water Resources, Shri Jai Prakash Narayan Yadav in response to a question by +Shri K.J.S.P. Reddy and Shri Navin Jindal in the Lok Sabha today.

6272. (3-3-2008) NEW DELHI : The anti-erosion measures are taken up by the respective State Governments through their own resources and according to their own priorities. Realizing the severity of sea erosion problems, a National Coastal Protection Project (NCPP) has been envisaged for seeking external funding. Based on details received from various States including Tamil Nadu, an approach paper was forwarded to Department of Economic Affairs for posing the same to an external funding agency, who in turn forwarded the same to Asian Development Bank (ADB) for consideration. Aide Memoire of the Fact Funding Mission of ADB mentions about a multi phase investment programme for a national project on sustainable coastal protection and management covering all maritime States. In the first phase, the ADB has agreed to provide Technical Assistance (TA) to the States of Goa, Karnataka and Maharashtra in preparing technically, economically, environmentally and socially viable investment proposal and introduce procedures for sustainable coastal protection and shoreline management under the Sustainable Coastal Protection and Management Project. This information was given by the Minister of State for Water Resources, Shri Jai Prakash Narayan Yadav in response to a question by Shri N.S.V. Chitthan in the Lok Sabha today.

6273. (3-3-2008) NEW DELHI : The Government today launched 'Dhan Laxmi'- a Conditional Cash Transfer Scheme for girl child wherein a significant amount will be provided to the family of girl child on fulfilling certain specific conditionalities-birth registration, immunization, school enrolement and delay marriage of the girl child till the age of 18 years. In addition an insurance cover to the tune of Rs. 1 lakh would be provided for the girl child at her birth. In all, cash package of around 2 lakh will be provided to the girl's family, preferably to the mother, through the scheme. Launching the scheme here today, Smt. Renuka Chowdhury, Minister for Women and Child Development said that objective of the scheme to provide a set of staggered financial incentives for families to encourage them for better upbringing of girl child and to educate her. She said that the scheme would also help to change the attitudinal mindset of the family towards the girl-by linking cash and non-cash transfers to her well-being. This will force the families to look upon the girl as an asset rather than a liability since her very existence would lead to cash inflow to the family. Initially the scheme is proposed to be piloted in 11 educationally backward blocks in 7 States. An outlay of Rs. 10 crores is proposed for 2008-09 benefiting 101970 girl children. Smt. Chowdhury also launched an public awareness campaign about women issues through Railway tickets. Initially 5 crore tickets will be printed carrying social messages to check female foeticide, child marriage, dowry, domestic violence, trafficking and harassment. She said that through tickets the messages will go upto the grassroot level. She also announced skill upgradation programme for women especially destitutes in private partnership under the programme about 100 women will be provided training in different trades and their employment will be facilitated. A leading health chain will also provide training in beauty culture and related fields. The Minister also launched online tracking of proposals submitted to the Ministry under various schemes for grant in aid in collaboration with National Informatics Centre (NIC). These schemes include working women's hostel scheme, Swadhar, Ujjawala, short stay homes, crèche and child welfare. The Ministry will also celebrate 3rd March to 8th March as women's week. The theme of the week-long celebration is ' Survival to Success : Celebrate her life'. Activities during the week include hoisting the Ananya Flag specially designed on women's empowerment, conference on prevention of trafficking, workshop on prevention of female foeticide, presentation of Stree Shakti Puraskaar, free health check-ups and nutrition exhibition. On 8th March, the International Women's Day special announcement will be made in flights, Rajdhani, Shatabadi and Metro trains and on telecommunication network. Request for these have been made to the concerned authorities.

6274. (3-3-2008) NEW DELHI : The Indian Navy is facing shortage of Sea Harrier aircraft. The ongoing upgrade of Sea Harrier programme has also temporarily affected the availability of the aircraft. Contract for the limited upgrade of Sea Harrier aircraft was concluded with M/s Hindustan Aeronautics Limited in March 2005 at a cost of Rs. 476.69 crore. The upgradation programme is expected to be completed by 2009. This information was given by Defence Minister Shri A K Antony in a written reply to Shri Sugrib Singh in Lok Sabha today.

6275. (3-3-2008) NEW DELHI : Compulsory Military Service The Government does not propose to make military service compulsory in the country. This information was given by Defence Minister Shri A K Antony in a written reply to Shri K.C. Singh Baba and others in Lok Sabha today.

6276. (3-3-2008) NEW DELHI : The Army within the framework of the Government's Counter Naxal Strategy is extending training and advice to Central Police Organisations (CPOs)/State Police Forces in Naxal affected States. 139 companies of State Police Forces / CPOs have been trained so far. There is no proposal to deploy Army in the Naxal affected areas. This information was given by Defence Minister Shri A K Antony in a written reply to Shri Nikhil Kumar in Lok Sabha today.

6277. (3-3-2008) NEW DELHI : The Committee on National Defence University has recommended establishment of an Indian National Defence University. This will include existing institutes namely National Defence College (Delhi), National Defence Academy (Khadakwasia), Institute of Defence Management (Secunderabad) and Defence Service Staff College (Wellington) and new institutes namely National Institute of Strategic Studies, College of National Security Policy, Institute for Advanced Technology Studies (Bangalore). No final decision on location of the proposed university has been taken as yet.

6278. (3-3-2008) NEW DELHI : Flight test programme of Light Combat Aircraft (LCA), Tejas is progressing as per the schedule. So far, 829 flight tests have been completed. Efforts are being made to accelerate the flight tests. Regular review meetings are being conducted involving Defence Research and Development Organisation (DRDO), Hindustan Aeronautics Limited (HAL), Indian Air Force (IAF) and other concerned agencies to take collective decisions and coordination. Presently, no need is felt for strategic partner. To complete the project at the earliest, a top level review is being conducted by the Chief of Air Staff once in every quarter and review by the Deputy Chief of Air Staff once in every month. So far, Rs. 4806.312 cr have been spent on development of various versions of Light Combat Aircraft. This information was given by Defence Minister Shri A K Antony in a written reply to Shri Adhalrao Patil Shivajirao, Shri K.S. Rao and Shri Ravi Prakash Verma in Lok Sabha today.

6279. (3-3-2008) NEW DELHI : A total of 46,926 cases were pending in the Supreme Court on 31st December, 2007. In the 21 High Courts across the country 37,00,223 cases were pending as on 30.9.07. Of these 30,00,118 were civil cases and 7,00,115 were criminal cases. High Court wise pendency is as under: Allahabad, 808226, Andhra Pradesh, 147537, Bombay, 367409, Calcutta, 279318, Chhattisgarh, 74701, Delhi, 76674, Gujarat, 110639, Gauhati, 59339, Himachal Pradesh, 26781, Jammu & Kashmir, 45374, Jharkhand, 49276, Karnataka, 104237, Kerala, 115750, Madhya Pradesh, 187677, Madras, 426347, Orissa, 227752, Patna, 102165, Punjab & Haryana, 255696, Rajasthan, 212451, Sikkim, 67 and Uttaranchal, 22807. Government has taken several steps including deciding to increase the strength of Judges in the High Courts and the Supreme Court, setting up of Fast Track Courts, setting up of special tribunals like the Central Administrative Tribunal, Income Tax Appellate Tribunals, etc. for facilitating reduction of pendency of cases in the Courts. Government also has under implementation a scheme of computerization of District and Subordinate Courts to facilitate speedier disposal of cases. Alternative modes of disposal including mediation, negotiation and arbitration have been encouraged. With a view to ensuring expeditious disposal of cases, the Civil Procedure Code has been amended, inter alia, limiting the number of adjournments that can be given to a party and the concept of 'Plea Bargaining' has been introduced through the Criminal Law (Amendment) Act, 2005. Through the Gram Nyayalays Bill, it is proposed to bring justice to the doorsteps of the rural people by creating over 5000 courts in the intermediate Panchayat level thereby reducing pendency.

6280. (3-3-2008) NEW DELHI : The Telecom Regulatory Authority of India (TRAI) in its report of 28.08.2007 on "Review of license terms and conditions and capping of number of access providers", had also included recommendations regarding spectrum allocation. The Authority has recommended among others, a revised subscriber based criteria to make more efficient use of spectrum taking into account technological features etc. Accordingly, the spectrum allocation criteria for public mobile telecom services have been revised. As per the relevant provisions of Unified Access Services license agreement, and eligibility critieria, the spectrum is allotted to the service providers, on first come first served basis subject to availability of spectrum which is assessed from time to time. The Wireless Planning & Coordination (WPC) Wing of Department of Telecommunications, Ministry of Communications & IT, is the national nodal agency for RF spectrum management, which includes allotment of spectrum, as per guidelines approved by the Government. This information was given by the Minister of Communications and Information Technology Shri A. Raja in a written reply to a question by Shri Bachi Singh Rawat "Bachda" in the Lok Sabha today.

6281. (3-3-2008) NEW DELHI : In order to give more attention to telecom services in rural areas, Government has undertaken the following schemes: Provision of Village Public Telephones (VPTs) in 66,822 uncovered villages under Bharat Nirman through subsidy support from Universal Service Obligation Fund (USOF). Setting up of 7871 Sharable Infrastructure Sites in 500 districts for provision of mobile services in rural and remote areas through subsidy support from USOF (Phase-I). Second Phase of the Mobile Infrastructure Scheme for setting up 11,049 additional towers to cover the remaining uncovered rural and remote areas of the country is likely to be launched shortly. For creation of general infrastructure for development of telephone facilities, Government has proposed to improve the OFC network between the Block Headquarters and District Headquarters. Subsidy support through USOF for Rural Director Exchange Lines (RDEL). An amount of Rs. 1450 crore is likely to be spent for this purpose during the current financial year.

6282. (3-3-2008) NEW DELHI : As per information from Software technology Parks of India (STPI) the software exports from STP units in Karnataka (registered with STPI, Bangalore) is around Rs. 48700 Crores, during 2006-07. Exports from STP Units of Southern region consisting of Tamil Nadu Karnataka, Kerala and Andhra Pradesh accounted for 61.59% of total export during 2006-07. The IT exports reported from STP units in Karnataka registered with STPI-Bangalore during 2005-06 was Rs. 37600 Crores contributing around 35% of exports from the country and during 2006-07 it was Rs. 48700 Crores contributing around 38% of exports from the country.

6283. (3-3-2008) NEW DELHI : Government of India releases funds for the various programmes connected with persons with disabilities mainly Non-Governmental Organisations, National Institutes, Artificial Limbs manufacturing Corporation of India and National Handicapped Finance and Development Corporation. During 2004-05, 2005-06 and 2006-07, Rs.130.55 crore, Rs.124.71 crore and Rs.122.19 crore were released. Since there is no earmarking of funds State-wise, actual releases are dependent upon timely receipt of proposals with complete set of documents. Taking into account past experience, the procedure for sanction of grant-in-aid to Non-Governmental Organizations has been streamlined from current financial year. The State Government had been advised to send consolidated proposals after getting them scrutinized by a multi-disciplinary committee. To ensure proper utilization of funds, periodic progress reports are obtained apart from audited statement of accounts, list of beneficiaries and utilization certificates. This information was given by the Minister of State for Social Justice and Empowerment, Smt. Subbulakshmi Jagadeesan in a written reply to a question in the Rajya Sabha today.

6284. (3-3-2008) NEW DELHI : India's exports during January, 2008 were valued at US $ 13140.71 million which was 20.47 per cent higher than the level of US $ 10907.72 million during January, 2007. In rupee terms, exports touched Rs.51739.82 crore, which was 7.00 per cent higher than the value of exports during January, 2007. Cumulative value of exports for the period April-January, 2008 was US $ 124190.41 million (Rs.500117.15 crore) as against US $ 102110.27 million (Rs.464532.19 crore) registering a growth of 21.62 per cent in Dollar terms and 7.66 per cent in Rupee terms over the same period last year. India's imports during January, 2008 were valued at US $ 22504.41 million representing an increase of 63.57 per cent over the level of imports valued at US $ 13757.93 million in January, 2007. In Rupee terms, imports increased by 45.28 per cent. Cumulative value of imports for the period April-January, 2008 was US $ 191604.13 million (Rs.771628.90 crore) as against US $ 147812.69 million (Rs.672514.33 crore) registering a growth of 29.63 per cent in Dollar terms and 14.74 per cent in Rupee terms over the same period last year. Oil imports during January, 2008 were valued at US $ 7711.78 million which was 60.81 per cent higher than oil imports valued at US $ 4795.46 million in the corresponding period last year. Oil imports during April-January, 2008 were valued at US $ 57023.33 million which was 16.49 per cent higher than the oil imports of US $ 48951.65 million in the corresponding period last year. Non-oil imports during January, 2008 were estimated at US $ 14792.62 million which was 65.05 per cent higher than non-oil imports of US $ 8962.47 million in January, 2007. Non-oil imports during April-January, 2008 were valued at US $ 134580.80 million which was 36.13 per cent higher than the level of such imports valued at US $ 98861.04 million in April-January, 2007.

6285. (3-3-2008) NEW DELHI : The Minister for Steel, Chemicals and Fertilisers Shri Ram Vilas Paswan today reviewed the progress of the new mega steel projects and brown-field expansion plans of existing manufacturers with all major steel producers of the country. Representatives of state governments were also present on the occasion. Later talking to newsmen Shri Paswan said, the consumption of steel in the country is increasing at a faster rate than the addition in capacity and there could be a short fall in production by 2020. Therefore, there is a need to remove the bottlenecks in the implementation of the projects. He, however, added that the country will produce 124 million tonnes of steel by 2011-12, exceeding its demand. The Minister said, land acquisition, extension of railway line, expansion of port facility, allocation of mines and speedy environmental clearance are among the major problems. Shri Paswan said, some of the promoters are even prepared to fund the extension of railway track for timely completion of the projects and the amount could be debited from the freight later. Shri Paswan said land acquisition and allocation of mines are two critical areas and depends upon the concerned state governments. Shri Paswan said, he would seek a meeting with the Prime Minister and request him to intervene on some of the issues. The Minister expressed satisfaction on the announcements made in the Union Budget 2008-09 on the steel sector. He said, the manufacturers have assured him that steel prices will comedown by about Rs.500 per tonne following a 2 percent reduction in the CENVAT.

6286. (3-3-2008) NEW DELHI : In the current Five Year Plan period, the outlay for construction of courts including High Courts through development of infrastructure, their modernization and computerization of all courts has been enhanced to Rs. 1470 crore. An outlay of Rs. 700 crore was provided in the Tenth Five Year Plan for modernization of all the courts including, computerization of the High Courts and the city courts, development of infrastructure facilities for the judiciary and the construction of High Courts. This information was given by Minister of Law and Justice, Shri H. R. Bhardwaj in written reply to a question in Rajya Sabha today.

6287. (3-3-2008) NEW DELHI : Following is the full text of the Suo Motu Statement on 'Foreign Policy-related Developments' by External Affairs Minister, Shri Pranab Mukherjee delivered in Lok Sabha today "Sir, I rise to apprise the House of developments related to foreign policy since the conclusion of the Winter Session last December. During this inter-sessional period, Government has made vigorous efforts to promote our objective of an external environment that enables India's accelerated development efforts and increases our strategic space. Prime Minister paid an official visit to the People's Republic of China, our largest neighbour, from 13 to 15 January 2008. He was received with great warmth. PM and Premier Wen Jiabao signed a joint document on "A Shared Vision for the 21st Century between the Republic of India and the People's Republic of China", that reflects the congruence of interests that we share on regional and international issues, and our willingness to work together in those areas. Prime Minister also took up the issue of trans-border rivers. The first meeting of the Expert Level Mechanism was held in September 2007. We have proposed to the Chinese side that we expand our cooperation in this area. We have also agreed to intensify high level exchanges with China. I will be visiting China this year and the Chinese Foreign Minister will also visit India. We will be holding the second annual defence dialogue as well as the second joint military exercise this year in an effort to continue deepening mutual understanding and trust between our Armed Forces. Our bilateral trade continues to show strong growth and both governments have revised the trade target to 60 billion dollars by 2010. Our Commerce Minister will visit China in April for the 8th meeting of the Joint Economic Group. On the boundary question, during Prime Minister's visit, both sides positively appraised the work of the Special Representatives in seeking a mutually acceptable framework for a settlement that will be based on the Agreement on Guiding Principles and Political Parameters signed in April 2005. Both sides have also agreed to maintain peace and tranquility in the border areas.

6288. (3-3-2008) NEW DELHI : In the field of technical education, the regulations of All India Council for Technical Education (AICTE) for entry and operation of foreign universities/institutions imparting technical education in India have been notified on 16 May, 2005. Under these regulations, the following institutes have been accorded approval by AICTE for conducting foreign university programmes in India: (i) Institute of Hotel Management, Aurangabad (Maharashtra) in collaboration with University of Hudderfield, United Kingdom. (ii) Asia Pacific Institute of Information Technology, Panipat (Haryana) in collaboration with Staffordshire University,, United Kingdom. (iii) Streenidhi Institute of Science & Technology, District Rangareddy, (Andhra Pradesh) in collaboration with Vaughn College of Aeronautics & Technology, New York, United States of America. (iv) IIMT Hotel Management College, Meerut, (Uttar Pradesh) in collaboration with Regency Institute of TAFE, Adelaide, Australia. A legislative proposal for regulating the entry and operation of foreign educational institutions in India is under consideration of the Government. This information was given by the Minister of State for Human Resource Development Smt. D. Purandeswari in a written reply in Rajya Sabha today.

6289. (3-3-2008) NEW DELHI : The Ministers of Social Development of South Asian countries, members of the South Asian Association for Regional Cooperation-SAARC (Afghanistan, Bangladesh, Bhutan, India, Maldives, Nepal, Pakistan and Sri Lanka) will participate in the 2nd Regional Forum being organized within the framework of UNESCO's programme for the Management of Social Transformations (MOST) on 5 and 6 March, 2008, at Vigyan Bhawan, New Delhi (India). The Regional Meeting is being co-organized by the Ministry of Human Resource Development, the Indian National Commission for Cooperation with UNESCO and UNESCO. Initiated in 2006 in Bhurban (Pakistan), the Forum of Ministers of Social Development from South Asia is the 3rd such Regional Forum in the series of four such forums established so far under the initiative of UNESCO's MOST programme. As is the case with preceding two Forums established for Latin America and Africa and the fourth established last year in the Arab region, it aims at reinforcing linkages between the research and policy-making communities by encouraging regional cooperation and exchange of experiences and best practices on national policies. For two days, participants will discuss the social sciences research policy linkage and in particular the contribution that social sciences can provide to the policy-making process, within the framework of the theme selected for the Second Forum, Transparency, Right to information and Social Development. On the first day, following the presentation of the Indian experience, where the law on the Right to Information (RTI 2005) recognizes the right of every citizen to access information and the obligation it represents for the Indian Government, the participants, including the Ministers, Members of Parliaments, Social Sciences Scholars, representatives of public institutions, UN Agencies and civil society will be invited to share their views during an open session, chaired by three panelists, *i.e.* Mr. Wajahat Habibullah, CIC, Mrs. Aruna Roy, well-known Indian political and social activist and Mr. Shekhar Singh, founder member, National Campaign for People's Right to Information. Shri Arjun Singh, Human Resource Development Minister would be chairing this meeting of the Regional Forum.

6290. (3-3-2008) NEW DELHI : Mahatma Gandhi once said, "I shall work for an India in which the poorest shall feel that it is their country, in whose making they have an effective voice, an India in which all communities shall live in perfect harmony. Women will enjoy the same right as men. This is the India of my dreams". India continues its efforts to make this dream a reality. The Eleventh Plan approach paper says: an important divide which compels immediate attention relates to gender. Special, focused efforts will be made to purge society of this malaise by creating an enabling environment for women to become economically, politically and socially empowered. The Union Budget 2008-09 has several proposals to cheer women. These have come at a time when International Women's Day is celebrated. Exemption limit for Women Tax Payers has been increased to Rs. 1,80,000 and for Senior Women Citizens to Rs. 2,25,000. The Railway Budget has announced free travel to girl students upto graduation level. This is called real empowerment as girls in rural areas will not hesitate to continue their education. Senior women citizens have to pay only 50 per cent of the cost to travel by trains paving the way for more travel and more integration. Women who have progressed tremendously play an important role both at home and outside but are yet to get their due recognition. This condition prevails mostly in rural areas where education still remains a dream. But continuous efforts like increased spending on education and health care have started yielding positive results. A Survey estimates the number of women in the age group of 15 to 49 years with no formal education at 41% as against 18% of men. The Government promises to change this during the Eleventh Plan period, 2007 to 2012. In the past also such concerns were expressed specially to the gender divide. Enrolment of girl child has been given preference in States like Kerala where the literacy rate is the highest in the country. In highly populated country like India schemes which are announced take a longer time to get implemented.

6291. (4-3-2008) NEW DELHI : Shri Pranab Mukherjee, the Union Minister for External Affairs released a Book entitled 'Traveling Through Conflict': Essays on the Politics of West Asia' authored by the Vice President of India, Shri Mohd. Hamid Ansari at a function here today. Addressing on the occasion, Shri Mukherjee said that he knows Shri Ansari for more than three decades and it is a privilege to have him as the Vice President of India. His career gave him familiarity with the Arab countries. Shri Mohd. Hamid Ansari, Vice President of India, gave an overview of the Book in detail and said that his personal knowledge of these countries reflect effectively in his writings. Shri Mani Shankar Aiyyar, Union Minister of Panchayati Raj, Youth Affairs & Sports read some excerpts from the

Book and said that Shri Ansari's analysis of West Asian countries sheds light on the basic causes of the disturbances in those countries. He also described Shri Ansari's contribution as a career diplomat an excellent one. A number of diplomats and foreign dignitaries were present on the occasion. Brought out by Pearson Education the Book is a collection of academic papers, book review essays and op-ed articles written over five years by an Indian diplomat with extensive experience of living and working in West Asian countries, sheds light on the root causes of recent and current turmoil. 'Traveling Through Conflict' deals with two broad themes: contemporary questions pertaining to religion and politics in the Muslim world, as well as their implications for state policy; and specific subjects in the politics of West Asian countries, especially in relation to Afghanistan, Iran, Iraq, Israel and Palestine, Saudi Arabia, the security of the Persian-Gulf, and proposed reforms.

6292. (4-3-2008) NEW DELHI : The Prime Minister, Dr. Manmohan Singh, has congratulated the Indian Cricket Team for its historic victory against Australia in the Commonwealth Bank Tri-Series.

6293. (4-3-2008) NEW DELHI : The President of India, Smt. Pratibha Devisingh Patil, has congratulated the Indian Cricket Team for its fabulous and historic victory in Brisbane today against Australia to win the Commonwealth-Bank Tri-Series. The President has said that this victory is based on teamwork and determination.

6294. (4-3-2008) NEW DELHI : Anemia has been recognized as one of the major public health problems in India. It occurs when the iron balance in the body is disturbed. Deficient intake of iron in our diet and/or low absorption and availability of iron from foods consumed is the principle cause of anemia. Though nutritional anemia affects all age and sex groups in India, it is particularly severe among pregnant women, lactating mothers and adolescent girls. More than half of the pregnant women suffer from Anemia. 13% are severely anemic (hemoglobin levels below 7gm./dl.). One in five of all the maternal deaths are attributed to anemia during pregnancy. More than half of the adolescent girls (50-60%) are anemic. A countrywide survey for estimating Hemoglobin among women (15-49 yrs) and children (0-3 yrs) was done for the first time in 1998-99 as a part of the National Family Health Survey (NFHS-II). In National Family Health Survey (NFHS)-III (2005-06), Hemoglobin (Hb) estimation was done among ever-married women in the age group 15-49 years, pregnant women. It was found that overall 56.1% of ever-married women had some degree of anemia while the overall prevalence of anemia among pregnant women was 57.8%. Anemia was more in Rural Areas *i.e.* 58.1%.

6295. (4-3-2008) NEW DELHI : A Notification amending the Foreigners Order, 1948 for implementing Advance Passenger Information System (APIS) from 1st

April, 2008 has been published in the Gazette of India on 24.01.2008. As per this Notification, the country representative/station manager of an airline landing in India shall provide information about the passengers on board and crew in electronic form, within fifteen minutes of taking off of the aircraft from the port of embarkation outside India, to the immigration authority at the port(s) of landing in India. The details of the passengers *viz.* name, gender, date of birth, nationality, passport details etc. are to be provided to the immigration authorities. APIS will facilitate expeditious immigration clearance coupled with enhanced security screening of the passengers. This information was given by Minister of State in the Ministry of Home Affairs, Shri Sriprakash Jaiswal in a written reply to a question in Lok Sabha today.

6296. (4-3-2008) NEW DELHI : Due to development of transport system by Delhi Metro Rail Corporation, some trees were removed with the prior approval directly from the Forest Department of Government of National Capital Territory of Delhi. However, compensatory plantation has been carried out by the Delhi Metro Rail Corporation, as per guidelines. The overall green coverage in New Delhi Municipal Council area has, in fact, increased during the last three years. Tree plantation is being carried out every year as per requirement and availability of space with the objective of improving environment and to compensate for the loss of trees/greenery due to various reasons. During the current year, Horticulture Department of New Delhi Municipal Council has taken action for planting 20,000 tree saplings. The plantation is carried out from saplings raised in the departmental nursery and through departmental staff and no separate allocation of funds is required for this purpose. However, the Horticulture Department of New Delhi Municipal Council was allotted the following amount during the last three years and the same is used for maintenance of horticulture feature including planting of saplings, trees, etc.

6297. (4-3-2008) NEW DELHI : The Ministry of Rural Development on the request of Hill States has decided that in the blocks bordering International boundary in the Hill States all habitations within a path distance of 10 kms will be treated as a cluster for the purpose of providing all weather connectivity by the year 2009. This will help in providing connectivity to large number of habitations in the hill and mountainous areas under the Pradhan Mantri Gram Sarak Yojana (PMGSY). Various hill states have been requesting the Ministry of Rural Development to modify the existing guidelines to cater the need of scattered habitations. As per the present guideline habitations within a path distance of 1.5 km in hilly areas are clubbed together for the purpose of determining the population size for PMGSY.

6298. (4-3-2008) NEW DELHI : Sports Minister, Mr. Mani Shankar Aiyar has joined the nation in congratulating the Indian Cricket Team on winning the Commonwealth Bank Series. He praised the players for their "magnificent" performance. Mr. Aiyar said the dedication and spirit with which the series has been played is brilliant. He said that this has been a fantastic cricket season for India with the junior cricket team also picking up the under-19 World Cup. The Minister said he hopes that this will serve as a motivation and inspiration for others sports as well.

6299. (4-3-2008) NEW DELHI : In order to ensure improved financial services for the welfare of minorities, Reserve Bank of India (RBI) issued a Consolidated Master Circular dated 05.07.2007 to all the Scheduled Commercial Banks (SCBs) advising them to take care to see that minority communities secure, in a fair and adequate measure, the benefits flowing from various Government sponsored special programmes. This Master circular also envisages creating a separate cell in each bank to ensure smooth flow of credit to minority communities and also covers the role of the lead bank in the 121 districts identified for purposes of' earmarking of targets and location of development projects under the Prime Minister's New 15 Point Programme for the Welfare of Minorities. Minority communities have also been included in the category of "Weaker Sections" for availing credit within the Priority Sector advances. In October 2007, Public Sector Banks (PSBs) have been directed by the Government to, step up lending to minorities from the level of 9% of total priority sector advances to 15% over the next three years, *i.e.*, upto the end of Financial Year 2009-10, This information was given by Shri Pawan Kumar Bansal, Minister of State for Finance in reply to a question raised by Shri D. Raja in the Rajya Sabha today.

6300. (4-3-2008) NEW DELHI : The Committee on Financial Inclusion headed by Shri C. Rangarajan, has recommended that the semi-urban and rural branches of commercial banks and Regional Rural Banks may set for themselves a minimum target of covering 250 new cultivator and non-cultivator households per branch per annum, with an emphasis on financing marginal farmers and poor non-cultivator households for achieving financial inclusion. The Committee has submitted its final report to Government of India on 04 January 2008. Meanwhile, based on the recommendations for the interim report of this Committee, the Government of India has decided to constitute the Financial Inclusion Fund (FIF)-for meeting the cost of promotional and developmental interventions and the Financial Inclusion Technology Fund (FITF) to meet the cost of technology adoption, with an overall corpus of Rs. 500 crore each, with initial funding to be contributed by the Central Government, Reserve Bank of India (RBI) and National Bank for Agriculture and Rural Development (NABARD). This information was given by Shri Pawan Kumar Bansal, Minister of State for Finance in reply to a question raised by Shri Rajkumar Dhoot in the Rajya Sabha today.

6301. (4-3-2008) NEW DELHI : As a part of the financial inclusion especially with a view to provide institutional credit to the poorer sections of the rural community, the National Bank for Agriculture and Rural Development (NABARD) has been advised to coordinate with the sponsor banks and Regional Rural Banks (RRBs) for the coverage of uncovered districts by RRBs, their branch expansion in uncovered/unserved areas and establishment of RRBs wherever feasible in the States/Union Territories not covered by RRBs. As a result thereof, 39 more districts have been covered during the current year thus making a total of 573 districts covered by RRBs. Further, licenses have been granted by the Reserve Bank of India for the opening of 321 branches in the covered/uncovered districts in the current financial year. The establishment of new RRBs is an ongoing process and depends upon viability and other factors. This information was given by Shri Pawan Kumar Bansal, Minister of State for Finance in reply to a question raised by Smt. Shobhana Bhartia and Prof. Alka Balram Kshatriya in the Rajya Sabha today.

6302. (4-3-2008) NEW DELHI : Besides putting in place a framework to classify Micro, Small and Medium Enterprises to bring out the Micro, Small and Medium Enterprises (MSME) continuum under the MSME Development Act, 2006, the Government (in the Ministry of MSME) has initiated some steps to enable the Micro and Small Enterprises (MSEs) to grow vertically rather than exhibit the current pattern of horizontal growth. These steps include, inter alia, (i) enabling MSEs to obtain 15% subsidy for adoption of 48 currently identified modern technologies by availing financial assistance of up to Rs 1 crore under the Credit Linked Capital Subsidy Scheme. (ii) assistance for the upgradation of infrastructure in industrial clusters under the Micro and Small Enterprises Cluster Development Programme (MSE-CDP). The Ministry of MSME has also announced the implementation of a 10 point initiative under the National Manufacturing Competitiveness Programme (NMCP) for enhancing the competitiveness of the manufacturing sector, particularly the SMEs. The implementation of this Programme is likely to assist in achievement of this objective as well. This information was given by Shri Pawan Kumar Bansal, Minister of State for Finance in reply to a question raised by Shri Narendra Mohan in the Rajya Sabha today.

6303. (4-3-2008) NEW DELHI : Shri L.K. Advani said here that I wish no disrespect to the President while I disagree with the draftsmen of the President's speech who have chosen to give themselves a lavish praise for otherwise a directionless, rudderless and a non performing government. This Government will shortly enter the fifth year of its governance. Its past four years have been marked by directionless, rudderless, non-performing governance whose only achievement has been to stay in power despite no achievements. The ruling combination's popularity is at the lowest depth. In the past 2 years it lost election in Bihar, Punjab, Uttarakhand, U.P. Gujarat and Himachal Pradesh. It lost even in Jharkhand and Goa and through a process of political manipulations managed to come to power. When the Congress did led UPA last scored a decisive victory in the election? And yet the arrogance of power is such that the UPA believes that it was born to rule indefinitely. The UPA is passing though a phase where it indulges in an attractive propaganda and then starts to buying its own propaganda. It lives in an illusion of its own glory, little realizing that the ground position is slippery and weak. The next election due is in Karnataka. If the government is so confident of its popularity why are they keen on perpetuating a constitutional fraud by postponing the Karnataka elections? The President's rule in Karnataka ends on 28th May, 2008 The poll should be held before that date. The Delimitation Commission recommendations on Karnataka were submitted on 23 March, 2007. The Govt. notified those 11 months late. Rule 24 of the Registration of Electorates Rules, 1968 stipulates that after a process of delimitation urgent fast track delimitation shall be done for election going States. Why is that not being done? Deliberate inefficiency cannot be a ground for postponing a poll. Smt. Indira Gandhi in the 42nd amendment to the Constitution had added the second proviso to Article 82. It mentioned that till such time the new delimitation takes effect, elections shall be held on the old delimitation. The mandate is clear. Enforce the new delimitation. By going slow the govt. is deliberately violating the law and using its own violation as a ground to continue President's rule under Article 356. Since you claim that your Budget has brought you high popularity, holding elections in Karnataka shall be the appropriate occasion to test such popularity. Why do you wish to run away from that. The UPA is in a pathetic situation where it has reduced itself to a situation where early poll in Karnataka seems a scary proposition. This Government is a threat to democratic and constitutional institutions.

6304. (4-3-2008) NEW DELHI : Some species of lower plant forms, not native to Antarctica, have been found. For example, a species of European grass (Agrostis stolonifera), a carnivorous beetle species, Poa annua (as seed plant) and Australian pollen taxa have been reported as alien species in Antarctica. A total of 439 species of lichens, 111 species of mosses, 4 species of mites, 7 species of tardigrads have so far been reported from Antarctic region. However, due to phenotypic plasticity in different species, it is difficult to trace the actual centre of origin of Antarctic species. It may be possible with genomic sequencing of these species in future. The data and research undertaken by different countries on alien species are shared under the aegis of SCAR (Scientific Committee on Antarctic Research). According to published reports and data available, many of these alien species have been responsible for significantly decreasing biodiversity at invaded sites and indirectly causing a change in adult body size in populations of its major prey species. Antarctica's harsh climate and ice cover protect against alien colonization, but on milder sub Antarctic islands like Marion Island and South Georgia Island which are getting warmer in recent decades are increasingly favourable sites for alien species to colonize and spread. This information was given by Union Minister for Science & Technology and Earth Sciences, Shri Kapil Sibal, in the Lok Sabha today.

6305. (4-3-2008) NEW DELHI : Developing and nurturing of human resource in Science & Technology has always been on top of the Government's agenda. A number of schemes have been instituted by the Government for encouraging Young Scientists, and also for nurturing talented students in the form of SERC Programme for Young Scientists including BOYSCAST Fellowships and Fellowships like Swarnajayanthi Fellowships, Shyama Prasad Mookerjee Fellowships, KS Krishnan Fellowships, Ramanna Fellowships and J.C. Bose & Rámanujam Fellowships for practicing young scientists & technologists, and CSIR programme on Youth for leadership in Science (CPYLS), Diamond Jubilee Research Interns Award Scheme, Junior/Senior Research Fellowships (JRF/SRF), Biotechnology Post Doctoral Research Associateship & Overseas Fellowships, Kishore Vaigyanik Protsahan Yojana (KVPY), National Science Olympaid Programme etc. for attracting and retaining young talented students in R&D. In addition, the young scientists including students have been exposed to new technologies through schools, workshops etc. to encourage them to discover and/ or experiment on new technologies including the emerging fields like nanoscience & nanotechnology, biotechnology etc. Most of these schemes have been operated in a liberalized manner from time to time based on the needs of the young scientists. In addition, the Government, in the XI Plan has launched a new scheme called INSPIRE (Innovation in Science Pursuit for Inspired Research). The main features of the proposed scheme will be: (1) innovation funding in schools (one million young innovators); (2) summer camp with science icons (for high performers); (3) assured opportunity schemes for proven talent force; and (4) retention of talent in public funded research through public-private partnerships. Further, another new scheme on Scholarships for Science in Higher Education (SHE) is being initiated in the XI Plan under which 10,000 fellowships of Rs.1,00,000/- per year for bright students in science streams during their B.Sc/ M.Sc courses would be provided. These initiatives are aimed at generating interest in youth to conduct more and more research and produce valuable results. The Government recognizes that a large number of scientists go abroad for higher studies and/or advanced research.

6306. (4-3-2008) NEW DELHI : During the XI Five year plan period, an allocation of Rs.30.00 crores is made under the Island Development programme of Ministry of Earth Sciences. This covers research pertaining to Andaman & Nicobar islands, Lakshdweep islands and adjoining seas. National Institute of Ocean Technology (NIOT) an autonomous institute under Ministry of Earth Sciences has developed technology for farming and fattening of mud crabs in floating cages and pens in brackish water lakes, canals and in the mangrove areas in Andaman. The technology has been transferred to fishermen in Andamans. The floating cellular cages designed and fabricated by NIOT for fattening crabs are used in Andaman & Nicobar Islands. Further, NIOT has designed, fabricated oceanic Fish Aggregating Devices (FADs) deployments in sea to increase fish catch. The oceanographic parameters of Andaman sea act as the benchmark for pollution free coastal environment towards monitoring of coastal ocean pollution in rest of the offshore areas of India and in this regard, samplings are carried out 4 times a year representing the seasonal variations. Under the project on development of drugs from sea, so far 413 marine organisms were collected from Andaman Sea out of which, 61 samples were found to be potent bioactive metabolites. After confirmation of activity in the repeat extractions, four extracts showed bioactivity at very low concentrations. During the last 3 years Rs. 609.41 lakhs have been spent by the Ministry of Earth Sciences for the Research on Andaman sea and nearby areas. This information was given by Union Minister for Science & Technology and Earth Sciences, Shri Kapil Sibal, in the Lok Sabha today.

6307. (4-3-2008) NEW DELHI : Rehabilitation Council of India (RCI), under the Ministry of Social Justice & Empowerment, which has been entrusted with the twin responsibility of standardizing and regulating the training of personnel and professionals in the field of rehabilitation and special education has so far recognised 215 colleges / institutes to conduct B.Ed. (Special Education Courses), a State-wise list of which is enclosed as Annexure. To meet the need of trained resource teachers RCI has launched a series of training programmes through distance mode of education and has also launched a channel dedicated to disability rehabilitation for facilitating the process of training and creating a pool of manpower. This information was given by the Minister of State for Human Resource Development Shri M.A.A. Fatmi in a written reply in Lok Sabha today.

6308. (4-3-2008) NEW DELHI : Congress spokesman Dr. Shakeel Ahmed said that I would like to thank all political parties of India for not disrupting the proceedings of the House for the last two days. Parliamentary business is going uninterrupted and debates are also going on in a cordial manner. I would also like to inform you that a thanksgiving rally will be held on 9th March at the Ramlila Grounds. The rally organized by the AICC will thank the Prime Minister, the Congress President, the Finance Minister and all the ministers and the UPA allies for bringing out a people-friendly budget. To a question on the Nuclear deal and when will it be operable? Dr. Ahmed said that the Foreign Minister has very clearly said that our talks with the IAEA is progressing successfully. We have gone into talks with the IAEA with the consent of the UPA-Left Coordination Committee and the Congress party and the UPA government has always kept the Parliament aware of the progress made in this regard and it is hoped that with this cooperation from the coordination committee we would overcome all the hurdles in sealing this deal. We believe that this deal is very much essential for the nation and its development and we hope we get the cooperation of the Left coordination committee. To a question that if the Left opposes this deal, will the UPA still go ahead with it? Dr. Ahmed said the government has gone to IAEA with the consent of the coordination committee of UPA and Left partners. So any further step that will be taken will only be after consultations with the coordination committee. To a question as to what is the tour itinerary of Shri Rahul Gandhi? Dr. Shakeel Ahmed said that as far as I know Shri Rahul Gandhi is going to Orissa from 7 to 10 March and the details of his tour will be known to you as soon as we are informed of it. To a question that Ramsethu is a matter of faith and not because of any scientific reasons as mentioned by the Supreme Court, what have you to say? Dr. Ahmed said that first of all I would like to clarify that the Ramsethu project was started during the NDA rule and four top leaders of the BJP were involved behind this project and they were Shri Arun Jaitley, Shri Chiru Navkarsar sahib, V.P Goel and Shatrughan Sinha. The plans were also sanctioned during the NDA rule and later a controversy arose and the UPA government has to decide on it. An official affidavit has been filed in the Supreme Court yesterday. Dr. Ahmed said that this project was initiated by the NDA and Shri Karunanidhi had subscribed to this idea of Sethusamudram project to the then prime minister Shri Atal Behari Vajpayee and now the controversy over this project is also being raised by the NDA and this is very clear and wherever it is a matter of faith the BJP should not play politics over it. As far as science is concerned it has got its own basis of foundation. To a question that Shri Rahul Gandhi has engaged MNCs to train the young entrants, are there not enough talented persons in our own organisation? Dr. Ahmed said as far as our knowledge is concerned nothing of that sort has happened. If something will come to our knowledge we will get back to you. To a question that the opposition has criticized the Budget, Dr. Ahmed said that for the BJP it is customary to give communal colour to any subject and have also tried to give communal colour to the Budget and Shri Advani has made a statement that this Budget is a communal Budget and for Shri Advani and BJP everything seems to be communal but Mohammed Ali Jinnah.

6309. (4-3-2008) NEW DELHI : Consequent upon reduction in excise duty on drugs and pharmaceuticals from 16% to 8%, vide Ministry of Finance (Deptt. of Revenue) Notification no. 4/2008-CE dated 01.03.08 and also in the rate of abatement on drugs and pharmaceuticals from 42.5% to 35.5% vide Ministry of Finance (Deptt. of Revenue), Notification no. 14/2008-CE (NT) dt. 01.03.08 the prices of scheduled formulation packs have been revised downwards by the National Pharmaceutical Pricing Authority (NPPA), Govt. of India. In exercise of the powers conferred under DPCO' 1995, National Pharmaceutical Pricing Authority (NPPA), Govt. of India through Gazette Notification S.O. no. 418(E) dated March 3, 2008 has revised the Equivalent Maximum Retail price (MRP) (inclusive of all taxes) of all Scheduled formulation packs downward. As per this notification, all manufacturers are required to reduce the Equivalent Maximum Retail Price (MRP) (inclusive of Excise duty & all taxes) by 4.58%. [For example: For an existing equivalent MRP of Rs. 100, the revised Equivalent MRP (inclusive of all taxes) shall be Rs.95.42]. The above reduction in the Equivalent MRP (inclusive of Excise duty and all taxes) shall take effect immediately in terms of above mentioned two notifications, both dated the 1st March 2008 of the Ministry of Finance (Department of Revenue). The reduction in prices of such scheduled packs shall however not apply on those categories of scheduled formulation packs where no excise duty has been actually paid to the Government and therefore no excise duty shall be chargeable in the MRP of these scheduled formulation packs.

6310. (4-3-2008) NEW DELHI : Article 21 A of the Constitution makes education a Fundamental Right for children in the age group of 6-14 years by providing that "the State shall provide free and compulsory education to all children of the age of six to fourteen years in such manner as the State may, by law, determine". Based on the recommendations of the High Level Group (HLG) comprising Minister of Human Resource Development, Finance Minister, Deputy chairman, Planning Commission and Chairman of the Prime Minister's Economic Advisory Council constituted by the Prime Minister in November, 2005 to consider the legal, constitutional and financial implications of the Right to Education, a draft Model Right to Education Bill, 2006 as well as the proposals to incentivise the States to adopt the Model Bill were circulated to the States for their comments.

6311. (4-3-2008) NEW DELHI : The National Council for Teacher Education (NCTE) has, vide NCTE (Recognition Norms & Procedure) Regulations, 2007 notified on 10 December, 2007, revised the norms for admission of students to B.Ed. programme and qualification for appointment of academic staff in colleges imparting such programmes. The norms, inter alia, provide that candidates with at least 45% marks, either in the Bachelor's Degree and/or in the Master's degree or any other qualification equivalent thereto, are eligible for admission to the programme. The norms relating to qualification for post of Principal and other teaching faculty have also been revised under the said Regulation. The Norms and Standards for B.Ed. Courses notified on 18.11.2002 alongwith the Regulations, 2002 prescribed 45% as the minimum marks in Bachelor / Master degree for admission to B.Ed. Course. This was subsequently raised to 50% in the Norms and Standards for B..Ed. Course notified on 21.07.2006. Due to references received from several states for lowering the minimum marks to 45% and restoring it to the norms of 2002, the Norms notified by NCTE in 2007 have restored the position stipulated in 2002. Acute shortage of candidates with Ph.Ds in Education discipline and insufficient number of candidates having Masters' degree with M.Ed, led to a large number of vacancies at various level in B.Ed. Colleges. In view of various suggestions received for lowering of basic qualifications for Principals, the norms and qualification requirement were relaxed to allow persons holding Master's Degree with B.Ed. (55% marks) for appointment as lecturer in B.Ed. Colleges. The NCTE continuously strives to ensure adherence to its Regulations, norms and standards by the various teacher training institutions, so as to maintain the desired quality in such institutions. In this direction, the Regulation of 2007 has stipulated that institutions running secondary level teacher training programmes like B.Ed.

and B.P.Ed., would have to obtain accreditation from the National Assessment and Accreditation Council (NAAC) with a 'letter grade B' developed by NAAC before seeking additional intake in these programmes. This information was given by the Minister of State for Human Resource Development Shri M.A.A. Fatmi in a written reply in Lok Sabha today.

6312. (4-3-2008) NEW DELHI : The Government has decided in September, 2005 to set up strategic storage of crude oil of 5 Million Metric Tonne (MMT) capacity at 3 locations viz, Vizag (1.0 MMT), Mangalore (1.5 MMT) and Padur, Udipi (2.5 MMT). The estimated capital cost (as per September 2005 prices) was Rs.2397 crore and the crude filling cost Rs.8870 crore (based on the then crude price of $ 55 per barrel). OIDB will finance the cost of building the strategic storage. To meet the cost of crude, the Government could consider a temporary increase in the cess on domestic crude and/or customs duty on imported crude, if necessary.

6313. (4-3-2008) NEW DELHI : Government has conveyed "in principle" approval to the Public Sector Oil Marketing Companies (OMCs) for expanding the product line by way of introduction of composite cylinders for marketing domestic LPG, subject to there being no subsidy element in the LPG to be marketed through these composite cylinders. To start with, Indian Oil Corporation Limited (IOC) along with Bharat Petroleum Corporation Limited (BPCL) and Hindustan Petroleum Corporation Limited (HPCL) intend to import some cylinders and do test marketing in selected cities. OMCs are procuring LPG cylinders from cylinder manufacturers who have valid manufacturing licences from the Bureau of Indian Standards (BIS) and the Chief Controller of Explosives (CCOE). LPG cylinders procured by OMCs meet the required quality standards. OMCs have reported that necessary approval of CCOE has been obtained for use of composite cylinders for LPG. The above information was given by the Minister of State for Petroleum & Natural Gas Shri Dinsha Patel in a written reply in the Rajya Sabha today.

6314. (4-3-2008) NEW DELHI : The approved outlay for all Oil PSUs during the XI Five Year Plan period (2007-2012) is Rs. 229071.59 crore. With this proposed investment, the Oil PSUs would undertake all activities in the oil and gas sector, such as, Exploration and Production; Refining and Marketing; Petrochemicals and Engineering. The proposed investment by Oil PSUs during the XI Plan period would help in meeting the growing energy needs of the Indian economy. By the end of XI Plan, the domestic crude oil production is estimated to increase to 206.76 Million Metric Tonnes (MMT) as against the X Plan production of 166.56 MMT. Similarly, the domestic Natural Gas production is likely to increase to 255.76 Billion Cubic Metres (BCM) as against the X Plan production of 158.86 BCM. From overseas sources, during the XI Plan, the production of crude oil and natural gas is targeted to be 35.51 MMT and 9.67 BCM respectively. The Refining Capacity is projected to go up to 240.96 Million

Metric Tonnes Per Annum (MMTPA) in the terminal year of XI Plan as against 148.97 MMTPA at the end of X Plan. In fact, the country is expected to have surplus refining capacity of about 108 MMTPA by end of XI Plan. The above information was given by the Minister of State for Petroleum & Natural Gas Shri Dinsha Patel in a written reply in the Rajya Sabha today.

6315. (4-3-2008) NEW DELHI : The Minister of Tourism and Culture Smt. Ambika Soni has said that Ministry of Tourism has announced a scheme to provide incentive to hotels of 1 to 3 star and Heritage Basic categories all over the country where the hotels projects have been commissioned and classified w.e.f. 01.04.2007 to 31.03.2008. In a written reply in the Rajya Sabha today she said, the incentive will be in the form of capital subsidy of Rs. 2.00 lakh per room subject to a maximum of Rs. 30.00 lakh to one star hotel, Rs. 3.00 lakh per room subject to a maximum of Rs.75.00 lakh to two star hotel, Rs. 3.00 lakh per room subject to a maximum of Rs.100.00 lakh to three star and Heritage Basic category hotels.

6316. (4-3-2008) NEW DELHI : The Minister of Tourism and Culture Smt. Ambika Soni has said that during the 10th Five Year Plan, an amount of Rs.6.25 lakh was sanctioned by Ministry of Tourism, Government of India to Andaman and Nicobar Islands for tourism related activities. In a written reply in the Rajya Sabha today she said, the Government of India has also allocated Rs.76.5 crore as additional Central Assistance under Tsunami Rehabilitation Programme for up-gradation of tourism in the Andaman and Nicobar Islands to be utilized in 3 consecutive years, *i.e.* 2006-07 to 2008-09.

6317. (4-3-2008) NEW DELHI : The Minister of Tourism and Culture Smt. Ambika Soni has said that Ministry of Tourism has assessed that there is a shortage of 30,000 hotel rooms in the city of Delhi and NCR of Delhi for Commonwealth Games 2010. In a written reply in the Rajya Sabha today she said, Ministry of Tourism is in constant touch with the various Land Owning Agencies like DDA, Ministry of Urban Development, Ministry of Civil Aviation, Railways etc. to identify additional hotel sites. These agencies and the State Governments of the NCR have also been advised to follow investor friendly land policies and single window approach for promoting hotel projects and also for allotting sites on revenue sharing basis, so that budget hotels are promoted. All these efforts are in the direction of filling the gap.

6318. (4-3-2008) NEW DELHI : Shri Kamal Nath, Union Minister of Commerce and Industry, has called for increasing the bilateral trade between India and Romania, considering the untapped opportunities for exploiting the potential for growth. This he said during the bilateral meeting with Mr. Varujan Vosganian, Minister of Economy and Finance, Government of Romania, here today. He further explained that Indo-Romanian trade which stagnated over the last decade is now on the upswing. Bilateral trade has grown from US $ 68 million in 2000 to US $ 430 million during 2006-07, and added that India has a vibrant SME sector and engagement by SMEs on both sides would strengthen the foundations of the trade relationship. The bilateral meeting was attended by Shri Ajay Shankar, Secretary, Department of Industrial Policy & Promotion; Shri G.K. Pillai, Commerce Secretary; Shri R.S. Gujral, Director General of Foreign Trade; senior officials from the Ministries of External Affairs, Petroleum & Natural Gas and Chemicals & Fertilisers and representatives from the industry organisations and apex chambers. During the meeting, Shri Kamal Nath stated that the Indian economy is one of the fastest growing economies in the world and it is also the fourth largest in terms of purchasing power parity. Both sides noted about the B-2-B engagement would take the bilateral trade relationship to higher levels. On FDI front, the Minister underlined that FDI policies have been further liberalised and many new sectors have been opened to FDI recently and on automatic route upto 100% in most sectors. Shri Kamal Nath informed the Romanian Minister that infrastructure sector in India is an opportunity for investment and has the promise of sustained high levels of returns. As regards multilateral trade, Shri Kamal Nath said that India remains committed to a rule-based multilateral trading system. The success of Doha Development Round of WTO negotiations is of paramount interest to India. At the same time, we need to ensure that structural anomalies in world trade are corrected. Major export items to Romania are: iron ore, drugs, pharmaceuticals & fine chemicals, machinery & instruments, processed minerals and plastic & linoleum products. The major import items from Romania are: iron & steel, machinery except electric & electronic, transport equipments, wheat and Metalifers ores & metal scrap.

6319. (4-3-2008) NEW DELHI : The Minister of Tourism and Culture Smt. Ambika Soni has informed the Rajya Sabha today that the Government has taken various steps to promote medical tourism in India which include promotion in overseas market through brochure, CDs, films and other publicity materials, introduction of new category of 'M'-Visa for medical treatment purposes to foreign tourists coming to India. In a written reply she said, a Task Force headed by Secretary (Health & Family Welfare) and officials of Ministry of Health & Family Welfare, Ministry of Tourism and experts in medical field has been constituted for promoting healthcare tourism in the country.

6320. (4-3-2008) NEW DELHI : Twenty one students of Sainik School Kunjpura are all set to join 120th course of National Defence Academy, Khadagwasla, scheduled to commence in June this year. In addition, four students of the previous batch have also qualified for Joining NDA thus taking the total number of achievers to 25. This is an enviable feat accomplished by this unique and premier institution of the State of Haryana. This is the best result in the last 40 years though the school was able to achieve similar success in the year 2006 when it could send 17 boys to NDA. A total of 587 students from the school have joined in the Officer Cadre of the Armed Forces through the National Defence Academy (NDA), till Jan 08. Besides NDA entry, a good number of students have joined as officers in the Armed Force through direct entry (*i.e.* through CDS, AFA and OTA etc.) Sainik School Kunjpura has given the country statesmen and leaders of the stature of Shri Bhupinder Singh Hooda, Chief Minister of Haryana and General Deepak Kapoor, Chief of Army Staff, besides a large number of luminaries in Armed Forces and other fields. The school is also privileged to have many of its alumni as Doctors, Engineers, Lawyers and Managers in corporate sector. An alumnus Sant Kumar, who is presently holding the rank of Colonel in the Army, had represented India in the 1980 Olympics held at Moscow.

6321. (4-3-2008) NEW DELHI : The Union Public Service Commission will conduct Interviews of candidates who have qualified in the written part of Engineering Services Examination, 2007 from 13th March, 2008 till 28th March, 2008. Interview letters to all the eligible candidates have been dispatched. If any eligible candidate has not received the call letter so far, he/she may contact UPSC on Telephone No. 011-23387402 or 011-23098591 (Extn. 4331). The candidates can also send fax messages on FAX No. 011-23387310. The date of interview for individual candidates is available at Union Public Service Commission Website at http://www.upsc.gov.in. Mobile phones and other such IT gadgets are banned in the Campus of UPSC Examination Halls.

6322. (4-3-2008) NEW DELHI : The Minister of Petroleum and Natural Gas Shri Murli Deora informed the Rajya Sabha today in a written reply that in Krishna Godavari basin, Oil and Natural Gas Corporation Limited (ONGC) started commercial oil and gas production in October 1998. In 2006-07, production by ONGC in onland areas of KG basin was about 602 tonnes per day of crude oil and 4 million metric standard cubic metres per day (MMSCMD) of natural gas. He told the House that in July 2008, additional natural gas of 40 MMSCMD from Krishna Godavari deepwater areas is likely to be produced by Reliance Industries Limited and NIKO Resources Limited Joint Venture. Shri Deora also informed that in Rajasthan, ONGC and Oil India Limited are producing natural gas at the rate of 0.75 MMSCMD. In second quarter of 2009, crude oil peak production of 6 million metric tones per annum is likely to be produced by Cairn Energy India Pty. Ltd. He added that 12 MMSCMD of natural gas is produced from Tapti field by British Gas Exploration Production India Limited (BGEPIL). The Minister further said that as on 1.4.2007, in KG basin, initially in place oil and gas reserves of 970.52 million metric tones of oil equivalent (MMTOE) have been established. In Rajasthan, initially in place oil and gas reserves of 330.36 MMTOE have been established.

6323. (4-3-2008) NEW DELHI : According to observations by Central Ground Water Board, the level of ground water is falling in certain parts of country. The main reasons for this fall are withdrawal of ground water in excess of annual recharge, increase in the demand for various types of uses, reduced recharge to aquifers due to urbanization and free electricity for extraction of ground water in some States. State Governments and Central Government have taken action for water harvesting and ground water recharge to arrest decline in the levels of ground water. The Ministry of Water Resources have a scheme on "Artificial Recharge to Ground Water through dugewells" in seven States of Tamil Nadu, Andhra Pradesh, Gujarat, Rajasthan, Maharashtra, Madhya Pradesh and Karnataka. This information was given by the Minister of State for Water Resources, Shri Jai Prakash Narayan Yadav in response to a question by Shri Mangani Lal Mandal in the Rajya Sabha today.

6324. (4-3-2008) NEW DELHI : Central Government has decided to provide 90% grant of the project cost to the projects included in Accelerated Irrigation Benefits Programme (AIBP) of the following categories (i) Major and medium projects benefiting drought prone/tribal./flood prone areas. (ii) Major/medium projects and surface water Minor Irrigation schemes in the special category States and Koraput, Bolangir and Kalahandi districts of Orissa State. (iii) Surface water minor irrigation schemes in non special category States benefiting drought prone/ tribal areas. Projects included in AIBP and falling in above categories are eligible for 90% grant under AIBP. New projects which could be included in AIBP as per guidelines of the programme and falling in above category are also eligible for 90% grant.

6325. (4-3-2008) NEW DELHI : Ministry of Water Resources, Government of India approved a Pilot Scheme *viz.* National Project for Repair, Renovation and Restoration of Water Bodies directly linked to Agriculture in January 2005 at a cost of Rs. 300.00 crore to be shared by the Centre and State in the ratio of 3:1 for the remaining period of X Plan. Under the scheme, project proposals in respect of 1098 water bodies for 26 districts in 15 States were approved at a cost of Rs. 299.92 crore. This information was given by the Minister of State for Water Resources, Shri Jai Prakash Narayan Yadav in response to a question by Shri Rajniti Prasad in the Rajya Sabha today.

6326. (4-3-2008) NEW DELHI : The scheme for Orissa Integrated Irrigated Agriculture and Water Management Project (OIIAWMP) has been forwarded by Ministry of Water Resources to Department of Economic Affairs who posed the same to Asian Development Bank (ADB). The scheme, interalia, includes thee projects namely: Improvement to Gohira Irrigation Project; Improvement to Remal Irrigation project; and Improvement to Sunei Irrigation Project. The activities also include works related to command area development. However, the Detailed Project Reports (DPRs) have been received from Govt. of Orissa by Central Water Commission during October/November, 2007 for appraisal and technical clearance. In the meanwhile the agreement for project preparatory technical assistance has been signed by the State Govt., Department of Economic Affairs and ADB in respect of above scheme. This information was given by the Minister of State for Water Resources, Shri Jai Prakash Narayan Yadav in response to a question by Ms. Pramila Bohidar and Shri B.J. Panda in the Rajya Sabha today.

6327. (4-3-2008) NEW DELHI : According to the University Grants Commission (UGC), 27 Government Colleges and 185 Private Colleges are functioning in Assam under Section 2(f) and 12(b) of the UGC act 1956. The details of All India Council for Technical Education (AICTE) approved Technical Institutions in the State of Assam with approved intake and teachers is enclosed. Kendriya Vidyalayas are composite co-educational schools having classes from I to XII. At present 50 Kendriya Vidyalayas are functional in the State of Assam. The total number of students in these Kendriya Vidyalayas is 18,248 (as on 30.9.2007) and 1,272 teachers are in position. Navodaya Vidyalaya Samiti has a mandate to establish one Jawahar Navodaya Vidyalaya (JNV) in each district of the country. These Vidyalayas are meant for imparting education to the children from Class VI to Class XII and are affiliated to CBSE. These Vidyalayas are co-educational and residential in nature. 27 JNVs have been sanctioned in the State of Assam. The details of functional JNVs in the State of Assam indicating the highest Class and students enrolment as on 31.12.2007. There is no provision to set up lower primary level JNVs in the country as well as in Assam. Hence, there are no students in the JNVs at lower primary level. There are 165 Post Graduate Teachers (PGTs), 180 Trained Graduate Teachers (TGTs) and 114 Misc. Category Teachers working in the JNVs in Assam. According to the Central board of Secondary Education (CBSE), as on 31st December, 2007 there are 136 Schools including 69 unaided independent private schools affiliated with CBSE. CBSE does not maintained the data about the total No. of teachers and No. of Students of its affiliated schools. However, No. of students registered with CBSE for board exam from the state of Assam during the year 2007-08 were 7188 (Class X), 5388 (Class XII), 7740 (class X) 6164 (Class XII) respectively.

6328. (4-3-2008) NEW DELHI : The Government has launched the Scheme of Fund for Regeneration of Traditional Industries (SFURTI) for development of around 100 clusters from khadi, village and coir sectors with a total plan outlay of Rs. 97.25 crore. The Scheme envisages need-based assistance for replacement of production equipment, setting up of common facility centres (CFC), product development, quality improvement, improved marketing, training and capacity building, etc. 118 clusters (33 from khadi, 59 from Village Industries and 26 from coir) have been approved for their development under this scheme. Under SFURTI, the Ministry of Micro, Small and Medium Enterprises (erstwhile Ministry of Agro and Rural Industries) does not receive any proposals directly from State/UT Governments. The cluster development proposals are received by the Nodal Agencies, *i.e.* Khadi and Village Industries Commission (KVIC) and Coir Board from Khadi Institutions, NGOs, institutions of the Central and State Governments and semi Government institutions with the consent of the State Governments. After examining the proposal, the same are forwarded by the Nodal Agency to the Scheme Steering Committee of SFURTI for consideration. This information was given by the Minister of Small Scale Industries and Agro & Rural Industries, Shri Mahabir Prasad in a written reply to a question in Lok Sabha today.

6329. (4-3-2008) NEW DELHI : Based on the results of the 3rd All India Census of Micro and Small Enterprises (MSEs) with 2001-02 as the reference year, the estimated share of MSEs in the total industrial production of the country during 2004-05, 2005-06 and 2006-07 have been 38.62%, 38.56% and 38.57% respectively. The share of employment generation in the MSE sector to the total industrial employment in the country has been estimated at 34.93 %. There has been significant increase in the production and employment generation in MSEs as may be seen from the table given below.

6330. (4-3-2008) NEW DELHI : There is no constraint in timely supply of turbines by Bharat Heavy Electricals Limited (BHEL) to hydel projects. Central Electricity Authority (CEA) in its report on "Assessment of preparedness of BHEL to meet the capacity addition requirement of Power Sector during the 11th Five Year Plan" has stated that "for hydro projects, no delay is attributable to supply and erection of power house equipment by BHEL" BHEL has enhanced its power generating equipment manufacturing capacity from existing 6,000 MW to 10,000 MW per annum as on 31.12.2007 and is further augmenting it to 15,000 MW per annum by end December 2009 to meet the emerging requirement of the country. This information was given by the Minister of State for Heavy Industries and Public Enterprises, Smt. Kanti Singh in a written reply to a question in Rajya Sabha today.

6331. (5-3-2008) NEW DELHI : According to the National Family Health Survey III (2005-06), 69.5% children in the age group 6-59 months are suffering from anemia of which 63% are in the urban areas and 71.5% in the rural areas. Anemia is a multifaceted problem. The important reasons for widespread anemia are inadequate intake and absorption of iron from cereal based diet, inadequate consumption of green leafy vegetables and citrus fruits, frequent pregnancies with shorter intervals, high prevalence of infections and infestations, faulty feeding practices and lack of dietary diversification. Apart from aforesaid factors, illiteracy, poverty and general economic and social development have a bearing on the incidence of anemia among people of our country. The State-wise prevalence of anemia in children can be seen at Annexure I. Government has initiated several measures to improve the health and nutritional status including anemia amongst the people. The various measures can be seen at Annexure II. This information was given by the Minister for Health & Family Welfare, Dr. Anbumani Ramadoss in a reply to a question in the Lok Sabha.

6332. (5-3-2008) NEW DELHI : The Prime Minister (Dr. Manmohan Singh) said in the Lok Sabha: Mr. Speaker, Sir, I rise to join all the Members of this august House in conveying our sincere thanks to the hon. President of India for her inspiring Address. Sir, in the 60th year of our Republic it is a matter of pride for us to have the first lady of the State a very distinguished woman and it was our privilege to listen to her inspiring Address. Sir, it is also a matter of satisfaction that over the last three days we have had a fascinating debate on the issues covered in the Rashtrapatiji's Address. While some of the hon. Members have expressed their satisfaction at the performance of the Government on many fronts, there have been others who have found fault with us on some fronts. This, for me, is the essence of democracy. Democracy is about debate, about argument and constructive criticism. Democracy is about acknowledging the existence of multiple view points, about tolerance for dissent and diversity, about respecting the opinions held by others without necessarily agreeing with them. The debate we have witnessed is in the best traditions of parliamentary democracy. This is what makes our nation unique and makes me hopeful for our collective future. I sincerely hope that we will have more of such debates and less disruption which has become a sad feature of our parliamentary democracy. Sir, as I listened to the various Members of this House and I drew considerable satisfaction from the fact that the vision of inclusive growth spelt out in the hon. President's Address is something about which there is almost unanimity on both sides of the House, that we need a strong resurgent growth to get rid of chronic poverty, ignorance and disease which still characterizes millions of our people in our country, something which is universally accepted.

6333. (5-3-2008) NEW DELHI : National Rural Employment Guarantee Scheme (NREGS) was launched in 200 districts with effect from 2.2.2006. The Scheme was extended to 130 additional districts with effect from 1.4.2007. The Government has notified all the remaining rural areas of the country for coverage under NREGS with effect from 1.4.2008. In accordance with Section 4 (1) of NREG Act, Every State Government is required to frame a Scheme, within one year from the date of enactment of the Act, for providing not less than 100 days of guaranteed employment in a financial year to every household in rural areas covered under the Scheme and whose adult members, by application, volunteer to do unskilled manual work. The Scheme so framed, must provide for the minimum features and facilities as specified in Schedule I and II of the Act respectively. This information was given by the Minister of State in the Ministry of Rural Development Shri Chandra Sekhar Sahu in reply to a written question in the Rajya Sabha today.

6334. (5-3-2008) NEW DELHI : Ministry of Rural Development requested CAG to undertake performance audit of the implementation of NREGA in phase I districts for the year 2006-07. Accordingly, CAG conducted audit in 68 districts of 26 States. CAG submitted its draft report on 17.12.2007 to the Ministry. The draft report was shared with all States. The States have given their responses to the observations made by CAG in the draft report. These have been sent to CAG. State responses are in the process of examination by CAG for finalisation of the performance audit report of NREGA.

6335. (5-3-2008) NEW DELHI : Water is a state subject and state governments are responsible for drinking water to the rural areas. To supplement the efforts of the state, financial assistance is rendered to the states through centrally sponsored, Accelerated Rural Water Supply Programme (ARWSP). The state governments are competent to plan, sanction and implement rural water supply schemes from the funds provided under ARWSP. Under ARWSP, unit of coverage for providing drinking water supply is habitation and not village. Based on the Habitation Survey-2003 conducted by States, as on 1.4.2007, State-wise status of coverage of habitations with provision of potable drinking water is at Annex-I.

6336. (5-3-2008) NEW DELHI : A meeting to review the progress of implementation of PMGSY of works in Bihar through the Nominated Central Agencies (NEAs) was held here today under the Chairpersonship of Secretary (RD) Dr. Rita Sharma. In her opening remarks Secretary (RD) termed the Pradhan Mantri Gram Sadak Yojana (PMGSY) as one of the most important programmes aiming at providing connectivity by way of all weather roads to the eligible unconnected habitations in the rural areas. She made special mention about certain important issues, viz; setting up of dedicating units, timely achievement of targets and periodical review of the progress and emphasized on the timely achievement of the targets by deputing adequate supervisory staff. The Agencies, while mentioning the difficulties including heavy floods, shortage of contractors; manpower etc as some of the impediments in the way of rapid progress were however assured to make all out efforts to achieve physical and financial targets to the maximum extent possible. The participating agencies included the National Rural Road Development Agency (NRRDA), the ministry officials From the NEAs, representatives from NHPC, NBCC, IRCON, CPWD and NPCC.

6337. (5-3-2008) NEW DELHI : Statistical analysis of the available earthquakes database does not indicate any apparent increasing trend in the earthquake frequency. With the densification of seismic network in recent times, it has become possible to detect lower magnitude earthquakes over India. India Meteorological Department (IMD) is the nodal agency in the country to monitor the earthquake activity on 24X7 basis and notify the magnitude and location soon after the occurrence of any earthquake in and around the country. The capability has been augmented recently in the wake of the Tsunami waves that struck the Indian coasts on 26th December, 2004. As part of the network augmentation, a Real Time Seismic Monitoring Network (RTSMN) consisting of 17 field stations has been set up with auto-location capability to provide timely input to the Tsunami Warning System in operation at Indian National Centre for Ocean Information Services (INCOIS),

Hyderabad. Providing information prior to the occurrence is not possible as on today, anywhere in the world as no prediction methodology exists. Global scientific community is making efforts to study the pre-cursory phenomena of earthquakes. This information was given by Union Minister for Science & Technology and Earth Sciences, Shri Kapil Sibal, in the Rajya Sabha today.

6338. (5-3-2008) NEW DELHI : India Meteorological Department (IMD) has been monitoring several parameters like temperature, rainfall, humidity and pressure for monitoring climate change over more than 100 years through a network of stations all over India. Atmospheric turbidity is measured from mid-seventies. Acidic components of atmosphere emanating from the industrial emissions manifested in the form of acidic components of sulphates and nitrates in rainwater has been monitored for the last 30 years. The Survey of India (SoI) has been monitoring sea-level through its network of tide-gauges installed over the Indian coasts.

6339. (5-3-2008) NEW DELHI : Congress spokesman Shri Manish Tewari said first I would like to congratulate, on behalf of the AICC, the Indian cricket team on winning the ODI Commonwealth Bank Tri Series by winning both the final matches by beating the Australians in Australia after 23 years. As you all know that my colleague Dr. Shakeel Ahmed announced yesterday that AICC General Secretary Shri Rahul Gandhi will be touring Orissa from 7 to 10 March. His main objective is to meet the people and also appeal to the youth to be present in large numbers. Yesterday the General Secretaries and Secrataries of the AICC met and it was decided that, apart from the rally which is going to be held on 9 March in Delhi, there will be more rallies to follow later in March and in April which would include rallies, conventions and meetings would be organized. The UPA government's achievements would be highlighted. On 10 March at 7 p.m. all PCC presidents and CLP leaders will meet and discuss with the respective state general secretaries and formalize the programme. To a question whether the Congress Party has any organization in Tamil Nadu and what can it do, Shri Tewari said the Congress Party has an organizational setup in every block of this country from Kashmir to Kanyakumari and from the North East to Gujarat. In some states we may be ruling and in some states we may not be ruling but that does not obviate the fact that we are a National Party. To a question on Elections in Karnataka that it may be deferred, Shri Tewari said it is for the Elections Commission to decide as to when the elections would be held in a particular state and we are ready to face the election. To a question on the claim that all the achievements of the UPA government belong to the Congress Party and second what about the re-entry of Shri S.M. Krishna, Shri Tewari said the Congress Party is a part of the UPA coalition which has taken people-friendly decisions over the past 4 ½ years. The Congress Party is a political organization hence it is legitimate that we conduct our political activities independently, so there is no question of ignoring anybody or not taking anybody along. We are endeavouring to take the message of the UPA government to the people. Second, it has always been the policy of the Congress Party not to comment on individuals who are holding high constitutional positions and the gentleman that you have referred to still continues to be where he is. To a question that governors keep shuffling between politics and constitutional office, what are your views, Shri Tewari said as far as my understanding goes there is nothing which bars that. People who come through a political process are people who graduate to occupying constitutional offices hence there is nothing which bars them from coming back to political activities. To a question that today was the hearing on the Sethusamudram project in the Supreme Court and the government has cited various scientific studies and does the Congress Party consider Ramjanambhoomi also as a matter of faith, Shri Tewari said first as far as the Sethusamudaram project is concerned, it could not be taken up a it was way down in the pecking order. As far as the government stand is concerned it has filed a detailed 60-page affidavit and what the government has endevoured to do is to bring before the Supreme Court the entire background of the entire matter. We have informed the Supreme Court that the project was approved when the NDA was in government, the alignment was approved when the NDA was in government. We have also informed the Supreme Court that the Archaeological Survey of India has not conducted any studies insofar as the Adam's bridge around the Sethusamudram is concerned. So we have apprised the Court of the situation as it stands and since the matter is subjudice, we have left it to the wisdom of the Court to decide one way or the other. Second, as far as Ramjanambhoomi is concerned it has already been discussed at length and it would require entire separate briefing sessions to revisit all the issues as it has various dimensions and it needs to be addressed in its entirety and that would require some time.

6340. (5-3-2008) NEW DELHI : ISRO has developed Automatic Weather Stations (AWS), capable of collecting in-situ weather data such as pressure, temperature, humidity, wind and rainfall on an hourly basis, and transmitting the same to a Central Station through INSAT communication satellites. 360 Automatic Weather Stations have been set up so far covering monsoon regions of South India and disaster-prone regions of North East. This information was given by the Minister of State in the Prime Minister's Office, Shri Prithviraj Chavan, in the Lok Sabha today. The Minister also informed that the Indo-Australian Workshop on remote sensing was held at Bangalore in December 2007 under the aegis of Indian National Academy of Engineering (INAE) and the Australian Academy of Technological Sciences and Engineering (AATSE). The workshop recommended joint working between scientists of the two countries in areas including calibration and validation activities; data assimilation in numerical weather prediction models; and hyperspectral data processing and analysis.

6341. (5-3-2008) NEW DELHI : A two-day International Workshop on Developing Methodology for Assessment of Enhancement of Forest Carbon stock due to conservation sustainable management of forests and increase in forest cover has been organized in New Delhi from this Friday. It aims to evolve a common strategy for developing modalities for accounting of incremental carbon due to forest conservation efforts and sustainable forest management by the developing countries. This has been organized after the Conference of Parties (COP) 13 of UNFCC under the Agenda of reducing emissions from deforestation and degradation (REDD) in developing countries where India argued for incorporating the concept of "compensated conservation" as a policy approach for compensating countries adopting forest conservation policies and measures. This has been organized by the Indian Council of Forestry Research & Education, Dehradun, Ministry of Environment & Forests. The outcome of COP 13 at Bali has been very encouraging for the country's practicing conservation policies for their forest resources. At the end of the Bali Conference role of conservation, sustainable management of forests and enhancement of forest carbon stocks found place in COP decisions on Bal Action Plan, and reducing emissions from the deforestation and degradation in developing countries. The task ahead now is to develop modalities and procedures for transparent and verifiable assessment of changes in forest cover, associated carbon stocks and green house gas emissions and also incremental changes in carbon stocks. The Workshop will have various technical sessions. Representatives from China, Costa Rica, Cameroon, Brazil, Pakistan, EU, Bolivia, Sri Lanka, Indonesia, Thailand, United States, Papua New Guinea, Bhutan, Nepal, Malaysia will participate. India and China has increased their forest covers. They are endeavouring to seek adequate compensation for maintaining and increasing forest cover resulting in locking of carbon in forest.

6342. (5-3-2008) NEW DELHI : A naval version of the Brahmos cruise missile was successfully tested off Andamans coast this morning. The missile was launched from the decks of INS Rajput at 10.30 AM and precisely hit a land target in one of the islands of Andaman and Nicobar. DRDO scientists said the missile met all flight parameters during its launch, flight and zeroed in on the designated target among the group of targets, destroying it with a thunderous blast. This mission is very important as it has established the sea to land attack capability of the formidable weapon system. It was the 15th successive successful launch of the Brahmos missile, developed jointly by India and Russia. The Indian Navy's Andaman & Nicobar Command provided the logistics support to the missile test. The command deployed ten ships, three aircraft and three helicopters for mission support. The parameters set for the mission were kept extremely difficult including the positioning of the target to achieve maximum output. The 100 percent success of the launch once again demonstrated the tremendous capability of BRAHMOS weapon system. The launch was witnessed by Dr. A. Sivathanu Pillai, CEO & MD of BrahMos Aerospace, along with the officiating Commander in Chief of the Andaman Command, Rear Admiral P.K. Nair along with other senior naval officers and defence scientists. The Defence Minister Shri A.K. Antony congratulated the Navy and team of scientists for the successful launch of BRAHMOS.

6343. (5-3-2008) NEW DELHI : The Ministry is implementing the scheme of National Lake Conservation Plan (NLCP) since June, 2001 for conservation and management of polluted and degraded lakes in urban and semi-urban areas. Under this Plan, the Ministry has so far, sanctioned 35 projects for conservation of 52 lakes at an estimated cost of Rs. 687.52 crore. The National Lake Conservation Plan is presently continuing and an outlay of Rs.63.21 crore (Revised Estimate) has been earmarked for the first year of the XI Plan *i.e.*, Annual Plan 2007-08, for the NLCP projects. For the financial year 2008-09, the out lay (Budget Estimate) for implementation of the NLCP projects is Rs.80 crore. Based on the response of the State Governments on prioritization of lakes and submission of proposals for their conservation; a requirement of Rs. 800 crore for ongoing and new projects had been estimated for the NLCP during the XI Plan. The proposals for new lakes are considered for sanction subject to their admissibility as per NLCP guidelines, pollution status, prioritization and availability of funds under the Plan This information was given by the Minister of State for Environment and Forests Shri Namo Narain Meena, in a written reply to a question by Shri Jual Oram, in the Lok Sabha today.

6344. (5-3-2008) NEW DELHI : Reports relating to poisoning of wild tiger, at times, are received from States. However, no definite trend can be inferred from such figures. The State (Assam) has reported mortality of three tigers on account of suspected poisoning (in Rajiv Gandhi Orang National Park and Hatikhuli Tea Estate near Kaziranga National Park). However, no confirmation in this regard has been received.

6345. (5-3-2008) NEW DELHI : Seven river valley and hydroelectric projects from Maharashtra have been accorded environmental clearance under the Environment Impact Assessment Notification of 2006. As on date, only one irrigation project, namely Jihe Kathapur Lift Irrigation Scheme in Satara District, Maharashtra is pending for environment clearance due to non submission of information by the project proponent. Generally, the final decision on projects is to be taken within 105 days after receipt of complete information. This information was given by the Minister of State for Environment and Forests Shri Namo Narain Meena, in a written reply to a question by Smt. Rupatai Diliprao Nilangakar Patil, in the Lok Sabha today.

6346. (5-3-2008) NEW DELHI : A Scheme for afforestation on non-forest lands by involving the Panchayati Raj Institutions has been mooted by the Ministry of Environment and Forests. The Scheme has not been approved yet, though the draft guidelines of the proposed Scheme have been circulated to States/Union Territories and concerned Ministries of Government of India for their comments. The Kerala Forest Department has been requested to resubmit the proposal after the scheme is approved and as per the approved Guidelines of the Scheme. This information was given by the Minister of State for Environment and Forests Shri S. Regupathy, in a written reply to a question by Shri P.C. Thomas in the Lok Sabha today.

6347. (5-3-2008) NEW DELHI : India as a developing country does not have any mitigation commitments, nevertheless, a sustainable development path is being followed through a range of policies and programmes to mitigate climate change and reduce carbon emissions, that include: The Human Development Report of the United Nations Development Programme (UNDP) has recommended to develop a multilateral framework for avoiding dangerous climate change under the "post 2012 Kyoto Protocol (KP)" that includes interalia: i) agree to global sustainable emissions pathway aimed at 50 percent reductions of greenhouse gas emissions by 2050 from 1990 levels ii) targets under KP implemented by developed countries, with a further agreement to cut greenhouse gas emissions by at least 80 percent by 2050, with 20-30 percent cuts by 2020. iii) Major emitters in developing countries to aim at an emissions trajectory that peaks in 2020, with 20 percent cuts by 2050. This information was given by the Minister of State for Environment and Forests Shri Namo Narain Meena, in a written reply to a question by Shri Prabodh Panda in the Lok Sabha today.

6348. (5-3-2008) NEW DELHI : The government has released nearly Rs 3 crores for the protection and management of Kaziranga National Park, Assam under the Centrally Sponsored Scheme-Development of National Parks and Sanctuaries during the last three years.

6349. (5-3-2008) NEW DELHI : Publications Division's latest book on space science titled-'Pioneer of Space Travel: Sunita Williams' was released by Secretary, Ministry of Information & Broadcasting Smt. Asha Swarup in a function here today. The book is written by renowned science writer and Sr. Scientist in Vigyan Prasar Dr. Subodh Mahanti. The book outlines the events that made Sunita Williams an icon. Smt. Swarup also inaugurated the renovated and remodelled Sales Emporium and Book Gallery of Publications Division. Conforming to the Division's modernization policy, the book gallery has computerized billing system in place and a spacious visitors' lobby to create a buyer-friendly ambience. Smt. Swarup said that in age of consumerism presentation of a book is as important as its content and the Division is successfully bringing out quality books that are attractive too. Talking about the book the Secretary said that Sunita Williams is an inspiration and a role model for the young generation. She is only the second woman astronaut of Indian origin after late Kalpana Chawla. This book not only informs about the life and work of Sunita Williams as an astronaut, but also tries to answer some questions on spaceflights and space travellers that arise in the readers' minds. Dr. Subodh Mahanti, the author of the book said that today's children going away from the world science and so through this book he had tried to increase their interest in one of the most challenging frontiers of science. Welcoming the guests, Addl. Director General (in-charge) of Publications Division

Smt. Veena Jain said that release of this book just a few days before the International Women's Day, is also a humble tribute to all women achievers. Joint Secretary (P&A) in the Ministry of Information & Broadcasting Smt. Stuti Kacker was also present on the occasion.

6350. (5-3-2008) NEW DELHI : Since there are no major industries and urban centres/towns located in and around Chilika lagoon, the lagoon water in general is unpolluted. Chilka Development Authority (CDA) is monitoring the water quality of the lagoon every month from 30 different Stations for various physico-chemical parameters, which are found to be within the permissible limits. No incidence of mass killing of fish, birds and dolphins due to pollution load has been reported. Financial assistance of Rs. 1785.2 lakhs was allocated to the State Government by the Ministry and 12th Finance Commission during the last three years (Annexure), out of which an amount of Rs. 1306.35 lakhs has been incurred for various developmental works which include catchment area treatment, community development, education awareness, fisheries development, hydrographic surveys, communication network, etc.

6351. (5-3-2008) NEW DELHI : The Government has received two proposal from the State Government of Gujarat for the project of Forest Development Agencies of Gir (East) and Gir (West). These Gir (West) and Gir (East) Forest Development Agencies have been received for Rs.224.86 lakh and Rs.254.18 lakh during the Tenth Five Year Plan. The Gujarat Forest Department has been requested to provide details of up-to-date wage rates and other requisite documents. The proposals shall be considered after receipt of requisite documents and suitable proposal from the State subject to availability of funds. This information was given by the Minister of State for Environment and Forests Shri S. Regpathy in a written reply to a question by Shri P.S. Gadhavi, Shri Bhupendrasinh Solani and Shri Mahesh Kanodia, in the Lok Sabha today.

6352. (5-3-2008) NEW DELHI : 983 families in Wyanad Wildlife Sanctuary in Kerala will be re-habilitated at a cost of Rs.85 crores. Government of India has received a proposal to this tune from Government of Kerala for relocation. The Government will process subject to the availability of funds, conformity of the proposal to the guidelines in vogue and fulfilment of necessary legal and administrative requirements after which the amount also will be decided. This information was given by the Minister of State for Environment and Forests Shri S.Regupathy, in a written reply to a question by Shri P.C. Thomas in the Lok Sabha today.

6353. (5-3-2008) NEW DELHI : The ecosystems are overburdened with environmental pressures from commercialization, excessive use of resources and indiscriminate dumping of industrial and agricultural wastes. The developmental activities are generally accompanied with use of natural resources and generation of waste if the environmental management measures are not integrated at the planning and design stage. To harmonize development with conservation and protection of environment, various legislative, regulatory and policy measures have been put in place. They include: Notification of the Environment (Protection) Act, 1986 and other related Environment Legislations including the Hazardous Waste (Handling and Management) Rules, 1989 and its amendment; Notification of industry specific environmental emission and effluent standards; Notification on Environment Impact Assessment, 2006 for prior environmental clearance. Adoption of the National Environment Policy, 2006, Conservation Strategy and Policy Statement on Environment and Development, 1992 and Policy Statement on Abatement of Pollution, 1992 etc. This information was given by the Minister of State for Environment and Forests Shri Namo Narain Meena, in a written reply to a question by Shri Ranen Barman and Shri Joachim Baxla in the Lok Sabha today.

6354. (5-3-2008) NEW DELHI : The objective of the proposed academy is to act as an umbrella organisation for all basic training needs of the Kerala Forest Department. It is proposed that the academy will conduct Refresher Training Courses for in-service frontline forest staff, Orientation Training for "to be promoted" officers, Executive Management Programmes for senior officers, Professional Training and Training of Trainers. The proposal envisages capital expenditure of Rs.13.75 crore and recurring annual expenditure of Rs. 4.35 crore. The Ministry of Environment & Forests does not have a scheme to support the proposed activity. This information was given by the Minister of State for Environment and Forests Shri S. Regupathy, in a written reply to a question by Shri P.Karunakaran and Shri P.C. Thomas in the Lok Sabha today.

6355. (5-3-2008) NEW DELHI : The glaciers of Himalayas are melting at an alarming pace; The Government is aware of this melting process Compilations of the data on secular movement of glaciers have revealed that the majority of the glaciers of the Himalayan region are passing through a phase of recession, which is a worldwide phenomenon. No abnormal rate of recession has been reported by Geological Survey of India (GSI). Even in the Himalayan region, the rate of recession in different climatic zones is found to be variable on average and in year to year basis. The retreat parameters of 35 glaciers show that 43% of the glaciers in the Himalayan region are retreating in the range of 10 to 20m/yr. The causative factors for this variable retreat may be subnormal snowfall, higher temperature during summer, less severe winter or a combination of all of them. It could also be attributed to the phenomenon of rise in temperature, global warming, a topic which is still under debate. No specific studies have been undertaken with regard to melting glaciers impact on environment and threats to the ecological system. Recession of the glaciers is a process which cannot be checked in absolute terms. The Geological Survey of India has carried out few pilot studies on retardation of ice melting. However, the thick supra-glacial morainic cover on majority of the Himalayan glaciers may not yield desired results. Thus artificial reduction in melting rate may not be possible because of its economic feasibility, scale of operation and pollution hazards. However, the Government of India has identified the possible measures for reducing the recession of glacier, which include conservation activities such as afforestation, removal of garbage, restriction on human interference on glaciers and promotion of sustainable eco-tourism. This information was given by the Minister of State for Environment and Forests Shri Namo Narain Meena, in a written reply to a question by Shri Kailash Meghwal, in the Lok Sabha today.

6356. (5-3-2008) NEW DELHI : The Polavaram Inter State irrigation project, was accorded environmental clearance on 25th October, 2005. This project involves the States of Andhra Pradesh, Orissa and Chhattisgarh, The National Environment Appellate Authority vide its order dated 19th December, 2007 has quashed the environmental clearance on the grounds that public hearing was not conducted in affected areas of Orissa and Chhattisgarh resulting in the denial of access to information and opportunities to the affected people to express their views/opinions etc. on the environmental impact of the project and the consequential violation of principles of Natural Justice. This information was given by the Minister of State for Environment and Forests Shri Namo Narain Meena in a written reply to a question by Shri Kinjarapu Yerrannaidu in the Lok Sabha today.

6357. (5-3-2008) NEW DELHI : The Minister of Petroleum and Natural Gas Shri Murli Deora is visiting Venezuela on 7-8 March, 2008 on an invitation from Mr. Rafael Ramirez Carreno, Minister of Energy, Government of Venezuela. Shri Deora is accompanied by Shri M.S. Srinivasan, Secretary (Petroleum & Natural Gas), Shri R.S. Sharma, CMD, ONGC and Shri R.S. Butola, MD, OVL. During his visit a joint venture agreement between the national oil company of Venezuela, PDVSA and ONGC is scheduled to be signed on 8th March, 2008 at Caracas. The proposed agreement comes in the wake of a hydrocarbon cooperation agreement signed between the Government of India and the Government of Venezuela on 5th March, 2005 in New Delhi in the presence of Prime Minister Dr. Manmohan Singh during the visit of the President of Venezuela to India. It may be pointed out that the Ministry of Petroleum and Natural Gas has been making efforts to promote collaboration between the national oil companies of India and other countries including Venezuela to obtain participation in exploration production assets abroad. The Government had on Monday (03.03.2008) approved a proposal to authorize OVL for formation of a Joint Venture Company with CVP/Petroleos De Venezuela S.A.(PDVSA), Venezuela for development of San Cristobal field located in Orinoco Oil belt, directly or through OVL's existing/new wholly owned subsidiary. The project will provide OVL an opportunity to obtain significant equity ownership (40%) in one of the largest Oil producing countries in partnership with the host National Oil Company of Venezuela. It will be the first OVL property in oil rich Venezuela and is expected to open up other business opportunities, especially in the Orinoco Heavy Oil belt where development opportunities are coming up.

6358. (5-3-2008) NEW DELHI : The sixth Pravasi Bharatiya Divas conference was organized at New Delhi on 7-9 January, 2008. The event was organized in partnership with the Government of National Capital Territory of Delhi and the Confederation of Indian Industry (CII). The theme for this year's PBD was "Engaging the Diaspora: the way forward". The Conference included plenary sessions on 'Social Development Challenges in India: Health & Education', 'Investment & Infrastructure', 'Trade & Business Opportunities', 'Developmental Challenges of States: Partnership Opportunities', 'Diaspora Philanthropy: Empowerment of Rural Women'. Concurrent Sessions on 'Knowledge Economy', 'Culture' and 'Challenges in Women Empowerment and Leadership' and Regional Working Sessions on 'Gulf', 'Asia-Pacific', 'Africa', 'Americas' and 'Europe' were also held as part of the Conference. In all, 1500 people participated in the conference. A list indicating the number of registered participants, country-wise, is enclosed. A highlight of the Pravasi Bharatiya Divas 2008 was a plenary session on 'Diaspora Philanthropy: Empowerment of Rural Women'. It was for the first time the potential of overseas Indian engagement through innovative schemes such as extension of micro-credit through self help group of women for their empowerment was discussed. The direct outcome of this session is a proposal to establish and promote an 'India Development Foundation' as an autonomous not-for-profit Trust. The foundation will serve as a credible institutional mechanism to lead overseas Indian philanthropic propensities into human development efforts in India. The Foundation will assist overseas Indians to contribute to the cause of education, health and rural development in their erstwhile home villages, districts or states in partnership with credible NGOs and philanthropic organizations engaged in the social development sector in the country. This information was given by the Minister of Overseas Indian Affairs, Shri Vayalar Ravi in a written reply to a question in Lok Sabha today.

6359. (5-3-2008) NEW DELHI : As per the report received from the High Commission of India in Kuala Lumpur, the Minister of Home Affairs of Malaysia has categorically denied any move to limit the intake of workers from India. However, it has been informed that all foreign priests have to now go through more stringent checks. The Malaysian Minister of Home Affairs has denied that Indian temple priests were being prevented from coming to Malaysia. Steps are also afoot for signing a bilateral Memorandum of Understanding on Labour & Manpower Development between Malaysia and India, which will provide for an institutional framework to facilitate employment, protection and welfare of Indian workers in Malaysia. Negotiations have been completed and the MoU has been finalized. The MoU will be signed after completing the internal procedure by both countries. This information was given by the Minister of Overseas Indian Affairs, Shri Vayalar Ravi in a written reply to a question in Lok Sabha today.

6360. (5-3-2008) NEW DELHI : An emigrant worker is required to pay a fee of Rs. 200/- as processing / service charges for grant of emigration clearance in the office of Protectors of Emigrants (POEs). The fee so collected is deposited in the relevant Revenue Head under the Consolidated Fund of India. During the period 2005 to 2007 an amount of Rs. 42.12 crore (approx) has been collected as the Emigration Fees by POE offices for processing of emigration clearance. The fee charged is for the processing / service being provided by the Government of India to the emigrant worker, and forms the part of the Government's revenue, the same is not used for expenditure on any purpose by the Ministry of Overseas Indian Affairs. This information was given by the Minister of Overseas Indian Affairs, Shri Vayalar Ravi in a written reply to a question in Lok Sabha today.

6361. (5-3-2008) NEW DELHI : During PBD 2008 held at New Delhi, Prime Minister of India announced the establishment of Prime Minister's Global Council of People of Indian Origin. This Council will comprise of people of Indian Origin from a variety of disciplines who are recognized as leaders in their respective fields, not only in their country of residence but globally as well. The council would serve as a high level platform for the Prime Minister to draw upon the experience, knowledge and wisdom of the best Indian minds wherever they may be based. The council would function as a sounding board and a 'think tank' to (a) effectively address the concerns and problems of Overseas Indians and (b) encouraging the Overseas Indians to share their expertise, experience and (c) to promote an environment for attracting the resources of Overseas Indians for development opportunities in India. The process of establishment of the council is underway and it is expected to start functioning before the next Pravasi Bharatiya Divas. This information was given by the Minister of Overseas Indian Affairs, Shri Vayalar Ravi in a written reply to a question in Lok Sabha today.

6362. (5-3-2008) NEW DELHI : At present, the Asian Highway (AH) route AH-2 near Siliguri passes through Banglabandha-Siliguri-Kakarbhitta. Further AH-48 presently extends from Thimphu-Phuentsholing-Border of India. The Government has approved in February 2008 the proposal for proposing to the Economic and Social Commission for Asia and the Pacific of the United Nations (UNESCAP) amendments to the above mentioned AH routes. The amendment to AH-2 involves inclusion of 'Phulbari' between the route passing through Banglabandha and Siliguri and defining the route of AH-2 at this location as ".... Banglabandha-Phulbari-Siliguri-Kakarbhitta.....". The other amendment includes providing link to Bhutan by extending route of AH-48 from "Thimphu-Phuentsholing-Jaigaon-Hasimara-Jalpaiguri-Phulbari", and consequently connect with AH-2 at Phulbari in India. This is envisaged to be of help in improving the international travel for trade and tourism among India, Bangladesh, Nepal and Bhutan. This is also envisaged at providing connectivity to the Capital of Bhutan, *i.e.* Thimphu, with India through the Asian Highway route. This information was given by the Minister of State for Shipping, Road Transport and Highways, Shri K.H. Muniyappa in a written reply in the Lok Sabha today.

6363. (5-3-2008) NEW DELHI : The Committee on Road Safety and Traffic Management constituted under the Chairmanship of Shri S. Sundar, former Secretary, the then Ministry of Surface Transport submitted its report to the Government of India on 20.2.2007. The main recommendations of the Committee include creation of National Road Safety & Traffic Management Board through an Act of the Parliament. The Board would have advisory as well as regulatory functions. Under regulatory functions the Board would set standards for the motor vehicles, and set standards for designing roads. In its advisory role, the Board will assist Central Government in the matters relating to road safety and traffic management and would promote road safety research, road user behaviour strategies, lay guidelines for establishing medical care and rehabilitation etc. Enabling provision has been proposed for creation of similar bodies at State level. The Committee has also recommended earmarking of atleast 1% of the total proceeds of cess on diesel and petrol for road safety fund. A note has been submitted for consideration of Committee of Secretaries (CoS). During 2006-07, out of the budget provision of Rs.14.80 crore an amount of Rs. 12.16 crore was spent for procurement of cranes & ambulances under the scheme National Highways Accident Relief Service Scheme (NHARSS). To improve the driving skills the scheme of Setting up of a Model Training Institute on Driving & Research has been launched in the Tenth Five Year Plan. Under this scheme Central Assistance is provided to State Govts./ NGOs for Capital investment for setting up such Institute. So far 13 institutes have been sanctioned out of which 2 institutes at Vijayawada, Andhra Pradesh and Sarai Kale Khan, NCT of Delhi have become operational.

6364. (5-3-2008) NEW DELHI : The Government does not propose to de-link the Vadinar area from the Kandla Port limit. Vadinar, which was earlier a part of the minor port of Salaya, was included in the limits of Kandla Port-a major port, by a Gazette Notification of the Union Ministry of Shipping and Transport, in 1978 with full agreement of the Government of Gujarat to establish an Offshore Oil Terminal at Vadinar within and under the jurisdiction of the Kandla Port Trust. The Government of Gujarat also through its Notification dated 1.5.1978, accordingly altered and declared the revised limits of the Ports of Salaya. By these two Notifications, the Government of India and the State Government of Gujarat had vested the jurisdiction of Vadinar with the Major Port of Kandla authority, *i.e.* the Kandla Port Trust without any precondition. The Kandla Port is fully empowered to enter into agreement with any other party within the provisions of Indian Ports Act and Major Port Trusts Act and therefore any compensation to the State

Government of Gujarat in this regard does not arise. This information was given by the Minister of Shipping, Road Transport and Highways, Shri T.R. Baalu in a written reply in the Lok Sabha today.

6365. (5-3-2008) NEW DELHI : Under the Indian Ports Act.,1908, responsibility for development of Non-Major Ports vests in the respective State Government. Maritime Boards are set up and funded by the Maritime State Governments for the development of Non-Major Ports and sectors related thereto. Out of the 9 Maritime States, 4 States viz, Gujarat, Maharashtra, Tamil Nadu and West Bengal have so far set up the Maritime Boards. This information was given by the Minister of Shipping, Road Transport and Highways, Shri T.R. Baalu in a written reply in the Lok Sabha today.

6366. (5-3-2008) NEW DELHI : Delhi-Dehradun National Highway has been identified for 4 laning under National Highway Development Project (NHDP) Phase III on Build, Operate & Transfer (BOT) basis. Widening to 4 lane work in Meerut-Muzaffarnagar section is in progress and delayed due to initial problem regarding tree cutting & land acquisition and is targeted to be completed by March, 2009. Widening to 4 lane work in Muzaffarnagar-Haridwar section could not be awarded as only single bid was received and the same was cancelled. For re-bidding of this section, updation of Detailed Project Report (DPR) as per new Model Concession Agreement (MCA) as decided by Public Private Partnership Appraisal Committee (PPPAC) is in progress. The Haridwar-Dehradun section is passing through Rajaji National Park and clearance is to be obtained from the Central Empowered Committee constituted by the Hon'ble Supreme Court of India. After clearance from Central Empowered Committee and PPPAC, bidding process is to be taken up for award of 4 laning work. This information was given by the Minister of State for Shipping, Road Transport and Highways, Shri K.H. Muniyappa in a written reply in the Lok Sabha today.

6367. (5-3-2008) NEW DELHI : The National Highways in the country are being kept in traffic worthy condition within the available resources. However, there have been damages to the National Highways due to overloading, rains, floods etc. Repair of National Highways is a continuous process and the repair works are taken up within the available resources depending upon the extent of damages, traffic density and inter-se priority of works.

6368. (5-3-2008) NEW DELHI : Execution of works on National Highways is being done by the implementing agencies of this Ministry *viz.* National Highways Authority of India (NHAI), State Public Works Departments (PWDs) and Border Roads Organization (BRO). In order to ensure that the execution of works conform to Ministry's specifications and relevant publications of Indian Roads Congress, the implementing agencies have well established quality control system. For ensuring quality during construction, supervision consultants/ independent engineers are appointed by NHAI. Test checks are also performed by Project Directors of various field units. In some projects NHAI is also employing technical examiners to confirm the quality. For works handled by State PWDs and BRO, the quality control checks are performed by field officials. The implementing agencies are exercising necessary quality control checks as per norms prescribed during construction. If any defects are observed, the same are got rectified with full quality control and re-tested. This information was given by the Minister of State for Shipping, Road Transport and Highways, Shri K.H. Muniyappa in a written reply in the Lok Sabha today.

6369. (5-3-2008) NEW DELHI : The women and Child Development Ministry is embarking on a massive national level awareness and sensitization programme on a sustained basis to check female foeticide. Besides NGOs media, entertainment industry, spiritual leaders and medical fraternity, youth will be involved in a big way as agents of social change in the campaign. The Ministry is also planning to institute awards for District Magistrates for their outstanding work to improve the male and female sex ratio in their Districts. Presiding over a workshop on the issue of female foeticide orgnaised as a part of weeklong celebrations of International Women Day. Smt. Renuka Chowdhury, Minister for Women and Child Development said that female foeticide is an extreme manifestation of violence against women. Media can play a very significant role to create awareness against this evil and to project women issues in a positive manner. She said that media should develop its own ethics to show positive aspects of women's empowerment and achievements of women in various fields. Participating in the workshop representatives of media, advertising sector and spiritual leaders asserted that all stakeholders should join together to sensitise masses about the role of the women and girl child in society. The Government's efforts would not suffice until people come forward to take the initiative in this regard, they said.

6370. (5-3-2008) NEW DELHI : There is no proposal under the consideration of Government for allocating funds directly to Panchayats. In furtherance of the commitment in the National Common Minimum Programme of the Government that funds going to the Panchayats are neither delayed nor diverted, the Ministry of Panchayati Raj constituted a Committee on Feasibility of Rapid Fund Transfer to Panchayats through Banking Channels. This Committee submitted its report in May, 2005. Taking into consideration the recommendations of this Committee, the Ministry of Panchayati Raj supports the position that financial inflows meant for Panchayats should first flow into the Consolidated Fund of State Governments, but should then be speedily transferred directly to the Panchayats through banking or treasury channels "without delay or diversion". At present, funds released under the Backward Regions Grant Fund Programme and funds released on the basis of recommendations of Twelfth Finance Commission conform to this pattern of fund flow. These funds are being utilized in various developmental works at the

Panchayat level, which would include expenditure on roads. This information was given by Shri Mani Shankar Aiyar, Minister of Panchayati Raj, Youth Affairs & Sports and DoNER in the Lok Sabha today in a written reply to a question by Shri Haribhau Rathod.

6371. (5-3-2008) NEW DELHI : Of the 24 States to which the provisions of Parts IX and IX-A of the Constitution apply, 18 States, namely, Andhra Pradesh, Arunachal Pradesh, Assam, Bihar, Chhattisgarh, Goa, Himachal Pradesh, Haryana, Karnataka, Kerala, Madhya Pradesh, Manipur, Orissa, Rajasthan, Sikkim, Tamil Nadu, Tripura and West Bengal have constituted District Planning Committees (DPCs) in accordance with Article 243 ZD of the Constitution. Article 243ZD of the Constitution mandates that there shall be constituted in every State at the district level a District Planning Committee to consolidate the plans prepared by the Panchayats and the Municipalities in the district and to prepare a draft development plan for the district as a whole. The establishment of District Planning Committees and the consolidation of draft district plans by DPCs in conformity with Article 243ZD of the Constitution is the "sine qua non" of the Backward Regions Grant Fund (BRGF). The Planning Commission has issued guidelines on 25th August 2006 for the preparation of participative district plans, which form part of the BRGF guidelines. The State-wise details of funds released during 2006-07 and 2007-08 against participative district plans that have been consolidated by DPCs is annexed. This information was given by Shri Mani Shankar Aiyar, Minister of Panchayati Raj, Youth Affairs & Sports and DoNER in the Lok Sabha today in a written reply to a question by Shri Braja Kishore Tripathy.

6372. (5-3-2008) NEW DELHI : A total requirement of around 25000 volunteers has been projected by the Organizing Committee (OC), Commonwealth Games, 2010 for deployment during the Games. A Committee has been constituted by the OC to select and train a good team of volunteers to be posted at various venues/ locations. The services of students from colleges, NCC, NSS, Scouts & Guides and other institutions are proposed to be utilized for this purpose. Out of these volunteers, the services of about 8700 volunteers will be utilized by the Delhi Police for traffic regulation, management of pedestrian flow at and around the venues, security supports, queue formation, help desks, parking assistance, frisking etc during the Commonwealth Games, 2010. Delhi Police have also envisaged a Special Training Programme for ingraining courtesy and politeness in the police personnel in the discharge of their duties, specially during the Commonwealth Games and a three months' trial class has already been organized successfully in this regard. In the next phase about 40,000 police personnel are proposed to be imparted training under capsule course of one year, from March 2008 in this regard. The Delhi Traffic Police is organizing training programmes for the personnel working at key locations in association with Delhi Tourism/ITDC. They are also planning to train the relevant stakeholders such as drivers of TSRs, Taxis and

Buses etc. This information was given by Shri Mani Shankar Aiyar, Minister of Panchayati Raj, Youth Affairs & Sports and DoNER in the Lok Sabha today in a written reply to a question by Dr. K. Dhanaraju.

6373. (5-3-2008) NEW DELHI : Panchayati Raj Institutions (PRIs) constitute the third tier of administration for local governance in rural India institutionalized by the 73rd Constitutional Amendment Act, 1992 which envisages, inter alia, implementation and monitoring of various developmental and welfare schemes launched by the Union Government and respective State Governments by the PRIs functioning as "Institutions of Local Self-Government" (Art. 243G). Various measures of empowerment of PRIs, including devolution of functions, functionaries and funds, have been undertaken by State Governments to enable PRIs to implement such developmental and welfare schemes effectively and efficiently. Empowerment of PRIs with emphasis on inclusive growth attendant with inclusive governance is a continuous process and the Ministry of Panchayati Raj is taking the required steps in this regard from time to time in consultation with State Governments. This information was given by Shri Mani Shankar Aiyar, Minister of Panchayati Raj, Youth Affairs & Sports and DoNER in the Lok Sabha today in a written reply to a question by Shri Bapu Hari Chaure and Shri Sanjay Dhotre.

6374. (5-3-2008) NEW DELHI : The approach to 11th Five Year Plan has assessed that while India's young demographic profile has the country favourably placed in terms of manpower availability, talent supply shortages are emerging. This is extremely disconcerting especially for the knowledge services sector, which over the last few years has emerged as a significant growth engine which demonstrated gains in terms of exports, employment and very visibly in urban development across several cities in the country. Research has shown that so far, only a tenth of the global addressable market for these services has been tapped. India is best positioned to take advantage of this opportunity with its early lead and strong fundamentals such as demographics, economics, and expertise. Yet the unsuitability of a large proportion of the talent pool in the country could lead to significant lost opportunities. The NASSCOM-McKinsey Report, 2005 Projections indicate that these will fall short by about 0.5 million suitable professionals by the end of the decade and in the absence of corrective action, this gap will continue to grow. However, if current trends are maintained, the IT and ITES sector will need an additional 1 million plus qualified people in the next 5 years. If the country is to capitalize on the huge opportunity in this and other areas of knowledge services, a major thrust is needed at all levels of education and skill development. Accordingly Government has decided to set up a National Skill Development Mission under which 1600 more ITIs and polytechnics, 10,000 vocational education schools and 50,000 skill development centres are planned proposed in Public Private Partnership mode in order to train 10 million persons per annum. This information was given by the Minister of State for Labour and Employment Shri Oscar Fernandes (Independent Charge) in a written reply in the Rajya Sabha today.

6375. (5-3-2008) NEW DELHI : The Millennium Declaration adopted by the General Assembly of United States in September 2000 reaffirmed its commitment to the right to development, peace, security and gender equality, to the eradication of many dimensions of poverty and to overall sustainable development. These are intended for the Member Countries to take efforts in the fight against poverty, illiteracy, hunger, lack of education, gender inequality, infant and maternal mortality, disease and environmental degradation. The approach paper to 11th Five Year Plan envisages creation of 70 million job opportunities in the next five years. It also provides a framework to restructure policies to achieve a new vision based on faster, more broad based and inclusive growth. It aims at making employment generation an integral part of the growth process and devise strategies to accelerate not only growth of employment but also wages of the poorly paid. Besides, Government of India has been implementing various employment generation and poverty alleviation programmes in both rural and urban areas to increase employment opportunities. Some of these are: Swarna Jayanti Shahari Rozgar Yojana (SJSRY); Prime Minister's Rozgar Yojana (PMRY); Pradhan Mantri Gram Sadak Yojana (PMGSY); Swarnajayanti Gram Swarozgar Yojana (SGSY); Rural Employment Generation Programme (REGP); Sampoorna Grameen Rozgar Yojana (SGRY) and National Rural Employment Guarantee Act, 2005. This information was given by the Minister of State for Labour and Employment Shri Oscar Fernandes (Independent Charge) in a written reply in the Rajya Sabha today.

6376. (5-3-2008) NEW DELHI : The 55th round of National Sample Survey Organisation Report has revealed that only 5% of the workforce in the age group 20-24 years has got training through formal sources. Government has taken up the following new schemes to provide skilled manpower to industry : Upgradation of 500 existing ITIs for providing highly skilled labour force in various industrial sectors. Upgradation of the remaining 1396 ITIs in Public Private Partnership mode. Establishment of new ITIs and strengthening of existing ITIs in the North Eastern States, Sikkim and J & K. Conducting of Short term Modular Employable Courses under "Skill Development Initiative". In addition, it has also been decided to set up a National Skill Development Mission under which 1500 new ITIs and 50,000 Skill Development Centres are planned in Public Private Partnership mode. This information was given by the Minister of State for Labour and Employment Shri Oscar Fernandes (Independent Charge) in a written reply in the Rajya Sabha today.

6377. (5-3-2008) NEW DELHI : The Group of Ministers (GoM) report on 'Reforming the National Security System' was presented to the Government in February 2001 in which amongst others, it was recommended to create the institution of Chief of Defence Staff (CDS). The Government approved the recommendations contained in the GoM report except those pertaining to institution of CDS for which it was decided that Government would take a view after consulting various political parties. The process of consultation with political parties was initiated in March 2006 when the Defence Minister wrote a letter to leaders of various national level political parties. Only five parties have replied. Reminders were issued to the parties that did not respond on this issue. This information was given by the Defence Minister Shri A K Antony in a written reply to Shri Rajeev Chandrasekhar in Rajya Sabha today.

6378. (5-3-2008) NEW DELHI : Government constantly reviews the security environment and accordingly decides to induct appropriate equipment for adequate defence preparedness. Various countries from which imports were made during the last five years include Russia, Israel, France, the USA, the UK, Germany, Canada, Italy, Sweden, Australia and Ukraine. This information was given by the Defence Minister Shri A K Antony in a written reply to Shri Sitaram Yechury in Rajya Sabha today.

6379. (5-3-2008) NEW DELHI : The overall deficiency of officers in the Army is around 24%. The deficiency has been continuing for some time. Presently, there is shortage of 11,153 officers, mainly in the ranks of Lt. Colonel and below. Several steps have been undertaken to create awareness among the youth on the advantages of taking up a challenging and satisfying career in the Army. A number of 'Image Projection Campaigns' have been launched in this regard. Awareness campaigns, participation in career fairs and exhibitions, preparation of publicity materials, advertisements in print and electronic media, counselling and motivational talks in schools, colleges and NCC camps are also some of the other measures taken up in this direction. This information was given by the Defence Minister Shri A K Antony in a written reply to Shri Janeshwar Mishra and Shri Bhagwati Singh in Rajya Sabha today.

6380. (5-3-2008) NEW DELHI : A total of ten (10) Indian Air Force's aircraft crashed during the calendar year 2007. In these accidents, three (3) Kiran, two (2) MiG-21, one (1) Mirage-2000, one (1) MiG-29 and one(1) Advance Light Helicopter were lost. Seven pilots were killed in these accidents. There was no civilian casualty. However, there was loss to civil property worth Rs.41,700/- in the accident which took place on 24.1.2007. A compensation of Rs. 41,700/- was paid in case of loss of the civil property in the accident which took place on 24.1.2007. Payment is made on the basis of loss assessment report by the local Revenue Officials duly countersigned by District Magistrate/Deputy Commissioner/Collector of the district. This information was given by the Defence Minister Shri A K Antony in a written reply to Shri Varinder Singh Bajwa in Rajya Sabha today.

6381. (5-3-2008) NEW DELHI : Indian Ocean Region faces security threats on account of territorial disputes, trade and goods movements along sealanes, low intensity maritime threats, economic offences from the sea, etc. There are reports of certain terrorists being imparted training and likelihood of their infiltration through sea routes. However, India's coastal waters are well guarded by Indian Navy and Coast Guard and therefore threat perception of any nature can always be taken care of. In order to meet the modernization requirement of the Indian Navy, procurement/acquisition of items are made from various indigenous as well as foreign sources, including Russia, France, Germany, USA, UK, Israel, etc. This information was given by the Defence Minister Shri A K Antony in a written reply to Shri Shreegopal Vyas in Rajya Sabha today.

6382. (5-3-2008) NEW DELHI : Orders for the development of Radar Computer-I & Radar Computer-II and their software for fitment on SU-30 aircraft received from Malaysia; upgradation of display processor for SU-30 MK (A) aircraft received from Algeria; and development of six numbers of Airborne Antennas also received from Poland. Two numbers of Battle Field Surveillance Radar-S2 have been supplied to Indonesia. To enhance global marketing of its products, Defence Research and Development Organisation (DRDO) has been regularly participating in important exhibitions organized at national and international levels. During the past, DRDO has participated in DEFEXPO India, Aeroindia, India International Trade Fair, Asean Aerospace & Defence Exhibition, Defence Service Asia, Africa Aerospace & Defence Exhibition, Indian Science Congress, Latin America Aero Defence, Defence Systems and Equipment International, etc. from time-to-time. This information was given by the Defence Minister Shri A K Antony in a written reply to Shri Shahid Siddiqui in Rajya Sabha today.

6383. (5-3-2008) NEW DELHI : Government has, on a review of existing policy, approved changes in the policy for Foreign Direct Investment (FDI) in the Civil Aviation Sector, Petroleum Sector and in Commodity Exchanges. The policy on FDI is reviewed on a continuing basis through an inter-ministerial consultation process with a view to rationalization / liberalization of the policy and taking into account stakeholders concerns.

6384. (5-3-2008) NEW DELHI : As per extant Policy, Foreign Direct Investment (FDI) up to 100% in allowed under the automatic route in the manufacturing sector subject to the sectoral Guidelines. FDI Inflows in the Manufacturing sector during April 2000 to December 2007 were US $ 19.038 million and during the same period in the Manufacturing sector in the North Eastern Region were US $ 1.44 million. Government has put in place a liberal, transparent and investor-friendly Policy to FDI. Under the liberalized environment, investment decisions, including choice of location, are taken by the entrepreneurs based on techno-economic and commercial considerations. Government has announced the 'North East Industrial and investment promotion policy (NEIIPP), 2007' with effect from 1-4-2007, under which a package of fiscal incentives and other concessions been notified for the North East Region This was stated by Dr. Ashwani Kumar, Minister of State for Industry, in a written reply in the Rajya Sabha today.

6385. (5-3-2008) NEW DELHI : On the 11th January, 2008, the World Bank has shared with us a report, *viz.*, DIR. This report is based on the review of five health sector projects which were being implemented during periods varying from 1997 till 2006 end. One project was under State health sector. In this report, the World Bank has mentioned deficiencies relating to procurement, oversight and implementation like collusion, bid rigging, deficiency in civil works, equipments not installed because of lack of staff etc. Majority of the deficiencies reported relate to decentralized procurements at the district level, which are implemented at the State level. The World Bank report suffers from several infirmities. Ministry of Health & Family Welfare has already conveyed its response on the infirmities in the methodology adopted by World Bank emphasizing that the World Bank did not discuss with any of the programme officers either during the review or before finalizing the review report. These discussions would have clarified most of the issues mentioned in the report. Had this been done, most of the inferences would have been different. Government of India is committed to elimination of any deficiencies or irregularities which are detected. Structural deficiencies which were noted in the earlier programmes have been taken care of in the successor programmes. It has been aware of some irregularities and has taken action, if required in the past.

6386. (5-3-2008) NEW DELHI : The Government of India has implemented National Rural Health Mission (NRHM) throughout the country to provide accessible, affordable, accountable, effective and reliable primary health care facilities especially to the poor and vulnerable sections of the population. Recently International Advisory Panel of NRHM led by Prof. Jeffery Sachs reviewed the progress of NRHM, in which it was concluded that the NRHM is the most ambitious public health programme in the world and its success is crucial for replication in other parts of the world especially in the year of the 30th anniversary of the Alma Ata declaration "Health For All". Further, Union Health & family Welfare Minister has enumerated the measures already being undertaken by the Ministry/States in areas of content of ASHA training, providing pregnancy kit in ASHA drug kit, Trauma Centres, importance of mothers milk, replication of best practices, focus on nutritional issues by the ASHA and AWW, introduction of new vaccines, efforts towards quality immunisation through cold chains/AD syringes, legislation for setting up of Tobacco Regulatory Authority etc. This information was given by the Minister of State for Health & Family Welfare, Smt. Panabaaka Lakshmi in a written reply to a question in the Lok Sabha.

6387. (5-3-2008) NEW DELHI : Out of an allocation of Rs.1,36,147 crore for the Department of Health & Family Welfare during the 11th Five Year Plan, Rs.89,478 crore has been earmarked for implementation of various programmes under National Rural Health Mission (NRHM). Additionally, Rs. 625 crore will be contributed by the Department of AYUSH to make a total of Rs.90, 103 crore for NRHM. In order to provide effective healthcare to the rural population throughout the country with special focus on 18 States, with poor health indicators and weak health infrastructure, the Government launched the National Rural Health Mission in April, 2005. Bihar is one of the high focus States identified under the Mission. The Mission adopts a synergistic approach by relating health to determinants of good health and the main objective is to provide accessible, affordable, accountable and reliable health care especially to the poor and vulnerable sections of the population. Further, the gaps in the existing scenario of rural health care are being addressed through involvement of the community, the Panchayati Raj Institutions and other non-governmental organizations. An Accredited Social Health Activist (ASHA) will act as a link between the community and the healthcare system.

6388. (5-3-2008) NEW DELHI : The Andhra Pradesh Health Sector Reforms Programme (APHSRP) was jointly developed by UK's Department for International Developments (DFID) and Government of Andhra Pradesh. The programme, which will cost £ 40 million over three years, was approved by DFID in June, 2007 and the exchange of letters with the Department of Economic Affairs was signed in September, 2007. The first tranche of £ 9.5 million was released to implement the agreed priorities of the AP Health Sector Reforms Strategy and Work Plan for 2007-08. The programme is being implemented by the Department of Health, Medical and Family Affairs, Government of Andhra Pradesh. A technical Cooperation Support Agency is expected to be in place by March, 2008. The health sector support will be provided over three years (2007-08-2009-10). It aims at increased use of quality health services, especially by the poorest people and in underserved areas.

6389. (5-3-2008) NEW DELHI : As per data compiled by Bureau of Police Research and Development (BPR&D) the number of Police personnel per one lakh of population in India as on 1.1.2006, is 1:142.69. (142.69 Police Personnel for every 1 lakh population) No information as to the police and population ratio of other countries is being compiled by BPR&D. However, as per the report prepared by UN Division for Policy Analysis and Public Affairs available on the web site of United Nations released on 31st March, 2005, such ratio in some of the countries are like, Italy (559.0), Mexico (491.8), Saudi Arabia (386.5) and Belgium (357.5) which have much higher Police-Population ratio than India (136.4) during the year 2002 for every 1,00,000 (one hundred thousands) population. As per the VII Schedule to the Constitution of India 'Police' and 'law and order' are State subjects. Therefore, the primary responsibility to decide about the composition of their police forces, as also modernizing and equipping them adequately, to face the challenges to internal security, is on the State Govts. However, the Central Government has been advising all the State Governments to fill up the existing vacancies of police personnel and outsource some of the non-core police duties which will also save manpower and promote police-community partnership. This information was given by the Minister of State in the Ministry of Home Affairs, Shri Sriprakash Jaiswal in a written reply to a question in Rajya Sabha today.

6390. (5-3-2008) NEW DELHI : The Central Government has recently approved the raising of 35 additional India Reserve (IR) battalions during the period 2007-08 to 2009-10, to be sanctioned, as per the internal security situation and requirements, to various States, including those affected by naxalite activities. In the 9 states, Andhra Pradesh, Bihar, Chhattisgarh, Jharkhand, Orissa, Maharashtra, Madhya Pradesh, Uttar Pradesh and West Bengal, where, for dealing with naxalite activities, assistance for the policing and operational needs of security forces is provided under the Security Related Expenditure (SRE) scheme of Ministry of Home Affairs, 26 IR battalions have already been sanctioned earlier. These have added to the capabilities of the State police forces in dealing with various law and order problems. For dealing with naxalite activities, States are being assisted in, and requested for, steps as are important for effective policing, which include filling up of vacancies in State police forces and the raising of specialized forces, trained in counter-insurgency and jungle-warfare. This information was given by the Minister of State in the Ministry of Home Affairs, Shri Sriprakash Jaiswal in a written reply to a question in Rajya Sabha today.

6391. (5-3-2008) NEW DELHI : To mark the 'International Women's Day (8th March)', a Blood Donation Camp was organized on 05 Mar 08 by Air Force Wives Welfare Association (Local) at Station Medicare Centre, Air Force Station, Race Course, New Delhi. Air Commodore S Misra, Air Officer Commanding Air Force Station New Delhi inaugurated the camp. The event was organized under the guidance and support of Dr. (Mrs) M Misra, President AFWWA (L) and Gp Capt SC Kabra, SMO, Air Force Station Race Course. Many Senior Air Force Officers, ladies and airmen attended the event and donated 186 blood units to Armed Forces Transfusion Centre, Delhi Cantt. The blood will be utilized for needy patients admitted to Army Hospital (R&R) and Base Hospital Delhi Cantt.

6392. (5-3-2008) NEW DELHI : The Minister for Steel, Chemicals and Fertilisers Shri Ram Vilas Paswan has urged the steel industry to exercise restraint on increasing prices. Delivering the inaugural address at the "Summit on Mining to Steel Making" organized by the Indian Chamber of Commerce here today, the Minister said every price hike should have some relevance with the rise in cost. He said, the government has accepted several of the recommendations of the steel ministry and these have been incorporated in the latest Union Budget. Noting that any price rise of steel indirectly affects basic consumer goods Shri Paswan asked the steel industry to appreciate the sensitive relationship. The Minister said, steel producers had responded positively to his request for partial roll back and urged the industry to ensure that any price reduction should be reflected in the retail prices. Shri Paswan said, the price monitoring committee can play an effective role only with the cooperation of all concerned. On the growth of the steel sector the Minister said, the government is alive to the problems of the steel sector and will take all steps to remove hurdles on increasing capacity. He said, Indian steel sector is set for rapid expansion with production likely to touch 124 million tonnes by 2011-12. He said, the consumption of steel is growing at 14-16 per cent at least for next 7 years. Therefore there is a need to expedite the ongoing steel projects. He said, one of the critical problems facing the growth of steel sector is the need for a sound policy on allocation of iron ore mines,. He said, the steel ministry has always favoured priority in allocation of iron ore mines to the domestic value addition in the country itself. He said, export of iron ore should be limited to the quantity only after meeting the domestic steel production. The Minister said, there is also a need for conservation of iron ore as well as its scientific use through better technologies and beneficiation methods.

6393. (5-3-2008) NEW DELHI : Agriculture Minister, Shri Sharad Pawar today called for sharing farm technology and experience among the SAARC countries to reduce poverty in the region. Cooperation in the agriculture sector is of special significance for this region as about 60 per cent of the people in South Asia are still dependent directly on agriculture for their livelihood and also because agriculture has been growing at mere 2 per cent per year, he said. Shri Pawar was addressing Conference on Science based Agricultural Transformation Towards Alleviation of Hunger and Poverty in SAARC Countries. Ministers, officials, scientists and farmers from SAARC countries will deliberate upon the issues relating to use of science in agriculture over the next three days. Sharing information about the vast network of research institutions and agriculture universities in India, the Agriculture Minister offered cooperation in agriculture R&D to other SAARC nations. Shri Pawar also highlighted the need for intra-region trade in South Asia, which is only 0.8 per cent of GDP as compared to nearly 27 per cent in the East Asia. He expressed the need to strengthen the South Asian Free Trade Area (SAFTA). The Agriculture Minister stressed that investments and regional cooperation in R&D must be at the top of policy agenda of SAARC countries. The Minister said, ' with agriculture becoming complex today, we need science and technology interventions at a much larger scale at all stages of agricultural chain. The urgency of enhancing agricultural productivity, bridging yield gaps and strengthening regional agricultural research, extension and farmer linkages can hardly be overemphasized.... It is well accepted that investments in R&D pay off handsomely with appreciable high internal rate of return. Given the agro-climatic advantages and availability of man power, there is potential to turn agriculture in the SAARC region into a dynamic sector with rapid technological innovation accelerating growth and reducing poverty.' The Conference has been organized jointly by the Agriculture Ministry, ICAR and IFFCO Foundation. Besides country representatives, Dr. M.S. Swaminathan, Shri Suresh Prabhu, MP, and Dr. Mangala Rai, DG, ICAR also address the Conference.

6394. (5-3-2008) NEW DELHI : The Indian textiles industry has been demanding various concessions, which include the refund of State and local levies, higher rates of Duty Entitlement Pass Book (DEPB) and Duty Drawback, etc., to cope with the adverse situation arising due to the recent appreciation of the Indian rupee vis-a-vis the US dollar. The Government has, in response, introduced several measures to provide relief to the affected exporters, which include increase in Duty Entitlement Pass Book and Duty Drawback rates, exemption from service tax on select services, reduction in interest rates of pre-shipment and post-shipment credit and faster clearance of arrears of terminal excise duties and Central Sales Tax. This information was given by the Minister of State for Textiles, Shri E.V.K.S. Elangovan, in the Rajya Sabha today, in a written reply to a question by Shri Mahendra Mohan. The Minister further informed that as per the latest available figures of World Trade Organization, India's share in world trade of textiles and clothing in 2006 was 4.3% and 3.3%, respectively.

6395. (5-3-2008) NEW DELHI : Shri Arjun Singh, Human Resource Development Minister has said that Even the most Impressive and Robust Economic Progress is Rendered Meaningless if Social Development Lags Behind. he also said that one of the most critical aspects of social development has to do with education. Provision of free and compulsory education for the relevant age group of 6 to 14 years has been mandated by our Constitution as a fundamental right, and we are in the process of making a law dedicated to this objective. He was inaugurating second Meeting of the Regional Forum of Ministers of Social Development of SAARC here today. Shri Singh further added Education is also a sector where each of our nations has a vital stake. Even though there are limits to public funding, and there may be temptations to opt for market determined policies on grounds of efficiency, education can be left to the market forces only at our peril. That is why in India we have a nine-fold allocation proposed for education in our 11th Five Year Plan over the 10th Plan. 'Expansion of opportunities must be accompanied by a concern for equity-particularly, in the access to education for the marginalized sections of populations. Apart from education, there are equally good reasons for focusing on the other social development issues-public health, for example' he added. As a sequel to the First Forum of Ministers on Social Development of South Asia who met on 26-27 May 2006 in Bhurban, Pakistan, this Meeting is the second in the series of UNESCO's and the Regions initiative to organise a network of Asian Ministers of Social Development. The purpose of the Forum is to establish a network among the countries of the region to address issues related to social justice and development in the overall theme of the social sciences research and its policy-linkages and in particular, the contribution that social sciences can provide to the policy making process. As agreed at Bhurban, India has been honoured by member countries by asking her to assume the Chair of the Forum for the current year. The theme selected for the Second Forum *i.e.* Transparency, Right to Information and Social Development' reflects the shared vision of good governance common to all the Governments of the region. The Ministers of Social Development of South Asian countries, from Afghanistan, Maldives, Ministers of Women, Children & Social Welfare from Bangladesh, Nepal and Sri Lanka and Minister of Education from Bhutan participated in the meeting. Mr. Skweyiya, Minister of Social Development of South Africa and the President of the Management of Social Transformation-MOST Programme and Mr. Pierre Sane' from UNESCO also spoke during the inauguration function.

6396. (5-3-2008) NEW DELHI : Several Indian companies engaged in publishing newspapers and periodicals dealing with news and current affairs have been allowed to bring in Foreign Direct Investment (FDI) subject to the maximum limit of 26% of their paid up equity capital. A large number of Indian companies publishing scientific/technical and speciality magazines/periodicals/journals have been permitted to bring in FDI up to the maximum limit of 100% of their paid up equity capital. Permission has been given for publication of 107 magazines/ journals in the speciality/scientific/technical sector by Indian companies having FDI. In addition, permissions have been granted for publication of 172 magazines/ journals as Indian editions of various foreign magazines/journals in the scientific/ speciality/technical sector. As such there are no factors preventing foreign media from entering India. This information was given by Minister of Information & Broadcasting and Parliamentary Affairs, Shri P. R. Dasmunsi in written reply to a question in Rajya Sabha today.

6397. (5-3-2008) NEW DELHI : During the current financial year [up to 22/ 02/2008] an amount of Rs. 17.5 crores has been spent by the Government on newspaper advertisements through DAVP. Central Government advertisements released through DAVP to newspapers, magazines, radio and TV, are meant to create awareness amongst the public, whereas internet facilities may not be accessible to a large majority of the public. DAVP does not issue any personal or political advertisement. The DAVP endeavours to right size the advertisement according to the content. An audit on how effective is Government's spending on communication is done through impact studies are undertaken from time to time, through professional communication research organisations. This information was given by Minister of Information & Broadcasting and Parliamentary Affairs, Shri P. R. Dasmunsi in written reply to a question in Rajya Sabha today.

6398. (5-3-2008) NEW DELHI : Exercise BRAZEN CHARIOTS, a Fire and Manoeuvre, Army-Air Force, combat exercise will be conducted by one of India's Desert Formations in the Desert Sector on 19 March. The exercise will be witnessed by a host of foreign dignitaries and Defence Attaches of friendly foreign countries. The exercise has been set to project the Manoeuvre Warfare Doctrine which has since been promulgated in the Indian Armed Forces and is seen as a breakaway from the traditional attritionist approach of the Army. The Army is putting to test all of its latest weapon system acquisitions, to include the state of the art missile firing tanks T-90 (Bhishma), all weather Air Defence Gun Missile Systems, Searcher UAVs and other electronic sensors and surveillance equipment. The Indian Air Force during this Exercise would be closely supporting the surface forces with its frontline fighter aircraft like the SU-30 Mk I and Jaguar, unleashing variety of ordnance. The exercise will also involve deployment of a comprehensive communication and data linking systems incorporating Battlefield Surveillance System and Force Multiplier Command Post. While the acquisition of hi-tech weaponry and war fighting support systems is an essential pre-requisite to success in battle, honing human skills to be able to apply infinite technology advancements in military hardware is a never ending challenge faced by modern armies of the world, the Indian Army being no exception. During the conduct of Exercise BRAZEN CHARIOTS, combat decisions taken at each level of command will be analysed for their ability to synergise the application of state-of-the-art weapon platforms to achieve optimum results aimed at causing pre-emption, disruption and dislocation of opposing forces.

6399. (5-3-2008) NEW DELHI : Army Wives Welfare Association (AWWA) runs a large number of schools for disabled children across the nation. These schools for disabled children are called 'AWWA ASHA SCHOOLS'. Under the guidance of President AWWA Mrs Kirti Kapoor, the Chairperson Mrs Renuka Sree Kumar organised a two day seminar on 03-04 Mar at Delhi Cantonment. A number of eminent research scholars and social workers were the guest speakers in the seminar who shared their thoughts on issues like 'Intervention for Primary Prevention', 'Inclusive Education for Disabled Children'. 'Threatening Diseases causing Disability in Childhood', 'Infant care of Children with Special needs' and many more covering the issues relating to upbringing of children with special needs. The two day seminar was interactive and gave a common platform to share points of views to both professional experts and representatives of the AWWA ASHA schools. The seminar gave an opportunity to develop a better understanding to empower the differently abled children as early as possible and an awareness of long term programmes to enable them to be an essential part of the mainstream. Confederation of Indian Industry representative Mrs Pamela Bhagat brought out the innumerable opportunities available to the differently abled in the private sector and highlighted the numerous initiatives taken up by industry to help people with special needs to join the mainstream.

6400. (5-3-2008) NEW DELHI : Following is the text of the address of the Vice President of India Mohd. Hamid Ansari at the presentation of the Saraswati Samman Awards for 2006 and 2007 at the National Museum here today: "Philanthropy as a social virtue and as a source of public good is inadequately appreciated in our country and insufficiently harnessed. It takes vision, courage and commitment to give away personal fortune to the society than to one's progeny. An enabling social environment helps it in considerable measure. As a society, and exceptions apart, we must do more on both counts. This evening we focus on what is an outstanding exception. The K. K. Birla Foundation deserves appreciation for promoting literature and the arts, and especially for its focus on literature in Hindi and other Indian languages. Language embodies the soul of a people and the diversity of our languages is expressive of the soul of India. The Saraswati Samman, along with the Vyas Samman, the Bihari Puraskar and the Vachaspati Puraskar have immensely contributed to recognition of excellence. The Foundation has also encouraged works in Hindi on Indian philosophy, culture and art through the Shankar Puraskar and has supported work on comparative Indian literature though fellowships.

6401. (5-3-2008) NEW DELHI : The Plan outlay for Maharashtra for the year 2008-09 was finalized at a meeting, here today, between the Deputy Chairman Planning Commission, Shri Montek Singh Ahluwalia and Chief Minister of Maharashtra, Shri Vilasrao Deshmukh. The Annual Plan size was agreed at Rs.25000 crores. This includes additional Central assistance of Rs.250 crores for projects of special interest to the State. Deputy Chairman, Planning Commission, Mr. Ahluwalia complimented the State for fiscal performance. He said performance in both human development and growth rate was satisfactory. The State is all set to achieve growth rate above national target for the Eleventh Plan. Against 3.8 per cent growth rate in Ninth Plan, the State has recorded growth of 8.2 per cent in the Tenth Plan. Improving urban infrastructure, housing, irrigation and agriculture should be given priority during the Eleventh Plan. Performance in agriculture and efforts aimed at accelerating socio-economic up-liftment of minority were appreciated. He said the Commission was keen to improve performance of Centrally sponsored programmes and invited suggestions on flexibility needed in the guidelines of these programmes. The Centre was keen to improve connectivity with Mumbai and Western Freight Corridor Construction Work was likely to begin this year. He said the State Government should supplement Centre's efforts to improve infrastructure. Public Private Partnership needs to be encouraged to accelerate this process. Attention was drawn to depleting forest cover, rural poverty and child sex ratio. It was pointed out that State needs to step up efforts in power sector as power shortage would hamper State's initiatives to encourage investment. The State was also advised to revisit rent control act as it could affect plans to make Mumbai an international financial centre. Emphasis should also be given to skill development and State should benefit from Centre's initiative in this regard. Briefing the Commission on State's performance and strategy for the Eleventh Plan, the Chief Minister said that infrastructure development would be taken up on BOT basis so as to release funds for social sector. Emphasis would be given to improving health, nutrition, education standards and economic growth of population so as to contain population growth rate. Balanced regional growth would be promoted and focused attention will be given to further increase agriculture production. To improve socio-economic indicators programmes like NRHM, SSA,

NREGS, Bharat Nirman, JNNURM, BRGF and ARWSP would be vigorously implemented. Thrust areas of Annual Plan would be poverty alleviation, employment generation, 20-point Programme, Minimum Needs Programme, Tribal Sub-plan, Special Component Plan, Programmes for Removal of Regional Imbalances and Infrastructure Development.

6402. (6-3-2008) NEW DELHI : The Department of Science & Technology is organizing a two-day National Conference on the theme of Showcasing Cutting Edge of Science & Technology by Women on 8-9 March, 2008. The conference will be inaugurated by the Hon'ble President of India, Smt. Pratibha Devisingh Patil on the International Women's Day. Shri Kapil Sibal, Minister for Science & Technology and Earth Sciences will preside over the function. The Venue of the conference is Vigyan Bhawan, New Delhi.

6403. (6-3-2008) NEW DELHI : Upon the invitation of Shri. Arjun Singh, Minister of Human Development Resource (MHRD) of the Republic of India, the Second Forum of Ministers of Social Development from South Asia met on 5 and 6 March 2008 in New Delhi, India. Ministers and High Level Officials from Afghanistan, Bhutan, Maldives, Nepal, Pakistan and Sri Lanka attended the meeting. The meeting was co-organized with UNESCO. H.E. Mr. Wasil Noor Mohmand, Deputy Minister of Labour Social Affairs, Martyrs and Disabled of Afghanistan, Ms Rasheda K.Chowdry, Honourable Adviser, Ministry of Women and Children Affairs, Bangladesh, H.E. Mr. Lyonpo Thinley Gyamtsho, Minister of Education, Royal Government of Bhutan, H.E. Shri Arjun Singh, Minister of Human Resource Development, and H.E. Mrs. Purandeswari, Minister of State for Human Resource Development, India, Ms Racheeda Ali, Deputy Minister of Planning and National Development, Maldives, H.E. Ms. Pampha Bhusal, Minister for Women, Children and Social Welfare, Nepal, H.E. Mr. Shahid Malik, High Commissioner, High Commission for the Islamic Republic of Pakistan, and H.E. Douglas Devananda, Minister of Social Services and Social Welfare, Sri Lanka, participated in the meeting. H.E. Mr. Zola Sidney Skweyiya, Minister of Social Development, South Africa, and President of the MOST Programme, as well as Mr. Pierre Sané, UNESCO's Assistant Director-General for Social and Human Sciences and the Representative of the Indian Council of Social Science Research (ICSSR), Prof. T.C.A. Anant also attended the meeting.

6404. (6-3-2008) NEW DELHI : The President of India has accepted the resignation of Shri S.M. Krishna as Governor of Maharashtra and has appointed Shri S.C. Jamir, Governor of Goa to discharge the functions of the Governor of Maharashtra in addition to his own duties, until regular arrangements for the office of the Governor of Maharashtra are made.

6405. (7-3-2008) NEW DELHI : The Union Cabinet today gave its approval to the following proposals : i) The amalgamation / merger of the Central Indian

Pharmacopoeia Laboratory (CIPL), Ghaziabad with Indian Pharmacopoeia Commission (IPC). ii) The transfer of staff, assets and liabilities including buildings and all other existing infrastructure belonging to the CIPL, Ghaziabad to the control of IPC; iii) To authorize the IPC to make use of the staff and infrastructure of the CIPL, Ghaziabad; iv) Creation and filling up of 13 restructured additional posts in the IPC in lieu of 38 vacant posts in CIPL, which would be abolished simultaneously; v) Upgrade the post of Director, CIPL from the scale of Rs. 14300-18300 to Rs. 18400-22400, so as to function as the Secretary-cum-Scientific Director of the IPC; vi) Filling up of the vacancies arising due to resignation, retirement etc., of the existing incumbents of the resultant 80 posts belonging to the original CIPL.

6406. (7-3-2008) NEW DELHI : The Union Cabinet today gave its approval for long-term reconstruction plan for restoration of damaged in the States of (i) Andhra Pradesh (ii) Gujarat (iii) Himachal Pradesh (iv) Karnataka (v) Kerala (vi) Madhya Pradesh (vii) Maharashtra (viii) Tamil Nadu and (ix) Uttar Pradesh, at a cost of Rs. 5368.37 crore to be implemented over a period of two years and release of Additional Central Assistance for implementing the Plan to the affected States as an additionality to Gross Budgetary Support. This will enable the affected States to undertake long-term reconstruction of the damaged infrastructure. The affected States will implement the Reconstruction Plan in a period of two years *i.e.* 2007-08 and 2008-09.

6407. (7-3-2008) NEW DELHI : The Union Cabinet today gave its approval to release of 50% share of the Central Government *i.e.*, Rs. 50 lakh towards contribution for the establishment of a Regional Rural Bank in the Union Territory of Pondichery to be sponsored by Indian Bank. This decision will assist in expanding the network of RRBs in uncovered areas. The Issued Capital of each stand-alone RRB is Rs. 1 crore and accordingly the proposed Issued Capital of the RRB to be established in UT of Pondichery be Rs. 1 crore.

6408. (7-3-2008) NEW DELHI : The Union Cabinet today gave its approval to release of a sum of Rs. 2615 crore (subject to actuals) as interest subvention to Public Sector Banks, Regional Rural Banks, Cooperative Banks and to NABARD for refinance to RRBs and Cooperative Banks at concessional rates to reimburse the amount of interest subvention for the decision that the farmer should receive short terms credit at 7% p.a. with an upper limit of Rs. 3 lakhs on the principal amount during 2007-08. The borrowers who avail short term crop loans up to Rs. 3 lakhs will be instantly benefited.

6409. (7-3-2008) NEW DELHI : The Union Cabinet today gave its approval to release of additional instalment of dearness allowance to the Central Government employees and dearness relief to pensioners due from 1.1.2008, in cash, at the rate of 6% over the existing rate of 41%. Thus, The rate of DA from 1.1.2008 will be 47%. The Central Government employees and pensioners will become entitled to higher amount of dearness allowance / relief respectively 1.1.2008. The combined impact on the exchequer on account of both dearness allowance and dearness relief would be of the order of Rs. 3297.12 crore in a full year and Rs. 3846.66 crore in the financial year 2008-2009 (for a period of 14 months from January 2008 to February, 2009).

6410. (7-3-2008) NEW DELHI : The Cabinet Committee on Economic Affairs today gave its approval for implementation of Panchayat Yuva Krida Aur Khel Abhiyan (PYKKA). Under the Scheme, each village Panchayat and each Block Panchayat would be given one time seed capital grant of Rs.1 lakh and Rs.5 lakh, respectively. In addition, while village panchayats would be given annual acquisition grant and annual operational grant at Rs.10000 and Rs.12000 per annum, respectively, block panchayats would be given Rs.20000 and 24000 respectively. Each block panchayat would also be provided annual competition grant of Rs.50000 for holding block level competitions and each district will be provided annual competition grant of Rs.3 lakh for holding district level competitions. Further, prize money would also be provided to the winners (first three positions) in block level and district level competitions. The Mission outlay for the 11th Five Year Plan is Rs.1500 crore. PYKKA aims at providing basic sports infrastructure and promoting games/sports in rural areas in a phased and time-bound manner through concerted efforts of all stakeholders, particularly the State Governments, panchayats, educational institutes, sports promotion bodies and youth clubs. Apart from contributing to public health, social inclusiveness, the promotion of indigenous games and the identification and nurturing of rural sports talent, PYKKA is also expected to stimulate the economic activities within the sports sector, as it would lead to an exponential growth in the demand for sports instructors, coaches, sports equipment and consumables and sports events and related support services.

6411. (7-3-2008) NEW DELHI : The Cabinet Committee on Economic Affairs today gave its approval for the following: (i) Implementation of the polio eradication strategy with estimated expenditure of Rs.2344.56 crore. (ii) The number of SNID (Sub National Immunization Day) rounds in high-risk States / areas and their coverage each year will depend upon the recommendations of IEAG made from time to time. (iii) The funding guidelines for Operational Cost will remain the same (a) the quantum of honorarium to vaccinators and supervisors will be increased from Rs.25/50 to Rs.75 respectively; (b) The cost of POL will be increased from Rs.400 per vehicle per day to Rs.650 per vehicle per day. (iv) The Department of H&FW will be permitted to negotiate with the World Bank and other external funding agencies and access external funds in order to bridge the gap between total requirements and availability so that reliance on domestic budgetary resources could be reduced to the minimum. Elimination of polio will improve the quality of lives of those otherwise affected by polio involving life long disability, thus improving national productivity and eliminating wasteful expense on treatment and rehabilitation.

6412. (7-3-2008) NEW DELHI : The Cabinet Committee on Economic Affairs today gave its approval for implementation of the Central Sector Plan Scheme of "Assistance to States/UTs for Conducting 18th Livestock Census" during the Eleventh Five Year Plan period (2007012) with an outlay of Rs.301.34 crore. The entire funding will be done by the Central Government. The approval would help in the collection of detailed data on livestock, poultry, agricultural implements & machinery and fishery statistics and infrastructure related to these sectors and their computerization and report publication. The Livestock Census data provides basis for planning and formulation of schemes aimed at bringing further development in the Animal Husbandry, Poultry and Fisheries Sectors. Data helps in taking up various research projects in this sector which ultimately guide in deciding the types of programmes to be initiated in the given situations. It provides necessarily required frame for planning and execution of Integrated Sample Surveys meant for annual estimation of various livestock products viz; milk meat, egg, wool.

6413. (7-3-2008) NEW DELHI : The Vice President of India Shri Mohd. Hamid Ansari released the book titled "War of Civilizations: India AD 1857"- (Volume I-The Road to Delhi; & Volume II-The Long Revolution) authored by the writer/ journalist Shri Amaresh Mishra at a function here today. Addressing on the occasion, the Vice President said that writing such a voluminous book is an extra-ordinary success. Referring to the sources in the book he said that these sources are well-authenticated. He said that 1857 revolt was a revolution which failed because it was not sufficiently organized and many people did not join it. Congratulating the author the Vice President said that he has done a great service to the nation. The book showcases a West, the West has never seen, an Asia which Asians are unaware of and a story of the 'Indian Mutiny' which has never been told before. The whole Asia-Europe conflict gets a new slant. Accessible to scholars, historians, lay readers, students of military adventure and battles, ideologies, action and drama, the story of 1857 resonates with smells and sounds of an Indian caravanserai, the auburn-gray picture of high sounding, Victorian England. The author Shri Amresh Mishra gave a brief description of the book. Former Ministers Shri K. Natwar Singh and Shri Salman Khurshid also addressed. Many dignitaries were present on the occasion.

6414. (7-3-2008) NEW DELHI : The Ministry of Rural Development has granted Rs.63.95 crore to the State Government of Bihar under the Revised Sub Mission Programme of Water Quality under Rajiv Gandhi National Drinking Water Mission (RGNDWM)-a Centrally Sponsored Programme of Accelerated Rural Water Supply Programme (ARWSP) during the current financial year (2007-08). The first instalment of Rs.200.17 lakh *i.e.* 45% of GOI share of Rs.442.82 lakh is being released to tackle 11 Iron ore affected habitations spread over two districts of

Purnea and Katihar. Secondly, Rs. 6194.83 lakh as part of first instalment of Rs.12805.00 lakh *i.e.* 45% of total GOI share of Rs.28457.48 lakh is being released to tackle 551 Arsenic and Fluoride affected habitations spread over 19 districts of the state. The State Government will ensure to provide State share for implementation of projects and revised guidelines on Sub-Mission of water quality shall be followed.

6415. (7-3-2008) NEW DELHI : The Ministry of Rural Development has authorized the National Rural Road Development Agency (NRRDA) for the drawl of Rs.105,96,00,000/- (One Hundred Five Crore Ninety Six lakh) as First Instalment of Phase-VI from the special window created in National Bank for Agriculture and Rural Development (NABARD) under RIDF towards payment for works taken up the Pradhan Mantri Gram Sadak Yojana (PMGSY) as Grants-in-Aid to the Sikkim Rural Road Development Agency, an autonomous agency for receiving the funds for the programme during the current financial year (2007-08). The grant is towards plan expenditure and is subject to the provisions of PMGSY Programme Guidelines and supplementary directions issued there under.

6416. (7-3-2008) NEW DELHI : The Home Secretary level talks between India and Myanmar began here today. The Indian delegation is being led by the Union Home Secretary, Shri Madhukar Gupta and the Myanmar delegation by their Deputy Minister of Home Affairs, Brig. Gen. Phone Swe. The discussions are taking place on various issues including security-related matters, smuggling of arms and narcotic drugs, effective border management, border trade and cross-border projects. This is the 14th round of annual Home Secretary level talks between the two countries. The talks would conclude on Monday. The previous round of talks was held in Myanmar in February last year.

6417. (7-3-2008) NEW DELHI : The celebrated scientist Marie Curie once said, "Life is not easy for any of us. But what of that? We must have perseverance and above all, confidence in ourselves. We must believe that we are gifted for something and that this thing must be attained." Over the years women in India have overcome the traditional mindsets and have excelled in professions like teaching, medicine and pure sciences. Women have made important contributions in all walks of life and made inroads into new fields like engineering and information technology. In India, of the women science graduates, 88 % of the science degree holders are in pure science,.8% in medicine and 3% in engineering and technology. Recently there has been a spurt of women joining the engineering and information technology fields and the number of women in computing and internet industries have also registered a sharp rise. Still the percentage of women scientists sustaining R&D careers in science is very low compared to the number of women postgraduates in science. This may partly be attributed to break in career due to marriage, child birth and rearing. Moreover in a country as large as India there are a lot of regional disparities depending on the socio-economic background which decide the choice of careers.

6418. (7-3-2008) NEW DELHI : The Defence Minister Shri AK Antony has commended the Armed Forces for leading the way in organ donation. Felicitating families of organ donors at a function here today, Shri Antony said that the men in uniform have also set example in organ donation, even in medico-legal cases. He lauded the medical fraternity for its efforts to treat patients suffering from liver related diseases and the research in this field. Shri Antony said that organ donation is crucial to the development of a vibrant transplant programme in our country. Shri Antony was speaking after inaugurating the 16th Annual Conference of the Indian National Association for Study of Liver (INASL), being organized this year by the Army Medical Corps. The three daylong conference is witnessing the coming together of the top doctors specializing in hepatic disorders and research, and organ transplants. After the welcome address by the eminent liver specialist Dr. YK Chawla, who is also the President of the INASL, the Director General of the Armed Forces Medical Services, Lt Gen Yogendra Singh addressed the gathering. On the occasion, a booklet containing vital information on the brain stem death and organ donation was released by Lt Gen S Mukherjee, the Director General of Medical Services of the Army. It may be recalled that the Army Medical Corps is doing yeoman service in the field of organ donation through Army Organ Retrieval and Transplant Organisation (AORTA). Just into its second year of being, AORTA's services have benefited several patients in need of organs, not only in the armed forces but also civilians. In some cases the organs from a single donor have given a new lease to life to five or more organ recipients. It has also undertaken the retrieval of organs from the donors who were involved in medico legal cases. In such cases it has received the cooperation of the Delhi Police, police from other states such as Uttar Pradesh and doctors from the forensic department of Safdarjung Hospital, New Delhi. This organization which operates from Army Hospital (R&R) has been guided by its Commandant, Maj Gen OP Mathew and Brig RP Choubey, Head of Gastrointestinal Surgery at that hospital. Director AORTA, Col AK Seth and his team introduced the families of the donors, who were felicitated by Shri AK Antony. Lt Col (Mrs) Pradhi Nambiar, the coordinator of this hugely successful programme, who is instrumental in explaining to the kin of the patients various aspects of organ donation, was also present. Armymen and personnel of the three forces have led the way in organ donation in the country, setting example by their service to humanity. Leading the way, an army officer Maj Sidharth Malik donated the organs of his little 18 month old son Shaurya Malik who fell off the balcony accidentally in December 2006. His eyes gave sight to two, while his kidneys saved the life of a 31 year old man. Major S.K. Singh of the Artillery Regiment agreed to donate his father's liver when doctors at the Army Research and Referral Hospital here pronounced him brain dead. The retired schoolteacher P.N. Singh (72) was brought here on January 9 last year and treated for two days for brain hemorrhage and a massive stroke. It was transplanted successfully on a 45-year-old Hyderabad-based man suffering from an end stage liver ailment. His cornea was also donated.

6419. (7-3-2008) NEW DELHI : Congress spokesman Smt. Jayanthi Natarajan introduced the newly appointed president of the All India Mahila Congress Smt. Prabha Thakur, MP, who is also a member of DEPCO apart from being past president and general secretary of Rajasthan Mahila Congress and also of Rajasthan Pradesh Congress Committee. Smt. Jayanthi said that the Congress President and the Prime Minister will be present at the rally which will be held on 9 March at the Ramlila grounds to focus attention on the tremendous support that is being extended to the farmers and the agricultural sector by the UPA government in pursuance of the promises under the Common Minimum Programme. On 10 March all CLP leaders and PCC presidents have been asked to come to Delhi to take this message to the farmers that this has been done for their welfare, to take advantage of all the benefits that have been extended to them by the UPA government. On 31 March there will be state level conventions in this regard and rallies will be held to highlight the achievements of the UPA government including extension of National Rural Employment Guarantee Scheme which will be attended by Central ministers, AICC leaders as well as the state leaders. Farmers conventions and rallies will also be held throughout March and April to highlight the benefits that have been extended to the farmers as also state level conventions on Tribal rights and the Tribal Rights Bill will be organised in Gujarat, Rajasthan, Maharshtra, Madhya Pradesh, Chhattisgarh, Jharkhand, Orissa, Karnataka and other states. These will be followed by district level conventions and workshops to guide Tribals and other forest dwellers on how to get pattas for land which has been allotted to them. To a question that your party in Tripura has suffered a crushing defeat and CPM general secretary Shri Prakash Karat said the Congress Party should learn a lesson for two reasons, one on the rejection of the economic policy and the other on the party joining hands with extremist forces, what is your response? Smt. Jayanthi said we accept the verdict of the people of Tripura in all humility and we certainly will examine the factors that have led to this. We would also like to reflect upon our comparative success in Meghalaya. But coming back to Tripura we strongly believe, from information coming back to us, that this is certainly due to local factors. It cannot, by any stretch of argument or logic, be extended to a referendum on economic policy. The most outstanding feature of the Budget was, in fact, the tremendous step taken towards waiving the loans of small farmers and by no means can this be construed as a rejection of a people-friendly Budget or a people-friendly economic policy. In a democracy there are wins as well as defeats. We take the defeats in our stride. We use our successes to continue our service to the people and we will do the same in this case as well. It is by no means any commentary or reflection on the UPA government at the Centre but entirely confined to localized factors. To a question that according to results the Congress Party is leading in Meghalaya, does it mean a popular mandate for the party and a better coordination with the Left? Smt. Jayanthi said the UPA-led coordination is an ongoing process which will continue at the Centre and you are aware that at the state level we have our differences, we have different governments and the national government of the UPA will continue its good work and continue with the joint mechanism. To a question on the Nuke-deal that whether the Congress Party stands by Shri Pranab Mukherjee's statement that the deal gets precedence and you need to take the Left along, Smt Jayanthi said we have taken a consistent stand that the nuke deal is very important for the welfare of the country and it is in the national interest and it will be our effort to make sure the deal goes through smoothly. However, we will make every effort to take all our allies with us and that is why the joint mechanism has been set up and that process will continue.

6420. (7-3-2008) NEW DELHI : The Union Minister of Shipping, Road Transport and Highways, Thiru T.R. Baalu has approved a sum of Rs. 497.58 lakh for road improvement works at National Highway-209 in the state of Tamil Nadu. The stretch between km 227/6-230/0 of this Highway in Satyamangalam town limit in Erode District would be strengthened on Dindigul-Pollachi-Coimbatore-Sathyamangalam-Bangalore road. NH-209 is an inter-state road connecting major cities and towns like Dindigul, Palani, Coimbatore, Sathyamangalm in Tamil Nadu and Chamraj Nagar, Kollegal, Bangalore in Karnataka. The riding surface of the stretch was badly damaged during the last monsoon. The riding surface is deteriorated, potholes, patches have developed in this stretch and therefore, it has become absolutely necessary to repair this stretch.

6421. (7-3-2008) NEW DELHI : In exercise of the powers conferred by Section 3 of Essential Commodities Act, 1955 (10 of 1955) the Central Government issued the Wheat (Stock declaration by Companies or Firms or Individuals) Order 2008 vide notification dated 11.2.2008. The order requires submission of return by a Company or Firm or Individual who purchases wheat in excess of 10,000 metric tonnes (total purchases made throughout the country) during the Rabi Marketing Season 2008-09 (April-March) shall furnish to the Secretary, Department of Food of the State from where maximum quantity has been purchased, a return in the Form at such interval as may be specified by the Central Government. In case the purchase of wheat exceeds 25,000 Metric Tonnes (total purchases made throughout the country), the return in the Form at such intervals specified therein shall be furnished to the Under Secretary (Policy-III), Department of Food & Public Distribution, Room No. 292, Krishi Bhawan, New Delhi-110001 (Fax No. 011-23782213, e-mail: uspy34.fpd@nic.in). The concerned State Governments with which the returns are filed by any Company or Firm or Individual in Form declaring purchase of wheat in excess of 10,000 Metric Tonnes shall submit a consolidated monthly report to the Under Secretary (Py-III), Department of Food and Public Distribution by the 10th of every month. Ministry of Consumer Affairs, Food and Public Distribution, (Department of Food & Public Distribution).

6422. (7-3-2008) NEW DELHI : The Minister of Health and Family Welfare, Government of Tamil Nadu, Thiru M.R.K. Panneerselvam along with senior officials from the State Health Department met the Union Health Minister, Dr. Anbumani Ramadoss today. The ongoing healthcare programmes in the State under the National Rural Health Mission (NRHM) and strengthening the mission further were discussed at the meeting. Welcoming the State Health Minister, Dr. Ramadoss congratulated the Government of Tamil Nadu on managing one of the finest public health systems in the country. He said the resources of the NRHM have been very effectively utilized by the State administration to improve the quality of services available in Government health facilities in the State. He further said that Tamil Nadu has set a very good example of making the public health sector so good that it has become the facility of first choice for many households. This shift is indeed remarkable as public systems are often criticized for poor quality services. The dramatic shift in institutional deliveries and other patient care services and the engagement of three staff nurses for round the clock in over 900 PHCs were appreciated by the Minister. Dr. Ramadoss assured that funds will be released to the State under NRHM activities along with the ongoing programmes of the Ministry. He said availability of funds will not be a constraint for upgradation, strengthening and creation of facilities. Congratulating the Health Minister of Tamil Nadu for having led this entire thrust on quality health services, Dr. Ramadoss said I am sure if the current thrust on healthcare in Tamil Nadu is maintained it will emerge as perhaps the finest example in the country in reaching health services to every household.

6423. (7-3-2008) NEW DELHI : The concept of Joint Forest Management (JFM) in India is a step towards increasing the productivity of forests, improving the stocking of forests and in turn increase the carbon stocks. This approach matches well with the objectives of National Environment Policy (NEP) 2006 which emphasize identification of climate change impacts on forests and the need to internalize the adaptations majors in respect to forest management. Inaugurating a two day international workshop on " Developing Methodology for Assessment of Enhancement of Forest Carbon Stocks due to Conservation, Sustainable Management of Forests, and Increase in Forests Cover", the Minister of State, for Environment & Forests Shri Namo Narayin Meena further explained that there are more than 22 million members in more than one hundred thousand JFM Committees in India covering 22 million hectares of forest area. India acknowledges the seriousness of threat of deforestation and is actively participating in the International efforts to reduce deforestation at global level, Shri Meena said the forest and tree cover in India has been stabilized since 1980s and shows steady improvement since then. Shri Meena said the progressive conservation oriented forest policies and aforestation programmes are contributing to reduction in carbon emission, stabilization and improvement of carbon stocks in forests together with conservation of biodiversity. Shri Meena explained that this forestry sector of India is making positive contribution in checking global climate change and in promoting sustainable development.

6424. (7-3-2008) NEW DELHI : The President of India, Smt. Pratibha Devisingh Patil has greeted the women of the country on the occasion of the International Women's Day, which is being celebrated on March 8th. In her message on this occasion, Smt. Patil has said, "On the occasion of International Women's Day, I extend my greetings and felicitations to all my sisters in their continuing role and their relentless effort in shaping the destiny of our country. Our women folk inspired by Mahatma Gandhi came out of their homes to take part in the freedom struggle. Beginning with their determined efforts in the days before our freedom, today our women continue to strive to transform the social order into a more just and equal one. Now, many gifted women are making their mark in their chosen professions and each one of them can assist in eliminating social evils like female foeticide, infanticide, dowry etc. They should come forward and help to educate the hapless underprivileged girl child. The empowerment of women is the most effective tool for development as well as poverty alleviation."

6425. (7-3-2008) NEW DELHI : Army Chief Gen Deepak Kapoor is undertaking a five days tour to Poland and Belarus from 10 to 14 March 2008. India shares good bilateral relations with Poland and Belarus and these have been strengthened over the years with regular exchange of visits at political and diplomatic levels. Both these countries are also keen to improve their defence relationship with India. The visit by Gen Kapoor will add the necessary impetus to the existing defence relationship and broad-base it into a mutually beneficial partnership. Our relations in the field of defence with Poland have graduated from military cooperation to a comprehensive defence cooperation to include courses, training for UN Peacekeeping Operations, exchange of observers on Army exs etc. The relations with Belarus have been on the rise at political and diplomatic levels; however the defence relationship is still at a nascent stage. The visit of Gen Kapoor will enhance the existing military equipment cooperation and will diversify it to other fields like exchange of visits, availing of courses, training for UN Peacekeeping Operations and conduct of joint sports and adventure activities. During his visit, Gen Kapoor will be interacting with the senior military and civilian defence hierarchy and will discuss various defence related issues to strengthen existing defence ties with these countries. While in Poland, he will be laying wreath at the 'Tomb of Unsung Soldier'. In addition, visits to the National Defence University, Service HQs and Operational Unit HQs have also been planned. In Belarus, the COAS will be visiting Defence Research Facilities and Military Academy apart from the historic Mir Castle, the national monument that has witnessed a number of historic wars. He will also be interacting with the State Military and Industrial Committee.

6426. (8-3-2008) NEW DELHI : A life of dignity, Below Poverty Line, Policies of the Government all these had little meaning for the Arnadan tribe, one of the earliest tribes in Malappuram District, Kerala. No amount of cajoling by the government officials would bring them near getting any welfare government schemes. Men either worked as labourers or resorted to minor thefts. Some of the women folks even took to prostitution for fetching additional income. Yet waves of change swept in 2006. It took Vasantha to take the bold step and to think differently. She purchased 12 goats. An amount of Rs. 37,700/- was released to her under the Central Government's Swarnjayanti Gram Swarozgar Yojana (SGSY). Rs 10,000/- was given as subsidy and Rs.27,700 loan from South Malabar Grameen Bank with five years as repayment period. The amount helped her in constructing a shelter for the goats too. This year in January she sold 8 goats for Rs. 8000/- and she paid Rs.6000/- to the bank. Now she has altogether 14 goats. The goats deliver mostly two kids every 6 months. Today Vasantha is very happy as she gets additional income by selling even the dung of goats which fetches Rs.15/- for 10 kg. She uses the goat milk for her family. Food for goats is not a concern at all as behind her courtyard is the vast Nilambur forest area. The success of Vasantha has led Shanta of same community also to follow suite. She applied for loan under SGSY scheme in 2007-08 and today has 6 goats. Today her husband Kannan who is a well known thief is mending his ways by taking the goats for grazing. There are many other families who are shyly joining the group of bold women who took the first step towards dignified living. Bounded by the Nilgiris hills on the East and the Arabian Sea on the west, the district of Malappuram literally means the land atop the hills, is remarkable for its unique natural beauty. In earlier times, Malappuram was the head quarters of European and British troops and later it became the head quarters of the Malabar Special Police (M.S.P). Recent times have seen the District making great strides in education and IT. But even today there are many who are illiterate or partially literate. But the Self Help Groups have helped the women to know their mettle and to utilize their talents. One such sight you can see when you reach the main junction in Karulai Panchayat. You will see a Board saying " Sneha Vanitha Hotel". The Hotel started in December 2006 when like minded 10 women from BPL families thought of making best use of their culinary talents and spare time. They received Rs 2,40,000/- under the SGSY Scheme. Out of this Rs 1,20,000 was subsidy and Rs. 1,20,000/- as Loan. " We knew how to feed others but today unknowingly we have learnt accounting also" says Shobhana, the team leader. Roughly we make Rs. 5000/- daily and after one year we have already paid Rs. 80,000/- she added. "Now I also earn additional income and support my family" said Biyakutty gaily. Great ! women have started setting up their targets and started harping on their resources.

6427. (8-3-2008) NEW DELHI: The Communist Party of India (Marxist) on Friday attributed the victory of the party and the Left Front in the Tripura Assembly elections to the record of the Left Front government and support of all sections of the people. "The people have rejected the opportunist alliance of the Congress with the extremist INPT. The Central Committee is confident that the new Left

Front government will continue the work of developing the State and raising the living standards of the people," the CPI(M) central committee which is meeting here said in a statement. The central committee said the people in Tripura have delivered more than 80 per cent of the seats to the CPI(M) and the Left Front who have won 49 out of the 60 seats in the Assembly compared to 41 in the last Assembly. "The stage has been set for the sixth Left Front government in the State," the central committee said. The CPI(M) general secretary Prakash Karat said with this victory, the Left Front has achieved a hat-trick of wins in three states-Tripura, West Bengal and Kerala. "The economic policies being followed by the Congress-led government at the Centre has been rejected by the people of Tripura," he said. CPI(M) Polit Bureau member Sitaram Yechury said: "Where we are in power, anti-incumbency does not work. In fact what works is pro-incumbency and that is it. And this is precisely the message people are continuously giving." CPI national secretary and MP D. Raja said the Left Front government would take Tripura on the path of rapid development and further progress. "This impressive victory is for the entire Left Front which will do its best to come up to the expectations of the people and the faith which they have reposed in us," Mr. Raja said.

6428. (8-3-2008) NEW DELHI : The Speaker of the Lok Sabha, Shri Somnath Chatterjee today inaugurated an exhibition on Nutrition Promotion put up by the Ministry of Women and Child Development as a part of International Womens' Day celebrations. Inaugurating the exhibition, Shri Chatterjee said that it was a matter of concern that a large number of children are the victim of various types of mal nutrition. The women who are the backbone of the family have also various types of nutrition deficiency. This requires mass awareness campaign and many more such exhibitions not only in the urban areas but in villages also, he asserted. Underlining the importance women empowerment in society, Shri Chatterjee expressed the hope that women reservation would become a reality during his tenure as Speaker. Listing the initiatives of Women and Child Development Ministry, Smt. Renuka Chowdhary, Minister of Women and Child Development said that the Government is making all efforts to bring nutritional and health awareness at the forefront of the activities of 'Anganbadis', campaigns were being planned to create the awareness at grassroot level, she added. Three-day exhibition showcases messages and information related to food and nutrition requirements. Live demonstration have been arranged of low cost nutritious recipes, instant health checkups of women and girls is being done by way of Body Mass Index. Cultural shows have also been arranged to give message on nutrition and health.

6429. (8-3-2008) NEW DELHI : Stree Shakti Puraskar for outstanding achievements in the area of women' empowerment were presented today by Smt. Sonia Gandhi, Chairperson of UPA. The award instituted by the Ministry of Women and Child Development carries a citation and an amount of Rs. 3 lakh.

Presiding over the function, Smt. Renuka Chowdhury, Minister for Women and Child Development said the programmes and policies initiated recently by the Government would bring forth perceptible improvement in the socio-economic status of women. A number of schemes have been implemented both for economic and social empowerment of women. Laws have been amended to check child marriage, domestic violence and to make women more empowered. 'Dhan Luxmi' has been recently launched to encourage the family of girl child and to check female foeticide by giving cash incentives and 'Ujjawala' for rehabilitation of trafficked victims. But that Government's efforts would not suffice until women come forward to assert themselves, she said. Presenting the awards Smt. Sonia Gandhi said that journey of empowerment of the women is challenging but it should not be stopped at any cost. Expressing concern over female foeticide, she said that the crime should be stopped and women should work for the society where there is not a single case of female foeticide and dowry death. Underlining the importance womens' welfare and empowerment, Smt. Sonia Gandhi said whenever there is a crisis in a society women are worst affected. Hence waiving off the farmers' loan would benefit women most. Recalling the initiative of Late Rajiv Gandhi for women reservations in Panchayats, she said that today more the 10 lakh women are successfully working in Panchayats, which is a symbol of women empowerment at grassroot level. Smt. Gursharan Kaur, wife of the Prime Minister, Dr. Manmohan Singh was also present on the occasion. The awardees of Stree Shakti Puraskar have shown that inspite of various odds, women, if given opportunities, can be trendsetters in any walk of the life. Smt. Shaik Shamshad Begum of Khammam, Andhra Pradesh was awarded for her support to self help groups. She alone formed village level organization with 400 members.

6430. (8-3-2008) NEW DELHI : Following is the text of the address of Vice President of India Shri Mohd. Hamid Ansari at the 'Annual Day Celebrations of Shri Ram College of Commerce' here today : "I am happy to be here today at the Annual Day Celebrations of the Shri Ram College of Commerce. The College has over the past eight decades emerged as a foremost centre of excellence in commerce education in the country. This can be attributed to the vision of its founder, Sir Shri Ram, and the initiative and drive of its faculty, students and alumni over the years. The College has done well in inculcating in students the spirit of entrepreneurship and innovation. As a citizen only partially initiated in the intricacies and mysteries of the world of business, I hesitated a good deal before accepting the invitation of the College to be here today. I am not an economist but like many others do understand a bit of the wider debate about what used to be known as 'political economy'. Business is not an exercise in a vacuum. The question, in other words, is of the environment in which business functions, its instruments of governance, and the manner in which it interacts with society. Some in this audience may have read Kautailya's Arthashastra and its chapter on the management of the state's treasury and economy. A great deal of commonsense advice is given there about how to achieve and sustain economic prosperity. He makes the interesting observation that 'just as elephants are needed to catch elephants, so does one needs wealth to capture more wealth'. In other words, wealth plays a role in the generation of wealth. What then is our wealth? In today's world, it is defined in terms of human and material resources. India is well endowed with both and the progress achieved by the country in the six decades of independence proves it in ample measure. The rate of growth in recent years has been particularly impressive. The momentum is set to continue. The interaction of the economy with the outside world stands enhanced in good measure. In this new setting, two aspects need particular attention.

6431. (8-3-2008) NEW DELHI : Dr. K. Vijaya Lakshmi has been awarded with National Award for Women's Development through Application of Science & Technology to recognize her outstanding contribution to solving environmental problems of the village communities especially the women by addressing issues concerning safe drinking water by development of a simple easy to use, field testing kit and community water filter. The Jal-TARA water testing Kits and Jal-TARA water Filter developed are being used for testing and treating water across rural India. This unique initiative involving women self help groups in Bundelkhand region helps to provide 'clean and safe water for the community. Her efforts have considerable reduced morbidity through waterborne diseases in this region. The award was conferred upon her by the President of India, Smt. Pratibha Devisingh Patil at the National Conference on Showcasing Cutting Edge Science & Technology by Women in New Delhi today. Dr. Vijaya Lakshmi, a Doctorate in Chemistry form Sri Venkateswara University, Tirupati, Andhra Pradesh, began her journey as environmental scientist 18 years ago at Development Alternatives. She is one of those rare scientists who have successfully made the journey from experiment and innovation in a research laboratory to applications in the field. Early in her career, she realized the criticality of using scrupulous scientific methods to identify, analyze and solve practical problems. She then applied frontline knowledge to solving the environmental problems of the village communities, the women and the poor. Issues concerning water quality, its health impacts especially on women and children intrigued her the most. She took upon the challenge of demystifying the science of water quality testing and purification and decided to make sure that the common person has access to simple, reliable, easy to operate tools. The Jal-TARA water testing Kits and Jal-TARA water Filter were developed which have now become very popular and are being used especially for testing millions of water samples and for treating gallons of water across India. She has meticulously built up a team and a facility at Development Alternatives, a technology oriented voluntary organization that is recognized worldwide for its innovation and large scale dissemination of science based techniques for raising the quality of the environment while providing day to day solutions for poor communities, particularly in safe drinking water. Due to her commitment the common person now has access to simple, reliable, easy to operate water-testing and purification tools. She is currently piloting a unique initiative involving Women Self Help Groups from 10 villages from Niwari and Jhansi districts of Bundelkhand region to provide 'clean and safe water for all and always'.

6432. (8-3-2008) NEW DELHI : Dr. Rani Bang has been awarded with National Award for Women's Development through Application of Science & Technology in recognition of her outstanding and pioneering contribution for the past two and a half decades on improving women's health in rural India through an innovative and powerful approach of research with the people and for the people. She has spearheaded the development of a comprehensive village health care programme which has now become a nationally and internationally acclaimed model. This innovative approach of empowering rural women to take care of their community's health has reduced the infant mortality in Gadchiroli, Maharashtra by over seventy five percent. The award was conferred upon her by the President of India, Smt. Pratibha Devisingh Patil at the National Conference on Showcasing Cutting Edge Science & Technology by Women in New Delhi. Dr. Rani Bang exemplifies an amalgamation of idealism, social service and scientific research. She has made landmark contribution to improving women's life in India and globally-as a gynecologist, as a research scientist and as a social activist. Dr. Bang completed her Medical Education (MD) in India with gold medal and at the Johns Hopkins School of Public Health, (MPH) in the US. Along with her husband, Dr. Abhay Bang, she founded the voluntary organization, SEARCH, (Society for Education, Action and Research in community Health) 22 years ago in one of the most underdeveloped districts, Gadchiroli, in the state of Maharashtra. There they live and work with the people in 150 villages to provide community-based health care and conduct research. They have established the now famous community health care and research centre 'Shodhagram' in this tribal area. From this remote place, they have evolved a very innovative and powerful approach of 'Research with the People' which has generated, time and again, new evidence and solutions to shape national and global thinking. By conducting the first ever study in two villages in Gadchiroli and publishing in the Lancet, Dr. Rani Bang first brought to the notice of the world that rural women had a large hidden burden of gynecological diseases. She subsequently trained the Dais in villages to make them village level health workers. With convincing evident she advocated the need for a comprehensive reproductive health care package for rural women in India. Dr. Rani Bang along with her husband and colleagues have developed a model for a village health care programme which is now being recognized nationally and internationally.

6433. (8-3-2008) NEW DELHI : Shri L K Advani leader of the opposition, Lok Sabha has sought immediate intervention by the centre to put an end to the unabated violence unleashed by CPM storm troopers against the BJP / RSS workers in Kerala. Shri Advani has taken up the issue with the Union Home Minister, Shri. Shivraj Patil. Responding to Mr. Advani's plea, Shri Patil has assured him that the centre has taken cognizance of this mindless violence and would take steps to restore normalcy in the violence torn districts of Kerala. Five BJP /RSS workers have been hacked to death by the CPM goons since the afternoon of March 5, 2008. Shri M P Sumesh a respected RSS worker was attacked when he emerged out of a hotel in Tellicherry town after having lunch. He has suffered multiple injuries on his legs, hands, face and head. He is in the Intensive Care Unit of Medical college Hospital, Calicut. The following day two more workers Shri Nikhil, a lorry cleaner, and Shri Satyan, a construction worker were killed in separate incidents. Shri Nikhil was pulled out off his lorry and killed on the spot. Shri Satyan was abducted from his work site and later his dead body was found with his head severed on a few kilometres away. It appears that CPM has trained its killer squads to kill political opponents in the most barbarous manner so that those differing from CPI(M) are terrified. In two separate incidents two more workers, Shri Vinayan and Shri Ranjit were attacked and are admitted in Medical College Hospital, Calicut.

6434. (8-3-2008) NEW DELHI : National Conference on Showcasing Cutting Edge Science & Technology by Women began in New Delhi today with the President of India, Smt. Pratibha Devisingh Patil calling upon women scientists to bring about significant change by working at the grassroot level for women's empowerment. Addressing the gathering which included a large number of women scientists from across the country and young science students at the Vigyan Bhavan, the first woman President of India said that the participation of women in the dynamic field of science is central not only in our efforts for gender equality but also to make women stakeholders of the future construct of the world. She lauded the efforts of the Ministry of Science and Technology in promoting women scientists. Union Minister for Science and Technology Shri Kapil Sibal who presided over the function pledged to continue with his endeavours to provide a level playing field to women scientists and announced that all DST Aided Institutions would.

6435. (9-3-2008) NEW DELHI : Following is the text of the Vice President of India, Shri Mohammad Hamid Ansari at the 18th World Congress of International Physicians for the Prevention of Nuclear War (IPPNW) here today. "I am happy to be here at the inauguration of the 18th World Congress of International Physicians for the Prevention of Nuclear War. The pioneering work of the organisation and its efforts for peace, health and development need no mention here; it has been awarded the Noble Peace Prize. Conferences of this nature help in better understanding of the causes of armed conflict, especially from a public health perspective, and build grassroots awareness of the immense health and environment consequences of nuclear war. The involvement of students and youth as part of these conferences brings in the much-needed dimension of spreading awareness among the future decision makers. This distinguished audience needs no reminding that the first resolution of the UN General Assembly of 24th January, 1946 was adopted unanimously and sought the elimination of atomic weapons and all other major weapons adaptable to mass destruction from national armaments and the control of atomic energy to ensure its use only for peaceful purposes. The horrors of the use of nuclear weapons have convinced all responsible nations that elimination of nuclear weapons is necessary. The International Court of Justice had in its advisory opinion of 8 July 1996 concluded that "there exists an obligation to pursue in good faith and bring to a conclusion negotiations leading to nuclear disarmament in all its aspects under strict and effective international control". The nuclear disarmament discourse has been enriched by the contributions of the Non-Alignment Movement, various members States including India and even the community of Non-Governmental Organisations. While there is agreement on the principle, the practical means and approaches necessary for realising this vision have been the subject of much debate and divergence of opinion. It was India that first proposed an end to nuclear testing in 1954. The principles for a Nuclear Non-Proliferation Treaty (NPT) were first proposed by India in 1965.

6436. (10-3-2008) NEW DELHI : The Ministry of New and Renewable Energy is implementing several programmes to promote use of solar energy devices and systems in the country including rural areas. The programmes are the Solar Photovoltaic Programme, Remote Village Electrification Programme, Solar Photovoltaic Water Pumping Programme, Solar Lantern Programme and Solar Thermal Energy Programme. Under these programmes, financial assistance is being provided on purchase/installation of dish type solar cookers, solar lanterns, solar home lighting systems, solar street lighting systems, solar pumping systems and solar power plants etc. The eligibility criteria and the quantum of support is different under different programmes. In addition to the above, a scheme on "Accelerated Development and Deployment of Solar Water Heating Systems in Domestic, Industrial and Commercial Sectors" is also being implemented under which soft loan is available to the beneficiaries through selected banks and Indian Renewable Energy Development Agency Ltd. for installation of solar water heating systems.

6437. (10-3-2008) NEW DELHI : The Government has been giving due encouragement to the renewable energy sector through a mix of fiscal and financial incentives that include capital/ interest subsidy, accelerated depreciation, nil/ concessional excise and customs duties. Further, benefit under Section 80-1A of Income Tax Act 1961 is available to undertakings setup for the generation or generation and distribution of Renewable power in India. This apart, preferential tariff for grid interactive renewable power is being given in most potential States. Avenues for cooperation in renewable energy sector are being explored with several countries that include, inter-alia, Brazil, Denmark, Germany, Japan, Iceland, Italy, Philippines, South Africa, Thailand and USA. Renewable energy products are already being exported mainly in the wind energy, small hydro, solar and biomass energy sectors. The prospects for such exports are expected to only improve with rising global oil prices. This information was given by the Minister of State for New And Renewable Energy, Shri Vilas Muttemwar, in a written reply to a question by Shri Shreegopal Vyas, Shri Balavant Alias Bal Apte and Shrimati Maya Singh in the Rajya Sabha today.

6438. (10-3-2008) NEW DELHI : The government has been encouraging private investment in renewable energy sector through a mix of fiscal and financial incentives that include capital/ interest subsidy, accelerated depreciation, nil/ concessional excise and customs duties. Further benefit under Section 80-1A of Income Tax Act 1961 is available to undertakings setup for the generation or generation and distribution of Renewable power in India. This apart, preferential tariff for grid interactive renewable power is being given in most potential States. A potential of 84,776 MW has been estimated from renewable energy sources such as wind, biomass, solar and small hydro in the country as per details given in Annexure. The grid-interactive power installed capacity from the renewable sources like wind, biomass, solar and small hydro in the country at the end of the 10th Plan, *i.e.*, upto 31.3.2007 was 10,250 MW which has reached 11,447 MW as on 31.01.08. A capacity addition of 14,000 MW is proposed during the 11th Plan. Most of this capacity is envisaged through private investment.

6439. (10-3-2008) NEW DELHI : The Government of India promotes setting up of commercial wind power projects in the country, including in the State of Tamil Nadu, by providing incentives such as concessional import duty for wind electricity generator sub-systems, excise duty exemption, ten years tax holiday on wind power projects, benefit of accelerated depreciation, term loan from Indian Renewable Energy Development Agency (IREDA) and identification of more potential locations by carrying out wind resource assessment studies. This apart, preferential tariff and grid evacuation facilities are provided for wind power in the State of Tamil Nadu. A wind power installed capacity of 7844 MW has been achieved upto 31.12.2007 in the country which includes 3712 MW in Tamil Nadu. Production of power from Ocean Energy has not been found to be cost effective on commercial scale. A capacity addition of 10,500 MW from wind power has been planned in the country during the 11th Plan period *i.e.* 2007-2012. The State Govt. of Tamil Nadu has planned a target of 2,500 MW from wind power during the 11 Plan period. An outlay of Rs.75 crore has been proposed during the 11th Plan to support wind resource assessment and demonstration projects in various States, R&D projects, etc. in the country. This information was given by the Minister of State for New And Renewable Energy, Shri Vilas Muttemwar, in a written reply to a question by Shri S. Anbalagan Rajya Sabha today.

6440. (10-3-2008) NEW DELHI : The Union Minister of Shipping, Road Transport and Highways, Thiru T.R. Baalu has said that the port sector in the country is poised to launch many projects to remove capacity constraints as well as to enhance operational efficiency and sector-specific human resource pool. Addressing the 5th Annual General Body Meeting of the Indian Institute of Maritime Studies (IIMS) here today, the Minister said that the business plans of all the Major Ports have been drawn up and several State Governments are also taking initiatives to develop non-major ports along their coastlines. The Minister said that this kind of huge expansion programme would lead to a burgeoning demand for trained and skilled manpower and by 2015, the shortage of marine officers is likely to nearly treble at 27,000 from 10,000 now. He said that we need to offer long term career and not just for 8 to 10 years span. Offering of long term career would be possible by having a Maritime University in position. Thiru Baalu said that when set up, Indian Maritime University would consolidate the present excellence in the maritime field and provide standardised education and training by creating a platform for integrated training. He said that it would give credit to ship board training, get diplomas/degrees while working on-board ships and provide a platform for research and innovation for the entire shipping industry for the benefit of all the stakeholders. Thiru Baalu expressed his happiness over the fact that the intake of students of all the Institutes under the IIMS has increased from 5,140 in 2005-06 to 6,299 during the year 2006-07 and the placement record of all the Pre-Sea Institutes under the IIMS has been successful. The proposed activities of the IIMS during the coming financial year, *viz.*, 2008-09, include procurement of new simulators as well as upgradation of the existing ones, augmentation of the capacity of hostel at all the four Institutes under the IIMS and procurement of training equipment for pneumatic lab and hydraulic lab to introduce new technology available in ships. The total expenditure of the IIMS was Rs.18.70 crores against the total revenue generated Rs.20.34 crores.

6441. (10-3-2008) NEW DELHI : The Monitoring Committee on RGGVY has accorded approval for 17 projects covering release of 631828 BPL connections with an outlay of Rs.37539.07 lakh for execution during 10th Plan period. Subsequently, six projects involving an outlay of Rs.17909.80 lakh for release of 206368 BPL connections have been approved for execution during Phase-I of 11th Plan period. Karnataka Govt. has submitted revised cost estimates of 17 sanctioned projects for execution during 10th Plan, of which the Monitoring Committee on RGGVY has accorded its approval for 10 projects and the balance 07 are yet to be approved. Funds under RGGVY are released in instalments commensurate with the progress reported by the implementing states/agencies, fulfilment of the pre-requisites as also availability of funds.

6442. (10-3-2008) NEW DELHI : Bihar Government has submitted 44 DPRs covering electrification of 14195 un-electrified villages, re-electrification of 10508 de-electrified villages and intensive electrification of 6069 electrified villages with an outlay of Rs.3345.68 crore. The implementing agencies have reported that electrification works in 12104 un-electrified villages (cumulatively) have been carried out as on 15th February, 2008. They have also reported release of 66799 rural household connections, including 52817 BPL household connections in Bihar under RGGVY. Bihar State so far (as on 25th February, 2008) has availed Rs.1288.23 crore under RGGVY. NHPC, the implementing agency of RGGVY project in Madhubani district, with concurrence of Bihar Government, has submitted two DPRs, one covering electrification of 16 un-electrified villages and re-electrification of 310 de-electrified villages under "Accelerated Electrification of One Lakh Villages and One Crore Households" which now stands merged with RGGVY. This project was sanctioned in March 2005. Subsequently, NHPC has submitted supplementary DPR of Madhubani district covering electrification of 221 un-electrified villages, re-electrification of 27 de-electrified villages and intensive electrification of 459 already electrified villages which is yet to be approved. Out of the four blocks, three blocks namely Lookaṇa, Ghoghardiha and Phulparas find coverage in both the DPRs whereas Khutonna is not appearing in either of the DPRs. However, village Khutonna with census code No. 0040200 has been covered in the supplementary DPR of Madhubani district. Sudyahi and Ghoonsahi villages have also not been covered in both these DPRs. This information was given by Union Minister for Power, Shri Sushilkumar Shinde in the Rajya Sabha today.

6443. (10-3-2008) NEW DELHI : The Ministry of Rural Development has granted Rs.6.14 crore and Rs.2.86 crore to the State Governments of Gujarat and Tamil Nadu respectively towards restoration of cut imposed while releasing second instalments of funds against the original allocation of Rs.18.144 crore and Rs.19.09 crore respectively under Rajiv Gandhi National Drinking Water Mission (RGNDWM)-a Centrally Sponsored Programme of Accelerated Rural Water Supply Programme (ARWSP) during the current financial year (2007-08). In the case of Tamil Nadu the sanctioned amount is to be delivered to the Tamil Nadu Water Supply and Drainage Board, Chennai. Up to 15% of the funds released under this sanction will be utilized for Operation and Maintenance and up to 5% of funds may be spent for taking sustainability measures. States have been have been requested to delegate powers for management of Rural Water Supply Schemes through the Panchayati Raj Institutions (PRIs). Priorities set in ARWSP guidelines and through other instructions issued from time to time shall be followed for coverage of rural habitations and rural schools.

6444. (10-3-2008) NEW DELHI : The Surplus power used to be available on a sustained basis in the Eastern Region (ER). During the current year, (April, 2007 to January, 2008), the energy and peak shortage in the Eastern Region has been of the order of 4.6% and 6% respectively. As compared to the Eastern Region the energy and peak shortage in the country as a whole is of the order of 9% and 15.2% respectively. The main reasons for shortage of power in the Eastern Region are inadequate capacity addition within the Region vis-a-vis the growth in demand, poor performance of generating units in some of the States and reduced availability of power during the winter months due to reduction of water inflows into Tala Hydro Power Stations.

6445. (10-3-2008) NEW DELHI : Replying to a written question whether the Government is contemplating to abandon the Sampoorna Grameen Rozgar Yojana (SGRY), National Food for Work Programme (NFFWP) as reported in a section of Media in the Lok Sabha to day, the Union Minister for Rural Development Dr. Raghuvansh Prasad Singh said that the Sampoorna Grameen Rozgar Yojana (SGRY), National Food for Work Programme (NFFWP) was launched in November 2004. With the launching of the National Rural Employment Guarantee Act (NREGA) in 200 identified districts with effect from 2nd February, 2006, the NFFWP and SGRY programmes were subsumed in these identified districts. The work started under SGRY and NFFWP and spilled over to the financial year 2006-07 were allowed to be completed by 30th June, 2006 by following the NREGA processes. SGRY programme in additional 130 districts was subsumed in NREGS in the year 2007-08. Incomplete SGRY works in these districts were allowed to be completed by 31st August, 2007 by following the NREGA processes. Detailed modifications were issued to SGRY guidelines on 1st August, 2007 which inter-alia stipulated that only those new works will be taken up under SGRY which are NREGA compliant to ensure smooth completion of such works as and when remaining districts are subsumed into NREGA.

6446. (10-3-2008) NEW DELHI : The estimation of poverty at the national and State level is done by the Planning Commission on the basis of the Sample Survey of Consumer Expenditure carried out by the National Sample Survey Organisation (NSSO) after an interval of 5 years approximately. The Ministry of Rural Development provides financial and technical support to the States and UTs to undertake BPL Census to identify the BPL households in the rural areas who could be targeted under its various programmes. The BPL Census is done by covering 100% rural households through door-to-door survey. The BPL Census 2002 has been conducted for the 10th Five Year Plan and 21 States and UTs have finalized and furnished the BPL list. The State Governments have been advised to post the BPL data for each district with details of individual BPL households on their website also. 158 Districts have already posted the village-wise BPL data on the website of this Ministry *i.e.* www.rural.nic.in also. This information was given by the Union Minister for Rural Development Dr. Raghuvansh Prasad Singh in reply to a written question in the Lok Sabha today.

6447. (10-3-2008) NEW DELHI : Shri Singhvi said we condemn unequivocally and unambiguously the violence unleashed in Delhi at the headquarters of the

CPM by several activists of the BJP, of the RSS and their associated organizations. We do so because for the Congress Party, fundamentally, violence has absolutely no place in democracy. Violence, climate of fear and lawless are non-negotiable. If the principle, an eye for an eye, is followed then Gandhiji's principle will inevitably follow and everyone will become blind. In particular it is deplorable that such lawlessness and violence has been unleashed in the capital, a place which sends a message not only to the whole nation but to the world at large. It creates a unavoidable climate of fear, of indiscipline and of insecurity. We are particularly shocked by the premeditated carrying of stones, other heavy objects which clearly reflects the premeditated mindsets and the clear intention to inflict injury. We are equally shocked and we believe that it really lets the cat out of the bag that the earlier statement of former BJP president Venkaiah Naidu, a statement clearly designed to provoke, to incite, where he referred to the possibility of counterpart actions like this being unleashed in Delhi, and this was two days ago. Therefore, in conclusion, we condemn the mode, the methodology, the motive and the mindset of those who indulge in such wanton violence. And those who breed this climate and attitude of intolerance and of confrontation deserve to be condemned not only by us but by the senior elements, even of the same parties and organizations to whom these elements belong. To a question on the violence in Kerala, Shri Singhvi said we do not support violence anywhere but first of all unless there is evidence, and we are not going into that evidence at this stage, two wrongs can never make a right. In any event, whatever happened anywhere, cannot, under any circumstances, be an excuse and justification for what happened in Delhi yesterday and that is why I said in the beginning, violence in such forms or any form, is non-negotiable and condemnable. To a question that are you willing for a judicial or parliamentary probe? Shri Singhvi said I think its not just a formality of asking for probes. The real issue is that civil society and political parties have to unanimously condemn such things that happened under our very nose in the capital. A probe is required if you have a doubt, or if you have an uncertainty. When under the gaze of the whole wide world, on full candid camera you have the faces, you have the names, you have the persona all depicted. So where is the need for a probe? Let us also not forget that there are senior officers of the opposition both in the Delhi government and at the Centre, the BJP. There are seven councillors, there are mayors who are present and filmed and captured in the process of this destruction which is completely inexcusable. They should be the guardians of the law here not as violators. To a question that BJP has shown photos of people being beheaded and limbs being cut up, your response?

6448. (10-3-2008) NEW DELHI : Under the Sarva Shiksha Abhiyan (SSA), an independent survey was commissioned in July-August 2005 which brought out that 1.34 crore children were out of school in the 6-14 years age group. This figure has reduced to 75.97 lakhs in March, 2007 as per State Government Reports. The State-wise details are in Annexure. Since, the remaining out of school children constitute "the most difficult to access group", context specific interventions for children who are "hard to reach", such as bridge courses, learning centres with flexible timings, seasonal hostels, home based education, mobile schools, have been taken up under the Sarva Shiksha Abhiyan Programme. The Government of India has undertaken orientation and capacity building workshops with States/UTs with illustrative case studies of good practices, to encourage State/districts to implement such context specific interventions. This information was given by the Minister of State for Human Resource Development Shri M.A.A Fatmi in a written reply in Rajya Sabha today.

6449. (10-3-2008) NEW DELHI : Payment of wages under NREGA through workers accounts in post offices had been taken up with the Department of Posts. Department of Posts has requested all Heads of Circles to take prompt measures for operationalisation of the accounts of wage earners in the Post Offices. Ministry has issued instructions to State Governments for proper coordination with the Department of Posts. Department of Posts has advised their State Offices to cooperate with the State Government to enable early operationalisation of wage payment through NREGA workers accounts in post offices wherever possible and not to charge service charges. This information was given by the Union Minister for Rural Development Dr. Raghuvansh Prasad Singh while replying to a written question whether the Government is contemplating to introduce smart or electronic cards and electronic transfer of money to beneficiaries to make the implementation of the National Rural Employment Guarantee (NREG) Scheme effective in the Lok Sabha today.

6450. (10-3-2008) NEW DELHI : Indian Renewable Energy Development Agency (IREDA), a non-banking financial company under the administrative control of this Ministry, is envisaging formation of a Special Purpose Vehicle to facilitate setting up a SEZ for production of renewable energy equipment. Presently IREDA is in the process of discussing the issue with State Governments and private sector parties. One of the possible locations under consideration is near Nagpur, however the final decision with regard to setting up a SEZ would depend on various techno-economic considerations of investors. This information was given by the Minister of State for New And Renewable Energy, Shri Vilas Muttemwar, in a written reply to a question by Shri B.K. Hariprasad in the Rajya Sabha today.

6451. (10-3-2008) NEW DELHI : The Sarva Shiksha Abhiyan (SSA) programme is being implemented in all districts of the country to achieve the goal of universalisation of elementary education in a mission mode. Various incentives including cooked mid day meal are being provided to ensure universal enrolment of children in rural areas, in the 6-14 years age group. Consequently 98 % of rural India has a primary school within one kilometre and remaining rural habitations have alternate schooling arrangements including Education Guarantee Scheme (EGS). World Bank (WB), Department for International Development (DFID) of

United Kingdom and European Commission (EC) have been providing partial financial assistance for the Sarva Shiksha Abhiyan (SSA) on reimbursement basis. Total reimbursements claimed by Government of India from these agencies in the last three years *i.e.* 2004-05, 2005-06 & 2006-07 have been Rs.1047.67 crore, Rs 2341.98 crore & Rs.1091.91 crore, respectively. Government of India has so far received an amount of Rs. 189.88 crores in 2007-08 as reimbursement from external funding agencies on account of the Sarva Shiksha Abhiyan. Central funds under Sarva Shiksha Abhiyan are released to all State/UTs on the basis of Annual Work Plan & Budget (AWP&B) submitted by State/UTs to the Government of India every year. A part of this expenditure of Government of India is reimbursed by external funding agencies. A rigorous system of monitoring of the SSA for tracking the performance of States, is in place which includes, inter alia, monthly and quarterly progress reports and review meetings, furnishing of annual elementary school statistics, field monitoring by 40 independent monitoring institutions and six monthly independent Review Missions. In addition, annual statutory audit of the State/UT SSA programmes are in place and concurrent financial reviews are also carried out. Wherever deficiencies in the implementation of the programme are noticed, such deficiencies are brought to the notice of the State Governments for corrective action. This information was given by the Minister of State for Human Resource Development Shri M.A.Fatmi in a written reply in Rajya Sabha today......

6452. (10-3-2008) NEW DELHI : 31 waste-to-energy based power projects aggregating to 68.62 MW capacity in eight States and 36 demonstration wind power projects aggregating to 70.9 MW capacity in nine States have been set up with Central Financial Assistance from Ministry of New and Renewable Energy. Moreover, commercial wind power projects of about 7844 MW capacity have been installed in the country through private investment. Resource Assessments are being carried out for power generation from wind and biomass resources in the country, including the backward and rural areas. Wind-solar hybrid systems and biomass gasifiers are being installed for meeting the energy requirements in various States, including the backward and rural areas. The Ministry is also implementing a programme for electrification of remote un-electrified census villages and un-electrified hamlets of electrified census villages through various new and renewable energy sources including biomass resources such as crop residues and agro-industrial wastes. Central Financial Assistance of Rs. 10.03 crore for waste-to-power projects and Rs. 1.90 crore for demonstration wind power projects has been provided by the Ministry to various States during the last two years. This information was given by the Minister of State for New And Renewable Energy, Shri Vilas Muttemwar, in a written reply to a question by Shri Jai Parkash Aggarwal in the Rajya Sabha today.

6453. (10-3-2008) NEW DELHI : The Ministry of New & Renewable Energy is implementing several schemes to popularize solar energy equipments, including use for house hold applications. In view of the high initial cost of the solar energy systems and devices, Central Financial Assistance is provided in the form of capital or interest subsidy. Apart from this, several fiscal and promotional incentives are also available. 6,50,000 sq. m. of collector area for solar water heating systems; 5,25,000 solar cookers; 4,79,869 solar lanterns; 2,23,595 solar home systems; 46,186 solar street lights; 4500 solar pumps; and, 3783 kWp capacity power plants were installed up to the end of the Ninth Plan. For the 11th Plan period, a target of 5 million sq. m. of collector area for solar water heating systems; 20,000 solar cookers; and, 50 MW solar photovoltaic systems has been set by the Ministry. No State-wise allocations are made. Apart from financial and fiscal incentives, publicity and awareness campaigns are organized. Some State Governments are providing additional subsidies apart from providing rebate in property tax and electricity tariff to the users of solar water heaters. Soft loans are also available for the manufactures for up-gradation of technology, besides rebate in excise and custom duties. The Bureau of Indian Standards have issued certain standards for solar cookers, flat plate collectors for solar water heating systems and solar photovoltaic modules. In addition, performance specifications for solar home systems, solar street lights and solar lanterns have also been announced. This information was given by the Minister of State for New And Renewable Energy, Shri Vilas Muttemwar, in a written reply to a question by Shri Balawant Alias Bal Apte, Shri Shreegopal Vyas and Shrimati Maya Singh in the Rajya Sabha today.

6454. (10-3-2008) NEW DELHI : There is a gap in the demand and supply of power in the country. The renewable energy sources such as wind, small hydro and biomass have contributed about 11274 MW to the capacity addition of power generation in the country. India receives solar energy equivalent to over 5,000 trillion kWh per year. The daily average solar energy incident over India varies from 4-7 kWh per square meter depending upon the location. Solar energy can be harnessed through two routes, namely solar photovoltaic (PV) and solar thermal, by direct conversion to electricity and heat energy respectively. Thus solar energy has potential to meet growing demand of energy. The high initial cost of solar energy devices and systems, and lack of sufficient awareness are the main reasons for low utilization of this resource. However, some of the solar energy systems are becoming cost competitive to the conventional alternatives, when compared over the life of the systems. Solar water heaters, solar cookers and photovoltaic systems for small power applications in remote areas are the examples. The Ministry has taken several steps to increase the utilization of solar energy in the country during the 11th plan, which include (i) expanded programmes of the Ministry to encourage utilization of solar energy systems through subsidy or soft loans, (ii) incentive to manufacturers, commercial users and power project developers, (iv) research and development to reduce the cost, improve the efficiency and performance of solar energy systems, (v) support to Akshaya Urja shops to provide additional channels for sale and after-sales servicing of solar energy systems, and (v) create awareness about the solar energy systems and their benefits. This information was given by the Minister of State for New And Renewable Energy, Shri Vilas Muttemwar, in a written reply to a question by Shri Dara Singh and Shri Ramdas Agarwal in the Rajya Sabha today.

6455. (10-3-2008) NEW DELHI : The Government of Gujarat had sent proposal for construction of hostel for SC boys during 2002-03 at Morbi and Mehsana for which central share of Rs.1,00,39,650/- was sanctioned. Out of this, Rs.77,00,000/- (Rupees seventy seven lakh only) were released during 2002-03 and remaining amount of Rs.23,39,650/- (Rupees twenty three lakh thirty nine thousand six hundred and fifty only) has been released during 2007-08. No proposal has been received for Government boys hostel at Idar. The Government of Gujarat had also sent the proposals for ideal residential schools at Mehsanna and Idar (Sabarkantha) during 2005-06. Grant-in-aid of Rs.87,08,500/- (Rupees eighty seven lakh eight thousand and five hundred only for ideal residential school at Idar has been released by the Ministry during 2007-08. This information was given by the Minister of State for Social Justice and Empowerment, Smt. Subbulakshmi Jagadeesan in a written reply to a question in the Rajya Sabha today.

6456. (10-3-2008) NEW DELHI : Following is the text of the address of the Vice President of India Mohd. Hamid Ansari at the Annual Day Celebrations of Lady Shriram College, here today: "I accepted Dr. Gopinath's invitation with some trepidation and kept hoping that the programme would require me to do no more than release a pigeon of peace, cut a ribbon, launch the college magazine and generally do the things that vice presidents of countries the world over are so well drilled to do. I discovered a bit late that I would have to sing for my afternoon cup of tea! Entrapment, however distasteful, does facilitate the thought process!! I decided to lean in favour of the contentious, to think aloud, and to explore the dimensions of the gender challenge to modern India. LSR, with its stated mission of 'empowering women to assume leadership', is an appropriate forum for such an endeavour. Ours is a land in the throes of change. The functional mantra is growth; the guiding principle is inclusive growth. The underpinning for both is the constitutional stipulation of equality and prohibition of discrimination on grounds of religion, race, caste, sex or place of birth. It is, according to Article 51A, a fundamental duty 'to renounce practices derogatory to the dignity of women'. In terms of principles, therefore, citizens of India should be a satisfied lot. In actuality, they are not. Their dissatisfaction is of various kinds and has many dimensions. Gender inequality is one of them. It affects half the population and is found in all parts of the country and at all levels of society. The journal Manushi, in its first editorial in January 1979, raised a question: Is it possible to talk of women as an undifferentiated mass? Its answer was in the affirmative: Despite factors dividing women from each other, 'if we look at the nature and basis of women's oppression, we discover that our sex determines our common predicament in a very fundamental way'. The editorial asserted that the initiative for an alternative has to come from 'toiling women' who alone are 'capable of providing the leadership and the militancy that is required to bring about radical changes in this unjust system'. It raised a battle cry: 'Let us re-examine the whole question, all the questions. Let us take nothing for granted. Let us not only redefine ourselves, our role, our image-but also the kind of society we want to live in'.

6457. (10-3-2008) NEW DELHI : Based on the Selected Educational Statistics 2004-05, against the all India Gross Enrolment Ratio (GER) of 93.54% at the elementary stage (Classes I to VIII, ages 6-14), the GER of Rajasthan is 102.67%. In Rajasthan, GER for SC students is 105.16% and is 96.33% for ST students as against national average of 98.79% and 102.36% respectively. For SC girls, the GER is 95.65% against national average of 90.29% and for ST girls it is 86.10% against national average of 95.82%. The GER figures at the elementary level for all States are given in the Annexure. The drop out rates in Rajasthan is 56.59% for all categories for Classes I-V. It is 52.90% for girls, 53.80% for SCs and 56.22% for STs. For Classes I-VIII it is 65.34% for all categories, 71.33% for girls, 71.97% for SCs and 69.14% for ST students. For Classes I-X, it is 73.87% for all categories, 80.72% for girls, 80.74% for SCs and 75.30% for STs. The Government of India has launched Sarva Shiksha Abhiyan in year 2001 to address these issues. This information was given by the Minister of State for Human Resource Development Shri M.A.A. Fatmi in a written reply in Rajya Sabha today......

6458. (10-3-2008) NEW DELHI : Sporadic instances of corporal punishment in schools have been reported in the media in the recent past. Education is a concurrent subject and school education primarily comes under the purview of the State Governments. Details of physical punishment in schools are not centrally maintained in this Ministry. Affiliation Bye-laws of Central Board of Secondary Education (CBSE), inter-alia, empowers school Managing Committee to place an employee under suspension if " he/she is charged with cruelty with any student or any employee of the school". CBSE has issued a circular to its affiliated schools not to resort to corporal/physical punishment of students. Government of India has issued an advisory on 17.12.2007 to State Governments to prohibit corporal punishment in schools under their jurisdiction. Corporal punishment has been strictly prohibited in schools run by Kendriya Vidyalaya Sangathan, Navodaya Vidyalaya Samiti and Central Tibetan School Administration, which are under the Ministry of Human Resources Development. This information was given by the Minister of State for Human Resource Development Shri M.A.A. Fatmi in a written reply in Rajya Sabha today.

6459. (10-3-2008) NEW DELHI : A study report by the National Sample Survey Organisation (NSSO) titled "Employment and Unemployment Situations in India" has revealed that in rural areas a woman's daily wage is less than that of a man, though both work equal hours. This disparity in wages could be attributed to existing social norms and practices as well as inadequate accounting of the overall work output of women in rural areas. However, for the payment of equal wages to women, Government is implementing the Equal Remuneration Act, 1976 which provides for payment of equal remuneration to men and women for the same work or work of a similar nature without any discrimination. This Act is being implemented by the State Governments for the areas under their jurisdiction and monitored by the Central Government. For the areas under the Central Governments, the Act is being implemented by the office of the Chief Labour Commissioner (Central). This information was given by the Minister of State for Labour and Employment Shri Oscar Fernandes (Independent Charge) in a written reply in the Lok Sabha today.

6460. (10-3-2008) NEW DELHI : The Government is not proposing to amend the Child Labour (Prohibition and Regulation) Act, 1986 to prohibit all forms of child labour. Considering the socio-economic conditions of the country and the nature and magnitude of the problem, Government is following a sequential approach of first covering children working in hazardous occupations/processes. This information was given by the Minister of State for Labour and Employment Shri Oscar Fernandes (Independent Charge) in a written reply in the Lok Sabha today.

6461. (10-3-2008) NEW DELHI : Industrial Training Institutes / Industrial Training Centres are set up under the administrative and financial control of the respective State Governments. No central assistance / grants are provided for running these ITIs. However, Central Government is providing assistance for upgrading 500 ITIs in the country, out of which assistance to 100 Government ITIs is met through domestic resources and 245 Government ITIs (out of 400 ITIs identified so far) from World Bank assistance, during the last three years Proposals for release of Central assistance from various States including the State of Karnataka are received and central assistance for their upgradation is released after scrutiny of the proposals. So far, central assistance of Rs. 8.66 crores has been released for upgrading 12 ITIs in the State of Karnataka. In addition, an amount of Rs.57.5 crore has been released for upgradation of another 23 ITIs of Karnataka as interest free loan under the scheme of Upgradation of 1396 Government ITIs through Public Private Partnership mode in the current financial year This information was given by the Minister of State for Labour and Employment Shri Oscar Fernandes (Independent Charge) in a written reply in the Lok Sabha today.

6462. (10-3-2008) NEW DELHI : Government has recently announced to set up a National Skill Development Mission under which 1500 more ITIs and 50,000 Skill Development Centres are proposed to be opened in Public Private Partnership mode to train about 10 million persons per annum. National Council for Vocational Training has formed a Sub Committee dealing with courses to consider inclusion of new trades under Craftsmen Training Scheme. A similar body has been recommended for apprenticeship training scheme by Central Apprenticeship Council. The members of Sub-Committee include Officers from Ministries, State Government, Industry association, Industry, Experts from relevant field. This information was given by the Minister of State for Labour and Employment Shri Oscar Fernandes (Independent Charge) in a written reply in the Lok Sabha today.

6463. (10-3-2008) NEW DELHI : The Airports Authority of India (AAI) has paid Interim Dividend of Rs.100 crore (One hundred crore) to the Government of India for the financial year 2007-08. The cheque was presented to the Minister of Civil Aviation, Shri Praful Patel by Chairman AAI, Dr. K. Ramalingam in the presence of Secretary Civil Aviation, Shri Ashok Chawla and other senior officers from Ministry of Civil Aviation and AAI. AAI has undertaken a number of projects to improve airport infrastructure in the country in view of ever growing traffic in civil aviation sector. During the current financial year 2007-08, *i.e.* is by 31 March 2008, AAI is likely to incur capital expenditure of more than Rs. 1900 crores in modernizing the airports and passenger facilities all across the country. AAI is also undertaking city side development of 35 non-metro Airports to meet the growing demand of civil aviation sector. AAI had earlier paid total dividend of Rs.172 crore (including interim Dividend of Rs.60 crore) for the financial year 2006-07 to Government. The Civil Aviation Minister on this occasion complimented AAI for their initiatives in modernizing the airport infrastructure in the country and emphasized the need for speedy implementation of ongoing projects to meet the growing traffic demand.

6464. (10-3-2008) NEW DELHI : Eleventh Five Year Plan allocation of Rs.2,69,873 crore has been made available for the Ministry of Human Resource Development [Rs. 1,84,930 crore for Department of School Education & Literacy and 84,943 crore for Department of Higher Education]. This constitutes 4.6 fold increase over the expenditure of about Rs.58,820 crore incurred during X Five Year Plan and 19.4% of the over all Central Plan allocation. The increased allocation provided during XI Five Year Plan is proposed to be utilized for expansion of existing institutions, opening of new institutions and improvement in the quality of education. The total Plan allocation for the Ministry of Human Resource Development for 2008-09 is Rs.34,400 crore(Rs.7,600 crore for the Department of Higher Education and Rs.26,800 crore for the Department of School Education & Literacy). The increased allocation during XI Plan is expected to be utilized for expansion of capacity to increase access while ensuring quality and inclusiveness and also to take steps for improving quality of education. This information was given by the Minister of State for Human Resource Development smt. D. Purandeswari in a written reply in Rajya Sabha today.

6465. (10-3-2008) NEW DELHI : The Scheduled Tribes and Other Traditional Forest Dwellers (Recognition of Forest Rights) Act, 2006, implemented by the

Ministry of Tribal Affairs, seeks to recognize and vest the forest rights and occupation in forest land in forest dwelling Scheduled Tribes and other traditional forest dwellers who have been residing in such forest for generations but whose rights could not be recorded. This was stated by the Minister for Tribal Affairs, Shri P.R. Kyndiah in a reply to a question by Shri dharma Pal Sabharwal in Rajya Sabha today. He further added that there is no case reported by the State/UT Government regarding eviction of forest dwellers belonging to Scheduled Tribes. Further, Section 4(5) of the Scheduled Tribes and Other Traditional Forest Dwellers Act, 2006 also provides that no member of a forest dwelling scheduled Tribe or other traditional forest dweller shall be evicted or removed form forest land under his occupation till the recognition and verification procedure is complete.

6466. (10-3-2008) NEW DELHI : As per the information received from Ministry of Health, the latest survey report of Registrar General of India (RGI-SRS 2001-03) published in the year 2006, the Maternal Mortality Ratio (MMR) for India is 301 per 100,000 live births which translates into about 77,000 maternal deaths per year or in other words 211 maternal deaths per day. This was stated by the Minister of State for Women and Child Development, Smt. Renuka Chowdhury in a reply to a question by Smt. Viplove Thankur in Rajya Sabha here today.

6467. (10-3-2008) NEW DELHI : India requires enormous investment in infrastructure sector and infrastructure projects have long gestation periods and, in most cases, are not financially viable on their own. The advantage of long tenure and low interest of Japanese ODA is beneficial to India for funding large infrastructure projects. This was stated by the Finance Minister, Shri P. Chidambaram at the Note Exchange ceremony, held here today for Japanese ODA Package of Yen 185.575 billion (equivalent to Rs.7074 crore approximately) for the second batch of FY 2007. In the presence of Finance Minister, the notes were exchanged between Shri Kumar Sanjay Krishna, Joint Secretary in the Ministry of Finance and Mr. Hideaki Domichi, Ambassador of Japan to India. Appreciating the increasing commitment of Japanese ODA to India since FY 2003-04, Shri P. Chidambaram said that with this commitment total ODA loan commitment from Japan in FY 2007 comes to JPY 225.13 billion (Rs.8582 crore or US $ 2.17 billion) and this is a 21.76% increase from last year's ODA commitment which was JPY 184.893 billion. This is also the highest ever ODA loan commitment from Japan to India and India continues to be the highest recipient of ODA from Japan, the Finance Minister added. Shri Chidambaram stated that this year's ODA package include projects which are very important to India, like the Delhi MRTS, Kolkata East-West, Hyderabad Outer Ring Road and Tamil Nadu Urban Infrastructure development Projects. He mentioned that inclusion of Hogenakkal Water Supply and Fluorisis Mitigation Project in the ODA package serves a long standing demand of the people of Tamil Nadu. Shri Chidambaram said that in the last few years relations between India and Japan have steadily progressed based on India-

Japan Global Partnership. The visits of the Indian Prime Minister to Japan in 2006 and the visit of the Japanese Prime Minister to India in 2007 have further strengthened the India-Japan Global Partnership by adding greater substance to the bilateral relations based on India-Japan Global Partnership, the Minister said.

6468. (10-3-2008) NEW DELHI : The Prime Minister reviewed the action taken by the Government to counteract the erosion of the Majuli Island in the Brahmaputra River on 29th October, 2007 at New Delhi. In the meeting, the reasons for erosion of Majuli Island due to Brahmaputra river and the actions needed to address the issue were reviewed. It was also indicated that there had been a gradual but steady erosion of the Island which has led to the reduction in Vaishnavite monasteries to 22 at present. The Brahmaputra Board has undertaken the measures for protection of Majuli Island from flood and erosion.

6469. (10-3-2008) NEW DELHI : The average annual precipitation is estimated as 4000 Billion Cubic Metre (BCM) in the country. After accounting for the natural process evaporation etc. The average annual water availability in the country is assessed as 1869 BCM. It is estimated that owing to topographic, hydrological and other constraints, the utilizable water is 1123 BCM which comprises of 690 BCM of surface water and 433 BCM of replenishable ground water resources. 629 BCM of water is being utilized for diverse purposes. Rest of the water could be considered to be flowing down to sea. The assessment of available water resources has been made river basin-wise. With a view to, optimally utilize the available resources, several measures for development and management of water resources are undertaken by the respective State Governments which include creation of storages, restoration of water bodies, rain water harvesting, artificial recharge to ground water and adoption of better management practices etc. Storage capacity of about 225 Billion Cubic Metre (BCM) has been created so far. As per present assessment, the total estimated storage capacity of the various projects under construction is about 64 BCM. Further, the State Governments have identified various other schemes for investigation and planning and the estimated storage for such schemes is about 108 BCM. State Governments conceive, plan and implement major, medium and minor schemes (both surface and ground water) for utilization of water resources. Government of India is providing central assistance to the State Governments through various schemes/programmes, such as Accelerated Irrigation Benefits Programme (AIBP); Command Area Development and Water Management (CADWM) Programme; National Project for Repair, Renovation and Restoration of Water Bodies directly linked to Agriculture etc. The Ministry of Water Resources encourages conservation of water including measures such as traditional water conservation practices, rainwater harvesting and recharge to ground water and adoption of better management practices. This information was given by the Minister of State for Water Resources, Shri Jai Prakash Narayan Yadav in response to a question by Chaudhary Bijendra Singh in the Lok Sabha today.

6470. (10-3-2008) NEW DELHI : As per the Report of Working Group on Water Resources for the XI Five Year Plan, the unapproved projects in the X Plan comprising of 90 major, 136 medium and 74 Extension, Renovation & Modernization (ERM) projects are likely to spill over into XI Plan. The latest estimated cost of these projects is assessed as Rs.122060.24 crore and expenditure incurred on these projects up to X Plan is assessed as Rs.41127.75 crore. Irrigation being State subject, the planning, execution and funding of irrigation projects is within the purview of the concerned State Governments. The Central Appraising Agencies (CAA) considers only those projects which are submitted by the State Government for appraisal to CAA. However, funding for expeditious completion of these projects being provided under Accelerated Irrigation Benefits Programme is not provided to unapproved projects. The time taken for completion of appraisal process for the project proposals received by CAA depends on the promptness with which the State Governments complies with the observations of the Central Appraising Agencies. This information was given by the Minister of State for Water Resources, Shri Jai Prakash Narayan Yadav in response to a question by Shri Ramesh Dube in the Lok Sabha today.

6471. (10-3-2008) NEW DELHI : Desilting of water bodies is required to be carried out by various agencies, particularly, the State Governments as part of regular operation and maintenance. The Ministry of Water Resources has not taken up any specific programme or scheme for "Desilting of Water Bodies". However, removal of deposited material in tanks or other water bodies or lakes etc. is taken up as site specific measure in respect of water bodies or lakes included under the scheme of the Ministry of Water Resources for "Repair, Renovation and Restoration of Water Bodies directly linked to Agriculture" and "National Lake Conservation Plan" of Ministry of Environment and Forests. The Ministry of Water Resources, Government of India approved project proposals in respect of 1098 water bodies for 26 districts in 15 States under Pilot Scheme for Repair, Renovation and Restoration of Water Bodies directly linked to Agriculture. Besides, the World Bank Loan Agreement has been signed with Tamil Nadu for Rs. 2182 crore to restore 5763 water bodies. Loan agreements in respect of the project in Andhra Pradesh for Rs. 835 crore for restoration of 3000 water bodies and the project in Karnataka for Rs. 259 crore for restoration of 1225 water bodies have also been signed with the World Bank. The components of the scheme, inter-alia, include activities related to desilting. The Ministry of Environment and Forests has informed that out of the proposals received so far, the Ministry has sanctioned projects for conservation of 52 lakes at a total estimated cost of Rs. 687.52 crore which generally include desilting as one of the components. This information was given by the Minister of State for Water Resources, Shri Jai Prakash Narayan Yadav in response to a question by Shri Rayapati Sambasiva Rao and Dr. K. Thanaraju in the Lok Sabha today.

6472. (10-3-2008) NEW DELHI : The paper of International Water Management Institute (IWMI) on "Biofuels and Implications for Agricultural Water Use: Blue Impacts of Green Energy" has explored the land and water implications of increased biofuel production globally and with special focus on China and India. The report concludes that, although of minor concern at global level, local and regional impacts could be substantial. However, nowhere in the paper, it has been mentioned that the vigorous use of biofuel plant can vanish the water resources in the country. This information was given by the Minister of State for Water Resources, Shri Jai Prakash Narayan Yadav in response to a question by Shri Chandra Mani Tripathi and Dr. Laxminarayan Pandey in the Lok Sabha today.

6473. (10-3-2008) NEW DELHI : In the carbon constraint world of today quest for new energy technologies assumes great importance in view of the inherent problems that exists in current energy systems. Talking on "Prospects of EU-India S&T Cooperation in the field of Renewable Energy-a perspective for India," Co-chair, India Dr. A. Ramachandran said because of growing concern about high oil prices, energy security and climate change has changed the focus on certain key areas of energy research around the globe. In this context this workshop is timely and most relevant in the context of India-EU framework of S&T cooperation. Dr. Ramachandran explained energy issues have become complex as they are inextricably linked to various economic, social and environmental aspects of development. Many of these issues transcend national boundaries. There is growing awareness among all stakeholders of the compelling necessity for the world as a whole to make a transition to clean energy technologies. Dr. Ramachandran appealed to incorporate a diversified portfolio of energy technology options along with the likely timeframe for the development and deployment, leading to sustainable energy pathways. He said renewable energy in India has made noteworthy progress under the stewardship of the Ministry of New And Renewable Energy but the overall impact remains relatively small. To make the share of renewable energy visible in the total energy makes, the national effort has to be scaled up several fold from the present level. Earlier, opening this two-day Indo-EU Energy Research Workshop Dr. T. Ramasami, Secretary, Department of Science & Technology said we have huge demand of energy whereas the supply is less and fossil fuels are decreasing. In this situation looking for renewable energy is not an option but it is necessity. Without putting any stress on environment and natural resources, we are looking forward to alternative renewable energy. Dr. Ramasami welcomed all delegates of EU Member countries, Scientists and experts and expressed hope that on this platform we will learn as well as share from each other and we will co-invest and co-generate values in the field of renewables. Mr. R Liberali, Director of Energy, DG Research expressed his views on perspective from the EU and said that the joint statement of last years India-EU summit reaffirm our common willingness to strengthen our cooperation to jointly meet the serious challenge of climate change and energy security. Within this context, he added that the joint action plan between India and the EU also stressed the importance of our S&T cooperation on low carbon technologies and in particular on new and renewable energy to achieve climate change and energy policy objectives. This will allow us to start a more focussed and concrete discussion and exchange of information on the areas of solar and wind technologies, biomass gasification and waste to energy. The two-day workshop has been organized by the Ministry of New & Renewable Energy.

6474. (10-3-2008) NEW DELHI : India and Myanmar have expressed strong desire that the common border between the two countries should be a region and symbol of peace and harmony so that the benefits out of various infrastructure projects and economic cooperation between the two countries can be fully realized. Both sides have agreed to work closely for achieving these objectives and, in this context, discussed various institutional mechanisms to strengthen security cooperation. The understanding was reached at the 14th National Level Meeting between India and Myanmar which began here last Friday and concluded today. The Indian delegation was led by the Union Home Secretary, Shri Madhukar Gupta, and the Myanmar delegation by their Deputy Minister for Home Affairs, Brig. General Phone Swe. At this meeting, various issues of mutual concern including those related to security, drug trafficking and border management were discussed. Later, the leader of the Myanmar delegation called on the Home Minister, Shri Shivraj Patil. The Home Minister recalled the strong and close bonds between the two countries and emphasized the importance of strengthening cooperation in the areas of security and border management as well as in the context of India's 'Look East' policy. Myanmar is a close and friendly neighbour with whom India shares a border of around 1650 kms. India-Myanmar bilateral relations are reflective of the multi-dimensional and traditional linkages between the two countries.

6475. (10-3-2008) NEW DELHI : Following is the situation of bird flu in West Bengal up to 10th March, 2008 (2.00 PM): After samples from Raghunathganj-II and Jiaganj blocks of Murshidabad districts testing positive as per update submitted on 7th March 2008, there are no further report from the High Security Animal Disease Laboratory, Bhopal of any sample testing positive from any part of the country, including West Bengal. Culling in a radius of five kilometers around the two new foci of infection has already commenced today *i.e.* 10th March 2008. While 22,440 birds are to be culled in Raghunathganj-II, the culling target in respect of Jiaganj is 27,200 birds. A total of 20 RRTs have been deployed in each of the two blocks. No unusual mortality was reported in West Bengal on 9th March, 2008. As per the latest report received from the Government of West Bengal, the cumulative figure of poultry culled in the state up to 9th March 2008 is 40.03 lakh. The cumulative figures of eggs and feed destroyed till the said date are 14,91,307 and 80,033 kg respectively.

6476. (10-3-2008) NEW DELHI : The Union Government is implementing a scheme Textile Workers Rehabilitation Fund Scheme (TWRFS) to provide relief to workers of closed textile mills. This information was given by the Minister of State for Textiles, Shri E.V.K.S. Elangovan, in the Lok Sabha today, in a written reply to a question by Shri Asaduddin Owaisi. The Minister further said that the Scheme has been in operation with effect from 15th September, 1986. It seeks to provide interim relief to textile workers rendered unemployed as a consequence of permanent closure of any particular portion or entire textile units. Assistance under the Scheme is payable to eligible workers only for the purpose of enabling them to settle in another employment. Such assistance is not heritable, transferable or capable of being attached on account of any other liabilities of the worker. The worker's eligibility shall cease if he takes up employment in another registered or licensed undertaking. The rehabilitation assistance will not be curtailed if the worker fixes himself in a self-employment venture. To avail the relief under this Scheme, any worker is eligible provided he/she has been engaged in a closed textile unit on the date of its closure continuously for five years or more and earning a wage equivalent of Rs. 2500 per month or less for the mills closed between 06.06.1985 to 01.04.1993 and Rs.3500 or less thereafter. They should be contributing to provident fund maintained by the Regional Provident Fund Commissioner of the State concerned. He further stated the cooperation and assistance of the State Governments is crucial in smooth functioning of this Scheme. The State Governments collect the details of the workers from the management/official liquidator/provident fund authorities etc. and forward the same to the concerned regional office of the Textile Commissioner. The State Governments also certify the relief claiming application of the individual workers

6477. (10-3-2008) NEW DELHI : As per the information received from Ministry of Health, the latest survey report of Registrar General of India (RGI-SRS 2001-03) published in the year 2006, the Maternal Mortality Ratio (MMR) for India is 301 per 100,000 live births which translates into about 77,000 maternal deaths per year or in other words 211 maternal deaths per day. This was stated by the Minister of State for Women and Child Development, Smt. Renuka Chowdhury in a reply to a question by Smt. Viplove Thankur in Rajya Sabha here today.

6478. (10-3-2008) NEW DELHI : Lack of skilled human resource will be the single largest deterrent to speedy development in the country, according to a recent McKinsey report. The sectors expected to drive job demand in India are manufacturing, IT&ITeS, retail, communication and transport. The manufacturing sector accounts for about 15% of India's Gross Domestic Product (GDP), while the share of the services' sector in the GDP of India has increased to 56% in 2006-07. The need to vocationalise education is higher than ever before. Meanwhile, India does have a problem. According to a Confederation of Indian Industries (CII) and Ministry of Labour and Employment report, although India has over 65% of its population below the age of 26 years, only 5% of the Indian labour force in the age group of 20-24 years has obtained vocational skills through the formal system while the percentage in industrialized countries varies between 60% and 96%. Almost 63% of school students drop out at different stages before reaching Class X. While only about 25 lakh vocational training seats are available in India, about 1.28 crore people enter the labour market every year. Most school dropouts do not have access to skill development, reducing therefore, their chances of employability. To address this country's increasing skills shortage, the government is setting a Rs 31,000 crore skill-development mission. This will help in extending training facilities to 1 crore people per month. During last year's Budget presentation in Parliament, the Finance Minister P. Chidambaram had announced that the government had taken up a programme for upgradation of 500 ITIs over a span of five years, starting from 2005. He said: "Revised courses in the first lot of 100 upgraded ITIs were started in August 2005 and in the second lot of 100 upgraded ITIs in August 2006. I expect that another 300 ITIs will be covered by August 2009. That would still leave 1,396 Government ITIs. I propose that the 1,396 ITIs be upgraded into centres of excellence in specific trades and skills under public-private partnership." Meanwhile, IT and BPO sector could employ 90 lakh people by 2010, according to a NASSCOM-McKinsey Report 2006. Manufacturing in the next decade in the country is expected to create 2.5 crore jobs. According to a recent CII-ICRIER study on Higher Education in India, the global IT off shoring market is to the tune of Rs 30,000 crore, "of which India may be able to garnet Rs 60 crore by 2010". The report also mentions that India could achieve Rs 16, 500 crore in merchandise trade by 2009-10, creating an additional 2.1 crore new jobs. As far as research is concerned, only 10% look to getting into research-a primary need for all industries for their future growth. Meanwhile, the additional 1% secondary education cess announced in last year's Budget is reported to have generated an additional revenue of Rs 5,300 crore, according to government sources, while the 2% education cess levied through the Finance Act 2004, yielded Rs 8, 748 crore in 2006-07, used primarily to finance the Sarva Siksha Abhiyan (Education for All) scheme of the government. Meanwhile, Last year, a Ma Foi survey (Global Search Services) predicted that over 10 lakh jobs would be created across sectors in India. Despite, its 100-crore population, imparting the right skills for an emerging market will test the country's institutions of learning. As far as higher education is concerned, the government aims to increase the enrolment rate from the estimated 10% of the population by the end of the Tenth Plan (2007) to 15% by 2011-12 in the Eleventh Plan. India has come a long way from 1950s, when the enrolment rate in higher education was a mere 0.7%. According to government figures, even a 5% net increase in the number of students will result in an additional increase of about 84 lakh during the period 2007-12. Of this, about 50 lakh will be in general education and the remaining in technical and professional education.

6479. (10-3-2008) NEW DELHI : The Government has announced a special package to promote the Jute Industry in the country. This information was information was given by the Minister of State for Textiles, Shri E.V.K.S. Elangovan, in the Lok Sabha today, in a written reply to a question by Shri Navjot Singh Sidhu. The Minister further stated that the Ministry of Textiles has launched the Jute Technology Mission (JTM), w.e.f. 2007-08 for a period of five years to promote the jute industry in the country. An amount of Rs 355.55 Crores has been allocated for the implementation of the schemes for the Mini Mission I to IV of the Jute Technology Mission during Eleventh Plan Period. The schemes of the Mini Mission I & II are being implemented by the Ministry of Agriculture and the schemes of the Mini Mission-III & IV are being implemented by the Ministry of Textiles.

6480. (10-3-2008) NEW DELHI : The National Pharmaceutical Pricing Authority (NPPA) have issued guidelines regarding reduction in prices of non scheduled formulation packs consequent to reduction in excise duty from 16% to 8% and the rate of abatement from 42.5% to 35.5% notified by the Ministry of Finance, (Department of Revenue) on 01.03.2008. This is to ensure that the benefit of the excise duty reduction announced in the Union Budget for 2008-09 is passed on to the Consumers. A copy of the guideline issued by NPPA is reproduced below:- Consequent upon the reduction in the rate of excise duty on medicines from 16% to 8% notified by the Ministry of Finance, Department of Revenue vide Notification No.4/2008 Central (Excise) dated on 01.03.2008 and the rate of abatement from 42.5% to 35.5% vide Notification No.14/2008-Central Excise (N.T.) dated 01.03.2008, all manufacturers and marketing companies of formulation packs are advised to ensure that the benefit of this excise duty reduction and the reduced rate of abatement is passed on to consumers through reduced Maximum Retail Price (MRP). Prices of all non scheduled packs must accordingly be reduced downwards by 4.58% except in those categories of non scheduled formulation packs where no excise duty has been actually paid to the Government and therefore no excise duty shall be chargeable in the MRP of such non scheduled packs. The National Pharmaceutical Pricing Authority (NPPA) expects that the above reduction in MRP would be complied with by way of reduced MRP and that necessary revised price lists would be submitted to NPPA forthwith.

6481. (10-3-2008) NEW DELHI : The Prince Andrew Albert Christian Edward, Duke of York and special Representative of Department of Trade & Investment, Government of UK, called on Dr. Ashwani Kumar, Minister of State for Industry, here today. During their bilateral meeting, useful exchanges took place on enhancing India-UK Trade & Investment flows. The visit coming right after the annual summit visit by the Prime Minister, Gordon Brown to New Delhi in January 2008 assumes special significance in respect of trade and investment relations. Dr. Kumar informed the Prince about the Government of India's focus on education and skill upgradation. Both sides recalled the warmth in the historical relationship between the two countries and expressed satisfaction on the current level of mutual engagement particularly by large MNCs of UK in India and of Indian MNCs in

UK. They called for an exponential increase in business contacts between SMEs and service sectors of both the countries in view of the limitless business potential that exists between the two countries. Dr. Ashwani Kumar mentioned the significance of major UK investments in India like Vodafone, Virgin, Huges, Marconi & E-com in Telecommunication sector, British Petroleum, Shell, Castrol, Cairns, British Gas in oil and gas sector, Scottish and New Castle, HSBC, Powergen, Aviva, Cadbury, GSK Pharmaceuticals, Johnson Matthey, Logica, Marks & Spencer, Standard Chartered Bank, Tesco, Unilever etc. Similarly, he mentioned the recent trend of Indian companies investing in the UK, which includes HCL, ICICI, Infosys, TCS, Thermax, Wipro and Wockhardt. During the bilateral meeting, Duke of York informed Dr. Kumar that British companies recognize that India would be at the centre of the Asian economic growth story and added that British companies are aware of the importance of India's favourable demographic profile being the major contributor of the growth of global economy. Keeping in view the overall outward investment profile of UK, Duke of York stated that there is tremendous scope for an exponential growth in not only trade but also in investments. He outlined comparative strength of UK in services sectors like legal and accountancy, R&D, financial, education, retail, innovation, infrastructure and green technologies. He hoped that India will take next level of steps for improved market access. He also assured Dr. Kumar that there would be no discrimination against Indian professionals for work visas in the UK. Dr. Ashwani Kumar reiterated India's commitment to the rule-based multilateral and equitable international trade regime for enlarging global business opportunity. UK is the third largest investor in India with cumulative FDI of US $ 4.13 billion. UK is also one of the major contributors of technology to India with 860 technical collaborations in the past 17 years.

6482. (10-3-2008) NEW DELHI : Government has an existing system of agricultural bio-security maintained through its Plan and Animal Quarantine systems. The import of agricultural commodities is regulated through 57 Plant Quarantine Stations covering the notified import entry points, airports, seaports, and land frontiers, and sixty in-land depots to carry out plant quarantine inspections and to facilitate safe import and export of plants and plant materials. The legislative framework is provided by the Plant Quarantine (Regulation of Import into India) order, 2003 issued under the Destructive Insects and Pests Act, 1914. The purpose and intent of this Act is to prevent the introduction of any insect, nematodes, weeds, fungus or other invasive and exotic pest, which is or may be destructive to crops. The import of plants and plant materials are regulated on the basis of a scientific Pest Risk Analysis to safeguard the native plants species from exotic pests. For Animal Quarantine there is a central legislation, entitled, "The Livestock Importation (Amendment) Act, 2001" The National Commission on Farmers recommended the setting up of a National Agricultural Bio-security System, a National Agricultural Bio-security Council for policy making and coordination, a National Centre for Agricultural Bio-security and a National Agricultural Bio-security Network. On the basis of the recommendations made by the National Commission on Farmers, Government of India formulated the National Policy for Farmers, 2007. This policy has the goal to strengthen the bio-security of crops, farm animals, fish and forest trees for safeguarding the livelihood and income security of farmers families and the health and trade security of the nation. This policy has laid down the establishment of an Integrated National Agricultural Bio-security System (NABS) covering crops, animal husbandry, fisheries, forestry and agriculturally relevant micro-organisms, with the objectives to (i) safeguard the income and livelihood security of farmers families, (ii) enhance national and local capacity in initiating proactive measures in monitoring and early warning, education, international cooperation, (iii) introduce an integrated bio-security package, and (iv) organize an integrated national agricultural bio-security programme with effective home and regional quarantine facilities. This information was given in the Lok Sabha today by Shri Kanti Lal Bhuria, Minister of State for Agriculture in a written reply.

6483. (10-3-2008) NEW DELHI : Following Measures have been taken to tackle problems of farmers adopting organic farming:-i) In collaboration with Food & Agriculture Organization (FAO) organic Package of Practices for important crops for 5 States have been prepared. ii) Efforts are being made to document available information on organic farming for farmers. iii) For promotion of marketing and dissemination of information about organic products a web based information portal is being launched, where farmers can post their details or organic products for marketing. Under NPOF efforts are being made to create awareness for organic products. iv) For facilitation of certification at affordable cost, assistance is being provided under the component of "Capacity Building through Service Providers" for Internal Control System (ICS) management & facilitation of certification. An assistance of RS. 200/- per farmer is provided to the agencies for such Service.

6484. (10-3-2008) NEW DELHI : To increase the production and improvement of quality of sugarcane, a Centrally Sponsored Scheme of Sustainable Development of Sugarcane Based Cropping System (SUBACS) under Macro Management Mode of Agriculture is under implementation in different States. The Scheme provides assistance for field demonstrations, training of farmers and extension workers, farm implements/machinery, heat treatment plant, production of planting material and drip irrigation. The Ministry of Consumer Affairs, Food and Public Distribution have taken various steps/measures to provide relief to sugar mills and sugarcane farmers. The important steps/measures taken are as under:-i) The Government has created a buffer stock of 50 lakh tonnes in 2007-07 sugar season, which would involve an annual subsidy amount of Rs. 880 crores (approx) to be borne from the Sugar Development Fund. The banks provide additional credit on creation of buffer stock. The buffer subsidy amount and the additional credit are to be used for payment of cane price including cane price arrears as a first priority.

ii) Export assistance is provided on internal transport, marketing and handling charges and ocean freight@ Rs. 1350/- per tonne for sugar factories located in coastal areas and Rs. 1450/- per tonne for sugar factories located in non-coastal areas for a period one year with effect from 10th April, 2007. This assistance provided shall also be used for payment of cane price arrears of farmers, as a first priority. iii) A special Scheme has been notified for extending financial assistance to sugar mills from the banks where full interest subvention (limited to 12%) will be provided to all banks for the total duration of the loan. This will help the mills towards payment of cane price including cane price arrears. iv) Making 5% blending of ethanol with petrol mandatory across the country, except in J&K, North Eastern States and Island Territories and to make 10% blending optional from October, 2007 and mandatory from October, 2008, excepting in the areas mentioned above; v) Reduction of customs duty from 7.5% to 5% on "denatured alcohol" and from 10% to 5% on molasses and to implement the same only when mandatory ethanol blending at 5% level is operationalised in the country; iv) Permitting sugar factories to produce ethanol directly from sugarcane juice to augment availability of ethanol and reduce over supply of sugar. This information was given in the Lok Sabha today by Shri Kanti Lal Bhuria, Minister of State for Agriculture in a written reply.

6485. (10-3-2008) NEW DELHI : Over 6.53 lakh farmers have been covered under the Livestock Insurance Scheme upto 28.2.08. Funds to the tune of Rs. 90.21 crore have been released to States by the Central Government. The Livestock Insurance Scheme is being implemented on a pilot basis in 100 selected districts across the country during 2005-06, 2006-07 and 2007-08. The scheme is being implemented through the State Livestock Development Boards. Under the scheme 50% subsidy on premium is provided by the Central Government to insure crossbred and high yielding cattle and buffaloes and rest of the premium to a beneficiary. The benefit of one time subsidy on premium to a beneficiary is restricted to two crossbred cows and buffaloes for a policy of maximum period of three years. The animal can be insured under the scheme for maximum of their current market value. Animals covered under any other insurance scheme/plan scheme will not be covered under this scheme. The premium rates may not exceed 4.5% for annual policies and 12% for 3 year policies (inclusive of additional risk factors). Further, the claims are to be settled by the insurance companies within 15 days on receipt of claims with the requisite documents. This information was given in the Lok Sabha today by Shri Taslimuddin, Minister of State for Agriculture in a written reply.

6486. (10-3-2008) NEW DELHI : The Insurance Regulatory & Development Authority (IRDA) has reported that vide its circular dated 01.01.2008, it has directed all insurance companies to provide policyholders the details of various charges deducted from the premium and the amount available for investment in each policy year at the time of purchasing the Unit Linked Insurance Plans. IRDA has reported that action would be taken against the insurance companies not complying with its instructions under Section 3 of the Insurance Act, 1938.

6487. (10-3-2008) NEW DELHI : Defence Research and Development Organisation is pursuing development of Airborne Early Warning and Control System (AWACS) at a cost of Rs. 1,800 cr with a probable date of completion in the year 2011. Development and manufacture of indigenous Radar is included in AWACS programme. The possibilities of marketing Indian technology for surveillance equipment in world markets have not been assessed. This information was given by Defence Minister Shri A K Antony in a written reply to Shri Naveen Jindal in Lok Sabha today.

6488. (10-3-2008) NEW DELHI : The Defence Minister Shri AK Antony will inaugurate the two-day International Maritime Search and Rescue Conference (IMSARCON 2008) here tomorrow. India acceded to the International Maritime Organisation Convention on Search and Rescue in 2001. The accession provided the much needed impetus for regional and international cooperation in SAR operations. The Indian Coast Guard is designated as the nodal agency for Maritime Search and Rescue in Indian Search and Rescue Region (ISRR) under the convention. It has been entrusted with the onerous task of ensuring the security of the Maritime Zones of India with a view to protect maritime and other national interests in such zones. Given India's strategic location, it is but natural that India plays a lead role in the Indian Ocean region. Consequently, the Indian Coast Guard has been playing a vital role in ensuring "Safety of Life at Sea" not only in the vast Indian Search and Rescue Region (ISRR) that extends over four million square kilometers, but also in adjoining Search and Rescue Regions whenever requested for assistance by the neighbouring countries. Close cooperation with our littoral neighbours is therefore essential for efficient coordination of Maritime Search and Rescue (SAR). The Indian Coast Guard's interaction has been formally institutionalised with Japan, Maldives, and South Korea. Further, a working relationship has been established with Bangladesh, Malaysia, Mauritius, Oman, Philippines, Seychelles, Singapore, Sri Lanka, Thailand, United States of America and Vietnam.

6489. (10-3-2008) NEW DELHI : National Aluminium Company Limited (NALCO) has announced an interim dividend of 45% on a paid-up capital of Rs. 644.31 crore, amounting to Rs. 289.94 crore for the financial year 2007-08. The dividend cheque for Rs. 252.67 crore on the 87.15% shares held by the Government of India was handed over to Shri Sis Ram Ola, Union Minister of Mines, by Shri C.R. Pradhan, CMD, NALCO in New Delhi today, in the presence of Shri J.P. Singh, Secretary, Ministry of Mines, and other senior officials of the Ministry and NALCO. The balance amount of Rs. 37.27 crores has been disbursed to other shareholders of the Company like banks, financial institutions and individual shareholders. The Minister expressed happiness at the increasing profits being incurred by NALCO. He announced that NALCO would soon become a Navratna Company and thus ruled out any talks about dis investment of the Company. He stressed that NALCO would remain a PSU and expressed hope that in the future would continue to achieve increasing profits and pay richer dividends to the Government.

6490. (10-3-2008) NEW DELHI : The Franchisee Scheme which entails setting up of Franchisee Outlets of postal network is already in existence. The Franchisee Scheme was launched in February 2007 in select urban areas for providing increased access to postal counter services in areas where opening of a Post Office was not possible as per prescribed norms. The scheme has now been extended to cover areas of new upcoming urban townships, special economic zones, major highway projects, upcoming new industrial centres, colleges, etc. The opening of Franchisee Outlets is in addition to opening of Post Offices wherever justified. Unemployed youth are not debarred from working as Franchisees of the Department. The applicant in this regard should fulfil the criteria for selection, such as minimum age requirement, educational qualification, etc. Criteria for selection of Franchisees are in view of the need to select persons with capacity to manage and market a range of products, along with a sense of the community needs and public aspects of the job and willingness to accept technological options. The preference is given to postal pensioners and those able to provide computers.

6491. (10-3-2008) NEW DELHI : The Government proposes to freeze the existing Corpus of Post Office Insurance Fund and convert it into dated securities over a period of three years. The future accretion to the fund are proposed to be invested as per the Insurance Regulatory and Development Authority (Investment) Regulations, 2000 and IRDA (Investment) (Amendment) Regulations, 2001, and further amendments thereto from time to time. The future accretion from the Post Office Insurance Funds are proposed to be invested as per the Insurance Regulatory and Development Authority (Investment) Regulations, 2000 and IRDA (Investment) (Amendment) Regulations, 2001, and further amendments thereto from time to time. To check proper utilization of funds firstly, the Government proposes that the funds will be given to the Fund Managers under "passive" or "non-discretionary" mode for investment as per IRDA (Investment) Regulations 2000. Secondly, an Investment Board will be constituted headed by Member (I &FS) Postal Services Board and consisting of other members such as financial experts, Actuary and Joint Secretary of Ministry of Finance. The Board will be the apex body for the purpose of laying down the policy guidelines and investment strategy, which will set the framework for the day-to-day decision on investment. Thirdly, there will be a Chief Investment Officer, who will be heading the Investment Division. He will execute the policy framework and structure of the investment decided by the Investment Board. This information was given by the Minister of State for Communications and Information Technology, Dr. Shakeel Ahmad in a written reply to an un-starred question in the Lok Sabha today.

6492. (10-3-2008) NEW DELHI : The Government has been implementing inter alia the Rural Employment Generation Programme (REGP) through the Khadi and Village Industries Commission (KVIC) for assisting the entrepreneurs in establishing village industry (VI) units, including the traditional leaf-cup/plate making units, in rural areas and small towns with population upto 20,000 by margin money assistance from KVIC and loans from public sector scheduled commercial banks, selected regional rural banks, cooperative banks, etc., for projects with a maximum cost of Rs. 25 lakh. Leaf-cup/plate making units are promoted under the 'Forest based industry (FBI) Group' of the village industries under the REGP. During 2006-07, margin money amounting to Rs. 1847.73 lakh was provided for various VI units under the FBI Group assisted during the year, generating 28,000 additional employment opportunities in the country. REGP is a Central Sector scheme and the approved grants for the scheme are released to the KVIC which, in turn, releases the funds (towards margin money assistance) to the banks against the projects sanctioned in each State/Union Territory (UT). During 2007-08, it has been targeted to assist the setting up of 1849 VI units under the FBI Group with a margin money assistance of Rs. 2113.13 lakh throughout the country. This information was given by the Minister of Micro, Small & Medium Enterprises, Shri Mahabir Prasad in a written reply to a question in Rajya Sabha today.

6493. (10-3-2008) NEW DELHI : The Government sought recommendations of Telecom Regulatory Authority of India (TRAI) on certain terms & conditions of Access Services Licences including the issue of limiting the number of Access providers in each service area. In its recommendations dated 28.08.2007, on "review of license terms & conditions and capping of number of access providers", TRAI has inter-alia recommended that there should be no cap on the number of access provider in any service area which has been accepted by the Government. Accordingly, the Government is granting new Unified Access Services (UAS) licences in all service areas in the country. Allocation of spectrum to the access services licensees is subject to availability. Grant of new UAS licences will ensure rapid expansion of tele-density and transformation of the telecommunications sector in a time bound manner to a greater competitive environment in both urban and rural areas. This information was given by the Minister of State for Communications and Information Technology, Dr. Shakeel Ahmad in a written reply to an un-starred question in the Lok Sabha today.

6494. (10-3-2008) NEW DELHI : As per the information tracked by, and reported to Indian Computer Emergency Response Team (CERT-In), Department of Information Technology, a number of Government websites have been hacked during the period January, 2005 to February, 2008; of which one pertained to a defence related pay office in January, 2006. The websites hacked included those belonging to Ministry of Railways, Air Cargo Customs (Mumbai), Forward markets Commission, National Institute of Health and Family Welfare, National Institute of Social Defence, Department of Administrative Reforms and Public Grievances, Wireless Planning & Coordination Wing, Bharat Sanchar Nigam Limited, Telecom Regulatory Authority of India, Department of Information Technology and Anthropological Survey of India.

6495. (10-3-2008) NEW DELHI : In their recommendation submitted to the Prime Minister in February, 2008; National Knowledge Commission (NKC) has, inter-alia, proposed as under:-"Since private schools play an important role in the provision of education, there is need for both enabling and regulating mechanisms to be developed and strengthened for them. There should be transparent, norm-based and straightforward procedures for the recognition of private schools, to reduce harassment and bureaucratic delay. There should also be transparent criteria as for the disbursement of aid from the government to some self-financing schools, especially those which cater to underprivileged children and clear norms with respect to the ability of school managements to raise resources from other sources. The monitoring of private schools, in terms of ensuring a transparent admissions process, regulation of fee structures, as well as meeting minimum set standards for quality of teaching and infrastructure also requires attention. The possibility of greater exchange between schools, including monitoring of one school by another, should be allowed and encouraged." Education being a concurrent subject, a majority of private schools come under the jurisdiction of State Governments. So far as Central Board of Secondary Education (CBSE) is concerned, affiliation of schools is a very transparent process and the requirements/norms have been specified in affiliation bye-laws. This information was given by the Minister of State for Human Resource Development Shri M.A.A. Fatmi in a written reply in Rajya Sabha today.

6496. (10-3-2008) NEW DELHI : National University of Educational Planning and Administration (NUEPA) collects elementary school statistics annually through the District Information System for Education (DISE) from all districts in the country. According to DISE data 2006-07, 45.04% students passed with 60% and above marks, at the exit classes of the primary stage. Girls have performed slightly better than boys, and the percentage of girls and boys passing with 60% and above marks is 45.12% and 44.96% respectively. At the upper primary level, 39.40% students passed with 60% and above marks. Under Sarva Shiksha Abhiyan, several activities have been undertaken to improve the quality of elementary education. This includes recruitment of 8.32 lakh additional teachers to improve the pupil teacher ratio, in service training of teachers for a period of 20 days every year, free distribution of textbooks for primary and upper primary classes to about 6.5 crore Scheduled Caste, Scheduled Tribe and girl students, academic support to primary and upper primary schools through 6395 Block Resource Centres and 68352 Cluster Resource Centres and regular evaluation of students. This information was given by the Minister of State for Human Resource Development Shri M.A.A. Fatmi in a written reply in Rajya Sabha today.

6497. (10-3-2008) NEW DELHI : In the report of the Public-Private Partnership (PPP) Sub Group on social sector brought out by the Planning Commission in 2004, a reference has been made about Public-Private Partnership in Mid-Day Meal Scheme & Computer Aided Learning at Elementary Level under Sarva Shiksha Abhiyan (SSA). The guidelines of the Mid-Day Meal Scheme provide for association of Voluntary Organisations who undertake to supply cooked mid-day meal and provide resource support to the programme through training and capacity building, monitoring & evaluation and research. Selection, identification of Voluntary Organizations for the above activities is done by implementing agency of scheme, *i.e.* State Governments/UT Administrations. No assessment has been made to the implementation of the programme through these organizations. A component of Computer Aided Learning (CAL) operated through PPP is funded under SSa. Eighty one private organizations are associated with CAL during the current year. No assessment of the role of private sector in elementary education has been undertaken under SSA. This information was given by the Minister of State for Human Resource Development Shri M.A.A. Fatmi in a written reply in Rajya Sabha today.

6498. (10-3-2008) NEW DELHI : A proposal to increase the retirement age of the Judges of the Supreme Court and the High Courts by three years is under examination of the Government. As regards increase in the retirement age of District/Subordinate Court Judges, it is the concern of the respective State Governments. This information was given by Minister of Law and Justice, Shri H. R. Bhardwaj in written reply to a question in Rajya Sabha today.

6499. (10-3-2008) NEW DELHI : The Scheduled Tribes and Other Traditional Forest Dwellers (Recognition of Forest Rights) Act, 2006, implemented by the Ministry of Tribal Affairs, seeks to recognize and vest the forest rights and occupation in forest land in forest dwelling Scheduled Tribes and other traditional forest dwellers who have been residing in such forest for generations but whose rights could not be recorded. This was stated by the Minister for Tribal Affairs, Shri P.R. Kyndiah in a reply to a question by Shri dharma Pal Sabharwal in Rajya Sabha today. He further added that there is no case reported by the State/UT Government regarding eviction of forest dwellers belonging to Scheduled Tribes. Further, Section 4(5) of the Scheduled Tribes and Other Traditional Forest Dwellers Act, 2006 also provides that no member of a forest dwelling scheduled Tribe or other traditional forest dweller shall be evicted or removed form forest land under his occupation till the recognition and verification procedure is complete.

6500. (10-3-2008) NEW DELHI : Kutir Jyoti Programme has been subsumed under Rajiv Gandhi Grameen Vidyutikaran Yojana (RGGVY), which was launched in April, 2005. Since then, 2027525 connections have been provided to BPL households as per norms of Kutir Jyoti Programme. During the financial year 2005-06 Rs.562.16 crore and during the financial year 2006-07 Rs.3381.13 crore were disbursed to States under RGGVY. This information was given by Union Minister for Power, Shri Sushilkumar Shinde in the Rajya Sabha today.

6501. (11-3-2008) NEW DELHI : The Prime Minister has sanctioned an assistance of Rupees two lakh from the Prime Minister's National Relief Fund to Shri Manjunath Kalmani who is hospitalized in the Safdarjung Hospital. As desired by the Prime Minister, a Senior Officer of the Prime Minister's Office visited Shri Manjunath in hospital today and handed over the cheque to the Hospital Authorities for his treatment. The Prime Minister has extended his best wishes to Shri Manjunath Kalmani and his family.

6502. (11-3-2008) NEW DELHI : Kendriya Vidyalaya Sangathan (KVS), a premier educational organization under the Ministry of Human Resource Development, Government of India concluded its celebration of International Women's Day here today. Union Minister of State for HRD Smt. D. Purandeswari was the Chief Guest at the programme while noted writer Shri Shiv Khera was the Guest of Honour. Speaking on the occasion, Smt. Purandeswari called upon the academicians and education experts to work for strengthening education of women in the country and work for their overall empowerment in all walks of life. Referring to various measures taken by Kendriya Vidyalaya Sangathan improving and facilitating girls education, the Minister emphasized the need to sustain these efforts in a big way. Shri Shiv Kera delivered an inspiring speech on the theme 'Living Treasure'. He said that the society should give highest regard to the women and constantly work towards their empowerment and welfare. In his welcome address, Shri Ranglal Jamuda, Commissioner, KVS recounted achievements of KVS specially in the field of girl education. He also talked about the new initiatives taken by KVS in the field of school education. The highlights of the today's programme were a chorus sung by music teachers of KVS highlighting the need of women empowerment and the performances of the winners of various inter Kendriya Vidyalaya competitions held at different levels during the month long celebrations. The winner students of the debate competition on the topic 'Gender Based Reservation will Retard the progress of the country' presented their repeat performance at the programme.. The young students enlivened the atmosphere with the recitation of beautiful poems. Smt. D. Purandeswari gave away the prizes to the winners of various competitions Smt. Pragya Richa Srivastava, Joint Commissioner (Admn.) Kendriya Vidyalaya Sangathan, proposed the vote of thanks.

6503. (11-3-2008) NEW DELHI : Delegates from SAARC countries are discussing the Use of Satellite Products in day-to-day Weather Forecasting Techniques at a four-day workshop organized by the India Meteorological Department in New Delhi. The workshop inaugurated today by Dr. P.S. Goel, Secretary, Ministry of Earth Sciences & Chairman, Earth Commission is being attended by about 16 foreign delegates from SAARC Countries *viz.* Afghanistan, Bangladesh, Bhutan,

Nepal, Maldives, Sri Lanka, Pakistan, besides a large number of participants from the host country India. Under the aegis of SAARC cooperation programme, Meteorology was one of the five areas chosen for cooperation since inception in 1981. The knowledge and expertise in the related field of Meteorology in the SAARC region is shared mostly through participation in the Seminars/ workshops hosted by Member States time to time. SAARC Countries have had more than a fair share of weather & weather related disasters. Accurate day to day weather forecasting including Early Warnings of Tropical Cyclones, Track Prediction and associated weather, Heavy Precipitation, Western Disturbances, Seasonal and Long range rainfall prediction, forecasting floods, snow & avalanche etc. are vital for the SAARC Region. The satellite data are very important for accurate forecasting and monitoring of these events especially the cyclones and floods and also other events causing severe disasters, thus proved very useful information in saving lives & property & therefore the economy of the country. The workshop aims at apprising working Scientists/Meteorologists of SAARC region with the use of meteorological data and imageries derived from the Satellite in day-to-day weather forecasting. INSAT data provides Earth Cloud Imageries in visible, Infrared and Water Vapour Bands. In addition, quantitative products such as Cloud Motion Vectors (CMVs), outgoing Longwave Radiation, Sea Surface Temperature and Quantitative Precipitation Estimates are also derived, which are vital inputs for weather forecasting. It is planned to launch probably by the end of this year an advanced dedicated Meteorological Satellite, INSAT-3D which will give a quantum jump in satellite meteorology.

6504. (11-3-2008) NEW DELHI : There has been no human case of Avian Influenza. During the recent outbreak of Avian Influenza in poultry in West Bengal, the Central Government initiated a series of actions to assist the State in the containment operations and restrict further spread of the disease. The contingency plan has been implemented in affected districts of West Bengal. The state of preparedness of the States of Jharkhand, Bihar, Orissa and Assam that share a common border with West Bengal were reviewed. Other States have also been put on alert. Information, education and communication campaign to sensitize the community was launched in the visual and print media. Adequate stock of Oseltamivir (the drug required for prevention and treatment), and personal protective equipments were made available to West Bengal and other States. Assistance to Government of West Bengal included deputing central Rapid Response Teams to all the affected districts, supply of 4,20,000 capsules of Oseltamivir, 6500 personal protective equipments, 6500 N-95 masks, 150 bottles of Tamiflu syrup, 20 ventilators for critical care support. Financial assistance of Rs. 94.38 lakh has also been granted to Government of West Bengal to carry out human surveillance using the World Health Organization Polio Surveillance model. This information was given by the Minister for Health & Family Welfare, Dr. Anbumani Ramadoss in a written reply to a question in the Rajya Sabha.

6505. (11-3-2008) NEW DELHI : The Hon'ble High Court of Delhi in CWP No. 813/2004 vide its order dated 06.09.2004 had set up a Committee to examine the provisions of Transplantation of Human Organs Act, 1994, and the Transplantation of Human Organs Rules, 1995. The report was submitted on 25.05.2005. A National Consultation was held on 18.05.2007 and the report was submitted in the second fortnight of August 2007. The recommended changes required amendments in the Transplantation of Human Organs Act, 1994 and the Rules framed there under. These changes are intended to facilitate genuine cases, increase transparency in transplantation procedures and to provide deterrent penalties for violation of the law.

6506. (11-3-2008) NEW DELHI : As per the HIV Sentinel Surveillance data, four districts in Orissa namely Anugul, Bolangir, Bhadrak and Ganjam have been identified as category 'A' districts *i.e.* districts having HIV prevalence of more than 1% among Antenatal women representing General Population. The probable reasons for spread of HIV infection in Ganjam and Bhadrak, which are coastal districts are (a) large scale out migration to far flung areas like ship breaking yards in Bhavnagar and various industries in Surat & Gandhi Nagar in Gujarat and Mumbai (b) number of National Highways and large number of truckers passing through the districts have increased the vulnerability of these districts. However, there is no evidence regarding the spread of HIV in these districts due to foreign tourist and infiltrators from Bangladesh. In order to check the spread of HIV/AIDS in the State, Government of India has launched the National AIDS Control Programme Phase III, through State AIDS Control Socieities with the goal to halt and reverse the epidemic in the country over the next 5 years by integrating programmes for prevention, care, support and treatment. However, the primary focus is given to preventive efforts focusing on high risk population consisting of female sex workers, men having sex with men, injectable drug users, truckers and migrant population. In order to make people aware about HIV/AIDS and promote safe behaviours, NACO and State AIDS Control Societies conduct regular IEC campaigns through mass media and inter-personal communication channel. During these campaigns, the information regarding availability of counselling and testing services is also provided to the community. A special train (Red Ribbon Express) has been launched on 1st December, 2007 to spread the HIV/AIDS awareness messages in various Rural areas. Rupees 15.06 crore have been allocated to Orissa State during the financial year 2007-08 for implementing the programme. This information was given by the Minister for Health & Family Welfare, Dr. Anbumani Ramadoss in a reply to a question in the Rajya Sabha.

6507. (11-3-2008) NEW DELHI : India is the World's second largest producer of leather footwear; with an estimated production of over 900 million pairs per annum. Of all the leather products, footwear has registered the highest growth rate of 18% CAGR (Compound Annual Growth Rate) in 2005-06. Exports in 2005-06 were valued at US$ 786.76 million, which accounts for 28% of total export of Leather products. In the last 5 years, India's overall footwear export has been growing at 12% per annum. India has one of the highest potential for footwear consumption, given the rapid increase in the disposable income among the younger population. However, presently, around 70-80% of footwear units are in unorganized sector and therefore, it is necessary to increase production capacities of footwear units in order to meet the increasing demand and to capture the available opportunities in global footwear market. In order to increase the production capacities, development of Footwear Complexes/Parks was encouraged by the Central Government and during the 10th Plan, financial assistance towards establishment of a Footwear Complex and a Footwear Component Park at Chennai under the Plan Scheme, Indian Leather Development Programme was provided. During the 10th Plan period training and marketing support were provided to primary workers and artisans thereby increasing employment opportunity in the sector. This Information was given by the Minister of State for Industry, Dr. Ashwani Kumar, in a written reply in the Lok Sabha Today.

6508. (11-3-2008) NEW DELHI : Shri Kamal Nath, Union Minister of Commerce and Industry, has said that the Indian economy is increasingly getting integrated with the world economy. India's share in the world exports has increased from 0.7% in 2001 to 1% in 2006. India's trade as a percentage of GDP has increased from 14.6% in 1990-91 to 21.2% in 2000-01 and 34.9% in 2006-07. This was stated by Shri Kamal Nath while inaugurating the 77th Annual General Meeting (AGM) of International Chamber of Commerce (ICC) India on the theme of "Global Economic Outlook: Impact on Asia", here today. "Indian merchandise exports have witnessed a sustained high growth rate of more than 20% per annum during the Tenth Plan. Exports reached a level of US $ 126.3 billion in 2006-07 registering a growth rate of 22.5% over the previous year. Against the target of US $ 160 billion for the year 2007-08, exports reached a level of US $ 111.1 billion during April-December 2007. With the present trend growth, exports during the current year are expected to reach a level of US $ 152-155 billion", Shri Kamal Nath said. Keeping the current international scenario in view, Shri Kamal Nath said that there is a need for a new architecture of international relations which should be based on trust and mutually beneficial integration. With economic power of the emerging markets accounting for a larger share of global GDP, China, India, Brazil, Russia and other crucial players need to be brought to the table of international policymaking. While commending the role of ICC, the Minister stated that ICC promotes an open international trade and investment system and the market economy. He further stated that the high growth of Indian exports during the recent years has been possible due to concerted efforts made by the government to reduce trade barriers, bring down transaction costs and facilitate trade accompanied by a favourable international environment. The Minister was quoting the World Bank publication "Doing Business 2008", that India has been rated as the top reformer in the Trading Across Borders in 2006-07. Shri Kamal Nath emphasized that the agenda for world trade negotiations need to be more receptive to the needs and sensibilities of the developing countries and LDCs, and added that agriculture should remain at the heart of the negotiations since the livelihood concerns of more than a billion resource poor farmers depend on it. He further added that a delicate balance between the defensive agenda on agriculture and the relatively offensive agenda on Services and NAMA.

6509. (11-3-2008) NEW DELHI : The Union Budget 2008-09 has attracted considerable attention on its debt waiver and relief for farmers, as its centerpiece, but more importantly its framework is designed to sustain India's robust growth momentum, during a period of turbulence in the world economy, with continuing efforts to hold prices at tolerable levels. Firstly, it seeks to stimulate domestic demand by injecting more purchasing power in the hands of the people and thus reverse the recent slowing trends, especially in manufacturing. This it does by the range of income tax concessions and indirect tax cuts on goods, which should promote consumption, help reduce production costs and result in lower end prices. The rise in demand would ensure that the economy retains vigour of investments. Relief to millions of small and marginal farmers on their debt burden also would contribute to demand in rural areas. Secondly, the budget makes substantial provisions for human resource development through education, health, employment, rural development and other social programmes in the pursuit of inclusive growth. Thirdly, to make growth sustainable over the medium and longer terms, the budget accords priority for infrastructure and development of skills on a national level, in view of the growing and changing needs of the economy and the gains India could reap from a "demographic dividend" over the next few decades.

6510. (11-3-2008) NEW DELHI : The breeds of dogs than can be trained and deployed in the forces for sniffing and other work are German Shepherd Dog (GSD), Labrador Retriever, Cocker Spaniel, St. Bernard (for snow rescue), Alsatian, Labrador and Dobermann There is no proposal to deploy street dogs in the forces. This information was given by the Minister of State in the Ministry of Home

6511. (11-3-2008) NEW DELHI: The Delhi State Committee of the Communist Party of India (Marxist) held a demonstration at Jantar Mantar here on Monday protesting against Sunday's attack at its party headquarters by BJP-RSS activists. The protesting speakers charged that the attack was pre-planned. They said it was not just an attack on the CPI (M) but also on democratic values and institutions. They alleged that the RSS-BJP was acting in this manner as because of frustration over the growing role of the CPI (M) in national politics and its steadfast defence of secularism. It was also pointed out that the BJP-RSS was not able to grow in areas where the CPI (M) was strong. The protesters demanded strict action against the culprits.

6512. (11-3-2008) NEW DELHI : The Government has not received any formal proposal from ULFA for direct talks. However, the Government is open to talks with any militant groups including United Liberation Front of Asom (ULFA) provided they shun violence and abide by the Constitution of India. This information was given by the Minister of State in the Ministry of Home

6513. (11-3-2008) NEW DELHI : Union Rural Development Minister Dr. Raghuvansh Prasad Singh has emphasized the need for concerted efforts for the timely completion of PMGSY projects. Presiding over a meeting to review the progress of implementation of Pradhan Mantri Gram Sadak Yojana (PMGSY) in the States of Jammu & Kashmir, Jharkhand, Kerala, Meghalaya, Nagaland, Tamil Nadu and Uttarakhand held here today he said in order to make the rural areas frequently accessible the construction of all weather roads under the Bharat Nirman comonent should be given utmost priority and no laxity or sluggishness is permissible in this regard. Earlier in her opening remarks Dr. Rita Sharma, Secretary (Rural Development) termed the Pradhan Mantri Gram Sadak Yojana (PMGSY) as one of the most important programmes aiming at providing connectivity by way of all weather roads to the eligible unconnected habitations in the rural areas. Expressing dissatisfaction over the slow progress she thrust upon the timely achievement of targets and asked the participating State Government functionaries to ensure the promised achievements fulfilled at the end of each quarter. She also emphasized on deputing adequate staff for this purpose. The State Government representatives while mentioning the difficulties termed the delay in the clearance of projects from the forest departments as one of the main impediments in the way of rapid progress. However it was assured by them of making all out efforts to achieve physical and financial targets to the maximum extent possible. Besides the Rural Development Ministry officials, representatives from the National Rural Road Development Agency (NRRDA) were also present in the meeting.

6514. (11-3-2008) NEW DELHI : The Ministry of Rural Development has allocated Rs. 1213330 lakh during the last four years (till 2007-08) for its Rural Housing projects under the Indira Awaas Yojana (IAY) Scheme. The total number of Houses constructed during this period stood at 1458367. An amount of Rs.134846.35 lakh was released as Second instalment during the financial year 2006-07. However, as per the guidelines of the Indira Awaas Yojana (IAY) Scheme, second instalment of funds is released only to those States/DRDAs who have spent at least 60% of the total available funds during the year including the amount of 1st instalment. Also, the construction of IAY houses is done by the beneficiaries themselves with a layout and type design of their own choice. As per "All India Report on Concurrent Evaluation of Indira Awaas Yojana (IAY)" conducted during 1998-1999, 86% of the beneficiaries have expressed satisfaction with the constructed houses. The Central allocation for the last three years and current year and amount released to various States/UTs as second instalment of funds under Indira Awaas Yojana during the year 2006-07, alongwith the amount utilized by them and the houses constructed, is given in the table enclosed.

6515. (11-3-2008) NEW DELHI : Based on the recommendation of the Board for Reconstruction of Public Sector Enterprises (BRPSE), the Government has approved the proposal for revival of 28 Central Public Sector Enterprises (CPSEs) involving a total assistance of Rs.8409.31 crore (*i.e.* cash assistance of Rs.1962.51 crore and non cash assistance of Rs.6446.80 crore) during the period 4.5.2005 to 3.1.2008. The concerned administrative Ministry identifies sick CPSEs and submits the proposal for their revival to BRPSE from time to time. BRPSE has considered and given its recommendation on 51 proposals for revival (including closure of 2 CPSEs) till 29.02.2008, out of which 28 proposals for revival have been approved. This information was given by the Minister of Heavy Industries & Public Enterprises, Shri Sontosh Mohan Dev in a written reply to a question in Rajya Sabha today.

6516. (11-3-2008) NEW DELHI : As per the data compiled by the Reserve Bank of India (RBI) from the scheduled commercial banks, the number of sick Micro, Small And Medium Enterprises (MSMEs) in the country as at the end of March 2007 (latest available) was 1,32,081. As per the data compiled by the RBI from the scheduled commercial banks, the number of sick MSMEs declined from 1,40,337 at the end of March 2006 to 1,32,081 at the end of March 2007. This information was given by the Minister of Micro, Small & Medium Enterprises, Shri Mahabir Prasad in a written reply to a question in Lok Sabha today.

6517. (11-3-2008) NEW DELHI : The Government of India has given top priority for promotion and use of bio-fuels, which included bio-diesel and bio-ethanol. Considering the importance of promotion and use of bio-fuels for transportation, stationery and other applications, the Government of India has issued a Notification in July 2006 giving specific responsibilities to various Union Ministries and Departments. The Government emphasizes use of non-edible oils such as Jatropha curcas, Pongamia Pinnata oils, etc. for production of bio-diesel and use of forest and non-forest wastelands for plantation of non-edible oil seed bearing plants. Ministry of Petroleum and Natural Gas vide Gazette Notification No. G.S.R. 580(E) dated 20.9.2006 has directed that subject to commercial viability, oil marketing companies shall sell 5 per cent ethanol blended petrol, as per Bureau of Indian Standards specification, in the notified 20 States and 4 Union Territories, comprising of the entire country except North Eastern States, J&K, Andaman & Nicobar Islands and Lakshadweep w.e.f. 1.11.2006. Oil Marketing Companies are procuring ethanol from indigenous producers through open tenders with validity for three years extendable by two more years. The Cabinet Committee on Economic Affairs (CCEA) decided on 9.10.2007 to make 10% blending optional from October, 2007 and thereafter mandatory from October 2008. To encourage production of bio-diesel in the country, the Ministry of Petroleum and Natural Gas announced a Bio-diesel Purchase Policy, in October 2005, effective 1.1.2006. The policy has identified 20 purchase centres of the public sector oil marketing companies (OMCs) all over the country. The OMCs would purchase bio-diesel meeting the standards prescribed by the Bureau of Indian Standards (BIS), from those bio-diesel manufacturers who register with them after satisfying the technical specifications, at a specified delivered price. Depending upon felt need and preparedness, the OMCs could also open more purchase centres. The Ministry of New & Renewable Energy has sponsored R&D projects on bio-fuels to some leading R&D Institutions. Process parameters for production of bio-diesel from jatropha curcas (Ratanjot) and Pongamia Pinnata (Karanja) have been optimized. Field trials on diesel car have been carried out with different levels of blend of bio-diesel produced from Jatropha and Pongamia with diesel. The vehicles response has been found to be comparable with diesel vehicles. A 200 litre capacity per batch-diesel reactor has been designed, fabricated and developed. The above information was given by the Minister of State for Petroleum & Natural Gas Shri Dinsha Patel in a written reply in the Rajya Sabha today.

6518. (11-3-2008) NEW DELHI : Panna-Mukta and Tapti (PMT) JV invited bids from the prospective buyers for sale of natural gas up to 4 million metric standard cubic metres per day (MMSCMD) for a period of two years from 1.4.2006. In response to JV's bid GSPC, one of the bidders offered the highest price of US $ 4.75/MMBTU for 4 MMSCMD gas. As per Production Sharing Contract (PSC) signed by the Government with PMT JV, the Government nominee for lifting of natural gas is GAIL. However, in view of lack of consensus on gas price between GAIL and PMT JV, the Government had allowed JV partners to market the gas directly initially for a period of one year with effect from 1.4.2005 and subsequently for another two years. However, to take care of the existing priority consumers in power and fertilizer sectors, GAIL continued to get major portion of the gas, while remaining gas was supplied in accordance with the bids received from the companies. The Government of Gujarat had represented to the Government of India. As per the PSC terms and provisions, Government nominee GAIL has the first right on natural gas produced from these PSCs. Accordingly, if GAIL is able to lift entire gas produced by PMT JV on terms, mutually agreeable to both the parties, GAIL may market the entire gas. The bids were invited from companies in 2006 in view of the lack of consensus on gas price between GAIL and PMT JV. The above information was given by the Minister for Petroleum & Natural Gas Shri Murli Deora in a written reply in the Rajya Sabha today.

6519. (11-3-2008) NEW DELHI : The Department of Scientific and Industrial Research (DSIR) in the Ministry of Science and Technology commissioned a study to "Institute for Studies in Industrial Development" on the subject-"Defining the Role of Government in Trans-nationalization Efforts of Indian SMEs: A Case Study of Indian Pharmaceutical Industry". The Institute, in the final report submitted to DSIR, has highlighted certain weaknesses of pharmaceutical small and medium enterprises (SMEs) in their endeavour towards trans-nationalization and exports.

These include: lack of expertise, training and finance for technological up-gradation and adoption of good manufacturing practices (GMP) by SMEs to meet global quality standards; limited exposure and expertise on IPR issues; limited adoption of information technology (IT) techniques in production and processes; low or negligible R&D expenditure which affects the ability of SMEs to offer innovative solutions; and the inability of SMEs to access finance on easy terms for import of capital goods and undertaking advertising and marketing activities. The steps taken or proposed to be taken by the Central Government to enable the small and medium pharmaceutical companies to face the stiff challenges posed by big pharmaceutical companies include: availability of financial assistance up to Rs.1 crore with 15% capital subsidy to small scale drug and pharma units for technology up-gradation under the credit linked capital subsidy scheme of Ministry of Micro, Small and Medium Enterprises (MSME); proposal of Department of Chemicals and Petrochemicals to extend 5% interest subsidy to pharma small scale units for technology up-gradation on the basis of Schedule 'M' of Drugs and Cosmetic Rules, 1945; support to high-risk pre-proof-of-concept research and late stage development in small and medium companies in the areas of agriculture, human and animal health, environment, diagnostics, immuno-biologicals and various industrial products like antibiotics, industrial enzymes, vitamins etc. under the Small Business Innovation Research Initiative (SBIRI) scheme launched by the Department of Biotechnology. Ministry of MSME has also taken a step to enable small and medium companies, in general to face challenges of stiff competition by formulating a National Manufacturing Competitiveness Programme (NMCP), worked out by the National Manufacturing Competitiveness Council (NMCC) in consultation with industry. Under this programme, a "major promotional package" has been announced to provide full support to the SMEs in the areas of credit, technological up-gradation, marketing and up-gradation of industrial infrastructure. This information was given by Union Minister for Science & Technology and Earth Sciences, Shri Kapil Sibal, in the Lok Sabha today.

6520. (11-3-2008) NEW DELHI : According to the official statistics, 0.8 percent of the GDP is spent on Research & Development in Science and Technology in the country. The Government has taken various measures to increase the expenditure on Science & Technology in the Country. These measures include higher allocation for scientific research from Plan to Plan for setting up of new institutions for science education and research, creation of centres of excellence and facilities in emerging and frontline areas in academic and national institutes, induction of new and attractive fellowships, strengthening infrastructure for R&D in universities, encouraging public-private R&D partnerships, national awards for outstanding R&D etc. Accordingly, the Government have enhanced XI plan allocation for Scientific Departments to Rs.75,304.00 crores from Rs.25,301.35 crores during X Plan. This information was given by Union Minister for Science & Technology and Earth Sciences, Shri Kapil Sibal, in the Lok Sabha today.

6521. (11-3-2008) NEW DELHI : The disaster forecast centres available today are adequate to cater to the requirements of the country. Disaster Forecast Centres have been set up in the country for different types of disasters. They are: (i) Cyclone Warning: Six cyclone warning centres have been established in the country covering both East and West coasts. (ii) Early Warning System for Tsunami: At Indian National Centre for Ocean Information Services (INCOIS), Hyderabad, an Early Warning Centre for Tsunami covering the entire coastline of the country has been set up. (iii) Flood Meteorological Offices: Ten such offices located, provide heavy rainfall warning to Central Flood Forecasting Division of Central Water Commission, which in turn issues the flood advisory/forecast. No earthquake forecasting centre has so far been established since it is not yet possible, anywhere in the world, to forecast earthquake. However, sixty seven earthquake monitoring centres are in operation across the country to detect and locate earthquakes occurring in and around the country. State-wise list of the Disaster Forecast Centres are enclosed in the annexure. Besides, the Government is also implementing an Urban Earthquake Vulnerability Reduction Project in 38 cities failing in Seismic Zones III to V and having a population of 5 lac or more. The project aims at reducing the vulnerability of these cities to earthquakes by preparation of response plans at various levels, training of architects and engineers in seismic safe construction practices, etc. National Disaster Management Authority (NDMA) has laid down guidelines for the 'Management of Earthquakes' in April 2007. The guidelines prescribe measures for Central Ministries and Departments and State Governments to prepare disaster management plans having specific components on earthquake risk management. Government also send advisories to State Government and Union Territory from time to time on disaster mitigation and preparedness measures including those relating to earthquake through adoption of modern building bye-laws. All new buildings and structures built after 30th June 2007 have to comply with the earthquake resistant building code and the National Building Code 2005.

6522. (11-3-2008) NEW DELHI : The Minister of Tourism and Culture Smt. Ambika Soni has said that centrally protected temples of national importance are in a fairly good state of preservation. They are conserved, preserved and maintained as per conservation norms subject to availability of resources. In a written reply in the Rajya Sabha today she said, entry to 116 centrally protected monuments, including temples that are not under worship, is ticketed. There is no proposal at present to levy any ticket or fee for entry to centrally protected temples under worship. The National Culture Fund set up by the Ministry of Culture vide notification dated November 28, 1996 provides an opportunity for individuals, NGO's and Corporate Houses to participate in the upkeep and maintenance of monuments. It is an important initiative for forging public-private partnership and mobilizing extra budgetary resources for the conservation of monuments.

6523. (11-3-2008) NEW DELHI : Rajya Sabha Shri Pawan Kumar Bansal, Minister of State for Finance affirmed in Rajya Sabha today that the Twelfth

Finance Commission has mandated that Rs. 20,000 crore of grant money for Panchayats from 2005-10 be disbursed by the State Governments within 15 days of receipt of money from the Central Government. Some States have reported delay in transferring of grants to Panchayats beyond the stipulated period of 15 days. As per guidelines framed by the Ministry of Finance for release and utilization of grants to local bodies recommended by the Twelfth Finance Commission, States shall constitute High Level Committee (HLC), headed by the state Chief Secretary to ensure proper utilization of grants and State Governments have to send utilization certificates. Utilisation reports have been received from 22 States in respect of grants released to them so far. As per the above guidelines, in addition to HLC constitute at State level, committees have also been constituted in the Government of India, headed by Secretary, Department of Expenditure; and another headed by Secretary, Ministry of Panchayati Raj to review the releases and utilization of grants by States. This information was given by Shri Bansal, in a written reply to a question by Shri S.M.Laljan Basha.

6524. (11-3-2008) NEW DELHI : Micro Finance Institutions (MFIs) are presently not regulated in the country. To regulate these MFIs, the Government has introduced a Bill in Lok Sabha on 20.3.2007 called "The Micro Financial Sector (Development and Regulation) Bill, 2007' to create environment friendly policy for micro-finance services in the country. The Bill is intended to provide a formal statutory framework for the promotion, development and regulation of the micro finance sector. As the MFIs are presently not regulated, the Data Reporting system does not generate such data. This information was given by Shri Pawan Kumar Bansal, Minister of State in the Ministry of Finance in the Rajya Sabha today in a written reply to a question by Shri Mahendra Mohan and Dr. (Smt) Najma A.Heptula.

6525. (11-3-2008) NEW DELHI : The Minister of Tourism and Culture Smt. Ambika Soni has said that her Ministry has asked the Ministry of Home Affairs to get the proposal regarding visa-on-Arrival be cleared. In a written reply in the Rajya Sabha today she said, at present, the Ministry of Home Affairs has not agreed to this scheme due to the prevalent security scenario.

6526. (11-3-2008) NEW DELHI : The cumulative inflation in terms of WPI (since 1st week of April, 2007 to February 23, 2008) was 4.33 per cent during the current financial year 2007-08, which is lower than 5.98 per cent as on 24 February, 2007 in the last financial year 2006-07. Containment of inflation remains high on the agenda of the Government. Anti-inflationary policies of the government include strict fiscal discipline, rationalization of duties of essential items, effective supply-demand management of essential commodities through liberal tariff and trade policies, and strengthening the public distribution system. The Monetary policy of Reserve Bank of India, while being conducive to economic growth, has attempted to contain inflationary expectations arising out of uncertainties in domestic and international environment. This information was given by Shri Pawan Kumar

Bansal, Minister of State in the Ministry of Finance in the Rajya Sabha today in a written reply to a question by Dr. V. Maitreyan.

6527. (11-3-2008) NEW DELHI : WPI is an economy-wide index covering 435 commodities. Weights of the commodities are derived based on the value of quantities traded in the domestic market. It is currently the most comprehensive measure of economy-wide inflation available with high frequency. The weights assigned to foodgrains, vegetables and milk in the commodities basket of WPI (1993-94= 100) is 5.01 per cent, 1.46 per cent and 4.37 per cent, respectively. Dearness Allowance is calculated on the basis of the average of preceding 12 months Consumer price index for Industrial Workers. It becomes due twice a year in January and July. Total 11 instalments of dearness allowances have become due from July 2002 to July 2007. The formula for calculation of dearness allowance has remained same. This information was given by Shri Pawan Kumar Bansal, Minister of State for Finance in reply to a question raised by Shri Vijaykumar Rupani and Smt. Hema Malini in Rajya Sabha today.

6528. (11-3-2008) NEW DELHI : The amount of subsidies during 2007-08 (RE) for food, fertilizers and-petroleum is estimated at Rs 64,929 crore. The food subsidies are largely designed to be' targeted to people below the poverty line (BPL), the other two subsidies, namely fertilizer and petroleum, particularly-the LPG are available to all users/consumers. A "study by Programme Evaluation Organisation (PEO) of the Planning Commission regarding Targeted Public Distribution System (TPDS) which covered 18 states reveals that though the offtake per household has shown improvement under TPDS, yet only about 57 per cent of the BPL households are covered by it. Further the report finds that only about 42 per cent of the subsidized grains issued by the Central Pool reaches the target group. Based on evaluation studies and feedback received from states, a nine point action plan has been jointly formulated by the Central and the State/ UT governments to strengthen the TPDS. These include regular reviews of the BPL and Antyodaya Ann Yojana (AAY) lists to ensure coverage of eligible families, involvement of Panchayati Raj Institutions in the public distribution system (PDS) operations, use of information technology, creating awareness among public about PDS operations, etc. This information was given by Shri Pawan Kumar Bansal, Minister of State for Finance in reply to a question raised by Smt. Syeda Anwara Taimur and Shri Vijay J. Darda in Rajya Sabha today.

6529. (11-3-2008) NEW DELHI : Only Doordarshan DD Direct Plus (DTH) is providing DTH services free of cost of the consumers. Private DTH service licensees are not providing their DTH service free of cost. Presently 42 TV channels are on DD Direct Plus, including 22 private channels and 20 DD channels. DTH platform of Doordarshan is being made available to the private TV channels for telecasting free to air channels, subject to the payment of carriage free and suitability of such channels for DD Direct Plus platform. This information was given by Minister of Information & Broadcasting and Parliamentary Affairs, Shri P. R. Dasmunsi in written reply to a question in Lok Sabha today.

6530. (11-3-2008) NEW DELHI : Sarva Shiksha Abhiyan (SSA) and Mid-Day Meal (MDM) programme are being reviewed on on-going basis through monthly returns & quarterly progress reports. In addition 41 independent monitoring institutions submit six monthly reports on performance of these programmes. Under SSA independent studies have been commissioned which include interalia, study on out of school children, National evaluation of Kasturba Gandhi Balika Vidyalaya (KGBV) programme, study on student & teacher absence and National Pupil Achievement Surveys. The latest biannual Joint Review Mission (JRM), the 7th JRM of SSA held in January 2008 has found the overall performance of States/ UTs under SSA, satisfactory.

6531. (11-3-2008) NEW DELHI : 105 Special Focus Districts were initially identified during the year 2005. The Schemes under Sarva Shiksha Abhiyan, however, target educationally backward blocks. Further, University Grants Commission (UGC) in 2007, has identified educationally backward districts mainly based on the criterion of Gross Enrolment Ratio (GER) less than National Average. The list of these educationally backward districts is annexed. The Government proposes to incentivise State Governments to establish one college in each of these districts during the XI Five Year Plan. These steps will significantly contribute in increasing the access of education alongwith inclusiveness in the educationally backward districts.

6532. (11-3-2008) NEW DELHI : As per the guidelines of the Accelerated Irrigation Benefits Programme in force, the funding pattern for major/medium projects and surface water minor irrigation schemes is as under: (i) Major/medium irrigation projects and surface water minor irrigation schemes of Special category States and Koraput, Bolangir and Kalahandi districts of Orissa are eligible for 90% grant of project cost included in AIBP. (ii) Major/mediun projects benefiting drought prone/tribal/flood prone area are eligible for upto 90% grant of project cost included in AIBP depending on extent of such area benefited from project and included in AIBP. (iii) Surface water minor irrigation schemes of Non Special Category States (which also includes Madhya Pradesh) eligible for inclusion in AIBP as per guidelines are also eligible for 90% grant. (iv) All other major/ medium projects are eligible for 25% grant of project cost included in AIBP. The balance cost is to be arranged by the State Governments from their own resources which may also be arranged by the State Governments by market borrowings for which approval of Government of India is not required. This information was given by the Minister of State for Water Resources, Shri Jai Prakash Narayan Yadav in response to a question by Smt. Maya Singh in the Rajya Sabha today.

6533. (11-3-2008) NEW DELHI : No proposal by Government of Gujarat on Central assistance for Safe Stage Works and improvement of Minor Irrigation

Schemes in Gujarat has been submitted to Government of India. However, during 2005-06, Government of Gujarat has submitted 42 Nos. of water bodies under Pilot scheme, *viz.* "National Project for Repair, Renovation and Restoration of Water Bodies directly linked to Agriculture" in two districts *viz.* Sabarkantha (17 Water Bodies) and Banaskantha (25 water bodies). The estimated cost of above schemes is Rs. 655.14 lakh and Rs. 766.53 lakhs respectively and has been approved by the Government of India under the Pilot Scheme. The Central Share of Rs.2.654 crore and Rs.3.10 crore has since been released for Sabarkantha and Banaskantha, respectively. This information was given by the Minister of State for Water Resources, Shri Jai Prakash Narayan Yadav in response to a question by Shri Keshubhai S. Patel in the Rajya Sabha today.

6534. (11-3-2008) NEW DELHI : Government of India has decided to take up 14 projects as National Projects. Out of these 14 projects, 9 projects are on the international rivers/their tributaries. Further, one of the proposed National projects namely, Ken-Betwa is river interlinking project. One of the National projects, namely, Upper Siang in Arunachal Pradesh envisages flood moderation benefits. This information was given by the Minister of State for Water Resources, Shri Jai Prakash Narayan Yadav in response to a question by Shri Mangani Lal Mandal in the Rajya Sabha today.

6535. (11-3-2008) NEW DELHI : Major share of ground water utilization in the country is for agricultural purposes. The studies conducted by Central Ground Water Board reveal that the water tables are dipping due to cumulative effect of domestic, agricultural and industrial uses, including withdrawals of ground water by soft drinks and bottled drinking water companies. The Central Ground Water Authority has issued guidelines for regulation of withdrawal of ground water in over-exploited, critical and semi-critical areas. States have been requested to take steps to implement these guidelines. This information was given by the Minister of State for Water Resources, Shri Jai Prakash Narayan Yadav in response to a question by Shri N.R. Govindarajar in the Rajya Sabha today.

6536. (11-3-2008) NEW DELHI : Government has taken various steps in the direction of water management to stop the flood in North Bihar coming from the rivers of Nepal. To control the floods in rivers Bagmati and Kamala-Balan in north Bihar, the Government has approved two schemes, namely, (i) Raising and Strengthening of Embankments along River Bagmati at an estimated cost of Rs.135.16 crore and (ii) Raising and Strengthening of Embankments along River Kamala at an estimated cost of Rs.52.09 crore. Government of India has initiated steps for creation of storages in the Nepal territory which will help in mitigating the problem of floods being faced in North Bihar. A Joint Committee on Water Resources (JCWR) headed by the Secretary's of Water Resources of India and Nepal already exists to address the water related issues including floods. A Detailed Project Report for the Sapt-Kosi High Dam project and Sun Kosi diversion scheme is under preparation jointly with the cooperation of the Government of Nepal. The Central Government has envisaged to make a comprehensive assessment of the feasibility of linking the rivers in the country starting with the southern rivers in a fully consultative manner. It would also explore the feasibility of linking sub-basins of rivers within the States, like Bihar. Six intra-state link proposals have been identified in Bihar by the State Government of Bihar, namely, (i) Kohra-Chandravat, (ii) Burhi-Gandak-None-Baya-Ganga, (iii) Bagmati-Burhi-Gandak through Belwabhar, (iv) Kosi-Ganga, (v) Kosi-Mechi (Indian portion) and (vi) Karmanasha-Suara links in Bihar. The State Government of Bihar has commenced the study of these Intra-State links. This information was given by the Minister of State for Water Resources, Shri Jai Prakash Narayan Yadav in response to a question by Prof. Ram Deo Bhandary in the Rajya Sabha today.

6537. (11-3-2008) NEW DELHI : Government has constituted a Coordination Committee chaired by the Prime Minister called Prime Minister's Council on Climate Change to coordinate national action for assessment, adaptation and mitigation of climate change. Realising the need for proper assessment of the effect of climate change on water resources and flow characteristics, research on specific issues including impact assessment of climate change on water resources has been undertaken by Ministry of Water Resources through Central Water Commission, Brahmaputra Board and National Institute of Hydrology with active participation of reputed academic institutes. This information was given by the Minister of State for Water Resources, Shri Jai Prakash Narayan Yadav in response to a question by Prof. Alka Balram Kshatriya and Shri Vijay J. Darda in the Rajya Sabha today.

6538. (11-3-2008) NEW DELHI : Addressing the distinguished delegates on the concluding day of the 18th World Congress of International Physicians for the Prevention of Nuclear War (IPPNW) today, the Union Minister for Health & Family Welfare, Dr. Anbumani Ramadoss said that no other time would be more apt than the present period to debate on a theme of peace, health and development in the context of nations acquiring increasing destruction abilities using nuclear weapons. Representatives and leaders from more than 59 countries are participating in the Conference jointly organised by International Physicians for the Prevention of Nuclear War (IPPNW) and Indian Doctors for Peace and Development (IDPD).

6539. (11-3-2008) NEW DELHI : Geological Survey of India (GSI) has discovered new deposits of Bauxite, Manganese and Iron Ore in the State of Orissa. This information was given by Dr. T. Subbarami Reddy, Minister of State for Mines in the Parliament today. Iron Ore has also been discovered in the States of Karnataka and Tamil Nadu and Graphite was discovered in Tamil Nadu. The other major mineral discoveries by GSI are: Gold deposits in Rajasthan, Jharkhand and Karnataka; Basemetal (copper, lead, zinc) in the States of Rajasthan, Maharashtra and Madhya Pradesh; Platinum Group of Metals in Karnataka; Limestone deposits in the States of Meghalaya and Tamil Nadu and Clay in Kerala

6540. (11-3-2008) NEW DELHI : The Minister for Civil Aviation, Shri Praful Patel informed the Parliament today the target date for completion of modernization process of the 35 non-metro airports by the Airports Authority of India (AAI), is March 2010. New Terminal Buildings expandable on modular basis are being constructed at Ahmedabad, Amritsar, Aurangabad, Agatti, Bhopal, Bhubaneshwar, Chandigarh, Dehradun, Goa, Jaipur, Lucknow, Indore, Khajuraho, Madurai, Mangalore, Port Blair, Ranchi, Raipur, Rajkot, Trivandrum, Trichy, Udaipur, Varanasi and Vishakhapatnam airports. Modification/expansion of existing Terminal Buildings is being undertaken at airports in Agra, Agartala, Coimbatore, Dimapur, Guwahati, Imphal, Jammu, Nagpur, Patna, Pune and Vadodara. Airside works including expansion and strengthening of runway for wide bodied aircraft operations, extension/new construction of Apron for more parking of aircrafts, link taxiways and parallel taxi tracks are being taken up at these airports as per requirement. At 24 of these airports, cityside development through Public Private Partnership is being undertaken. Bids for pre-qualification have been received for Amritsar and Udaipur airports.

6541. (11-3-2008) NEW DELHI : The Minister for Civil Aviation, Shri Praful Patel informed the Parliament today that civil aviation industry in the country is facing a shortage of type rated pilots. In order to bridge the gap between the demand and availability of pilots, 944 foreign Pilots have been engaged by various airline operators. The airline-wise breakup of Indian and foreign pilots as on 1st January 2008 is Indigo-88, 84; Paramount Airways-03,11; Blue Dart-06,10; Spice Jet-152, 53; Air Deccan-324, 141; Alliance Air-65,40; Go Air-52, 14; Kingfisher Airlines-419, 110; Jet Airways-799, 276; Jet Lite-230, 13; Air India-622, 66 and Air India Express-44, 79. The Government has taken various steps to reduce the gap between demand and supply of skilled Indian pilots. These include conditionally increasing the age-limit to 65 years for pilots, upgradation and modernization of training infrastructure of the Indira Gandhi Rashtriya Uran Akademi (IGRUA) to enhance its training capacity from 40 to 100 pilots per year, setting up of a world class flying training institute at Gondia, Maharashtra for training 100 cadets and assistance to flying clubs by allocating trainer aircraft through Directorate General of Civil Aviation/Aero Club of India.

6542. (11-3-2008) NEW DELHI : The Minister for Civil Aviation, Shri Praful Patel today informed the Parliament about the setting up of the Cargo Hub at Nagpur. He said that, the Union Cabinet in its meeting held on 17th January 2008 has accorded 'in principle' approval to the proposal for transfer of Dr. Ambedkar International Airport, Nagpur to a Joint Venture Company (JVC) of Airports Authority of India (AAI) and Maharashtra Airport Development Company Limited (MADC) for upgradation of the airport to a world class Multi modal International Passenger and Cargo Hub with the directions that (i) the Indian Air Force(IAF) will continue to use its existing facilities in Nagpur till appropriate alternative arrangements are put in place and that any transfer of land of the IAF to the Joint Venture will take place only after concurrence by the Ministry of Defence and (ii) a Committee comprising of Cabinet Secretary, Finance Secretary, Secretary, Ministry of Civil Aviation and Chief Secretary, Government of Maharashtra will examine the financial structure of the proposed JV and related issues. As per a Techno Economic Feasibility Study (TEFS) got conducted by the Government of Maharashtra, the cost of Multi-modal International Hub Airport (MIHAN) Project has been estimated at Rs. 2581 crores to be spent over 30 years. Revenue to the extent of Rs. 5280 crores has been projected by 2035. Project contemplates setting up of a multi-modal cargo Hub backed by economic value addition activities such as Special Economic Zone (SEZ) etc.

6543. (11-3-2008) NEW DELHI : The Minister for Civil Aviation, Shri Praful Patel, today informed the Parliament about the Bilateral Air Services Agreement between India and Pakistan. As per his statement, bilateral air services consultations between India and Pakistan were held on 14-15 February, 2008 at Rawalpindi in Pakistan. As per the MoU signed between the two sides during the talks, the capacity entitlements for the designated airlines of each side have been increased from 12 flights per week to 28 flights per week. Also, Islamabad and Chennai have been granted as additional points of call for the designated airlines of India and Pakistan respectively. According to the agreement reached during the above talks, each side could now designate up to three airlines. Before the agreement, Indian Airlines was the only designated Indian carrier and Pakistan International Airlines, Shaheen Air International and Air Blue were the designated airlines of Pakistan.

6544. (11-3-2008) NEW DELHI : The Minister for Civil Aviation, Shri Praful Patel today informed the Parliament about the airports charges at Hyderabad & Bangalore airports. As per Concession Agreements signed by Government of India (GOI) with Hyderabad International Airport Limited (HIAL) and Bangalore International Airport Limited (BIAL), both the Airport Companies are allowed to levy the following regulated charges-(i) Landing, Housing and Parking Charges (Domestic & International) (ii) Passenger Service Fee (Domestic & international) and (iii) User Development Fee (Domestic & International). For the first year of operation the Landing & parking Fee and Passenger Service Fee will be at rates applicable at other airports in India. For the Hyderabad airport Government of India has approved levy of Rs. 1000/- as ad-hoc UDF on international departing passengers. Actual quantum of UDF for domestic and international passengers as well as other regulated charges in respect of both Hyderabad and Bangalore airports would be fixed up only after the receipt of final audited project cost from them. As per the provisions of the Concession Agreement entered into by BIAL and the Government of India (GOI), UDF can be levied by BIAL on departing international and domestic passengers. The quantum of the fee has not been specified in the Concession Agreement, and the fee is to be determined at a level which would enable BIAL to recover its cost. Pursuant to the above provision of Concession Agreement, BIAL had proposed to levy a UDF of Rs. 675/- and Rs. 995/- on departing domestic and international passengers respectively. The proposal of BIAL is under examination. BIAL has been advised by the GOI that pending finalization of the final audited project cost, BIAL may levy ad-hoc UDF only on the departing international passengers and not on the domestic passengers. Once the final audited project cost is received from BIAL, the Government would fix the UDF to be charged. The Minister also informed that consequent to the increase in traffic at the new airport, BIAL has also made additional investments for increasing the capacity of the new airport. Thus, the scope for cost recovery would also undergo a change. India's airport charges are one of the lowest when compared to many other countries. Transport Research Laboratory (TRL, Australia conducted a study on aeronautical charges (Feb. 2006) and has positioned countries on the Index of 1 (least expensive) to 100 (most expensive) on the basis of their aeronautical charges (Landing, Parking, TNLC and PSF). India's position on that scale is 22nd which is lower than the New York (88), Frankfurt (72), London (58), Bangkok (36), Singapore (32), Hong Kong (32), Kuala Lumpur (28) and Dubai (23).

6545. (11-3-2008) NEW DELHI : The dropout rate at elementary level (class I to VIII) during 2004-05 was 50.8 per cent. The main reasons for children dropping out, inter-alia, include distance to school, social and cultural barriers to girls education, inadequate school infrastructure, teacher vacancies, teacher absenteeism, skewed teacher deployment, lack of community involvement, etc. Central Government has decided to implement a centrally sponsored scheme for universalization of access to and improvement of quality of education at secondary stage during the 11th Five Year Plan. The objective of the scheme is to make secondary education of good quality available, accessible and affordable to all young persons by providing one secondary school within 5 kilometre of every habitation. the proposed scheme envisages: (i) provision of necessary infrastructure and resources for the existing secondary schools and for improvement in quality of learning in the schools; (ii) provision for filling the missing gaps in the existing secondary schools system; (iii) provision of extra support for education of girls and children of disadvantaged sections of the society; and (iv) a holistic convergent framework for implementation of various schemes in secondary education. Some of the major components of the proposed scheme are, (i) new schools buildings, (ii) additional rooms including classrooms, laboratories, computer room, library room, toilet etc., (iii) teaching-learning aids, (iv) school grant (v) teachers' in service training (vi) additional teachers, (vii) research and innovation, (viii) curricular reforms and (ix) examinations reforms etc. The Planning Commission has allocated Rs. 20,120 crore for the 11th Five Year Plan for various components of this scheme. This information was given by the Minister of State for Human Resource Development Shri M.A.A. Fatmi in a written reply in Lok Sabha today.

6546. (11-3-2008) NEW DELHI : The Government has decided to establish Programme Generating Facility Centres in various cities of the country. In all, 34 such centres will be set up. Of these, 33 are those of All India Radio and one at Tirupati (AP) is of Doordarshan. This information was given by Minister of Information & Broadcasting and Parliamentary Affairs, Shri P. R. Dasmunsi in written reply to a question in Lok Sabha today.

6547. (11-3-2008) NEW DELHI : The Telecom Regulatory Authority of India (TRAI) recommendations on 'Headend-in-the-sky' (HITS) are under examination of the Ministry of Information & Broadcastingin consultation with other Ministries/ Departments in order to formulate policy guidelines. HITS is a digital delivery platform to distribute multiple channels via satellite straight to cable operators. The essential difference between a HITS operator and the operation of Multi-System Operator (MSO) is that the former transmits the bundle of channels to the cable operators using a satellite, whereas the latter does the same through a cable. HITS operator's area of coverage spans the whole country, whereas the MSO's area of coverage is confined to a limited geographical area (typically a town or a city) close to his headend. Cable operators subscribing to services of a HITS operator will be able to provide a large number of channels with better picture quality & choice of channels to their subscribers than the conventional analog services. The introduction of HITS services will speed up the process of migration from analog to digital mode of transmission and distribution of television signals resulting in benefits to all stakeholders including subscribers, cable operators, broadcasters & the Government. The policy of "Headend-in-the-Sky" (HITS) is under finalization. However, no time frame could be given on such policy issues. This information was given by Minister of Information & Broadcasting and Parliamentary Affairs, Shri P. R. Dasmunsi in written reply to a question in Lok Sabha today.

6548. (11-3-2008) NEW DELHI : As per Article 3 of the Schedule containing terms & conditions of License Agreement, a DTH licensee has to share 10% of the gross revenue every year as license fee. Out of six DTH licensees only three operators are providing their services so far. Dish TV India Ltd. which started its services in October, 2003 has paid Rs. 2,04,87,187/- for 2004-2005; Rs. 2.5 crores for 2005-2006 and Rs. 10 crores for 2006-2007. M/s Tata Sky started its services in financial year 2006-2007 and has paid Rs. 8,84,90,208/- as license fee. M/s Sun Direct TV Pvt. Ltd. started its services in December, 2007. The license fee will be due at the end of the current financial year and is to be paid by licensees within one month of the end of the financial year. This information was given by Minister of Information & Broadcasting and Parliamentary Affairs, Shri P. R. Dasmunsi in written reply to a question in Lok Sabha today.

6549. (11-3-2008) NEW DELHI : Following is the text of the special address delivered by the Minister of State for Defence Shri MM Pallam Raju at the inauguration of the two day International Maritime Search and Rescue Conference (IMSARCON-2008), here today:-For many centuries there were no organised efforts to offer assistance to shipwreckedo mariners, and hapless victims who perished in appalling conditions within sight and sound of horrified bystanders ashore. The earliest known attempts of rescue and recovery were undertaken in China where the use of river lifeboats was first recorded in 1708. It would be more than 50 years before such organized humanitarian efforts emerged in Europe but in 1767 the 'Institution for the Recovery of Drowned Persons' was established in Netherlands, while in 1774 the English took up the cause with the establishment of the 'Royal Humane Society'. From these early beginnings came such organisations as the Shipwreck Institution (UK), the Societye Humaine de Boulogne (France), the Asilo dos Naufragos (Portugal) and The Massachusetts Humane Society (USA). However, the methods of rescue at sea continued to remain primitive in the absence of adequate means of communications, coordinated response system and global synergy for launching effective response. The importance of international cooperation in shipping was recognized by maritime nations owing to incidents of ships taking refuge in foreign ports in the event of bad weather and their proceeding to the aid of others in distress, irrespective of their nationality. Thus in 1889, an International Maritime Conference in Washington discussed a proposal to set up a permanent international body to cater to the needs of shipping. This followed the establishment of a number of other international organizations except a body for shipping. The establishment of a permanent international maritime commission was not considered expedient as the shipping industry was suspicious of any attempt to control its activities and restrict its commercial freedom. Although the obligation of ships to go to the assistance of vessels in distress was enshrined both in tradition and in international treaties (such as the International Convention for the Safety of life at Sea (SOLAS), 1974, there was no international system covering search and, rescue operations. In some areas there was a well established organization able to provide assistance promptly and efficiently, in others there was nothing at all.

6550. (11-3-2008) NEW DELHI : Nine Central Universities and one Indian Institute of Technology (IIT) are presently in operation in the North East Region. Whole no Central University or IIT is presently in operation in the Fifty Scheduled Areas, a Bill for setting up the Indira Gandhi National Tribal University with headquarters at Amarkantak (Madhya Pradesh) falling in the Fifth Scheduled Area has since been passed by both the Houses of Parliament as also assented to by the President. The proposed University shall have powers to establish such number of its regional centres, *viz.* off-campuses constituted by the University and functioning as part of the University, in the areas inhabited by tribal population, as are, in the opinion of the University, necessary for furtherance of its objects, thereby covering the Scheduled Areas of ten States as well. The existing Guru Ghasidas University, Koni, Bilaspur, is proposed to be converted into a Central

University. In addition, the Government proposes to open new Central Universities, IITs, Indian Institutes of Management, National Institutes of Technology, etc. during the XIth Plan. Some of these Institutes could be located in the Fifth Scheduled Areas. This information was given by the Minister of State for Human Resource Development Smt. D. Purandeswari in a written reply in Lok Sabha today.

6551. (11-3-2008) NEW DELHI : By virtue of Press Note 2 (2000 series) dated the 11th February 2000 of the Ministry of Commerce and Industry, Government has allowed Foreign Direct Investment (FDI) upto 100% on the automatic route in the Education Sector, subject to notified Sectoral policy and equity caps. All India Council for Technical Education (AICTE) already has regulations in place for the entry and operation of foreign universities/institutes imparting technical education in India. A legislative proposal for regulation of entry and operation of foreign educational institutions in India is under consideration of the Government. The University Grants Commission has constituted a Committee under the Chairmanship of Prof. K.B. Powar, former Secretary General of Association of Indian Universities, to formulate the Action Plan for identifying various modes of public-private participation to promote higher education. This information was given by the Minister of State for Human Resource Development Smt. D. Purandeswari in a written reply in Lok Sabha today.

6552. (11-3-2008) NEW DELHI : While the Government does not have any proposal to impose a "user fee", the Planning Commission, in the XI Plan document, has, inter-alia, suggested that since most university students come from top 10% of the population by income levels, they would be able to pay fees amounting to 20% of the operative cost of general higher education. The fees for professional courses could be much higher. The fee levels should, therefore, be increased gradually in existing institutions but the new norms could be implemented in new institutions from the start. An additional cess of 1 per cent on Central taxes is being levied with effect from the financial year 2007-08 to fund Secondary Education & Higher Education and for the expansion of capacity of the existing institutions. The University Grants Commission (UGC) has constituted a Committee to formulate regulations for admission and fee structure for self-financing, private, professional institutes including deemed to be universities, and also for self-financing and aided courses in aided Universities/Colleges. This information was given by the Minister of State for Human Resource Development Smt. D. Purandeswari in a written reply in Lok Sabha today.

6553. (11-3-2008) NEW DELHI : A Scheme for 'Strengthening of Boarding and Hostel facilities for Girl Students of Secondary and Higher Secondary Schools' has been implemented by the Ministry of Human Resource Development since 1993. Under the scheme, a maximum grant of Rs. 10,000/- per boarder per year was provided to voluntary organizations for running girls' hostels. A one time grant of Rs. 3000/- per boarder was also provided to NGOs. Voluntary Organizations from all States/UTs, including Union Territory of Andaman and Nicobar Islands, were eligible for assistance under this scheme subject to fulfilment of requisite conditions. Based on an evaluation of the scheme conducted by the 'Tata Institute of Social Sciences', it has been decided to revise the scheme for implementation during 11th Five Year Plan. This information was given by the Minister of State for Human Resource Development Shri M.A.A. Fatmi in a written reply in Lok Sabha today.

6554. (11-3-2008) NEW DELHI : The decision to establish the South Asian University in India was taken at the 14th SAARC Summit and an Inter-Governmental Agreement for establishing South Asian University has been signed. Subsequently, an Inter Governmental Steering Committee was set up to finalize the modalities for operationalisation of the University. The Inter Governmental Steering Committee at its first meeting in May 2007 had agreed to establish a Project Office for the main campus of the University. The Office will be responsible for acquisition of land, overseeing construction, drawing up Charter, Byelaws, business plans etc. of the south Asian University. It was agreed that the Project Office will be headed by an interim CEO from the host country with appropriate academic and administrative credentials and experience of running a large institution/university. The Government has already initiated action in this regard. This information was given by the Minister of State for Human Resource Development Smt. D. Purandeswari in a written reply in Lok Sabha today.

6555. (11-3-2008) NEW DELHI : The total approximate earnings of Indian Railways on originating basis during 1st April 2007-29th February 2008 were Rs. 64032.18 crore compared to Rs. 56013.42 crore during the same period last year, registering an increase of 14.32 per cent. The total goods earnings have gone up from Rs. 37958.28 crore during 1st April 2006-29th February 2007 to Rs. 43300.89 crore during 1st April 2007-29th February 2008, showing an increase of 14.07 per cent. The total passenger revenue earnings during first eleven months of the financial year 2007-08 were Rs. 17934.67 crore compared to Rs. 15497.36 crore during the same period last year, registering an increase of 15.73 per cent. The revenue earnings from other coaching and sundry amounted to Rs. 2796.62 crore during April 2007-February 2008 compared to Rs. 2557.78 crore during the same period last year, showing an increase of 9.34 per cent. The total approximate number of passengers booked during April 2007-February 2008 were 6099.26 million compared to 5801.15 million during the same period last year, showing an increase of 5.14 per cent. In the suburban and non-suburban sectors, the number of passengers booked during April 2007-February 2008 were 3372.75 million and 2726.51 million compared to 3212.15 million and 2589.00 million during the same period last year, an increase of 5.00 per cent and 5.31 per cent respectively.

6556. (11-3-2008) NEW DELHI : Following is the text of the inaugural address delivered by the Defence Minister Shri AK Antony to the two day International Maritime Search and Rescue Conference (IMSARCON-2008), here today:-I am delighted to be amidst you today, at this International Conference on Maritime Search and Rescue being organised by Indian Coast Guard. Since times immemorial, human civilisations have thrived on the banks of rivers and looked to the sea for resources and adventure. Gradually, the seas turned into a medium of trade and commerce, transport and exploration. Strong powers began the process of colonisation, bringing into existence, a new world order. Mankind's dependence on the seas for sustenance has never ceased to exist. In fact, it is bound to increase further, as the resources available on land are depleting at a fast pace. As we increase our maritime activities, we must take care of our common environment and of all life forms-human, as well as marine. The Coast Guard is the national coordinating authority for maritime search and rescue. It is an onerous responsibility. For this very reason, it is not prudent for the Indian Coast Guard, or the Coast Guard of any other country to perform this task alone. There are several constraints like time, money, resources and at times, even technology. All national and international agencies related to search and rescue should pool in their efforts and experience to achieve optimum results. The vagaries of nature affect the seafaring vessels much more than any other mode of transportation. Natural hazards apart, sea-lanes are today increasingly at the risk of attacks by terrorists, pirates and agents of transnational crimes. I am sure this Conference will identify ways and means to provide timely help to those in distress and trauma at sea. The Indian Coast Guard has saved thousands of lives since its inception. Most of the saved people were foreign sailors, sailing vessels under varied flags. However, the Indian Coast Guard must not rest on its laurels. It has the responsibility of guarding an area of about 4.6 million square kilometres. That's twice the area of our country's landmass.

6557. (12-3-2008) NEW DELHI : World Economic Forum (WEF) has released its Travel and Tourism Competitiveness Report 2008 on 4th March 2008. In addition to other information, the report provides the ranking of 130 countries according to travel and tourism competitiveness index. This is the second report and the first one was released in 2007. According to the latest report the overall index for India is 65 in 2008 as it was in 2007. However there are glaring shortcomings in the two reports. Out of the 71 indicators considered for compilation of the index in 2008, only 46 indicators were used in 2007. Further, hard data have been used only for 42 indicators out of 71 and for others the results of Executive Opinion Survey conducted by WEF have been used. Surprisingly, the details of the methodology of the Survey such as sample size, selection of executives, etc. are also not given in the report. Because of the perception bias of the respondents in the opinion surveys, the results of such surveys have to be seen from a wholistic perspective unlike the piecemeal interpretation which has been done in certain sections of the press which is quite inappropriate. Growth of tourism in India has to be appreciated in its entirety, and a piecemeal analysis does not do justice either to the situation or to those drawing inferences from incorrect analysis. India has shown an impressive performance in the tourism sector with foreign tourist arrivals growing at about 12.4% and foreign exchange earnings in dollar terms growing at about 34% over the previous year. Incredible India is not only attracting an increasingly a large proportion of the world tourism market but has also been able to capture the high end tourists who are spending a longer duration in India. This is evident from the UN WTO's latest report which indicates that even though countries like Indonesia, Thailand, Singapore may be having larger number of foreign tourist arrivals but the foreign exchange earned per foreign tourist of India which stood at about $ 1920 was much higher than that of Indonesia ($ 905), Thailand ($ 830) and Singapore ($ 835) & Malaysia ($ 520). These facts confirm that India is attracting travelers across the globe who are spending more time and money as compared to the other South East Asian countries. Considering India's tremendous potential and the high growth scenario for the future, the Ministry of Tourism has been coordinating with other Ministries and other organs of the Government to ensure that constraints related to infrastructure, connectivity, visas etc. are removed.

6558. (12-3-2008) NEW DELHI : Under Pradhan Mantri Gram Sadak Yojana (PMGSY), as per programme guidelines, the first instalment amounting to 50% of the cleared value of projects or annual allocation whichever is lower is released subject to fulfilment of conditions, if any, stipulated earlier. The release of 2nd instalment is subject to utilisation of 60% of the available funds and completion of at least 80% of the road works awarded in the year previous to the preceding year and 100% of the awarded works of all the years preceding that year, and fulfilment of other conditions, if any, stipulated while releasing the previous instalment. The release of the second instalment in a year is also subject to submission of Utilisation Certificate for the funds released earlier, year-wise in the form prescribed, Certificate by the Bank Manager indicating the balance amount on date of issue of the Certificate and the interest credited, Certificate regarding the requisite physical completion of works, Audited Statement of Accounts etc. For ensuring high level of quality in works, PMGSY programme guidelines have the provision for three tier Quality Control Mechanism. The first two tiers of the Quality Control Structure are overseen by the State Quality Coordinators, appointed by the State Governments. The first tier of quality control mechanism is in-house quality control at the level of executing agencies. The field laboratories are established by the Contractors and mandatory tests on the quality of material and workmanship are conducted under the supervision of Programme Implementation Units (PIUs). Quality Control Handbooks have been prescribed and test records are maintained by the PIUs in the prescribed Quality Control registers. The second tier provides for quality monitoring by the State Governments through independent State Quality Monitors (SQMs). SQMs are deployed to ensure that quality issues are properly being attended to at the first tier. The third tier of this arrangement consists of quality monitoring of works through random inspection by independent National Quality Monitors (NQMs).

6559. (12-3-2008) NEW DELHI : Replying to a written question whether Government proposes to extend the National Rural Employment Guarantee Scheme the Minister of State in the Ministry of Rural Development Shri Chandra Sekhar Sahu to day told Rajya Sabha that Government has decided to extend NREGS to all the remaining rural areas in the country with effect from 1.4.2008. A notification to this effect was issued on 28.9.2007. Accordingly, States have been directed to take up preparatory arrangements for new districts like IEC, printing and procurement of statutory documents, training of officials and non-officials and preparation of perspective plans. A sum of Rs. 163.12 crore has been released to the States for the purpose. NREGS is demand driven. All rural households are entitled to get employment under the Act on demand. It is, therefore, not possible to make an estimate of the additional families likely to be covered.

6560. (12-3-2008) NEW DELHI : Drawback is a rebate of duty or tax, as the case may be, chargeable on any imported materials or excisable materials used or taxable services used as input services in the manufacture of export goods. It is paid to the exporters after export of goods. Under the provisions of Customs Act, 1962 the drawback is to be recovered if the sale proceeds in respect of such export goods are not realized within the time allowed under the Foreign Exchange Management Act, 1999. Presently, the monitoring of realization of export proceeds in respect of goods exported under the Drawback Scheme is being done on the basis of Export Outstanding Statement (XOS) received from the RBI. The XOS is a consolidated half-yearly statement giving details of all export bills outstanding beyond the period prescribed for realisation. However, following the issuance of RBI's instructions dispensing with submission of declarations for export of goods of value not exceeding US $ 25,000 it is observed that a large number of export consignments presently fall outside the purview of monitoring mechanism through XOS in as much as, the shipment details of goods valued upto Rs. 10 lakhs (approx) are no longer reported through this statement. In view of this, particularly considering that under the statute the drawback payment is ultimately linked to the realisation of export proceeds, it has become necessary for the Department of Revenue to put in place an in-house monitoring mechanism to monitor the realization of proceeds for exports made under the Drawback Scheme. Extensive consultations were held in this regard with field formations and the trade bodies, *viz.* Federation of Indian Export Organisations (FIEO), Apparel Export Promotion Council (AEPC), Council for Leather Exports (CLE), Engineering Export Promotion Council (EEPC), Export Promotion Council for Handicrafts (EPCH), Delhi Exporters Association and others. Taking note of suggestions received from the trade and after examination of the issue, a software "BRC (Bank Realisation Certificate) module" has been developed for monitoring realization of export proceeds in respect of Drawback Shipping bills. Under this module, the exporters will submit a certificate from the authorized dealer(s) providing details of shipment which remain outstanding beyond the prescribed time limit including the extended time, if any, allowed by the authorized dealer/RBI on quarterly basis. The status holders and other exporters who are permitted to realize export proceeds within a period of 12 months or more may submit these certificates once in six months. The certificates have to be furnished port-wise. The software shall issue alerts against the shipping bills where the BRC/negative statement has not been furnished by the exporter within the prescribed date.

6561. (12-3-2008) NEW DELHI : Following is the text of the statement of Minister for Civil Aviation, Shri Praful Patel in Parliament today regarding the Hyderabad and Bangalore Airports: "The Governments of Andhra Pradesh and Karnataka in 1990's approached the Central Government with request to construct Greenfield airports at Hyderabad and Bangalore respectively. This was due to the traffic growth and the constraints at the existing airports. In the Year 2000, the Task Force on infrastructure recommended setting up of new international airports at Bangalore and Hyderabad and closure of the existing airports once the new airports become operational. Based on the recommendation, the Central Government approved the proposal. This decision was taken so as to ensure financial viability of the new airports. The State Governments decided to implement the projects through Public Private Partnership (PPP) and selected private partners through international competitive bidding. To implement the projects, Joint Venture Companies were set up with 74% equity by the private companies and 13% each by the respective State Governments and Airports Authority of India (AAI). Government of India (GOI) entered into a Concession Agreement with these Joint Venture Companies (JVC) in 2004. The Concession Agreements entail obligations of the JVCs regarding the implementation of the projects and require them to construct, develop and maintain the airports as per the standards stipulated in these agreements. On its part, GOI is obliged to close down all commercial civil aviation operations at the existing airports once the new airports are made operational. The Concession Agreement specifies the consequences of default by each party. The existing airports at Hyderabad and Bangalore would continue to remain operational for general aviation, defence purposes, national emergencies etc. Further the interests of the AAI employees at these airports will be fully protected. I would also like to inform the Hon'ble members that all reserved activities such as security, immigration, customs and air traffic control would continue to be under government control at the new airports."

6562. (12-3-2008) NEW DELHI : The Quick Estimates of Index of Industrial Production (IIP) with base 1993-94 for the month of January 2008 have been released by the Central Statistical Organisation of the Ministry of Statistics and

Programme Implementation. The General Index stands at 279.7, which is 5.3% higher as compared to the level in the month of January 2007. The cumulative growth for the period April-January 2007-08 stands at 8.7% over the corresponding period of the previous year. 2. The Indices of Industrial Production for the Mining, Manufacturing and Electricity sectors for the month of January 2008 stand at 184.8, 299.5, and 223.0 respectively, with the corresponding growth rates of 1.8%, 5.9% and 3.3% as compared to January 2007. The cumulative growth during April-January, 2007-08 over the corresponding period of 2006-07 in the three sectors have been 4.6%, 9.2% and 6.3% respectively, which moved the overall growth in the General Index to 8.7%. 3. In terms of industries, as many as fifteen (15) out of the seventeen (17) industry groups (as per 2-digit NIC-1987) have shown positive growth during the month of January 2008 as compared to the corresponding month of the previous year. The industry group 'Jute and Other Vegetable Fibre Textile (except cotton)' have shown the highest growth of 281.1%, followed by 18.7% in 'Leather and Leather & Fur products' and 13.1% in 'Basic Chemicals & Chemical Products (except production of Petroleum & Coal)'. On the other hand, the industry group 'Wood and Wood Products; Furniture and Fixtures' have shown a negative growth of 4.6% followed by 3.8% in 'Machinery and Equipment other than Transport Equipment'. 4. As per Use-based classification, the Sectoral growth rates in January 2008 over January 2007 are 3.5% in Basic goods, 2.1% in Capital goods and 7.0% in Intermediate goods. The Consumer durables and Consumer non-durables have recorded growth of (-)3.1% and 10.1% respectively, with the overall growth in Consumer goods being 7.0%. 5. Alongwith the Quick Estimates of IIP for January 2008, the indices for December 2007 have undergone the first revision and those for October 2007 have undergone the second (final) revision in the light of the updated data received from the source agencies. 6. Statements giving Quick Estimates of the Index of Industrial Production at Sectoral, 2-digit level of National Industrial Classification (NIC)-1987 and by Use-based classification for the month of January 2008, along with the growth rates over the corresponding month of previous year, including the cumulative indices and growth rates, are enclosed.

6563. (12-3-2008) NEW DELHI : The ambient noise levels in the national Capital city of Delhi are monitored during the day and night by the Central Pollution Control Board (CPCB) as well as by the Delhi Pollution Control Committee (DPCC). Uneven trend has been observed with regard to ambient noise levels in the city showing an increase in some places and decrease in others. As per the available data, while the ambient noise standards are exceeded marginally in some places the situation in Delhi is however not very alarming. This information was given by the Minister of State for Environment and Forests Shri Namo Narain Meena, in a written reply to a question by Shri Madhu Goud Yaskhi, Shri Eknath M.Gaikwad, Shri Anirudh Prasad Alias Sadhu Yadav and Shrimati Nivedita Mane in the Lok Sabha today.

6564. (12-3-2008) NEW DELHI : India and the European Union have agreed to strengthen cooperation in the area of new and renewable energy on the basis of common interest and mutual benefit under the EU-India Science and Technology Cooperation Agreement. Both sides attach high priority to sustainable development of energy systems to jointly meet the challenges of energy security and climate change. At a Workshop held at New Delhi, the two sides identified strategic areas and topics for research and technology development cooperation in solar photovoltaics, solar thermal power generation, wind energy, biomass and waste-to-energy. Apart from these areas, the Indian side also expressed interest for cooperation in hydrogen, fuel cells and biofuels. Science and Technology cooperation in the renewable energy sector would include joint studies and research; technology and product development; setting up of pilot demonstration units; capacity building covering testing, standards, best practices, exchange of information and experts, training etc. Mechanisms and instruments for cooperation could include participation of India in the EU Framework Programme, Technology Platforms for Renewable Energy, European Industrial Initiatives and Specific International Cooperation Actions. The Framework Programmes are the main instrument of the European Commission for funding research. Energy, including renewable energy, is an important focus area. Under the Seventh Framework Programme which runs from 2007 to 2013, it has been decided to issue an India-EU Call for Research and Technology Development proposals in renewable energy in the areas identified at the Workshop. Cooperation between research institutions in various EU countries and Indian research institutions would be on the basis of co-investment of resources, including funding to the tune of Rs.30 crores each by the European Commission and the Government of India. The Workshop was organized by the Ministry of New and Renewable Energy in association with the Directorate General Research of the European Commission and the Department of Science and Technology. It was attended by scientists and experts and delegates from leading institutions who are active in renewable energy research and technology development, apart from officials from both the sides.

6565. (12-3-2008) NEW DELHI : At national level the World Wetlands Day was observed on 2nd February 2008 at Fatehapur near Pong Dam in Himachal Pradesh, which is one of the Ramsar sites. Minister of State for Environment and Forests was the chief guest. On this occasion, prizes were also distributed to winners of various painting, essay and declamation contests. A small brochure on wetlands of Himachal Pradesh was also released on this day. Deepar Beel is one of the identified wetlands under National Wetland Conservation Programme from Assam apart from recently identified Urpad Beel Wetland. Other wetlands from North East include Loktak (Manipur), Rudrasagar (Tripura), Tamdil & Palak (Mizoram), Khechuperi, Tamze, Tembao, Phendang, Gurudokmar, Tsomgo (Sikkim) and Umiami Lake (Meghalaya). An amount of Rs 249.70 lakhs has been released for conservation of wetlands in North-East Region during the last three years for activities like catchment area treatment, fisheries development, removal of weeds, biodiversity conservation, socio-economic aspects, survey & demarcation, raising of horticulture plantations, education and awareness, etc. This information was given by the Minister of State for Environment and Forests Shri Namo Narain Meena, in a written reply to a question by Shri M.K. Subbain the Lok Sabha today.

6566. (12-3-2008) NEW DELHI : The mining activity is covered under the provisions of the Environment (Protection) Act, 1986 through a notification, dated 14th September 2006 on Environment Impact Assessment (EIA) under which environmental clearance is required to be obtained for mining projects having area equal to 5 hectare and above. The mining activity is also regulated under the provisions of the Air (Prevention and Control of Pollution) Act, 1981 and the Water (Prevention and Control of Pollution) Act, 1974 in terms of air and water pollution respectively by the concerned State Pollution Control Board (SPCB)/ Pollution Control Committee (PCC) of the UT. Further, under section 23 (1) of the Mines & Minerals (Development and Regulation) Act, 1957, powers have been delegated to the respective State Governments / UT Administrations for preventing illegal mining, transportation and storage of minerals. While there is no general information regarding mining being undertaken not in accordance with the legal provisions, as and when such specific references related to mining in specific areas are received the same are referred to the concerned Authority/ SPCB/ PCC. In regard to mining of boulders from river bed in district Saharanpur of the State, Uttar Pradesh, a reference is received by the ministry and the same has been referred to the Central Pollution Control Board for further examination. This information was given by the Minister of State for Environment and Forests Shri Namo Narain Meena, in a written reply to a question by Shri Rasheed Masood in the Lok Sabha today. Shri Rasheed Masood

6567. (12-3-2008) NEW DELHI : The Government proposes to increase the forest cover in the country, during the Eleventh Plan by 5 percentage points. No State-wise target has been fixed by the Government. The Ministry of Environment and Forests is implementing a number of schemes, including the National Afforestation Programme scheme and the Grants-in-Aid for Greening India scheme, which contribute to increase in forest and tree cover in the country. The Ministry has also mooted Gram Van Yojana scheme for afforestation of non-forest lands involving Panchayati Raj Institutions during the Eleventh Five Year Plan. Besides, tree planting is one of the permissible activity in the schemes of other Ministries including Integrated Watershed Management Programme, National Rural Employment Guarantee Scheme, National Bamboo Mission, etc. This information was given by the Minister of State for Environment and Forests Shri S. Regupathy, in a written reply to a question by Shri Ananta Nayak Shri Bhartruhari Mahtab in the Lok Sabha today.

6568. (12-3-2008) NEW DELHI: Congress spokesman Sh. Manish Ṭewari said that the All India Congress Committee would like to place on record its deepest sense of sorrow over the loss of innocent lives yesterday in Lahore. We condemn the terrorist attack which has led to 28 people losing their lives and more than 180 people getting injured. The whole region is very concerned about the sectarian strife which has been continuing in Pakistan. We hope that the new government which takes office in Pakistan would be able to bring the situation under control though this is not the occasion and it has never been our intent to politicize any incident which involves the loss of human lives but there has to be a realization that terror does eat the hands that feeds it. I hope the new government in Pakistan would energise the anti-terror mechanism which was institutionalized in 2006 at the initiative of Prime Minister Dr. Manmohan Singh and steps would be taken to extradite those who are wanted by the Government of India and continue to live in Pakistan. As you all know that the employees of the Airports Authority of India are on strike resulting in disruption in flights at many airports and we are of the opinion that for the progress of the nation the infrastructure of the nation has to be upgraded. Therefore I would like to appeal to the unions of the AAI to withdraw their strike and come to a settlement after having talks with the government. By striking work and causing inconvenience to passengers would not help the strikers in any way. You are all aware that the question hour was again adjourned today. We have been repeatedly pointing out that Parliament must be allowed to function as the question hour is a very important and integral part of the parliamentary process in which the issues of the common people living across India get resolved through this interactive process. We would like to place on record once again that we strongly condemn the cult of violence which is being perpetrated by the BJP not only in Delhi but in various other parts of the country. In a democracy there may be differences but there is no place for political violence. Political issues need to be settled through debate and dialogue and if anybody takes law into his own hands then he must be prepared to face the consequences of his act. To a question that Shri Rahul Gandhi said that he wants a transparent culture in the Party and we need to strengthen those processes, Shri Tewari said the constitution of the Congress Party does have a laid down process which clearly states as to how the process within the Party has to function. However there is always scope for improvement and we are open to that. And since the general secretary has expressed a view to strengthen those processes I think it's a welcome view and the Congress Party has always had the strength to introspect and imbibe processes which not only strengthen it internally but also help in its outreach to the people. To a question that are you aware what the Karnataka Congress has said on the airport shifting, Shri Tewari said we are cognizant of what the Karnataka unit of the Congress Party has said.

6569. (12-3-2008) NEW DELHI : The eco sensitive zones need to be declared in order to provide better sanctity to protected areas; as an additional tool to strengthen the buffers and corridors around the Protected Area network; and to check the negative impact of industrialization and unplanned development in and around Protected Areas. In this background the Indian Board for Wildlife in its XXI meeting held on 21st January 2002 under the Chairmanship of Hon'ble Prime Minister had adopted a 'Wildlife Conservation Strategy-2002' in which one of the action point envisaged to notify lands falling within 10 km. of the boundaries of National Parks and Sanctuaries as Eco-fragile zones under the Environment (Protection) Act, 1986. After concern raised by the State Governments like Himachal Pradesh, Rajasthan and Goa, over applicability of the 10 Kms range from the Protected Area boundary and informed that most of the human habitation and other areas including important cities in these States would come under the purview of eco-sensitive zone and will adversely affect the development, it has been decided that the delineation of eco-sensitive zones would have to be site specific and relate to regulation, rather than prohibition, of specific activities. The decision was communicated to all the State Governments for compliance. Only the States of Assam, Haryana, Karnataka, Sikkim, Chattisgarh and Goa have so far submitted the proposal for declaration of eco-sensitive zones around Protected Areas. This information was given by the Minister of State for Environment and Forests Shri S.Regupathy, in a written reply to a question by Shri Asaduddin Owaisi in the Lok Sabha today.

6570. (12-3-2008) NEW DELHI : Of the ten ongoing forestry projects funded externally, nine are funded by Japan Bank of International Cooperation and one project by the World Bank. The total project outlay of these projects is about Rs 4977 crores spread over ten different States. The details of these projects, their total outlay, project period and objectives are annexed. In the State of Karnataka, the Karnataka Sustainable Forest Management and Biodiversity Conservation Project is being implemented with the total project cost of Rs. 745 crores including 131.734 crores as State share. An amount of Rs. 157.951 crores has been claimed as reimbursement from JBIC till 19th February 2008. The objectives of the project are to increase forest cover, to manage forests sustainably, conservation and protection of protected areas, to support JFPM and village communities, development of natural resources on degraded forests sites, to develop enabling policy environment to achieve the sustainable forest management objectives. The project period is 2005-06 to 2012-13.

6571. (12-3-2008) NEW DELHI : The International Coral Reef Initiative (ICRI), a partnership among governments, international organizations, and non-governmental organizations throughout the world, has designated 2008 as the International Year of the Reef (IYOR 2008). The Government has issued the Coastal Regulation Zone Notification, 1991. Under the Notification, mangroves, corals and coral reef areas are classified as Coastal Regulation Zone-I (i). No developmental activities in these areas, other than those permissible under the Notification, can be taken up. For implementing and enforcing the said Notification, the Government has constituted one National and State/Union Territory level

Coastal Zone Management Authorities under Environment (Protection) Act, 1986. These Authorities have been delegated with necessary powers under the aforesaid Act to take punitive action against violations. The Ministry of Environment & Forests also has a National Committee on Mangroves & Coral Reefs to oversee their conservation & management. Some species of fishes are included in Schedule I Part II A of Wildlife (Protection) Act, 1972 and any trade of the scheduled species is not allowed under the provisions of the Act. However, the Chief Wildlife Warden of the concerned State/Union Territory Governments, with the prior permission from the Director, Wildlife Preservation, Government of India can permit the collection of such Scheduled species for research purpose. Besides, the Department of Animal Husbandry, Dairying & Fisheries is regulating the import of exotic aquatic species including ornamental fishes through the National Committee on Introduction of Exotic Aquatic Species into Indian Waters. This information was given by the Minister of State for Environment and Forests Shri Namo Narain Meena, in a written reply to a question by Shrimati Maneka Gandhi in the Lok Sabha today.

6572. (12-3-2008) NEW DELHI : The bio-diversity of the Western Ghats is not yet fully explored. The exploration of the area is carried out by the Botanical Survey of India; Zoological Survey of India; 'Centre of Ecological Sciences' under the Indian Institute of Science, Bangalore and many other regional institutions. The technical man power of the Botanical Survey of India and the Zoological Survey of India have been strengthened. In order to protect the biodiversity of the region, a number of National Parks, Wildlife Sanctuaries, Tiger Reserves and Elephant Reserves have been notified. In addition, the parts of Nilgiri and the Augasthiyamalai areas have been designated as Biosphere Reserves. Ex-situ conservation of rare and endemic plants has been promoted through botanic gardens and the centres of ex-situ conservation. This information was given by the Minister of State for Environment and Forests Shri Namo Narain Meena, in a written reply to a question by Shri Shriniwas Dadasaheb Patil in the Lok Sabha today.

6573. (12-3-2008) NEW DELHI : The Government has approved to set up the Rajiv Gandhi Regional Museum of Natural History at Sawai Madhopur, Rajasthan at an estimated cost of Rs. 40 crores. The foundation stone of the Museum was laid by Hon'ble Vice President of India on 23rd December, 2007 and is expected to be opened to the public by 2011. It will serve as a non-formal centre for Environment Education and creation of public awareness on conservation of nature and natural resources through potential medium of exhibits and educational activities. It would also provide an understanding of the diversity of life on the earth, the factors responsible for their well being, man's dependence upon nature and the necessity to maintain our ecological heritage and to ensure sustainable development with special emphasis on the Western Arid region of India. This information was given by the Minister of State for Environment and Forests Shri

Namo Narain Meena, in a written reply to a question by Shri Sugrib Singh, Shri Nand Kumar Sai And Shri Kishanbhai V. Patel in the Lok Sabha today.

6574. (12-3-2008) NEW DELHI : The Government set up the Expert Committee on the impacts of Climate Change on 7th of May 2007 to cope up with challenges posed to biodiversity due to global warming and climate change. Dr. R. Chidambaram, Principal Scientific Adviser to Government of India is chairman of this committee. It will study the impacts of anthropogenic climate change on India including impacts on Bio diversity and to identify the measures that we may have to take in the future in relation to addressing vulnerability to anthropogenic climate change impacts. A high level coordination Committee chaired by Prime Minister called Prime Minister's Council on Climate Change to coordinate national action for assessment, adaptation and mitigation of climate change was constituted on 6th of June 2007 to evolve a coordinated response to issues relating to climate change at the national level and to provide oversight for formulation of action plans in the area of assessment, adaptation and mitigation of climate change. This information was given by the Minister of State for Environment and Forests Shri Namo Narain Meena, in a written reply to a question by Shri K.J. S. P. Reddy in the Lok Sabha today.

6575. (12-3-2008) NEW DELHI : The Government has recently decided about decentralization in the sphere of green clearance. The Environment Impact Assessment (EIA) Notification issued vide SO 1533 (E) dated 14th September, 2006 provides for decentralization of prior environmental clearance required under the provisions thereof. The EIA Notification has categorized the projects / activities requiring prior environmental clearance into two categories-Category 'A' and Category 'B', based on the potential of impacts on human health and natural and man made resources and their spatial extent. The Category 'A' projects are required to obtain prior environmental clearance at the central level in the Ministry of Environment & Forests and Category 'B' projects from the State / Union Territory Environment Impact Assessment Authority. This information was given by the Minister of State for Environment and Forests Shri Namo Narain Meena, in a written reply to a question by Shri G.M. Siddeswara in the Lok Sabha today.

6576. (12-3-2008) NEW DELHI : The Genetic Engineering Approval Committee (GEAC) has approved the confined experimental field trials of genetically modified (GM) paddy developed by M/s. Maharashtra Hybrid Company, Mumbai during Rabi-2007 to generate biosafety and agronomic data at 11 locations. They are Anand in Gujarat, Bhandara and Rajgad in Maharashtra, South 24 Parganas and Midnapur in West Bengal, Gaya in Bihar, Ranchi in Jharkhand, Davangere and Mandya in Karnataka and Tanjore and Coimbatore in Tamil Nadu. As no experimental field trials on GM Paddy are being conducted in proximity to basmati growing area. The basmati rice producing areas does not get destroyed. To prevent the possible contamination due to gene flow during experimental field trials, the GEAC, in accordance with the Indian Minimum Seed Certification Standards, 1988, stipulates stringent norms which include a minimum of 200 m isolation distance as well as biological and physical barriers. The Government has also taken a decision not to permit transgenic research in crop commodities such as Basmati where international trade may be affected. This information was given by the Minister of State for Environment and Forests Shri Namo Narain Meena, in a written reply to a question by Shri Subrata Bose in the Lok Sabha today.

6577. (12-3-2008) NEW DELHI : There is no report of tiger presence in Sariska. As per the recent (2008) All India Tiger Estimation using the refined methodology, tiger presence has been reported in the Kuno Wildlife Sanctuary of Madhya Pradesh. The tiger population is estimated around 32 in the Ranthambhore Tiger Reserve of Rajasthan, which encompasses the Kaila Devi Wildlife Sanctuary, at times frequented by transient tigers. This information was given by the Minister of State for Environment and Forests Shri S. Regupathy, in a written reply to a question by Shri Mohan Sing in the Lok Sabha today.

6578. (12-3-2008) NEW DELHI : The principal outcome of the thirteenth Conference of Parties (COP-13) of the United Nations Framework Convention on Climate Change (UNFCCC) at Bali in December 2007 was to launch a comprehensive process called Bali Action Plan (BAP) that would enable the full, effective and sustained implementation of the UNFCCC through long-term cooperative action, now, up to and beyond 2012. It is expected that an agreed outcome would be reached and a decision adopted regarding BAP, at the fifteenth Conference of Parties (COP-15) to be held in December 2009. As decided by the Prime Minister's Council on Climate Change, the National Action Plan on Climate Change is being prepared and that would consider approaches to address the concerns of climate change.

6579. (12-3-2008) NEW DELHI : As per the information provided by Central Pollution Control Board, the coal mines, coal washeries, thermal power plants, chemical factories, located in the vicinity of the river Damodar, discharge their wastewater into the river Damodar after necessary treatment. The effluent discharged by these industries is regularly monitored by the respective State Pollution Control Board of Jharkhand and West Bengal to check compliance with the prescribed standards. Action is taken against the defaulting units as per the provisions of the Water (Prevention and Control of Pollution) Act, 1974 and Environment (Protection) Act, 1986. The Government of India is implementing the National River Conservation Plan (NRCP) for abatement of pollution of river Damodar from domestic sewage in the towns of Bokaro-Kargali, Chirkunda, Dugdha, Jharia, Ramgarh, Sindri, Sudamdih and Telmachu in the State of Jharkhand and Raniganj, Asansol, Andal and Durgapur in the State of West Bengal. The various schemes undertaken include Interception & Diversion (I&D) of sewage, installation of

Sewage Treatment Plants (STP), Low Cost Sanitation (LCS) Units, Improved Wood Crematoria (IWC) among others. Four projects relating to LCS at Bokaro-Kargali, Ramgarh, Sudamdih and Telmachu towns in the State of Jharkhand have been completed. An expenditure of Rs. 6.31 Lakh has been incurred in the State of Jharkhand during the last three years out of earlier funds provided to the State for the implementation of these projects. No further requirement of funds has been received from the State Government. In the State of West Bengal, ten projects have been sanctioned, out of which eight projects consisting of LCS and IWC each at Raniganj, Asansol, Andal and Durgapur towns have been completed. An expenditure of Rs. 2.23 crore has been incurred in execution of these projects during the last three years out of the amount of Rs. 3.0 crore allocated for the period. Conservation of rivers is a dynamic activity with the ever increasing pollution load due to rapid urbanization and increase in population. Review of the strategies of conservation policy and identification of additional towns and rivers is a continuous process. Due to continuous increase in the population of the towns located along the banks of the rivers resulting in increased pollution load, and gap in the availability of financial resources to take up works commensurate with the requirements, there is likely to be persistent divergence between the tackled pollution load and the actual pollution load. This information was given by the Minister of State for Environment and Forests Shri Namo Narain Meena, in a written reply to a question by Shri Tek Lal Mahto in the Lok Sabha today.

6580. (12-3-2008) NEW DELHI : The fourth assessment reports of the Intergovernmental Panel on Climate Change (IPCC) brought out in 2007, provide information on global impacts of projected climate change on various regions of the world and provides information on the impacts such as Ecosystems, Food, Fibre and Forest products, Coastal systems and low-lying areas, Industry, Settlement, Society and Health across the world. In general these reports do not state impacts on India but give on a global regional basis.

6581. (12-3-2008) NEW DELHI : The Union Minister of Shipping, Road Transport and Highways, Thiru T.R. Baalu has approved two proposals for road repair works in Jammu and Kashmir at a cost of Rs. 25.93 crore under the Central Road Fund (CRF) Scheme. A sum of Rs. 19.97 crore has been sanctioned for widening and upgradation of 21 km stretch of Bugroo Khan Saheb Dood Pathri Road (ODR) in Budgam district of the state. An amount of Rs. 5.96 crore has also been sanctioned for improvement and upgradation of 16 km. of Kaluchak Purmandal Road in Jammu District.

6582. (12-3-2008) NEW DELHI : The Tourism & Cultural Minister Smt. Ambika Soni has said that better inter ministerial coordination is needed for further promotion and growth of tourism sector in the country. Chairing the first meeting of the reconstituted National Tourism Advisory Council (NTAC) here today, she said Planning Commission can be an appropriate platform in this regard on issues such as connectivity etc. Responding to Members' suggestions on Visa on Arrival issue, the Minister said her Ministry has taken up the matter with the Home Ministry and it is assured by the Home Ministry that once the work of upgradation of airports is complete, the issue would be decided. She said India has witnessed arrival of 5 million tourists in the year 2007 with a foreign exchange earnings of 12 billion dollars. She urged the members of NTAC to come forward with their suggestions to help the tourism sector in a sustainable manner. Referring to some recent media reports about safety and security of tourists in the country, the Minister said she is most concerned about these unfortunate incidents. She said although law and order is a state subject, the Ministry of Tourism had taken up the issue of safety and security of tourists with State Governments. She also said that ten states had already deployed tourist police and some more are in the process of doing so. A tourist-friendly and sensitive security organization of ex-servicemen is being proposed to effectively deal with cases of harassment and misbehaviour in destinations frequented by tourists.

6583. (12-3-2008) NEW DELHI : At present, 2,58,770 Youth Clubs / Mahila Mandals all over the country are affiliated to Nehru Yuva Kendras. The state-wise details of Youth Clubs/Mahila Mandals is at annex. The Budget proposals for 2008-09 provide for the establishment of a Nehru Yuva Kendra in each district headed by a District Youth Coordinator. Grants are released to the Nehru Yuva Kendra Sangathan on an annual basis for meeting expenditure on Establishment and Regular Programmes. Funds were released to the tune of Rs. 33.52 crores in 2004-05, Rs. 36.74 crores in 2005-06 and Rs. 36.00 crores in 2006-07. During the current year, permission has been granted to NYKS to carry forward and utilise the surplus grant of Rs. 63.91 crores lying with them, accumulated since the inception of NYKS in 1987. This information was given by Shri Mani Shankar Aiyar, Minister of Panchayati Raj, Youth Affairs & Sports and DoNER in the Lok Sabha today in a written reply to a question by

6584. (12-3-2008) NEW DELHI : The 73rd Constitutional Amendment incorporated Part IX covering Article 243 and Articles 243A to 243O in the Constitution of India. All 24 States to which the provisions of Part IX of the Constitution apply have enacted Panchayati Raj legislation. The State Panchayati Raj Acts define the contours of implementation of Panchayati Raj in different States. In pursuance of Article 243B of the Constitution, all States to which provisions of this constitutional amendment apply (except Jharkhand) have constituted Panchayats. All the States have provided for the reservation of seats for SC, ST and women in conformity with Article 243D. The States of Bihar and Madhya Pradesh have amended their State Acts to provide for 50% reservation to women and Sikkim provides for 40%. Except Jharkhand (where Panchayat elections have not been held as the quantum of reservation for STs is sub judice before the Supreme Court), elections to Panchayats in all the States/UTs have by and large, been held regularly in conformity with Article 243E. Also, all the States have constituted State Election Commissions which have the mandate to ensure compliance with the provisions enshrined in Article 243F. In conformity with Article 243 K, all State Governments have constituted State Election Commissions to ensure free and fair elections to the PRIs on the completion of each five year cycle and also to fill the casual vacancies that may arise during the cycle. Article 243 G provides for devolution, that is, the empowerment of Panchayati Raj Institutions to function as institutions of self government for the twin purposes of (i) making plans for economic development and social justice for their respective areas, and (ii) implementing programmes of economic development and social justice in their respective areas, for the subjects devolved to the PRIs, including those listed in the Eleventh Schedule, and subject to such conditions as the State may, by law, specify. The formal devolution through State legislation needs to be translated into the actual transfer of activities relating to devolved functions to Panchayats at different levels through executive orders, instructions and administrative arrangements. Such transfer of powers and responsibilities will need to be matched by the corresponding transfer of funds and functionaries so that Panchayats can perform their role as institutions of self-government in the spirit of the 73rd Constitutional Amendment. The position in this regard varies from State to State. In the spirit of Article 243H, State Governments have been regularly pursued to provide untied grants to the Panchayats from the Consolidated Fund of the States and to open a Panchayat sector window in their State budgets to supplement the resources of the Panchayati Raj Institutions. In pursuance of Article 243M of the Constitution, Parliament has enacted the Provisions of Panchayats (Extension to the Scheduled Areas) Act, 1996. This Act extends the provisions of Part IX of the Constitution to the Fifth Schedule areas of nine States, *i.e.*, Andhra Pradesh, Orissa, Chhattisgarh, Jharkhand, Rajasthan, Madhya Pradesh, Gujarat, Himachal Pradesh and Maharashtra that are listed in the Fifth Schedule to the Constitution. All the States concerned have enacted conformity legislation related to this Act.

6585. (12-3-2008) NEW DELHI : A comprehensive national interactive portal- "Punarbhava.in" window for taking care of the education, communication and rehabilitation needs of persons with disabilities was jointly launched by the Minister of Social Justice & Empowerment, Smt. Meira Kumar and the Minister of State for Communication & IT, Dr. Shakeel Ahmed here today. On the Occasion, Smt. Meira Kumar said that by inaugurating the national interactive web portal on disability, we mark our bid to enhance public access to information and knowledge about disability and rehabilitation. She further said that the plan for the portal is to provide all related information regarding different disability issues at one platform. This will enable persons with disabilities, NGOs, professionals, policy makers, students, parents, community works and all other stakeholders to access information relating to the disability sector. Some of the key features of the web portal include the setting up of a National Disability Register, a repository of all Govt. orders, legal instruments on disabilities. We will also have a repository of books in text, audio and multimedia mode that will be available for downloading on request. Details of information on manpower available in the sector, both of professionals and persons with disabilities is also envisaged. On the occasion, the SAFA-Screen Access for All was launched and the Handbook on Social Welfare Statistics-2007 was released by the Minister. Smt Meira Kumar said that the SAFA will enable a large number of people with disabilities, specifically those with visual impairment to not only operate a computer using speech output support for the windows environment in 13 Indian languages, but will also enable them to browse the net, check email, use excel and other software and search for information independently. Giving the outline of The Handbook on Social Welfare Statistics-2007 she said that The Handbook on Social Welfare Statistics-2007 is yet another initiative of our Ministry to collate all the data relating to our various programmes for providing for social justice and empowerment of the marginalized sections of our society. The Handbook contains social welfare statistics relating to schemes and programmes implemented by my Ministry as well as other Ministries of the Government of India working for the socially disadvantaged sections of population during the Tenth Plan Period. Besides, the data on social indicators pertaining to population, demographic trends, literacy levels and employment status are added. The Minister of State for Communication & IT, Dr. Ahmed said "My Ministry is committed to serve the disadvantaged in the country in order to build an inclusive society, and this of course includes persons with disability. Initiatives like these help in building a strong society that knows how to take care of its people". The Secretary of Social Justice & Empowerment was also present on the occasion.

6586. (12-3-2008) NEW DELHI : Governments procurement agencies have so far procured 20.85 million tonne rice in the current kharif marketing season. This is one million tonne more than the procurement achieved on March 12, 2007 (19.83 MT). In the entire marketing season last year (October 2006-September-2007) 25.08 MT rice was procured. States procuring more than one million tonne rice in the current kharif season include: Punjab (7.69 MT), Andhra Pradesh (3.3 MT), Chhattisgarh (2.64 MT), Uttar Pradesh (2.52 MT), Haryana (1.56 MT) and Orissa (1.46 MT).

6587. (12-3-2008) NEW DELHI : Government has set up a network of about 50 tidal gauges all along Indian coast line for continuous monitoring of sea level. Besides, Coastal zone vulnerability zonation maps are being generated for various sectors along the Indian Coast. Reports indicate that the sea surface temperatures (SST) and the upper ocean heat content in the Arctic Ocean have been steadily increasing. Few climate stations that have records extending back beyond 50 years, indicate that the Arctic region warmed up by about 1-20C between 1910 and 1945. A number of stations showed further warming over the past two decades. The SST recorded in 2007, is reported to have been about 3.50C warmer than the 100 year average. The average volume of Arctic Ice is 20,000 Km3, compared to the Antarctic Ice volume (30,000,000 Km3). Since the quantity of ice in Arctic is very small compared to Antarctic, Arctic sea ice melting does not increase the water level of the oceans significantly. Since melting of the ice cover on the Arctic Ocean does not affect sea level significantly, the coastal areas will not be adversely affected. This information was given by Union Minister for Science & Technology and Earth Sciences, Shri Kapil Sibal, in the Rajya Sabha today.

6588. (12-3-2008) NEW DELHI : There is no proposal to set up dedicated facilities in the Major Ports for handling textile cargo. Also, there is no proposal to have uniform tariff rates across all the ports in the country. This information was given by the Minister of Shipping, Road Transport and Highways, Shri T.R. Baalu in a written reply in the Lok Sabha today.

6589. (12-3-2008) NEW DELHI : Jawaharlal Nehru Port Trust (JNPT) has acquired about 2584 hectares of land and as per approved Coastal Zone Management Plan (CZMP), about 1200 hectares is balance for future development such as operational activities, commercial/social facilities, residential facilities for Project Affected Persons (PAPs) etc. The Jawaharlal Nehru Port proposes to set up SEZ/EPZ for the port based industries in the above mentioned balance developable land. The port has invited applications for appointment of Consultants to advise on the creation of a port based Special Economic Zone/Export Processing Zone at JNPT. Taking into consideration the existing traffic and future traffic potential, the selected consultant would be required to formulate an appropriate planning concept and develop a master plan for appropriate land use for the area within SEZ project so as to have a synergy with the port operations. The port will allow commercial activities directly related to the port activities only and no manufacturing industry is proposed to be set up in the port. Due care would be taken at the planning stage itself to ensure that there is free flow of port traffic and there is no delay in handling of cargo. This information was given by the Minister of Shipping, Road Transport and Highways, Shri T.R. Baalu in a written reply in the Lok Sabha today.

6590. (12-3-2008) NEW DELHI : As part of the on-going process of development, it is planned to construct Deep Draught Iron Ore Berth and Deep Draught Coal Berth at Paradip Port at a total estimated cost of Rs.892.60 crore. The projects are at tendering stage. Plan for Development of Southern Dock Complex at the Port is also at preliminary stage. This information was given by the Minister of Shipping, Road Transport and Highways, Shri T.R. Baalu in a written reply in the Lok Sabha today.

6591. (12-3-2008) NEW DELHI : The Government has taken various steps for promotion of micro and small enterprises in the country, particularly the first generation entrepreneurs through Entrepreneurship Development Programmes. This was stated by Shri Mahabir Prasad, Minister for Micro, Small & Medium Enterprises (MSME) while chairing the Fourth Meeting of the National Board for Micro, Small & Medium Enterprises (NBMSME) here today. The main agenda for the fourth meeting of the NBMSME was Establishing of Entrepreneurship Development Institutes by State Governments and issues of concern for MSMEs. Shri Prasad said, Entrepreneurship Development is one of the key elements for promotion of micro, small & medium enterprises and is a major means for inclusive growth. The Minister said, to undertake and facilitate this task on a regular basis, the Ministry of Micro, Small & Medium Enterprises has set up three national level Entrepreneurship Development Institutes (EDIs). Besides, the Ministry has also been implementing an important scheme, *viz.*, Scheme for Assistance for Strengthening of Training Infrastructure and new Entrepreneurship Development Institutes. Under this scheme a maximum of one crore rupees assistance is given to new Entrepreneurship Development Institutes as also to existing institutes. Expressing satisfaction that the General Budget 2008-09 has made a provision of Rs.2,000 crore Risk Capital Fund for Small Industries Development Bank of India (SIDBI), the Minister said that some more proposals would be taken up during the budget discussions. Some of the Members raised the issue of extending collateral free loans upto Rs.5,00,000 to the MSME Sector (both manufacturing and services enterprises) to which Shri Prasad said the Reserve Bank of India (RBI) had already issued a circular on 21st September 2007 to all scheduled commercial banks that they should extend collateral free loans up to Rs.5,00,000 to the units of MSME Sector as defined under MSMED Act 2006. RBI advised all scheduled commercial banks to issue necessary instructions to the branches/ controlling offices in this regard, the Minister added. Some of the Members raised the issue of steel price hike, which was affecting the micro and small industries. The Minister assured the Members that the issue would be taken up at the appropriate level. Representatives of MSME Associations and Trade Unions, from all over the country and senior officials of various ministries from the central as well as the state governments participated in the daylong deliberations.

6592. (12-3-2008) NEW DELHI : At present, there are 271 medical colleges in the country, out of which 138 are in the Government sector and remaining 133 medical colleges are in the private sector. State-wise details in this regard can be seen at Annexure-I. The MBBS students intake capacity of these medical colleges is about 31,172 and the number of seats available in various PG medical courses is approximately 11,005 annually. As to the number of reserved seats in MBBS and PG medical courses, the data is not centrally maintained. However, at the State level, the State Governments follow their reservation policy. And in the All India Quota against these seats, 15% seats are reserved for SC candidates and 7.5% for ST candidates. The number of medical colleges recognized since April 2004, is 27, the details of which can be seen at Annexure-II. The Central Government encourages starting of new courses and increase of seats in MBBS and PG medical courses. For this purpose, the concerned institutions are required to apply to the Central Government for permission as per the Regulations framed under Indian Medical Council Act, 1956, after obtaining Essentiality Certificate from the State Government, Consent of Affiliation from University concerned etc. Such applications received from the medical colleges are evaluated by the Medical Council of India and on its recommendations and taking into consideration various factors, the Central Government takes appropriate decision to grant necessary permission in this regard from time to time.

6593. (12-3-2008) NEW DELHI : The Governing Body of All India Institute of Medical Sciences (AIIMS) in its meeting on 20.12.2007 have discussed the issue of debarring doctors who seek voluntary retirement from AIIMS for practicing within 35-40 Kms radius of AIIMS and desired that the issue should be examined on priority and brought before the next Governing Body meeting of AIIMS for consideration. A clause is being inserted in the retirement orders that the concerned faculty member is required to take NO OBJECTION from the AIIMS in the event of his/her accepting any commercial employment within two years from the date of his/her voluntary retirement in accordance with Rule 10 of CCS (Pension) Rules, 1972. This information was given by the Minister of State for Health & Family Welfare, Smt. Panabaaka Lakshmi in a written reply to a question in the Lok Sabha.

6594. (12-3-2008) NEW DELHI : Section 8 of the "The Cigarette and Other Tobacco Products (Prohibition of Advertisement and Regulation of Trade and Commerce, Production, Supply and Distribution) Act, 2003" provides for display of specified health warnings which includes pictorial warning on a package of cigarettes or any other tobacco products. The Cigarette and Other Tobacco Products (Packaging and Labeling) Rules, 2006 has been notified, which are to come into force w.e.f. 17th March 2008. This information was given by the Minister of State for Health & Family Welfare, Smt. Panabaaka Lakshmi in a written reply to a question in the Lok Sabha.

6595. (12-3-2008) NEW DELHI : Review of the programme is an ongoing activity, which is being done regularly. The World Bank reviews the programme biannually along with other donor partners. The last World Bank review mission came in December 2007. In addition, the programme is reviewed externally every three years by Joint Monitoring Mission comprising of international experts from WHO, International Union Against TB and Lung Diseases (IUATLD), World Bank, DFID, Netherlands TB Association and CDC, Atlanta etc. Such reviews took place in the years 2000, 2003 and 2006. The latest World Bank review in December 2007, observed that with case detection and treatment success rate at 70% and 84% respectively, Revised National TB Control Programme (RNTCP) has almost achieved the global targets of 70% case detection and 85% treatment outcome of smear positive cases. This highly satisfactory result is a proof of the professionalism and dedication of RNTCP staff. The overall progress needs now to be sustained and more attention should be devoted to poor performing districts / states still below targets. RNTCP has also made commendable progress in challenging areas like TB/HIV collaboration where a good referral system has now been put in place. The institutional strengthening process in Central TB Division is proceeding well and collaboration with the National Rural Health Mission (NRHM) is bearing fruit. The targets fixed by the Government during the 10th plan period for the National TB Control Programme have been achieved. Entire country has been covered under DOTS Strategy by March 2006. The international Joint Monitoring Mission (JMM) in October 2006, has hailed it as the fastest expansion of DOTS in the world. The target and achievements of case detection and cure rates in 10th five year plan can be seen at Annexure. The performance of the programme and its impact is being monitored regularly. Till date, the RNTCP has placed more than 82 lacs patients on treatment thus saving more than 14 lacs additional lives. As per the WHO report 2007, the death rates due to TB have declined from 42 per 100,000 population in 1990 to 29 per 100,000 population in 2005 and prevalence of tuberculosis (old and new cases) has declined from 570 cases per 100,000 population in 1990 to 299 cases per 100,000 population in 2005. Involvement of more than 260 medical colleges, more than 2500 NGO's, 150 corporate health facilities and more than 18000 private practitioners in the implementation of RNTCP, has increased the access of programme services. The programme is well on its way to achieve MDGs (Millennium Development Goals) related to tuberculosis.

6596. (12-3-2008) NEW DELHI : The main recommendations of the Committee inter alia include (i) Removal of stagnation at Senior Administrative Grade (SAG) and Higher Administrative Grade (HAG) level; (ii) enhancement of retirement age to 62 years; (iii) Terminal benefits of additional 5 years of service over and above 5 years already admissible under Pension Rules; (iv) Permission to attend International Conferences/Symposia once in 2 years with financial assistance of Rs.1.00 Lac per case (v) Enhancement of NPA to 30%; and (vi) Enhancement of Book/Research/Academic Allowance. The age of retirement of Specialist doctors of Central Health Service has already been enhanced to 62 years. Orders for allowing Central Health Service (CHS) Doctors to attend International Conferences/ Symposia once in 2 years with financial assistance of Rs.1.00 Lac per case has also been issued. The proposal for allowing Terminal benefits of additional 5 years of service over and above 5 years already admissible under Pension Rules was taken up thrice with Department of Pension and Pensioner's Welfare but not agreed to by that Department. While the action towards implementation of other recommendations was in progress, Department of Expenditure, Ministry of Finance have in the meantime issued instructions vide OM No.5/16/2006-E.III.A dated 21.12.2006 that all cases involving upgradation of pay-scales, grant of fresh non-functional scales, new allowances, enhancement of existing allowances are to be brought before the 6th Central Pay Commission. Accordingly the issues relating to enhancement of Non Practicing Allowance, increase of Annual Allowance or Book/Research/Academic Allowance and the proposal for enhancement of age of superannuation of General Duty Medical Officers sub-cadre have been referred to 6th Central Pay Commission. This information was given by the Minister of State for Health & Family Welfare, Smt. Panabaaka Lakshmi in a written reply to a question in the Lok Sabha.

6597. (12-3-2008) NEW DELHI : The Major centrally sponsored Health and Family Welfare Programmes under implementation for the last three years include inter-alia, National Rural Health Mission (NRHM), National Cancer Control Programme (NCCP) and National AIDS Control Programme. NRHM cover under its gamut the National Programmes relating to Vector Borne, Blindness Control, Leprosy Eradication and Tuberculosis Control. The success achieved in respect of the above major programmes can be seen at Annexure.

6598. (12-3-2008) NEW DELHI : As on March 2007 there is a shortfall of 1410 doctors at Primary Health Centres across the country. A total of 7352 PHCs are functioning without lab technicians. The PHCs are run by the State/UT Governments. Under National Rural Health Mission [NRHM], funds are released to States/UTs Governments for upgradation and strengthening of Primary Health Centres including contractual appointment of staff. The State/UT Governments are however required to incorporate their requirement in their annual NRHM Programme Implementation Plans.

6599. (12-3-2008) NEW DELHI : To make the world better for the persons with disability, a comprehensive national interactive portal-punarbhava.in, is jointly launched by the Ministry of Communication & IT and the Ministry of Social Justice & Empowerment here today. The Minister of State for Communication & IT, Dr. Shakeel Ahmed along with Smt. Meira Kumar, Union Minister for Social Justice and Empowerment launched the web portal. On this occasion, Dr. Ahmed said "My Ministry is committed to serve the disadvantaged in the country in order to build an inclusive society, and this of course includes persons with disability. Initiatives like these help in building a strong society that knows how to take care of its people". This is the first ever initiative in India where two Government of India organizations have joined hands for reaching the un-reached and providing them opportunities to fully participate in the social life and become productive members of society. This unique web portal by Media Lab Asia and Rehabilitation Council of India is likely to bring a revolution in the way of persons with disabilities, their parents, NGOs, community members, rehabilitation professionals and a variety of other individuals associated with disabled access information on Government Acts/National policies on disability, institutions working in this field, assistive devices available, educational courses and employment opportunities.

The portal is categorized mainly into three segments: the first segment will be a National Disability Register that will give statistical information on the disabled population in India. The second segment of the portal covers the resources which include available online courses, catalogues knowledge repository of audio video and Braille files in Indian languages, books related to disability and news magazine. The third segment is proposed to have Grievance Redressal mechanism through Web Court. In future, this will redress the complaints related to Chief Commissioner for Persons with Disabilities, National Trust, and Rehabilitation council of India etc. It also proposes to provide transaction assistance. Dr. Shakeel Ahmed also released a screen reading software-SAFA (Screen Access for All) for the education and computer literacy of visually impaired.

6600. (12-3-2008) NEW DELHI : Although violence and militancy continue in some parts of the country, the overall situation has remained largely under control. There has been a significant improvement in so far as the situation in Jammu & Kashmir is concerned. In the North Eastern Region, the situation has improved considerably in some States such as Tripura and Meghalaya, while coordinated measures are being taken to check and control the activities of militant groups in the other affected States in the region *viz.* Assam, Manipur and Nagaland. In the naxal-affected areas also, the overall level of extremist violence has more or less remained at a similar level in the last few years and, has in fact, shown improvement in a number of areas barring a few major incidents in some States like Chhattisgarh, Jharkhand, etc. As far as terrorism in the hinterland is concerned, some incidents have occurred in different States. Action taken by the Government to tackle terrorism includes urging the State Governments to take focused and coordinated measures to deal with the situation and providing all possible help in this regard. Close coordination is being maintained between the Central and State agencies, including regular sharing of information and intelligence. As a result, a large number of terrorist modules have been busted and possible major terrorist incidents averted. Institutional arrangements have also been put in place so that sharing and analysis of information and intelligence can be done on a continuing basis in a systematic and coordinated manner. The State Governments have also been urged to strengthen the State police forces by filling up vacancies and improving the police-population ratio, as also to take special measures to strengthen their intelligence set-up. Assistance for these purposes is given under the Police Modernisation Scheme under which the States have also been asked to prepare sub-plans for strengthening intelligence-related arrangements for which the assistance of Central agencies is also provided. All this is in addition to deployment of Central forces to assist the civil authorities in the States, liberal sanctions for raising of India Reserve (IR) battalions and assistance for general and specialized training for State security forces. This information was given by the Minister of State in the Ministry of Home Affairs, Shri Sriprakash Jaiswal in a written reply to a question in the Rajya Sabha today.

6601. (12-3-2008) NEW DELHI : A need is being felt to augment the strength of the Delhi Police keeping in view the increasing population of Delhi as well as the Commonwealth Games slated to be held in Delhi in the year 2010. The Commissioner of Police of Delhi has made a presentation to the Ministry of Home Affairs regarding manpower requirement of Delhi Police. Strengthening of the police forces is a continuous process. The strength of Delhi Police is reviewed from time to time and additional manpower is sanctioned depending upon the requirement of personnel and availability of resources. In September 2007, 5000 posts of various ranks were sanctioned for Delhi Police to make arrangements for increasing population of Delhi and for Commonwealth Games, 2010. This information was given by the Minister of State in the Ministry of Home

6602. (12-3-2008) NEW DELHI : The Ministry of Home Affairs is considering a proposal for construction of roads along the India-Nepal and India-Bhutan borders. The development of border roads along the India-Nepal border would improve border infrastructure thereby leading to enhanced connectivity and promote cross-border economic integration and development of the area. This would also be helpful in effective patrolling and communication and check trans-border crimes and anti-national activities. This will also facilitate better movement of border guarding forces. This information was given by the Minister of State in the Ministry of Home

6603. (12-3-2008) NEW DELHI : Government promulgated Defence Procurement Procedure (DPP) 2006 with effect from 1st September, 2006 to ensure expeditious procurement of the approved requirements of the Armed Forces in terms of capabilities sought and time frame prescribed. Procedure for implementing Offset Provisions is part of DPP-2006. Offset clause is applicable for all procurement proposals where indicate cost is Rs. 300 crore or more and the schemes are categorized as 'Buy (Global)' involving outright purchase from foreign/India vendors an 'Buy and Make with Transfer of Technology' *i.e.* Purchase from foreign vendor followed by Licensed Production. A uniform offset of 30% of the indicative cost of the acquisition in 'Buy (Global)' category acquisitions and 30% of the foreign exchange component in 'Buy and Make' category acquisitions will be minimum required value of the offset. The Defence Acquisition Council may, after due deliberations, also prescribe varying offset percentages above 30% for difference classes of cases or for individual cases depending upon the factors involved such as strategic importance of the acquisition or technology, enhanced ability of Indian defence industry to absorb the offset, export potential generated etc.

6604. (12-3-2008) NEW DELHI : Contracts and supplementary agreements comprising of repair and re-equipping, logistics supports, shore infrastructure, training of ships' crew, repair and technical documents etc. were signed with Russia on 20th January, 2004 for acquisition of "Admiral Gorshkov" with delivery schedule in August 2008. The cost of repair and modernization of Admiral

Gorshkkov including Logistic Support, Training and documentation is US Dollar 974 million. It is, however, apprehended that delay may take place in the delivery of the ship. The existing contract with Russia is still valid. The process of examination of the scope and necessity for additional works projected by the Russian side has been initiated. This information was given by the Defence Minister Shri AK Antony in a written reply to Shri SS Ahluwalia in Rajya Sabha today.

6605. (12-3-2008) NEW DELHI : Bharat Electronics Limited (BEL), a defence PSU has developed Air Borne Com ECM System for demonstration to IAF. About Rs. 2.5 crores investment was made for the same by BEL through its own fund. This information was given by the Defence Minister Shri AK Antony in a written reply to Shri Tapan Kumar Sen and Shri Mohammed Amin in Rajya Sabha today.

6606. (12-3-2008) NEW DELHI : No private agency providing mobile services has approached Army to vacate airwaves for offering high speed services. Wireless Planning and Coordination Wing (WPC) in Ministry of Communication and Information Technology is the agency concerned for this purpose. This information was given by the Defence Minister Shri AK Antony in a written reply to Shri PR Rajan in Rajya Sabha today.

6607. (12-3-2008) NEW DELHI : The Government has signed a Letter of Offer & Acceptance with the US Government for the procurement of six C-130J-30 aircraft for the Indian Air Force. The estimated value of the aircraft along with associated ground support equipment, ground handling equipment and the role equipment is 962,454,677 US$. A letter of Offer & Acceptance has also been signed with the US Government for procurement of weapons and equipment for the Special Forces of the Army. This information was given by the Defence Minister Shri AK Antony in a written reply to Shri Dharam Pal Sabharwal in Rajya Sabha today.

6608. (12-3-2008) NEW DELHI : Government constantly review the security environment and accordingly decide to induct appropriate equipment including aircraft for Navy for adequate defence preparedness. Reconnaissance aircraft are required for maritime surveillance. Sea Harrier aircraft are used for air defence of the fleet. The need for reconnaissance aircraft has increased in the present context. The number of reconnaissance and Sea Harrier aircraft in the Navy has decreased over the past years. However, this shortfall is being met by induction of additional Dornier aircraft, procurement of MiG-29 K and Long Range Maritime Reconnaissance aircraft. Limited upgrade of Sea Harrier aircraft undertaken through M/s Hindustan Aeronautics Limited is expected to be completed by 2009. This information was given by the Defence Minister Shri AK Antony in a written reply to Ms. Sushila Tiriya in Rajya Sabha today.

6609. (12-3-2008) NEW DELHI : Three airmen of the Indian Air Force (IAF), were arrested by the Government Railway Police (GRP) Gomoh on the written complaint made by a lady co-passenger on Dec. 27, 2007 for misbehavior while they were travelling by Delhi-Bhubaneshwar Rajdhani train. A case against all the three was registered under section 354/34 IPC and is being investigated by GRP Gomoh. The next hearing by judicial Magistrate (Railway) Dhanbad is on 03rd April 2008. The airmen have been released on bail on 28 Dec. 2007. In a Formal Investigation, conducted by Air Force Station Kalaikunda in January 2008, one airman has been blamed for improper behaviour with the lady co-passenger. All three have been blamed for not reporting the matter to Air Force authorities in time about the said incident. After approval by competent authority, it is proposed to take action against the blamed airmen, for the lapses established. If the airmen are subsequently convicted by the Criminal Court further appropriate action will also be taken accordingly under the Air Force Laws. This information was given by the Defence Minister Shri AK Antony in a written reply to Shri Harish Rawat and Shri Santosh Bagrodia in Rajya Sabha today.

6610. (12-3-2008) NEW DELHI : Indian Railways have carried 714.25 million tonnes of revenue earning freight traffic during the first eleven months (*i.e.* April 2007-February 2008) of the current financial year 2007-08. The freight carried shows an increase of 58.90 million tonnes over the freight traffic of 655.35 million tonnes actually carried during the corresponding period last year, reflecting an increase of 8.99 per cent. During the month of February 2008, the revenue earning freight traffic carried by Indian Railways was 70.54 million tonnes. There is an increase of 8.87 million tonnes over the freight traffic of 61.67 million tonnes actually carried by the Indian Railways during the same period last year, reflecting an increase of 14.38 per cent.

6611. (12-3-2008) NEW DELHI : The Government of India launched the Technology Mission on Cotton (TMC) in February, 2000 in 9th Five Year Plan, with the objective of improvement in the production, productivity and quality of cotton and reduction in cost of cultivation, in order to provide abundant supply of good quality cotton at competitive prices to the textile industry and a remunerative return to the farmers. The scheme is functional in Maharashtra State also including Vidarbha region. The mission consists of four mini missions, which are being jointly implemented by the Ministry of Agriculture and the Ministry of Textiles.

6612. (12-3-2008) NEW DELHI : The Government of India has introduced Integrated Handloom Development scheme, Marketing and Export promotion Scheme, Handloom Weavers' Comprehensive Welfare Scheme, Mill Gate Price Scheme and Diversified Handloom Development Scheme to be implemented during the XI Five Year Plan. This information was information was given by the Minister of State for Textiles, Shri E.V.K.S. Elangovan, in the Rajya Sabha today, in a written reply to a question by Shri Datta Meghe He further stated that these schemes will enable the handloom weavers to enhance production, productivity and efficiency of the handloom sector and enhance their income and socio-economic status by upgrading their skills and providing infrastructural input and marketing support. DHD scheme include the components, with a view to create awareness among the weavers about modern colours, fashions etc., to promote handloom industries. Regarding growth in the handloom sector, the Minister informed that this sector is highly decentralized in nature and therefore the production in handloom is estimated on the basis of domestic delivery of hank yarn in Kgs. During the last three years handloom production has maintained a positive growth. Since 2004-05, a consistent increase in production of handloom fabrics has been witnessed with the production rising from 5722 mn sq. mtre in 2004-05, 6263mn sq.mtre, in 2005-2006, 6536 mn.sq.mtr in 2006-07. During the current year, 2007-08 (upto January) also, the production of fabrics has reached to 5797 mn.sq.mtre (Prov) and it is anticipated to reach upto 7865 mn sq. mtre upto March, 2008.

6613. (12-3-2008) NEW DELHI : The Ministry of Labour and Employment has introduced a bill in the parliament for security of unorganised sector workers. The Unorganised Sector Workers' Social Security Bill was examined by the Standing Committee of the Parliament and received recommendations. These recommendations are being considered and the views of the Government would soon be placed before the Parliament. Copy of the draft Bill as well as the highlights of the Bill are contained in the note that has been circulated to the Members. This information was given by the Minister for Labour and Employment Shri Oscar Fernandes at the Consultative Committee Meeting here today. The Minister said that the numbers and percentage of unorganized sector workers has gone up on the past few years. As per the latest date, it is 94 per cent. Hence, there is all the more need to address issues relating to this segment of the workforce. So far, social security has been provided to certain segments of unorganized sector workers through various welfare schemes, which include health care, education, housing and recreation facilities. Thus, non-coal mine workers, beedi workers and cine workers are being provided assistance through funds created out of cess collected under respective legislations. However, the coverage so far has been miniscule in the context of large number of unorganized sector workers. Shri Fernandes further said that one of the major insecurities for workers in the unorganized sector is the inability of the worker to find the funds for medical care for themselves, and their family members. It has been clearly recognized that health insurance is one way of providing protection to poor households against the risk of having to incur heavy expenditure on health care disproportionate to their income. Such contingencies, unavoidable as they are, lead to further impoverishment and indeed destitution of poor households. The Minister also informed that in the tune with the announcement made by the Prime Minister, the Ministry of Labour and Employment launched the Rashtriya Swasthya Bima Yojana on 1st October, 2007. The benefits of the scheme will start accruing, in phases, to BPL workers from 1st April, 2008. All the BPL families in the unorganized sector will be covered in the next five years under the 'Rashtriya Swasthya Bima Yojana'. 1.2 crore BPL families will be added each year till all 6 crore such families are covered. The Government would contribute 75 per cent of the estimated annual premium of Rs. 750/- subject to a maximum of Rs. 565/- per family per annum. Additionally, the cost of smart card would be borne by the Central Government. Respective State Governments could contribute 25 per cent of the annual premium as well as any additional premium in case of higher benefits. The administrative and other related cost of administering the scheme would be borne by the respective State Governments. The National Old Age Pension Scheme (Indira Gandhi National Old Age Pension Scheme) has been expanded to coer all BPL citizens above the age of 65 years with effect from 19th November 2007. The scheme is being implemented by Ministry of Rural Development, he added. The Members who participated in the meeting were: Shri Gurudas Dasgupta, Shri. Dawa Narbula, Shri. Bapu Hari Chaure from Lok Sabha; Shri Balihari Babu and Mohammed Amin from Rajya Sabha.

6614. (12-3-2008) NEW DELHI : In exercise of the powers conferred by clause (1) of article 222 of the Constitution of India, the President, after consultation with the Chief Justice of India, is pleased to transfer Shri Justice S. Ashok Kumar, Judge, Madras high Court as Judge, Andhra Pradesh High Court and to direct him to assume charge of the office of the Judge of the Andhra Pradesh High Court on or before 25th March, 2008.

6615. (12-3-2008) NEW DELHI : In exercise of the powers conferred by clause (1) of article 224 of the Constitution of India, the President is pleased to appoint (i) Shri Siddharth Mridul and (ii) Shri Manmohan to be Additional Judges of the Delhi High Court, in that order of seniority, for a period of two years with effect from the dates they assume charge of their respective offices. The President has also appointed (i) Shrimati Sabina and (ii) Shri Jora Singh to be Additional Judges of the Punjab and Haryana High Court, in that order of seniority, for a period of two years with effect from the dates they assume charge of their respective offices.

6616. (12-3-2008) NEW DELHI : Health status of the people has been of prime concern to the Government. There has been some improvement in the quality of health care over the years but wide inter-state, male-female and rural-urban disparities in outcomes and impacts continue to persist. While population stabilization is in the Concurrent List, health is a State subject. The reproductive and child health services reach community and household levels through the primary health care infrastructure. Inadequacies in the existing health infrastructure have led to gaps in coverage and outreach services in rural areas. The Finance Minister, Shri P.Chidambaram in the Budget has set ambitious goals for 2008-09 and has proposed to allocate Rs. 16,534 crore for the Health Sector (including NER). This marks an increase of 15 per cent over the allocation of Rs. 14,363 crore in 2007-08.

6617. (13-3-2008) NEW DELHI : The Cabinet Committee on Economic Affairs today gave its approval for providing the relief against the outstanding dues of RITES Ltd. and IRCON International Ltd. on outstanding dues for projects executed in Iraq in 1980's on deferred payment basis in the following manner: (i) RITES and IRCON will be paid the balance amounts as per the approved exchange rate of Rs.47.86 per US$ at which private exporters were paid, to maintain the parity in treatment of all the exporters; (ii) RITES and IRCON will be paid balance amounts of Rs.117.75 crore and Rs.16.06 crore respectively in cash through additional budget allocation provided by Ministry of Finance to M/o Railways for this purpose and (iii) RITES and IRCON will be paid interest in cash @ 8.75% per annum effective from 1st October 2001 on Rs.117.75 crore and Rs.16.06 crore respectively till principal and interest both are paid by additional budget allocation in addition to above stated balance amount of Rs.117.75 crore and Rs.16.06 crore. It would project the creditability of the Government to help exporters: solve liquidity problem of project exporters who have faced unprecedented situation due to their money being held up; increase competitiveness of Indian project exporters to bid in international market; maintain parity in treatment among all the exporters, and facilitate to determine best share value for forthcoming IPOs.

6618. (13-3-2008) NEW DELHI : The Cabinet Committee on Economic Affairs today gave its approval for Implementation of the Scheme of Development Support for coffee by the Coffee Board during the XIth Plan with an outlay of Rs.310 crore in the following manner: (i) Payment of replanting subsidy @ 25%, 30% and 40% to the coffee growers having holdings of more than 10 hectares, 2 to 10 hectares, and up to 2 hectares, respectively, for an outlay of Rs.100 crore subject to the condition that subsidy would be available only to individual growers and not to the cooperative corporate entities engaged in plantation; (ii) Payment of subsidy of 20% towards quality upgradation, and pollution abatement and 25% towards water augmentation, restricted to individual growers having holding size of 20 hectares, for an outlay of Rs.40 crore; (iii) To extend financial incentives in North East Region for planting and aftercare and also supply of coffee seedlings/shade saplings for an outlay of Rs.20 crore; (iv) Expansion of the area under coffee in Non-Traditional Areas and tribal sector for an outlay of Rs.45 crore; (iv) Implementation of programmes of capacity building for all stakeholders in coffee sector for an outlay of Rs.10 crore; (v) Implementation of welfare support to labours and tiny growers for an outlay of Rs.5 crore; (vii) Providing interest subsidy at the uniform rate not exceeding 5% to growers on working capital loans for an outlay of Rs.90 crore, subject to the following conditions: (a) The interest subsidy will be limited to a ceiling of Rs.50,000 per Arabica coffee grower and Rs.40,000 per Robusta coffee grower. (b) The interest rate, after allowing interest subsidy should not be lower than 7%. (viii) Comprehensive evaluation of the scheme will be done by an independent agency after two years with regard to the parameters of the scheme and scales of subsidy. The Scheme of Development Support is aimed to provide support to coffee growers to improve farm productivity by way of replanting senile coffee blocks; to support water augmentation, quality improvement of the product to augment grower realization, and pollution abatement; to support coffee development in North-East Region and in Non-Traditional Areas *viz.* Andhra Pradesh and Orissa; to build capacity among various stakeholders in the Indian coffee sector; to extend welfare support to coffee sector workers as well as tiny coffee growers; and to provide interest subsidy to growers on working capital loans to provide some relief from fast increasing production costs.

6619. (13-3-2008) NEW DELHI : The Cabinet Committee on Economic Affairs today gave its approval for the "Export Development and Promotion of Spices Scheme" with an outlay of Rs.192.69 crore for implementation during 11th Plan period by the Spices Board. The Scheme is a continuation of similar scheme implemented by the Spices Board during Xth Plan period with some modifications in contents and outlay. The main thrust of the scheme is to promote high tech and high end value addition in spice processing / packing and quality control facilities for producing the quality products; setting up of spices park having common processing facilities and world class infrastructure for facilitating growers and exporting community to improve the quality of spices and motivate new entrepreneurs, promote product research to establish the health and medicinal values of spices; support spice processors in the north East and organic spice producers elsewhere to enter into high-end value addition; trade promotion activities *e.g.* market research, surveys, mounting trade delegations, trade fair participation, publicity programmes etc. and strengthening market/trade information services. Apart from other assistance, financial assistance to 150 exporters in the general area and 10 exporters in North East / Special areas to produce value added spice products of international standards and quality; to meet part of their expenditure on trade promotion activities like packaging development / bar coding etc, 100 exporters will be supported. For providing common facilities for cleaning, grading, packing and storing, the scheme will have six such centres for quality improvement and value addition.

6620. (13-3-2008) NEW DELHI : The Cabinet Committee on Economic Affairs today gave its approval for implementation of Tea Quality Upgradation and Product Diversification Scheme, with an outlay of Rs.230 crore by the Tea Board during 11th Plan period subject to the condition that an independent evaluation of the subsidy component of orthodox tea would be undertaken before March, 2009. The scheme is expected at act as a catalyst for tea manufacturing units to invest in process modernization/upgradation; create facilities for dual manufacture of tea (orthodox and CTC); improving the standards of manufacturing and packaging, value addition, production of speciality teas; and acquiring ISO/HACCP and Organic certification etc. The improved price realization owing to better quality/value addition of the produce, both in domestic and international markets would benefit the growers. Besides, increase in the production of orthodox tea will result in additional export as it has very less demand in the domestic market.

6621. (13-3-2008) NEW DELHI : The Cabinet Committee on Economic Affairs today gave its approval for implementing the project for modernization strengthening of Intellectual Property Offices at an estimated cost of Rs.300 crore in the 11th Five Year Plan. The modernized Intellectual Property Offices would be able to provide infrastructure necessary for a vibrant intellectual property regime which would be able to address the concerns of reliability, effectiveness, transparency and user-friendliness of the procedures and capable of handling increased workload. The scheme also provides for the infrastructure required by the Patent Office to operate as an International Searching Authority and International Preliminary Examining Authority under the Patent Cooperation Treaty and enable the Trade Marks registry.

6622. (13-3-2008) NEW DELHI : The Cabinet Committee on Economic Affairs today gave its approval to M/s. SKIL Infrastructure Limited (SKIL), Mumbai to accept foreign investments upto US$50 million (Rupees 195 crore approx.) from Ashoka Investment Holdings Limited, Mauritius (Ashoka) and Ambadevi Mauritius Holding Limited (Ambadevi) together referred to as 'AIG Funds', constituting upto 5% of the fully diluted share capital of the company.". The approval will be subject to the following conditions: (i) a downstream investment being in compliance with Press Note No.9 of 1999; (ii) adherence to the Ministry of Finance Press Release of 30.04.2007 on issuance of Preference shares. With the approval, FDI amounting to Rs.195 crore approximately will be received in the country.

6623. (13-3-2008) NEW DELHI : The Union Cabinet today gave its approval to the new National Mineral Policy, 2008, in principle, recommended by the High Level Committee together with the modifications on the basis of consultations with State Governments, inter-ministerial consultations and in line with the recommendations of the GOM and also gave its approval for setting up an independent dispute resolution mechanism, namely Mining Administrative Appellate Tribunal (MAAT). The implementation of the new National Mineral Policy, 2008 would likely to attract FDI to the value of US$ 250 million per annum in the mining sector by the end of five year. An amendment Bill will be introduced during Budget Session for bringing about suitable amendments in the Mines and Minerals (Development and Regulation) Act, 1957, the MCR Rules, 1 960 and MCDR, 1988 to give effect to the new National Mineral Policy, 2008. MATT will be made fully operational within six months.

6624. (13-3-2008) NEW DELHI : The Union Cabinet today gave its approval to the following proposals : (i) To amend the Resolution constituting the PESB by specifying that the candidates from State Public Sector Enterprises and the

Private Sector subject to fulfilling the eligibility criteria, will also be considered as non-internal candidates along with the candidates of the other Public Sector Enterprises, for a period of five years. (ii) iii) DOP&T to lay down modalities for overseeing the prescription of recruitment norms by the PESB. (iv) Prescription of norms for development of the system of quantifiable parameters to be adopted by PESB in making selections. The existing selection policy laid down in Resolution dated 3rd March, 1987, covers only candidates from the Central PSUs. The amendment will allow making the best talent available to Central PSUs, which is very much necessary in the present liberalized economic scenario. It would infuse more transparency and objectivity into the selections in PSUs.

6625. (13-3-2008) NEW DELHI : The Union Cabinet today gave its approval for introduction of a Bill, namely, the Compensatory Afforestation Fund Bill, 2008 in Parliament for the purpose of establishment of a Compensatory Afforestation Fund and for 1. Creation of Compensatory Afforestation Fund (CAF) by the Ministry of Environment and Forests. 2. Creation of Compensatory Afforestation Fund Management and Planning Authority (CAMPA) by the Ministry of Environment and Forests. 3. Utilization of Funds for "Green India" and other afforestation activities. 4. Creation of one post of Chief Executive Officer (CEO) of the rank of Inspector General of Forests. 5. Enabling CAMPA for creation of SPV with approval of competent Authority. 6. Apprising the Supreme Court through an affidavit of the action taken in compliance of the orders of the Supreme Court. It will give effective transparent functioning of the authority for the management of afforestation funds. The funds will be utilized for a massive afforestation programme to increase tree cover through Green India. The principles of environmental conservation would be better handled. The accountability of the implementing authority will be increased. Independent and concurrent Monitoring of the works will be done.

6626. (13-3-2008) NEW DELHI : The Union Cabinet today gave its approval to increase the Authorized Capital of Food Corporation of India from Rs. 2500 crores to Rs. 3500 crores. The enhancement of authorized capital of FCI will enable the Ministry of consumer Affairs, Food & Public Distribution to release funds allocated by the Planning Commission under the Plan Scheme for construction of storage godowns in North East, J&K, H.P. & other newly emerging procuring States etc. and Integrated Information System on Foodgrains Management (IISFM).

6627. (13-3-2008) NEW DELHI : The Union Cabinet today gave its approval for allowing duty-free market access to India for eight million pieces of garments per calendar year from Bangladesh without any sourcing condition, in modification of the earlier Cabinet approval given at its meeting held on 29th December, 2005 for market access for eight million pieces of garments from Bangladesh with the sourcing condition for six million pieces and without any sourcing condition for two million, as per the procedure set down in the MOU signed between the two countries on 16.9.2007. This is expected to correct to some extent the trade imbalance of Bangladesh with India.

6628. (13-3-2008) NEW DELHI : The Union Cabinet today gave its approval for signing of the Agreement between India and Tajikistan for the Avoidance of Double Taxation and the Prevention of Fiscal Evasion with respect to taxes on income. Double Taxation Avoidance Agreements aim to avoid and reduce burden of double taxation on the same tax payer in two countries in order to promote international trade and investments between the two countries. The proposed Agreement will stimulate the flow of investment, technology and services from India to Tajikistan and vice versa. It will also provide tax stability to the residents of India and Tajikistan and facilitate mutual economic cooperation.

6629. (13-3-2008) NEW DELHI : The Atmospheric Brown Cloud (ABC) refers to the high loading of pollutants in the atmosphere consisting of mixture of anthropogenic sulphates, nitrates, organics, black carbon, dust, fly ash particles, and natural aerosols such as sea salt and mineral dust. The brownish colour of cloud is due to the absorption and scattering of solar ultraviolet radiation by black carbon; soil derived dust, fly ash and nitrogen oxide. The ABC phenomenon occurs over several world regions, and is seasonal phenomenon. The precise impacts of pollutant loading over monsoon rain and agriculture are still under study, and an international programme has been initiated by the world community to better understand the origins, inventories and impacts of Atmospheric Brown Cloud. The Government has taken several measures to reduce the pollutant loading like introduction of tightened emission norms for vehicles, improvement in fuel quality in transport sector, use of cleaner fuels, introduction of electrostatic precipitators in thermal power plants, introduction of biogas plants and improved biomass stoves especially, in rural areas. These measures are aimed to improve the air quality by reducing the pollution loading. A programme named INDOEX (Indian Ocean Experiment)-undertaken during 1996-1999 with the participation of the Indian scientists, has drawn the attention of the international community on issues pertaining to pollution. The preliminary investigation of effects of pollution loading on rains was undertaken for India with the help of a model.

6630. (13-3-2008) NEW DELHI : The objective of the Post Matric Scholarships scheme for SCs is to provide financial assistance to the Scheduled Castes students for all recognized courses pursued in recognized institutions. The financial assistance includes maintenance allowance, reimbursement of non-refundable compulsory fee charged by educational institutions, Book Bank facility and other allowances. The scholarships are available for studying in India only and are awarded by the State Governments/Union Territory Administrations to which the students actually belong. The scholarship is paid to the students whose parent's/guardian's income from all sources does not exceed Rs. 1.00 lakh per annum. The Scheme is implemented by the State Governments and Union Territory Administrations, which receive 100% central assistance from the Government of India for the total expenditure under the scheme, over and above their respective Committed Liability. However, in the case of North Eastern States, the Government of India meets 100% expenditure, without applying the concept of the Committed Liability. This information was given by the Minister of State for Social Justice and Empowerment, Smt. Subbulakshmi Jagadeesan in a written reply to a question in the Lok Sabha today.

6631. (13-3-2008) NEW DELHI : Reports of exploitation and ill-treatment of Indian workers working in Gulf countries, Malaysia and a few African countries are received in Ministry of Overseas Indian Affairs and Indian Missions from time to time. The problems faced by the overseas Indian workers mainly relate to contractual violations by employers such as non-payment / delayed payment of salary, non-availability of medical facilities, proper food, unhygienic living conditions etc. In such cases, if registered recruitment agency is involved, action is taken under the provision of Emigration Act, 1983, leading to suspension and cancellation of their registration certificate (RC). 27 RCs have been suspended/ cancelled during 2007. In respect of unregistered recruiting agents, the complaints are referred to concerned State Police Authorities/ Protector of Emigrants for investigation and appropriate action as per provisions of the law. 7 prosecution sanctions have been issued during 2007. In respect of complaint against foreign employers, such foreign employer is placed in the Prior Approval Category. 334 Foreign employers have been placed under such category. The following policy measures for protection and welfare of Indian workers have been taken by this Ministry:- (i) Bilateral Labour MoUs have been signed with UAE in December, 2006 and with Kuwait in April, 2007. An additional protocol with Qatar was signed in November, 2007. These provide for an agreed broad framework for exchange of views leading to better protection of Indian workers while they are employed abroad. (ii) Age restriction of 30 years has been made mandatory for all women emigrants holding ECR passports seeking employment abroad. (iii) Government has decided to prescribe the minimum wage for women household service workers emigrating to the ECR countries. The minimum wage will be fixed by the Indian Missions concerned in the range of US $ 300-350, after taking into account the prevailing market wage in that country and is intended to serve as a bench mark for the Indian Missions for attesting work contracts and for the Protectors of Emigrants before granting emigration clearance. (iv) Introduction of a pre-departure orientation and skill-upgradation programme for potential emigrants to enhance their empowerment. (v) A massive media campaign has been launched to educate the potential emigrants. (vi) Overseas Workers Resource Centre has been established with a toll-free helpline to help the emigrants. (vii) The Emigration Act, 1983 is in the process of being amended to further strengthen the safeguards for the emigrants. This information was given by the Minister of Overseas Indian Affairs, Shri Vayalar Ravi in a written reply to a question in Rajya Sabha today.

6632. (13-3-2008) NEW DELHI : The foreign visitors will now have to pay the entry fee for the ticketed monuments of Archaeology Survey of India (ASI) in Indian rupee only. The decision has come into effect from 28th February, 2008. Now the visitors from foreign countries will be charged Rs. 250 (for ticketed World Heritage Sites) and Rs. 100 (for other ticketed monuments) per person. In another decision the Government has decided that visitors from SAARC (Bangladesh, Nepal, Bhutan, Sri Lanka, Pakistan, Maldives and Afghanistan) and BIMSTEC countries (Bangladesh, Nepal, Bhutan, Sri Lanka, Thailand and Myanmar) will pay an entry fee of Rs. 10 (for ticketed World Heritage Sites) and Rs. 5 (for other ticketed monuments) per person. Same charges are applicable to Indian citizens. This decision has come into effect from 5th March, 2008.

6633. (13-3-2008) NEW DELHI : The Premier of South Australia, Mr. Mike Rann, during his meeting with Shri Kamal Nath, Union Minister of Commerce and Industry, here today, discussed various matters including the stepping up of bilateral trade and economic cooperation between the two countries. Both sides agreed that there is vast scope for increasing the bilateral trade, considering the untapped opportunities for exploiting the potential for growth. The Premier has invited Shri Kamal Nath to visit Australia during May 2008 for the 11th India-Australia Joint Ministerial Commission. Both sides discussed about the market access-sending teams of experts to each other's country to address quarantine, food safety, certification and standardization issues. South Australia currently has investment from Indian companies *viz.*, Reliance Industries, Sterlite Industries, Indage Group and Minda, in the areas of mining, wine and tooling amongst others. During the discussions, Shri Kamal Nath informed the Premier that FDI policies in India have been further liberalised and many new sectors have been opened recently and added that infrastructure sector in India is an opportunity for investment. Australia is ranked as the 18th largest source of foreign investments in India. The percentage share of total approvals for top sectors attractive investment into India from Australia has been in the areas of fuels (37.03%); metallurgical industries (33.81%); telecom (15.33%); transportation (2.96%) and chemicals-other than fertilisers-(2.91%). In recent years, the bilateral trade shows a healthy growth trend and the total trade between India and Australia during 2006-07 was US $ 7932.79 million as compared to US $ 5769.14 million during 2005-06 showing a growth of 37.5%. Major items of India's exports to Australia are: gems & jewellery, manufactures of metals, machinery & instruments, cotton yarn, fabrics, made-ups etc., while India's imports from Australia are: gold, coal, coke & briquettes, Metalifers ores and metal scrap.

6634. (13-3-2008) NEW DELHI : The Ministry of Environment and Forests proposes to take up plantation over 6 million hectares of degraded forests of the country in two Phases by utilizing the money collected under Compensatory Afforestation Fund Management and Planning Authority (CAMPA). This has been known as "Green India Programme". The money collected under CAMPA besides being used to partly finance the Green India Programme would be mainly used for site specific schemes approved for taking up compensatory afforestation, artificial regeneration (plantation), natural assisted regeneration, forest management, protection, infrastructure development, wildlife protection and management. These activities besides greening the country would also help in mitigating the adverse effects of climate change. The State Government of Rajasthan has informed that Prosopis Juliflora had not been planted in Rajasthan during the last 10 years except on few refractory sites where other species would not come up. While Prosopis Juliflora is acting as an impenetrable barrier to biotic interference thereby contributing towards conservation of bio-diversity, there are a few areas where it has become menace to plants and wildlife. Therefore, its eradication in such areas has been taken up. Under the proposed Green India Programmer the implementation would be done through the mechanism of Joint Forest Management using the Forest Development Agencies (FDAs). This information was given by the Minister of State for Environment and Forests Shri S. Regupathy, in a written reply to a question by Shri. Lalit Kishore Chaturvedianddr gyan prakash pilania in the Rajya Sabha today.

6635. (13-3-2008) NEW DELHI : According to the information provided by Delhi Jal Board, Government of NCT of Delhi, it has evolved the concept of laying interceptor sewer along the three major drains in Delhi to prevent the flowing of untreated sewage into river Yamuna. The salient features of the proposal are: Laying of interceptor sewers along the three major drains namely, Najafgarh, Supplementary and Shahdara; augmentation of existing capacity of STPs at the mouth of Delhi Gate and Dr. Sen Nursing Home Drain; interception of 13 other drains into the Bela Road and Ring Road Trunk Sewers after their rehabilitation; and construction of additional Sewage Treatment Plants after utilization of full capacity of the existing STPs. As reported, the proposal is technically feasible as it takes care of the untreated sewage from unsewered areas and will allow only discharge of treated effluent into river Yamuna. The tentative cost of the project is about Rs. 1300 crore. This information was given by the Minister of State for Environment and Forests Shri Namo Narain Meena, in a written reply to a question by Shrimati Hema Malini in the Rajya Sabha today.

6636. (13-3-2008) NEW DELHI : GAIL is pursuing opportunities for setting up of petrochemicals projects in other countries. Currently, GAIL is looking for investment opportunities in Middle East, Russia, CIS and African countries. GAIL has signed Memorandum of Understanding (MoU) with Reliance Industries Limited on 4th December, 2007. The major area of cooperation agreed in the MoU is setting up gas-based Petrochemical Complexes in gas rich countries. MoU between GAIL & Oil India Limited (OIL) has been signed on 27th December, 2007. GAIL and OIL agreed inter alia to examine various opportunities available in the petrochemicals sector in India as well as abroad. GAIL and ITERA Oil and Gas Company have signed an MoU on 13th February, 2008 and agreed to participate in methane based Petrochemicals projects in Russia. The above information was given by the Minister of State for Petroleum & Natural Gas Shri Dinsha Patel in a written reply in the Lok Sabha today.

6637. (13-3-2008) NEW DELHI : Indian Oil Corporation (IOC) has signed an agreement with Maruti Suzuki India Limited (MUL) for marketing of lubricant as Maruti Genuine Oil in the country. The salient features of the agreement are as under:-(i) Agreement is valid till 31.03.2009. (ii) Agreement is for marketing of Maruti Genuine Oil for all the Maruti vehicles through Maruti authorized service stations, Maruti authorized dealers and other marketing channels of IOC like Retail Outlets, bazaar counters, etc. (iii) The agreement allows IOC to use Maruti's trade mark as Maruti Genuine Part (MGP) in respect of product on the terms and conditions mutually agreed, for which license fee is payable by IOC. With this agreement, IOC will be able to generate sales revenue of approx. Rs. 50 crores per year. The above information was given by the Minister of State for Petroleum & Natural Gas Shri Dinsha Patel in a written reply in the Lok Sabha today.

6638. (13-3-2008) NEW DELHI : The Centrally Sponsored Scheme of post-matric scholarship for students belonging to the minority communities form class XI up to Ph. D., and technical and vocational course of Industrial Training Institutes/ Industrial training Centres (affiliated with NCVT) of class XI and XII level, has been launched. The details/ guidelines for the scheme are available at website "www.minorityaffairs.gov.in" The last date for receipt of applications from students was 29.02.2008. The feasibility of further enhancing the scope and coverage of the scheme is being examined. Any enhancement that might take place will include Andhra Pradesh. This information was given by the Minister of Minority Affairs Shri A.R. Antulay in reply to a written question in the Lok Sabha today.

6639. (13-3-2008) NEW DELHI : Replying to a written question whether the Government proposes to have the concept of a sub-plan for the Muslim community to ensure their development on the lines of the sub-plan for the scheduled tribes, the Minister of Minority Affairs Shri A.R. Antulay today informed the Lok Sabha the report of the Working Group on empowerment of the minorities suggested various schemes including creation of a separate Minority Sub-Plan for the 11th Five Year Plan. A view has not been taken on this. The Planning Commission has advised that the issue required wider consultation.

6640. (13-3-2008) NEW DELHI : The Planning Commission has constituted an autonomous Assessment and Monitoring Authority (AMA) to evaluate the extent of development benefits accruing to different socio-religious communities (SRCs) through various programmes; to visit various places to have first hand information about conditions of Minorities; and to give directions to the concerned Central

Ministries/ Departments, State Governments, U.T. Administrations to implement effectively the programme for Minorities. No State level branch is envisaged. This information was given by the Minister of Minority Affairs this important by A.R. Antulay in reply to a written question whether the Government is considering to constitute an autonomous Assessment and Monitoring Authority (AMA) to evaluate the extent of development benefits, which accrue to different Socio-Religious Categories (SRCs) through various programmes based on Sachar Committee Report.

6641. (13-3-2008) NEW DELHI : The monitoring of water quality of river Ganga under the Ganga Action Plan indicates that the water quality of river is not complying with the desired standards in stretches along the towns of Kanpur and Varanasi, but meeting with the norms in its stretch along the Haridwar town. The levels of Fecal Coliforms (bacterial indicator for health concerns) are also reported to be exceeding the maximum permissible limit of 2500 MPN (Most Probable Number) per 100 milliliter at many of the monitoring stations along river Ganga except in upstream locations of Haridwar. Indian Council of Medical Research and National Institute of Communicable Diseases under the Ministry of Health & Family Welfare, Government of India, are reportedly neither aware nor have conducted any study or survey regarding the Ganga river becoming a reservoir of virulent forms of bacteria, Escherichia coli. Since 1985, with the implementation of Ganga Action Plan (GAP) for pollution abatement activities in the identified polluted stretches of river Ganga,, a total sewage treatment capacity of 1765.34 million litres per day has been created so far for Ganga and its major tributaries. Despite phenomenal increase in the urban population along the banks of the river leading to increased pollution loads, the water quality of river Ganga has shown discernible improvement in terms of organic pollution at major locations, over the pre-Action Plan water quality This information was given by the Minister of State for Environment and Forests Shri Namo Narain Meena, in a written reply to a question by Dr. (Shrimati) Najma Hepttulla, in the Rajya Sabha today.

6642. (13-3-2008) NEW DELHI : Based on a survey conducted under the guidance of the Central Pollution Control Board (CPCB) it has been estimated that about 1,46,000 tons of waste from electrical and electronic equipment [WEEE] is generated annually in the country. According to WEEE Directives of the European Union (EU), waste electrical or electronic equipments which include all components consumables etc. after use are to be disposed off as per the provisions of their National Law enforced. Further, EU directives focus on the restriction of the use of certain hazardous substances in electrical and electronic equipments which has come into force with effect from January, 2007. These directives provide for the reduction and elimination of hazardous substances used in electrical and electronic equipments. The Ministry of Environment and Forests have notified the Hazardous Waste (Management and Handling) Rules, 1989 as amended in 2003 which regulate the generation, collection, storage, treatment, disposal as well as export and import of hazardous wastes, which include e-waste. The processes generating hazardous wastes are listed in Schedule 1 of these rules. The residues and wastes generated from the operations in electronic industry are already considered as hazardous wastes and are included at S.No.31 of Schedule 1 of these rules. Further, the import and export of e-waste is also regulated under Schedule 3 of these rules. As per the provisions of these rules, the import of e-waste is regulated under Schedule 3 of these rules wherein Electrical and Electronic Assemblies are covered under category A 1180 in the list A and B 1110 in list B of the Schedule 3. The import of such waste is permitted only for direct reuse and not for recycling of final disposal. The Ministry of Environment and Forests had also constituted a Task Force to finalise the Guidelines for Environmentally Sound Management of E-waste for the State Pollution Control Boards and Pollution Control Committees of the Union Territories and the industries for handling e-waste. Guidelines have since been finalised for the Environmentally Sound Management of E-waste. This information was given by the Minister of State for Environment and Forests Shri Namo Narain Meena, in a written reply to a question by Shri B. J. Panda and Ms. Pramila Bohidar in the Rajya Sabha today.

6643. (13-3-2008) NEW DELHI : The Government has asked the Bangalore International Airport Pvt. Ltd. (BIAL) to consider a suitable date after 10th May, 2008 for the opening of new airport at Devanahalli, Bangalore. It will be recalled that the anticipated date for the opening of the airport was 30th March, 2008. However, because ATC services will not be available by 30th March, 2008, the Ministry of Civil Aviation has regretted its inability to accept that date for the opening of the airport. Given the status of the availability of ATC services, the Ministry has directed BIAL to consider a suitable date after 10th May, 2008 for the airport opening. Earlier, the Ministry had intimated the anticipated date for opening of 30 March, 2008 to the various Central Government Agencies which are responsible for the performance of Reserved Activities at the airports. While all agencies had confirmed their readiness, the AAI had reservation about the availability of ATC by 30th March, 2008. Delays in the construction of ATC facilities including the Control Tower, Technical Block, office accommodation of AAI personnel and issues like electricity supply, house-keeping, air-conditioning at the ATC facilities were the reasons for this delay.

6644. (13-3-2008) NEW DELHI : In exercise of the powers conferred by clause (1) of article 222 of the Constitution of India, the President, after consultation with the Chief Justice of India, is pleased to transfer Shri Justice S. R. Singharavelu, Judge, Madras High Court as Judge, Orissa High Court and to direct him to assume charge of the office of the Judge of the Orissa High Court on or before 26th March, 2008.

6645. (13-3-2008) NEW DELHI : In exercise of the powers conferred by clause (1) of article 224 of the Constitution of India, the President is pleased to appoint Shri Shinde Sambhaji Shiwaji, to be an Additional Judge of the Bombay High Court, for a period of two years with effect from the date he assumes charge of his office.

6646. (13-3-2008) NEW DELHI : The President of India has accepted the resignation of Shri Mukut Mithi as Lt. Governor of Pondichery and has appointed Lt. Gen. (Retd.) Bhopinder Singh, Lt. Governor of Andaman & Nicobar Islands to discharge the functions of the Lt. Governor of Pondichery in addition to his own duties, until regular arrangements for the office of the Lt. Governor of Pondichery are made.

6647. (13-3-2008) NEW DELHI : Development and improvement of Ahmedabad-Dandi Heritage Route (NH-228) having a length of 386 km has been planned to be taken up in two phases with the fund available from Gross Budgetary Support (GBS) through the State Government. In the first phase, improvement of riding surface, widening of carriageway wherever feasible, within the available Right of Way (ROW) are proposed to be taken up under the Annual Plan of the year 2008-09. In Phase-II, upgradation of road to two-lane with paved shoulders, construction of bridges, missing links, bypasses etc are proposed to be taken up. These works would be undertaken after finalization of Detailed Project Report (DPR). The tentative completion period of Phase-I works is about two years and for Phase-II works is about three to four years. There is no separate budget provision for the development of NH-228 at present. This information was given by the Minister of State for Shipping, Road Transport and Highways, Shri K.H. Muniyappa in a written reply in the Rajya Sabha today.

6648. (13-3-2008) NEW DELHI : The Minister of State in the Ministry of Shipping, Road Transport and Highways, Shri K.H. Muniyappa informed the Rajya Sabha today that the construction of 4-lane Gwalior bypass has been taken up on BOT(Annuity) basis. In a written reply, he said that the bypass connects NH 3 at chainage km. 103.000 and NH-75 at chainage km. 16.00 and the total length of the bypass is 42.03 km. The work has commenced in April 2007. The total cost of this project is Rs. 300.93 crore and an amount of Rs. 22.77 crore has been spent on this project upto January 2008. The project is scheduled to be completed in October 2009.

6649 (13-3-2008) NEW DELHI: The political killings in the Kannur district of Kerala disrupted proceedings in Parliament for the third consecutive day on Wednesday with the Bharatiya Janata Party taking the offensive this time. Citing the Kerala High Court's observation that Central intervention was needed to end the cycle of violence in Kannur, the BJP demanded the dismissal of the State Government. The matter was raised in the Lok Sabha at the start of the day's proceedings, resulting in a verbal duel between the BJP and the Communist Party of India (Marxist). Reprimanding the members for their behaviour and murdering democracy, the Speaker adjourned the House within minutes for two hours.

6650. (13-3-2008) NEW DELHI : During the current financial year 2007-2008, an expenditure of Rs. 1776.58 crore has been incurred against an allocation of Rs. 2168.64 crore up to the end of February 2008 for the development of National Highways in the country, which is about 82% of the allocation. The Ministry of Shipping, Road Transport & Highways is primarily responsible for the development and maintenance of the National Highways in the country. State-highways and roads leading to National Highways are the responsibility of the respective State Governments. This information was given by the Minister of State for Shipping, Road Transport and Highways, Shri K.H. Muniyappa in a written reply in the Rajya Sabha today.

6651. (13-3-2008) NEW DELHI : The Minister of Tourism and Culture Smt. Ambika Soni informed the Lok Sabha today that her Ministry has launched a Scheme titled 'Earn While You Learn' with a view to inculcate appropriate tourism travel traits and knowledge amongst trainees to enable them to work as 'student volunteers'. The salient features of the Scheme are: (i) College-going students pursuing graduation courses or graduates in the age group of 18 to 25 years would be eligible for the training programme. (ii) The Indian Institute of Tourism & Travel Management (IITTM) would conduct the programme and select the candidates through a written test. (iii) The duration of each programme would be 21 working days. (iv) The course content has been finalized by the IITTM in consultation with the Archaeological Survey of India, the Institute of Archaeology and eminent academicians. This information was given in a written reply.

6652. (13-3-2008) NEW DELHI : The Minister of Tourism and Culture Smt. Ambika Soni informed the Lok Sabha today that a comprehensive review of the Protected Area Permit / Restricted Area Permit (PAP/ RAP) regime to relax the restrictions imposed to visit some locations in the concerned State / UTs, from the tourism perspective has been undertaken by the Ministry of Home Affairs. Specific proposals in this regard have been received from the concerned State Governments / UTs. In a written reply she said, these proposals are examined from the tourism and security perspectives with the concerned State Governments / UTs and an appropriate decision expedited in the matter by the Ministry of Home Affairs. Protected Areas: The Protected Areas are those areas falling between the 'Inner Line' and the International border of the State. (i) Whole of Arunachal Pradesh (ii) Parts of Himachal Pradesh (iii) Parts of Jammu & Kashmir (iv) Whole of Manipur (v) Whole of Mizoram (vi) Whole of Nagaland (vii) Parts of Rajasthan (viii) Whole of Sikkim (partly Restricted & partly in Protected area) (ix) Parts of Uttarakhand. Restricted Areas: Under the Foreigners (Restricted Areas) Order, 1963 the following areas have been declared as 'Restricted Areas'. No foreigner can enter or stay in the restricted areas without obtaining a permit from the competent authorities. (i) Andaman & Nicobar Island-entire Union Territory (ii) Sikkim-Part of the State. A foreigner is not normally allowed to visit a Protected / Restricted Area unless it is established to the satisfaction of the Government that there are exceptional reasons to justify such a visit.

6653. (13-3-2008) NEW DELHI : The Minister of Tourism and Culture Smt. Ambika Soni has said that as per the Action Plan adopted for celebrating 'India China Year of Friendship Through Tourism' both countries agreed to open their tourism offices in each other's country. China has already opened its tourism office in New Delhi in August, 2007 and Government of India has approved the opening of India Tourism Office in Beijing, China. This information was given to the Lok Sabha in a written reply.

6654. (13-3-2008) NEW DELHI : The Minister of Tourism and Culture Smt. Ambika Soni has said that the Epigraphy Branch, Archaeological Survey of India (ASI) has formulated plans to digitize nearly 74,000 estampages (impressions of inscriptions on paper) from its collection. In a written reply in the Lok Sabha today she said, the process of digitization involves scanning of transcripts, indexing of the scanned copies and preparation of a database.

6655. (13-3-2008) NEW DELHI : Congress spokesman Dr. Shakeel Ahmed said that tomorrow (14th March) the Congress president, Smt. Sonia Gandhi will be completing ten years in office. On this occasion we feel happy and proud and because of her able leadership since taking over the reigns of the party in 1998 she gave stability to the party by moving among the people of the country in her tours and by initiating people oriented programmes and today the Congress-led UPA government is at the Centre. On behalf of the AICC and the Congress Party we would like to congratulate our party president and hope that she continue to lead the party for a long time. Yesterday the Supreme Court refused to take action on a plea filed regarding the issue in Meghalaya. The issue was that the governor called the single-largest party which had emerged during the elections to form the government. Some people who were accusing the Congress Party and the state governor of showing partiality because of Congress Party being in power at the Centre has been proved wrong and the apex court too has given its decision in this direction and we applaud this decision. Today the Congress President, Smt. Sonia Gandhi approved the names for the biennial elections to the Rajya Sabha and Legislative Council. The list was released to the electronic and print media. To a question that does the Congress Party endorse the suggestions made by Shri Rahul Gandhi, Dr. Ahmed said the suggestions were very reasonable and valid. Shri Rahul said the upper limit of two hectare land for the loan waiver scheme should be increased and the cutoff date of 31st March should be looked into since the harvesting season varies. And as far as the endorsement is concerned Shri Rahul Gandhi spoke on behalf of the Party and his views according to the Party were valid suggestions. To a question whether it is true that the Orissa government has lodged a protest against Shri Rahul Gandhi for spending the night out and not informing the state government about it, Dr. Ahmed said no protest or official complaint was lodged. The matter was raised in the Orissa Assembly and the government of India and the Orissa government are in consultation and I don't think there will be any problem or controversy.

6656. (13-3-2008) NEW DELHI : Shri Arjun Singh, Minister for Human Resource Development will inaugurate on Friday KRITI 2008-A Mega Exhibition of Crafts by Jan Shikshan Sansthans (14-18 March, 08) at Pragati Maidan, New Delhi. National Literacy Mission of the Ministry of Human Resource Development in collaboration with National Handicrafts and Handlooms Museum, Ministry of Textiles have put up this mega exhibition of crafts. These products are being exhibited in 50 stalls at National Handicrafts and Handloom Museum, Pragati Maidan, which are being manned by the beneficiaries themselves. About 100 Jan Shikshan Sansthans shall be participating and displaying their products. On this occasion cultural programmes are being arranged on daily basis. The exhibition shall be open from 10.30 a.m. to 7.00 p.m. from March 14 to 18, 2008. Other dignitaries visiting the exhibition include Ministers of State for Human Resource Development, Md. A.A.Fatmi (18.3.2008) and Smt. D.Purandeswari (16.3.2008), Shri Arun Kumar Rath, Secretary, Department of School Education & Literacy (15.3.08), Shri R.P.Agrawal, Secretary, Department of Higher Education (17.3.08) and other senior officials of the Ministry and other Government Departments.

6657. (13-3-2008) NEW DELHI : Government provides sports scholarship to encourage talented children in sports. It also provides financial assistance @ Rs.75,000 per district for organizing district level school sports competitions. Apart from the above, the Sports of Authority of India operates the National Sports Talent Contest Scheme for the identification and nurturing of talented young sportspersons. It also adopts schools having good sports performance. However, in recognition of the inadequecy of sports facilities in rural India, especially at the sub-district level, Government have recently approved the Panchayat Yuva Krida aur Khel Abhiyan (PYKKA) which aims at broad-basing of sports by way of creation of sports infrastructure at grassroots level in all village panchayats and block panchayats in a phased manner over a period of ten years and organizing sports competitions at block and district levels. Schools will form important component of PYKKA and will be made the hub of sports activities in the panchayats wherever feasible. This information was given by Shri Mani Shankar Aiyar, Minister of Panchayati Raj, Youth Affairs & Sports and DoNER in the Rajya Sabha today in a written reply to a question by Shri Ajay Singh Chautala.

6658. (13-3-2008) NEW DELHI : The Core Committee Meeting to draft the charter on issues related to Panchayati Raj began in the capital today. About 120 participants drawn from panchayat representatives from all states are attending the meeting. Each state team comprises of women, SC and ST representatives.

Addressing the opening session of the meeting Mr. Mani Shankar Aiyar, Minister for Panchayati Raj called upon the participants to give their voice a shape of words in the charter and put forth their views on what is required for Panchayats. Mr. Aiyar said that the stage of this meeting belongs to the panchayat representatives and they should feel free and independent to put their ideas and opinions on paper. He said that the draft charter should be the views and voice of the state representatives who are participating in this meeting. The Minister said that 5 sub-committees will be formed from amongst the participants which will look into the issues of powers of panchayats, economy of panchayats, officials and their role in panchayats, preparation of plans and on how to make panchayat family more effective. Once the draft charter is formulated, it will be circulated to about 2.5 lakh Gram Panchayats all over the country so that all of them get a chance to deliberate on it and give their views. Thereafter the draft would be presented during the Panchayat Convention to be held in April 22-24, 2008 for finalisation and final charter would then be given to the Prime Minister and the UPA Chairman. The Core Committee Meeting will conclude on 14th March 2008.

6659. (13-3-2008) NEW DELHI : Land being a State subject, primarily, it is for the State Governments to take steps to cater for the increasing demand for houses in cities and towns. The Union Government has however formulated the National Urban Housing & Habitat Policy (NUHHP), 2007, which was laid in both Houses of the Parliament on 7.12.2007. This information was given by the Minister of State for Housing & Poverty Alleviation Kumari Selja in the Rajya Sabha today, in a written reply to a question by Ms. Sushila Tiriya. The Minister further informed that the Policy has been widely publicized and has been forwarded to all States/Union Territories. The Policy seeks to bridge the gap between need and supply of housing and infrastructure and inter-alia provides for forging various types of partnerships between public, private and cooperative sectors for accelerated growth in the Housing Sector and sustainable development of habitat. According to the estimations of the Technical Group constituted by the Ministry for assessment of the urban housing shortage at the end of the 10th Five Year Plan, the total housing shortage in the country is 24.71 million. During the 11th Five Year Plan period, the total urban housing requirement including the backlog and additional requirement is estimated as 26.53 million dwelling units, the Minister added.

6660. (13-3-2008) NEW DELHI : With a view to ameliorate the living condition of urban poor, Ministry of Housing & Urban Poverty Alleviation is already implementing an urban poverty alleviation programme named Swarna Jayanti Shahari Rozgar Yojana (SJSRY) on all India basis since 1.12.1997. The scheme strives to provide gainful employment to the urban unemployed and underemployed poor through, firstly, encouraging the setting up of self-employment ventures by those who have not studied beyond 9th standard and, secondly, by providing wage employment by utilizing their labour for construction of socially and economically useful public assets. The implementation of Swarna Jayanti Shahari Rozgar Yojana rests on the foundation of community empowerment. This programme focuses on establishing and promoting community organizations and structures to provide supporting and facilitating mechanism for local development. Towards this end community organizations like Neighbourhood Groups (NHGs), Neighbourhood Committees (NHCs), and Community Development Societies (CDSs) are set up in the target areas. The scheme of Swarna Jayanti Shahari Rozgar Yojana (SJSRY) is being implemented on all India basis, in all urban towns/cities including the city of Delhi. This information was given by the Minister of State for Housing & Poverty Alleviation Kumari Selja in the Rajya Sabha today, in a written reply to a question by Shri Shreegopal Vyas.

6661. (13-3-2008) NEW DELHI : The Government of India has launched the Jawaharlal Nehru National Urban Renewal Mission (JNNURM) on 3rd December, 2005 to give focused attention to integrated development of urban infrastructure and services in cities with emphasis on provision of basic services to the urban poor including housing, water supply, sanitation, road network, urban transport, development of inner (Old) city areas etc. The Mission envisages central assistance of Rs.50, 000 crore as reform linked Central assistance over the Mission period of seven years beginning from 2005-06.

6662. (13-3-2008) NEW DELHI : MPD-2021, notified on 7.2.2007, inter alia, prescribes the Development Control Norms for buildings in residential plotted housing on different size of plots in respect of maximum ground coverage, Floor Area Ratio (FAR) and maximum height of the building as 15 metres. These parameters subject to fulfilment of other terms and conditions, determine the number of floors which could be constructed on a given size of plot. However, the matter is subjudice and the Supreme Court in W.P. No. 4677 of 1985 in the case of M.C. Mehta Vs. Union of India & others vide its Orders dated 7.5.2007 and 23.7.2007 has permitted additional floors only on those cases where construction were permissible on the basis of the MPD-2001 as modified in 1998 and such cases where additional floor has been sanctioned and constructed before 7.5.2007. By virtue of these orders, additional floor without dwelling unit is allowed only on plots measuring 250 sqm. and above in size and facing 24 m and more wide roads. Applications which do not fulfil these parameters are not being entertained at present. MPD-2021 provides that 100% Ground coverage and 350 FAR shall be eligible for regularization of construction already existing as on 22.9.2006 on payment of charges as per the Notification, in respect of plot size upto 175 sqm.

6663. (13-3-2008) NEW DELHI : In the 10th Five Year Plan, Department of Posts proposed to computerize 7700 Departmental Post Offices. By the end of the 10th Plan, 8263 Departmental Post Offices were computerized thereby exceeding the target. In the 11th Plan, Department of Posts has a proposal to computerize remaining 17598 Departmental Post Offices and 64000 Extra Departmental Post Offices. Till date, 8726 Departmental Post Offices have been computerized. In view of the above, there is no delay in computerization of Post Offices. The Department of Posts has also set up internet kiosks in Post Offices and Railway Mail Service Offices in a few major cities to enable the customer to browse Internet and access different services. Internet kiosks have been established at some selected offices in Andhra Pradesh, Kerala and Maharashtra Circle. This information was given by the Minister of State for Communications and Information Technology, Dr. Shakeel Ahmed in a written reply to an un-starred question in the Rajya Sabha today.

6664. (13-3-2008) NEW DELHI : Videsh Sanchar Nigam Ltd. (VSNL), is not resorting to performance evaluation of the SC/ST employees of the Company as a prelude to retrenchment. The Company has a System of carrying out an annual performance review for all its employees and this is similar to the process adopted by many organizations. The performance is evaluated against specific objectives/ job carried out and not on the basis of caste/creed/religion etc. The statement that 75% of the people have been rated as unfit/marginal is incorrect. The employment of new employees is done as per the needs of the business and the same is on merits and qualifications after a thorough and objective selection process. There is no undertaking given by VSNL to the Centre at the time of disinvestment to protect SC/ST employees on roll at that time. However, at the time of disinvestment, an assurance was given in writing by Panatone (the Strategic Partner), that no employee in VSNL would be retrenched for a period of two years instead of one year as provided in the Shareholders Agreement, and that the present salary, wages and prerequisites would not be altered and no adverse change would be made in the retirement benefits which the employees on the rolls of VSNL were eligible. These assurances have been fulfilled and complied with. Further it is clarified that the Central Government is not a majority shareholder in the company and holds only 26.12% stake. This information was given by the Minister of State for Communications and Information Technology, Dr. Shakeel Ahmed in a written reply to an un-starred question in the Rajya Sabha today.

6665. (13-3-2008) NEW DELHI : Thirty three (33) railway stations have been identified for development as Model Stations on Northeast Frontier Railway out of which following 15 stations fall in North East States including Assam: 1. Kokrajhar, 2. Gosaingaonhat, 3. Srirampur, 4. Rangiya, 5. Tezpur, 6. New Bongaigaon, 7. Guwahati, 8. Kamakhya, 9. Dimapur, 10. Silchar, 11. Dharmanagar, 12. Lumding, 13. Dibrugarh, 14. New Tinsukia and 15. Jorhat Town. Minimum Essential Amenities as per norms have already been provided at these stations. Under the Model Station Scheme further facilities planned to be provided at these stations as per norms depending upon category of the stations are as under : Retiring room, Waiting room (with bathing facilities), Cloak room, Enquiry Counter, National Train Enquiry System (NTES), Inter Voice Response System (IVRS), Public Address System/Computer based announcement, Book stalls/other stalls of essential goods, Refreshment room, Parking/circulatory area with lights, Washable apron with jet cleaning, Electronic Train indicator board, Public phone booth, Touch Screen Enquiry system, Water vending machines, Water coolers, Signages, Modular Catering Stalls, Automatic Vending Machines, Pay & Use Toilets, Unreserved Ticketing System (UTS), Computerization of complaints etc. Development of railway stations is a continuous process and is undertaken as so warranted by increase in traffic depending upon availability of funds and other relative priorities. Further stations would accordingly taken in hand for development during the Eleventh Five Year Plan. This information was given by the Minister of State for Railways, Shri R. Velu in a written reply in Lok Sabha today.

6666. (13-3-2008) NEW DELHI : The annual installed production capacities of Integral Coach Factory (ICF) and Rail Coach Factory (RCF) are being augmented from 1000 coaches to 1500 coaches per annum, each respectively. The production in the above two factories will be 3000 coaches per annum after augmentation. It is estimated that BEML can additionally manufacture approximately 450-500 coaches per annum. Further, supplementing the acquision of coaches by way of outsourcing some EMU/MEMU and DEMU coaches, through tendering, is also planned. A new coach manufacturing unit is being set up at Rai Bareilly with a manufacturing capacity of 1000 coaches per annum. In addition, to meet requirements beyond this level, it has also been announced to set up a new rail coach factory in the State of Kerala, in the Railway Budget 2008-09. This information was given by the Minister of State for Railways, Shri R. Velu in a written reply in Lok Sabha today.

6667. (13-3-2007) NEW DELHI: Though the United Progressive Alliance (UPA) and the Left parties have an edge in the electoral college for Presidential elections, the Communist Party of India (Marxist) is hopeful of a "maximum possible" consensus on a candidate who subscribes to democratic and secular values. "The point is not in having an edge and going in for a contest. We want to have maximum possible support for a candidate with secular credentials who will safeguard our Constitutional rights. In a few days, we hope to arrive at a decision. Consultations are on," CPI (M)'s Polit Bureau member and MP Sitaram Yechurysaid here on Saturday. (According to a PTI report, Mr. Yechury met UPA chairperson Sonia Gandhi on Saturday.) Mr. Yechury refused to discuss the merits or demerits of the names suggested by newspersons-Bhairon Singh Shekhawat, Somnath Chatterjee, Pranab Mukherjee, Sushil Kumar Shinde, Karan Singh-and refuted suggestions that some of the names were aired by Prime Minister Manmohan Singh during meetings with Left leaders. He reserved comments on whether a candidate suggested by the Congress would be acceptable to the Left. But pointed out that in the past the Left had supported the candidature of Shankar Dayal Sharma and K.R. Narayanan whose names were proposed by the Congress. On the possibility of Bahujan Samaj Party (BSP) leader Mayawati insisting on a Dalit as the next President, he said this was a "simplistic" notion because she had fought the Uttar Pradesh Assembly elections on the slogan of accommodating the upper castes. However, the UPA-Left would retain the edge even if the BSP did not seek a consensus but the margin with the National Democratic Alliance would come down. He said the Left was striving for a third alternative forged through mass struggles and shared ideological values on issues such as communalism.

6668. (13-3-2008) NEW DELHI : Government has allowed Navratna and Miniratna CPSEs to invest in SEBI regulated public sector mutual funds subject to fulfilment of certain conditions. Investments of surplus funds by Navratna and Miniratna CPSEs in schemes of such mutual funds, having equity investments, should not exceed 30% of the available surplus funds of the concerned CPSE. Further, the Board of Directors of these CPSEs will decide the guidelines, procedures and management control systems for investment in such mutual funds in consultation with the administrative Ministries. The quantum of profit from such investments is dependent upon the performance of the schemes of mutual funds in which investments have been made. CPSEs which compete with private sector enterprises are on a level playing field with them in terms of investment options. This information was given by the Minister of Heavy Industries & Public Enterprises, Shri Sontosh Mohan Dev in a written reply to a question in Lok Sabha today.

6669. (14-3-2008) NEW DELHI : The Prime Minister, Dr. Manmohan Singh interacted with many delegations from the city of Varanasi, including a delegation of weavers led by Dr. R.K. Mishra, MP. The Prime Minister mentioned that the following issues would be pursued by the Government soon for the benefit of the people of Varanasi and weavers of Varanasi. Decisions on these would be taken soon. 1. Public Transport for Varanasi-Varanasi is a major city and deserves top class public transport. Varanasi is included in the Jawahar Lal Nehru National Urban Renewal Mission (JNNURM). Under the JNNURM, the Central Government would be willing to fund a major public transport project for Varanasi. Adequate funds would be provided to enable Varanasi to have a modern transport system in keeping with its importance as a Heritage City. The State Government will be requested to forward a project to Government of India and a decision will be taken on this proposal favourably. The Government of India will provide all possible support for preparing the project. 2. Heritage Development of Varanasi-Varanasi is one of the few cities included in JNNURM, which have an ancient heritage value. The Ministry of Tourism also has taken up Varanasi under its Mega Projects Scheme for tourism development. Budget-2008 also has a provision for tax concessions to hotels in districts with heritage monuments. The State Government would be requested to form a Group of Experts to prepare a Heritage Development Plan for Varanasi which would be funded from the JNNURM and other sources. 3. Development of a Mega Cluster for Silk Weavers-Varanasi is one of the six locations chosen for infrastructure development under the Mega Cluster Scheme announced in Budget 2008. Under this, Rs. 70 crores will be provided to Varanasi to improve the infrastructural facilities for weavers through better storage facilities, weaving facilities, production facilities, health facilities, training and design facilities, etc. 4. Health Insurance for Weavers-Over one lakh weavers from Varanasi are being covered under the weavers' health insurance scheme. There are also a large number of powerloom workers. They could be covered under the Rashtriya Swastiya Bima Yojana, to be launched on 1st April 2008. We will work with the State Government on this. 5. Payment of overdue electricity bills-The Prime Minister is aware of the problems being faced by weavers on account of overdue electricity bills. The government is working to see how relief could be provided to weavers from the burden of past electricity bills.

6670. (14-3-2008) NEW DELHI : Consumer activist Dr. Sheetal Kapoor said here that "a customer is the most important visitor on our premises. He is not dependent on us. We are dependent on him. He is not an interruption in our work-he is the purpose of it. We are not doing him a favour by serving him. He is doing us a favour by giving us the opportunity to serve him", said Gandhiji. Consumers today want value for money, a product or service that would meet reasonable expectations, should be safe in use and full disclosure of the product specification. These expectations are termed as 'Consumer Rights'. 15 March is observed as the World Consumers' Day.

6671. (14-3-2008) NEW DELHI : Defence PSU Bharat Electronics Ltd (BEL) has paid Rs 36.41 cr to the Government towards 60% Interim Dividend for 2007-08. Shri V V R Sastry, Chairman and Managing Director, BEL, presented the Interim Dividend cheque for Rs 36,41,37,600 (Rs Thirty six crore forty one lakh, thirty seven thousand six hundred) to the defence minister, Shri A K Antony here today. This is the fourth consecutive year that the Navratna Company is paying interim dividend. BEL has been making profits continuously for more than four decades. The company's dividend payment has been continuously rising and the company paid a dividend of 180% for the year 2006-07. The turnover of the company has been steadily increasing over the years. During 2006-07, BEL achieved a turnover of Rs. 3,952.69 crores, which amounts to a Compounded Annual Growth Rate (CAGR) of 16% over the last 5 years. 81% of the turnover accrued from indigenously developed products and upto 85% of the turnover comes from products sold to the Armed Forces. BEL has more than 350 products to its credit. The product range includes small components costing a few rupees to huge systems costing more than Rs. 50 to 60 crores. Starting with a single Unit at Bangalore in 1954, BEL now has nine Units across the country, all of them are ISO 9001:2000 and ISO 14001 certified for Environment Management System. BEL became a Mini Ratna Category I company in February 2002 and ascended to the Navratna status in June 2007, granting it more financial and operational autonomy. International recognition has also come BEL's way. It has been named as the top Indian company in the Electrical and Electronic equipment sector by

Dun and Bradstreet India and ranked as 58th in the list of top 100 defence companies in the world for 2007 by US-based 'Defence News' magazine.

6672. (14-3-2008) NEW DELHI : The Vice President of India Shri Mohd. Hamid Ansari released a book entitled "The Republic of Science-Golden Jubilee Vignettes" edited by Prof. Ranjit Nair at a function here today. Addressing on the occasion, the Vice President said that we are living on a past glory as far as Science is concerned. He expressed his concern that not enough talent is going to scientific research and foundational science whereas India's contribution is great in the field of Science. He called upon the people to motivate students at the entry at school and university level. The Vice President said that such kind of books should be brought out in Hindi language also for a wider dissemination of information and wished the Centre for Philosophy and Foundations of Science (CPFS) all success for bringing out such a book. Prof. Ranjit Nair, Director of CPFS and Prof. Mrinal Miri also addressed.A number of dignitaries were present on the occasion. Brought out by the Centre for Philosophy and Foundations of Science (CPFS), the book comprises of lectures by key contributors to the development of Science and technology in India and provide insider's perspective complementing historical analyses.` It focuses attention on the strengths and weaknesses, successes and failures, attainments and expectations of science and technology in the fifty years of the Republic. Dealing with individuals, institutions and initiatives, the book evaluates the social, cultural and intellectual consequences of India's tryst with her scientific destiny.

6673. (14-3-2008) NEW DELHI : The Delhi Jal Board (DJB) has informed that a study was conducted by Price Water House Cooper in the year 2003-04. In the study, no ranking was given to Delhi's water management. The study conducted by Tata consulting Engineers, advised construction of 53 additional Under Ground Reservoirs (UGRs) and Booster Pumping Stations (BPSs) in Delhi for rationalizing the water supply to different areas of National Capital. About 14 of these Under Ground Reservoirs (UGRs) are already commissioned. Another 9 Under Ground Reservoirs (UGRs) are likely to be commissioned this year. After commissioning of the Under Ground Reservoirs (UGRs), the supply of water shall be made through the Under Ground Reservoirs (UGRs) and the direct tappings from the trunk mains shall be removed. Besides for improving water management, Delhi Jal Board has already placed a supply order for 305 bulk meters to be installed on all the major distribution points and after installation of these bulk meters, a precise water accounting would be possible and the non revenue water identified area-wise. The incidence of Non Revenue Water is also because of poor metering. In absence of meters, the supply is being billed on flat rate basis and under this system the water billed is much less than the actually being consumed. Steps for procurement of domestic meters have been initiated. DJB has also engaged a Consultant for survey and preparation of document for out-sourcing maintenance including leakage management of water mains (about 500 Kms. long). It is expected that leakages from water mains shall be efficiently managed after award of this work. Various other short-term/long-term measures taken/proposed to be taken to enhance the water availability in Delhi include construction of independent lined canal from Munak to Haiderpur, construction of recycling plants, development of tube-wells in the National Capital Region, additional allocation from surplus Ravi Beas water, construction of up-stream storage projects. etc. This information was given by the Minister of State for Urban Development, Shri Ajay Maken in a written reply to an un-starred question in the Lok Sabha today.

6674. (14-3-2008) NEW DELHI : Urban Transport is a State subject. However, realizing the seriousness of rapidly growing problem of urban transportation, Government has approved National Urban Transport Policy (NUTP) in April, 2006. The Policy provides guidelines to the States/cities to design their urban transport strategies. The Government is providing Central financial assistance for urban transport projects through various schemes like Jawaharlal Nehru National Urban Renewal Mission (JNNURM), scheme of Ministry of Finance for financial support to Public Private Partnership in Infrastructure and budgetary support, etc. Further, to address the various issues of urban transportation, advisory letters have been issued to all States/UTs for prioritizing investment in public transportation, non-motorised mode of transport, running of city bus service on Public Private Partnership (PPP) model, integration of land use and transport planning, developing parking policy and using intelligent transport system for integration across various modes of transport and traffic management etc. This information was given by the Minister of State for Urban Development, Shri Ajay Maken in a written reply to an un-starred question in the Lok Sabha today.

6675. (14-3-2008) NEW DELHI : There are 27 locations in the coastal areas of the country which have potential for harnessing wind. The wind surveys were carried out at 71 locations in the states of Andhra Pradesh, Gujarat, Goa, Karnataka, Kerala, Maharashtra, Orissa, Pondicherry, Tamil Nadu and West Bengal, Lakshadweep, and Andaman & Nicobar Islands. A wind power capacity of 7844 MW has been installed in the country as on 31.12.2007 including potential coastal areas. A target of 10,500 MW wind power capacity has been planned in the country during the Eleventh Five Year Plan period including in potential coastal areas. Strategy for promoting wind power projects through private sector investment is being continued during the 11th Plan by providing various fiscal incentives such as concessional import duty on certain components of wind electric generator, excise duty exemption, ten years' tax holiday on income generated from wind power projects, benefit of accelerated depreciation, loan from Indian Renewable Energy Development Agency (IREDA). Technical support is provided by the Centre for Wind Energy Technology (C-WET) by way of detailed wind resource assessment to identify further potential sites. Besides this, higher tariff is being provided for wind power in all the potential States. This information was given by the Minister of State for New And Renewable Energy, Shri Vilas Muttemwar, in a written reply to a question by Shri J.M. Aaron Rashid and Shri Dushyant Singh in the Lok Sabha today.

6676. (14-3-2008) NEW DELHI : Cost audit of the companies is carried out under section 233B of the Companies Act, 1956 and the compliance thereof is monitored in the Ministry of Corporate Affairs. All the companies mentioned in part (a) of the question are engaged in the manufacture of pharmaceutical products. National Pharmaceutical Pricing Authority has been availing cost audit reports of these companies from this Ministry for regulatory action by them. In addition, Department of Expenditure has also been using such cost audit reports for cost/ price studies. The Government undertakes investigations as per the provisions of the law whenever any specific allegation warranting investigation is noticed. This information was given by the Minister of Corporate Affairs, Shri Prem Chand Gupta, in a written reply to a question by Shri Chandrakant Khaire, in the Lok Sabha today.

6677. (14-3-2008) NEW DELHI : The Competition Commission of India was established in October, 2003 but could not be duly constituted under the Competition Act, 2002 due to legal challenge before the Supreme Court. The Supreme Court delivered its judgement in the matter in January, 2005. Keeping in view the ruling of the Apex Court and the need to provide an appropriate institutional structure for regulation of competition in India, some amendments were proposed to the Competition Act, 2002. These proposals were included in the Competition (Amendment) Act, 2007 which was approved by the Parliament in Monsoon Session, 2007 and has since been enacted. The Competition Act, 2002, as amended, provides that the Commission shall consist of a Chairperson and not less than two and not more than six other members. There shall also be a Competition Appellate Tribunal to hear and decide appeals against the orders of the Commission and to decide on matters relating to compensation. The Commission presently comprises only one Member and as such is not in a position to take up enforcement functions under the Competition Act. The Competition Appellate Tribunal is yet to be established. Action has since been initiated to duly constitute the Commission and the Competition Appellate Tribunal and provide necessary infrastructure and staff. The Commission is likely to become fully operational during 2008-09. This information was given by the Minister of Corporate Affairs, Shri Prem Chand Gupta, in a written reply to a question by Shri Prabodh Panda, Shri K.S. Rao, Shri S.K. Kharventhan: in the Lok Sabha today.

6678. (14-3-2008) NEW DELHI : The Government is encouraging setting up of energy generation projects from biomass including rice husk and coconut shells through various technological routes such as combustion, gasification and cogeneration. A cumulative capacity of about 1400 MW has been installed as on

31.12.2007 for generation of energy from biomass mainly in the States of Andhra Pradesh, Bihar, Chattisgarh, Gujarat, Haryana, Karnataka, Madhya Pradesh, Maharashtra, Punjab, Rajasthan, Tamil nadu, Uttar Pradesh and West Bengal. Further, a target for adding about 2000 MW biomass power installed capacity has been proposed during the 11th Plan period. This information was given by the Minister of State for New And Renewable Energy, Shri Vilas Muttemwar, in a written reply to a question by Shri K.C. Pallani Shamy, in the Lok Sabha today.

6679. (14-3-2008) NEW DELHI : Ministry of Urban Development has prepared a new Centrally Sponsored Scheme (CSS), *viz.* "National Mission Mode Project on e-Governance in Municipalities" for implementation in 423 cities and towns having population of one lakh and above over a period of five years. The Scheme has been designed to cover 8 services/management functions within urban local bodies, *i.e.* (i) Registrations and issue of birth and death certificate, (ii) Payment of property tax, water supply and other utility bills and Management of utilities that come under ULBs, (iii) Grievances and suggestions, (iv) Building plan approvals, (v) Procurement and monitoring of projects including E-procurement and Project/ward works, (vi) Health programme including Licenses and Solid Waste Management, (vii) Accounting system, and (viii) Personnel Information System. The total estimated Central share for implementation of the scheme is Rs.676 crore. The Cabinet Committee on Economic Affairs (CCEA) considered the proposal for implementation of this scheme in 423cities/towns on January 24, 2007 and directed that the proposal be considered as pert of the Eleventh five Year Plan. The Planning Commission was accordingly requested to consider the scheme as part of the Eleventh Five Year Plan.

6680. (14-3-2008) NEW DELHI : In view of the apprehension raised on the retrospective amendment to section 271 of the Income-tax Act, proposed in the Finance Bill, 2008, empowering the assessing officer to, inter-alia, levy penalty in case of concealment of income, the Ministry of Finance has issued the following clarification. In the context of levy of penalty under section 271 of the Income-tax Act, there has been an ongoing dispute between the Income-tax department and taxpayers on whether an assessing officer is required to record his satisfaction before initiating penalty proceedings. The Income-tax department has held the view that no separate satisfaction is required to be recorded before initiating penalty proceedings. In the case of Commissioner of Income-tax Vs. S.V. Angidi Chettiar (44 ITR 739; 1962), the Supreme Court has, while dealing with penalty under section 28 of the Indian Income-tax Act, 1922, held that "satisfaction before conclusion of proceeding under the Act, and not the issue of a notice or initiation of any step for imposing penalty is a condition for the exercise of the jurisdiction". The same matter came up once again before the Calcutta High Court in the case of Becker Gray And Company (1930) Limited Vs. Income-tax Officer, Central Circle-I, Calcutta, And Others (112 ITR 503; 1977). Relying on the Supreme Court decision in the above case, the Calcutta High Court held that "It is true that the Income-tax Officer should be prima facie satisfied before the penalty notice is issued, but it does not mean that he is required to record such satisfaction in writing in every case." Following these decisions, wherever additions are made, assessing officers have, without separately recording any satisfaction, been issuing directions for initiating penalty proceedings.

6681. (14-3-2008) NEW DELHI : Indian Renewable Energy Development Agency (IREDA), a non-banking financial company is envisaging formation of a Special Purpose Vehicle to facilitate setting up a Special Economic Zone (SEZ) for production of renewable energy equipment. IREDA is discussing the issue with interested State Governments and Private Sector. Maharashtra, Tamil Nadu, Karnataka, Madhya Pradesh and Chhattisgarh have evinced interest to facilitate setting up of such SEZs. However, the final decision to set up a SEZ would depend on various techno-economic considerations of investors. This information was given by the Minister of State for New And Renewable Energy, Shri Vilas Muttemwar, in a written reply to a question by Shri J.M. Aaron Rashid, Shri Girdhari Lal Bhargava, in the Lok Sabha today.

6682. (14-3-2008) NEW DELHI : Under the solar energy programmes of the Ministry of New and Renewable Energy a total of 74,203 solar home lighting systems, 11,328 solar street lighting systems, 83,378 solar lanterns, 659 solar pumps, 956 kWp capacity of solar PV plants and 57,532 solar cookers have been installed during the last three years. A state wise list of these systems is given in Annexure. The programme on solar water heaters is implemented through Banks and other financial institutions, therefore, state wise details are not maintained. During the last three years about 10 lakh square metre solar thermal collector area has been installed in the country, mainly for solar water heaters. These systems are estimated to save about 608 million units of electricity in a year. Recently the Ministry of New and Renewable Energy has announced a demonstration programme to support mega watt size grid interactive solar power generation projects, up to a maximum capacity of 50 MW, in the country. Any registered company, as project developer, would be eligible to set up solar power projects on build, own and operate basis. Proposal from each project developer with a maximum aggregate capacity of 5 MW, either through a single project or multiple projects of a minimum capacity of 1 MW each, would be considered. A maximum of 10 MW capacity solar power generation projects would be considered in a State. Preference would be given to the projects from the States where the State Electricity Regulatory Commissions (SERCs) have announced or are in the process of announcing tariff for solar power. For projects approved and commissioned by 31st December, 2009, the Ministry will provide generation based incentive up to Rs.12 per kWh for solar photovoltaic power and Rs.10 per kWh for solar thermal power fed to the grid by the solar power project developers, after taking in to account the tariff provided by the SERC or the utility. The Ministry will also provide incentive to the concerned utility and the State Nodal Agency, which will be involved in implementation and monitoring of the projects in that State. Investment of about Rs. 1,000 crore is expected by public and private sectors through installation of 50 MW capacity solar power plants during the 11th plan period. This information was given by the Minister of State for New And Renewable Energy, Shri Vilas Muttemwar, in a written reply to a question by Shri Balashowry Vallabhaneni, Shri Chandra Bhushan Singh, Shri Dushyant Singh in the Lok Sabha today.

6683. (14-3-2008) NEW DELHI : So far, 615 small hydro projects (up to 25 MW) aggregating 2108 MW have been set up in the country. Uttarakhand tops the list with 89 small Hydro Projects followed by 72 in Karnataka and 68 Arunachal Pradesh. More than five thousand sites have been identified in the country to install hydro projects in small capacities. They will have 14204 MW total capacity. This process of identification of potential sites for mini / micro / small hydro projects and their survey is carried out by the respective State Governments and Agencies. State-wise details of the number of potential sites identified and their estimated potential is given in Table-1. State-wise details of numbers and aggregate capacity of small hydro power projects upto 25 MW which are installed is given in Table-2. To set up any mini, micro or small hydro projects up to 25 MW station capacity, no clearance is required from the Central Government.

6684. (14-3-2008) NEW DELHI : Based on the recommendations of the National Commission on Farmers headed by Prof. M.S. Swaminathan, as contained in the Revised Draft National Policy for Farmers, submitted by the Commission, the Government has approved the National Policy for Farmers 2007 which has also been laid on the Table of the House in November 2007. Various recommendations made by the Commission for revival of agriculture and allied sectors, as accepted by the Government, have been incorporated in the National Policy for Farmers. These include asset reforms in respect of land, water, livestock, fisheries and bioresources; support services and inputs like application of fronitier technologies; agricultural biosecurity system; supply of good quality seeds and disease-free planting material; issue of soil health passbooks to the farmers and integrated pest management system; region and crop specific implements and machinery; support services for women like crèches, child care centres, nutrition, health and training; timely, adequate and easy reach of institutional credit at reasonable interest rates and farmer-friendly insurance instruments; use of Information and Communication Technology and setting up of farm schools to revitalize agricultural extension; coverage of farmers under a comprehensive national social security scheme; effective implementation of MSP across the country and establishing community foodgrain banks; development of agricultural market infrastructure and terminal markets for agriculture; curriculum reforms in agricultural universities; special categories of farming like organic farming and contract farming; rural non-farm employment initiative for farm households; and integrated approach for rural energy, etc. A very few recommendations of NCF contained in the Revised Draft National Policy for Farmers have not been incorporated in the National Policy for Farmers 2007. These include, inter alia, (i) fixation of Minimun Support Price (MSP) at least 50% higher than the weighted average cost of production-as MSP is recommended by the Commission for Agricultural Costs & Prices (CACP) on objective criteria considering variety of relevant factors and a mechanical linkage between MSP and cost of production maybe counter-productive; (ii) Public Distribution System (PDS) to be made universal-as PDS is a targeted scheme where even off take for BPL families is short against allocation for BPL categories; (iii) establishment of Indian Trade Organisation and National Livestock Development Council at the National level-as the concerned Departments of Government of India opposed to their establishment; (iv) setting up of Agricultural Risk Fund, Market Price Stabilization Fund and Gram Panchayat Mahila Fund-as Ministry of Finance opined that these should be proposed as schemes to be funded through the normal budgeting process. Many of the provisions contained in the National Policy for Farmers 2007 are already under implementation by various Central Ministries and Departments and the States through several on-going schemes and programmes. These include, inter alia, Bharat Nirman for improving rural infrastructure and irrigation potential; National Rural Employment Guarantee Scheme carrying a legal guarantee of employment; Swaranjayanti Gram Swarozgar Yojana to promote self-employment among the rural poor; National Rural Health Mission; Accelerated Irrigation Benefit Programme to complete more irrigation projects; pilot projects to repair, renovate and restore water bodies and groundwater recharge programme to divert rainwater into dug-wells; revival of agricultural extension system, reforms in agricultural marketing and development of market infrastructure; establishment of National Horticulture Mission, National Rainfed Area Authority, National Fisheries Development Board, National Bamboo Mission, etc.; expansion of institutional farm credit at reduced rate of several other initiatives. Government of India has recently launched two new schemes *i.e.* National Food Security Mission to improve production and productivity of foodgrains and Rashtriya Krishi Vikas Yojana to incentivize States to increase public investment in agricultural so as to achieve the targeted growth rate in agriculture.

6685. (14-3-2008) NEW DELHI : Pursuant to the Resolution adopted on 29.5.2007 by the National Development Council (NDC), a new State Plan scheme of Additional Central Assistance (ACA) for agriculture & allied sectors, namely, Rashtriya Krishi Vikas Yojana (RKVY) has been launched during 2007-08 with an envisaged outlay of Rs. 25,000/- crore during the 11th Five Year Plan. The broad objective of RKVY is to incentives the States to increase public investment to achieve 4% growth rate in agriculture and allied sectors in the 11th Five Year Plan. The new scheme requires the States to prepare District and State Agriculture Plans and maintain, or increase, the share of expenditure in agriculture and allied sectors in the State's total Plan expenditure. The allocation of funds to the States is based on the net un-irrigated area, gross State agricultural product to be attained by the end of 11th Plan, and increase in the State Plan expenditure in agriculture and allied sectors.

6686. (14-3-2008) NEW DELHI : India produces around 111.77 million MTs of vegetables and 57.73 million MTs of fruits, which accounts for nearly 11.90 per cent and 10.90 per cent of country's share in the world production of vegetables and fruits, respectively. While the India's share in the global market in vegetable and fruits stands at 1.70 per cent and 0.50 per cent, respectively. Most of the agricultural commodity markets generally operate under the normal forces of demand and supply. The buying and selling of agricultural produce takes place in the market yards where numbers of market functionaries are involved. The share of producer in consumers price depend upon the types of marketing channels followed in sales transactions by the farmers. The studies indicate that the share of producers varies from 56 to 83 per cent in food grains and 79 to 95 per cent in pulses, 65-96 per cent in oilseeds and 33 to 75 per cent in case of fruit and vegetables. In order to provide the remunerative prices to the farmers, there is a need to eliminate the chain of middlemen etc., by introducing innovative marketing channels like direct marketing, contract farming, etc. and removal of controls on movement and storage of agricultural produce across the country which will facilitate functioning of common Indian market. Keeping this in view, a Model Law on agricultural marketing has been formulated by the Ministry of Agriculture and circulated to all the States/Union Territories for making necessary amendment in their respective Agricultural Produce Market Committee (APMC) Act in order to guide them in removal of legal barriers, which introduce inefficiencies and monopoly controls in the functioning of agricultural markets. It redefines the role of present Agricultural Produce Market Committee to promote alternative marketing system, contract farming, direct marketing and farmers/consumers markets. Most of the State Governments have since initiated the process of amendment of APMC Act on the lines suggested in the model law, which will facilitate competitive marketing. Since agriculture marketing is a State subject, it is for the State Governments to amend the APMC Act, wherever required, to provide for alternate marketing channels to the farmers through direct marketing, contract farming and setting up of markets in cooperative and private sector to enable him to decide the channel which provide him the best remunerative price for his agricultural produce.

6687. (14-3-2008) NEW DELHI : Union Minister for Agriculture, Consumer Affairs, Food and Public Distribution, Shri Sharad Pawar today lauded the consumer fora for protecting consumers rights and called upon States to create necessary infrastructure for proper functioning of these fora. Shri Pawar was addressing the

Conference of Presidents of State Commissions & Secretaries in-charge, Consumer Affairs in State/UT Governments here today. The Conference was inaugurated by Lok Sabha Speaker, Shri Somnath Chatterjee. Shri Pawar said 'we are the only country in the world which has exclusive fora for the consumer complaints redressal in this form. As per reports received, despite constraints the overall performance of consumer fora is commendable, and the disposal of 88% of cases registered, which is over 29 lakh cases.' Highlighting the need to strengthen the consumer fora, the Minister said that unless the consumer fora function effectively, the fledgling consumer movement would hit a roadblock. In this regard he called upon States to create necessary infrastructure for effective functioning of these fora. He said, ' in order to supplement the efforts of the States/UTs in strengthening and meeting critical gaps in infrastructure of the consumer fora, we have another scheme titled 'Integrated Project on Consumer Protection' where additional financial assistance is being extended to States/UTs. I am confident that after this inadequate infrastructure should not be a cause now which could come in the way of disposal; I am however told that many State Governments have not yet come forward to take advantage of the scheme. Many of them have been slow in providing even land or proper premises for these fora. There are many vacancies in a number of States. This is surprising as the Government of India scheme provides liberal assistance to States for creating infrastructure which under the Act is the responsibility of the State. I hope, States will address these issues on priority.' Minister of Law & Justice, Shri H.R. Bhardwaj, Secretary, Consumer Affairs, Shri Yashwant Bhave and President, National Consumer Disputes Redressal Commission, Justice M.B. Shah also addressed the Conference. The Conference is held as part of Silver Jubilee Celebration of the World Consumer Rights Day. This year's theme of the Day is "Junk Food Generation" to draw the attention of the society towards the menace of junk food. All the Speakers highlighting the growing influence of Junk Food on the society especially by younger generation. Calling for a movement against unethical marketing of unhealthy food, Shri Pawar said that the ingredients of the food products should be clearly known to the consumers along with the information regarding quality, quantity and purity. He also wanted the producers of such eatables to publish the likely health hazards.

6688. (14-3-2008) NEW DELHI : The Ministry of Tribal Affairs has been implementing a 100% centrally funded scheme *viz.* 'Development of Primitive Tribal Groups (PTGs)' for the conservation and overall development of PTGs. The scheme is extremely flexible and it enables taking up activities like housing, land distribution, land development, agricultural development, cattle development, construction of link roads, installation of non-conventional sources of energy for lighting purpose, social securing including insurance or any other innovative activity meant for the socio-economic development of PTGs. During current plan period, the scheme is being implemented with the help of comprehensive 'Conservation-cum-Development (CCD) Plan for PTGs', aiming at habitat development, formulated by various State Governments and Union Territory Administration of Andaman & Nicobar Islands, on the basis of requirement assessed through base line surveys. This was stated by Shri P.R. Kyndiah, Minister of Tribal Affairs in a reply of a question by Shri Mohan Jena in Lok Sabha today. He further added that as per information submitted by the State government, there are 13 PTG communities living in the State of Orissa. The total population of PTGs of Orissa was 58225 as per 1991 census. The PTG-wise population figure of 2001 census is not available. However, the population of PTGs of Orissa, as per Base Line Survey conducted by the State Government during 2007 is 78519. As per CCD Plan submitted by State Government of Orissa for the 11th Plan period, for the Mankirdia PTGs inhabiting Jashipur block of district Mayurbhanj, the State Government has identified certain priority areas *viz.* provision for providing cultivable land, housing, health facilities, residential education, connectivity, drinking water system and irrigation facilities, for attention. The Ministry has released Rs. 10.00 crore during current financial year for the development of PTGs of Orissa including Mankirdia PTGs, he added.

6689. (14-3-2008) NEW DELHI : The Ministry of Women and Child Development is running 'Swadhar-A Scheme for women in difficult circumstances' to cater to the requirements of various types of women in distress in diverse situations including destitute old women and widows. This was stated by Smt. Renuka Chowdhury, Minister for Women and Child Development in a reply to a question by Shri Kashiram Rana and Shri Harikewal Prasad in Lok Sabha today. She further added that the package of services made available under the Scheme includes provision for food, clothing, shelter, health care counselling and legal support, social and economic rehabilitation through education awareness generation, skill up gradation and behavioural training. The Scheme also supports a help-line for women in distress.

6690. (14-3-2008) NEW DELHI : Congress spokesman Shri Abhishek Singhvi said the Congress Party is proud of the completion of 10 years of leadership as Congress President by Smt. Sonia Gandhi. Theses were the words engraved on the silver plaque presented to the Congress President by members of the Congress Working Committee this morning at 10 Janpath. The sequence was that flowers were presented to Smt. Sonia Gandhi followed by the presentation of a shawl and that in turn was followed by the presentation of the silver plaque. Thereafter, the members of the CWC presented a resolution which had been drafted by the members of the CWC and that resolution was read out by Shri Pranab Mukherjee at the residence of the Prime Minister yesterday evening and the Prime Minister subsequently also spoke this morning. The Congress President left for Hyderabad in the morning for the inauguration of an airport. Shri Singhvi said why are we happy, why are we proud? There are many reasons and the reasons are too long to list. But we would like to say that the unity of purpose with which the Congress Party has been tied, with one golden thread, since 1998 under her leadership, is the compassionate approach to inclusive governance which is the hallmark of Smt. Sonia Gandhi's approach. The self-sacrificing, self-effacing approach to both power and politics, which is truly unique and, of course, for rejuvenating a party, for creating a pan-Indian footprint for the party after the dark days of 1997 and 1998 and last, but no the least, a consensual, a collective and collegiate approach to decision-making. As you know, and this is not merely in terms of arithmetic or politics, but the Congress Party expanded its footprint from three states to 16 states at one time. We have come to power in the Central government. Smt. Sonia Gandhi is and remains our chief mascot. She has enthused, energized and enlivened the Party and there is no parallel example not only in Indian politics but in the global politics to compare with the spontaneous self-sacrificing spirit of her approach to pelf, power, position and politics. Whether it is her spontaneous hearkening back to the people, after the office of profit or saying no to the positions of power not only in 2004 but also in 1991, these are events, these are memories and these are feelings unique to Indian politics and we as the Congress Party cherish it. To a question that will Smt. Sonia Gandhi lead the prime ministerial candidate in 2009 also, Shri Singhvi said we will see in 2009. The Congress Party MPs will decide, the Party itself will decide and before that the people of India will decide about the Congress Party. So let's not jump to any figures, conclusions or comments. To a question that if Smt. Sonia Gandhi is the mascot what is Shri Rahul Gandhi? Shri Singhvi said Shri Rahul Gandhi is an extremely important, charismatic political leader of the Congress Party who contributes to energizing and enlivening the Congress Party. To a question as to what is the Prime Minister? Is he a mascot? Shri Singhvi said the Prime Minister is the Prime Minister of the country, he is the UPA Prime Minister of this country and we are proud of having a Prime Minister like that.

6691. (14-3-2008) NEW DELHI : During the year 2006-07, domestic steel industry consumed about 68.504 million tonne of iron ore (Estimated), whereas 93.79 million tonne of iron ore was exported (Provisional). Government has been receiving pleas from some sectors especially steel manufacturers for regulating the export of iron ore. Government of India has imposed an export duty of Rs. 300/- per tonne on export of all varieties of Lumps and on export of iron ore fines having Fe content more than 62%. Export duty of Rs. 50/- per tonne has been imposed on iron ore fines having Fe content 62% and below. This information was given by the Minister of State for Steel, Dr. Akhilesh Das in a written reply in the Rajya Sabha today.

6692. (14-3-2008) NEW DELHI : There has been an increase in number of Foreign Institutional Investors (FIIs) and sub-accounts operating in the Indian stock markets. Over the last six months, their number has increased from 1100 FIIs and 3388 sub-accounts registered as at end September, 2007 to 1303 FIIs and 3877 sub-accounts as at end February, 2008. The Securities and Exchange

Board of India (SEBI) has informed that it has started to implement the measures approved by it in October 2007 to streamline the participation of Foreign Institutional Investors (FIIs) in the Indian Stock Market.

6693. (14-3-2008) NEW DELHI : As per Advanced Estimates of Central Statistical Organisation (CSO), the Gross Domestic Product (GDP) at factor cost at constant (1999-2000) prices in the year 2007-08 is likely to attain a level of Rs.31,14, 452 crore as against GDP of Rs.28,64,310 crore for the year 2006-07. Accordingly, the growth in GDP during 2007-08 is estimated at 8.7 per cent as compared to growth rate of 9.6 per cent in 2006-07. The Government does not set year-specific growth targets. The growth rate in 2007-08 declined due to a general slowdown in most of the sectors except electricity, community services and me composite category "trade, hotels, transport and communications". The deceleration in the growth of agricultural sector is attributed to the slackening in the growth of rabi crops. The slower growth of consumer durables was the most important factor in the slow down of manufacturing sector. Overall, there was a deceleration in the growth of public and private consumption which affected the growth of the services sector, including construction. The National Development Council has endorsed an average growth of 9 per cent per annum in GDP for the Eleventh Five Year Plan period (2007-2012). This information was given by Shri Pawan Kumar Bansal, Minister of State for Finance in reply to a question raised by Shri Amitava Nandy in Lok Sabha today.

6694. (14-3-2008) NEW DELHI : Reserve Bank has taken a number of initiatives for bringing the financially excluded population into the formal financial system. The major initiatives include, advising banks to make available a basic banking 'no-frills' account with low or nil minimum balances, simplified know your customer (EON) procedure for opening accounts, introduction of a General Purpose Credit Card (GCC) facility up to Rs. 25,000/- at rural and semi-urban branches of banks, advising the State Level Bankers Committee (SLBC) to identify one district for 100 % financial inclusion, etc. Further, in certain less developed states, such as those in North Eastern Region, Bihar, Chhattisgarh and Uttarakhand, Working Groups appointed by the Reserve Bank have made specific recommendations for financial inclusion, strengthening financial institutions and improving currency and payments systems. Besides, the Rangarajan Committee on Financial Inclusion has also submitted its final report to Government of India on 4é1 January, 2008. Meanwhile, based on the recommendations for the interim report of this Committee, the Government of India (Gol) has already taken a number of steps for implementation of this report. One of the important steps is the decision to constitute the Financial Inclusion Fund (FIF) for meeting the cost of promotional and developmental interventions and the Financial Inclusion Technology Fund (FITF) to meet the cost of technology adoption, with an overall corpus of Rs. 500 crore each, with initial funding to be contributed by the Central

Government, Reserve Bank of India (RBJ.) and National Bank for Agriculture and Rural Development (NABARD). This information was given by Shri Pawan Kumar Bansal, Minister of State for Finance in reply to a question raised by Dr. K.S. Manoj in Lok Sabha today.

6695. (14-3-2008) NEW DELHI : The Government has decided to ensure that farmers receive Short Term Credit at 7% with an upper limit of Rs.3 lakh on the principal amount since 2006-07. Public Sector Banks, Regional Rural Banks (RRBs) and Cooperative Banks are being provided interest subvention on their own involvement of funds @ 2%. The Government is also providing interest subvention to NABARD for providing concessional refinance to RRBs and Cooperative Banks for the purpose. This scheme continues for the years 2007-08 and 2008-09. The Government of Gujarat informed that the cost of funds of Cooperative Banks in Gujarat are on the high side and therefore they are not in a position to implement the scheme.

6696. (14-3-2008) NEW DELHI : Pharma units are eligible for general small-scale industries excise duty exemption scheme. As such, units having clearance value upto Rs 4 crore in the preceding financial year are eligible for full excise duty exemption on their first clearances upto Rs 1.5 crore in a financial year, subject to certain conditions. In the States of Uttarakhand & Himachal Pradesh, new units or units undertaking substantial expansion are fully exempt from excise duty, while such units in the North East, Jammu & Kashmir and Kutch are entitled for refund of duty paid in cash. Government had received requests for increasing eligibility limit under SSI exemption Scheme for pharma units and enhancing the exemption limit. Government had also received requests for reducing the normal rate of excise duty from 16% to 8%/4% on pharmaceutical products including drugs. In the budget 2008-09, the issue of excise duty on pharma products was examined and excise duty on pharmaceutical products including drugs has been reduced from 16% to 8%. The tax-exemption under small scale exemption scheme was also examined and it was decided not to make any change for the present. This information was given by Shri S.S. Palanimanickam, Minister of State for Finance in reply to a question raised by Smt. Botcha Jhansi Lakshmi in Lok Sabha today.

6697. (14-3-2008) NEW DELHI : The Election Commission of India yesterday (13.03.08) has announced certain bye-elections to the House of People and State Legislative Assemblies, including a bye-election to the 76-Meerut Parliamentary Constituency in Uttar Pradesh. It has now been brought to the notice of the Commission that the Hon'ble High Court of judicature of Allahabad has, in writ petition no. 9750 of 2008 (Md. Shahid Akhlaq Vs. Union of India and Others) vide its Order dated 20.02.08 granted an Order to maintain Status quo as on that day (20.02.08) regarding the seat declared vacant by the Hon'ble Speaker in the House of People. Accordingly the bye-election announced for 76-Meerut shall not be held for the time being. The Commission has also received an intimation yesterday regarding the Uttar Pradesh Assembly seat for 373-Muradnagar being vacant with effect from 13.03.08 due to the resignation of the sitting member thereof. It has been decided to hold bye-election for this seat also along with other Lok Sabha/Assembly seats of Uttar Pradesh as per programme announced vide Commissions Press Note no. No. ECI/PN/08/2008 dated: 13th March, 2008.

6698. (14-3-2008) NEW DELHI : Dr. Shakeel Ahmed, Minister of State for Communication & Information Technology reviewed the activities of the Department of Posts in a meeting of the Consultative Committee of the Parliament attached to his Ministry in New Delhi yesterday. He thanked the MPs for their support in confirming the minutes of the last meeting held on 28.12.2007 on Rural Telephony. A Power Point presentation on "Energizing the Rural Postal Network" was made which was followed by the discussion on the same. He assured the Members of the Committee that provision of postal facilities in the rural and remote areas of the country is receiving high priority in the Department of Posts. He apprised them about the initiatives taken by his Department to revitalize and energize its rural postal network. 'Out of a total network of 1,55,204 Post Offices, 1,39,046 Post Offices are functioning in rural areas with average coverage of 22.61 sq.km per rural Post Office. Since Independence, the Department has expanded its network by over 664 per cent, thereby becoming the largest postal network in the world" he said. He further added that 3,000 new Branch Post Offices are to be opened in 11th Plan. Out of 2000 departmental post offices to be opened in 11th Plan, some will be in rural areas. Office equipments will be provided to 10,000 rural branch offices while 50,000 pillar letter boxes will be installed in villages having branch post offices. In the current Five Year Plan, all departmental Post Offices and 64,000 Extra Departmental Post Offices will be computerized. These computerized Post Offices will be connected to the National Data Centre. The Department has been mobilizing savings from rural areas for Small Savings Bank and National Savings Certificates, disbursing pensions, undertaking verification of Electoral rolls. etc. as part of its agency and retail functions. Members cutting across party lines stressed the need for enhancing the postal network in rural areas, especially in North-Eastern States. The meeting was chaired by the Minister of State for Communication & IT, Dr. Shakeel Ahmad and attended by senior officials of the Ministry, MTNL and BSNL. The Members of Parliament who attended the meeting include S/Shri Narayan Chandra Borkataky (BJP), Dr. Laxminarayan Pandey (BJP) Smt. Sangeeta Kumar Singh Deo (BJP), Shri Vanlalzawma (MNF), Shri Munshiram (RLD), Kunwar Rewati Raman Singh (SP) and Shri A. P. Abdullakutty (CPI(M) from Lok Sabha and Prof. Ram Deo Bhandari (RJD) from Rajya Sabha.

6699. (14-3-2008) NEW DELHI : Stressing the need on rural telephony Shri A. Raja, Minister for Communication and IT said that "Low penetration in rural areas has been a cause of concern, but now since last one year, rural telephony has come on fast tract. During the last one year, rural tele-density has increased from 2 per cent to nearly 8 per cent. Much of the growth is driven by wireless technology". While inaugurating the conference on "Emerging Trends in Wireless Technologies and Services" organized by PTC India Foundation here today, he further added that our target of 25 per cent rural tele-density will require lot of collective efforts by the Government and the industry. Initiatives of USO Fund for setting up towers in rural areas and sharing of infrastructure are some of the steps in this direction. Projecting India as a trendsetter in the field of telecommunications among the developing countries, the Minister said that competition between different technologies has become quite fierce and has led to considerable debate. But as long as such debate helps the telecom sector, the industry and the users, it should be welcome. Although voice telephony is important, but more emphasis should be put to increase the penetration of Broadband connections, which is presently alarmingly low at 3 million broadband connections only. Broadband connectivity is essential for supporting applications for socio-economic development of the masses. "Technologies have become available in recent years that do not require the layout of parallel networks. A common backbone network once available and spread up to all the district headquarters of the country, access to villages could be through wireless as key for rapid growth, while copper or fiber optic cable would be equally cost effective in certain cases. This includes broadband over 3G cellular or WiMAX, corDECT, broadband over power line (BPL) etc", the Minister said. On the occasion, the Secretary, Communications, Shri S. Behura said that broad guidelines for 3rd Generation mobile services and Broadband Wireless Access Services have been announced recently. With this, the level of broadband penetration in the country, especially in rural areas will be addressed. Introduction of BWA services will enhance the penetration as well as growth in broadband subscribers. He further said that as radio frequency spectrum is a limited natural resource, the complexity and complication involved with accommodating new technologies require thoughtful consideration of number of issues like techno-economic, radio regulatory, etc. including balancing of conflicting and competing requirements. Practically all frequency bands are shared amongst different types of radio-communication services for variety of applications and technologies. While considering the spectrum requirements of new emerging wireless technologies, the legitimate and genuine requirements of existing technologies and services cannot be ignored. Hence, the Government's endeavour is to make room for accommodating new wireless technologies with adequate protection to existing operations. The two-day Conference (14&15 March, 2008) was also addressed by Shri S.D. Saxena, Chairman, PTCIF and a presentation on 'Broadband Internet'/ WiMax-3G was given by Shri R. Shivakumar of Intel Technology.

6700. (14-3-2008) NEW DELHI : A revised scheme namely "Project for establishment of trauma care facilities along National highways" during the 11th

Five Year Plan has been envisaged to develop a network of Trauma centres along the Golden Quadrilateral, North-South and East-West corridors of the National Highways to help the accident victims. The revised project envisages the availability of the life support ambulances every 50 Km. along with the National Highways. It also provides for three categories of Trauma centres, *viz.* L-I, L-II and L-III. The trauma care network has been so designed that no trauma victim has to be transferred for more than 50 Km. and a designated trauma centre is available at every 100 Km. The proposed budget estimate for the scheme during the current financial year (1007-08) is Rs.42.73 crores and 34 hospitals in 6 States have been identified for upgradation in the 1st phase. This information was given by the Minister of State for Health & Family Welfare, Smt. Panabaaka Lakshmi in a written reply to a question in the Rajya Sabha.

6701. (14-3-2008) NEW DELHI : As on March, 2007, out of a total of 22370 functioning Primary Health Centres (PHCs) across the country, 964 PHCs are functioning without a doctor, 3073 PHCs are functioning without a pharmacist, 7352 PHCs are functioning without a lab technician, 10522 PHCs are functioning with labour room and 9273 PHCs are functioning with operation theatre. The PHCs are run by the State/UT Governments. Under National Rural Health Mission (NRHM), funds are released to States/UTs Government for upgradation and strengthening of Primary Health Centres including contractual appointment of staff, construction of buildings and provision of infrastructure. The State/UT Governments are, however, required to incorporate their requirements in their annual NRHM Programme Implementation Plans. This information was given by the Minister of State for Health & Family Welfare, Smt. Panabaaka Lakshmi in a written reply to a question in the Rajya Sabha.

6702. (14-3-2008) NEW DELHI : Safety is the prime concern of Indian Railways and all possible steps are undertaken on a continuing basis to prevent accidents which include timely replacement of over-aged assets, adoption of suitable technologies for up-gradation and maintenance of track, rolling stock, signaling and interlocking systems, safety drives and inspections at regular intervals to monitor and educate staff for observance of safe practices. As a result, there has been a declining trend in the number of accidents from 473 in 2000-01 to 234 in 2005-06 and further to 195 in 2006-07. Though the definition of accident varies in different railway systems of different countries, on Indian Railways, the number of accidents per million train kilometer which is an important universally accepted safety indicator, have shown continuous reduction from 0.55 in 2001-02 to 0.44 in 2002-03, 0.41 in 2003-04, 0.29 in 2004-05, 0.28 in 2005-06 and 0.23 in 2006-07. During the last ten years from 1997-98 to 2006-07, 3450 persons including 1539 passengers lost their lives in 3483 consequential train accidents on Indian Railways and 58.25 per cent of these accidents were attributed to railway staff failure. Of the 3483 consequential train accidents, 1959 were involving passenger trains. This information was given by the Minister of State for Railways, Shri R. Velu in a written reply in the Rajya Sabha today.

6703. (14-3-2008) NEW DELHI : Railway has sanctioned a pilot project namely Satellite Imaging for Rail Navigation (SIMRAN) for real time passenger information system. This project is being developed by utilizing Global Positioning System (GPS). This project is being carried out jointly by Research Designs & Standards Organisation (RDSO), Lucknow and Indian Institute of Technology (IIT) Kanpur. The pilot project is sanctioned for development of hardware and software for providing real time information to the passengers.

6704. (14-3-2008) NEW DELHI : The individual plastic card to be issued shall have the name of member and relationship to Government employees/pensioner. Photo of each member and a unique serial number to identify the cardholder with linkage to the other members of family, entitlement of ward for treatment in CGHS empanelled hospitals. Individual card would enable family members to use the card conveniently. It enables availing of CGHS facilities in other cities; enable maintenance of medical history of CGHS beneficiaries. The data of CGHS beneficiaries would also be updated. This work is being done through National Informatics Centre Services Incorporated (NICSI), a subsidiary of National Informatics Centre (NIC). This information was given by the Minister of State for Health & Family Welfare, Smt. Panabaaka Lakshmi in a written reply to a question in the Rajya Sabha.

6705. (14-3-2008) NEW DELHI : According to the estimates released by the Office of Registrar General of India, the life expectancy at birth for Indian males and females corresponding to the mid year 2003 is 62.3 and 63.9 years respectively, giving an overall life expectancy as 63.2 years. Further, as per the report "State of the World's Children, 2008, published by UNICEF, the life expectancy at birth for Japan and USA are 82 and 78 years respectively in 2006. Statement-I gives the Life Expectancy at birth for selected countries including India. To improve primary health care system and provide medical facilities to citizens in rural areas, the Government has initiated comprehensive health sector reforms. The National Rural Health Mission (NRHM) is the main vehicle for these reforms and is a flagship programme of the Government. It is being operationalized throughout the country, with special focus on 18 states, which includes 8 Empowered Action Group States (Bihar, Jharkhand, Madhya Pradesh, Chhattisgarh, Uttar Pradesh, Uttaranchal, Orissa and Rajasthan), 8 North-East States, Himachal Pradesh and Jammu & Kashmir. The main aim of NRHM is to provide accessible, affordable, accountable, effective and reliable primary health care facilities, especially, to the poor and vulnerable sections of the population. NRHM seeks to strengthen the Public Health delivery services at all levels. The interventions/initiatives launched under the NRHM aim to reduce mortality and morbidity so that the life expectancy of the people will improve. The Infant Mortality Rate of India and some selected countries is annexed at Statement-I. Government of India has initiated several measures to bring down the Infant Mortality Rate in the country.A major initiative is the implementation of the Integrated Management of Neonatal and Childhood Illness (IMNCI) strategy, which adopts a holistic approach to the management of the commonest causes of neonatal and childhood mortality-sepsis, acute respiratory infections, diarrhoea, measles and malaria, all compounded by malnutrition. IMNCI is to be implemented throughout the country in a phased manner. In addition, thrust is being given to ensure institutional deliveries and train health personnel on essential newborn care so that skilled attendance at birth is available and all newborns receive specialized care. Efforts to deliver newborn, both facility based as well as home based, are being made. Micronutrient supplementation with Vitamin A, Iron Folic Acid and Zinc, Infant and Young Child Nutrition are being stressed. Immunization is one of the major thrust areas of the ongoing Reproductive & Child Health Programme. The National Rural Health Mission, launched in April, 2005 for a period of 7 years (2005 to 2012) is an overarching initiative with a holistic approach which provides multiple strategic additionalities, like provision for health infrastructure upgradation and a health care worker for every 1000 population, among others and has envisaged reduction in Infant Mortality as one of the prime goals to be achieved. This information was given by the Minister of State for Health & Family Welfare, Smt. Panabaaka Lakshmi in a written reply to a question in the Rajya Sabha.

6706. (14-3-2008) NEW DELHI : The declining sex ratio is a matter of great concern and calls for concerted action from all quarters. In order to contain the menace of female foeticide and ushering in a healthy sex ratio in the Country, the Central Government enacted the Pre-Conception & Pre-Natal Diagnostic Techniques Act, 1994. The Act, inter alia, provides for stringent action against individuals and genetic laboratories/ clinics offering sex determination services. Similar penalty provision also exists for those who seek such services. Various mechanisms have been evolved at the national, State and district levels to ensure strict compliance of the provisions of the Act by all stakeholders through periodic inspection and monitoring. The advent of Internet e-communication has emerged as a new threat in this regard. It has been reported that some of the overseas agencies are freely posting advertisements pertaining to sex determination services and wares. For instance, websites like the www.GenSelect.com, www.4-gender-selection.com, www.pregnancystore.com etc., are offering sex determination kits called the 'baby Gender Mentor Home DNA Test Kit', that help the buyer determine the sex of the foetus through DNA analysis at home. The matter was referred to the Ministry of Communications & IT to block the offending websites. But, that Ministry expressed the view that such an action did not render the promoters of such sites completely ineffective as they could re-emerge and be available for the viewers again under a new nomenclature and in a new avatar. To identify the people involved, the issue was then taken up with the Department of Revenue, Ministry of Finance, to trap the people importing the sex determination kits pandered by the offending overseas websites into the Country. The Ministry of Health requested the Customs Department for details of the individuals or organizations who have imported the sex determination (Gender Testing) kits from abroad to facilitate the Government to proceed further against such people under Section 23 (3) of the PC & PNDT Act and also to intercept and not release such articles under Sub-Section (2) (k), (u) & (v) of Section 11 under Chapter IV of the Customs Act, 1962 (52 of 1962), vide the Government's letter dated 29.11.2007 and 5.1.2008. In response to the Government's above request, the Customs Department have suitably alerted their field formations not to release the imported Gender Testing Kits and to take appropriate action under the Customs Act. This information was given by the Minister for Health & Family Welfare, Dr. Anbumani Ramadoss in a reply to a question in the Rajya Sabha.

6707. (14-3-2008) NEW DELHI : The Sex Ratio (SR) (number of females per thousand males) has increased from 927 to 933 from 1991 to 2001. However, the Child Sex Ratio (CSR) has declined from 945 to 927 during the same period. Some of the reasons commonly put forward to explain the consistently low levels of sex ratio are son preference, neglect of the girl child resulting in higher mortality at younger age, female infanticide, female foeticide, higher maternal mortality and male bias in enumeration of population. Easy availability of the sex determination tests may also be proving to be catalyst in the process, which may be further stimulated by pre-conception sex selection facilities. The Government has taken action on strengthening the Pre-Conception & Pre-Natal Diagnostic Techniques Act (PC & PNDT Act) as well as creating awareness on the issue through various IEC mechanisms. Some of the steps taken by the Government to improve the Child Sex Ratio in the Country are constitution of the Central Supervisory Board under the Chairmanship of Union Minister of Health & Family Welfare, whose function, inter alia, is to review and monitor implementation of the Act and rules made thereunder and recommend to the Central Government changes in the said Act and rules and to create public awareness against the practice of pre-conception sex selection and pre-natal determination of sex of foetus leading to female foeticide; constitution of the National Inspection & Monitoring Committee for undertaking field visits periodically across the country, and constitution of the National Support & Monitoring Cell for effective implementation of the Act, training of Judiciary, publication of Annual Reports, Frequently Asked Questions (FAQs), On-Line Complaint facility on the Ministry's Website, organizing sensitization workshops/seminars, launching of 'Save the Girl Child' campaign, seeking cooperation from the NGOs/religious leaders, etc.. Further, under the National Rural Health Mission, Auxiliary Nursing Midwife (ANM) and Accredited Social Health Activist (ASHA) are being sensitised on the issue. Also, funds have been provided to all States/UTs under the Rural Child Health programme for implementation of the Act and related activities. This information was given by the Minister of State for Health & Family Welfare, Smt. Panabaaka Lakshmi in a written reply to a question in the Rajya Sabha.

6708. (14-3-2008) NEW DELHI : The Government is cognizant of the fact that consumption of alcohol in excessive amounts can lead to social economic and health related problems. A study conducted by NIMHANS for WHO published in the year 2006 shows that nearly 30% of adult men and less than 5% of women consume alcohol giving a male to female ratio of 6:1. Alcohol use is higher in poor communities. The average age of initiation has reduced from 28 years during the 80s to 20 years in recent years. Alcoholism could lead to liver disease and brain damage, gastro intestinal diseases, peptic ulcer, pancreatic diseases, nervous system related diseases, alcoholic dementia, alcoholic memory loss, peripheral nerve damage, muscle damage, cancer of several body organs, hypertension and coronary heart diseases etc. Besides severed health problems, accidents also take place resulting in head injuries and hospitalization. The policy with regard to sale and distribution of alcohol is within the purview of the State Governments. Therefore, the efforts made to contain the damage done by alcoholism vary from State to State. The business of alcohol is a controlled one and without a licence issued by the respective State Government, no one can sell alcoholic beverages. Selling of alcoholic beverages to minors is prohibited. A high rate of State excise duty is levied to dissuade people from consuming alcohol. Advertisements of alcoholic beverages have been banned by the Government. Apart from this, clinical care, building awareness, counselling and rehabilitation is made available through de-addiction centres and counselling centres run/funded by the Government. This information was given by the Minister for Health & Family Welfare, Dr. Anbumani Ramadoss in a reply to a question in the Rajya Sabha.

6709. (14-3-2008) NEW DELHI : The meeting of Parliamentary Consultative Committee for the Ministry of Coal was held under the Chairmanship of Dr. Dasari Narayan Rao, Minister of State for Coal, last evening. In his remarks, the Minister said, a number of measures have been taken by the coal companies to prevent illegal mining which include, apart from conducting raids and seizing illegally mined coal, fencing of unused work areas, filling up of rat holes, sealing of exposed coal by dumping of overburden material, digging trenches, creation of concrete walls, regular and surprise raids by CISF and the security personnel of the coal companies, collection of intelligence, installation of check-posts, filling of FIRs in police stations and close liaison with the State Government authorities. Ministry of Coal has been pursuing this matter with the State Governments concerned on regular basis. Illegal mining has serious consequences for the States in terms of loss of revenue, environmental hazards, law and order problems, unscientific exploitation and resultant wastage of a precious natural resources, safety hazards etc, he said. The Minister further said that he has discussed the issue with the Chief Ministers of Jharkhand and West Bengal who agreed to look into the matter and to instruct the administrative machinery for taking effective steps. Besides this, the State Governments have also initiated some concrete steps. Government of Jharkhand has constituted Task Forces at the State and District levels. In West Bengal also, Task Forces have been constituted at the State and District levels. Joint action for prevention of illegal mining has been initiated by the coal companies and District Collectors. The Minister said, the Central Government has constituted a Committee to look into the various aspects of illegal mining of coal. The Committee is headed by the Minister and has representation from the States of West Bengal and Jharkhand at the level of Minister-in-charge of Mining and Leaders of opposition in the Legislative Assemblies. Some of the members suggested the formation of a Special Task Force to check the menace. Others felt that illegal mining had been thriving with the connivance of police and some bureaucrats and suggested that stern action is warranted against those found involved in the mal-practice. Special Central Illegal Vigilance Team should be formed for surprise checks and raids on illegal mining. The members felt that social security issues involving miners need to be tackled on a priority basis. Those who attended the meeting included S/Shri Baisagopal Choudhury, Dharmendra Pradhan, C.S. Dubey, B.P. Mehta, Manik Singh, Ghuran Ram, Rajiv Ranjan Singh, Furkan Ansari and N.K. Chaudhary, all MPs, Senior officers from the Coal Ministry, Coal India Limited and its subsidiaries were also present in the meeting.

6710. (14-3-2008) NEW DELHI : The allocations under Swarna Jayanti Shahari Rozgar Yojana (SJSRY) have been fully utilized by the Ministry during the last three years. During the course of implementation of the scheme, it was observed that the guidelines of the scheme of Swarna Jayanti Shahari Rozgar Yojana (SJSRY) need modification to make it more focused and effective in tackling the needs of urban poor. This information was given by the Minister of State for Housing & Poverty Alleviation Kumari Selja in the Lok Sabha today, in a written reply to a question by Shri Asaduddin Owaisi. The Minister further stated that accordingly proposals have been prepared for revising the guidelines of Swarna Jayanti Shahari Rozgar Yojana (SJSRY) will focus on self employment of urban poor with entrepreneurial and other support through Micro Business Centres and also on high quality skill upgradation of the urban poor. As per prescribed procedure, the proposal for revision of the guidelines will be placed before the competent authority for approval in due course of time. The Minister also informed that it is expected that the revised Swarna Jayanti Shahari Rozgar Yojana (SJSRY) will effectively help the urban poor in setting up enterprises and also getting high quality skill training so that they can earn enough to run their family decently and rise above the poverty line. Ministry has already pressed upon States/UTs to gear up the machinery for effective implementation of Swarna Jayanti Shahari Rozgar Yojana (SJSRY) and utilize the funds released to them under the scheme. Swarna Jayanti Shahari Rozgar Yojana (SJSRY) is the only urban poverty alleviation scheme targeting exclusively the urban poor living below poverty line.

6711. (14-3-2008) NEW DELHI : More than one million houses have been approved so far under the Sub-Mission of Basic Services to the Urban Poor (BSUP) of Jawaharlal Nehru National Urban Renewal Mission (JNNURM) and Integrated Housing and Slum Development Programme (IHSDP) with a total project cost of Rs.20416 Crore. This information was given by the Minister of State for Housing & Poverty Alleviation Kumari Selja in the Lok Sabha today, in a written reply to a question by Shri Asaduddin Owaisi. The Minister further stated that to speed-up the submission of detailed project reports for approval by the Sanctioning Committee at the Central level, 59 capacity building/training programmes have been conducted by the Ministry of Housing & Urban Poverty Alleviation for State and Urban Local Body officials and other stakeholders. State Governments are coming forward with a large number of projects for seeking Additional Central Assistance for the upliftment of the urban poor. The Minister further informed that Hon'ble Prime Minister has addressed the Chief Ministers of all States to accord priority to slum development and provision of basic amenities to the urban poor under JNNURM. The Minister for Housing & Urban Poverty Alleviation has also taken up the matter with Chief Ministers from time to time. To facilitate effective implementation of programmes, the Government is providing support for strengthening project management at the State and local levels, the Minister added.

6712. (15-3-2008) NEW DELHI : In an effort to connect dreams of today with the actions of tomorrow, the Union Minister for Science & Technology and Earth Sciences, Shri. Kapil Sibal, had a face-to-face interaction with about one hundred Young Scientists from across the country at a brainstorming session in New Delhi today. The event organized by the Ministry of Science and Technology at the Indian National Science Academy was attended by bright and performing Young Associates of all the National Science Academies (INSA, IASc, NASI, INAE) and CSIR Young Scientist awardees who described it as a unique opportunity where the Minister sought suggestions on various issues of S&T for building a vision for the country. Addressing the young minds, Shri Kapil Sibal called for connecting science with larger issues that touch the mankind and common man. Emphasizing the need for touch of irreverence and challenging attitude among scientists he said that Climate Change, technologies for mitigation and adaptation with a wide spread effect are the areas to be looked into. The Young Scientists, on the other hand, came out with several suggestions for policy framework, research and career development which would serve as Vision for Indian Science. Some of these included reaching the available solutions to solving problems on a given time frame by refocusing priorities, creation of new mindset to link research with wealth generation, creating excitements in schools and colleges to attract talented youth to science and research and retention and career opportunities, access to science information as mission, inclusion of social scientists in the main stream of S&T sector and linking youth to community work and linking knowledge of the lab to the people in field etc.

6713. (15-3-2008) NEW DELHI : The Core Committee to draft the charter for Panchayat Convention to be held in April 2008 has unanimously passed the draft charter after two day deliberations (13th and 14th March) in the capital. The committee agreed that flexibility for some modifications to include more ideas and views should be kept in the draft. Speaking on the occasion, Minister for Panchayati Raj, Mr. Mani Shankar Aiyar said that this is a significant step towards inclusive growth through inclusive governance.

6714. (15-3-2008) NEW DELHI : The Ministry of Rural Development has provided adequate funds to Government of West Bengal under National Rural Employment Guarantee Act (NREGA). In the year 2007-08 upto 15th February, 2008, the total available funds with West Bengal, which includes the opening balance and contribution from the state was Rs. 1235.14 crore. Against this the expenditure has been Rs. 688.48 crores which is only 55.74% of total available fund During this period 3984711 households have been provided employment against the demand of 4045887 households. This low expenditure has been because of the low persondays generated which is on average only 18 days per households till now. Analysis based on the trend of actual expenditure, the number of persondays generated and cost per person days indicates that the state would have required Rs. 89.81 crore for March, 2008. Against this the State has Rs. 544.66 cores as unspent balance. This would still leave the state with a surplus of Rs. 456.86 crores.

6715. (16-3-2008) ADILABAD: All India Congress Committee secretary and Nizamabad MP Madhu Yaskhi Goud on Saturday called the Communist Party of India (Marxist) as the prime stumbling block for the formation of a separate Telangana State. He said taking advantage of its key role in the coalition at the Centre, the CPI (M) has ensured Telangana remained a distant dream. Answering questions at a meet the press programme here, the MP referred to a challenge made by CPI (M)'s Sitaram Yechury at Hyderabad recently. He quoted the latter as saying "I will dare the Congress introduce the (Telangana State) Bill in the Parliament" during his Hyderabad visit to illustrate the left party's opposition to the idea of carving out a separate State. Talking about the demand for separate Rayalaseema and coastal Andhra raised by a section of leaders, Mr. Yaskhi Goud said the demand was being raised only to hinder formation of Telangana. Only a handful of leaders voiced their opinion on the subject to create hurdles for Telangana formation, he explained. The AICC secretary likened the current year to the Quit India movement. He said separate Telangana should be possible during 2009.

6716. (16-3-2008) NEW DELHI : BJP National President Shri Rajnath Singh has appointed the Election-Incharges of certain States. Shri Arun Jaitley has been made the election incharge of Karnataka. Shri M Venkaiah Naidu has been made the election incharge of Madhya Pradesh and Rajasthan and Shri Ravi Sahankar

Prasad will be the election incharge of Chhattisgarh. Shri Rajnath Singh has also constituted a seven member core-group from the election management committee announced earlier. Shri M Venkaiah Naidu would be the convenor of this core-group. The other members of this core-group are Dr. Murali Manohar Joshi, Shri Jaswant Singh, Smt Suhsma Swaraj, Shri Arun Jaitley, Shri Ram Lal and Shri Ananth Kumar. Shri Ananth Kumar has been appointed the Secretary of the election management committee and the core group committee.

6717. (16-3-2008) BANGALORE: The attack on Communist Party of India (Marxist) State secretary V.J.K. Nair's residence recently is an indicator to the people of Karnataka on what the future of politics will be like if the Bharatiya Janata Party is voted to power, according to CPI(M) Polit Bureau member Brinda Karat. Speaking to presspersons after visiting Mr. Nair's house here on Saturday, she said that Sangh Parivar politics showed "no civilised norms of behaviour", and the top leaders of BJP and RSS were even justifying the attack. There had been widespread condemnation of the attack from all quarters, cutting across party barriers, and the BJP and the Sangh Parivar were isolated, she said. While the BJP was trying to garner sympathy by projecting that they were denied their chance to come to power, incidents like this showed that they deserved none, said Ms. Karat. The Government should immediately bring to book those responsible for the attack, she demanded. Mr. Nair's wife, Rajamma, who was threatened at knifepoint and was alone when the house was ransacked, said that the police dogs had traced the culprits' track to an RSS office at Ramachandrapura. G.V. Srirama Reddy, former MLA, said that rather than carry the investigation forward on this specific lead, the police were busy making inquiries in Kannur in Kerala over Mr. Nair's credentials. He said party leaders would meet Governor Rameshwar Thakur soon to demand that the investigation be speeded up.

6718. (16-3-2008) LUCKNOW: Uttar Pradesh Chief Minister Mayawati on Saturday reiterated her government's support for trifurcation of the State and said a letter had been sent to Prime Minister Manmohan Singh for creating three States of Purvanchal, Bundelkhand and Western Uttar Pradesh. Addressing party workers on the occasion of the 74th birth anniversary celebration of Bahujan Samaj Party founder Kanshi Ram at the party headquarters here, the Chief Minister said the letter was written on Saturday. Ms. Mayawati said this in reference to the Prime Minister's statement in Varanasi on Friday asking the State government to take the initiative for the formation of the separate State of Purvanchal. The Chief Minister released the English version of her book, "A Travelogue of My Struggle-Ridden Life and Bahujan Movement, Part 1 and 2". The treatise, in the form of an autobiography, recounts her experiences as a politician, as well as the Bahujan movement. Later, presiding over the Kanshi Ram Birth Memorial function in the City Montessori School auditorium, the Chief Minister unveiled projects, including 74 bridges worth Rs. 215 crore and 31 urban water supply schemes costing about Rs.41 crore. Ms. Mayawati also laid the foundation stone for a Tourism Management

Institute and an Environment Bhavan, both named after the BSP founder. Describing Kanshi Ram as the biggest "messiah" of the dalits and the downtrodden, after Bhim Rao Ambedkar, Ms. Mayawati said the BSP founder devoted his life towards the betterment of the underprivileged sections. He instilled a feeling of pride and self-confidence in them, she added. She said the credit for the formation of the present government with absolute majority went to the party's founder.

6719. (16-3-2008) NEW DELHI: The Communist Party of India (Marxist) on Saturday demanded a probe into the "dubious" purchase of a 36-year-old U.S. naval warship, which the Comptroller and Auditor General (CAG) said was made without physical assessment. In a statement here, the CPI(M) Polit Bureau also wanted the government to come out with a statement in Parliament and give an assurance that "such dubious defence purchases will not be resorted to in future." The CAG report tabled in Parliament severely censured the Navy for buying USS Trenton, now named INS Jalashwa. "The country would like to know why the government is going in for such defence deals with the United States. Is it due to the pressure of the Bush administration to buy U.S. arms and defence equipment," the CPI(M) asked. It said the CAG report raised various "disturbing issues" like "why the ship of 1971 vintage was bought when the U.S. Navy itself had concluded in 2003 that it was not suitable for modernisation and should be decommissioned in 2006." The report questioned why the $ 50-million deal was "finalised after only a visual inspection" and why were "restrictions on offensive deployment accepted and permission given to the U.S. to conduct an inspection and inventory of all articles transferred under the end-use monitoring clause." Pointing out that six Indian sailors died aboard this ship due to a gas leak, the Polit Bureau said the CAG report also asked whether the authorities were "not aware that ships of this class had suffered similar problems in the past and three U.S. sailors had lost their lives."

6720. (17-3-2008) NEW DELHI : Replying to a written a question about the steps Government has taken to implement Prime Minister's 15 point programme for minorities and whether there is a programme to improve the housing condition of minorities, the Minister of Minority affairs Sh. A.R. Antulay today informed Rajya Sabha that the Prime Minister's New 15 point Programme for the welfare of Minorities was announced in June, 2006. The programme provides for earmarking of 15% of targets and outlays for minorities under schemes included in the programme and considered amenable to such earmarking. The details of the scheme are available on the ministry at www.minorityaffairs.gov.in. The programme, inter-alia includes the Integrated Housing & Slum Development Programme (IHSDP) and the Indira Awaas Yojana (IAY), both of which have earmarking of targets for minorities.

6721. (17-3-2008) NEW DELHI : Indian Air Force's special force 'Garud' conducted a week long joint exercise with the National Security Guards named

'Black Eagle-I'. The exercise was conducted in two phases from 07 Mar 08 to 14 Mar 08. The first phase was conducted at Garud Regimental Training Centre (GRTC) and the second phase was conducted at NSG Force Headquarters at Manesar. The aim of the exercise was to develop compatibility between the Special Forces on each other's tactics, techniques and procedures and hone their collective skills for special missions. The exercise cultiminated with a capability demonstration by joint forces at NSG Manesar on 14 Mar 08. This demonstration was witnessed by the Chief of Air Staff Air Chief Marshal FH Major and Director General of National Security Guards Shri Jyoti Krishan Dutt IPS. Senior officers from IAF and NSG were also present during the occasion.

6722. (17-3-2008) NEW DELHI : There is huge potential for cultivation of mushroom in the country. India, with varied agro-climatic, abundant raw materials (about 600 millions tonnes agro-waste/annum) and manpower, has huge potential for production of different types of mushrooms in various regions and seasons throughout the year. At present India is producing about 1,00,000 tonnes/annum. For enhancing horticulture production including mushroom, two Centrally Sponsored Schemes namely National Horticulture Mission and Horticulture Technology Mission for North Eastern and Himalayan States, are being implemented in the country. The schemes aimed at increasing production and productivity of horticultural produce including mushroom in the country to meet the growing demand in the domestic as well as export market. However, there is some variation in power tariffs and income tax on cultivation of mushrooms in different States depending upon the classification of mushrooms. This information was given in the Lok Sabha today by Shri Kanti Lal Bhuria, Minister of State for Agriculture in a written reply.

6723. (17-3-2008) NEW DELHI : ESIC has set up one super speciality hospital at ESIC Model Hospital Complex, Kollam, Kerala. It is proposed to start Cardiology and nephrology super-speciality services in this Hospital. Rest of the super specialties will be added as per the need. ESI Corporation proposes to set up zonal super-speciality hospitals in various parts of the country. As a pilot project, zonal super speciality hospital for South Zone is being set up at ESI hospital, Sanath Nagar Complex, Hyderabad (A.P.). Based on the experience, super speciality hospitals will be set up in other parts of the country. At present, there is no proposal for setting up of super speciality hospital in Tamil Nadu. Super speciality hospital at Sanath Nagar, Hyderabad is likely to be operational after three years. Based on the experience of Sanath Nagar Super Speciality Hospital, decision regarding setting up of more super speciality hospitals will be taken. This information was given by the Minister of State for Labour and Employment Shri Oscar Fernandes (Independent Charge) in a written reply in the Lok Sabha today.

6724. (17-3-2008) NEW DELHI : There are the Employees' Provident Fund and Miscellaneous Provisions Act, 1952 including the Employees' Pension Scheme,

1995 (in the specified establishments and employing 20 or more persons) and The Workmen's Compensation Act, 1923 (for persons employed in factories, mines, plantations, mechanically propelled vehicles, construction works and certain other hazardous occupations) for the social and economic security of the workers. There is no distinction between a regular and a casual worker under both the Acts. However in the Contract Labour (Regulation & Abolition) Act, 1970 there is no provision for any compensation to the victims of the family in case of death of the former. The Employees' Provident Fund and Miscellaneous Provisions Act, 1952 aims at providing social and economic security to industrial and other workers covered under the Act and their dependents in casse of their premature death. Under the said Act the Employees' Pension Scheme, 1995 provides for pensionary benefits to the victims family. The Workmen's Compensation Act, 1923 provides for payment of compensation to workmen and their dependents in case of injury and accident (including certain occupational disease) arising out of and in the course of employment and resulting in disablement or death. The Act applies to railway servants and persons employed in any such capacity including persons employed in factories, mines, plantations, mechanically propelled vehicles, construction works and certain other hazardous occupations. Minimum rates of compensation for permanent total disablement and death have been fixed at Rs. 90,000/- and Rs. 80,000/- respectively. Maximum amount for death and permanent total disablement can go up to Rs. 4.56 lakh and Rs. 5.48 lakh respectively depending on age and wages of workmen. Though there is no specific scheme to inform the workers, there are various tripartite fora through which such messages are discussed and disseminated. This information was given by the Minister of State for Labour and Employment Shri Oscar Fernandes (Independent Charge) in a written reply in the Lok Sabha today.

6725. (17-3-2008) NEW DELHI : A project titled: "A study of health hazards/ environmental hazards resulting from the use of chrysotile asbestos in the country" is under way with National Institute of Occupational Health, Ahmedabad. The total cost of the project is Rs. 59.66 lakhs. Out of this, Government of India (Ministry of Chemicals and Fertilizers) is contributing Rs. 43.66 lakhs and the balance of Rs. 16 lakhs is contributed by the Asbestos Cement Product Manufacturer Association to ensure cooperation and involvement of the industry. This information was given by the Minister of State for Labour and Employment Shri Oscar Fernandes (Independent Charge) in a written reply in the Lok Sabha today.

6726. (17-3-2008) NEW DELHI : The Employees' State Insurance Corporation is examining the proposal to provide Unique Identification Numbers to Insured Persons covered under the ESI Scheme. This information was given by the Minister of State for Labour and Employment Shri Oscar Fernandes (Independent Charge) in a written reply in the Lok Sabha today.

6727. (17-3-2008) NEW DELHI : The benefits under the 'Rashtriya Swasthya

Bima Yojana' scheme for BPL families in unorganised sector will start accruing from the first of next month. This information was given by the Minister of State for Labour and Employment Shri Oscar Fernandes (Independent Charge) in a written reply in the Lok Sabha today. The Scheme was launched on 1st October, 2007. The unorganized sector worker and his family (a unit of five) will be covered under the scheme. The total sum insured will be Rs. 30,000/- per family per annum on a family floater basis.

6728. (17-3-2008) NEW DELHI : The Department of Biotechnology, Ministry of Science & Technology, Government of India today celebrated its 22nd Foundation Day. Inaugurating the function organized in New Delhi to mark the occasion, Shri Kapil Sibal, Union Minister for Science & Technology and Earth Sciences appreciated the initiatives taken by the Department of Biotechnology for promoting biotechnology in India through various schemes/programmes. Recalling the efforts of the visionary leader late Rajiv Gandhi who set up the Department in 1986, the Minister said that in a short span of 22 years the Biotechnology Department has made great contribution to nation building. He, however, stressed the need for expanding the physical and technical sources of the Department in near future so as to meet emerging challenges effectively. The Minister informed the gathering that new institutions are being located in 4 technology clusters namely Agri-Food Technology at Mohali, Punjab; Health Science Biotechnology at Faridabad, Haryana; Animal Science and Biotechnology in Hyderabad and Marine Science and Technology in Tamil Nadu. Observing that the influx of woman in biotechnology sector is unprecedented and that over 100 companies in the sector are run by young technocrats, Shri Sibal projected that by the end of 11th Plan the biotechnology sector would be worth 10 billion dollars. Reiterating the commitment of the government to promote rapid growth in biotechnology he said 1000 positions of Ph.D. would be created in next five year. He also emphasized that biotechnology has great potential in delivering social goods for health care, agriculture/animal productivity, employment generation, and contribution to national economy. National Bioscience Award for Career Development, Innovative Young Biotechnologist Awards and DBT Biology Scholarships (for students scoring highest marks in biology at 10+2 level in central and state board examinations and opting for biological courses at graduate level) were also given away on the occasion. Several dignitaries, Directors of premier institutions, Government officials, Scientists and Students were present on the occasion.

6729. (17-3-2008) NEW DELHI : Replying to a written a question about the name of states in which Prime minister's new 15-point programme for the welfare of minorities is implemented and whether the programme is implemented in Goa also. The Minister of Minority Affairs A.R. Antulay the schemes included in the New 15 point Programme are centrally sponsored schemes, which are operated by the Central Ministries/ Departments concerned. The programme provides for earmaking of 15 % of targets and outlays under schemes included in the programme and considered amenable to earmarking. The details of the schemes are available on the website of the Ministry at www.minorityaffairs.gov.in. Financial assistance is provided to States/Uts as per the guidelines of the concerned scheme. This information was given by the Union Minister of Minority Affairs Shri A.R. Antulay in reply to a written question in the Rajya Sabha today.

6730. (17-3-2008) NEW DELHI : Recently a scheme for promotion of employment in the private sector, for persons with disabilities including visual impaired has been sanctioned by the Government, which envisages payment of employer's contribution to Employees Provident Fund (EPF) and Employees State Insurance (ESI) for the first three years for employment of persons with disabilities. The benefit of the scheme is for the persons with monthly wages up to Rs.25,000/- per month. A provision of Rs.15.00 crore has been made in the budget of the Ministry during 2008-09 for the scheme.

6731. (17-3-2008) NEW DELHI : In response to commitment contained in the National Common Programme to initiate a dialogue with Industry and other Associations to fulfil the aspirations of the Scheduled Castes and Scheduled Tribes youth, a Group of Ministers was formed. The Group met five times and also held with the representatives of Apex Industry Associations in private sector on this issue. To carry forward the process of dialogue, a Coordination Committee has been constituted under the Chairmanship of the Principal Secretary to the Prime Minister. This Committee is serviced by the Department of Industrial Policy and Promotion. The Committee has held discussions with representatives of Apex Industry Chambers/Associations under the chairmanship of Principal Secretary to the Prime Minister. The discussions primarily centred around the measures by industry for enhancing skill development and increasing employability. This information was given by the Minister of State for Social Justice and Empowerment, Smt. Subbulakshmi Jagadeesan in a written reply to a question in the Rajya Sabha today.

6732. (17-3-2008) NEW DELHI : Government of India has approved the continuation of the scheme in 11th Plan for attaining the goal for providing access to electricity to all households. Capital subsidy of Rs.28,000 Crores for electrification of about 1.15 lakh unelectrified villages and electricity connections to 2.34 crore BPL house holds has been sanctioned at this stage. The Panchayat institutions would be associated in the management of rural distribution through franchisees after completion of RGGVY works. RGGVY Guidelines have stipulated that electrification works under the sanctioned projects are to be executed on turn-key basis. The guidelines have also specified the qualification requirements for such turn-key contractors. Panchayats and Local Bodies can also participate in such tenders in case they satisfy the stipulated qualifying requirements. The rural electrification policy has stipulated that "The Gram Panchayat/Village Council or equivalent shall issue the first Certificate at the time of the village becoming eligible for declaring it "electrified". Subsequent to the village being declared as "Electrified", the Gram Panchayat shall certify and confirm the electrified status of the village as on 31st March each year". This information was given by Union Minister for Power, Shri Sushilkumar Shinde in a written reply to a question by Shri C. Perumal in the Rajya Sabha today.

6733. (17-3-2008) NEW DELHI : Replying to a written a question whether there is any official definition of minority, minister of Minority Affairs Shri. A.R. Antulay today informed Rajya Sabha that section 2(C) of the National Commission for Minorities (NCM) Act, 1992, defines "minority" as "Minority for the purposes of this Act, means a community notified as such by the Central Government." Accordingly the Central Government has notified five religious communities, *viz.*, Muslims, Christians, Sikhs, Buddhists and Zoroastrians (Parsis) as minority communities. He also informed that there are cases of recognition of minorities are pending in courts and there are no special minorities amongst the said minorities.

6734. (17-3-2008) NEW DELHI : The planning Commission estimates the incidence of poverty at national and state level form the large sample survey on household consumer expenditure conducted by the National Sample Survey Organisation (NSSO) at an interval of approximately five years. Based on this, the percentage of population living below the poverty line for the minorities had been estimated for the year 1999-2000. the corresponding estimate of the number of number of persons living below the poverty line is not available. This information was given by the Union Minister of Minority Affairs Shri A.R. Antulay in reply to a written question in the Rajya Sabha today.

6735. (17-3-2008) NEW DELHI : The Government has formulated schemes to provide incentives to farmers for the optimum use of improved and modern agricultural technology and other inputs in order to increase production and to cut production cost. The main schemes are-A. The Centrally Sponsored Scheme ¡§Support to State Extension Programmes for Extension Reforms¡¨ launched during 2005-06, aims at delivery of farmer driven extension services for disseminating information on modern agriculture technologies and other support services, which may help increase production and productivity through a new institutional arrangements in the form of ATMA. ATMA have active participation of farmers/ farmer groups, NGOs, KVKs, PRIs and other stakeholders operating at the district level and below. ATMAs have been established in 565 districts. Over 18 lakhs farmers have been benefited in different extension activities, so far. Farmer oriented activities under the scheme includes Trainings, Demonstrations, Exposure Visit, Group Mobilization & Capacity Building, Exhibition, Information Technology, Research-Extension-Farmer linkages. An amount of Rs.240.65 Crore has been released so far during last 3 years and a provision of Rs.298.00 Crore has been made for 2008-09. B. The Centrally Sponsored Scheme on ¡§National Horticulture Mission (NHM)¡¨ is being implemented for the holistic development of horticulture sector duly ensuring forward and backward linkages with the active participation of all the stake holders. Under the scheme, assistance is being provided to the farmers for taking up various activities related to horticulture such as area coverage, rejuvenation of senile orchards, protected cultivation organic farming, promotion of integrated nutrient management/integrated pest management and bee-keeping. Besides assistance is also being provided for creation of water resources and infrastructure for post harvest management and markets. An amount of Rs.1575.29 Crore has been released to the State Horticulture Mission and National Level Agencies during 2005-06 and 2006-07. An outlay of Rs.1150.00 Crore was earmarked for implementing the scheme during 2008-09. C. A Central Sector Scheme ¡§Post Harvest Technology & Management¡¨ formulated to implementation during 11th Plan aims at establishment of units for transfer of primary processing, technology, value addition, low cost scientific storage, packaging units and technologies for bi-product management, demonstration of technologies, training of farmers, entrepreneurs and scientist. The outlay of the scheme for 11th Plan is Rs.40.00 Crore. D. A Centrally Sponsored Scheme on ¡§National Bamboo Mission¡¨ has been launched across the country for implementation in the last quarter of 2006-07 with 100% central assistance at a total cost of Rs.56,82,300/ - thousand including a outlay of Rs.7,00,00/- thousand during 2006-08 (10th Plan) and next four years of the 11th Five Year Plan. The Mission activities are spread over a period of 5 years and they are at present implemented in 25 States. E. A Centrally Sponsored Scheme on ¡§Micro Irrigation¡¨ has been launched in January, 2008, during 10th Plan for covering a total area of 6.2 lakh hac. under Micro Irrigation. The scheme is launched to achieve greater Water Use Efficiency resulting in enhanced productivity and better quality of produce. Under this scheme drip and sprinkler irrigation is being promoted on a large scale. Assistance is provided to all categories of farmers @ 50% for drip/sprinkler system implementation and @ 75% for training and demonstration. The drip and sprinkler irrigation system is being implemented in each district of the State for both horticulture crops as well as non-horticulture crops. F. A Centrally Sponsored Scheme on ¡§National Food Security Mission (NFSM)¡¨ has been launched in the country to enhance the production of rice, wheat and pulses by 10, 8 and 2 million tones, respectively by the end of 11th Plan. The mission aims at increasing production of rice, wheat and pulses through area expansion and productivity enhancement, restoring soil fertility and productivity, creating employment opportunities, and enhancing farm level economy to restore confidence of farmers of targeted districts.

6736. (17-3-2008) NEW DELHI : Muslims, Christians, Sikhs, Buddhists and Zoroastians (Parsis) have been notified as minority communities under section 2 (C) of the National Commission for Minorities Act 1992. Details of religious minorities including percentage growth of population are available in the "Census of India 2001-The First Report on Religion Data" published by Registrar General and Census Commissioner of India and also on the website www.censusindia.gov.in.

The growth rate during 1991-2001 is variable. This information was given by the Union Minister of Minority Affairs Shri A.R. Antulay in reply to a written question in the Rajya Sabha today.

6737. (17-3-2008) NEW DELHI : NTPC Ltd. is setting up a coal based Thermal Power Project of 750 MW (3x250 MW) at Salakati in Kokrajhar District (Part of Bodo Territorial Autonomous District) in Assam at the site of existing non-operational Bongaigaon Thermal Power Station (4x60 MW). In this regard, a Transfer Agreement has been executed amongst NTPC Ltd., Government of Assam and Assam Power Generation Corporation Ltd. (APGCL) for transfer of the existing infrastructure of 240 MW (4x60 MW) Bongaigaon Thermal Power Station of APGCL in Assam to NTPC Ltd. and setting up of new 3x250 MW power station at the same location by NTPC Ltd. Notification in respect of transfer of assets was issued by Government of Assam on 13.11.2007. All necessary key inputs and clearances including environmental clearance from the Ministry of Environment & Forests have been tied-up/obtained for the project. Site specific studies have been completed. Preparation for commencement of main plant activities has started. Main Plant Equipment packages have been awarded on BHEL in February 2008. Work on the project has already commenced. Investment approval has been accorded by NTPC Board on 30.01.2008 at current estimated cost of Rs.4375.35 Crores. An expenditure of Rs. 86.85 lakhs has been incurred in the project so far. 16 employees have been posted at Bongaigaon Thermal Power Project as on 31.01.2008. This information was given by Union Minister for Power, Shri Sushilkumar Shinde in a written reply to a question by Shri Urkhao Gwra Brahma in the Rajya Sabha today.

6738. (17-3-2008) NEW DELHI : The constitution (One Hundred and Third Amendment) Bill to confer constitutional status on the National Commission for Minorities was introduced in the Lok Sabha in December, 2004. The Bill includes a definition of 'minority'. The recommendations of the Standing Committee on Social Justice and Empowerment regarding the Bill have been considered but some other related issues are still under examination. This information was given by the Union Minister of Minority Affairs Shri A.R. Antulay in reply to a written question in the Rajya Sabha today.

6739. (17-3-2008) NEW DELHI : The following measures have been taken by the Government in order to promote export of sugar: (i) Export assistance is being provided to defray expenditure on internal transport, marketing and handling charges and ocean freight @ Rs. 1350/- per ton for sugar factories located in coastal States and Rs. 1450/- per ton for sugar factories located in non-coastal States (subject to actuals for export by road/rail to neighbouring countries) for a period of one year with effect from 19th April, 2007. The amount involved is Rs. 300 crore (approx) which is to be borne from the Sugar Development Fund. This assistance shall be used for payment of cane price arrears of farmers as the first priority. (ii) The requirement of obtaining release orders for the purpose of export has been dispensed with, with effect from 31st July, 2007 till 30th September, 2008. This would help the sugar factories to undertake exports expeditiously and improve their liquidity position. Major buyers of sugar from India are-Afghanistan, Bangladesh, China, Djibouti, Egypt, Indonesia, Iran, Kenya, Pakistan, Portugal, Singapore, Somalia, Srilanka, Syria, Tanzania, UAE and Yemen Repubic. This information was given today by Dr. Akhilesh Prasad Singh Minister of State for Agriculture, Consumer Affairs, Food and Public Distribution in written reply in the Lok Sabha.

6740. (17-3-2008) NEW DELHI : A nine-day Akash missile campaign was held in December 2007. Air Force user flight trials were conducted during 11-20 December 2007 at Interim Test Range (ITR) Chandipur and all trial objectives were met completely. Air Force is processing the case for procurement of Akash Missile System from the designated Production Agency based on their user trials. Army has informed that they will take a final view on inducting the Akash Weapon System after studying the report of Air Force User trials. The campaign has conclusively established the readiness and effectiveness of Akash Weapon System in area defence role against flying targets under various flying condition including engaging target in "ripple" mode. This information was given by Defence Minister Shri A K Antony in a written reply to Shri Braja Kishore Tripathy and Shri K S Rao in Lok Sabha today.

6741. (17-3-2008) NEW DELHI : The Hindustan Aeronautics Limited (HAL) has signed a MoU with Boeing to source sub-system for fighter aircraft and helicopters. An MoU has been signed by HAL with Boeing in December 2007 which envisages exploration of business opportunities principally relating to defence related work packages. The proposal regarding procurement of Long Range Maritime Reconnaissance (LRMR) aircraft is in progress. Such MoUs are expected to benefit HAL through enhanced export opportunities, development of new technologies and processes; and implementation of best practices and skills for global competitiveness. This information was given by the Minister of State for Defence Production Rao Inderjit Singh in a written reply to Shri Sugrib Singh and others in Lok Sabha today.

6742. (17-3-2008) NEW DELHI : As per information available from Indian Veterinary practitioners Registers (IVPR) maintained by Veterinary Council of India, a total of 50,650 registered veterinary practitioners are available in the country as on 31.3.2007 which is within the norms recommended by National Commission on Agriculture. As per the recommendation of National Commission on Agriculture (1976) there should be at least one veterinarian for every 5,000 cattle unit by 2000 AD. Veterinary Services is a state subject and new veterinary hospitals, dispensaries, polyclinics are being set up by the respective State/Union Territory Governments depending upon livestock population in a particular area and availability of resources with the State/Union Territory Governments. This information was given in the Lok Sabha today by Shri Kanti Lal Bhuria, Minister of State for Agriculture in a written reply.

6743. (17-3-2008) NEW DELHI : A MiG-27 aircraft crashed at Hashimara airbase in West Bengal on 31st January, 2008. A total of two MiG-27 aircraft crashed during the last two financial years *i.e.* 2005-2006, 2006-2007 and the current financial year *i.e.* 2007-2008 (till 10th March, 2008). No pilot or co-pilot lost their life in these accidents. Each crash is investigated through a Court of Inquiry and remedial measures are undertaken accordingly. The average financial loss incurred due to crash of one Mig-27 aircraft is Rs. 6,79,00,000/-. This information was given by Defence Minister Shri A K Antony in a written reply to Shri Mohan Singh in Lok Sabha today.

6744. (17-3-2008) NEW DELHI : The Minossrity concentration districts have been identified on the basis of both concentration of minority population and the relative backwardness of the districts vis-à-vis the national average in respect of socio-economic and basic amenities parameters. Sriganganagar qualifies in terms of population but the indices of its socio-economic and basic amenities parameters are above the national average. As far as Jaisalmer district is concerned, it does not qualify in terms of the population criteria. The Chairman, Rahasthan State Commission for Minorities has been informed suitable. This information was given by the Union Minister of Minority Affairs Shri A.R. Antulay in reply to a written question in the Rajya Sabha today.

6745. (17-3-2008) NEW DELHI : Landmine Monitor Report of 2007 was released during the Ottawa Convention Meeting held at Anman, Jordan in November, 2007. The Report gives details about use and stockpile of anti-personnel mines of all countries in the World. Mines were laid as per operational plans dictated by need during OPERATION PARAKARAM. On demobilization of troops, demining operations for the mines laid during the Operation commenced in November, 2002. Demining operations have been completed in all areas, except those required for operational reasons. Cases of 353 civilian land mine casualties (61 killed and 292 injured) have been sanctioned ex-gratia compensation in accordance with the extant guidelines. This information was given by Defence Minister Shri A K Antony in a written reply to Kumari Mehbooba Mufti in Lok Sabha today.

6746. (17-3-2008) NEW DELHI : The Government has signed a Letter of Offer & Acceptance with the US Government for the procurement of six C-130J-30 aircraft for the Indian Air Force. The estimated value of the aircraft along with associated ground support equipment, ground handling equipment and the role equipment is 962,454,677 USD. The delivery of these aircraft is likely to be completed by December 2011. This information was given by Defence Minister

Shri A K Antony in a written reply to Shri Hansraj G. Ahir and Shri Milind Deora in Lok Sabha today.

6747. (17-3-2008) NEW DELHI : 475 Exhibitors from 31 countries including 273 international companies participated in the Defexpo India 2008. Approximately 40,000 business visitors visited the exhibition. 3,490 business inquiries were generated during the exhibition and 21 MoUs were signed. These are likely to further boost the expert of defence items from India. However, no purchase agreements were signed by the government during Defexpo India 2008. Defence Procurement Procedure (DPP) 2006 and Defence Procurement Manual (DPM 2006) under implementation with effect from 1st September 2006, provide for direct dealing with Original Equipment Manufacturers (OEMs) or Authorised Vendors or Government sponsored Export Agencies (applicable in case of countries where domestic laws do not permit direct export by OEMs). Further, the procedures inter-alia incorporate provisions for penalties being imposed if any seller engages any individual or firm, whether Indian or foreign whatsoever, to intercede, facilitate or in any way recommend to the Government of India or any of its functionaries, whether officially or unofficially, to the award of the Contract to the Seller.

6748. (17-3-2008) NEW DELHI : The DBT Biology Scholarships are awarded from the combined merit list of toppers in Biology/Biotechnology from Central Board of Secondary Education (CBSE), Council for Indian School Certificate Examinations (CISCE) and State Boards. The students who pursue Biological Sciences at graduation level after 10+2 are eligible for Scholarship. This year, the Department has increased the number of scholarships from 77 to 100 *i.e.* 44 from CBSE, 4 from CISCE and 52 scholarships @ 2 scholarships each from 26 State Boards. The scholarship amount has also been increased from Rs.15,000/- to Rs.20,000/- as one time award from the year 2007. In addition, awardees are provided with one gold plated medal and a certificate. Union Minister for Science and Technology and Earth Sciences, Shri Kapil Sibal awarded the scholarships for 2007 at a function in New Delhi today to mark the 22nd Foundation Day of the Department of Biotechnology (DBT). The 98 awardees selected for award of DBT Biology Scholarships include 44 from CBSE, 4 from CISCE and 2 each from 24 State Boards and 1 each from remaining 2 State Boards.

6749. (17-3-2008) NEW DELHI : Joint exercises with friendly foreign countries are considered on case to case basis based on our need to engage them as directed by our National Security Guidelines. During the last one year joint exercises were conducted with France, USA, UK, Singapore, Russia, Thailand, China, Mongolia, Oman and Maldives. The expenses incurred on conduct of these exercises are determined by the nature and complexity of the exercise for which specific expenditure sanction is issued with the approval of the competent authority. Joint exercises benefit the Indian Army by enhancing its capability through exchange of best practices and procedures and exposure to advanced technologies. Joint exercises also build interoperability, mutual understanding and give impetus to the ongoing Military to Military Cooperation. This information was given by Defence Minister Shri A K Antony in a written reply to Shri Milind Deora in Lok Sabha today.

6750. (17-3-2008) NEW DELHI : Nine Bioscientists were honoured today with the National Bioscience Awards for Career Development to recognize outstanding contributions of young scientists below 45 years of age in basic and applied research in the areas of biosciences and biotechnology including agricultural, biomedical and environmental sciences with potential for application/product and technology development. Each award carrying a cash prize of Rs.1.00 lakh and a trophy along with a citation and a project research grant of Rs.9.00 lakhs for 3 years for career development was presented by Union Minister for Science and Technology and Earth Sciences, Shri Kapil Sibal at a function held in New Delhi to mark the 22nd Foundation Day of Department of Biotechnology.

6751. (17-3-2008) NEW DELHI : The overall Plant Load Factor (PLF) of Central Sector Thermal Power Stations (coal & lignite) and nuclear power plants in the country during the current financial year (April, 2007-February, 2008) was 86.4% and 46.6% respectively. The performance of power plants (generation, PLF etc.) is dependent on a number factors like installed capacity, age of the units, past performance, planned outages, availability of water/fuel (both quantity and quality), etc. While availability of water during monsoon and non-monsoon season as well as irrigation requirements influence performance of hydro-power stations, the quality and availability of fuel have a bearing on the performance of thermal power stations. Therefore, the actual performance of some power plants, mostly in the state sector, is at variance with their normal working capacity.

6752. (17-3-2008) NEW DELHI : Government, vide Press Note 2 (2000 series) dated 11.2.2000 of the Ministry of Commerce and Industry (department of Industrial Policy and Promotion) has allowed FDI up to 100%, on the automatic route in the Education Sector, subject to the sectoral rules/regulations as may be applicable. This information was given by the Minister of State for Human Resource Developmen Smt. D. Purandeswari in a written reply in Rajya Sabha today.

6753. (17-3-2008) NEW DELHI : The demand for flowers in the domestic and international market is increasing rapidly. The production of loose flowers increased from 0.66 million tones during 2004-05 to 0.92 million tones during 2006-07, while the production of cut flowers increased from 952 million nos. to 3290 million nos. The export of floriculture has increased from Rs.210.99 crores to Rs.649.84 crores during the same period. The Ministry of Agriculture is implementing two Centrally Sponsored Schemes namely Technology Mission for Integrated Development of Horticulture in North Eastern & Himalayan States and National Horticulture Mission, for increasing production & productivity of horticultural crops including flowers. Under these schemes, assistance is provided to the farmers for area expansion, production of quality planting materials of elite cultivars, adoption of new technologies, integrated pest management, integrated nutrient management, etc. Besides, National Horticulture Board is implementing schemes which provide assistance for production of horticultural crops including flowers. APEDA is also provided financial assistance to registered exporters for export of floriculture produce under the schemes for market development, infrastructure development, quality development, research & development and transport assistance. In the best growing periods (Nov.-Feb.) quality of the Indian flowers is comparable to the Kenyan flowers in the same segment. Some of the varieties grown in India has been rated to be of higher quality than their counterparts growing the same variety in Kenya. On a longer growing period Kenyan flowers are more consistent in overall quality than flowers from Indian as Kenya enjoys a more stable climate. Ethiopia grows flowers in higher altitudes which have a different quality (bigger buds and stronger stems) but suffer from low production due to the low temperatures. APEDA has set up a market facilitation centre at the Netherlands and it is providing awareness amongst its registered growers of the possibilities and chances that exist in the market. APEDA has also introduced a scheme for recognition of floriculture units that covers all the quality parameters which an export floriculture unit should possess. This information was given in the Lok Sabha today by Shri Kanti Lal Bhuria, Minister of State for Agriculture in a written reply.

6754. (17-3-2008) NEW DELHI : Replying to a question whether Government has decided to set up a fund for enlistment of minorities in the country and whether any guidelines for spending the money form the fund have been prepared, the minister of Minority Affairs A.R. Antulay today informed Rajaya Sabha that no fund has been set up for upliftment of the minorities. However, a number of schemes meant exclusively for the minorities have been approved and funds provided for them like the merit-cum-means scholarship for technical and professional courses at undergraduate and post gradate level, (ii) pre-matric scholarship form class XI upto Ph. D level including technical and vocational courses of Class XI and XII level (iii) pre-matric scholarship scheme form class I to class X, and (iv) Coaching and allied scheme. The corpus fund of the Maulana Azad Education Fundation has been augmented to Rs. 250 crore, the authorized share capital of National Minorities Development Corporation (NMDFC) has been raised form Rs. 650 crore to Rs. 750 crore and the paid up equity of the Central government in NMDFC raised form Rs. 375.36 crore to Rs. 445.36 crore in 2007-08. a multi-sectoral development programme for 90 minority concentration districts is on the anvil.

6755. (17-3-2008) NEW DELHI : The Ministry of New and Renewable Energy supports Research, Design and Development(RD&D) activities in New and

Renewable Energy including solar energy in the country. Comprehensive guidelines for supporting and accelerating pace of Research, Design and Development leading to eventual manufacture and deployment of various Renewable Energy Systems including solar energy have been put in place. In this regard, about 600 RD&D projects have been financially supported in the aforesaid technology areas. During the 10th Five Year Plan period an expenditure of Rs. 72.65 crore has been incurred on research and development in New and Renewable Energy. An amount of Rs. 600 crore has been tentatively allocated for Research, Design and Development in New and Renewable Energy for the 11th Five Year Plan. The Ministry has launched some new schemes in addition to implementation of ongoing schemes to encourage large scale use of solar energy in the country during the 11th Five Year Plan Period. The new schemes include 'Development of Solar Cities' and 'Demonstration Programme on MW size Grid Solar Power Generation'. In addition, Research and Development thrust areas for solar and other New and Renewable Energy Technologies for the 11th Five Year Plan period have also been identified and publicized through newspaper and website advertisements for further intensifying research and technology development in this area. Promotional measures taken by the Government and other associated agencies include publicity and awareness campaigns, amendment of building bye-laws for making the use of solar water heaters mandatory in certain categories of buildings, rebate in property tax/ electricity tariff to the users of solar water heaters, etc. In addition, various other types of fiscal and financial incentives are proposed to continue to be provided for promoting the use of various solar energy systems and devices in the country during the Eleventh Plan. This information was given by the Minister of State for New and Renewable Energy, Shri Vilas Muttemwar, in a written reply to a question by Shri N.R.Govindarajar in the Rajya Sabha today.

6756. (17-3-2008) NEW DELHI : The Sarva Shiksha Abhiyan (SSA) programme is being implemented in all districts of the country to achieve the goal of universalisation of elementary education in a time bound manner, in a mission mode. Consequently since the launch of SSA all the out of school children in the 6-14 age group in the country (who numbered 320 lakh in 2001-02), have been brought in the ambit of elementary education except 75.97 lakh out-of-school children (as on 31.03.2007), who represent the difficult to reach category. Central Budget support of Rs. 10,671 Crore was provided in Budget Estimates 2007-08 for implementation of SSA. This was enhanced to Rs. 13,171 crore in the Revised Estimates 2007-08. An amount of Rs.11,336.38 crore has already been released to States/UTs as on 10.03.2008. Cumulative achievements made for key targets under SSA up to 31.12.2007 are given at Annexure. Under SSA programme 11.32 lakh teachers have been sanctioned up to 2007-08 against which 8.80 lakh teachers have been recruited till 31.12.2007. This has led to improvement in national average of Pupil Teacher Ratio (PTR) from 38:1 in 2005-06 to 36:1 in 2006-07 at primary level & from 34:1 to 32:1 at upper primary level in the corresponding period. This information was given by the Minister of State for Human Resource Development Shri M.A.A. Fatmi in a written reply in Rajya Sabha today.

6757. (17-3-2008) NEW DELHI : The Union Minister of Shipping, Road Transport and Highways, Thiru T.R. Baalu has approved a total sum of Rs. 401.12 lakh for road improvement works at National Highway-208 of Kollam-Thirumangalam Road in the state of Tamil Nadu. An amount of Rs. 297.02 lakh has been approved for strengthening the stretch between Kottaivasal and Puliyari in Tirunelveli district in Tamil Nadu on NH-208. This road is an important National Highway of interstate connectivity. It starts from Kollam (Kerala State) and passes through many important towns like Shengottah, Tenkasi, Sivagiri, Rajapalayam and terminates at Thirumangalam. It also connects two important tourism centres of Coutrallam and Madurai. The riding surface of the road was badly damaged during the monsoon season and cracks are developed and signs of distress are noticed in this stretch. Hence, it has become necessary to strength this stretch. An amount of Rs 94.98 lakh has been approved for reconstruction of minor bridges in Vasudevanallur and Sivagiri of NH-208 in Thirunelveli district. The minor bridges in this stretch are narrow and are in damaged condition. It is very difficult to pass over heavy vehicular traffic. Therefore, the reconstruction the bridges has been approved. An amount of Rs. 29.12 lakh has also been approved for improvement of Y-Junction located at Chintamani Junction near Puliyangudi of NH-208 in Thirunelveli district. The traffic intensity in this road is very heavy and the vehicles find it very difficult to negotiate this portion which is located on an acute curve. Hence, it becomes absolute necessary to improve the junction.

6758. (17-3-2008) NEW DELHI : The Railways have generated Rs. 42696.22 crore of revenue earnings from freight traffic during the first eleven months (*i.e.* April 2007-February 2008) of the current financial year 2007-08 as compared to Rs. 37648.87 crore during the corresponding period last year, registering an increase of 13.41 per cent. Railways carried 714.25 million tonnes of freight traffic during April 2007-February 2008 as compared to 655.35 million tonnes carried during the corresponding period last year, reflecting an increase of 8.99 per cent. The Net Tonne Kilo Metres (NTKM) went up from 429093 million during the months of April 2006-February 2007 to 461368 million during April 2007-February 2008, with an increase of 7.52 per cent. The earnings from freight traffic during the month of February 2008 was Rs. 4404.22 crore, compared to Rs. 3571.62 crore during the corresponding period last year showing an increase of 23.31 per cent. Railways carried 70.54 million tonnes of freight traffic during the month of February 2008 as compared to 61.67 million tonnes of freight traffic during the corresponding period last year, registering an increase of 14.38 per cent. The Net Tonne Kilo Metres (NTKM) went up from 39880 million during the month of February 2007 to 45936 million during February 2008, showing an increase of 15.19 per cent. Of the total earnings during the month of February 2008, Rs. 1610.94 crore came from transportation of 29.31 million tonnes of coal, followed by

Rs. 748.34 crore from 11.96 million tonnes of iron ore, Rs. 365.56 crore from 3.84 million tonnes of foodgrains, Rs. 358.19 crore from 7.09 million tonnes of cement, Rs. 266.43 crore from 3.16 million tonnes of petroleum oil and lubricant (POL), Rs. 238.64 crore from 2.29 million tonnes of iron & finished steel, Rs. 179.35 crore from 2.71 million tonnes of fertilizers, Rs. 172.19 crore from 2.31 million tones of container service, Rs. 69.52 crore from 1.01 million tonnes of raw material for steel plants except iron ore and Rs. 395.06 crore from 6.86 million tonnes of other goods.

6759. (17-3-2008) NEW DELHI : The Congress Party would like to endorse, reinforce and reiterate strongly the concern of the Central government in respect of the distressing situation in Tibet. As you are aware, the Central government has spoken through its spokespersons, it has spoken through the Hon'ble Foreign Minister in the Lok Sabha and the Congress Party wishes to repeat and put on record first, the concern about violence expressed, second, the unsettled situation in the entire region, third, the deaths of innocent persons, emphasis added, fourth, the dire necessity to take recourse to non-violent means to bring peace and stability in that autonomous region of China. The Congress Party associates with each of those concerns, adopt those concerns and hopes and wishes that a better and more stable situation will prevail there at the earliest possible. There is a limit to the hypocrisy and the opportunism of the BJP, of the leader of the opposition in the BJP. The leader of the opposition, Shri Advani, in a remarkable, unprovoked statement has accused the Congress Party of promoting corruption. This is truly amazing because Shri Advani does not give a single specific example or instance. Indeed for four long years no such credible or specific example, with facts has been furnished by the entire opposition. And this sudden unprovoked attack on a false issue comes by no less a person than the deputy prime minister of a government which established new milestones and scaled new heights as far as corruption was concerned. It was the NDA government which made catch-words and by-words out of Tehelka which was not a mere allegation but a capturing on candid camera about no less than the president of that ruling party itself. Shri Advani has forgotten that apart from his own party and its president, one of the principal supporting parties, their president Smt. Jaya Jaitley was also captured on camera. No less than the defence minister of the NDA is embroiled in extremely serious allegations, including the Barak deal. There is the HUDCO scam and there are so many of them it is too long to list. And yet Shri Advani's party has the audacity to talk of corruption and its promotion by the UPA or the Congress Party. It is obvious that he needs to do his home work better, his research better. Those who understand know very well the difference between night and day for example, as far as the PMO is concerned, they know and understand the nepotistic allegations and ambience and activities of the then PMO or the roles which the relatives played in that PMO and the comparison, for example only, I am giving with the current PMO. This is nothing but a sad and sorry, a pitiable example of ulta chor kotwal ko dante. It is hypocrisy at its worst, it is opportunism at its worst, apart from being totally baseless. To a question that your government is in power for four years, what action has your government taken? Shri Singhvi said first, you must continue to make the distinction and not forget the distinction between the accused and the prosecutor. You are now talking about the supposed inaction by the prosecutor. There is a difference. Second, as far as we are concerned, and perhaps you are not aware that the CBI, to whom the Barak case has been entrusted, is in an advanced stage. Charges are being filed and arrests have been made. Unlike those who break the law in the previous government we believe in following the law and prosecuting them. And as far as Tehelka is concerned they not only broke the law and were recorded in camera while talking of corruption. Later a cover up operation was started by the same NDA government to compound the felony and a commission was established which was captured on camera. For five long years no FIR was filed. Today proceedings have started, FIRs have been filed. To a question that Shri Advani has also accused the Nehru/Gandhi family of appropriating the Congress Party and treating it as family fiefdom, what is your reaction? Shri Singhvi said is it surprising? It is Shri Advani and his party which have fought elections on these issues and have done everything possible to mislead the public. They forget that each of these are validated by huge democratic majorities and electoral verdicts. It reflects nothing but his and his party's frustrations and animus against individuals. To a question that leaving aside the Barak scam there are so many other scams, what about them? Shri Singhvi said different actions are being taken in different fora. There is a case pending about HUDCO in the Supreme Court, there is a Barak investigation going on. In Tehelka case only after the Commissions were over action could be taken over the ATR. But do not forget the five years of obfuscation, of stalling, of delay and obstruction with the previous government. To a question that you are accusing the NDA of buying Barak what about your government and what about the CAG report? Shri Singhvi said we have accused nobody of anything. It is a case of the pot calling the kettle black because they are accusing us of corruption with these incidents. As far as your allegations are concerned they are in the realm of some speculation. And as far as the CAG report is concerned it has not yet passed a final discussion. There is an Act of CAG let that report be discussed after which action will be taken. To a question that Shri Sitaram Yechuri has alleged that your government is responsible for BSNL not fulfilling its duty in Tamil Nadu? Shri Singhvi said it's a democratic country, it's a democratic parliament and Shri Yechuri is entitled to air his views and that doesn't mean that the Congress Party or the UPA agrees with his views.

6760. (17-3-2008) NEW DELHI : The Ministry of Tribal Affairs has formulated a draft National Tribal Policy in order to address the issues concerning tribals *viz.* lower Human Development Index, poor infrastructure, diminishing control over the natural resource base, persistent threats of eviction from their natural habitat, exclusion from mainstream society, inequality in distribution of wealth and opportunities, non-empowerment, and inadequate implementation of Constitutional provisions, and to ensure their active and informed participation in development. After extensive consultation with various stakeholders, the final draft of Policy was placed before the Union Cabinet for approval on 31st May 2007. The Union Cabinet has referred it to a Group of Ministers for harmonization with the National Rehabilitation Policy. The Policy is yet to be finalized. This was stated by Shri P.R. Kyndiah, Minister for Tribal Affairs in a reply to a question by Shri Kanjibhai Patel in Rajya Sabha today.

6761. (17-3-2008) NEW DELHI : In order to prohibit child marriages and to make the provisions of the Act more effective and punishment more stringent for offenders, a new legislation 'The Prohibition of Child Marriage Act, 2006' has been enforced w.e.f. 1.11.2007. This was stated by Smt. Renuka Chowdhury, Minister for Women and Child Development in a reply to a question by Shri Abu Asim Azmi in Rajya Sabha today. She further added that the Child Marriage Restraint Act, 1929 is repealed with the enforcement of the said Act. As per the said Act, the marriageable age for girls is 18 years and for boys 21 years. Enhancement in punishments for male adults marrying a child and persons performing, abetting, promoting, attending a child marriage with imprisonment up to two years and fine up to one lakh rupees as well as appointment of Child Marriage Prohibition Officers in each State/UT and also awareness generation and advocacy measures which are continuously being undertaken by the Ministry of Women and Child Development will help in prohibiting child marriages, she added.

6762. (17-3-2008) NEW DELHI : To fulfil the commitments towards welfare of tribals, the Government enacted the Scheduled Tribes and Other Traditional Forest Dwellers (Recognition of Forest Rights) Act. The Rules framed under this Act have also been notified recently. The Act and the Rules are meant for recognition and vesting of forest rights in the forest-dwelling Scheduled Tribes and other traditional forest dwellers. The major rights that are granted under the Act include, the right to cultivate forest land to the extent under occupation, the right to own, collect, use and dispose of minor forest produce, rights inside forests like grazing etc. which are traditional and customary. The Act enjoins upon these beneficiaries the duties for protecting wild life, forest and their bio-diversity also. This was stated by Shri P.R. Kyndiah in a reply to a question by Shri Praveen Rashtrapal in Rajya Sabha today. He further added that the Ministry is also implementing a number of development programmes both in the Central Sector and Centrally Sponsored Sector for the welfare and upliftment of Scheduled Tribes and for the development of the areas where Scheduled tribes reside, he added.

6763. (17-3-2008) NEW DELHI : The Ministry of Tribal Affairs launched a new initiative in the year 2005-06 for the development of forest villages under Special

Central Assistance to Tribal Sub Plan (SCA to TSP), under which infrastructure work relating to basic services and facilities, *viz.* approach roads, healthcare, primary education, minor irrigation, rainwater harvesting, drinking water, sanitation, community halls, etc. and activities related to livelihood are taken up for implementation. Under the programme, the Ministry of Tribal Affairs has so far sanctioned and released Rs. 45,924.71 lakh for 2,388 forest villages/ habitations spread in 11 States. In addition, the scheme of Grant-in-Aid to State Tribal Development Cooperative Corporations (STDCCs) for Minor Forest Produce (MFP) operations aims at ensuring remunerative prices to tribals engaged in the collection of MFP. Further, the Scheduled Tribes and Other Traditional Forest Dwellers (Recognition of Forest Rights) Act, 2006, enacted by the Parliament, has been notified for operation with effect from 31.12.2007. The Act seeks to recognize and vest certain forest rights in forest dwelling Scheduled Tribes and other traditional forest dwellers who have been residing in such forests for generations but whose rights could not be recorded to ensure (a) tenurial security, providing them relief against the physical and psychological alienation from land belonging to them; (b) livelihood, in terms of agriculture and ownership of minor forest produce, including right to collect, use, and dispose the same; and (c) traditional and customary rights. This was stated by Shri P.R. Kyndiah, Minister of Tribal Affairs in a reply to a question by Shri Jai Parkash Aggarwal in Rajya Sabha today.

6764. (17-3-2008) NEW DELHI : The Government of West Bengal has already completed resuscitation of the river for a length of 24.3 K.M. within Indian Territory in the district of North 24 Parganas at a cost of Rs. 24.88 Crore (Approx.). For the balance portion of approximate 20 km. length, from Angrail BSF Bridge to Kalanchi BSF Bridge, which forms common border between India and Bangladesh, Government of West Bengal prepared a scheme amounting to Rs. 23.59 crore for desilting/dredging of river Ichhamati for better drainage and flood management. As the river Ichhamati forms the international border between India and Bangladesh, the matter has already been taken up by Government of India with Bangladesh during 36th meeting of Indo-Bangladesh Joint Rivers Commission (JRC) held at Dhaka in September, 2005 to work out the modalities for undertaking desilting/dredging work. A joint field visit by Ministers of Water Resources of both the countries (India and Bangladesh) was also undertaken in September, 2006 to assess situation on the ground. This information was given by the Minister of State for Water Resources, Shri Jai Prakash Narayan Yadav in response to a question by Shri Ajoy Chakraborty in the Lok Sabha today.

6765. (17-3-2008) NEW DELHI : The average annual precipitation is estimated as 4000 Billion Cubic Metre (BCM) in the country. After accounting for the natural process of evaporation etc., the average annual water availability in the country is assessed as 1869 BCM. Owing to topographic, hydrological and other constraints, the utilizable water is assessed as 1123 BCM. With a view to augment the utilizable water resources, various measures such as utilization of surplus flood water by transfer to water short area through inter-linking of rivers, rainwater harvesting and ground water recharge have been envisaged. This information was given by the Minister of State for Water Resources, Shri Jai Prakash Narayan Yadav in response to a question by Shri Adhir Chowdhury in the Lok Sabha today.

6766. (17-3-2008) NEW DELHI : The Government of India has laid due emphasis on the Irrigation Sector. The National Common Minimum Programme (NCMP) states that "UPA Government will ensure that public investment in irrigation is stepped up in a significant manner at the very earliest". The NCMP further states that "Irrigation will receive the highest investment priority and all on-going projects will be completed according to strict time schedule". An outlay of Rs.2,32,311 crore has been provided for the irrigation, command area development & water management and flood control in the XI Plan against the X Plan outlay of Rs.95,743 crore. Water being a State subject, the projects for irrigation development are conceived, planned and implemented by the State Government as per their own priority. The States submit the proposals for seeking central assistance under Accelerated Irrigation Benefit Programme (AIBP). This information was given by the Minister of State for Water Resources, Shri Jai Prakash Narayan Yadav in response to a question by Shri Nand Kumar Sai, Shri Kishanbhai V. Patel and Shri Sugrib Singh in the Lok Sabha today.

6767. (17-3-2008) NEW DELHI : The average annual water availability in the country is assessed as 1869 billion cubic metre (BCM) but the utilizable water is estimated to be about 1123 BCM. Full utilization of all the available water is not possible primarily due to topographic, hydrological and other constraints. With a view to augment the utilizable water resources, various measures such as utilization of surplus flood water by transfer to water short area through inter-linking of rivers, rainwater harvesting and ground water recharge have been envisaged. This information was given by the Minister of State for Water Resources, Shri Jai Prakash Narayan Yadav in response to a question by Shri Raghunath Jha in the Lok Sabha today.

6768. (17-3-2008) NEW DELHI : Variable rates are being charged by some States for water supply from State owned tubewells for agricultural purpose as per information available. Ministry of Water Resources has not constituted the "Expert Committee to rationalize the water charges for agricultural purposes in various parts of the country". However, the Planning Commission constituted an Expert Group headed by Member, Planning Commission on 'Ground Water Management and Ownership'. The Expert Group has inter-alia suggested measures for creating incentives for more efficient energy and water use. This information was given by the Minister of State for Water Resources, Shri Jai Prakash Narayan Yadav in response to a question by Shri Ravichandran Sippiparai in the Lok Sabha today.

6769. (17-3-2008) NEW DELHI : During the last three years the Government has taken various steps to develop and promote use of alternative fuels like ethanol, bio-diesel and hydrogen for transport applications. The Ministry of Petroleum and Natural Gas (MoP&NG) has mandated the use of 5% Ethanol Blended Petrol (EBP), subject to commercial viability in the entire country except North-Eastern States, Jammu & Kashmir, Andaman & Nicobar Islands and Lakshdweep with effect from 1st November 2006. As a result, release of 5% EBP has commenced at all locations in 15 States and 4 Union Territories. The Government has further decided that since 9th October 2007, 5% blending of ethanol with petrol will be mandatory and 10% blending will be optional and thereafter mandatory from October 2008. The modalities for implementation are being worked by the MoP&NG in consultation with stakeholders. A broad based programme for research & development, production and utilization of bio-diesel is under implementation by different Ministries. The Ministry of New and Renewable Energy (MNRE) has prepared a Draft National Policy on Bio-fuels. Under its ongoing Research, Development and Demonstration Programmes, MNRE has supported field trials of different blends of bio-diesel in diesel cars, use of hydrogen as fuel in motorcycles and three-wheelers and introduction of hydrogen-compressed natural gas (CNG) blends in different vehicles. In addition, support is also being provided for development & promotion of battery operated vehicles. This information was given by the Minister of State for New and Renewable Energy, Shri Vilas Muttemwar, in a written reply to a question by Shri S. Anbalagan in the Rajya Sabha today.

6770. (17-3-2008) NEW DELHI : An agreement was signed between Department of Posts and Centurion Bank of Punjab here today to provide foreign exchange services to the public. Although the Department has full fledged money changing licence this is the first time that the Department is entering the foreign exchange market. To start with the foreign exchange services is to be run as a pilot project covering the 31 Post Offices spread across 23 large cities, towns and villages in 11 States. The project will facilitate both the encashment of foreign exchange and transfer of money in foreign currency. While the main foreign exchange business will be operated by the Centurion Bank of Punjab, the Department of Posts officials will operationalise the scheme after training imparted by the Bank. An agreement was signed today by Shri J. Panda of the Department of Posts and Shri Sudarshan Motwani of Centurion Bank of Punjab in the presence of Shri Anil Jaggia, Chief Operating Officer of the Bank and Shri I.M.G. Khan, Secretary, Department of Posts launching the services. Speaking after the launch of the project Shri Anil Jaggia described this project as "one more step towards financial inclusion of our rural population". Depending on the success of the pilot project the bank hopes to reach out this scheme to thousands of cities and towns across the country. The select Post Offices will be hubs around which the bank hopes to sensitize rural population about the liberalized foreign exchange norms. Shri I.M.G. Khan, Secretary, Posts emphasized the initiatives taken by the Department of Posts to leverage the great strengths which lies in the network of Post Offices and the knowledge of people by postal departmental staff. He said with the induction of the new technology plan and the strengths available with the Postal Services they would be able to open up partnerships with all types of organizations which will be of great benefit to the people.

6771. (17-3-2008) NEW DELHI : To attract corporate/private investment in renewable energy sector, the Government is providing a mix of fiscal and financial incentives that include capital/ interest subsidy, accelerated depreciation, nil/ concessional excise and customs duties. Further benefit under Section 80-1A of Income Tax Act 1961 is available to undertakings setup for the generation or generation and distribution of Renewable power in India. This apart, preferential tariff for grid interactive renewable power is being given in most potential States. The grid-interactive power installed capacity from renewable energy sources such as wind, biomass, solar and small hydro in the country at the end of the 10th Plan, *i.e.*, upto 31.3.2007 was 10,250 MW which has reached 11,447 MW as on 31.01.08. A capacity addition of 14,000 MW from renewable energy sources is proposed during the 11th Plan. This information was given by the Minister of State for New and Renewable Energy, Shri Vilas Muttemwar, in a written reply to a question by Shri Tariq Anwar in the Rajya Sabha today.

6772. (17-3-2008) NEW DELHI : Recently the Ministry of New and Renewable Energy has announced a demonstration programme to support mega watt size grid interactive solar power generation projects, up to a maximum capacity of 50 MW, in the country. Any registered company, as project developer, would be eligible to set up solar power projects on build, own and operate basis. Proposal from each project developer with a maximum aggregate capacity of 5 MW, either through a single project or multiple projects of a minimum capacity of 1 MW each, would be considered. A maximum of 10 MW capacity solar power generation projects would be considered in a State. Preference would be given to the projects from the States where the State Electricity Regulatory Commissions (SERCs) have announced or are in the process of announcing tariff for solar power. For the projects approved and commissioned by 31st December, 2009, the Ministry will provide generation based incentive up to Rs.12 per kWh for solar photovoltaic power and Rs.10 per kWh for solar thermal power fed to the grid by the solar power project developers, after taking in to account the tariff provided by the SERC or the utility. The Ministry will also provide incentive to the concerned utility and the State Nodal Agency, which will be involved in implementation and monitoring of the projects in that State. This information was given by the Minister of State for New And Renewable Energy, Shri Vilas Muttemwar, in a written reply to a question by Shri Amar Singh in the Rajya Sabha today.

6773. (17-3-2008) NEW DELHI : Under the Allocation of Business Rules, the Ministry of New & Renewable Energy has been given the responsibility of setting up of a National Bio-fuel Development Board. The proposal for setting up of the Board including its draft Terms of Reference and composition has been submitted for necessary approvals. The Ministry of Agriculture is providing subsidy through National Oilseeds and Vegetable Oils Development (NOVOD) Board to the farmers, Non-Governmental Organizations (NGOs), individuals etc. for production of Tree Borne Oilseeds (TBOs), including bio-fuel crops, under the Integrated Development of Tree Borne Oilseeds Scheme. Under this scheme, 30% credit linked subsidy is being provided, which is linked with 50% term loan to be taken from bank, and 20% beneficiary share in the form of land, labour etc. Further, the Ministry of Rural Development has provided financial assistance to the tune of Rs.49.00 crore to 9 identified States in 2005-06 and Rs.49.50 crore to 15 States in 2006-07 for the purpose of raising jatropha/pongamia seedlings and plantation of the same under the ongoing States/Central Sector area development programmes. This information was given by the Minister of State for New And Renewable Energy, Shri Vilas Muttemwar, in a written reply to a question by Shri Tariq Anwar in the Rajya Sabha today.

6774. (17-3-2008) NEW DELHI : Ministry of Finance had raised some queries on issues, inter-alia, related to usage of dual technology spectrum under the existing telecom access services licence(s) and necessary information has been provided to the Ministry of Finance. This information was given by the Minister of State for Communications and Information Technology, Dr. Shakeel Ahmad in a written reply to a unstarred question in the Lok Sabha today. Telecom service providers holding Unified Access Services (UAS) licence or Cellular Mobile Telecom Services (CMTS) licence as well as registered Cable TV operators can provide IPTV services without requiring any further licence subject to certain conditions. Moreover the Minister said that the "Committee on allocation of spectrum in a practicable and scientific manner" has given certain recommendations and the Government has taken a decision on the Report of the Committee. Spectrum to the CMTS/UAS licensees is allotted as per the relevant provisions of their licence agreement and eligibility criteria for additional spectrum, subject to availability. The present criteria for allocation of additional spectrum has been issued after review in January, 2008.

6775. (17-3-2008) NEW DELHI : Shri Alok Rawat took charge as Secretary, Union Public Service Commission, here today. Before joining UPSC, he was Principal Secretary, Planning and Development cum Development Commissioner cum Principal Secretary (PIME-NDC), Govt. of Sikkim, since June, 2005. Shri Rawat joined the IAS in 1977 and belongs to the Sikkim cadre. He has held diverse assignments in his 30 years of rich administrative experience. From June 2000 to June 2005, Shri Alok Rawat was Joint Secretary in the Ministry of Road Transport and Highways, Govt. of India. He has also worked as Joint Secretary in the Ministry of Defence, Govt. of India. Shri Rawat held various posts in Govt. of Sikkim, including Resident Commissioner, Commissioner cum Secretary,

Information & Public Relations, and Finance Secretary, as also other district-level field postings. Shri Rawat did his graduation in Physics in the year 1974 from Lucknow University. In 1989, he did his post graduation in Development Studies from United Kingdom and in 1997 he did a one-year course on National Security.

6776. (17-3-2008) NEW DELHI : Union Public Service Commission (UPSC) has declared the results of the Civil Services (Main) Examination, 2007 held by the UPSC in October-November, 2007. The result includes the roll numbers of the candidates who have qualified for Personality Test for selection to the Indian Administrative Service, Indian Foreign Service, Indian Police Service and other Central Services (Group 'A' and Group 'B'). The result is available on the UPSC's website: http://www.upsc.gov.in. The candidature of these candidates is provisional subject to their being found eligible in all respects. The candidates would be required to produce the original certificates in support of their claims relating to age, educational qualifications, community, physical disability etc. at the time of the Personality Test. They are, therefore, advised to keep the said prescribed certificates ready. Personality Test of these candidates would commence from 31st March, 2008. The date and time of Personality Test is being intimated to the qualified candidates individually. The date and time of Personality Test in respect of candidates fixed for P.T. from 31.03.2008 to 09.04.2008 would be displayed on the Commission's Website on 25th March, 2008 onwards and in respect of remaining P.T. dates, the same would be displayed on 2nd April, 2008 onwards. The candidates who do not receive communication with regard to their Personality Test by the dates indicated above, should immediately contact the office of the Commission through letter or on Phone Nos. 23385271, 23381125, 23098543 or Fax No. 011-23385345, 011-23387310, 011-23384472. The Personality Tests would be held in the Office of the Union Public Service Commission, Dholpur House, Shahjahan Road, New Delhi-110069. No request for change in the date and time of the Personality Test intimated to the candidates will be entertained under any circumstances. The candidates are advised to intimate change in their address, if any, to the Commission immediately through letter or Fax at Telephone numbers indicated above. The mark-sheets of candidates who have not qualified, shall be put on the Commission's Website within one month from the date of publication of this result and would remain available on the Website for a period of 60 days.

6777. (17-3-2008) NEW DELHI : The National Policy on Education 1986 (as modified in 1992) recognizes the need to develop a system of education to express and promote the country's unique socio cultural identity and to meet the challenges of the times. Education has been recognized as fundamental to all round development, contributing to national cohesion, scientific temper and independence of mind and spirit. The National System of Education envisages a common educational structure (10+2+3) and is based on a national curricular framework.

6778. (17-3-2008) NEW DELHI : As per the latest available information, there are 2,55,696 cases pending in the Punjab and Haryana High Court as on 30th September, 2007. As reported by the High Court of Punjab & Haryana, there were 2,65,072 cases pending as on 30.06.2007 out of which 68,114 cases were pending for that 10 years and 66,473 cases for less than 10 years but more than 5 years. Government has taken several steps including deciding to increase the strength of Judges in the High Courts. Government is implementing a scheme for computerization of District & Subordinate Courts, which includes upgradation of the information and communication technology infrastructure of the High Courts. Alternative modes of disposal including mediation, negotiation and arbitration have been encouraged. With a view to ensuring expeditious disposal of cases, the Civil Procedure Code has been amended, inter alia, limiting the number of adjournments that can be given to a party. Classification and Grouping of cases involving common question of law is also done in the High Courts for speedy disposal of pending cases. This information was given by Minister of Law and Justice, Shri H. R. Bhardwaj in written reply to a question in Rajya Sabha today.

6779. (17-3-2008) NEW DELHI : The All India Council for Technical Education (AICTE) has notified certain regulations vide Notification No. 37-3/Legal/AICTE/2005 dated 16.5.2005 for regulating entry and operation of foreign universities/institutions in India for imparting technical education. A list of institutions running technical education programmes with foreign collaboration without AICTE approval is given in the Annexure. The above list has been displayed on the AICTE's website www.aicte.ernet.in for information of students and the general public. Public Notices have also been issued in leading newspapers cautioning students against these unapproved institutions. This information was given by the Minister of State for Human Resource Development Smt. D. Purandeswari in a written reply in Rajya Sabha today.

6780. (18-3-2008) NEW DELHI : Annual Plan of Goa for the year 2008-09 was approved in a meeting, here today, between the Deputy Chairman, Planning Commission, Shri Montek Singh Ahluwalia and the Chief Minister of Goa, Shri Digambar Kamat, here today. The Annual Plan size was agreed at Rs.1737.65 crores, which includes additional Central assistance of Rs.35 crores for projects of special assistance to the State. Deputy Chairman, Planning Commission, Mr. Ahluwalia in his remarks said the State had impressive achievements both in social sector and economy. He said the economy of the State has shown a trend growth rate of over 10 per cent per annum which clearly shows that the State is ready to leap forward to the next stage of development and aim at achieving higher standards of development and social justice during Eleventh Plan period. He said the State has been having growing emphasis on public private partnership in all sectors of infrastructure and provision of infrastructure was rightly priority of the government. He said emphasis should continue on exploiting the opportunities arising from tourism and mining industries. Agro-tourism, agro processing and organic farming needs more focused attention. He said this would supplement tourism industry while generating employment. Mr. Ahluwalia said the social indicators of the State like literacy, birth rate, death rate, infant mortality rate are very impressive. Even per capita income of the State is not only highest in the country but almost three times the average of the country. Attention was drawn to significant gender gap and high drop out rates at secondary level of education. Quality of education also needs focused attention. The State government was also complemented for setting up one of the best health care infrastructure including network of hospitals both in urban and rural areas. Briefing the Commission on the performance of the State and focus of development during Eleventh Plan, Mr. Digambar Kamat said the focus would continue on social sector with increased participation of private sector. He said against a growth rate of 6.9 per cent reached during Ninth Plan period, the State has recorded a growth of 8.4 per cent in Tenth Plan. It would aim at a growth of 12.1 per cent in the Eleventh Plan which would include agricultural growth of 7.7 per cent, industry at 15.7 per cent and services at 9 per cent. Women self-help groups are being encouraged to take up income generating activities. To achieve higher growth rate in industry, food processing & agro based industries, IT & IT enabled services pharmaceuticals & bio-tech industries and tourism would be given priority. He said the State government would work to make Goa a modal State with high focus on knowledge and tourism. To facilitate better health facilities, a universal medical scheme would be introduced shortly. He requested Planning Commission for additional support in improving sewerage system and road network to meet pressures on the system due to increased flow of tourists.

6781. (18-3-2008) NEW DELHI : A Turkish delegation of businessmen and representatives of major construction companies, led by Shri Kursat Tuzmen, State Minister for Foreign Trade of Turkey called on Shri T.R. Baalu, the Minister for Shipping, Road Transport and Highway here today. The meeting was held in a cordial atmosphere. Both the Ministers exchanged views regarding business opportunities available in shipping, ports and road transport sectors of their respective countries. Shri Baalu stated that there is a good possibility of development of chemical transportation by sea between India and Turkey, which should be explored by both the countries. He further said that general cargo/container trade business has a good potential for trade between the two countries. Shri Baalu urged the Turkish Minister to ask the Turkish shipyards to participate in the global tenders floated by Shipping Corporation of India for acquisition of vessels.

6782. (18-3-2008) NEW DELHI : The Government is considering revising the foreign investment limits in various subsectors of Broadcasting. In her keynote address at CASBAA India Satellite Forum, Secretary (I&B) Smt. Asha Swarup said that we are of the opinion that the composite limits for FDI and FII, both direct and indirect can be kept at 74% in the case of infrastructure and platform services like teleports, DTH, HITS and satellite radio. Already 100% foreign investment is allowed in the case of non-News and current affairs channels and channels permitted under the Downlinking Policy. No changes are proposed in the 26% limit for News and current affairs channels and 49% for cable operators. On Conditional Access System (CAS), the Secretary said that the Government at present is in the process of analyzing the impact and success of the CAS implementation in the four metros so that appropriate lessons can be drawn for its further extension and if need be suitable improvements can be made in the present regime to make it more acceptable to stakeholders. The Government has since received three survey and evaluation reports on CAS. These studies were conducted by BECIL, IIMC and a consumer organization VOICE, she said. Smt. Swarup said, there is need for a better enforcement mechanism at the local level to ensure that pay channels are made available only in an encrypted format and violations if any at the level of MSOs and cable operators are punished and dealt with severely. The Government will welcome any suggestions on this issue. For improved penetration, the cost of set top boxes needs to be brought down and it has to be ensured that MSOs and cable operators ensure compliance to the quality of service regulations laid down by TRAI, she added. The Secretary remarked that the group on digitalization and introduction of CAS has selected fifty five cities which include all the cities with a million plus population, some cities located in the proximity of the cities to the existing CAS cities. It has also included all the State capitals, which would not come under any of the above criteria. The Group has also suggested a three-year roll out plan ending September 2011, for these fifty five cities. A sunset period for regulation especially w.r.t tariff regulation is also proposed by the group. The Government is actively considering the recommendation and has started in the action with stakeholders at its level. However it will take some time before a final view is taken on its applicability. She said, price cap in the CAS areas are not forever and can be reviewed at an appropriate time. The fact that there has been a substantial growth in the number of both free to air and pay channels with over 300 private channels now and about 80 more applications under consideration with applications not only from the existing but also new players is an indication that despite the tariff regime the business of broadcasting is lucrative. TRAI has also indicated that the need for regulation will go once effective competition develops with alternative modes of content availability so that consumer interest remains protected. She said that the attempt of the Government is to introduce new service providers to ensure effective competition and to create new avenues for investment and growth of the industry. On digitalization Smt. Swarup said that a national digitalization plan for India will have to be voluntary in all steps and will have to provide for simultaneous provision of analogue and digital service. Broadly speaking our aim should be to phase out analogue transmission by the end of the Twelfth Plan *i.e.* 2017, she said.

6783. (18-3-2008) NEW DELHI : The Government has introduced a bill in Lok Sabha on 20.03.2007 called "The Micro Financial Sector (Development and Regulation) Bill, 2007" to create environment friendly policy for micro-finance services in the country. The Bill is intended to provide a formal statutory framework for the promotion, development and regulation of the micro finance sector. As of now, there is no plan of the Government to establish any micro finance institution However, a large number of micro finance organisations in the private sector are operational across the country, including Telangana, and provide micro credit services to the disadvantaged sections of the population including artisans, craftsmen and agriculturists. This information was given by the Minister of State for Finance Shri Pawan Kumar Bansal in a written reply to a question in the Rajya Sabha today.

6784. (18-3-2008) NEW DELHI : As per extant guidelines, the interest rate on education loans upto Rs.4 lakh should not exceed the Benchmark Prime Lending Rate (BPLR) of the | banks and for loans above Rs.4 lakh it should not exceed BPLR+1 per cent. Certain features have been built into the education loan scheme to reduce the burden of interest on the student. There is a repayment holiday/ moratorium, during the period of the course plus one year or six months after getting a job, whichever is earlier. Furthermore, the interest is to be debited quarterly/half yearly on simple basis during the repayment holiday/ moratorium period to further ease the interest burden on the student. This information was given by the Minister of State for Finance Shri Pawan Kumar Bansal in a written reply to a question in the Rajya Sabha today.

6785. (18-3-2008) NEW DELHI : The Government of India has launched the National Food Security Mission (NFSM) and the Rashtriya Krishi Vikas Yojana (RKVY) with a view to rejuvenate agriculture and improve farm incomes. It is envisaged that these initiatives along with better implementation of some ongoing schemes, covering irrigation, agriculture credit, insurance, marketing and other inputs, will help in achieving a four per cent annual growth in agricultural sector during the Eleventh Five Year Plan The NFSM, a Centrally Sponsored Scheme, with an Eleventh Plan outlay of Rs.4,883 crore, aims at increasing food grains production of rice, wheat and pulses through area expansion and productivity enhancement; restoring soil fertility and productivity; creating employment opportunities; and enhancing farm level economy to restore confidence of farmers in the targeted districts of the country. The RKVY, with an allocation of Rs 25,000 crore for the Eleventh Five Year Plan, aims at incentivising the State Governments to increase public investment in agriculture and allied sectors and support focused interventions to reduce the yield gaps in important crops. In the proposal for the Union Budget 2008-09, the Government has announced a Scheme of debt waiver and debt relief for farmers which would cover all agricultural loans disbursed by scheduled commercial banks, regional rural banks and cooperative credit institutions up to March 31, 2007 and overdue as on December 31, 2007. The Government estimates that about 3 crore small and marginal farmers and about 1 crore other farmers will benefit from this scheme. The total value of proposed debt waiver and debt relief is estimated at around Rs.60,314 crore. This information was given by the Minister of State for Finance Shri Pawan Kumar Bansal in a written reply to a question in the Rajya Sabha today.

6786. (18-3-2008) NEW DELHI : The maximum limit of deposit in Monthly Income Scheme has been enhanced to Rs. 4.50 lakh in single account and Rs. 9.00 lakh in joint account with effect from 1st August, 2007. Apart from Monthly Income Scheme, the maximum limit of deposit/balance is applicable only to (i) Post Office Savings Accounts (ii) Public Provident Fund and (iii) Senior Citizens Savings Scheme. There is no upqer limit of deposit in respect of any other small savings scheme. Proposals for increasing the maximum limit of balance in Post Office Savings Account and Public Provident Fund were recently considered by the Government. Interest on Post Office Savings Account is exempt from the income-tax. This exemption was provided in the context of similar deduction under Section 80Lof Income Tax Act, 1961 for interest from savings account with a bank, which has been withdrawn from the assessment year 2006-07. Therefore, enhancement of deposit veiling for the Post Office Savings Accounts was not found feasible as it would have widened the disparity between the two and led to higher revenue loss. Similarly, as the interest accruing on deposits in Public Provident Fund accounts is exempt from the income-tax, enhancement in the maximum deposit limit was not found feasible for the reason that it would result in revenue loss. The Senior Citizens Savings Scheme was launched on 2nd August 2004. The maximum limit of deposit under the Scheme is Rs. 15 lakh in single/ joint account, which is considered adequate. This information was given by the Minister of State for Finance Shri Pawan Kumar Bansal in a written reply to a question in the Rajya Sabha today.

6787. (18-3-2008) NEW DELHI : The Screening Committee of Ministry of Information and Broadcasting has cleared 1616 (1184 for AIR and 432 for Doordarshan) vacancies for direct recruitment under Annual Direct Recruitment Plan (ADRP) till now. There is a shortage of specialized manpower in AIR and Doordarshan as no recruitment is taking place because the status of Prasar Bharati employees is under consideration of GOM. A few retired personnel have been engaged on contract basis for a limited period to ensure that important and specialized works of Prasar Bharati does not suffer. After clearance of the vacancies for direct recruitment by the Screening Committee under ADRP, Prasar Bharati has initiated action to fill up these vacancies at the earliest. This information was given by Shri P.R. Dasmunsi, Minister for Information and Broadcasting & Parliamentary Affairs in a written reply to a question in the Parliament today.

6788. (18-3-2008) NEW DELHI : Telecom Regulatory Authority of India (TRAI) has recommended that at least three channels excluding All India Radio (AIR) will be given to three different entities. Once this condition is met in any district, the existing operators/permission holder can bid for the remaining channels and may be declared successful for any channel where his bid is highest subject to the condition that maximum number of channels to a permission holder in the district will not be more than 50% of total channels in the district. TRAI has also recommended that FDI including Foreign Institutional Investment for FM Radio broadcasting permission holders may be enhanced to 26% from the present level of 20% for those who want to broadcast news and to 49% for those who do not opt for news broadcasting. Recommendations of TRAI have been received in the Government on 22.2.2008. A view has not been taken on them. This information was given by Shri P.R. Dasmunsi, Minister for Information and Broadcasting & Parliamentary Affairs in a written reply to a question in the Parliament today.

6789. (18-3-2008) NEW DELHI : The Government proposes to take action against tobacco and liquor companies indulging in 'surrogate' advertising in print, electronic and outdoor media. The Ministry of Information and Broadcasting has recently issued a Notification dated 25.02.2008 amending the Cable Television Networks Rules, 1994 to the effect that no advertisement shall be permitted which promotes directly or indirectly production, sale or consumption of cigarettes, tobacco products, wine, alcohol, liquor or other intoxicants. Failure to comply will entail action as per the provisions of the Cable Television Networks (Regulation) Act, 1995 and rules framed there-under. As far as the Press in India is concerned, the Press Council of India, a statutory autonomous body have laid norms for Journalistic Conduct. Article 13(2)(b) of the Press Council Act 1987 states that- No advertisement shall be published, which promotes directly or indirectly production, sale or consumption of cigarettes, tobacco products, wine, alcohol, liquor or other intoxicants. This information was given by Shri P.R. Dasmunsi, Minister for Information and Broadcasting & Parliamentary Affairs in a written reply to a question in the Parliament today.

6790. (18-3-2008) NEW DELHI : The names of NGOs and details of funds released during the last three years to these NGOs State-wise and Union Territory-wise under the scheme "Innovative and Experimental Education" of Sarva Shiksha Abhiyan by Govt. of India are annexed. Centres for Innovative & Experimental (I&E) projects were run by NGOs for covering hard to reach children in the age group 6 to 14 years for achievement of goals of Universalization of Elementary Education (UEE). No complaints regarding diversion/misutilization of funds by NGOs have been received during the last 3 years. This information was given by the Minister of State for Human Resource Development Shri M.A.A. Fatmi in a written reply in Lok Sabha today.

6791. (18-3-2008) NEW DELHI : The Vice President of India Shri Mohd Hamid Ansari will inaugurate the plenary session of the World Water Day function organised by the Ministry of Water Resources in Vigyan Bhawan here on 20th

March 2008. Prof. Saifuddin Soz, the Union Minister for Water Resources and Shri Jai Prakash Narayan Yadav, the Minister of State for Water Resources will address on the occasion. Important issues related to 'Integrated Water Resources Development and Management (IWRDM)' like water quality, water supply, health etc. will be discussed to facilitate combined discussions in the day long sessions of the function. Eminent experts and stakeholders in the field of Water Resources will participate with suggestion for firming up the strategies in the water sector. Ministry of Water Resources organized programmes on various issues concerning water sector in partnership with concerned Ministries of Government as well as Non-Government Organizations (NGOs) preceding the World Water Day. Workshops were organised on data base management, Ground Water Regulation and Management, Conjunctive use of Surface and Ground Water, Eco-system security, Technology transfer, investment in Water sector, Corporate social responsibility as well as civil society participation in the context of IWRDM. Many Resident Welfare Associations (RWAs) have been invited to participate in the programme to make the discussions broad based with the involvement of civil society. In pursuance of the United Nations General Assembly Resolution, 22nd March is observed every year as the World Water Day, however, this year the UN has decided to observe the World Water Day on 20th March 2008.

6792. (18-3-2008) NEW DELHI : Following is the full text of the Suo Motu Statement regarding Sarabjit Singh delivered by External Affairs Minister, Shri Pranab Mukherjee in the Lok Sabha today: "I rise to inform Hon'ble members of the issue of Sarabjit Singh, an Indian national in Pakistani custody facing a death sentence. The media have reported that his mercy petition has been turned down by the President of Pakistan. We have received no formal intimation of this from the Government of Pakistan. But according to press reports, the black warrant has been issued and the sentence will be carried out on 1st April 2008. Our High Commission in Islamabad has sought details from the Government of Pakistan. 2. The Supreme Court of Pakistan, in a judgement on 18 August 2005 had upheld award of death sentence to Sarabjit Singh for causing explosions at various places in Pakistan. At our instance, Consular access to Sarabjit Singh was provided by Government of Pakistan for the first time on August 30, 2005 to the Indian High Commission. Thereafter his national status was confirmed. A review petition against the death sentence was also filed in the Supreme Court of Pakistan. The petition was dismissed by the Supreme Court in March 2006. A mercy petition was thereafter filed with the President of Pakistan which now, according to news reports, has been turned down. Throughout this period, Government of India have continued to urge the Government of Pakistan to take a sympathetic and humanitarian view of this case. 3. Hon'ble Members are aware that since my January 2007 visit to Pakistan, both Governments have put in place certain institutional arrangements, including a new Agreement on Consular Access and a joint Judicial Committee, in order to facilitate the resolution of consular issues. A delegation of family members of missing Indian defence personnel was also able to visit Pakistan last year. These initiatives may lead to an improvement of the situation for our prisoners. 4. It is in this context and in the same spirit that we appeal to the Government of Pakistan to treat Sarabjit Singh's case with clemency on humanitarian grounds."

6793. (18-3-2008) NEW DELHI : The details of the schemes and programmes proposed to be implemented by the Ministry of Human Resource Development (Department of School Education & Literacy and Department of Higher Education) during XI Five Year Plan alongwith their allocations is annexed. Prior state's/union territories-wise allocations are not made. This information was given by the Minister of State for Human Resource Development Smt. D. Purandeswari in a written reply in Lok Sabha today.

6794. (18-3-2008) NEW DELHI : The Union Public Service Commission will hold the National Defence Academy and Naval Academy Examination (II), 2008 on 17th August, 2008 for admission to Army, Navy and Air Force Wings of NDA for 122nd Course and Naval Academy for 42nd 10+2 (Executive Branch) Course commencing from 30th June, 2009. For details regarding the, Syllabus and Scheme of the examination, Centres of examination, Guidelines for filling up application form etc. aspirants must consult the Detailed Notice of the examination published in the Employment News/Rozgar Samachar dated 15th March, 2008. In case of any guidance/information/clarification regarding their applications, candidature etc. candidates can contact UPSC's Facilitation Counter near 'C' gate of its campus in persons or over Telephone No. 011-23385271/011-23381125/011-23098543 on working days between 10.00 hrs. to 17.00 hrs. The Commission also has Website at address: http:/www.upsc.gov.in over which the candidates can obtain details of the examination as well as information about registration of their applications, venue of the examination and results etc.

6795. (18-3-2008) NEW DELHI : The Government has with immediate effect prohibited export of all edible oils. Notification No. 85 dated 17.3.2008 has been issued in this regard. It may be recalled that before the ban imposed by the above Notification, export of edible oils was free. But with the Notification No. 85 dated 17.3.2008 export of all edible oils has been prohibited with immediate effect. The ban imposed by Notification No. 85 dated 17.3.2008 will be applicable for a period of one (1) year from the date of Notification No. 85 dated 17.3.2008. Also, transitional arrangements allowed under Para 1.5 of Foreign Trade Policy, 2004-2009, shall not be applicable to the ban imposed vide Notification No. 85 dated 17.3.2008. Vide Notification No. 84 dated 17.3.2008, export of Basmati rice has also been allowed through the ports of Mundra and Pipavav in addition to ports notified earlier. Vide Notification No. 82 dated 5.3.2008, the Central Government had notified that export of both basmati and non-basmati will be allowed through the four (4) ports of Kandla, Kakinada, Kolkata and JNPT Mumbai only. Now the Government vide Notification No. 84 dated 17.3.2008 has allowed export of basmati rice through the ports of Mundra and Pipavav also. It may be clarified that export of Non-Basmati rice will not be allowed through the ports of Mundra and Pipavav. Directorate General of Foreign Trade (DGFT), Ministry of Commerce & Industry New Delhi, dated 18th March, 2008

6796. (18-3-2008) NEW DELHI : Shri Kamal Nath, Union Minister of Commerce and Industry, has invited the Turkish Companies to explore the Indian markets and make investments, especially in the infrastructure sector as it has the promise of sustained high levels of returns, and added that Indian companies are also committed to make investments in Turkey. This he said during the bilateral meeting with Mr. Kursad Tuzmen, Turkish State Minister for Foreign Trade, here today. Both sides agreed that India and Turkey could collaborate in R&D and their commercial spin-offs in the fields of bio-technology, nano-technology and information technology. The meeting was attended by Shri Ajay Shanker, Secretary (Industrial Policy & Promotion); Shri G.K. Pillai, Commerce Secretary and senior officials from the Ministry of Commerce and Industry and representatives from the industry. Indian investments in Turkey are in diverse sectors *viz.*, railway construction, electricity transmission, pipelines, consultancy services for earthquake emergency, hydro-carbon, CNG conversion and IT services. Turkish investments in India are in sectors of tourism & travel, home textile products, construction/ maintenance of roads etc. During the discussions, both sides agreed to strengthen the bilateral trade relationship particularly in the small & medium enterprises (SME) sector. Shri Kamal Nath stated that Indo-Turkish trade is now on the upswing and the bilateral trade has grown from US $ 1193 million in 2005-06 to US $ 1653 million during 2006-07. Both sides noted that considerable untapped opportunities remain and both countries are seriously working at exploiting this potential for growth. It is felt that B-2-B engagement would take the bilateral trade relationship to higher levels and government on both sides need to facilitate B-2-B engagement and act as catalyst. India's exports to Turkey largely consist of manmade yarn fabrics, made-ups, transport equipments, cotton yarn, fabrics, drugs & pharmaceuticals & fine chemicals, plastic & linoleum products etc. The main imports from Turkey are petroleum, crude products, machinery except electrical & electronics, inorganic chemicals, spices etc.

6797. (18-3-2008) NEW DELHI : With a view to create awareness in respect of conservation and efficient use of water, Ministry of Water Resources has sanctioned Farmers' Participatory Action Research Progammes (FPARPs) aimed at dissemination of technologies to increase yield and income per drop of water at an estimated cost of Rs. 24.4685 crores through 5000 demonstrations across 26 States/UTs. In addition to this, the scheme of artificial recharge to ground water through dugwells has been approved for implementation in the States of Tamil Nadu, Karnataka, Andhra Pradesh, Maharashtra, Gujarat, Madhya Pradesh and

Rajasthan. This information was given by the Minister of State for Water Resources, Shri Jai Prakash Narayan Yadav in response to a question by Shri Pyarelal Khandelwal in the Rajya Sabha today.

6798. (18-3-2008) NEW DELHI : Congress spokesman Dr. Shakeel Ahmed said that for the last two months since the start of school examinations there has been a spate of suicides by students reported in newspapers which is certainly a matter of concern. These incidents are not only happening in Delhi but throughout India. Yesterday this issue was raised in Parliament by our young MPs Sandeep Dikshit and Priya Dutt. The Congress Party wants that the people who are concerned with education should take cognizance of the growing incidence of suicides. They should see that the education does not put so much pressure on students which forces them to take such extreme steps. The Congress Party is concerned and expects that the educationists and other authorities in the field of education will take note of it. The other issue of concern is the rising prices. During the last few days prices of essential commodities have been on the rise and the Congress Party expresses its concern. The rise in prices depends on quite a few issues. The price of food grains in the international markets also reflects on the price rise. There is a shortage of food grains in the international markets resulting in rise in price rise globally. When the UPA government came to power at the Centre the price of oil per barrel at that time was 36 dollars per barrel and today the price of oil is a little more than 111 dollars per barrel. But the Finance Minister has hinted that we will take every action at our command in capping the prices of essential commodities. It is the Centre which bears the brunt whenever prices rise but the fact of the matter is that whenever prices in the international markets go up it does get reflected in the Indian markets as well. The states are also to blame for this. In states where there is hoarding involved and where the law enforcing agencies are lacking in their duties concerning this issue the Centre should not be blamed. The Finance Minister has committed that we will take all steps to control the price rise of essential commodities and we welcome this step. To a question that your Party is expressing concern could this be due to elections in Karnataka or are these crocodile tears? Dr. Ahmed said this is concerning "human tears" and we are showing our concern because the sufferer mostly is the last man of the society. To a question that for the last 3 years you have been harping on the price rise issue and that even after the working committee meetings nothing fruitful has emerged, is this not utter failure on the part of the government? Dr. Ahmed said I do not agree to what you are saying. If you go back about two or three months the inflation rate was less than 4%. It is said that when the growth rate is more than 6.5 and inflation rate is near about 4.5 then it is considered to be normal. About 3 months back the growth rate was 8.8 and 9% and according to the Economic Survey it was 8.8 and the inflation rate was less than 4%. Therefore you cannot say that nothing has happened. Recently it was about 5.1% and therefore the Congress Party has expressed its concern and we want the government to pay more attention towards this issue. To a question that there is a political vendetta against CPM-ruled states, there is meager supply of food grains to the PDS and that the budget by Shri Chidambaram is a failure, Dr. Ahmed said we totally disapprove the charge that there is a political vendetta against Kerala or any other state. Everybody in the country is praising the budget presented by Shri Chidambaram and according to us Shri Chidambaram is a successful Finance Minister. And as far as the question of less supply of food grains to the PDS is concerned the issue relates to lifting capacities, however we will have to look into the matter. To a question that BSNL is not being allowed by the government to function properly in Tamil Nadu, Dr. Ahmed said the government is trying to increase the share of the public sector companies *i.e.*, BSNL and MTNL and we have added more than 15 million new connections in the last two years. Hence there is not an iota of truth in this statement. Yesterday when I was replying to a question in the Lok Sabha I categorically stated that the government was trying to strengthen both BSNL and MTNL. There are some court cases pending and keeping this in mind we are totally committed for the growth of public sector companies. To a question that Shri Ram Vilas Paswan is fielding a candidate who is involved in the murder of Gulshan Kumar, can he be allowed to contest the elections? Dr. Ahmed said that in Bihar we have decided to support Shri Ram Vilas Paswan's candidate. It was the print media that reported that he was involved in the murder and was acquitted. And if a person is acquitted in a criminal case, he/she is free to contest any election. To a question that Taslima Nasreen has accused Shri Pranab Mukherjee of pressurizing her to leave this country and blocking all medication to her and that she described it as a chamber of death and also not allowing her to go to Kolkatta to pack her bags to go abroad, your reaction? Dr. Ahmed said we disapprove the charges made by her. She was kept in India as a guest for so long with the permission of the government. The government cannot force any state to allow any person who poses law and order problems to allow that person to continue to live in the country.

6799. (18-3-2008) NEW DELHI : The Ministry of Water Resources has set up a Sub-Committee to formulate a policy for water for industries which provides the framework for regulation as well as incentive for economic use for large users of ground water. The Sub-Committee has submitted its report to the Ministry. The Sub-Committee in its report has discussed the National Water Policy provisions, ground water scenario in the country, water requirement for industrial uses, need for artificial recharge to ground water, etc. This information was given by the Minister of State for Water Resources, Shri Jai Prakash Narayan Yadav in response to a question by Smt. Shobhana Bhartia and Shri Vijay J. Darda in the Rajya Sabha today.

6800. (18-3-2008) NEW DELHI : It has come to the notice of the Government that large scale land transactions have taken place in the border areas of Rajasthan. The State Government of Rajasthan has been directed to conduct a detailed inquiry covering all aspects of this issue and to initiate suitable administrative, legal and criminal actions, accordingly. The detailed report from the State Government of Rajasthan is still awaited. This information was given by the Minister of State in the Ministry of Home

6801. (18-3-2008) NEW DELHI : Model Production Sharing Contract (MPSC), which forms basis of signing of Production Sharing Contract (PSC) with successful bidder is prepared by the Ministry of Petroleum & Natural Gas in consultation with stakeholders and industry bodies so as to take care of their concerns, which is duly approved by Empowered Committee of Secretaries (ECS). The MPSC as approved by ECS is finally vetted by Department of Legal Affairs before launch of new round of New Exploration Licensing Policy (NELP). After award of the block to the successful bidder, the PSC is signed between the Government of India and successful bidder(s) on mutually agreed terms. In the event of any dispute in the adherence to terms of the Contract, the PSC provides for an Arbitration clause. The above information was given by the Minister of State for Petroleum & Natural Gas Shri Dinsha Patel in a written reply in the Rajya Sabha today.

6802. (18-3-2008) NEW DELHI : The Hindustan Paper Corporation Ltd.(HPC) a Central Public Sector Enterprises intends to form a subsidiary to set up a new Paper Mill at Jagdishpur, Distt. Sultanpur (Uttar Pradesh) at an estimated cost of Rs.2742 crore (constant cost basis). The subsidiary company will have 51% equity holding by HPC and shall raise balance 49% equity from the capital market at an appropriate premium through IPO. Government has agreed to provide a loan of Rs.255 crore to HPC at an interest rate of 8% p.a. enabling HPC to subscribe by way of promoters' 51% contribution as equity in the new subsidiary company. To set up a Special Purpose Vehicle (SPV) in the form of Co-operative Society under the Multi-State Co-operative Societies Act 1984 for carrying out farm forestry activities for ensuring sustained raw material availability for the project. The Post of Managing Director for Jagdishpur Paper Mill Ltd. has been created. Name of the new subsidiary company as accepted by Registrar of Companies, Kanpur (UP) is Jagdishpur Paper Mills Limited, and application for registration of the company as per Companies Act has already been filed. This information was given by the Minister of State for Heavy Industries & Public Enterprises, Smt. Kanti Singh in a written reply to a question in Rajya Sabha today.

6803. (18-3-2008) NEW DELHI : A growth rate of 12% has been envisaged for the MSE sector during the Eleventh Five Year Plan (2007-12). This has been stated by Shri Mahabir Prasad, Minister for Micro, Small & Medium Enterprises in a written reply in Lok Sabha today. He said the Government implements various schemes and programmes to enable micro and small enterprises (MSE, formerly known as SSI) to enable them tc compete in the global market and strengthen their export competitiveness. Such programmes and schemes, inter alia include assistance for participation in international exhibitions/fairs, reimbursement for obtaining bar-code certification, etc. under its Market Development Assistance (MDA) Scheme. In addition, other support measures such as organising training programmes on packaging for exports, assistance for technology upgradation under Credit Linked Capital Subsidy Scheme (CLCSS), incentives for obtaining ISO/9000-14001, etc. are included to promote export competitiveness of the MSE sector. During the year 2005-06, Indian MSE sector accounted for approximately 33% of the total exports from the country.

6804. (18-3-2008) NEW DELHI : A National Biotechnology Department Strategy having been approved by the Government of India, action has been taken for implementation of some major decisions such as Establishment of an independent National Biotechnology Regulatory Authority, Increased Public Private Partnership programmes, improved quality of Human Resource, creation of Centres of Excellence and other infrastructural facilities, new legislation for protection of IP in public funded R&D. A number of major new initiatives have been launched- Under the Public Private Partnership-SBIRI Scheme a total of 35 projects have been supported so far and 8 Centres of Excellence projects have been supported across the country. (i) Two new centres-Centre for translational research in health science and technology and UNESCO regional centre for science, education and innovation have been approved. (ii) Special human resource initiative for quality improvement have been taken, such as setting up of Star colleges, teachers training programmes, etc. This information was given by Union Minister for Science & Technology and Earth Sciences, Shri Kapil Sibal in a written reply to a question by Shri Sugrib Singh in the Lok Sabha today.

6805. (18-3-2008) NEW DELHI : The Government has mounted a special scholarship scheme titled "Innovation in Science Pursuit for Inspired Research (INSPIRE)" to attract talented youth to study and careers with science. The main features of the INSPIRE are: a) Scheme for Early Attraction of Talents for Science (SEATS) providing Science innovation scholarship of Rs.5000 for a total of one million young learners of the age group 10-15 years once in their school career and mentorship through global science leaders including Nobel Laureates and Indians leaders in science at a summer camp for the top 1% performers in the Class X examination every year for period of five years; b) Scholarships for Higher Education (SHE) for the age group of 17-22 years @ Rs. 1 lakh per year for continuing science education at B.Sc. and M.Sc. levels for 10,000 candidates and c) Assured Opportunity for Research Careers (AORC) for 1000 young researchers in the age group of 22-32 years for 5 years to pursue doctoral research in science backed by an assured career opportunity scheme for another period of five years on completion of their Ph. D. The INSPIRE Programme, as it offers Science as a career option by providing necessary opportunities to youth with aptitude for science and a desire to innovate, in addition to reasonable financial assistance, would help in producing more science students and Ph.Ds and help in increasing the stock of the scientific community necessary for meeting future challenges including preventing the brain drain. The scheme also envisages that the available number of scholarships would be distributed to students from various Boards based on total number of students taken their examinations in the respective Boards including West Bengal. The total allocation for the entire 11th Five Year Plan is Rs.2250 crores for the INSPIRE Programme and is presently at various levels of Government approval. This information was given by Union Minister for Science & Technology and Earth Sciences, Shri Kapil Sibal in a written reply to a question by Shri S.K. Kharventhan in the Lok Sabha today.

6806. (18-3-2008) NEW DELHI : The Ministry of Women and Child Development will launch a nationwide campaign create nutritional awareness in the country. State level nutritional reviews will be held annually and efforts will be made for district-wise mapping of high malnutritional areas. Briefing the members of the Parliamentary Consultative Committee attached to her Ministry here today, Smt. Renuka Chowdhury, Minister for Women and Child Development said that her Ministry has proposed nutritional education as a part of school curriculum, inclusion of core module on nutrition in the induction training programmes of all the Government officers including Indian Administrative Services. She said that breast-feeding should be recognized as food security for infants and breast-feeding education should be considered as a priority programme like immunization in both health and nutrition sectors. Expressing concern over prevalence of malnutrition, especially among women and children, Smt. Chowdhury said that the Government is working on a multi-sectoral approach for its prevention and control. Nutritional awareness in the rural and urban slums would be created through the field units of Food and Nutrition Board (FNB) by using local dialects and regional languages. Capacity building and programmes would be run for village workers, Panchayat members and Anganwadi workers. The Ministry of Women and Child Development was also recasting Integrated Child Development Programme and nutrition counselling to take care of supplementary nutrition of children and lactating mothers and now Anganwadi would be sanctioned on demand, she said. Participating in the meeting, Members of Parliament stressed the need of continuous monitoring of ICDS and other Government's programmes related with nutritional support and health. They said that district level officers should be made responsible to check incidents of malnutrition in their areas. Member participated in the meeting include: Ms. Priya Dutt, Shri Viplov Thakur, Smt. Supriya Sule, Shri Sriniwas D. Patil, Shri Laxminarayan Sharma, Shri C.K. Chandrappan, Shri P. Satheedevi and Shri S.I. Shervani.

6807. (18-3-2008) NEW DELHI : The Minister of Tourism and Culture Smt. Ambika Soni has said that Government is considering to grant visas on arrival to promote tourism. However, at present, Ministry of Home Affairs has not agreed to the proposal regarding Visa-on-Arrival scheme due to the prevalent security scenario. In a written reply in the Rajya Sabha today she said, Indian Missions abroad including those in Western cities grant visas expeditiously in keeping with the relevant norms. Visas are granted on the same day or the next day of the receipt of application except in the case of applications which require prior approval of the Government. The Minister said, at present 24 Missions / Posts have already started outsourcing of collection of visa application forms. Tourists intending to visit India are provided prompt and courteous services when they visit Indian Missions/ Posts abroad for seeking Indian visas.

6808. (18-3-2008) NEW DELHI : The Minister of Tourism and Culture Smt. Ambika Soni informed the Rajya Sabha today that to increase the flow of foreign tourists to India from China, the Government has approved the opening of India Tourism Office in Beijing. In a written reply she said, providing of accommodation to tourists is primarily a private sector activity However, to facilitate augmentation of budget category accommodation for tourists, the Government has asked all the State/UT Governments and other land owning agencies including Indian Railways to allocate land for building hotels, especially in the budget category. They have also been advised to follow investor-friendly land policies, adopt single window approach for promoting hotel projects, allot sites on revenue sharing basis, grant extra FAR/FSI for hotels, permit extra commercial usage in the hotels etc. so that budget hotels are promoted. Further, in order to increase the number of rooms in the budget category, Ministry of Tourism has floated schemes for the approval of Guest Houses and Incredible India Bed & Breakfast Establishments. She said, the number of Chinese tourist arrivals to Goa at present is negligible. Smt. Soni said, development and promotion of tourism is primarily the responsibility of the State/UT Governments. However, the Government plays the role of a facilitator and catalyst to promote tourism in different parts of the country, including Goa. The activities undertaken by the Government include providing financial assistance to State/ UT Governments for tourism-related projects, co-ordination with various Central Ministries, undertaking centralized media campaigns, participation in fairs and exhibitions, printing and distributing brochures, etc.

6809. (18-3-2008) NEW DELHI : The Defence Minister Shri AK Antony today dedicated the Equipment Accounting On Line System (EQUOLS) to the Nation at a formal ceremony at Air Force Auditorium, New Delhi. The Marshal of IAF Arjan Singh, Chief of the Air Staff Air Chief Marshal Fali Major, The Chief of Army Staff General Deepak Kapoor were present at the occasion. The Indian Air Force holds a diverse fleet of aircraft, radars and various other associated equipment. An automated IT based material management system was required to account for the IAF's inventory and stores. The IAF's Accounts branch alongwith Tata Consultancy Services have developed a material management system based on Information Technology called the 'EQUOLS'. Before implementing the EQUOLS, all transactions were being done manually using vouchers, manual stock record cards etc and was a tedious and cumbersome forces. The EQUOLS system would be advantageous from the point of view of transparent, accurate, faster transactions at the same time providing for online auditing and provisioning of realistic future demands. In his address at the ceremony, Shri Antony said, "Information Technology has transformed the world into a global village. Physical distances have ceased to exist. Technological advancement has had an impact on every field-aerospace being no exception. Thus we must make optimum use of strengthening our capabilities". He further said, " I welcome Tata Consultancy Service, the strategic partner in this project. Military industry partnership is necessary and must be encourage more and more. I am sure this alliance will be strengthened in the years to come. I congratulate the IAF for this initiative and wish you all the best for the future". The 'EQUOLS' has been implemented in two phases namely the pilots site and sense phase site. The initial implementation was at 27 pilot sites and thereafter the application was installed at remaining sites. So far, over 17.5 million entries have been transfered from manual records to the EQUOLS application. This task was achieved over last six months. The transferred data has been subjected to a very thorough scrutiny by the staff of Defence Accounts Department.

6810. (18-3-2008) NEW DELHI : The Prime Minister, Dr. Manmohan Singh has assured the textile industry that the Government will pay the closest attention to devise appropriate strategies to further promote the growth and the competitiveness of this vital national industry. The Prime Minister stated this while delivering the inaugural address at the Golden Jubilee Celebrations of the Confederation of Indian Textile Industry (CITI), here today. The inaugural session was attended by Shri Shankersinh Vaghela, Union Minister of Textiles, Shri E.V.K.S. Elangovan, Minister of State of Textiles and key representatives of the textile industry. In making our textile industry globally competitive especially after Multi-Fibre Agreement (MFA) regime, the Prime Minister said that the UPA Government has focused on three imperatives namely the need to ensure a stable policy environment; the need to support modernization through financing technological upgradation and to help build global brands for Indian textiles. Recognizing the problems faced by the exporters due to the strengthening of rupee, the Prime Minister expressed confidence that the exporters have the enterprise and business acumen to deal with this challenge and improve their competitiveness. He said that the Government has also taken steps to help mitigate the loss of competitive advantage while ensuring that our external economic management is stable and sustainable. Giving the details of fiscal measures taken by the Government to strengthen the textile sector, Dr. Manmohan Singh said that the excise duty structure has been completely transformed with large scale concessions. Customs duty for a number of textile machinery items have been reduced and hosiery and knitwear items have been dereserved from the small scale sector. The Technology Upgradation Fund has been extended into the 11th Plan and the scheme for Integrated Textile Parks in Public-Private Partnership mode has also been expanded. He said that as a result of these measures India is also becoming a major outsourcing hub. The Prime Minister reiterated that the new growth areas like Technical Textiles will be actively promoted and a Technology Mission on Technical Textiles will be launched to support growth in this area. Stating that the challenge in the 11th Plan is to increase the skill base to make the sector competitive, the Prime Minister said that the National Skill Development Mission has already identified this as a thrust area. He emphasized the need of innovative responses to increase jobs in the country and the textile industry and suggested the idea of linking guaranteed employment for a certain number of days in a policy frame-work that can meet the genuine demands of the sector. The Prime Minister stated that the textile sector has been a major pillar of our industrial economy for more than one reason but importantly because of its employment potential. He said "Our Government will come forward and address all your legitimate concerns as long as we can work together to generate more employment".

6811. (18-3-2008) NEW DELHI : In a meeting of Prime Minister's Council on Trade and Industry, a suggestion emerged that private sector may be given a role in primary education. The framework for implementation of Sarva Shiksha Abhiyan (SSA) programme, being implemented at elementary level, provides for participation of private sectors within the broad parameters of State policy. SSA and centrally sponsored schemes like 'Integrated Education for Disabled Children' (IEDC) and 'Strengthening of Boarding and Hostel facilities for Girl Students of Secondary and Higher Secondary Schools' envisage a vibrant partnership with non governmental organisations. The role of the private sector is to supplement the effort of the Government. In addition to expansion of private schools, there is need to improve quality in Government schools, Central Government has been implementing Sarva Shiksha Abhiyan (SSA) at the elementary level since 2001-2, inter-alia, with the objective to focus on elementary education of satisfactory quality. It has also been decided to implement a centrally sponsored scheme for universalisation of access to and improvement of quality of education at secondary stage during the 11th Five Year Plan. These schemes primarily focus on improving access and quality of Government schools. This information was given by the Minister of State for Human Resource Development Shri M.A.A. Fatmi in a written reply in Lok Sabha today.

6812. (18-3-2008) NEW DELHI : According to the information furnished by the University of Delhi, some organizations have objected to the inclusion of an essay titled 'Three Hundred Ramayans: Five Examples and Three Thoughts on Translation' by late Shri A.K. Ramanujam in the suggested readings for the concurrent course on 'Culture in India: Ancient' in the B.A. (Honours) programme of the University alleging that it contained derogatory references to the Hindu gods and goddesses. In view of the reservations expressed, the University has constituted a Committee of eminent scholars, consisting of Prof. B.D. Chattopadhyaya, Prof. R.N. Mishra, Prof. M.G.S. Narayanan, Prof. Kapila Vatsyayan and Prof. M.K. Dhawalikar, to review the matter and give their views/opinion on it. This information was given by the Minister of State for Human Resource Development Smt. D. Purandeswari in a written reply in Lok Sabha today.

6813. (18-3-2008) NEW DELHI : The States/UTs on the basis of household surveys/updation identify out of school children, on an annual basis. The number of out of school children has declined from 320 lakhs in 2002 to 75.97 lakhs as on March, 2007 in 6-14 years age group. The State-wise details of out of school children as on March, 2007 as per the State reports, is given in Annexure-I. The Sarva Shiksha Abhiyan (SSA) is a programme for Universalization of Elementary Education, wherein interalia, one of the goals of the SSA is to bring all children in school/Education Guarantee Centre/Alternative schooling system. State-wise details of total central govt. releases under the SSA and expenditure incurred during 10th Plan Period is given in Annexure-II. This information was given by the Minister of State for Human Resource Development Shri M.S.A. Fatmi in a written reply in Lok Sabha today.

6814. (18-3-2008) NEW DELHI : The Prime Minister has informed the Punjab Chief Minister, Shri Prakash Singh Badal that the Government of India has taken up the matter regarding Shri Sarabjit Singh with the Pakistan government at the highest levels. In a reply to a letter from Shri Badal, the Prime Minister assured him that the Government of India is making all possible efforts to seek a reprieve for Shri Sarabjit Singh.

6815. (18-3-2008) NEW DELHI : The Union Government, exercising powers conferred upon it by the provisions of the Indian Medical Council Act, 1956, has recognized Post Graduate medical qualifications being awarded in Australia, Canada, New Zealand, United Kingdom and United States of America, with the condition that these degrees should be recognized in the respective country for enrolment of medical practitioners in the concerned specialties. This recognition has been notified in the Official Gazette on 10th March 2008.

6816. (18-3-2008) NEW DELHI : Union Rural Development Dr. Raghuvansh Prasad Singh has emphasized the need of promoting in Hindi in the day to day working of his ministry for better performance and speedy communication specifically with the rural masses. Presiding over to the Hindi Consultative Committee meeting of his Ministry held here today Dr. Singh said though best efforts are being done in the Ministry, it will take time to have a hundred percent achievement in bring out the entire work done in Hindi. He said use of local languages will be promoted while making posters and pamphlets for publicity campaigns in the rural areas of the country. He expressed the hope that the recommendations and guidelines of the consultative committee will be followed accordingly. The members of the committee opined for better and simple form use of Hindi in the working of the ministry. It was advised that the employees and officers should be motivated and instructed to use more and more Hindi in the official proceedings. Members also voiced for cash incentives and prizes to the ministry official working proficiently in Hindi. The members also vouched for translations of papers in Hindi and regional languages on reciprocal basis so as to promote Hindi in the Non-Hindi speaking areas. They also mooted for the financing of NGO's evolved in the work of Hindi promotion. The member who participated in the meeting were Shri Rajendra Avasthi, Shri Giridhari Lal Bhargava, Shri Jai Prakash & Shri D.K. Adi Kesavuau (all MPs Lok Sabha) Dr. S Parth Sarathi, Prof. B.D. Kadam, Dr.Tejasasvini Kattimani, Shri Sayed Mahmud Saidu, Prof. S.B. Madhav Rao, Shri Umakant Rai Pralyankar and Shri Santosh Kumar Sharma. The Sectary Rural Development Dr. Rita Sharma gave vote of thanks and expressed the hope that her ministry will be able to cope up to the suggestions made by the committee.

6817. (19-3-2008) NEW DELHI : The Home Minister has condemned the recent killing of some innocent persons by militants in various incidents in Manipur. Following is the text of his statement: "I strongly condemn the recent killing of innocent persons by extremists in Manipur. I convey my condolences to the kin of the deceased and pray for speedy recovery of the injured. These are acts of cowardice, perpetrated with the intention to disturb social harmony and create panic among people. The Ministry of Home Affairs is in touch with the Manipur Government which has been asked to take all steps to nab the culprits, provide security to vulnerable sections and avoid recurrence of such incidents. Every citizen of the country has the fundamental right to live in any part of the country. Government of India will provide all possible assistance to the concerned State Governments to effectively deal with the elements which try to infringe this right."

6818. (19-3-2008) NEW DELHI : Addressing the 4th CII-EXIM Conclave on India-Africa Project Partnership 2008, here today, Shri Kamal Nath, Union Minister of Commerce and Industry, has stressed that India keenly anticipates a deeper and closer engagement with Africa and is eager to work together for greater mutual prosperity. Agriculture and food processing are key sectors for cooperation, as both sides are prone to food shortages, lack of diversification in crops, and low agricultural productivity, he added. Dr. Ali Mohamed Shein, Vice President of the Republic of Tanzania, delivered the Special Address. The Conclave was also attended by senior officials from the Ministry of Commerce and Industry, representatives from Exim Bank of India, Confederation of Indian Industry (CII) and Federation of Indian Chamber of Commerce & Industry (FICCI). Shri Kamal Nath said that India's strategic global engagements depend much on its strong relations with Africa and with a view to further strengthen the relationship the first India-Africa Summit meeting will be held in New Delhi on 8th April, 2008. He further stated that the government also desires to forge a robust, effective and mutually beneficial economic relationship with Africa. He hoped that this Conclave will set the stage for a bilateral and multilateral trade agreements between India and countries as well as regional blocks like SACU, COMESA, SADC, EAC in Africa. India's exports to Africa during 2006-07 stood at US $ 8.4 billion, while imports aggregated US $ 11.4 billion, having almost doubled since previous year. Exports to Africa are regionally diversified with East, Southern and West Africa accounting for US $ 2.5-3 billion each. The Commerce Minister said that India needs to expand and diversify the import basket from the continent. "Project partnership is a key in this effort. It will help strengthen local skill resources, expand infrastructure availability and lay the foundation for strong and sustainable economic cooperation between India and Africa. Our mutual goals of poverty alleviation, human development and economic growth can be addressed in part through project partnerships", Shri Kamal Nath said.

6819. (19-3-2008) NEW DELHI : The Ministry of Rural Development has issued instructions to all the States for the smooth transition of Sampoorana Grameen Rozgar Yojana (SGRY) to National Rural Employment Guarantee Act (NREGA). This follows a decision of Government to extend the NREGA to all the rural areas of all the remaining districts of the country from the first of next month. Accordingly the SGRY programme will be discontinued in the districts on starting of NREG programme therein and such districts will not get any allocation under SGRY form the next financial year. Therefore the SGRY works have to be completed by the close of current financial year on the 31st of this month. Henceforth the SGRY account will be closed on 31.03.2008. There would be a budget head only for the Employment Guarantee Scheme (EGS). The unspent amount under SGRy as on 31.03.2008 will be transferred to EGA account. All SGRY projects will be closed on 31.03.2008 and no work would be carried out by following the SGRY processes. There would be no extension of time under SGRY for completion of these woks beyond 31.03.2008. Closure means the measurement is complete on as is where is basis on the cut-off date and physical and financial assessment of the work completed and the value of work done be made. On this basis, payments are to be made and works treated as closed. Any expenditure incurred form SGRY fund after 31.03.2008 shall be on the state account. Full details at the time of the closure of the project should be brought on the record and must be sent to the MoRD. Those incomplete works which are permissible under NREGA can be taken as new projects under NREGA. No expenditure is permissible selection of works as laid down in NREGA. No expenditure is permissible on such works which were sanctioned prior to 31.03.2008 but have not yet commenced. Fresh sanctions for taking of completion of incomplete permissible works as new projects in NREGA shall be subject to permissibility of the project under NREGA and further subject to other terms and conditions indicated below: (a) The list of such works shall be duly approved by Gram Sabhas and PRIs as laid down in NREGA. (b) Only job card holders demanding employment will be employed as labour. The overall ratio of 60:40 of wage and material will be maintained at the district level and no contactor/machinery to be used. Muster rolls will have to be maintained as prescribed under NREGA. These works will be included as works for providing employment and so will count towards the 100 days entitlement of the job card holders working on them and be recorded in their job cards. The list of incomplete SGRY works will be displayed on the office of the Village/Intermediate/ district Panchayat and the offices of PO/DPC so that the information on such works is transparent. Each district will have to certify for all such incomplete SGRY works which are permissible under NREGA that: (a) The expenditure already incurred is properly accounted. (b) Work was actually sanctioned with in the authorized allocation of the district. For works which are not permissible under NREGA, State may fund this from other available resource of states and central government programmes. States will bear the entire cost of such SGRY works, which were sanctioned after 31.03.2008 as these are specifically prohibited.

6820. (19-3-2008) NEW DELHI : Rajya Sabha Replying to a written a question whether the Government is considering to establish Drinking Water Quality Testing Laboratories in all districts of the country, Minister of State in the Ministry of Rural Development Shri Chandra Sekhar Sahu today informed the Rajya Sabha that as per the existing guidelines, the Central Government is funding the State Governments for establishing district water quality testing laboratories, wherever such facility is not available in the districts. In Gujarat State, all the 25 districts have been sanctioned with one district water testing laboratory. No proposal from Government of Gujarat for establishment of water quality testing laboratories is pending with the Government of India.

6821. (19-3-2008) NEW DELHI : Replying to a written a question the number of houses constructed during the last three years under Indira Awaas Yojana (IAY) particularly in backward rural regions of the country along with the details of open and constructed area allotted to houses, Minister of State in the Ministry of Rural Development Shrimati Suryakanta Patil informed the Rajya Sabha today that with a view to providing housing facility to the homeless rural people, the Ministry of Rural Development is implementing Indira Awaas Yojana (IAY) Scheme throughout the country, except Delhi and Chandigarh, under which financial assistance is provided to the rural BPL households for construction of a house. As per the information furnished by the Registrar General of India, based on 2001 Census, the total housing shortage in rural areas in the country was 148.34 lakh as on 1.4.2001. The rural housing shortage in Delhi was reported to be 7200. Since inception of the Scheme in 1985-86, 174.14 lakh houses have been constructed under the Scheme. A statement showing State-wise number of houses constructed under IAY during the last three years and the current year, is at Annexure.

6822. (19-3-2008) NEW DELHI : Replying to a written a question whether it is a fact that the Pradhan Mantri Gram Sadak Yojana (PMGSY), a part of the Centre's Bharat Nirman designed to upgrade rural infrastructure, is set to hit a roadblock owing to funds shortage, Minister of State in the Ministry of Rural

Development Shrimati Suryakanta Patil today informed the Rajya Sabha that it is not true. For the year 2008-09, Ministry of Rural Development has proposed allocation of Rs.15,000 crore for the implementation of the Pradhan Mantri Gram Sadak Yojana (PMGSY), against which outlay of Rs. 14,530 crore has been provided. This includes Rs. 7000 crore to be drawn as loan from the Rural Infrastructure Development Fund (RIDF) window of National Bank for Agriculture and Rural Development (NABARD).

6823. (19-3-2008) NEW DELHI : Speaking at the inauguration function of the Trauma Care Centre Building at the Dr. Ram Manohar Lohia Hospital today, the Union Minister for Health & Family Welfare, Dr. Anbumani Ramadoss said even though trauma victims were being treated in this hospital earlier also, their quality of care will now make giant strides because of provision of all the modern facilities and availability of doctors belonging to different specialties round-the-clock. Congratulating all those who have contributed to the commissioning of this facility, the Minister added, it will be an important milestone in the development and achievements of the hospital. Smt. Shiela Dikshit, Chief Minister, Delhi, and Smt. Panabaka Lakshmi, Minister of State (HFW) and were also present at the function including senior officials from the Ministry and the Hospital.

6824. (19-3-2008) NEW DELHI : Water quality of major rivers namely, Ganga and Gomti in the eastern part of Uttar Pradesh and Ganga in the State of Bihar is monitored at 15 locations by the Central Pollution Control Board. The Biochemical Oxygen Demand (BOD), a key indicator of water quality is complying with the designated water quality criteria at most of the locations in Ganga except at Allahabad, Varanasi and Ghazipur. As regards the river Gomti, the BOD is not complying with designated criteria at Jaunpur and Varanasi. Rapid urbanization and inadequate collection and treatment of sewage, leading to discharge of large part of untreated sewage have been among the main reasons causing pollution in these rivers. Pollution abatement works have been undertaken in the towns located in the eastern part of Uttar Pradesh namely, Allahabad, Varanasi, Mirzapur, Mugalsarai, Ghazipur and Chunar located on the banks of the river Ganga, and Jaunpur and Sultanpur located on the banks of the river Gomti. In Bihar, pollution abatement works have been undertaken in the towns namely, Arrah, Barahiya, Barh, Bhagalpur, Buxar, Chapra, Fatwah, Munger, Patna, Sultanganj, Hajipur, Kahelgaon and Mokamah along the banks of the river Ganga. The works include Interception and Diversion of Sewage, Sewage Treatment Plants, Low Cost Sanitation, Improved Wood Based/Electric Crematoria, River Front Development etc. So far, 142 projects have been completed along with creation of sewage treatment capacity of 297.8 million liters per day in these towns of eastern part of Uttar Pradesh and the State of Bihar, and total expenditure of Rs. 22.10 crore has been incurred during the last three years. As per the water quality monitoring done by the reputed institutions in the country, in spite of the phenomenal increase in urban centres along the banks of the river, the water quality of river Ganga has shown discernible improvement at most of the locations over the water quality prior to implementation of Ganga Action Plan. This information was given by the Minister of State for Environment and Forests Shri Namo Narain Meena in a written reply to a question by Shri Harikewal Prasad and Shri Giridhari Yadav in the Lok Sabha today.

6825. (19-3-2008) NEW DELHI : A number of Siberian birds migrate annually to different States in India for wintering. Though there is no specific report of smuggling of birds, but possibility of some isolated cases of bird smuggling cannot be ruled out. The steps taken by Government in this regard are as follows: Legal protection has been provided to endangered birds, including migratory birds against hunting and commercial exploitation under the provisions of the Wildlife (Protection) Act, 1972. The Wildlife (Protection) Act has been amended and made more stringent. The punishments in cases of offences have been enhanced. The Act also provides for forfeiture of any equipment, vehicle or weapon that is used for committing wildlife offence. The Wildlife Crime Control Bureau has been set up for control of poaching and illegal trade in wildlife and its products. The Central Bureau of Investigation (CBI) has been empowered under the Wildlife (Protection) Act, 1972 to apprehend and prosecute wildlife offenders. Crucial habitats of various species of birds have been notified as National Parks and Sanctuaries. Some of the important wetlands have also been notified as Ramsar Sites and World Natural Heritage Sites. Financial and technical assistance is extended to the State/ Union Territory Governments under Centrally Sponsored Schemes for the development of National Parks & Sanctuaries and conservation of wetlands for providing better protection to wild animals. This information was given by the Minister of State for Environment and Forests Shri S. Regupathy in a written reply to a question by Shri Raghuraj Singh Shakya in the Lok Sabha today.

6826. (19-3-2008) NEW DELHI : The urban areas in the county has a population of 27.8%. It would be practically not possible to assess the environmental damages/ changes that are occurring within these areas precisely due to various developmental activities that are being undertaken therein. As per the report titled "State of Forest Report, 2005" by Forest Survey of India, released recently, a comparison of forest covers of the country between the present and preceding assessment (2003) shows that there is a marginal loss of 728 sq km during the period 2002-2004. Hence, there has been no major change in the forest cover in the country. All major developmental projects that are listed in the schedule to the Environmental Impact Assessment Notification, 2006 attract the provisions of the said Notification. If felling of trees is essential for implementation of any developmental projects being considered for grant of environmental clearance (EC) under the notification in non forest areas, generally, plantation of trees at the minimum ratio of 1:2 is prescribed in the environmental clearance. The Forest (Conservation) Act, 1980 also provides for compensatory afforestation over equivalent non forestland or double the degraded forest area to mitigate the loss of forestland for non forestry purpose. This information was given by the Minister of State for Environment and Forests Shri Namo Narain Meena in a written reply to a question by Shri C. Kuppusami and Shri M.P. Veerendra Kumar, in the Lok Sabha today.

6827. (19-3-2008) NEW DELHI : The Government of India is following a case by case approval of genetically modified products for which extensive rules and guidelines have been framed for evaluating their environmental and health safety. Only those transgenic crops which are found to be safe for the environment as well as human consumption are approved for environment release. The 'Rules for Manufacture, Use, Import, Export and Storage of Hazardous Micro Organisms/ Genetically Engineered Organisms or Cells Rules, 1989 notified under the Environment (Protection) Act, 1986 has been in force since 1990. This information was given by the Minister of State for Environment and Forests Shri Namo Narain Meena in a written reply to a question by Shri K. Subbarayan in the Lok Sabha today.

6828. (19-3-2008) NEW DELHI : The Indian Armed Forces personnel are deployed in six UN Peace Keeping Missions *viz.*, Congo, Lebanon, Ethiopia-Eritrea, Sudan, Golan Heights and Ivory Coast, at present. A total of 8887 Indian Armed Forces' personnel are presently deployed in UN Peacekeeping operations and UN Headquarters, New York. The terms and conditions of the personnel deployed in these missions are governed by the orders/instructions issued by the UN and Government of India including Memorandum of Understanding/Letter of Assist signed between UN and Government of India. Each peacekeeping mission is governed by UN mandate which is reviewed from time to time. This information was given by the Defence Minister Shri A K Antony in a written reply to Smt. Jaya Bachchan in Rajya Sabha today.

6829. (19-3-2008) NEW DELHI : Shri Prakash Javadekar born on 30th January 1951, has been a crusader through his life. A devoted full time worker of BJP since its inception in 1980, he is presently the national spokesperson of the party. He was Executive Chairman of the State Planning Board of Maharashtra during BJP-Shiv Sena rule from 1995-1999. He was able to get NGOs and Experts participation in preparation of 10th Five Year Plan of Maharashtra. He was elected to the State Legislature Council form 1990-2002 from Pune Graduate Constituency twice. He was appointed Chairman of IT Task Force of Government of Maharashtra. During his tenure he formulated IT Policy for the state. He was also appointed as Chairman of the Working Group on "IT for Masses" of Government of India in 2000. The report of the working group prove to be a catalyst in many of the policy changes. He is Chairman of the NGO called "Gram Shakti", which has successfully completed watershed development project in 11 villages of Kolvan Valley in Mulshi Tehsil of Pune District (Maharashtra). It also completed successful people participation in World Bank aided water scheme around Pune city. Before joining BJP, he was ABVP activist and student leader in Pune and was elected to the University Senate. He organised struggle against emergency rule and was imprisoned for 16 months during 1975-1977.

6830. (19-3-2008) NEW DELHI : The names of countries with which India has conducted joint defence exercises in the last two years are USA, France, UK, Oman, Russia, Singapore, Thailand, China, Maldives and Mongolia. These exercises have helped in enhancing interoperability with defence forces of friendly foreign countries and in increasing military to military cooperation. This information was given by the Defence Minister Shri A K Antony in a written reply to Smt. Jaya Bachchan in Rajya Sabha today.

6831. (19-3-2008) NEW DELHI : Government promulgated Defence Procurement Procedure (DPP-2006) with effect from 1st September, 2006 to ensure expeditious procurement of the approved requirements of the Armed Forces in terms of capabilities sought and time frame prescribed. DPP-2006 provides for review of the procurement procedure after every two years in the light of the practical experience gained in its implementation. To encourage participation by Indian companies and strengthen the domestic technical/industrial base, Capital Acquisitions have been categorized in the Defence Procurement Procedure-2006 as under:-Acquisitions covered under the 'Buy' decision. Buy would mean an outright purchase of equipment. Based on the source of procurement, this category would be classified as 'Buy (Indian)' and 'Buy (Global)'. 'Indian' would mean Indian vendors only and 'Global' would mean foreign as well as Indian vendors. 'Buy Indian' must have minimum 30% indigenous content if the systems are being integrated by an Indian vendor. Acquisitions covered under the 'Buy & Make' decision would mean purchase from a foreign vendor followed by licensed production/indigenous manufacture in the country. Acquisitions covered under the 'Make' decision would include high technology complex systems to be designed, development and produced indigenously. This information was given by the Defence Minister Shri A K Antony in a written reply to Shri Ramdas Agarwal in Rajya Sabha today.

6832. (19-3-2008) NEW DELHI : Congress spokesman Shri Manish Tewari said we welcome the decision of the government of Pakistan to give a reprieve to Shri Sarabjit Singh. We do hope and pray that this reprieve would be converted into a permanent relief and his plea for clemency would be accepted by the government of Pakistan. On 10th of March, 2008 the BJP Government in Gujarat was compelled to withdraw the Freedom of Religion Amendment Bill 2006 in the wake of vociferous protests by Civil Society and the decision of the Governor of Gujarat to withhold assent to the said Bill as it was violative of Article 25 (a) of the Constitution of India. It is extremely reprehensible that the BJP Government of Rajasthan has introduced afresh a; Freedom of Religion Bill in the Rajasthan Assembly especially when an earlier Bill on the same subject introduced by it in 2006 is still pending consideration of the President of India. This act of the Rajasthan Government not only tantamount to defiance of Constitutional authorities but also goes against the grain of the law as laid down by a Constitution bench of the Supreme Court of India. In the matter of 'Purushothaman Nambudiri Vs. State of Kerala (AIR 1962 Supreme Court 694). Supreme Court has held that: "Article 201 then deals with the procedure which has to be adopted when a Bill is to be assented to by the President. Under the said Article the President shall declare either that he assents to the bill or that he withholds assent therefrom. The proviso lays down, inter alia, that the President may direct the Governor to return the Bill to the House together with such message as is mentioned in the first proviso to Article 200, and when a Bill is so returned the House shall reconsider it accordingly within a period of six months from the date of receipt of such message, and if it is again passed by the House with or without amendment it shall be presented again to the President for his consideration." "If we look at the relevant provision of Arts. 200 and 201 from this point of view it would be significant that neither Article provides for a time-limit within which the Governor or the President should come to a decision on the Bill referred to him for his assent. Where it appeared necessary and expedient to prescribe a time-limit the Constitution has made appropriate provisions in that behalf (vide : Art. 197(1)b and 2(b)). In fact the proviso to Art.201 requires that the House to which the Bill is remitted with a message from the President shall reconsider it accordingly within a period of six months from the date of the receipt of such message. Therefore, the failure to make any provision as to the time within which the Governor or the President should reach a decision may suggest that the Constitution makers knew that a Bill which was pending the assent of the Governor or the President did not stand the risk of lapse." This act of introducing a fresh Bill on the same subject raises a grave Constitutional question and clearly exposes that the BJP has no respect for Constitutional Institutions and Constitutional propriety. The BJP which allows no opportunity to pass in tom-toming its commitment to decency and morality in politics does not allow these basic Constitutional niceties which form the bedrock of the Indian democratic system to stand in the way of implementing the Agenda of the RSS when in office. The decision of the BJP Government in Rajasthan to introduce a fresh Bill on the same subject on which a live Bill is pending consideration of the President is clearly an attempt to try and communalize the situation ahead of the Assembly Elections in November, 2008 as the Rajasthan BJP Government has no achievement worth the name to take to the people.

6833. (19-3-2008) NEW DELHI : In 2007 some stray incidents of sale of ration meant for soldiers posted in Siachen came to the notice. However, based on intelligence report of the Army, police carried out raids on civilian shops at village Chumathang on 11.7.2007 and subsequent raids lasting upto 20.7.2007 in some shops in Nubra Valley. Certain quantities of special rations were recovered. 11

FIRs (3 in Police Station, Leh, 02 in Police Station, Nyoma and 6 in Police Station, Nubra) were registered by J&K Police under Section 409, 411 Ranvir Penal Code during the raids from 11th to 20th July 2007. Two Courts of Inquiry have been ordered to investigate into the incident. This information was given by the Defence Minister Shri A K Antony in a written reply to Shri Lalit Kishore Chaturvedi and Dr. Gyan Prakash Pilania in Rajya Sabha today.

6834. (19-3-2008) NEW DELHI : Presently there is a shortage of 11,153, 1,430 and 1,368 officers in Army, Navy and Air Force respectively. However, no survey has been conducted by the Government of India. There have been shortfalls in the intake of cadets in Indian Military Academy (IMA) (DE) at Dehradun. The shortfall in recruitment of officers in the services can be partly attributed to the change in the socio-economic environment, the change in career preferences and availability of employment opportunities in other sectors. Several steps have been taken by the three Services to attract more talented youth to join the Defence Forces. All officers including those in Short Service Commission (SSC) have been made eligible to hold substantive rank of Captain, Major and Lieutenant Colonel after 2, 6 and 13 years of reckonable service respectively. In addition to the above, 750 posts of Lieutenant Colonels have been upgraded to Colonel's rank. The tenure of SSC officers has also been extended from 10 years to 14 years. The Armed Forces have undertaken sustained image projection and publicity campaign to create awareness among the youth on the advantages of taking up a challenging and satisfying career. Candidate-friendly recruitment procedure to attract more number of candidates and a focused publicity drive in various institutions to attract potential candidates have been undertaken. Awareness campaigns, participation in career fairs and exhibitions, advertisements in print and electronic media, counselling and motivational talks in schools, colleges and NCC camps are also some of the other measures in this direction. In addition, the commitment and bravery of the Armed Forces is consistently projected through the electronic and print media. The Government has also appointed VI Central Pay Commission to go into the question of revision of pay and allowances etc. of all the Government servants including the Armed Forces. The three-Services have presented a joint memorandum to the Pay Commission suggesting revision of pay and allowances and other service conditions. The matter has also been discussed with the Pay Commission by the three Service Chiefs and officers in the Ministry of Defence. This information was given by the Defence Minister Shri A K Antony in a written reply to Shri Dara Singh in Rajya Sabha today.

6835. (19-3-2008) NEW DELHI : At present only one project *i.e.* NAG, third Generation Anti Tank Missile is under development as part of Integrated Guided Missile Development Programme. The probable date completion is December 2008. User Trials of NAG third generation anti-tank missile is scheduled during 2nd half of 2008. This information was given by the Defence Minister Shri A K Antony in a written reply to Shri S K Khabir Uddin Ahmed in Rajya Sabha today.

6836. (19-3-2008) NEW DELHI : 23rd of March is celebrated as the World Meteorological Day throughout the World. This day is of special significance to National Meteorological Services in all the countries and special programmes are organized to communicate to the public the importance of various aspects of climate and weather in our lives. This year the theme is "Observing our planet for a better future". On the occasion, the India Meteorological Department, IMD, will open all its offices in different cities of India for students and public to come and see for themselves the activities that are undertaken to collect meteorological data and issue weather forecasts. The observatory also will remain open to the public for viewing operational activities related to Weather Forecasting. In his message, the Director General of Meteorology, India Meteorology Department, AVM Ajit Tyagi has expressed hope that all Members of the World Meteorological Organization will recognize the importance of "Observing our planet for a better future" and its potential global impacts on their lives, their security and their prosperity as well as to the development of much needed climate applications to address some of the major challenges of the major challenges.

6837. (19-3-2008) NEW DELHI : The Government continues to give utmost importance in supplementing the efforts of the State Governments to provide sanitation facilities to the rural masses. The scheme of Central Rural Sanitation Programme was revised in 1999 and "Total Sanitation Campaign (TSC)" launched. The programme has been continued in the XI Plan period and now scaled up to cover 582 rural districts of the country. During the last three years, the programme has been enhanced to include the component of solid and liquid waste management and provision of revolving fund to each district. To encourage the Panchayati Raj Institutions (PRI) to take up sanitation promotion and attain 100% open defecation free environment, incentive scheme Nirmal Gram Puraskar (NGP) has been launched. During 2004-05, 39 PRIs from 6 States received NGP. This number had further increased to 769 PRIs in 2006 and to 4959 PRIs in 2007. Intensive monitoring, awareness and education campaigns, Capacity building activities are being taken up by each State to improve implementation. The Center has also enhanced the budget allocation for TSC in the last three years, from Rs. 400 crore in 2004-05 to Rs. 700 crore in 2005-06, Rs. 800 crore in 2006-07 and Rs. 1060 crore in 2007-08. The reason for poor sanitation is mainly the problem of open defecation, which was the only form of sanitation for the majority of the population in rural areas. This practice is prominently due to the traditional behavioural pattern and lack of awareness of the people about the associated health hazards. To tackle this issue, the Total Sanitation Campaign (TSC) has been restructured to a community led and people centred approach. The programme gives emphasis on Information, Education and Communication (IEC) for demand generation for sanitation facilities. It also lays emphasis on school sanitation and hygiene education for bringing about attitudinal and behavioural changes for relevant sanitation and hygiene practices from young age itself. The programme also develops convergence with National Rural Health Mission (NRHM) and Sarva Sikhsha Abhiyan (SSA) for awareness creation and hygiene education among the people and children in the rural areas This information was given by the Minister of State in the Ministry of Rural Development Shri Chandra Sekhar Sahu in reply to a written question in the Rajya Sabha today.

6838. (19-3-2008) NEW DELHI : The 11th Five Year Plan has given time bound goals in respect of Infant Mortality Rate (IMR), Maternal Mortality Rate (MMR) and Total Fertility Rate (TFR), which are in consonance with targets set under the National Population Policy, 2000 and National Rural Health Mission (NRHM). Better performing 15 States/UTs, which constitute about 44% of the population in 2001, have already achieved the replacement level TFR of 2.1. 10 States, which constitute about 14% of the population, are hopeful of achieving the replacement level in the near future as they have attained TFR between 2.4 and 2.9 by 2010. Remaining States/UTs namely, Bihar, Uttarakhand, Chhattisgarh, Jharkhand, Madhya Pradesh, Rajasthan, Uttar Pradesh, Meghalaya, Tripura and Dadra & Nagar Haveli, which constitute about 42% of the total population, may take longer period to achieve this goal. India was the first country globally in 1952 to launch Family Planning programme, emphasizing fertility regulation for reducing birth rates to stabilize the population at a level consistent with the requirement of national economy. During the seventies, the family planning programme was focused mainly on terminal methods and the programme received a set back due to the rigid implementation of a target based approach. Since April 1, 1996, the 'Target Free Approach' has been adopted all over India with a focus on decentralized participatory planning. Under this new approach, attention is being paid to enlarging family welfare services and ensuring community participation at the grass-root level. The family welfare programme is now fully voluntary and the main effort of the Government has been to provide service and to encourage the citizens by information, education and communication to use such services. It gives choice to the couple to adopt the size of their family by adopting the family welfare methods best suited to them. The Government is providing central assistance to the States/UTs under NRHM and second phase of Reproductive and Child Health (RCH-II) programme for implementation of various family welfare activities to achieve population stabilization in the country. Under the NRHM emphasis has been laid to provide accessible, affordable, accountable, effective, reliable and quality primary healthcare through creation of a cadre of Accredited Social Health Activities (ASHA), improved hospital care, decentralization of programme to district level to improve intra and inter-sectoral convergence and effective utilization of resources. As a part of NRHM, fixed day services both for terminal and spacing methods of family planning in all the upgraded Primary Health Centres, Community Health Centres, District Hospitals and Sub-District Hospital has been taken up in all the States/UTs. The enhanced package of compensation for loss of wages to persons who undergo sterilization has been introduced since September 2007.

6839. (19-3-2008) NEW DELHI : Replying to a written a question whether Government has promised to provide drinking water to all in the rural areas by 2012, Minister of State in the Ministry of Rural Development Shri Chandra Sekhar Sahu, today informed the Rajya Sabha that water is a State subject and State Governments are responsible to provide drinking water to the rural areas. To supplement the efforts of the state, financial assistance is provided to the States through centrally sponsored, Accelerated Rural Water Supply Programme (ARWSP). The State Governments are competent to plan, sanction and implement rural water supply schemes from the funds provided under ARWSP. Government is committed to enable the rural population to have access to safe drinking water in adequate quantity throughout the year. Accordingly, Bharat Nirman Programme with drinking water supply as one of the six components, has been launched in 2005 to be completed by March, 2009 for building rural infrastructure, under which, it is envisaged to cover 55,067 uncovered habitations, about 3.31 lakh slipped-back habitations and to address 2.17 lakh quality-affected habitations. Regarding Sanitation facilities in schools and anganwadi centres, as part of the "Total Sanitation Campaign", proposals for construction of toilets in all rural schools and anganwadi centres have been approved for 584 districts, the central share of the project cost is Rs. 8538.97 crore out of which Rs. 3076.81 crore has been already released by the Government. The proposal envisages providing at least one unit each for each of the schools and separate toilets for boys and girls in co-educational schools. Moreover, new schools in rural area are covered under Sarva Shiksha Abhiyan (SSA), Ministry of Human Resource Development. States have been impressed upon to cover all the schools by the end of 2007-08 with drinking water and sanitation facilities.

6840. (19-3-2008) NEW DELHI : 21 States and UTs (including Rajasthan) have finalized the BPL list on the basis of BPL Census 2002, and the details are given at Annexure-I. The Government of Rajasthan have already posted the New BPL list on the portal http:bpl2002.raj.nic.in. For BPL Census 2002, the Ministry had issued the guidelines to the States and UTs requesting them to identify the total number of BPL rural households in such a way that it should be equal to the Poverty Estimates 1999-2000 or the Adjusted Share worked out by the Planning Commission which ever is higher. Another 10% flexibility is allowed to account for the transient poor. Therefore, the States and UTs were informed their upper limit for identification of BPL households. Generally, the BPL Census is conducted in the beginning of the Five Year Plan, however, the results of BPL Census 2002 conducted for the 10th Five Year Plan could not be finalized because the Hon'ble Supreme Court had passed a stay order. The stay was vacated only on 14.2.2006 after which the BPL lists were approved by the Gram Sabhas. The Ministry had already issued the guidelines that in order to redress the public grievances with regard to their status in BPL list, the option of two-stage appeal mechanism can always be availed which is a continuous process and the BPL list continues to be relevant. This was stated by the Minister of State in the Ministry of Rural Development Shrimati Surya Kanta Patil, in reply to a written question in the Rajya Sabha today.

6841. (19-3-2008) NEW DELHI : The Comptroller & Auditor General (CAG) was requested by the Ministry to undertake performance audit of NREGA for the year 2006-07 in 68 phase I districts. In its draft report submitted to the Ministry by CAG, some irregularities have been reported in the implementation of NREGS. These mainly relate to procedures such as application for employment, issue of dated receipts, job card formats, muster rolls, maintenance of record registers. The draft report has been examined in the Ministry and has also been shared with all the States. The States have given their responses to the observations made by CAG in the draft report. These have been sent to CAG. State responses are in the process of examination by CAG for finalisation of the performance audit report of NREGA. In addition, complaints have also been received from various quarters regarding irregularities in the implementation of NREGA. State-wise details of the complaints along with the action taken by the Ministry there on have been put on the website www.nrega.nic.in under the heading "Complaints". Suggestions have been received from various quarters for effective implementation of NREGA. These relate to payment of wages through Bank/ Post office accounts of NREGA workers and revision of guidelines and formats under NREGA. Steps taken by the Government for effective implementation of NREGA are: Awareness generation; People's participation; Transparency;Strict vigilance and monitoring; and MIS/e-knowledge network

6842. (19-3-2008) NEW DELHI : State-wise status of ASHA can be seen at Annexure. Accredited Social Health Activists (ASHA) is a health activist in the community to create awareness on health, its social determinants and mobilize the community towards local health planning, increased utilization and accountability of the existing health services. Her roles and responsibilities are (i) to create awareness ii) to counsel iii) to mobilize the community and facilitate them in accessing health and health related services iv) to work with the Village Health & Sanitation Committee of the Gram Panchayat. v) Escort and company pregnant women and children requiring treatment vi) Provide primary medical care for minor illness vii) To act as a depot holder for essential provisions viii) To inform about births and deaths and ix) to promote construction of household toilets under total sanitation campaign.

6843. (19-3-2008) NEW DELHI : Child Labour is a complex socio-economic problem, which needs sustained efforts over a long period of time. Considering the nature and magnitude of the problem, government is following a sequential approach of first covering children working in hazardous occupations/processes. The National Plan of action for elimination of child labour includes project based plan of action covering families of child labour in general developmental programmes and strict enforcement of the Child Labour (Prohibition and Regulation) Act, 1986. Government is implementing the National Child Labour Project (NCLP) Scheme in 250 districts of the country. Under the Scheme, children withdrawn from identified hazardous work are put into Special Schools, where they are provided with accelerated bridging education, vocational training, nutrition, stipend and health care facilities etc., before they are mainstreamed into regular education system.

6844. (19-3-2008) NEW DELHI : The Major Centrally Sponsored Health and Family Welfare Programmes including inter-alia, National Cancer Control Programme (NCCP), National AIDS Control Programme, National Programmes relating to Vector Borne, Blindness Control, Leprosy Eradication, Tuberculosis Control and other programmes under National Rural Health Mission (NRHM), are under implementation in various states of the country including Karnataka.

6845. (19-3-2008) NEW DELHI : Government is committed to elimination of child labour and Government's commitment is reiterated whenever the child labour issue is discussed in ILO conferences at Geneva and elsewhere. With a view to providing social security to unorganised sector workers, the Unorganised Sector Workers' Social Security Bill, 2007 has been introduced in Rajya Sabha on 10.09.2007. Child Labour is a complex socio-economic problem, which needs sustained efforts over a long period of time. Considering the nature and magnitude of the problem, Government is following a sequential approach of first covering children working in hazardous occupations/processes. For the elimination of child labour, Government is implementing the National Child Labour Project (NCLP) Scheme in 250 districts of the country. Under the Scheme, children withdrawn from hazardous work are put into Special Schools, where they are provided with accelerated bridging education, vocational training, nutrition, stipend and health care facilities etc., before they are mainstreamed into regular education system. State Governments are the appropriate Government for implementation of the provisions of the Child Labour (Prohibition & Regulation) Act, 1986 for the areas coming under their jurisdiction. This information was given by the Minister of State (Independent Charge) of the Ministry of Labour and Employment, Shri Oscar Fernandes in a written reply in the Rajya Sabha today.

6846. (19-3-2008) NEW DELHI : India and the USA have discussed areas of collaboration in health care and thereafter several MOU/Agreements have been signed for various Indo-US collaborative efforts. Details of such agreements and areas of collaboration can be seen at Annexure. India has developed the infrastructure and expertise in basic as well as clinical research. However, there are various areas in health research, which are marked by complex technologies and multi-disciplinary involvement. In some areas where US has more experience than India, joint collaboration focus is on transfer of technology through training of the research staff in the US and in Indian laboratories, who will then implement this training using the infrastructure available in India. Under various Indo-US collaborative research activities, ICMR. has been conducting studies and making efforts to help Government of India to develop various strategies in Health sector such as capacity building in the field of emerging and re-emerging diseases, developing HIV Vaccine, containing Kala-azar, development of network for surveillance of human Influenza, Rota-Virus and Haemophilus Influenza B. Agencies like Centres for Disease Control and Prevention (CDC), USA and the Indian agencies *viz.* National Institute of Communicable Diseases (NICD) and Indian Council of Medical Research (ICMR) shall partner in the network of disease surveillance activities to derive maximum benefit from the collaboration. This information was given by the Minister of State for Health & Family Welfare, Smt. Panabaaka Lakshmi in a written reply to a question in the Lok Sabha.

6847. (19-3-2008) NEW DELHI : On the basis of information published in World Competitiveness Year Book 2007 by Institute of Management and Development, Lausanne, Switzerland, the labour productivity measured in terms of Gross Domestic Product (Purchasing Power Parity) per Person Employed per Hour in India during 2006 has been worked out to be US$4.16, which is lower than Singapore (US$25.92), Japan (US$ 31.10), China-Mainland (US$6.02) and Republic of Korea (US$19.78). As per the information furnished by Ministry of Overseas Indian Affairs, Indian workers are in great demand in some of the developed as well as developing countries. Every year about 6-7 lakh workers travel to various countries seeking job opportunities. Countries in the Middle East and South East Asia offer tremendous opportunities for the Indian skilled workers. The major trades in demand include electricians, plumbers, carpenters, drivers, welders, fitters, machine operators coming from China and other countries. In order to address the issue, during 2006-07 the Central Government in consultation with State Governments launched a new scheme for skill upgradation and pre-departure orientation of the prospective emigrants. The training includes familiarization with the good working practices, safety norms and use of tools. The trainees are also given exposure on personality needs and how they should conduct themselves while they are working in the overseas establishments. This will help skilled workers in sharpening of their skills in tune with emerging market needs. This information was given by the Minister of State (Independent Charge) of the Ministry of Labour and Employment, Shri Oscar Fernandes in a written reply in the Rajya Sabha today.

6848. (19-3-2008) NEW DELHI : For upgradation of Government ITIs in the Country the Central Government has launched a new Scheme "Upgradation of 1396 Government ITIs through Public Private Partnership" : The first batch of 300 ITIs has been taken up for upgradation at a cost of Rs. 750.00 Cr. in 2007-08. Under this Scheme an Industry Partner is associated with each ITI to lead the process of upgradation. An Institute Management Committee (IMC) is set up in the ITI with the Industry Partner or its representative as the Chairperson and the Principal of the ITI as the member Secretary. The IMC is registered as a Society and an interest free loan of upto Rs. 2.5 Cr. is given directly to the IMC Society. The loan is repayable by the IMC Society over a period of 30 years. For 2007-08, four Government ITIs in the State of Orissa *viz.* ITIs at Puri, Cuttack, Umerkote, and Chhatrapur (Women) have been covered under this Scheme and interest free loan of Rs. 10 Cr. has been released to them at a rate of Rs. 2.5 Cr. per ITI. This information was given by the Minister of State (Independent Charge) of the Ministry of Labour and Employment, Shri Oscar Fernandes in a written reply in the Rajya Sabha today.

6849. (19-3-2008) NEW DELHI : Ministry of Labour and Employment is implementing a scheme titled "Skill Development Initiative" which aims to train, test and certify skills of one million persons during the next five years with an outlay of Rs.550 crore. Government has decided to set up a National Skill Development Mission under which 1500 more Industrial Training Institutes and 50,000 Skill Development Centres are planned to be set up in the next five years in Public Private Partnership mode to train about 10 million persons per annum. This information was given by the Minister of State (Independent Charge) of the Ministry of Labour and Employment, Shri Oscar Fernandes in a written reply in the Rajya Sabha today.

6850. (19-3-2008) NEW DELHI : Reliable estimates of employment and unemployment are obtained through quinquennial labour force surveys conducted by National Sample Survey Organisation. Last such survey was conducted during 2004-05. As per two most recent quinquennial rounds of surveys on employment and unemployment, unemployment rate on usual status basis has marginally increased from 2.2% to 2.3% during 1999-2000 to 2004-05. This was due to the fact that the pace of growth in labour force at 2.97% per annum exceeded the rate of growth of work force at 2.95% per annum. The increase in labour force is mainly attributed to the fact that working age population grew faster than total population and labour force participation rate increased particularly, among women during 1999-2000 to 2004-05. However, overall employment opportunities on usual status basis during the same period have increased from 397 million in 1999-2000 to 459.10 in 2004-05. Government has been implementing various employment generation schemes and poverty alleviation programmes of which, some of the important ones are Prime Minister's Rozgar Yojāna (PMRY); Swarna Jayanti Shahari Rozgar Yojana (SJSRY); Swarnajayanti Gram Swarozgar Yojana (SGSY); Sampoorna Grameen Rozgar Yojana (SGRY); Rural Employment Generation Programme (REGP) and National Rural Employment Guarantee Act, 2005 (NREGA) etc. for generating gainful employment opportunities in the country. This information was given by the Minister of State (Independent Charge) of the Ministry of Labour and Employment, Shri Oscar Fernandes in a written reply in the Rajya Sabha today.

6851. (19-3-2008) NEW DELHI : The proposal for setting up of AIIMS-like institutions was approved by CCEA on 16.3.2006. The initial bid process for selection of Project Consultant proved to be unresponsive. The offer of short listed Architectural Design Consultant for preparing enlarged concept design was rejected due to the exorbitantly high price quoted by the selected designer. Therefore, the whole process had to be initiated de novo in December 2006. Several methodological changes were made to ensure progress keeping in mind the complexity of building 6 such institutions simultaneously and lack of capacity for taking the whole project as one. Therefore, it was decided that each AIIMS site would be taken as a separate and independent project instead of clubbing all six together. The construction of housing complex was also separated from that of Hospital and Medical College. The Design-DPR consultants have been selected for each site through an open competitive bidding. The layout / master plans for the AIIMS sites at Bhopal, Bhubaneshwar, Jodhpur, Raipur and Rishikesh have been approved. Approval of layout / master plan for Patna site is expected this month. The Consultants are in the process of preparing architectural design, which is expected to be finalized by May 2008. The detailed project report (DPR) would be ready by May-June 2008. Thereafter, tenders would be invited for selection of contractor for civil construction work. In so far as construction of residential complex (housing & hostel) is concerned, bids were invited for selection of turnkey Developers. However, bid process was successful only for Jodhpur site and work has been awarded to M/s. Rajasthan State Road Development Corporation, a PSU of Government of Rajasthan. Work is in progress. The work relating to construction of residential complex at Rishikesh and Patna has been entrusted to HLL and for Bhubaneshwar and Raipur to HSCC. Tender process has been initiated for selection of contractors for Bhubaneshwar and Raipur sites by HSCC. For Bhopal site, housing complex work is being awarded alongside the hospital-medical college complex.

6852. (19-3-2008) NEW DELHI : The ESI Corporation is exploring the feasibility of starting Medical Colleges, Nursing Colleges and Para-Medical Training Schools under ESI Medical Scheme. A consultant has been appointed on 29.02.2008 for submitting the feasibility report on the proposal. A letter has also been received from Government of Kerala requesting for taking necessary steps for starting a medical college at ESI Hospital, Paripally in Kollam District. A Sub-Committee constituted by the ESIC had recommended amending the ESI Act, 1948 for facilitating imparting of medical and para-medical education with a view to improving quality of services provided under the ESI Scheme. The ESIC has approved the recommendation in its meeting held on 22.02.2008. Further action can be taken only after the proposed amendment to the ESI Act is carried out and on the basis of feasibility report. This information was given by the Minister of State (Independent Charge) of the Ministry of Labour and Employment, Shri Oscar Fernandes in a written reply in the Rajya Sabha today.

6853. (19-3-2008) NEW DELHI : The Primary health care services in rural areas are provided through a network of a three-tier infrastructure of Sub Centres [SCs],

Primary Health Centres [PHCs] and Community Health Centres [CHCs]. As on March 2007 there are a total of 145272 Sub-centres, 22370 PHCs and 4045 CHCs functioning in the country. As on March, 2007, there is a shortfall of 21157 Health Worker [Female]/ANM at Sub Centres & Primary Health Centres, 77615 Health Workers[Male] at SCs, 7142 Health Assistants [Female]/LHVs at PHCs, 6261 Health Assistants [Male] at PHCs, 1410 Doctors at PHCs, 9455 Specialists at CHCs, 1398 Radiographers at CHCs, 4910 Pharmacists at PHCs and CHCs, 9795 Laboratory Technicians at PHCs and CHCs and 17262 Nurse Midwife/Staff Nurse at PHCs & CHCs. These centres are run by the States/UTs Governments and the staff is also recruited by them. Under National Rural Health Mission [NRHM], funds are released to States/UTs Governments for upgradation and strengthening of Primary Health Centres including contractual appointment of staff, construction of building and infrastructure. The State/UT Governments are however required to incorporate their requirement in their annual NRHM Programme Implementation Plans. This information was given by the Minister of State for Health & Family Welfare, Smt. Panabaaka Lakshmi in a written reply to a question in the Lok Sabha.

6854. (19-3-2008) NEW DELHI : A comprehensive review of the Protected Area Permit/Restricted Area Permit regime has been undertaken with a view to relaxing the restrictions imposed to promote tourism in the concerned States/Union Territories. Specific proposals in this regard have been received and are being invited from the concerned State Governments/UTs. These proposals are being/ will be duly examined from the tourism and security perspectives with the concerned State Governments/UTs and an appropriate decision will be expedited in the matter. This information was given by the Minister of State in the Ministry of Home.

6855. (19-3-2008) NEW DELHI : Government is aware that large scale land transactions have taken place in the border areas of Rajasthan. The Rajasthan Government has initiated a detailed inquiry into these transactions with the intention of identifying the purchasers and ascertaining the bona fides/motives behind such transactions. Preliminary enquiries indicate that lands have also been purchased by parties not belonging to Rajasthan. The Government of Rajasthan has since placed four sub-registrars under suspension for procedural violations and have started disciplinary action against other officials. While speculation linked to expectations about improved highway connectivity, new projects of irrigation and prospects of oil and gas finds may be a factor for accelerated investments in land in these areas, a definitive conclusion/analysis will be possible only after completion of the detailed enquiry being undertaken by the Government of Rajasthan with the support of the Central Government agencies. A high level review on the subject matter has also been held in the Ministry of Home Affairs and the issue is being closely monitored in coordination with the State Government from time to time. This information was given by the Minister of State in the Ministry of Home.

6856. (19-3-2008) NEW DELHI : It is planned to construct a Mega Terminal to handle extra large container ships at Chennai Port as part of the on-going process of development. The project is at its conception stage. This information was given by the Minister of Shipping, Road Transport and Highways, Shri T.R. Baalu in a written reply in the Lok Sabha today.

6857. (19-3-2008) NEW DELHI : A Panamanian registered vehicle M.V. Rezzak vessel was reported missing while navigating from Russia to Turkey. It was not an Indian ship. The vessel during its voyage in the Black Sea apparently encountered rough weather conditions due to the prevailing gale force winds. The last position report from the vessel was received on 18th February, 2008. Since then, no further information is known about its whereabouts. The company which hired the ship was "Carbofer, General Trading S.A".Turkey and the Company which operated the ship was "CMR Denizcilik ve Ticaret A.S, Turkey. An investigating officer of the Directorate General of Shipping, Mumbai is in Turkey and is taking part in the investigation into this incident which is being conducted by the Flag state Panama in Turkey. This information was given by the Minister of Shipping, Road Transport and Highways, Shri T.R. Baalu in a written reply in the Lok Sabha today.

6858. (19-3-2008) NEW DELHI : The Policy for the Maritime Sector, which is under finalization, seeks to combine vision and strategy for the sector through harmonious and coordinated development of our maritime assets including the ports, shipping, inland water transport systems and the ship building and ship repair industries. The locations for setting up deep-sea-ports have not been identified. This information was given by the Minister of Shipping, Road Transport and Highways, Shri T.R. Baalu in a written reply in the Lok Sabha today.

6859. (19-3-2008) NEW DELHI : A Standing Committee comprising both Chairman of Mumbai Port Trust and the Chief Secretary of Government of Maharashtra with their respective officers as members is being constituted to look into the various issues of Mumbai Port Trust vis-à-vis development of Mumbai city; issue. The Ministry of Shipping Road Transport and Highways proposes to issue the necessary notification after finalizing the terms of reference of the Committee. This information was given by the Minister of Shipping, Road Transport and Highways, Shri T.R. Baalu in a written reply in the Lok Sabha today.

6860. (19-3-2008) NEW DELHI : The mineral production from mining and quarrying sector in December 2007 increased by 4.48% as compared to that of the preceding month. Similarly the mineral sector has shown a positive growth of 4.84% during the current financial year *i.e.* April-December 2007 as compared to that of the previous year. The mineral production in December 2007 was also higher by 3.01% as compared to that of the corresponding month of previous year. The total value of mineral production (excluding atomic & minor minerals) in the country during December 2007 was Rs.7943 crore. The contribution of coal was the highest at Rs.3498 crore (44%). Next in the order of importance were: petroleum (crude) Rs.1605 crore, iron ore Rs.1294 crore, natural gas (utilized) Rs.796 crore, lignite Rs.186 crore and limestone Rs.181 crore. These six minerals together contributed about 95% of the total value of mineral production in December 2007. Production level of important minerals in December 2007 were: coal 435 lakh tonnes, lignite 27 lakh tonnes, natural gas (utilized) 2752 million cu. m., petroleum (crude) 29 lakh tonnes, bauxite 1712 thousand tones, chromite 392 thousand tonnes, copper conc. 14 thousand tonnes, gold 222 kg., iron ore 165 lakh tonnes, lead conc. 11 thousand tonnes, manganese ore 214 thousand tonnes, zinc conc. 89 thousand tonnes, apatite & phosphorite 134 thousand tonnes, dolomite 362 thousand tonnes, limestone 156 lakh tonnes and magnesite 22 thousand tonnes. A nominal production of diamond was also reported in the current month. In December 2007 the output of apatite & phosphorite increased 34.19%, lead conc. 28.61%, magnesite 13.87%, manganese ore 11.86%, lignite 10.51%, coal 9.24%, zinc conc. 5.81%, iron ore 5.50%, gold 5.21%, petroleum (crude) 2.09% and natural gas (utilized) 1.89%. The production of copper conc. maintained the level of preceding month. Whereas the production of limestone decreased 1.39%, dolomite 2.44%, chromite 8.40% and bauxite 14.42 percent.

6861. (19-3-2008) NEW DELHI : The allocation of funds from Central Road Fund (CRF) for each State /Union Territory (UT) is finalized at the beginning of the financial year. All the States/UTs are provided with one-third of their allocation of CRF, which is maintained as reserve by the States/UTs. This is replenished by subsequent releases based on receipt of utilization certificates for the amount previously released and the progress of works. As such, there is no delay in this regard. This information was given by the Minister of State for Shipping, Road Transport and Highways, Shri K.H. Muniyappa in a written reply in the Lok Sabha today.

6862. (19-3-2008) NEW DELHI : The compensation to the deceased/injured in a road accident is given on the basis of Structured Compensation Formula prescribed under II Schedule of the Motors Vehicle Act, 1988 on no-fault principle basis. The amount is calculated on the basis of number of factors such as age of the victim, income, number of dependents etc. If the road accident victim/legal heir is not satisfied with the amount of compensation, he may approach Motor Accidents Claims Tribunal/Civil Courts for higher compensation on fault principle. The details regarding compensation paid to the accident victim are not compiled in the Ministry of Shipping, Road Transport and Highways as the compensation is paid by the Insurance Company. This information was given by the Minister of State for Shipping, Road Transport and Highways, Shri K.H. Muniyappa in a written reply in the Lok Sabha today.

6863. (19-3-2008) NEW DELHI : No proposal for construction of Road Over Bridge (ROB) on National Highway No.24 has been received from Railways

Authorities and State Government of Uttar Pradesh. However, construction of a 4-lane ROB in Km.181 of Hapur-Moradabad Section of National Highway No.24 is in progress. On National Highway No.24, all existing two lane ROBs are to be widened to 4 lane and all existing level crossings including at Mirganj/Fatehganj in Bareilly district are to be replaced with 4 lane ROB as part of 4 laning work under National Highway Development Project (NHDP) Phase III/other projects. This information was given by the Minister of State for Shipping, Road Transport and Highways, Shri K.H. Muniyappa in a written reply in the Lok Sabha today.

6864. (19-3-2008) NEW DELHI : The Union Government has initiated a process to adequately compensate those villagers who lost their land in connection with the construction of National Highway-52 from Rupai (Tinsukia district) to Dirak Gate bordering Arunachal Pradesh. A sum of Rs.266.44 lakh on account of land compensation pertaining to construction of National Highway-52 in between Km. 848 (3.0 Km ahead of Dirak) to Km. 875.76 (Rupai) has been deposited with the Deputy Commissioner, Tinsukia for disbursement to affected villagers and the amount of compensation for the stretch from Km. 845 to km. 848 has not yet been communicated by Deputy Commissioner, Tinsukia. This information was given by the Minister of State for Shipping, Road Transport and Highways, Shri K.H. Muniyappa in a written reply in the Lok Sabha today.

6865. (19-3-2008) NEW DELHI : Four-laning of National Highway (NH)-9 in Andhra Pradesh is being taken up in a phased manner. Hyderabad-Machillipatnam section of this NH is being taken up for four-laning by National Highways Authority of India (NHAI) on Build, Operate and Transfer (BOT) basis under National Highway Development Project (NHDP) Phase-III. Four-laning in a length of 31 km from Hyderabad to Sangareddy is in progress on BOT basis. These works are targeted for completion by December, 2011. Consultancy services for examining the viability of 4/6 laning of Sangareddy-Zaheerabad section of this NH on Design, Build, Finance and Operate (DBFO) pattern is under progress. Further action in this regard will depend upon the outcome of the said study. This information was given by the Minister of State for Shipping, Road Transport and Highways, Shri K.H. Muniyappa in a written reply in the Lok Sabha today.

6866. (19-3-2008) NEW DELHI : The Ministry of Shipping, Road Transport and Highways is carrying out the construction and resurfacing works on National Highways through the agencies namely, the State Public Works Departments, Border Roads Organization and National Highways Authority of India. The contractors are selected and appointed by the agencies following transparent competitive bidding procedure by open invitation of bids. Both domestic and international contracting firms are engaged depending on the size & nature of the work and meeting the organizational, financial and technical requirements. This information was given by the Minister of State for Shipping, Road Transport and Highways, Shri K.H. Muniyappa in a written reply in the Lok Sabha today.

6867. (19-3-2008) NEW DELHI : An amount of Rs. 15.00 crore has been allotted for Urdu channel of Doordarshan for the year 2007-08. Twenty one Urdu knowing persons have been given contract jobs in this channel. Effective packaging, outsourcing quality software from top producers from the field of production, film-making, culture, literature and media are some of the steps taken to popularise the channel. DD Urdu is already available in Doordarshan's free to air DTH service. In addition to that Prasar Bharati has notified DD Urdu channel for mandatory carriage by the cable operators/multi system operators (MSOs) in all States and Union Territories. This information was given by Shri P.R. Dasmunsi, Minister for Information and Broadcasting & Parliamentary Affairs in a written reply to a question in the Parliament today.

6868. (19-3-2008) NEW DELHI : A regulatory mechanism is proposed for broadcasting sector. The proposed Broadcast Services Regulation Bill has provisions for constitution of Broadcasting Services Regulatory Authority. The proposed Bill does not compromise the freedom of expression as guaranteed in our Constitution. The Government has been consulting stakeholders including News Broadcasters Association on the proposed Bill. This information was given by Shri P.R. Dasmunsi, Minister for Information and Broadcasting & Parliamentary Affairs in a written reply to a question in the Parliament today.

6869. (19-3-2008) NEW DELHI : The Government has decided to continue the scheme for Integrated Textiles Parks (SITP) in the 11th Five year Plan, taking into consideration, the response to the scheme and the opportunities for the growth of textile industry in the quota free regime. The scheme targets industrial clusters / locations with high growth potential, which require strategic interventions by way of providing world-class infrastructure support. The project cost will cover common infrastructure and buildings for production / support activities (including textiles engineering, accessories, packaging), depending on the needs of the Integrated Textile Park (ITP). There will be flexibility in setting up ITPs to suit the local requirements.

6870. (19-3-2008) NEW DELHI : The Marketing Support & Services Scheme is being implemented during the 11th Plan Period with the aim to provide direct marketing outlets to the craftpersons for participation in various marketing events/ melas for augmenting their sales. This information was given by the Minister of State for Textiles, Shri E.V.K.S. Elangovan, in the Rajya Sabha today, in a written reply to a question by Ms. Pramila Bohidar and Sh. B.J. Panda. He further stated that the scheme has three broad components *i.e.* Domestic Marketing, International Marketing and Publicity. A sum of Rs.97.19 lakhs have been sanctioned to various implementing agencies under the scheme to the State of Orissa during 2007-08. In addition 6 exhibitions has been sanctioned to various agencies. The Minister further said that the aim of the scheme is to provide more marketing outlets to craftpersons which indirectly create more employment channels and not to provide full time job.

6871. (19-3-2008) NEW DELHI : As per the Report of the Working Group on Textile and Jute Industry for the Eleventh Five Year Plan (2007-12), the estimated employment in the textile industry is expected to increase from 33.17 million persons as on 31.3.2006 to 45.19 million persons by the terminal year of the Eleventh Plan. Employment in the allied industries is expected to increase from 54.85 million persons to 60.20 million persons. Consequently, the total employment in the textile sector including allied industries is projected to increase to 105.39 million persons in 2011-12 from the present level of 88.02 million persons, resulting in a net addition of 17.37 million persons. The vision projected by the textile industry envisages that cloth production would grow at 12% and the total turnover at 16% per annum during the Eleventh Five Year Plan and reach a level of US$ 115 billion by the terminal year of the Eleventh Plan. In order to achieve the projected level of growth, it is necessary to address the various handicaps of the manufacturing sector such as deficiencies in transport infrastructure, inadequate power supply, inflexible labour laws etc. In addition to making concerted efforts to address such handicaps, the Government is implementing specific schemes such as Technology Upgradation Fund Scheme (TUFS), Scheme for Integrated Textile Parks (SITP) etc. with a view to modernizing the textile industry and enabling the industry to benefit from economies of scale and integrated production. This information was given by the Minister of State for Textiles, Shri E.V.K.S. Elangovan, in the Rajya Sabha today, in a written reply to a question by Smt. N.P. Durga.

6872. (19-3-2008) NEW DELHI : Addressing the Indo-Turkish Business Summit titled "A New Beginning for Turkish-Indian Relations: Business and Investment Opportunities, here today, Dr. Ashwani Kumar, Minister of State for Industry, has called for increasing the trade and investment flows between India and Turkey. He said that GDP in both the countries is dominated by private sector and find similarities in pluralist, secular democracy and free market economy, which enabled four times growth of trade between 2002-03 to 2006-07 at US $ 1.6 billion. The Seminar was also addressed by Mr. Kursad Tuzmen, Turkish Minister of State for Foreign Trade and Foreign Contacting Services, and attended by senior officials from the Ministry of Commerce and Industry and representatives of apex chambers from both the countries. During the course of discussion, Dr. Ashwani Kumar, flagged four key aspects of policy framework *i.e.*, agriculture & rural development; infrastructure education; and health care for stepping up growth and at the same time make growth more inclusive, he Indian investments in Turkey are in diverse sectors *viz.*, railway construction, electricity transmission, pipelines, consultancy services for earthquake emergency, hydro-carbon, CNG conversion and IT services. Turkish investments in India are in sectors of tourism & travel, home textile products, construction/maintenance of roads etc. India's exports to Turkey largely consist of manmade yarn fabrics, made-ups, transport equipments, cotton yarn, fabrics, drugs & pharmaceuticals & fine chemicals, plastic & linoleum products etc. The main imports from Turkey are petroleum, crude products, machinery except electrical & electronics, inorganic chemicals, spices etc.

6873. (19-3-2008) NEW DELHI : The Tourism and Culture Minister Smt. Ambika Soni has said that any proposal for inclusion of Disability Studies in academic discipline should be supported as it will create awareness in the society about the needs and rights of the physically challenged persons. Inaugurating a three day "National Congress on Disability Studies in Secondary and Higher Education in India" here today she said, attitude has to be changed towards the physically challenged persons as they are challenged in a limited sense only and can do wonders in other areas of their expertise or interests. She said people at work place, society and in the country as a whole must be sensitized about the needs of the physically challenged and their rights within the Constitutional framework. Referring to the socially and economically disadvantaged groups in the country, Smt. Ambika Soni said we must work towards creating an inclusive society where every person would contribute in the growth and development of the country. She said a public awareness campaign for creating such an inclusive growth is the need of the hour. The Union Ministries of Tourism and Culture are sensitive to the special needs of challenged people. All the World Heritage Sites are in the process of being provided special facilities for such people. Other important monuments will also be provided with facilities which would improve access to these monuments to people with special needs. This would enable them to appreciate the heritage of this country in the same manner as other citizens. The Tourism Ministry is also encouraging the hotels and other tourism related infrastructure to be developed in a manner that people with special needs can also use them as effectively as others. Both the ministries will keep making further efforts in this direction.

6874. (19-3-2008) NEW DELHI : Vice Admiral Nirmal Verma will take over as the Flag officer commander-in-chief of the Eastern Naval Command from Vice Admiral Raman P Suthan, who in turn will take over as Vice Chief of Naval Staff on completion of an illustrious tenure as C-in-C of the Eastern Naval Command. The Eastern seaboard has gained prominence in the recent past and this is witnessed by the increasing engagement with immediate regional neighbours like Bangladesh, Indonesia, Malaysia, Myanmar, Singapore, Thailand and other states of South East Asia. Vice Admiral Nirmal Verma was commissioned into the Indian Navy on 01 Jul. 1970. An alumnus of the National Defence Academy, he is a specialist in Communications and Electronics Warfare. During his career spanning over 37 years, he has served in various afloat and shore appointments. As a Communications specialist, he has served as the Fleet Communication Officer of the Western Fleet, and at the Directorate of Naval Signals. His command tenures include INS Udaygiri (Leander Class Frigates), INS Ranvir (Destroyer) and the Aircraft Carrier INS Viraat. He has also commanded the Indian Naval Academy, INS Mandovi.

The Flag Officer is a graduate of the Royal Naval Staff College, Greenwich, UK, and thereafter served as the Head of the Training Team at Defence Services Staff College, Wellington. He is also a graduate of the US Naval War College, after which he has served as Senior Directing Staff (Navy) at the National Defence College, New Delhi. He has been the Chief of Staff of the Indian Navy's Eastern Naval Command and the Flag Officer Commanding Maharashtra Naval Area. The Flag Officer later served at Naval Headquarters as Assistant Chief of Naval Staff (Policy and Plans). On being promoted to the rank of Vice Admiral, he was appointed Chief of Personnel in Nov 2005. He took over as Vice Chief of Naval Staff on 30 Nov 06. Vice Admiral Suthan, who was earlier the Deputy Chief of Naval Staff and at present is the C-in-C of the Eastern Naval Command, brings with him excellent operational training and admin planning experience that would be crucial to shaping the Navy of tomorrow.

6875. (19-3-2008) NEW DELHI : An emigrant Indian worker holding (ECR) category passport and going for employment in any of the ECR country has to seek emigration clearance under the Emigration Act, 1983, from the offices of Protectors of Emigrants (POEs) under the administrative control of this Ministry. Cases of workers going abroad on visit/transit visas and taking up employment in that country have come to the notice of this Ministry and Indian Missions from time to time. Whenever such instances are reported, the Missions take up the matter with the local government there to redress the grievances of the workers and extends all help for repatriation of such workers back to India. Gulf Countries from time to time declare Amnesty for illegal migrants either to regularize their stay or leave the country without penalty. On declaration of such Amnesty the Indian Missions take up the matter with local authorities either for regularizing the stay of such workers or issue of emergency certificates for their deportation back to India. This Ministry coordinates with the Ministries of Home Affairs and Civil Aviation for ensuring their safe passage back to India.

6876. (20-3-2008) NEW DELHI : Government has been keeping a close watch on the domestic and international prices of essential commodities, particularly food items such as wheat, rice, pulses, and edible oils so as to keep inflation under check. It has also taken appropriate fiscal measures from time to time to achieve this objective. Full exemption from customs duty available to wheat has been extended beyond the expiry date of 31st December, 2007 and wheat flour has also been fully exempted from customs duty. Over the last six months, the international price of rice has increased sharply from US $ 430 (August 2007) to US $ 590 (February 2008) (FAS US Gulf). Domestic retail price in Delhi markets increased from Rs.15 to Rs.18 per kg over the same period. Owing to a surge in demand, international prices of edible oils have also continued to exhibit a sharp and steady upward trend in recent months. For instance, the international price of crude palm oil (fob Malaysia) has increased from US$ 770 PMT in the last week of August, 2007 to about US$ 1220 PMT in the last week of February, 2008. During the same period, the international price of sunflower oil (c.i.f. Rotterdam) has increased from US$ 947 to US$ 1695 PMT-an increase of about 79%. An increase of this order has obviously put pressure on domestic prices of edible oils despite two rounds of reductions in customs duties on palm oil in April, 2007 (by 10 percentage points) and again in July, 2007 (by 5 percentage points). Wholesale prices of RBD palmolein (Mumbai) have increased from Rs.4500 per quintal in August 2007 to Rs.5820 per quintal in February, 2008. Over the same period, price of sunflower oil (Mumbai) has increased from Rs. 4900 per quintal to Rs. 8250 per quintal and of mustard oil (Delhi) from Rs. 4960 per quintal to Rs. 6330 per quintal.

6877. (20-3-2008) NEW DELHI : The Cabinet today gave its approval for taking up the development of Anandpur Sahib and Talwandi Sabo as Commemorative Projects under the Ter-Centenary celebrations of Guru-ta-Gaddi of Shri Guru Granth Sahib in 2008. The Cabinet also gave its approval for funding the above development projects as a special grant of Rs. 17957.77 lakhs to the Punjab Government [for Anandpur Sahib Rs. 9973.77 lakhs and for Talwandi Sabo Rs. 7984 lakhs] as part of Ter-Centenary celebrations of Guru-ta-Gaddi of Shri Guru Granth Sahib at Nanded, 2008. The decision will enable the commemoration of the events which are presently mostly focused at Nanded. Development of Talwandi Sabo and Anandpur Sahib in Punjab which are important places associated with Guru Gobind Singhji and place of pilgrimage will also be given significance in the commemoration. State Government of Punjab to whom grant will be released, will be asked to complete the projects within the commemoration year *i.e.* by October, 2009.

6878. (20-3-2008) NEW DELHI : The Cabinet Committee on Economic Affairs today gave its approval to the Statutory Minimum Price (SMP) for sugarcane at Rs.81.18 per quintal for a basic recovery of 9 per cent subject to a premium of Rs.0.90 for every 0.1 percentage point increase in the recovery above that level for sugar season 2008-09. The SMP is based on the recommendations of Commission for Agricultural Costs and Prices (CACP). It will ensure a minimum price to cane growers.

6879. (20-3-2008) NEW DELHI : Under the Negotiable Instruments Act, State Governments may notify and declare any 15 holidays in their States including three National Holidays, namely, Republic Day, Independence Day and Birthday of Mahatma Gandhi. It has been ascertained that the Kerala State Government has declared 21st March, 2008 (Good Friday) as a Holiday under the Negotiable Instruments Act. Hence, all banks will be closed in Kerala on 21st March, 2008.

6880. (20-3-2008) NEW DELHI : The Orissa Government has requested the Rural Development Ministry to allocate additional funds of Rs.200 crore for the speedy implementation of the National Rural Employment Guarantee Act (NREGA). The demand came in a meeting held between the Union Rural Development

Minister Dr. Raghuvansh Prasad Singh and the Orissa Chief Minister Shri Navin Patnayak here today. Dr. Singh assured Shri Patnayak of all possible help for the different rural schemes under implementation in the State. The issue of BPL Survey list also came up in the meeting as Orrisa Chief Minister vouched for the continuation of work on the 1997 BPL list as the 2002 BPL survey list was not finalized in the State. However, the Rural Development Minister stressed that work on the basis of 2002 list has to be done as per the Planning Commission requirements.

6881. (20-3-2008) NEW DELHI : National programme of Mid Day Meal in Schools, earlier called National Nutritional support to Primary Education was launched as a Centrally Sponsored Scheme on 15th August 1995 in 2408 blocks in the county. By the year 1997-98, the programme was introduced in all blocks in the country. It was extended in 2003 to cover children studying in centres of Education Guarantee Scheme (EGS) and Alternative and Innovative Education (AIEs). From October 2007 it has been extended to children studying in classes VI to VIII in 3479 Educationally Backward Blocks (EBBs) in the country. From 2008-09, the programme will cover all children studying at upper primary stage in all areas across the country. Budget 2008-09 provides Rs.8000 crore for this programme. During the year 9.7 crore children at primary stage and 4.20 crore children at upper primary stage are expected to be covered under the programme.

6882. (20-3-2008) NEW DELHI : There are 12 Major Ports, namely, Kolkata, Paradip, Visakhapatnam, Ennore, Chennai, Tuticorin, Cochin, New Mangalore, Mormugao, Jawaharlal Nehru, Mumbai and Kandla Ports. These Major Ports are under the control of the Central Government. In addition, there are 200 Non-major Ports (earlier known as Minor Ports) which are under the overall jurisdiction of the respective Maritime State Governments. Development of infrastructure in the major ports is an on going activity, keeping in view the demands of maritime trade. The activities, performance, productivity and the profitability of the Major Ports vary depending on a number of factors including their location, infrastructure, labour, resources and cargo profile. In the absence of a common base for measurement, it is thus not feasible to rank them. The aggregate capacity in the 12 Major Ports which was 389.50 million tonnes per annum (MTPA) as on 31.3.2004 reached a level of 504.75 MTPA as on 31.3.2007, involving capacity addition of 115.25 MTPA during the three years period through various developmental activities, mainly, construction of new berths, expansion of existing berths and improvement in productivity. The aggregate capacity is expected to go upto 528.75 MTPA by 31.3.2008 and 1016.55 MTPA by the end of the Eleventh Five Year Plan period mainly through projects for berth development, procurement/ modernization and upgradation of cargo handling equipment. During the Eleventh Plan period, a Plan outlay of Rs.1227.74 crores, Rs.1254.79 crores and Rs.1448.20 crores are envisaged for the expansion and development of Ennore, Chennai and Tuticorin Ports respectively. In addition, private investment to the extent of

Rs.5300 crores, Rs.833.50 crores and Rs.5115.08 crores are also envisaged in the three ports respectively during the Eleventh Plan period. The capacities in the three Ports are planned to be enhanced to 64.20 MTPA, 73.50 MTPA and 63.98 MTPA by the end of the 11th Plan period.

6883. (20-3-2008) NEW DELHI : A High Power Steering Group under the Chairmanship of the Minister (Shipping, Road Transport & Highways) with the Union Minister of Tourism & Culture as Co-Chairperson was set up to formulate a cruise shipping policy with the objective of making India a major cruise tourism destination for attracting the right segment of foreign cruise tourists and for popularising cruise shipping, facilitating creation of requisite infrastructure and creating a conducive environment. The policy is under finalization in consultation with the concerned Ministries. This information was given by the Minister of Shipping, Road Transport and Highways, Shri T.R. Baalu in a written reply in the Rajya Sabha today.

6884. (20-3-2008) NEW DELHI : The Port Business Plans with a 20 year perspective for the 12 Major Ports have been prepared. Consultants, selected through the international competitive bidding process were engaged by the respective ports for the purpose. The Port Business Plans address the long term vision, goals and strategy of Ports; current Port capabilities and recent performance; competitive situation and outlook; new business opportunities and demand forecast; removing barriers to Ports performance; required investment in Port facilities and equipment; required improvements in hinterland connectivity; financing future investment requirements. Ports declared as Major Ports under the Indian Ports Act, 1908 are under the administrative control of the Central Government. All other ports, including private ports, collectively known as Non-Major Ports are under the overall jurisdiction of the respective Maritime State Governments. This information was given by the Minister of Shipping, Road Transport and Highways, Shri T.R. Baalu in a written reply in the Rajya Sabha today.

6885. (20-3-2008) NEW DELHI : A proposal for Rehabilitation-cum-Financial Restructuring of Hindustan Shipyard Limited (HSL) is under consideration of the Government. A Group of Ministers (GoM) constituted in this regard, has considered it and made certain recommendations The recommendations of the GoM shall be placed before the Cabinet Committee on Economic Affairs (CCEA) for consideration and approval. This information was given by the Minister of Shipping, Road Transport and Highways, Shri T.R. Baalu in a written reply in the Rajya Sabha today.

6886. (20-3-2008) NEW DELHI : There is a proposal for setting up two international size shipyards, one on the East Coast and another on the West Coast of India. An international size shipyard may build and repair ships upto the size of Very Large Crude Carrier (VLCC) which has a carrying capacity of 300,000

Tonnes (DWT). The shipyard may be located in a place which has 10-12 metres water depth at the jetty. The international size shipyard may have at least two and preferably three big dry docks (2 for building and 1 for repair), a quayside length of at least 2.5 kms and various support facilities for building and assembly of ships.

6887. (20-3-2008) NEW DELHI : 21 Projects for development of Inland Water Transport sector were received from the Govt. of Kerala under Centrally Sponsored Scheme [CSS]. Out of these, one project namely "Revival of Veli-Kovalam stretch of TS canal" was sanctioned at a cost of Rs 362.22 lakhs and initial release of Rs.65.30 lakhs was also made during 2004-05 to the State Government. Five projects could not be processed for sanction for want of information sought from the State Government. Remaining fifteen (15) projects could not be sanctioned as CSS was discontinued from April last year by the Planning Commission. This information was given by the Minister of Shipping, Road Transport and Highways, Shri T.R. Baalu in a written reply in the Rajya Sabha today.

6888. (20-3-2008) NEW DELHI : The Government has declared three rivers/ canal system, as National Waterways namely (i) the Ganga from Allahabad to Haldia (1620km) (ii) the Brahmaputra from Sadiya to Dhubri (891km) and (iii) the West Coast Canal from Kollam to Kottapuram along with Champakara and Udyogmandal canals (205km). Basic infrastructural facilities for shipping and navigation namely navigational channel, navigational aids, and terminals are being provided on these National Waterways.

6889. (20-3-2008): AMRITSAR: In a bold statement on Wednesday, the wife of Sarabjit Singh said the family did not want him repatriated from Pakistan if it meant India releasing some terrorists in exchange. "Myself and my daughters would never like Sarabjit freed in exchange for any hardcore Pakistani terrorist lodged in Indian jails," Sarabjit's wife, Sukhpreet Kaur, told PTI. Ms. Kaur said that for the family, "nothing is above the nation and we can't go against the interests of our motherland."

6890. (20-3-2008) NEW DELHI : The 23rd meeting of the Board of Approval for Special Economic Zones (SEZs) was held on 20th March, 2008 to consider proposals for setting up of Special Economic Zones and also approve other miscellaneous requests pertaining to SEZs. Chairman informed the members of the Board that so far formal approvals have been granted for setting up of 449 SEZs out of which 206 have been notified as on date. In this meeting, 9 proposals for setting up SEZs, including 1 proposal for conversion of In-Principle approval to Formal Approval were considered.

6891. (20-3-2008) NEW DELHI : According to consultancy firm Takashi Mobile, website of OFCOM (Telecom Regulator of United Kingdom) and information available on internet, Mobile Virtual Network Operators (MVNOs) are operational in Belgium, Denmark, Finland, The Netherlands, Norwey, France, Germany,

United Kingdom and United States. MVNO business models are in the process of being launched in some other countries, namely Portugal, Spain, Italy, Croatia, The Baltics, Chile and Austria. Mobile Virtual Network Operator is a new kind of service and as per Section 11 of the Telecom Regulatory Authority of India (TRAI) Act, 1997, the Government is required to seek recommendations of TRAI on need and timing for introduction of new service providers and regarding terms and conditions of license to be granted to such service providers. As on date, no decision in this regard has been taken by the Government. This information was given by the Minister of State for Communications and Information Technology, Dr. Shakeel Ahmed in a written reply to an un-starred question in the Rajya Sabha today.

6892. (20-3-2008) NEW DELHI : 143 numbers of National Highway projects under National Highway Development Project (NHDP) as well as 34 number of projects with State PWD each costing more than Rs. 5.00 crore are lagging behind the schedule due to problems associated with acquisition of land, shifting of utilities, delay in environmental and forest clearance, poor performance of some contractors and law & order and insurgency problems in some States. The Government closely monitors the progress of the construction works of National Highways at various levels through quarterly reviews and also has taken steps like appointing senior officers as nodal officers for resolving problems, constituting a Committee of Secretaries to address inter-ministerial and central-state issues and has taken action against defaulting contractors in order to ensure completion of National Highways works as per stipulated time frame. This information was given by the Minister of State for Shipping, Road Transport and Highways, Shri K.H. Muniyappa in a written reply in the Rajya Sabha today.

6893. (20-3-2008) NEW DELHI : This Ministry of Shipping, Road Transport & Highways is primarily responsible for the development and maintenance of National Highways in the country. The Ganga Expressway Project is a State road project to be taken up by Government of Uttar Pradesh on Public-Private-Partnership (PPP) mode. State Government did not propose to seek any support from Central Government. Government of Uttar Pradesh has reported that land is a State subject, but they have sought clearance from Department of Road, Transport & Highways for construction of the expressway on the suggestion of the Ganga Flood Control Board and in their view, the proposed expressway would not be a competing road to any on-going projects of National Highway Authority of India (NHAI). This Ministry is of the view that the proposed expressway would not generally present a problem for the projects of NHAI but that the impact in the stretch of about 200 km beyond Kanpur on National Highway No. 2 would need to be carefully assessed. This information was given by the Minister of State for Shipping, Road Transport and Highways, Shri K.H. Muniyappa in a written reply in the Rajya Sabha today.

6894. (20-3-2008) NEW DELHI : The Government had announced 1,000 km of expressway along the corridors of Vadodara-Mumbai (400 km) and six others from which the balance 600 km were to be selected. Delhi-Jaipur was one such corridor. Further decision for Delhi-Jaipur expressway is yet to be taken. However, Delhi-Jaipur section has been approved for six laning and the Build, Operate and Transfer (BOT) concession for the project has been awarded in February, 2008 under National Highways Development Project (NHDP) Phase-V. This information was given by the Minister of State for Shipping, Road Transport and Highways, Shri K.H. Muniyappa in a written reply in the Rajya Sabha today.

6895. (20-3-2008) NEW DELHI : 4 laning of Patna-Muzaffarpur section of NH 19 & 77 has been included under NHDP Phase III in the State of Bihar on BOT (Toll) mode. Bids for 4 laning of Patna-Muzaffarpur Section of NH 19 & 77 were invited in June 2005 under old Model Concession Agreement (MCA) for which no response was received. Bids were again invited for the second time in June 2007 on the basis of new MCA with the last date of submission of bid as 20.08.2007. But, no response was received this time also. As there is no response of bidders on toll based BOT bid for the project stretch, Government has accorded approval for changing the mode of upgradation of Patna-Muzaffarpur Section of NH 19 & 77 from BOT (Toll) to BOT (Annuity). This information was given by the Minister of State for Shipping, Road Transport and Highways, Shri K.H. Muniyappa in a written reply in the Rajya Sabha today.

6896. (20-3-2008) NEW DELHI : Department of Commerce, Ministry of Commerce & Industry, Government of India launched the Price Stabilisation Fund Scheme in April 2003 for the benefit of growers of Tea, Coffee, Natural Rubber and Tobacco. The objective of the Price Stabilisation Fund Scheme is to provide financial relief to the growers when the prices of these commodities fall below a specified level. The scheme is based on the principle of contribution from the growers and from the Government depending upon boom / normal / distress years, with a provision for withdrawal by the growers during the distress year. The contribution of the participant grower as well as that of the Government is credited to the savings bank account of the participant grower opened for this purpose with nationalized banks. The Price Stabilisation Fund Trust, Department of Commerce, Government of India has announced the Price Spectrum Band for the year 2007 for Rubber, Coffee and Tea. The Price Spectrum Band for each commodity has been calculated on the basis of Seven Years' Moving average of International price for the commodity. The annual average domestic price for Tea was Rs.64.66/kg during 2007 and it has been categorised as 'Normal Year" for Tea. The annual average domestic price for Coffee Arabica during 2007 was Rs.112.70/kg and it has been categorised as 'Boom Year" for Coffee Arabica. The annual average domestic price for Coffee Robusta was Rs.75.76/kg during 2007 and it has been categorised as 'Boom Year" for Coffee Robusta. The annual average domestic price for Rubber was Rs.90.06/kg during 2007 and it has been categorised as 'Boom Year" for Rubber. As no tobacco grower is enrolled under the scheme, Price Spectrum Band for tobacco has not been fixed. On the basis of Price Spectrum Band 2007, 15289 Tea growers would receive financial assistance of Rs.0.76 crore from the PSF Trust during 2008-09. Price Stabilisation Fund Trust, Ministry of Commerce and Industry, New Delhi, March 20, 2008.

6897. (20-3-2008) NEW DELHI : Lieutenant General SPS Dhillon, Deputy Chief of Army Staf (Information System and Training) addressed the contingent of Fifth Battalion the Garhwal Rifles (5 Garhwal Rifles), Tenth Battalion the Assam Regiment (10 Assam Regiment), Sixth Battalion the Sikh Light Infantry (6 Sikh Light Infantry), Headquarters 301 Infantry Brigade, Level III Hospital and 19 Recce and observation Flight, earmarked to represent the country in The Democratic Republic of Congo, Africa, as part of the United Peace Keeping Mission MONUC. 5 Garhwal Rifles was raised on 01 Feb 1962. The battalion has been nominated for the coveted UN Mission for their outstanding performances in 1971 War, Op Battle Axe in Mizoram, Op Rakshak in the state of Jammu & Kashmir during 1993-95, Op Rhino in Assam, Op Vijay and Op Parakram. For their heroic acts performed during the 1971 War, the battalion was conferred Battle Honour 'Hilli' and Theatre Honour 'East Pakistan' by the President of India. The battalion has been the proud recipient of the Chief of the Army Staff unit Citation for their meritorious performance in Op Rakshak during 1993-95 in the state of Jammu & Kashmir. The gallant troops of this unit have also won a number of individual awards which includes 01 Kirti Chakra, 04 Veer Chakras, 05 Shaurya Chakras, 21 Sena Medals, 01 Vishist Seva Medal, 07 mentioned-in-dispatches, 56 COAS' Commendation Cards, 03 VCOAS' Commendation Cards, 27 Army Commanders' Commendation Cards, 01 AOC-in-C Commendation Card and two DG NCC's Commendation Cards. 10 Assam Regiment, raised on 01 Mar 1981, has earned its coveted place on the Mission for its outstanding performances in Op Blue Star, Op Falcon, Op Rakshak I & II in the state of Jammu & Kashmir during 1995-97, Op Vijay and Op Rhino. The battalion has been the proud recipient of the Chief of the Army Staff Unit Citation for their meritorious performance in Operation Rakshak during 1995-97 in the state of Jammu & Kashmir. Soldiers and officers of this excellent outfit have also earned one SC, one VSM, seven SM, one Mentioned-in-Dispatch, 38 COAS Commendation Cards, 01 VCOAS Commendation Card and 15 Army Commander's Commendation Cards. 19 R&O Flight was raised on 01 Dec. 1974 at Jodhpur. Since its raising it has participated in all major operation during which includes Op Meghdoot, Op Trident and Op Falcon. 19 R&O Flight played a sterling role during Op Vijay and for it's outstanding performance was awarded the coveted COAS Unit Citation. The gallant troops of the Flight have been awarded won 01 SC, 03 VSM, 01 YSM, 02 Sena Medal, 01 Mention-in-Dispatch, 11 COAS Commendation Card and 03 GOC-in-C Commendation Card. In addition to the above mentioned meritorious battalions troops of 6 SIKH LIGHT INFANTRY battalion are being rotated after completion of six months and selected personnel of 301 Infantry Brigade and Level III Hospital are getting induct4ed in the mission area. The Deputy Chief of Army Staff (Information System and Training) while addressing the troops praised the outstanding work done by the Indian contingents in several United Nations Peace Keeping Operations in the past and expected to live up to their standards. He reminded them of the challenging tasks ahead and exhorted them to demonstrate their tradition of selfless dedication, devotion and humanitarian approach for ensuring peace in Democratic Republic of Congo, Africa.

6898. (20-3-2008) NEW DELHI : Active participation of States in horticulture-sector schemes and convergence of schemes of different Ministries have started bearing fruits and the high growth in this sector will be visible from 2008-09. This was underlined by Agriculture Minister, Shri Sharad Pawar, while reviewing the progress of National Horticulture Mission and the National Horticulture Board here today. Charting the investments made and support given by the Mission and the Board in the last few years, Shri Pawar informed that the Horticulture Mission has been extended to 340 districts and Rs. 8809 crore have been earmarked for it in the XI Plan. The Horticulture Board has assisted 7035 projects for area expansion and 209 for cold storage in 2006-07. He expressed satisfaction that the National Horticulture Mission has been able to achieve convergence of programme of different Ministries. He elaborated that 'the Ministry of Rural Development has taken initiative to provide road connectivity in NHM clusters for linking with markets under the Prime Minister's Grameen Sadak Yojana. The Ministry of Food Processing Industries has initiated dialogue for operationalising food processing units in NHM clusters. There is a close coordination between Ministry of Health and Family Welfare for the development of Medicinal Plants. The Krishi Vigyan Kendras and State Agriculture Universities are being closely involved in providing technical support and expertise for the mission activities apart from directly implementing some key activities such as production of quality planting material, demonstration of technologies and training of farmers. The ICAR has been closely involved in developing a package for responding to the Bacterial Blight Disease in Pomegranate, which has affected large areas in the States of Maharashtra, Karnataka and Andhra Pradesh. Special incentives have also been provided under the NHM to contain the Blight infestation in pomegranate.

6899. (20-3-2008) NEW DELHI : The reports regarding India Global Youth Tobacco Survey (GYTS) and the India Global Health Professional Student Survey (GHPSS) were released today by the Union Minister for Health & Family Welfare, Dr. Anbumani Ramadoss. These Reports prepared on the basis of extensive surveys done on behalf of the Ministry of Health & Family Welfare and World Health Organization reflect that there is a high prevalence of tobacco use among students, school personnel and also medical students. The Surveys were done during 2006 among students in the age group of 13-15 years, school personnel and 3rd year Medical / Dental students. The findings from these surveys highlight the need for targeted interventions among youth and children. It also highlights the need for sensitization of the school personnel and the health professionals as they play a prominent role in bringing awareness about the harmful ill effects of tobacco amongst the youth and other segments of society.

6900. (20-3-2008) NEW DELHI : The status of women in India has been subject to great many changes over the past few millennia. Women in India now participate in all activities such as education, politics, media, art and culture, service sector, science and technology, etc. Our Constitution guarantees equal rights for men and women. The Constitution is firmly grounded in the principles of liberty, fraternity, equality and justice. It contains a number of provisions for the empowerment of women. Women's right to equality and non/discrimination are defined as justiciable fundamental rights. The Constitution explicitly clarifies that affirmative action programmes for women are not incompatible with the principle of non-discrimination on the grounds of sex. The Government of India has always attached great importance to the protection and promotion of the human rights of women and is committed to achieving it. National plans and policies have consistently reflected a vision of progress that is not narrowly confined to expanding incomes, but gives a central place to the achievement of human rights, freedoms and well-being for all.

6901. (20-3-2008) NEW DELHI : The ambient air quality is monitored at 7(seven) locations in the National Capital Territory (NCT) of Delhi by the Central Pollution Control Board (CPCB) under the National Ambient Air Quality Monitoring Programme (NAMP). These locations include residential areas, industrial areas and traffic intersection. As per the monitored data, the levels of sulphur dioxide and carbon monoxide in the ambient air are showing a decreasing trend. The nitrogen dioxide levels decreased during the year 2007 in comparison to 2006. The concentration of the Suspended Particulate Matter (SPM) in residential and Industrial areas indicates mixed trend during 2001-2007. Sophisticated equipments for 3 (three) Continuous Ambient Air Quality Monitoring Stations (CAAQMS) and 7 (seven) PM2.5 Samplers have been procured by the CPCB for monitoring of gaseous pollutants including fine particulate matter for assessing the ambient air quality in the NCT of Delhi. This information was given by the Minister of State for Environment and Forests Shri Namo Narain Meena, in a written reply to a question by Shri Dharam Pal Sabharwal, in the Rajya Sabha today.

6902. (20-3-2008) NEW DELHI : According to a study conducted by the Central Pollution Control Board (CPCB), the stretch of river Yamuna between Wazirabad and Okhla in Delhi is among the most polluted stretches of major rivers across the country. It has been reported that the volume of wastewater generated from Delhi accounts for about 79 per cent of the total wastewater generated from major towns located along the banks of river Yamuna. Due to large scale extraction of water from the river upstream of Wazirabad barrage at Delhi for various uses, the flow of river in Delhi stretch mainly comprises of the wastewater flow from the surrounding areas during the non-monsoon period. The groundwater quality monitored by CPCB at the selected locations of Delhi area indicates that at Prahladpur, the concentration of toxic metals exceeds the drinking water quality standards prescribed by the Bureau of Indian Standards (BIS) during the pre-monsoon period. However, the groundwater quality improves in the post monsoon period due to recharge. Government of India has launched Yamuna Action Plan (YAP) for the abatement of pollution in river Yamuna with the assistance of the Japan Bank for International Cooperation in a phased manner. YAP, Phase-I was launched in April, 1993, and declared closed in February, 2003. The second phase of YAP was commenced in December, 2004. The total approved cost of both the phases of Yamuna Action Plan is Rs.1339 crores and expenditure incurred so far under both the phases is 719.76 crores. In addition to the YAP, the Government of NCT of Delhi has also taken up large scale pollution abatement works for river Yamuna from its own resources. A total of 269 schemes have been implemented in 21 towns of the three States of Delhi, Uttar Pradesh and Haryana and 753.25 million litres per day of sewage treatment capacity has been created so far under both the phases of YAP. The works completed under YAP include interception and diversion of raw sewage, setting up of Sewage Treatment Plants, creation of low cost sanitation facilities, setting up of electric/improved wood crematoria and River Front Development. This information was given by the Minister of State for Environment and Forests Shri Namo Narain Meena, in a written reply to a question by Shri Ekanath K. Thakur in the Rajya Sabha today.

6903. (20-3-2008) NEW DELHI : As reported by Ministry of Water Resources, Government of India, ground water level has declined in some parts of the country. As per the assessment of ground water resources carried out jointly by the Central Ground Water Board (CGWB) and the States in 2004, the ground water resource assessment units (Blocks/ Mandals/ Talukas) in various states of the country are categorized as Over-exploited, Critical and Semi-critical based on the stage of ground water development and the long term water level declining trend either in pre-monsoon or post-monsoon or both during the past decade (1995-2004). Out of 5723 such assessment units, 839 units have been categorized as 'Over-exploited', 226 units are reported to be 'Critical' whereas 550 units have been identified as 'Semi-critical'. Information regarding the instruction of the Hon'ble High court on conservation of ponds is not available with the Ministry of Water Resources. As per information from Ground Water Department, Government of Uttar Pradesh, a total of 51488 ponds have been restored / conserved. Government of India has undertaken steps to check depletion in the level of ground water by adopting measures through rain water harvesting and artificial recharge. These include circulation of a Model Bill for enactment of suitable legislation, circulation of manual to formulate area specific schemes, preparation of Master Plan for artificial recharge, constitution of Central Ground Water Authority under the Environment (Protection) Act, 1986 for regulation and control of ground water management and development, implementation of Central sector schemes for study of artificial recharge to ground water in the country during IX & XI Plans etc.

6904. (20-3-2008) NEW DELHI : A multi-billion shrimp seed multiplication centre is being established to produce Pathogen-free seed of shrimp. The Multiplication Centre will be established in Srikakulam district of Andhra Pradesh with technology from M/s Moana Technolgies Hong Kong. It would bring genetically improved shrimp, SPF-shrimp, and produce about three billion post-larvae at full capacity in about three years. This is expected to bring in a new approach for quality seed management, enhanced productivity and profitability in Indian aquaculture. An agreement for the above project was signed between the National Fisheries Development Board and M/s Moana Technologies, Hong Kong at New Delhi today in the presence of Shri Sharad Pawar, Union Minister for Agriculture. The Minister is also the Chairman of Governing Body of National Fisheries Development Board. Shri Pawar lauded the pioneering effort and said that this would greatly help the shrimp farmers in the years to come. Dr. Pradeep Kumar, Secretary, Department of Animal Husbandry, Dairying & Fisheries, gave details of the project that would establish the multiplication centre. Indian shrimp farming is mainly based mainly on black tiger shrimp, Penaeus monodon. While the present annual production through culture is of the order of 1.2 lakh tonnes, the main problem has been the availability of quality seed. White spot syndrome virus disease has been a major problem. The biosecure multiplication centre seed will produce seed free from this pathogen.

6905. (20-3-2008) NEW DELHI : The ambient air quality is monitored at 7 (seven) locations in the National Capital Territory (NCT) of Delhi by the Central Pollution Control Board (CPCB) under the National Ambient Air Quality Monitoring Programme (NAMP). These locations include residential areas, industrial areas and traffic intersection. As per the monitored data, the levels of sulphur dioxide and carbon monoxide in the ambient air are showing a decreasing trend. The nitrogen dioxide levels decreased during the year 2007 in comparison to 2006. The concentration of the Suspended Particulate Matter (SPM) in residential and Industrial areas indicates mixed trend during 2001-2007. Sophisticated equipments for 3 (three) Continuous Ambient Air Quality Monitoring Stations (CAAQMS) and 7 (seven) PM2.5 Samplers have been procured by the CPCB for monitoring of gaseous pollutants including fine particulate matter for assessing the ambient air quality in the NCT of Delhi. This information was given by the Minister of State for Environment and Forests Shri Namo Narain Meena, in a written reply to a question by Shri Dharam Pal Sabharwal, in the Rajya Sabha today.

6906. (20-3-2008) NEW DELHI : The Ministry of Environment and Forests have notified the Hazardous Waste (Management and Handling) Rules, 1989 as amended in 2003 which regulate the generation, collection, storage, treatment, disposal as well as export and import of hazardous wastes including e-waste. The processes generating hazardous wastes are listed in Schedule 1 to these Rules. The residues and wastes generated from the operations in electronic industry are already considered as hazardous wastes and are included at S.No.31 of Schedule 1 to these Rules. As per the provisions of these Rules, the import of e-waste is regulated under Schedule 3 to these Rules wherein Electrical and Electronic Assemblies are covered under category A 1180 in the list A and category B 1110 in the list B of Schedule 3. The import of such waste is permitted only for direct reuse and not for recycling or final disposal. The Ministry of Environment and Forests had also constituted a Task Force to finalise the Guidelines for Environmentally Sound Management of e-waste for State Pollution Control Boards and Pollution Control Committees of the Union Territories and the industries for handling e-waste. The Guidelines for environmentally sound management of e-waste have since been finalized. This information was given by the Minister of State for Environment and Forests Shri Namo Narain Meena, in a written reply to a question by Shri D.Raja in the Rajya Sabha today.

6907. (20-3-2008) NEW DELHI : The World Conservation Union has listed 247 Indian plant species as threatened, including 45 species which are critically endangered. In order to ensure sustainability of these plant species, the Government has taken several steps to protect and propagate the flora of the country through creation of Protected Areas like National Parks/ Wildlife Sanctuaries and Biosphere Reserves for in-situ conservation. The Government is also extending financial support to the Indian Botanic Garden, Howrah, Botanic Garden of the Indian Republic, NOIDA, associated gardens of Botanical Survey of India and other institutions under the scheme of 'Assistance to Botanic Gardens' for promoting ex-situ conservation. The Government has enacted the Wildlife (Protection) Act,1972 and Biological Diversity Act, 2002 with the aim of conservation and sustainable utilisation of flora of the country This information was given by the Minister of State for Environment and Forests Shri Namo Narain Meena, in a written reply to a question by Dr. Abhishek Manu Singhvi and Shri Vijay J. Darda in the Rajya Sabha today.

6908. (20-3-2008) NEW DELHI : Elite lifestyles and behaviour patterns including consumption patterns contribute to 'Global Warming' across various countries in the same manner. An organisation called "Green Peace India" published a report in November 2007 with the title 'Hiding behind the poor'. This report is stated to be based on face-to-face surveys of 819 households from the seven different income classes across the four metros, medium and small towns and rural areas for energy consumption patters. According to the report, the average CO2 emissions of an individual from the highest income group is 4.5 times that of one from the lowest income group. The report also states that this wealthy class is just 1% of the population. The report states that the high carbon intensity of electricity is due to a 67% share of coal (as the major fossil fuel) in the production of electricity and recommends that government should revise its electricity generation plans. It also recommends that Indian Government should develop a carbon tax system under which the use of fossil fuels shall be taxed. The Government of India is aware of its responsibilities and though as per United Nation Framework Convention on Climate Change (UNFCCC) and Kyoto Protocol, thereunder India has no mitigation commitments, however, India is following a sustainable development path through a range of policies and programmes to mitigate climate change and thereby reduce emissions. Some of the measures include: ensuring energy conservation and improved energy efficiency in various sectors as well as setting up of Bureau of Energy Efficiency; promoting use of renewable energy; power sector reforms and active renewable energy programme; use of cleaner and lesser carbon intensive fuel for transport; fuel switching to cleaner energy; afforestation and conservation of forests and promotion of clean coal technologies. Lastly, through the regime of differentiated duties and tariffs, superfluous consumption is sought to be curbed. This information was given by the Minister of State for Environment and Forests Shri Namo Narain Meena, in a written reply to a question by Smt. Hema Malini and Shri Vijay Kumar Rupani, in the Rajya Sabha today.

6909. (20-3-2008) NEW DELHI : The Ministry of Environment & Forests, Government of India is implementing the Centrally Sponsored Scheme of National Lake Conservation Plan (NLCP) since June, 2001 on 70:30 cost sharing basis between the Central Government and the respective State Government with its objective to restore and conserve the polluted and degraded lakes in urban and semi-urban areas in the country. In order to identify polluted and degraded lakes across the country, a study was carried out at the instance of Planning Commission. A list of 62 lakes across the country (including Bindusagar Lake in Orissa) requiring conservation, was prepared under the study. The State Governments were asked to review this list and to prioritize the lakes in their States for submission of proposals under NLCP. New lakes under the Plan are sanctioned on the basis of their prioritization, admissibility and availability of funds under NLCP. The proposal received from the State Government of Orissa for 'Conservation and Management of Bindusagar Lake' only in Bhubaneshwar has since been sanctioned in March, 2006, at an estimated cost of Rs.3.50 crore. This information was given by the Minister of State for Environment and Forests Shri Namo Narain Meena, in a written reply to a question by Shri B.J. Panda and Ms. Pramila Bohidar in the Rajya Sabha today.

6910. (20-3-2008) NEW DELHI : The developing countries have been demanding for quite some time that cost effective and easily accessible technologies for reducing emissions should be transferred to developing countries at the earliest. The same was reiterated at the thirteenth Conference of Parties (COP-13) to the United Nations Framework Convention on Climate Change (UNFCCC) held at

Bali in December 2007. Under the Bali Action Plan, it has been further stated that enhanced action for effective mechanisms and removal of obstacles, need to be considered including provision of financial and other incentives for, scaling up of the development and transfer of technology to developing countries in order to promote access to affordable environmentally sound technologies including their deployment and diffusion.

6911. (20-3-2008) NEW DELHI : The Scheduled Tribes and Other Traditional Forest Dwellers (Recognition of Forest Rights) Act, 2006 for recognition and vesting of occupation and habitation rights on forest land to the forest dwelling Scheduled Tribes and other traditional forest dwellers has already been notified for operation with effect from 31.12.2007. The rules for carrying out the provisions of the Act have also been notified on 1.1.2008. Copies of the Act and the rules are available on the website (www.tribal.gov.in) of the Ministry of Tribal Affairs. The Scheduled Tribes and Other Traditional Forest Dwellers (Recognition of Forest Rights) Act, 2006 is a Central Act and extends to the whole of India, except the State of Jammu & Kashmir. After operationalisation of the Act, the Central Government has addressed all the States and the UT Governments on 11.1.2008 to constitute various Committees under the Act and also initiate necessary action for recognition & vesting of forest rights in the forest dwelling Scheduled Tribes and other traditional forest dwellers under the Act, as per a time bound schedule. This information was given by the Minister of State for Environment and Forests Shri S. Regupathy, in a written reply to a question by Shri Jesudasu Seelam in the Rajya Sabha today.

6912. (20-3-2008) NEW DELHI : The National Institute of Occupational Health (NIOH), Ahmedabad has been entrusted with a study on environmental and health impacts of the usages of Chrysotile Asbestos with an objective to find out the concentration of asbestos fibres in the work zone and to assess the health status of the workers and the residents in the vicinity of the industry. The study is in progress in major Asbestos based products manufacturing units located in Kolkata, Silvasa, Vapi and Hyderabad. Out of a total of Rs. 59.66 lacs allocated for the study by Ministry of Chemicals and Fertilizers, the Asbestos Cement Products Manufactures Association has contributed Rs. 16 lacs. Since the NIOH study is still under progress, no report was presented before the Chemical Review Committee of Rotterdam Convention held at Geneva during March, 10-13,2008. This information was given by the Minister of State for Environment and Forests Shri Namo Narain Meena, in a written reply to a question by Shri B.K. Hariprasad in the Rajya Sabha today.

6913. (20-3-2008) NEW DELHI : To improve the performance of the Indian contingent in the Commonwealth Games, 2010, extensive discussions have been held with all stakeholders and a Scheme for providing state of art training, foreign exposure, scientific backup, equipment etc. at an estimated cost of Rs. 802.00

crore has been drawn up for the elite sportspersons in all the disciplines of the Commonwealth Games, 2010. The selection process of above Scheme envisages that the Sports Authority of India, in consultation with the National Sports Federations of the concerned discipline, will prepare the list of core probables with complete profile of each sportspersons for the consideration of a "Monitoring Committee" and a "Steering Committee" constituted at the Government level, where these lists of core probables will be finalized. These core probables will undergo state of art training and exposure and closer to the Games, based on their performance, the Indian teams which will represent India at the Commonwealth Games will be selected from out of these core probables. This information was given by Shri Mani Shankar Aiyar, Minister of Panchayati Raj, Youth Affairs & Sports and DoNER in the Rajya Sabha today in a written reply to a question by Shri O.T. Lepcha.

6914. (20-3-2008) NEW DELHI : The Central Government does not directly send financial assistance to Gram Panchayats: funds meant for Panchayati Raj Institutions are routed through State Governments. The previous SGRY has been subsumed in NREGA and under NREGA at least fifty percent of the expenditure is mandatorily required to be allocated to the Panchayat at the village level. NREGA also provides for district panchayats to approve the district shelf of projects. The actual financial powers of the District Panchayats are determined through such regulations and executive roles issued there under. In respect of NREGA at least fifty percent is mandatorily required to be allocated to the panchayat at the village level, and NREGA provides for district panchayats to approve the district shelf of projects. This information was given by Shri Mani Shankar Aiyar, Minister of Panchayati Raj, Youth Affairs & Sports and DoNER in the Rajya Sabha today in a written reply to a question by Shri Rudra Narayan Pany.

6915. (20-3-2008) NEW DELHI : Wishing you all a remarkable confluence of festivals. Let me convey on behalf of the Congress President and the entire Congress family a unique confluence of Holi, the Prophet's birth and death anniversary, Christ's crucification and the Parsee New Year. Book release functions should not be converted into political bashing sessions. And if you want to berate the Congress, you must get your facts rights, you must get your history right. The BJP, Mr. Advani, Mr. Jaswant Singh – all want to rewrite history. Jaswant Singh has said that Jinnah's action or his turning to the Muslim League or the partition of the country was all due to because of and attributable to the Congress. In other words, Jaswant Singh has said that all blame for Jinnah's action or inaction or deeds are attributable to the Congress. I want to ask, through you friends, what has happened to the Prime Minister in waiting and Prime Minister in waiting's party that they all find virtuous in Jinnah suddenly. The repository of all virtues is Jinnah and none in India, Indians or in the Congress Party. After Advani's spirited defence of Jinnah's secularism, we now have Jaswant Singh's spirited attribution of all Jinnah's deeds to the Congress. Why this great urge of the BJP to defend Jinnah, to give a clean chit to Jinnah by the Bharatiya Jinnah Party. Perhaps it is because like the Prime Minister in waiting, the Bharatiya Jinnah Party has also many chief ministers in waiting. Perhaps one of those chief ministers in waiting is Jaswant Singh. If that is so he should fight his battles in Rajasthan and not attack the Congress at book release functions. The same Jaswant Singh wrote a book some months ago and all of us are still waiting for the identity of the mole. The mole has vanished into the mole hill. I want to say let not your anti-Congressism become pro-Jinnahism. Let not your hatred for the Congress belittle or destroy democratic discourse by distorting facts and history. Let us look at that history. We all know what the Sangh Parivar, Hindu Mahasabha and àll the elements of that parivar were doing from 1900 to 1950. Where were they and what were their footprint on the Indian freedom movement. Let me give you one example. The Hindu Mahasabha, forbearers and forefathers of those who speak today, as early as 1915 was spitting venom against large groups of this country, against the Congress for standing by all the citizens of India as equal. An example in 1950, H S Lalchand, writing for Hindu Mahasabha, called self obligation in politics, called upon all Hindus to align with British imperialists to crush/ to fight the Muslims. Indian Nationalism was not important. Fighting part of Indian citizenry was. As early as 1915 at meetings under the auspices of Sangh parivar's forefathers, it was proclaimed that Hindus and Muslims were different nations. And that was the seed of partition. Today Mr. Jaswant Singh from Mr. Advani's platform accuses the Congress for Jinnah's partition. The seeds of those partition were sowed by none else that the forbearers of the Sangh Parivar itself. We all know their views regarding Gandhi. We all know the association of Gandhi's assassin with the particular brand of philosophy reflected by Golwakar. We all know how Gowdse worshipped Golwakar. Who were these anti-Gandhi forces? These anti-Gandhi forces are none other than today's pro-Jinnah forces. And why this new thinking, this new philosophy and the new urge from all quarters of the Bharatiya Jinnah Party to resurrect Jinnah. We will advice Mr. Advani, we will advice Mr. Jaswant Singh to read Jinnah's own writing to see if they bear out the deep regard and appreciation which they have for Jinnah. Book releases do not create Prime Ministers. Shedding crocodile tears when the Babri Masjid fell only reflects the hypocrisy and do not make you a nationalist. These do not change history or facts or truth. Both Mr. Advani and Mr. Jaswant Singh deliberately and consciously want to ignore the Congress contribution to the Indian freedom struggle. They want to do this by remembering Jinnah, they want to this by attributing all the faults, may be of Jinnah or others, to the Congress Party.

6916. (20-3-2008) NEW DELHI: Facing a stringent attack from Opposition members in the Rajya Sabha, the government on Wednesday said it could "neither mend nor end" the India-U.S. nuclear agreement as it was in dialogue at the International Atomic Energy Agency. Responding to a short duration discussion on foreign-policy related developments, Union External Affairs Minister Pranab Mukherjee initially did not refer to the deal as, he said, there was nothing to report. However, when the Opposition and Left members insisted that he state the government's position, Mr. Mukherjee said, "Leader of Opposition Jaswant Singh said we should either mend it or end it, but we are at a stage that neither it can be ended nor it can be mended because we are in dialogue," he said. Noting that there was some advancement in talks on the India-specific safeguards agreement at the IAEA, the Minister said, "whenever the procedure is over, if it is over," the government will come to Parliament. Dismissing the charge that Parliament was not being taken into confidence, Mr. Mukherjee said Prime Minister Manmohan Singh had assured members that whenever any stage (of negotiation) was completed, the government would share it. "[The UPA-Left Coordination Committee] is an internal arrangement. We have to carry their conviction and share some information with them." Refuting the charge of the government "diluting" India's foreign policy, Mr. Mukherjee asserted that there was "continuity" and India was not in isolation. There were no basic changes but only certain adjustments and reallocation of priorities in the context of the changing world. For instance, when the Non-Aligned Movement was formed, there was no World Trade Organisation. When such changes take place, they were bound to be reflected in the foreign policy he said. On the differences of perception with China on Arunachal Pradesh, he said: "We have representatives of Arunachal Pradesh in Parliament. When the Prime Minister visits the State and declares a package, it is consistent with our policies.

6917. (20-3-2008) NEW DELHI : The 23rd meeting of the Board of Approval for Special Economic Zones (SEZs) was held on 20th March, 2008 to consider proposals for setting up of Special Economic Zones and also approve other miscellaneous requests pertaining to SEZs. Chairman informed the members of the Board that so far formal approvals have been granted for setting up of 449 SEZs out of which 206 have been notified as on date. In this meeting, 9 proposals for setting up SEZs, including 1 proposal for conversion of In-Principle approval to Formal Approval were considered.

6918. (20-3-2008) NEW DELHI : Ms Deepa Jain Singh, IAS, (Haryana 1971) today took over as the Secretary of the Department of Ex-Servicemen Welfare (ESW), Ministry of Defence. Before joining the Department of Ex-Servicemen Welfare, Ms Singh was the Secretary, National Commission for Minorities. She has also served in various key departments and Ministries of Central Government and Haryana State including the post of Addl Secretary cum Financial Advisor, Ministry of Information and Broadcasting.

6919. (20-3-2008) NEW DELHI : The President of India, Smt. Pratibha Devi Singh Patil in her message on the occasion of Milad-un-Nabi, which is being observed tomorrow, has said:-"On the auspicious occasion of the birthday of Prophet Mohammad, I convey my greetings to all my countrymen. The message of Prophet Mohammad Sahib has great relevance in today's world. May his teachings of universal love, service to humanity and compassion inspire us all to lead righteous lives."

6920. (20-3-2008) NEW DELHI : The Indian Army and the Indian Air Force jointly executed the Air Land Battle doctrine at Pokharan Field Firing Ranges during Exercise "Brazen Chariots" Yesterday. This doctrine is based on manoeuvre and rapid response to disrupt enemy's decision cycle. It is also associated with the idea of an extended battlefield, intended to disrupt and delay the enemy's follow on echelons. Organic weapons of the Army may not always be capable of achieving this objective due to their limited range and mobility. This can most effectively be carried out by air power. The probability of future conventional wars being short, swift and intense has necessitated a shift in focus of land battle to manoeuvre warfare. The Air Land doctrine stresses on the fundamental shift away from the past attrition style of warfare to one of air arm making a significant contribution to the success of battle. It progressively recognizes that the inherent flexibility, variety and reach of airpower makes it a prime contributor to the future war. During the exercise, the latest array of weaponry were fielded by the Indian Army and the IAF, in a joint and synergistic Air-Land battle setting. In addition the IAF's ability and reach to para drop Special Forces and Para Troopers with heavy combat and logistic loads was being integrated in this exercise. The joint operations with ground forces demonstrated the synergy and team spirit. During the exercise fighters transport aircraft and helicopters including SU-30, MIG 21, MIG 27, IL 76, AN 32, MI-17 and MI-35 aircraft unleashed its firepower of a variety of weapons on simulated targets like artillery gun positions, company defended localities, communication nodes, logistics camps and armoured depots. The Army Aviation was also used for tactical mobility of land forces during the exercise. The Exercise involved engagement of an air target by shoulder fired air defence missiles, special heliborne operations, firing of multi barrel launcher batteries, helidrop, deployment and firing of a mortar battery and conduct of airborne operations. Unmanned Aerial Vehicle (UAV) with electronic sensors were also used to provide necessary support to these simulated operations. Exercise BRAZEN CHARIOTS, was witnessed by senior military dignitaries of about 60 countries.

6921. (20-3-2008) NEW DELHI : The President of India said here that "On the joyous occasion of Holi, the festival of colours, I convey my greetings and good wishes to all my countrymen. The festival of Holi brings joy and happiness, which imbibes the spirit of friendship among people of all faiths. On this occasion, let us ensure that the less advantaged in society do not remain untouched by the spirit of celebration. As the festival of colours is marked by mingling of diverse colours, so let our various cultural diversities come together in celebration, instilling a sense of unity amongst us all".

6922. (20-3-2008) NEW DELHI : The Aeronautical Authorities of the Republic of India and the People's Republic of China met in New Delhi on 19-20 March, 2008 for consultations on air service matters. It has been decided by both the sides that the designated airlines of both the countries will be entitled to operate to any 3 beyond points with not more than 2 points in one region. However, the intermediate points and beyond points and the exercise of traffic rights to/from these points shall be agreed upon by the two aeronautical authorities of the two countries. The Indian delegation has specified the United States of America and Canada as one region, Australia and New Zealand as the second region and Asia as the third region for the three beyond times for the Indian carriers to operate the agreed services. For China, Africa is one region, Middle-East (including Gulf Area) is a second region and Europe the third for the three beyond points for operations of the Chinese carriers. It has been agreed that the designated airlines of India may operate beyond China to San Francisco with full 5th freedom traffic rights. The Chinese side shall be allowed to nominate a beyond point in India with full 5th freedom traffic rights, at their discretion at a later date. Both sides have come to an agreement that the designated airlines of each country shall be entitled to exercise beyond 5th freedom traffic rights on not more than 14 frequencies to all the beyond points put together. The Chinese delegation has forwarded to the Indian side the complete set of documents regarding the operation of the Great Wall Airlines from Shanghai to Mumbai and Chennai. The Indian side will forward these documents to the concerned authorities in the Indian Government for appropriate action. The Indian delegation was headed by Shri R.K. Singh, Joint Secretary, Ministry of Civil Aviation and the Chinese delegation was headed by Mr. Li Jiang Min, Director General, Department of International Affairs and Cooperations, CAAC, Peoples Republic of China.

6923. (20-3-2008) NEW DELHI : Minimum wages for workers have not been prescribed by the local laws in the Gulf countries, and the wages are determined by the contracts between the employer and the worker. However for effective protection and welfare of women emigrants, Government of India has decided to ensure a minimum wages since they are in the most vulnerable category. The minimum wage are fixed by the Indian Missions concerned in the range of US$ 300-350 per months after taking into account the prevailing market wage in that country.

6924. (20-3-2008) NEW DELHI : Shri Sushilkumar Shinde, Union Minister of Power, has stressed that the country expects the power sector to provide uninterrupted power supply to the consumer and thereby keep the national economy on fast track. Stating this at the National Awards Presentation Function to Power Utilities for Meritorious Performance during 2006-07, here today, he informed that both Government of India and State Governments have been continuously attempting to improve the performance of power sector. "There has been improvement in all fields of the power sector. However, due to the increasing demand of energy, the country is still facing energy shortage of 9.5% and peak demand shortage of 15.8%". The function was attended by the Shri B.K. Chaturvedi, Member (Power), Planning Commission; Mr. Anil Razdan, Secretary, Ministry of Power; and Shri Rakesh Nath, Chairman, Central Electricity Authority, apart from the senior officials from the Ministry of Power.

6925. (20-3-2008) NEW DELHI : The Vice President of India Shri Mohd. Hamid Ansari has said that the last three decades have witnessed an impressive effort to provide access to safe drinking water to Indian households. It is heartening that while only 38 per cent of households had access to drinking water in 1981, that figure has gone up to 78 per cent by 2001. Much of the progress has been in rural areas, with the number of households having access to drinking water going up from a mere 26 per cent in 1981 to 73 per cent in 2001. Delivering inaugural address at the World Water Day 2008 Function organised by the Ministry of Water Resources here today, the Vice President said that this is a result of National Water Policy according the highest priority to drinking water in the planning and operation of the water resources system as also the success of the 'Accelerated Rural Water Supply Programme'. The Vice President said that the provision of sanitation facilities continues to remain a major challenge and an important Millennium Development Goal and only a third of our population has coverage with improved sanitation. This is far lower than the global coverage of 58 per cent, the developing countries' coverage of 49 per cent and even that of sub-Saharan Africa of 36 per cent. The Vice President said that ensuring rapid economic growth and undertaking targeted interventions have been the principle instruments in our poverty alleviation strategy. It is vital that our people have access to basic facilities including clean drinking water and improved sanitation for inclusive and sustainable growth. This should not be seen nearly as essential public services from the welfare perspective, they are critical determinants of economic opportunities for our citizens and pre conditions for sustainable long-term growth. The Vice President said that water conservation and replenishment is increasingly assuming a global dimension. Global warming and climate change have immediate and dire consequences for the availability of water. He hoped that the Government will continue to emphasise provision of safe drinking water and access to improved sanitation keeping in view the developmental, environmental and public health aspects.

6926. (20-3-2008) NEW DELHI : According to consultancy firm Takashi Mobile, website of OFCOM (Telecom Regulator of United Kingdom) and information available on internet, Mobile Virtual Network Operators (MVNOs) are operational in Belgium, Denmark, Finland, The Netherlands, Norwey, France, Germany, United Kingdom and United States. MVNO business models are in the process of being launched in some other countries, namely Portugal, Spain, Italy, Croatia, The Baltics, Chile and Austria. Mobile Virtual Network Operator is a new kind of service and as per Section 11 of the Telecom Regulatory Authority of India (TRAI) Act, 1997, the Government is required to seek recommendations of TRAI on need and timing for introduction of new service providers and regarding terms and conditions of license to be granted to such service providers. As on date, no decision in this regard has been taken by the Government. This information was given by the Minister of State for Communications and Information Technology, Dr. Shakeel Ahmed in a written reply to an un-starred question in the Rajya Sabha today.

6927. (20-3-2008) NEW DELHI : Government is very much aware that broadband connectivity is very essential for the development of the country as knowledge based society. Some of the major steps taken and proposed to be taken by the Government to proliferate broadband in the country are given below: Broadband policy has been announced by the Government during 2004 for accelerated growth of Broadband applications, contributing growth of GDP and enhancement in quality of life through societal applications including tele-education, tele-medicine, e-governance, entertainment as well as employment generation. In order to bring provisioning of broadband connectivity to rural areas under the purview of Universal Service Obligation Fund (USOF), the Indian Telegraph Rules have been amended, stream IV has been added under the title "Provision of broadband connectivity to villages in a phased manner". The USOF is working on a scheme for providing financial assistance by way of subsidy for the broadband active infrastructure such as BTS (Base Transceiver Station) and by utilizing the existing passive infrastructure available with the Telecom service providers. State owned Public Sector Unit, Bharat Sanchar Nigam Limited has identified around 25,576 rural exchanges and has placed order of 1.6 million ports for deployment of broadband services and rural areas. The Government has approved a Common Services Centres (CSCs) Scheme for providing support for establishing 100,000 Common Services Centres in 600,000 villages of India. The Scheme, as approved by the Government of India, envisions CSCs as the front-end delivery points for Government, private and social sector services to rural citizens of India, in an integrated manner. The objective is to develop a platform that can enable Government, private and social sector organizations to align their social and commercial goals for the benefit of the rural population in the remotest corners of the country through a combination of IT-based as well as non-IT-based services.

6928. (20-3-2008) NEW DELHI : The Ministry is concerned about affordability of houses for different sections of society. In order to address the issue of affordability of houses for all sections of society, the first urban area specific housing policy-the National Urban Housing & Habitat Policy (NUHHP), 2007 has been formulated, which has been laid on the Table of both Houses of the Parliament on 7.12.2007. The Policy seeks to set in motion a process for providing "Affordable Housing for All" particularly for Economically Weaker Section (EWS) and Low Income

Groups (LIG) through various types of public-private partnerships and development of various financial and operational innovations. Renewal Mission (JNNURM) launched by the Government in the year 2005 caters for provisions of housing and basic services to urban poor in 63 specified cities and also for non-specified cities. Also a provision has been made in the budget of 2007-08 to provide for interest rate subsidy scheme for loans to Economically Weaker Sections (EWS) and Low Income Groups (LIG). A Task force has also been set up by this Ministry to look into various aspects of providing "Affordable Housing for All" and to recommend ways and means of enhancing accessibility of EWS/LIG categories to housing with suitable governmental support and developing innovative financial instruments for bringing flexibility in the housing market and making recommendations as to fiscal, spatial incentives for increasing supply of houses. This information was given by the Minister of State for Housing & Urban Poverty Alleviation, Kumari Selja in the Rajya Sabha today, in a written reply to a question by Shri Tariq Anwar.

6929. (20-3-2008) NEW DELHI : In order to address the issue of affordability of houses for all sections of society, the first urban area specific housing policy, the National Urban Housing & Habitat Policy (NUHHP), 2007 has been formulated, which has been laid on the Table of both Houses of the Parliament on 07.12.2007. The Policy seeks to set in motion a process for providing "Affordable Housing for All" particularly for Economically Weaker Section (EWS) and Low Income Groups (LIG) through various types of public-private partnerships and development of various financial and operational innovations. According to the estimations of the Technical Group constituted by the Ministry for assessment of the urban housing shortage at the end of the 10th five Year Plan, the total housing shortage in the country is 24.71 million. During the 11th Five Year Plan period, the total urban housing requirement including the backlog and additional requirement is estimated as 26.53 million dwelling units. 'Land' and 'colonisation' being State subjects, State Governments have to take steps for implementation of initiatives envisaged in the Policy. The Policy has been widely publicized and has been forwarded to all States/Union Territories as well as to various Ministries of the Central Government and other implementing agencies. This information was given by the Minister of State for Housing & Urban Poverty Alleviation, Kumari Selja in the Rajya Sabha today, in a written reply to a question by Shri B.J. Panda & Ms. Pramila Bohidar.

6930. (20-3-2008) NEW DELHI : A new Consular Agreement is being finalised with Pakistan to replace the existing protocol to ensure expeditious release of and consular access to prisoners. A Judicial Committee comprising superior judges from both countries has been set up to address such issues. This information was provided by Minister of External Affairs Shri Pranab Mukherjee, in a written reply to a question in the Rajya Sabha today. The present arrangement between India and Pakistan on grant of Consular Access and the release of each other's nationals in custody is governed by the provisions of the Protocol on Consular access of 2 November 1982. In his reply, Shri Mukherjee also stated that the Government is concerned that 372 fishermen and an estimated 199 prisoners are in jails in Pakistan, many of whom have not been granted consular access despite prolonged periods in custody. On the issue of Pakistani prisoners lodged in Indian jails for minor offences, the Minister informed that on occasion there has been delay in repatriation of Pakistan prisoners as travel documents were not provided to them in time by the Government of Pakistan.

6931. (20-3-2008) NEW DELHI : Following is the text of the inaugural address of Vice President of India Shri Mohd Hamid Ansari at the 'World Water Day 2008 Function' organised by Ministry of Water Resources here today : "I am happy to be with you on this important occasion of World Water Day, celebrated globally since 1993. It is also appropriate that this year we focus on issues related to Sanitation with 2008 being declared the International Sanitation Year. Scriptures describe the act of creation. They say that in the beginning the earth was a formless void, covered with water. Even today 70% of the surface of our earth is water. Water is life giving and life sustaining. It is a vital resource that is finite and vulnerable. At one end of the spectrum, it is recognised as an integral component of environmentally sustainable development. At the other end, water and sanitation constitute an important component of public health. Its provision is important both for economic and human development. Water conservation and replenishment is increasingly assuming a global dimension. Global Warming and climate change have immediate and dire consequences for the availability of water. The last three decades have witnessed an impressive effort to provide access to safe drinking water to Indian households. It is heartening that while only 38% of households had access to drinking water in 1981, that figure has gone up to 78% by 2001. Much of the progress has been in rural areas, with the number of households having access to drinking water going up from a mere 26% in 1981 to 73% in 2001. This is a result of our National Water Policy according the highest priority to drinking water in the planning and operation of the water resources system as also the success of the 'Accelerated Rural Water Supply Programme'. Provision of sanitation facilities continues to remain a major challenge.

6932. (20-3-2008) NEW DELHI : The Union Minister of Shipping, Road Transport and Highways, Thiru T.R. Baalu has approved a central assistance of Rs. 80 lakh for implementing a pilot project of the Bangalore Metropolitan Transport Corporation (BMTC) for executing an online GPS/ GPRS based vehicle-tracking system. The project being envisaged at a total cost of Rs. 3.31 crore would involve 500 vehicles in the first stage on pilot basis. The BMTC is currently implementing online GPS with GPRS based vehicle tracking system on Build-Own-Operate and Transfer basis. While approving the assistance to BMTC for implementing the project which is one of the first of its kind in India, Thiru Baalu noted that the effort of BMTC is definitely a positive one and would help setting an agenda for other States to work in the direction of improving the public transport system. The benefits of GPS system are many such as it ensures schedule adherence by the bus crew, facilitates control over deviation, provides traffic loading information, helpful in driving pattern analysis and supports billing process etc. The BMTC has been asked by the Union Ministry of Shipping, Road Transport and Highways to provide the consultation for this pilot project to other States without charging any fee and also provide a quarterly report to the Centre on the progress made on the project. The BMTC would provide access to the officials of the Department of Road Transport & Highways to oversee the implementation of the project, as and when required.

6933. (20-3-2008) NEW DELHI : The Vice-President of India Mohd. Hamid Ansari has greeted the people of our country on the sacred and auspicious occasion of Milad-Un-Nabi that marks the birth of Prophet Mohammad. In his message, the Vice President said that Prophet Mohammad showed us the glorious path of righteousness, compassion, brotherhood and tolerance. Milad-Un-Nabi is an occasion for remembering the life, teachings and example of Prophet Mohammad. On this occasion, let us pray that God bestows his blessings on all of us for good health, progress and prosperity and inspire us to work for the welfare of the poor and the downtrodden, the Vice President said.

6934. (20-3-2008) NEW DELHI : The Vice-President of India Mohd. Hamid Ansari has greeted the people of our country on the joyous occasion of Holi, the festival of colours. In his greetings, the Vice President said that Holi, marking the advent of spring, is celebrated across the country with cheerfulness and zest. This festival portrays our great tradition of 'Unity in Diversity' by transcending all distinctions and bridges the social gap by uniting us all in a joyful celebration of sprinkling of colours. Let us celebrate this festival in its true spirit to strengthen the social fabric and promote national integration, the Vice President said.

6935. (21-3-2008) NEW DELHI : Bharat Heavy Electricals Limited (BHEL) has paid an interim dividend of 90 per cent on the enhanced equity capital post-bonus, for financial year 2007-08 to the Government. In this regard, a cheque of Rs. 298 crore on the equity (67.72%) held by the Government of India was presented here today to Shri Sontosh Mohan Dev, Union Minister for Heavy Industries and Public Enterprises, by Shri K. Ravi Kumar, CMD, BHEL. Senior officials of the Ministry and BHEL were also present on the occasion.

6936. (21-3-2008) NEW DELHI : The major task before the country is to rehabilitate the degraded forests, increasing productivity, enhancing contribution of forests towards poverty alleviation of the people living in and around forests and to enhance the area under forests. Addressing the World Forestry Day celebration today, Shri S Regupathy, Minister of State for Environment and Forests further said that India is actively participating in different forest related international processes. India has highlighted the gaps in the implementation of sustainable forest management in the decisions of Bali Conference on Climate Change and other international forums. Referring to this year's theme "Forest and Climate Change", Shri S Regupathy said the process of economic growth and development through industrialization and urbanization has led to the emission of Green House Gases (GHG) into the atmosphere leading to a rise in global temperature. Carbon di-oxide is the dominant GHG accounting for about half of the total global warming contribution by all GHG together. The CO2 is released mainly from burning of fossil fuels and urbanization. We have to work very hard to increase land area under forest and achieve one-third area of the country under forest and tree. Elaborating the principal aim of the National Forest Policy, the minister said its aim is to provide environmental stability and ecological balance including atmospheric equilibrium, which are vital for sustenance of all life forms-human, animal and plants, by conserving the natural heritage of the country. India's forests are primarily considered as social and environmental resources. The institutional framework of forest development is shifting from regulatory to participatory mode of administration and will be more people oriented in future. Earlier in his key-note address, Dr. R K Pachauri, TERI, said that forests are our biggest treasure. Today there are many stresses and challenges on forest sector. Application of science can help in increasing forest cover and development of forests.

6937. (21-3-2008) NEW DELHI : The Prime Minister, Dr. Manmohan Singh has greeted the nation especially the Parsi community on the occasion of Navroz, the New Year of the Zorastrians. In a message, the Prime Minister said that the festival is an occasion to celebrate the diversity of our country. It marks a new beginning and inspires us to rejoice in the spirit of harmony and goodwill. 'May the festival bring happiness, health and prosperity to all', the Prime Minister added.

6938. (21-3-2008) NEW DELHI : The Prime Minister, Dr. Manmohan Singh has greeted the people on the festive occasion of Holi. In a message, the Prime Minister said that the festival symbolizes the different shades of life and inspires us to rejoice in the glory of nature in all its varied colours. The festival symbolizes the country's spirit of togetherness, harmony and tolerance. 'May the festival bring gaiety, happiness health and prosperity to all', the Prime Minister wished.

6939. (23-3-2008) NEW DELHI : As the first-ever India-Africa conclave organised by the Ministry of External Affairs approaches, the Union Commerce Ministry has, for the first time, taken the initiative to establish systems for the direct imports of rough diamonds from Africa. To kick-start this initiative, the Minister of State for Commerce, Shri Jairam Ramesh is leading a high-powered delegation to Namibia and Angola beginning March 26th. Joining him are senior representatives of the Gems and Jewellery Export Promotion Council (GJEPC). India must buy rough and uncut diamonds directly from these and other African countries, Shri Jairam Ramesh said on the eve of his six-day trip. He also said that in the next couple of months, he would be visiting other important diamond producing countries like South Africa and Botswana as well. He emphasised that in future India will find it difficult to source rough diamonds unless it demonstrates to African nations that it will collaborate actively in helping them move up the value-chain and assist in value-addition in these producing countries itself. The Africanisation of the diamonds processing industry is not a threat to India but a great opportunity which we must proactively embrace, Shri Jairam Ramesh explained. India's estimated imports of rough diamonds in 2007/08 is around $ 10 billion, while estimates of exports of cut and polished diamonds in 2007/08 are about $ 14 billion. It is the world's largest importer of roughs and exporter of cut and polished diamonds with over 90% market share. "I started this initiative largely because the diamonds cutting and polishing trade is very employment-intensive and provides livelihoods to over 10 lakh families in our country", Shri Jairam Ramesh added. Rough diamonds are procured presently through a variety of sources with the bulk of it coming into India through Antwerp in Belgium. Shri Ramesh pointed out that it is in India's long-term interests to establish direct relationships with supplier countries, cutting out all the middlemen. He said that he had opened a dialogue with all major diamond producing countries and Alrossa, the Russian diamond producing company has recently sold roughs directly to Indian buyers. The quantities are small and need to be built up quickly, the Minister of State of Commerce said.

6940. (23-3-2008) NEW DELHI : Agni 1 (A1) missile, a strategic Surface-to-Surface missile, with a range capability of 700 km was successfully launched today at 10.15 hrs from Island Launch Complex off Dhamra, Orissa by Army unit. The missile had a textbook performance in terms of range, accuracy and lethality. A1 was developed by ASL, the premier missile development Laboratory of Defence Research & Development Organisation (DRDO) in collaboration with Defence Research and Development Laboratory, Hyderabad and Research Center Imarat, Hyderabad and integrated by defence Public Sector Undertaking, Bharat Dynamics Limited, Hyderabad. This has been an effort of consortium of DRDO labs *viz.* Vehicle Research & Development Establishment, Ahmednagar and Research & Development (Establishment), Interim Test Range, Chandipur and major public and private industries. Shri Avinash Chander, Programme Director and Director, ASL said that the performance of all the subsystems of A1 *viz.*, Explicit Guidance, Re-Entry structures, Avionics and Payload has been outstanding, confirming the robustness and maturity of Long Range Missile Technology in DRDO. It is a major milestone in the preparedness of Army unit in the strategic deployment of A1 system. Dr. V.K. Saraswat, CCR&D (MSS) participated in the launch and congratulated the team members for their dedicated and professional work towards achieving this success. Shri A.K. Antony, Defence Minister and Shri MM Pallam Raju, Minister of State for Defence have congratulated the scientists and the operations team of Strategic Force Command for outstanding achievements and adding yet another milestone in the preparedness of the country in the area of strategic defence.

6941. (24-3-2008) NEW DELHI : With a view to enabling institutional and retail investors to plan their investment in a better manner and also for providing transparency and stability in the Government securities market, it has been decided to continue with the system of releasing an indicative calendar for issuance of Government of India securities. Accordingly, an indicative issuance calendar for issue of dated securities for the first half of the year 2008-2009 covering the period from April 1, 2008 to September 30, 2008 (as given below) is being issued in consultation with the Reserve Bank of India.

6942. (24-3-2008) NEW DELHI : The Minister of State for Defence Shri M M Pallam Raju has called upon the Defence Research and Development Organisation (DRDO) to find ways and means to attract talent and retain them. Addressing the gathering after inaugurating 'DARPAN", a permanent exhibition set up at the Recruitment and Assessment Centre (RAC) here today, Shri Pallam Raju commended the centre for undertaking campus selection from reputed institutes and the recent induction of NRIs through video conferencing. He called upon the DRDO to encourage students and experts to visit the exhibition and take a glimpse at the DRDO's vast areas of research and products. Shri Pallam Raju hoped that an international workshop planned by the RAC this year will help formulate a reliable methodology in scientific recruitment and assessment. Earlier Dr. M Natarajan, Scientific Advisor to the Defence Minister and Secretary, Defence Research and Development, said that the time has come for the DRDO to offload certain tasks to the industry. He also suggested that a policy must be devised for scientists to migrate from the DRDO to industry and back. Speaking on the occasion, Dr. W Selvamurthy, Chief Controller (R&D), highlighted the products developed by DRDO, ranging from missiles to readymade meals, and the spinoffs to the industry. The exhibition 'Darpan' displays several models of DRDO's products including Prithvi and Agni missiles, radars and Electronic Warfare systems, MBT Arjun, torpedoes and NBC suits. An interactive Audio-Visual presentation takes visitors on a journey down the DRDO's fifty years' history.

6943. (24-3-2008) NEW DELHI : Provision of safe drinking water is considered today as fundamental to good governance to promote good health and welfare of the people. The States strive to resolve the issue involved in making safe drinking water accessible to all and to tackle the ever increasing concerns of depletion of ground water tables and quality problems that affect its sources. Considering the magnitude of the problem, the Central Government supplements the efforts of the State Governments in this regard. The Vice President of India Shri Mohd. Hamid Ansari has said that the last three decades have witnessed an impressive effort to provide access to safe drinking water to Indian households.

It is heartening that while only 38 per cent of households had access to drinking water in 1981, that figure has gone up to 78 per cent by 2001. Much of the progress has been in rural areas, with the number of households having access to drinking water going up from a mere 26 per cent in 1981 to 73 per cent in 2001. Speaking on the occasion of the World Water Day 2008 organised by the Ministry of Water Resources, the Vice President said that this is a result of National Water Policy according the highest priority to drinking water in the planning and operation of the water resources system as also the success of the 'Accelerated Rural Water Supply Programme'. He further added that the provision of sanitation facilities continues to remain a major challenge and an important Millennium Development Goal and only a third of our population has coverage with improved sanitation. This is far lower than the global coverage of 58 per cent, the developing countries' coverage of 49 per cent and even that of sub-Saharan Africa of 36 per cent. Shri Ansari said that ensuring rapid economic growth and undertaking targeted interventions have been the principle instruments in our poverty alleviation strategy. It is vital that our people have access to basic facilities including clean drinking water and improved sanitation for inclusive and sustainable growth. This should not be seen nearly as essential public services from the welfare perspective, they are critical determinants of economic opportunities for our citizens and pre conditions for sustainable long-term growth. He said that water conservation and replenishment is increasingly assuming a global dimension. Global warming and climate change have immediate and dire consequences for the availability of water. He hoped that the Government will continue to emphasise provision of safe drinking water and access to improved sanitation keeping in view the developmental, environmental and public health aspects.

6944. (24-3-2008) NEW DELHI : Bharat Earth Movers Limited (BEML), a premier Public Sector Company under Ministry of Defence and engaged in the manufacture and supply of Heavy Earth Moving Equipment for the Mining and construction Sector, Heavy Duty Trucks for Defence forces and Rail and Metro Coaches to the Indian Railways, has declared an all-time high Dividend of 55 % as Interim Dividend for the financial year 2007-08. The company's Chairman and Managing Director Shri VRS Natarajan presented the cheque for Rs. 12,37,50,000/- (Rupees twelve crores thirty seven lakhs and fifty thousand only) to the Defence Minister Shri AK Antony in New Delhi, today as interim dividend for 54% of company's shares held by the Government of India. Speaking on the occasion, the Defence Minister complimented the efforts of BEML and hoped for its bright future. Secretary (Defence Production), Shri Pradeep Kumar, Secretary (Defence Production) was also present on the occasion. During the last year BEML had paid 40% as interim dividend for an amount of Rs. 9 crores for 61.2 % of company's shares held with Government of India. BEML is set to achieve beyond its MoU Sales target of Rs. 2765 crores for the financial year 2007-08 and the order book position is expected to cross Rs. 4000 crores by the end of the current account year.

6945. (24-3-2008) NEW DELHI : The first ever Kerato-Refractive Surgery (Lasik Surgery) Centre of The Armed Forces was inaugurated at Army Hospital (R&R), here today by Lt Gen Yogendra Singh, Director General Armed Forces Medical Services in the presence of Maj Gen OP Mathew, Commandant, Army Hospital (R&R). Lasik surgery will help in correction of complex refractive errors and the problems of the anterior surface of the eye ball. Lt Gen Yogendra Singh brought out that a long standing need of the service clientele has been fulfilled. Maj Gen OP Mathew said that the dept of Ophthalmology at Army Hospital (R&R) is now equipped to offer competent management of the eye diseases available at any nationally reputed eye center in the country.

6946. (24-3-2008) NEW DELHI : India and New Zealand today agreed to increase cooperation in agriculture and sort out issues relating to bio-security at the earliest. In the delegation-level discussions held here today, Agriculture Minister, Shri Sharad Pawar proposed to have an 'umbrella agreement' to raise level of cooperation and expand cooperation into a range of issues in the agriculture sector. The Agriculture, Bio-Security, Fisheries and Forestry Minister of New Zealand Mr. Jim Anderton is on a visit to India on the invitation of the Agriculture Minister Shri Pawar. India and New Zealand already have an MoU on plant quarantine issues. A tripartite MoU among Indian Council of Agricultural Research, Land Care Research and Massey University, New Zealand is also being discussed and will be signed as soon as all the clearances are available. The proposed umbrella agreement between Ministry of Agriculture, India and Ministry of Agriculture, New Zealand will cover agriculture and allied activities including food processing, agricultural research, phytosanitary issues relating to trade in plants and animal products, engagement of private sector of both the countries and exchange of information in the areas of mutual interest. The proposed agreement would supplement other efforts being made by the two governments to strengthen cooperation and encourage trade. Shri Sharad Pawar and Mr. Anderton agreed that there is tremendous potential for cooperation between the two countries considering complementarity between agriculture, horticulture, environment and related areas. The visiting New Zealand team is scheduled to hold discussions with the Agriculture Minister of Maharashtra later this week.

6947. (24-3-2008) NEW DELHI : The Ministry of Information & Broadcasting, keeping in mind the Delhi High Court Order dated 28.02.2008 in W.P. (C) No. 9610/2007 in the matter of Ravi Dev Gupta V/s. Union of India and Another, has decided not to declare the India-South Africa test cricket series starting from March 26, 2008 as sporting event of national importance for the purpose of sharing of broadcast signals with Prasar Bharati. The Sports Broadcasting Signals (Mandatory Sharing with Prasar Bharati) Act, 2007 has provided for mandatory sharing of sports signals by right owners for all such events which are notified by the Central Government under Clause (s) of sub-section (1) of Section 2 of the said Act and after following the procedure prescribed under the provisions of said Act and rules made thereto.

6948. (24-3-2008) NEW DELHI : The BJP takes serious exception and note to the spiraling prices of essential food items including daily groceries to fuel to edible oils to fruits & vegetables. The wholesale price based inflation index has breached RBI's comfort zone and risen to 5.92% this week indicating an all time high. The country which still has to tide over the severe bout of inflation spell witnessed in August, 2007 is witnessing another unchecked substantial gallop. At the retail level the situation is grimmer. The average price of sugar has risen by 6 percent, 25 percent for rice, 33 percent for edible oil and while most of the price of house hold items has doubled. All this is in addition to the prices of diesel and petrol having been raised eight times in the tenure of UPA government. Apparently this is the instant outcome of the so called tom-tommed budget rolled out by Chidrambram recently. The rising inflation with a faltering economy leaves no room for the government to tinker with fiscal policies and worst is yet to come. The government has fallen in its own trap of populism and appeasement. All this is happening while the country is headed first time by a Prime Minister who is an Economist and a Finance Minister who claims to be better then him. The walloping inflation is the gift of the UPA Government to the country in an election year.

6949. (24-3-2008) NEW DELHI : The advances in information and communication technology provide great opportunities to enhance teaching and learning in higher education by both on campus and distance education. The Open University System was initiated in the country to augment opportunities for higher education as an instrument of democratizing education and also to make it a lifelong process. The first Open University in the country was established by Andhra Pradesh in 1982. In 1985, the Indira Gandhi National Open University (IGNOU) was established under an Act of Parliament. The IGNOU has designed, developed and delivered high quality academic programmes in the Humanities, Sciences and Social Sciences as well as in professional areas like Computer Applications, Engineering, Management, Nursing and Tourism. Most of the University's programmes are structured on modular pattern, leading to the award of certificates, diplomas and degrees. The Open University programmes have proved to be highly cost effective. The current indications are that their cost is much lower than the cost normally incurred by the traditional system on comparable programmes. The Open Universities arrive at lower cost through economics of scale since their fixed costs get distributed over a large number of students. EDUSAT the first Indian satellite built exclusively for serving the educational sector is a collaborative project of the Ministry of Human Resources Development, Indira Gandhi National Open University, and the Department of Space/ Indian Space Research Organization. It is mainly intended to meet the demand for an interactive satellite based distance education system for the country. It strongly reflects India's commitment to use space technology for national development especially for the development of the population in the remote and rural locations. Outlay and Projected Outcome 2008-09 of Distance Learning is at Annexure.

6950. (24-3-2008) NEW DELHI : India and Vietnam have signed a Memorandum of Understanding (MoU) for bilateral cooperation in security matters which, among others, would include international terrorism, illicit drug trafficking and trans-national crime. The MOU was signed here today following delegation-level talks between the Union Home Minister, Shri Shivraj Patil and the visiting Vietnamese Minister for Public Security, General Le Hong Anh. During the delegation-level talks, the two sides reviewed the on-going initiatives and discussed issues relevant to wider and enhanced cooperation in security-related matters. Capacity-building and training issues were substantially addressed. General Le Hong Anh is visiting India with a team of senior officers on the invitation of the Union Home Minister, Shri Shivraj Patil. The visit has further catalysed the momentum in high-level exchanges between the two countries. Shri Shivraj Patil had earlier paid an official visit to Vietnam from 8th to 10th October last year. During the visit, a Treaty on Mutual Legal Assistance in Criminal Matters between India and Vietnam was signed. The Treaty facilitates widest measures of mutual assistance in prevention, investigation and prosecution of crime, service of summons and other judicial documents, execution of warrants and other judicial commissions, and tracing, restraint, forfeiture and confiscation of proceeds and instruments of crime. During the visit, India had agreed to impart training to officers of Vietnam in investigation of bank fraud cases, organised crimes, money laundering, economic offences, drug trafficking, cyber crime and scientific investigation. Two courses have since been conducted and more are likely to be conducted shortly. India had also agreed to set up in Vietnam a laboratory on cyber forensic at an estimated cost of 2.2 crore rupees in a phased manner. The components of this project are being put together in a prioritized manner.

6951. (24-3-2008) NEW DELHI : Shri Abhishek Singhvi said a leader should always lead from the front. A leader should not equivocate or pass on the buck. Shri Advani's autobiography or should I call it hagiography follows a simple principle: whatever good happened is attributable to me; whatever went wrong is attributable to you or. Or better still whatever good happened is attributable to me. Whatever did not happen or should have happened is attributable to Shri Vajpayee. Take for example Kandahar which is mind-boggling that no less a person than the home minister of India did not know that the foreign minister of India was going to Afghanistan. To put it mildly this is mind-boggling. What kind of home minister was Shri Advani? Was he trying to be the loh purush, who like those historical figures, neither heard the evil in his government nor saw the evil in his government nor spoke evil in his government. But when evil is happening in your own government not to see it, not to hear it, is a mark of incompetence not of virtue, not of nobility. What is the level of competence of a government whose home minister is not even asked, when the country is going through one of its greatest national security crisis. What kind of government we have had, what kind of cabinet did we have, what kind of security we have been through where the essential elements of the Kandahar episode were not even put much less cleared. And Shri Advani, what did you do when you did come to know before the foreign minister left? Did you take any steps? Did you protest? Did you record your objection? It's easy to be silent in a book. The book is the silence of hypocrisy. It is only silence and hypocrisy which we get from the book. This book is written to conceal more than it reveals. This book is written to propound the thesis, the thesis of deceit which says 'heads I win, tails you loose'. There are several examples. Take the example of Shri Advani's new-found love and support for Shri Modi. This support, this great love, the declaration that he alone stood by Shri Modi during 2002 Godhra is made for the first time after 2004. Even if we ignore the pre-2004, Shri Advani has timed his declaration of support in 2008 after Shri Modi's Gujarat victory and a possible contention of the top slot in the BJP by Shri Modi. Thus Shri Advani knows which side of the bread is buttered. The book is nothing but a desperate attempt, to be accepted at least, as a prime minister in waiting if not as the prime minister. But he takes care, which is the main purpose of the book, in his public statement after the book to add that as far as prime minister-in-waiting is concerned first it is me and then it is you and you of course here is Shri Modi. Take a third example – Agra. Shri Advani again takes credit for what was universally acknowledged to be a fiasco. It is only Shri Advani's self-serving book which can take credit like an ostrich in the sand for an obvious fiasco. Only he can be so blind to the reality of Agra that he can first claim credit for it and then dissociate himself from his fiasco. These are few of the many examples, the few admitted extracts and statements of Shri Advani himself taken from the book for which you do not have to waste your time of reading 1000 pages but we can say that it is time he came down from self-serving hagiographies to real life and reality. To a question that Shri Advani has referred to your Party and Smt. Gandhi for sacrificing prime ministership because of differences in the Party, Shri Singhvi said Shri Advani, first is entitled to raise this question if and only if either he or Shri Vajpayee or any other person in his party from 1900 to 2008 can ever claim a similar sacrifice. First let him show that for any post much less the post of the prime minister and then let him ask the question. Second, it is for Smt. Gandhi and the public to answer this question not for Shri Advani.

6952. (24-3-2008) NEW DELHI : The Prime Minister, Dr. Manmohan Singh, laid the foundation stone of Pragati Phase III Power Project at Bawana in Delhi today. Shri Sushil Kumar Shinde, Minister of Power, Shri Tejender Khanna, Lt. Governor of Delhi, Smt. Sheila Dixit, Chief Minister of Delhi and other dignitaries were present on the occasion. In his address, the Prime Minister said that Rs.4000 crore project will meet the power required for Delhi to host the Commonwealth Games. The gas-based project is an environment friendly project and helps control pollution. Referring to widening energy basket, the Prime Minister emphasized that his Government is committed to further development of nuclear energy which is also environment friendly source of power. He urged the citizens in general and Delhiites in particular to improve energy efficiency. The Prime Minister called upon the young people of our country to start a new campaign for conservation of energy and asked them to think new ways of dealing with some of our energy problems. He also hoped that the construction technologies being used for the Commonwealth Games will be resource-efficient and energy-efficient.

6953. (24-3-2008) NEW DELHI : The draft Manual of Patent Practice and Procedure of the Patent Office has been uploaded on the website of the Office of the Controller General of Patents, Designs & Trade Marks (www.ipindia.nic.in) seeking comments/suggestions from the users and stakeholders. The Manual provides detailed information on the practices and procedures followed by the Patent Office for processing of the patent applications. The objective of the Manual is to provide guidelines to the users and also to the officials of the Patent Office in order to maintain uniformity and transparency in dealing with various issues under the Patents Act, 1970. The Manual, however, does not constitute rule making and hence do not have the force and effect of law. While the Manual may be regarded as a handbook, it does not impose any particular line of action and cannot be quoted to that end. The Manual has been so formatted as to reproduce the various sections of the Patents Act, 1970 with relevant rules of the Patents Rules, 2003 followed by the explanations. The explanations given are supported by citations from the decisions of the various courts of India including the Supreme Court of India and the decisions of other Countries in order to provide legal support to the explanation. The draft Manual consists of XXV Chapters covering, inter alia, issues related to origin and history of patent system in India, interpretation of definitions, patentable subject matter including non-patentable inventions, opposition proceedings, working of patents and compulsory license and guidelines to the users for filing of the patent applications etc. There are four annexures to the manual, detailing the lists of Fees applicable for various proceedings, Fees in respect of applications filed under Patent Cooperation Treaty (PCT), Forms to be used for various proceedings and Case laws referred to in the manual. The highlight of the current draft Manual is that the explanations are supported, wherever possible, by relevant judicial pronouncements. Therefore, this will provide more authoritative position to deal with a particular issue under the Patent Law. The draft Manual will be finalized in the light of the comments/ suggestions received from the users and stakeholders and would eventually replace the earlier edition of the manual. The last date for furnishing comments/suggestions to the Office of the Controller General of Patents, Designs and Trade Marks, S M Road,

Antop Hill, Mumbai-400037 was 25 March, 2008. However, in order to get more feedbacks from the stakeholders, the time for furnishing comments/suggestions has been extended to April 15, 2008. Department of Industrial Policy & Promotion, Ministry of Commerce and Industry, New Delhi, March 24, 2008

6954. (24-3-2008) NEW DELHI : The Union Ministry of Tribal Affairs has signed MoU with University of Delhi and the Ministry of Development of North Eastern Region (MDONER) for setting up of 500 seats girls hostel for tribal and North East students including Sikkim. The hostel to be set up at Dhaka Housing Complex of University of Delhi will have all the modern facilities including energy efficient building, solar water heating and rainwater harvesting. Besides blocks for 500 students with accompanying faculties, the hostel will have one provost flat, two warden flats, two resident tutor flats and twelve servants' quarters. Construction is expected to be completed by 30th September, 2009. Out of approved construction cost of Rs. 23.33 crore, 40% will be shared by the Ministry of Tribal Affairs and remaining 60% by the Ministry of Development of North Eastern Region. The Ministry of Tribal Affairs has already released Rs. 2.6 crore in the first week of March, 2008, from its share. Land for the hostel will be provided by the University as per the norms of UGC. A committee comprising of representatives from the Ministry of Tribal Affairs, the Ministry of DONER and Delhi University will regularly monitor the progress of construction works and meet at least every quarter for inspection and to discuss the related issues to ensure timely completion of the project.

6955. (25-3-2008) NEW DELHI : Prime Minister Dr. Manmohan Singh telephoned Pakistan Prime Minister Syed Yousuf Raza Gilani this evening and greeted him on his assumption of office. Dr. Singh expressed the hope that India-Pakistan relations can evolve to become the "best ever" and he also hoped Mr. Gilani would build on the initiatives taken by his predecessors, former Prime Ministers Benazir Bhutto and Nawaz Shariff and also that of President Pervez Musharaf to improve bilateral relations. Earlier in the day Prime Minister Singh also wrote a letter to Prime Minister Gilani.

6956. (25-3-2008) NEW DELHI : The Defence Minister Shri AK Antony has asked DRDO scientists to 'shed old mindsets' and reorient themselves to face the challenges brought in by rapid pace of changes taking place in every sphere of life in a globalised world. Addressing DRDO scientists after a day's tour of its cluster of laboratories in Hyderabad today, Shri Antony said, DRDO will have to actively increase its interaction with both the public and private sectors for technology transfers and R & D in view of the policy of the government to give the private industry an enhanced role in the defence sector. A major instrument to implement this is our offset policy which requires foreign vendors involved in large projects to actively invest in Indian firms and joint ventures, he said. The Defence Minister dwelt at length on the changing times and their myriad dimensions on security, economy and organizations. " The political and economic dynamics of relationships between the countries, today, both regional and global, are constantly changing. On the one side, this forces us to constantly reappraise conventional and non-conventional threats to our national security. On the other, the impact of globalization requires that we reassess and adjust to new economic relationships." Shri Antony said, DRDO can not remain insulated from the changes taking place around it and has to re-configure and adjust itself to the changing environment. " Rapid advances in science and technology require that the DRDO adjusts its organizational structure and goals to new situations and new requirements and in the process shed old mindsets. The DRDO will have to actively increase its interaction with both the public and private sectors for technology transfers and R & D so that products which have civilian applications can be productionised. And all this without losing sight of the DRDO's primary mandate which is in support of the country's defence preparedness." Shri Antony said the Rama Rao Committee Report which has looked at these issues is under consideration of the government. He congratulated the DRDO scientists for the successful launch of the Agni-1 missile on Sunday which was executed entirely by the user-the Army. Accompanied by the DRDO chief Shri M Natarajan and other distinguished scientists of the organization including Dr. VK Saraswat and Dr. Avinash Chander, Shri Antony visited the Missile Complex, constituted by the premier laboratories of Research Centre Imarat (RCI), Defence Research & Development Laboratory (DRDL) and Defence Electronics Research Laboratory, specializing on Electronic Warfare. During interactions with the scientists, Shri Antony said, in the long run, India must reduce considerably its dependence on foreign suppliers for its strategic requirements. In this respect, he called for synergy among the DRDO, the PSUs and the private sector.

6957. (25-3-2008) NEW DELHI : Annual Plan size for Madhya Pradesh for the year 2007-08 was approved today at a meeting between the Deputy Chairman, Planning Commission, Shri Montek Singh Ahluwalia and Chief Minister of Madhya Pradesh Shri Shivraj Singh Chouhan. The Plan outlay was agreed at Rs.14182.61 crores which include onetime additional Central assistance of Rs.150 crores for projects of special interest to the State. In his comments on the performance of the State, Deputy Chairman, Planning Commission, said the State needs to have more attention on human development. Social sector needs priority and efforts should be aimed at improving human development index with policy initiatives for creating investor friendly environment. He said the State Government should avail benefits available under various social sector schemes. Efforts should be made to improve performance in various programmes under Bharat Nirman. He said priority should be given to schemes related to Bundelkhand area. Power sector should get focused attention as achievement of higher growth rate in Eleventh Plan could be constrained due to power shortage. The Chief Minister Mr. Chouhan informed the Commission that thrust areas of development policy would be eliminating hunger, mal-nutrition and abject poverty. Livelihood opportunity would be created through generating economic activities based on natural resources. A number of new initiatives have been taken to improve social protection. These include Mukhya Mantri Mazdoor Suraksha Yojana, integrated livelihood programme and Din Dayal Antodya Upchar Yojana. Fiscal reforms are being pursued with focused attention to ensure good governance. State Government is working to facilitate investments and creating more physical and social infrastructure. He said addressing needs of disadvantage including women, SCs/STs and disabled is on the prioty agenda of the government. Efforts are on to reduce dependence on agriculture in rural areas and for this purpose allied areas are being given priority. He said States with higher forest cover than national average should be compensated.

6958. (25-3-2008) NEW DELHI : The Vice President of India Shri Mohd. Hamid Ansari released a book titled "Anatomy of Abduction" authored by senior journalist Shri V. Sudarshan at a function here today. Addressing on the occasion, the Vice President said that this book can be read in many ways *viz.* as a thriller, as an exercise to investigative reporting or as a serious commentary on Government's crisis management and negotiating skills. He hoped that more such books would come out in future. Congratulating Shri Sudarshan for his remarkable book, the Vice President said that he has presented a complete overview of Government of India's crisis management in handling the abduction crisis. Shri E. Ahmed, the Minister of State for External Affairs also addressed. A number of dignitaries were present on the occasion.

6959. (25-3-2008) NEW DELHI : Power Finance Corporation Ltd (PFC) and Indian Renewable Energy Development Agency Ltd (IREDA) signed a Memorandum of Understanding (MoU) today *i.e.* on 25th March, 2008 for facilitating joint financing of renewable energy, energy efficiency & conservation and medium & large hydro projects. The MoU was signed by Shri Shyam Wadhera, Director (Projects), PFC and Shri Debashish Majumdar, CMD, IREDA in presence of senior PFC and IREDA officials. PFC and IREDA shall cooperate to leverage their respective strengths and competencies built over the years for facilitating financing of renewable energy, energy efficiency & conservation and medium & large hydro projects for mutual benefit. At present the installed capacity of electric power from renewable energy sources in India is 10,209 MW and keeping in view the potential, Ministry of New and Renewable Energy, Govt. of India has set for itself a goal to add an additional 14,000 MW capacity of grid quality power through non-conventional renewable resources from commercially exploitable resources by the end of 11th Five Year Plan.

6960. (25-3-2008) NEW DELHI : The Minister for Civil Aviation, Shri Praful Patel today received the Report of the Committee under the Chairmanship of Shri Ajay Prasad which had been set up for formulating a Master Plan for Next

Generation Futuristic Air Navigation Services. The Committee had been set up on 20th March, 2007.

6961. (25-3-2008) NEW DELHI : Healthcare is a major concern for the Governments around the world. Globalization brings with it increasing threats to health including SARS, Avian Flu, HIV/ AIDS, Humanitarian Emergencies and Bio-terrorism. These and other threats to health know no boundaries as in an age of wide spread global trade and travel, new and existing diseases can cross national borders and threaten our collective security. At a more basic level the promotion of health is a fundamental value by itself, a vital public good and a basic human right. Instruments such as the Human Development Index have forced governments to redefine development. The importance of Universal access to health including water, sanitation and nutrition are essential to a balanced development.

India has both substantial achievements as well as a daunting unfinished agenda in the health sector. Longevity in the country has more than doubled since Independence in 1947, Infant Mortality Rate has fallen by 70% points, Malaria has been contained, Small pox and Guinea worm have been completely eradicated and Leprosy and Polio are nearing elimination. In the preceding 5 years over 500, 000 deaths have been averted due to the up scaling of the Directly Observed Treatment Short Course (DOTS).

6962. (25-3-2008) NEW DELHI : The Union Public Service Commission will be conducting the National Defence Academy and Naval Academy Examination (I), 2008 on 20th April, 2008 at 41 Centres all over the country. Admission Certificates to the admitted candidates have been dispatched. Similarly, letters of rejection to the applicants who did not comply with various essential conditions of the examination have also been issued. If any applicant has not received any one of the above-mentioned communications, he may contact UPSC Facilitation Counter on Telephone Nos. 011-23381125, 011-23385271 and 011-23098543 between 10:00 a.m. to 5.30 p.m. on all working days.

6963. (25-3-2008) NEW DELHI : The Ministry of Rural Development has granted Rs.138.15 crore to the State Government of Uttar Pradesh as 2nd instalment under Tranche-II of World Bank Assisted Projects under the Pradhan Mantri Gram Sadak Yojana (PMGSY)during the current financial year (2007-08). This amount will be given to the Uttar Pradesh Grameen Sadak Vikas Abhikaran, which is the Autonomous Agency for receiving the funds for the programmes under the scheme. The grant is towards plan expenditure and will, accordingly be subject to the conditions laid down from time to time in the guidelines of the Pradhan Mantri Gram Sadak Yojana (PMGSY) and supplementary directions there under.

6964. (25-3-2008) NEW DELHI : The Ministry of Rural Development has granted Rs.64.55 crore to the State Government of Assam as first instalment of

Central Share of Rs.143.44 crore to tackle 3092 water quality affected rural habitations in the State under the Revised Sub Mission Programme of Water Quality under Rajiv Gandhi National Drinking Water Mission (RGNDWM)-a Centrally Sponsored Programme of Accelerated Rural Water Supply Programme (ARWSP) during the current financial year (2007-08). The State Government will ensure to provide State share for implementation of projects and revised guidelines on Sub-Mission of water quality shall be followed.

6965. (25-3-2008) NEW DELHI : GAIL (India) Limited here today signed Annual Memorandum of Understanding with the Government of India for performance targets of GAIL for the Financial Year 2008-09. The MoU was signed by Mr.M.S. Srinivasan, Secretary, Ministry of Petroleum & Natural Gas on behalf of Government of India and Dr. U.D. Choubey, Chairman and Managing Director, GAIL on behalf of the company. Senior officials from the Government and Directors of GAIL were also present on the occasion. During the FY 2008-09, to achieve the Excellence in performance, the Company has been assigned a target for Gas Transmission of around 81.5 MMSCMD of natural gas from domestic sources and through LNG route. It includes the Gas Marketing target of around 70 MMSCMD. The MoU also provides for an 'Excellent' production target of 390 TMT of Polymers (HDPE & LLDPE) and 1,260 TMT of Liquid Hydrocarbons. The Company's performance will be assessed on key financial parameters and also dynamic and sector / enterprise-specific parameters such as Gas Sourcing, E&P and CBM, City Gas Projects, Pipeline Projects Implementation, Business Development & Globalization, Safety, Customer Focus, Quality Management etc.

6966. (25-3-2008) NEW DELHI : The Department of Personnel & Training (DOP&T) will organize the first seminar in the series of quarterly seminars that it intends to organize, to dwell upon professional and valuable inputs on modern subjects beneficial to the officers and staff of Central Secretariat Services (CSS). The maiden seminar in the series, titled 'HR Management (HRM): Revisited' will be inaugurated by Shri Suresh Pachauri, Minister of State, Ministry of Personnel, Public Grievances and Pensions in New Delhi tomorrow. The main aim of the seminar is to sensitize the officers and staff towards changes in the management techniques and the latest developments in the HR sector. Knowledge of modern HR practices will broaden the horizon of the officers and staff of Central Secretariat. Apart from the Minister, other participants at the seminar would be Shri Satyananda Mishra, Secretary (Personnel), Dr. Pritam Singh and Prof. Abha Chaturvedi, both from MDI Gurgaon, Dr. Santrup Misra, Director, Aditya Birla Management Corporation Ltd, Shri Hasmukh Adhia, Principal Secretary, Government of Gujarat etc. The speakers will elaborate the ground realities of government services and the improvements that can be accommodated into it so that the government machinery becomes more responsive to the needs of the people at large. With the advent of globalization and consequent liberalization of the country's policies, it becomes important that the grass-root levels of the Government machinery is groomed well so that the staff manning these posts become receptive to the changes in the world and enabled to initiate and implement new concepts in their day-to-day working. A major initiative taken in this direction has been the implementation of the cadre training programme for all the officers and staff across the board, irrespective of the levels at which they are working in the Government of India. This initiative has been implemented recently. DOP&T is optimistic about fruitful results of the newly introduced programmes.

6967. (25-3-2008) NEW DELHI : Shri Kamal Nath, Union Minister of Commerce and Industry, during his meeting with Mr. Jim Anderton, the New Zealand Minister for Agriculture, Forestry, Bio-Security and Fisheries, who called on him here today, has called for further strengthing of the bilateral ties between India and New Zealand. Observing that technical cooperation need to be put on the priority agenda, both India and New Zealand agreed to provide the enabling environment for achieving further cooperation. Shri G.K.Pillai, Commerce Secretary and senior officials from both sides were also present during the bilateral talks. The collaboration and investment from New Zealand has been rising continuously. From August 1991 to June 2007 Government has approved 50 FDI proposals from New Zealand with an equity participation of Rs. 3,922.2 (US$ 100.5) million). New Zealand ranks 37th in the list of countries in terms of cumulative FDI approved from August 1991 to June 2006. The top sectors attracting FDI (from August 1991 to June 2007) from New Zealand are Services Sector (57.65%), Food Processing Industries (28.37%), Telecommunications (12.83%), Boilers and Steam Generating Plants (0.52%), and Electrical Equipments (including computer software & electronics) (0.36%). Top sectors attracting FDI inflows (from January 2000 to June 2007) from New Zealand are Power (90.79%), computer software & Hardware (4.44%) and Trading (2.17%). As regards Technical collaborations, New Zealand has been granted 20 technical collaborations since, 1991. Top sectors attracting technology from New Zealand are-Electrical Equipments (including computer software & electronics) and Metallurgical Industries. Top FDI Inflows received (from January 2000 to June 2007) from New Zealand through Indian Companies are M/s. Estel Conversion Lab Pvt. Ltd., M/s. Applied Thermal Technologies India P. Ltd., M/s. Island Stone India Pvt. Ltd., M/s. Ibex Gallagher Pvt. Ltd., M/s. Q.E.D. India (P) Ltd., M/s. Light Office Software Pvt. Ltd., M/s. Good World Communication Services P. Ltd., and M/s. Ind Medica Ltd.

6968. (26-3-2008) NEW DELHI : Shri Kamal Nath, Union Minister of Commerce and Industry, during his bilateral meeting with Mr. Miguel Jorge, Brazilian Minister for Development Industry and Foreign Trade here today, has stated that India realizes the importance of Latin America and Caribbean and Indian Government has initiated a special programme, FOCUS LAC, to encourage trade relations between India and Latin America and Caribbean. The Minister further stated that, "Brazil being the largest trading partner in Latin America has special importance for India. Over the years, Brazil has emerged as our biggest partner in the LAC region with our bilateral trade crossing 3 billion marks in 2007. Bilateral trade has jumped to US$ 3.12 billion in 2007 from merely US$ 488 million in 2000. However, I feel that considering the huge opportunities of mutual interests, the volume of trade is still low and it could be enhanced manifolds by efforts of governments and trade bodies of our two countries. In the recent India-Brazil Joint Commission Meeting in April 2007, both the governments have set a target of US$ 10 billion by 2010 and we are working towards achieving this target." Senior officials from both the sides were also present on the occasion. As regards investments, Shri Kamal Nath informed that, "Our mutual investments have also increased in recent years, particularly in the field of information technology, biotechnology and pharmaceuticals. The Indian pharmaceutical companies have made a success story of their entry in Brazil. Almost all the major pharma players of India have established their presence in Brazil with supply of bulk drugs, finished formulations and establishment of manufacturing units and joint ventures. Areas of mutual interests between our countries cover pharma, aviation, engineering products, agriculture based industries including equipments and food processing industries, energy including ethanol, chemical products, auto parts and vehicles and two wheelers, IT, banking and urban infrastructure. South-South cooperation is an integral part of our bilateral relationship. India and Brazil have demonstrated their determination in reformulating the big questions that affect foreign policy and trade at the international level. India and Brazil must continue to be close partners in the UN, WTO and other international fora on issues such as social development, health care, sustainable economic development and poverty alleviation."

6969. (26-3-2008) NEW DELHI : The Minister of Social Justice and Empowerment, Smt. Meira Kumar has launched "Nirmaya" a Health Insurance Scheme for the welfare of persons with Autism, Cerebral Palsy, Mental Retardation and Multiple Disabilities here today. Addressing on the occasion, she said that a large number of persons will be benefited in terms of getting quality medical services in their respective areas through this scheme. She further said that it is a cashless scheme, under this persons need not pay even a penny for the services offer to them if they are admitted in hospital for an expenditure upto Rs. 1 lakh. Even transport arrangement also has been made for this purpose to reach the hospitals. The scheme also covers OPD services. The premium of the insurance scheme is paid by the National Trust for the Below Poverty Line persons. The above poverty line persons can also avail this facility by paying the suitable premium, she added. Smt. Meira Kumar announced that the Ministry is launching this scheme in 10 districts on pilot basis; Central Delhi-Delhi, Kaimur-Bihar,

Chandigarh-Haryana, Jabalpur-Madhya Pradesh, Agartala-Tripura, Raeareny-UP, Erode-Tamil Nadu, Ernakulam-Kerala, Ahmedabad-Gujarat and Bhageshwar in Uttarakhand. The Minister distributed photo ID cards to the first 20 specially-abled people. A film on Gyan Prabha Awardees was also shown on the occasion. Smt. Subbulakshmi Jagadeesan, the Minister of State for Social Justice & Empowerment, Smt. Poonam Natarajan, Chairperson of National Trust and Smt. Veena Chhotray, the Secretary of SJ&E were also present in the function.

6970. (26-3-2008) NEW DELHI : Union Rural Development Minister Dr. Raghuvansh Prasad Singh has thurst upon the quality work and timely completion of Pradhan Mantri Gram Sadak Yojana (PMGSY) works in the states. Presiding over to the 9th meeting of the Governing Body of National Rural Roads Development Agency (NRRDA) here today Dr.Singh said that projects under the flagship programme Bharat Nirman should not get delayed and there should be no compromise on the quality of works being rendered. He asked the State Governments to inform the Ministry of the Rural Development of the Action taken in respect to the slow pace of works. There should be penalty clause also for the delay and the defaulters should be made accountable, the Minister added. Dr. Singh advocated for the enhanced people's participation in the quality control measures and called for bringing in transparency in the process. He advised the States for a joint monitoring mechanism comprising of the elected representatives for the Parliament and State Legislature as well as the local bodies. He laid stress on the maintenance aspect of the roads constructed under PMGSY and called for yearly maintenance. He also pressed for the development of a software for this purpose. The minister suggested that the roads constructed under PMGSY should not be over burdened in terms of heavy vehicular traffic. He also mooted for a grievance redressal mechanism during the process of implementation of scheme. The meeting was attended by the Secretary Rural Development Dr. Rita Sharma, Special Secretary Shri Atul Chaturvedi along with the representatives from the Ministry of Finance, Panchayati Raj, the Planning Commission, the NRRDA, CRRI and officials from different States.

6971. (26-3-2008) NEW DELHI : The Ceremonial Changing of Guard takes place at Rashtrapati Bhavan every Saturday, excluding closed holidays. This ceremony can be watched by the general public from the pavement outside South Block. Due to the advent of summer, this Ceremony will now begin at 0800 hrs every Saturday, from March 29th onwards, except on closed holidays as mentioned above.

6972. (26-3-2008) NEW DELHI : The BJP has noted with serious concern the recent developments in Tibet. The use of indiscriminate violence by the Chinese armed forces to forcibly crush the voice of the people of Tibet is a serious development. The entire global community has begun to voice its apprehension about the manner in which force is being used against the protestors. The anguish and suffering of Tibet and its people, eloquently expressed by His Holiness the Dalai Lama in pain imbued words, is a call to the conscience of all humanity. In this context, it is indeed shameful to note that the Government of India, instead of expressing concern against the use of force by the Chinese government, is adopting a degrading policy of blatant appeasement towards China with scant regard to the country's national honour and foreign policy independence. Reports suggest that the Government of India has cancelled a proposed call by the Vice President of India on His Holiness when he is expected to visit Delhi in the near future. Why is the government adopting such a nationally humiliating and pusillanimous policy full of indecision at the cost of neglecting the country's prestige? The BJP condemns this and expects the UPA to candidly explain to the country the rationale behind this policy of irrationality. The illuminating thought and person of Lord Buddha, born in India and finding enlightenment here, has lent a unique kinship to the relations between India and Tibet. For centuries these relations are entirely spiritual in content and practice. Tibet is one of the important and last surviving repositories of the great thought and teachings of Lord Buddha and has for at least the last 13 centuries been the custodian of an important school of Buddhist thought. India cannot and must not disconnect with this invaluable and indeed unique spiritual linkage. India must give voice to its concerns; correctly, unequivocally and unambiguously. This is not any interference. It is standing up, by India, for preserving that which is our own, and that which is India's contribution to all humanity-Tibet's Buddhist culture and civilization. This is our bounden duty and our very "Dharma". Let us not forget that the "Chakra" which adorns independent India's flag, on cloth or engraved on stone is a Buddhist symbol of the "Dharma Chakra". How can we adopt the symbol but ignore the reality?

6973. (26-3-2008) NEW DELHI : The Union Minister of Shipping, Road Transport & Highways Thiru. T.R. Baalu was presented a Demand Draft for Rs. 16.50 crore (Rs. 16,49,82,750/-) crore here today towards the interim dividend for 2007-08 by Capt. S.S. Tripathi, Chairman and Managing Director of the Dredging Corporation of India (DCI), a Public Sector Undertaking under the administrative control of the Ministry of Shipping, Road Transport & Highways. The Board of Directors of the Company declared an interim dividend of 75 per cent for the year 2007-08 on the paid-up capital of the Company involving an amount of Rs. 21.00 crore. The total turnover of the company during the year 2006-07 was a record Rs. 622.09 crore. The profit before tax for the year stood at Rs. 206.39 crore. The Profit after tax for the year was also a record at Rs. 188.73 crore. As per the unaudited results for the period of nine months ended on 31st December 2008, the turnover is Rs. 514.42 crore, profit before tax is Rs. 116.85 crore and profit after tax is Rs. 105.36 crore. The paid-up capital of the Company is Rs.28.00 crore divided into 2,80,00,000 equity shares of Rs.10/- each of which 78.56% *i.e.*, 2,19,97,700 shares are held by the President of India. The Dredging Corporation of India (DCI) was established in 1976 to provide integrated dredging service to the Major Ports of the country. The DCI a Mini Ratna category-I Public Sector Undertaking was upgraded to Schedule 'B' from 'C' during the year 2002. The clients of the Company include Major Ports, non-major ports, Indian Navy, State Governments, etc.

6974. (26-3-2008) NEW DELHI : Command Hospital (Central Command) Lucknow has bagged the Raksha Mantri's Trophy for the Best Command Hospital for the year 2007. The Defence Minister Shri AK Antony presented the trophy and a cheque of Rs 2 lakhs to the Commandant of the Hospital Maj Gen AKS Bararia in New Delhi today. Shri AK Antony congratulated Major Gen Bararia on winning the trophy and appreciated the Armed Forces medical services for its yeomen services to the nation. He directed the Armed Forces Medical Services (AFMS) to improve the condition of the field hospitals so that they are able to provide better services to Jawans in insurgency affected areas. Earlier, welcoming the dignitaries at the award ceremony Lt Gen Yogendra Singh Director General Armed Forces Medical Service & Senior Colonel Commandant of the Army Medical Corps assured that the Armed Forces medical services will be always ready to face any challenge and will continue to provide high quality medical care. The Armed Forces Medical Services provide comprehensive medical care to the Army, Navy and the Air Force. The comprehensive medical cover spans the entire spectrum of preventive, curative and rehabilitative services to the serviceman, ex-servicemen and their families. Headed by the Director General Armed Forces Medical Services, the Armed Forces Medical Services have always excelled in their role whether in combat medical support or providing the most advanced and specialised treatment at state of the art medical facilities. In addition the Armed Forces Medical Services have always been among the first responders in situations like disasters and natural calamities, whether within the country or abroad. The medical services provided by our UN Missions and other relief teams have generated tremendous goodwill among the international community. The Armed Forces medical services cover the length and breadth of the country with a network of 127 hospitals and 87 field medical units. The Raksha Mantri's Trophy was instituted in 1989 to recognize excellence in patient care among the Command Hospitals of the Army and equivalent hospitals in the Navy and Air Force. Admiral Sureesh Mehta, Chief of Naval Staff, Gen Deepak Kapoor, Chief of Army Staff, Defence Secretary Shri Vijay Singh, Smt Deepa Jain Singh, Secretary Ex-Servicemen Welfare and other senior civil and military officers of Ministry of Defence also graced the occasion.

6975. (26-3-2008) NEW DELHI : India and Finland have signed an Agreement on Cooperation in Science & Technology that provides for a broad based framework of cooperation in the areas of research, development and innovation policies between the two countries with renowned cutting-edge technologies. The agreement was signed by Mr. Kapil Sibal, Union Minister of Science & Technology and Earth

Sciences and Mr. Mauri Pekkarinen, Finnish Minister of Economic Affairs, in Helsinki on 25 March 2008. Speaking on the occasion Shri Sibal said that the Way forward for the bilateral relations is to set up an innovation industrial R&D fund enabling technology access to market for mutual benefit of the people of India and Finland. Mr. Mauri Pekkarinen termed the visit of the Indian Minister as a big event in the bilateral relations between India and Finland. During his visit Mr. Sibal will also be calling on Finnish Prime Minister Mr. Matti Vanhanen and Mrs. Sari Sarkomaa, Minister of Education besides visiting a number of leading research institutions. Bilateral relations with Finland, an important member of the European Union with proven technological capabilities in ICT, Biotechnology, industrial machinery and paper industry, have assumed a dynamic edge following the exchange of Prime Ministerial visits in 2006. The India-EU Summit meeting took place in Helsinki in October 2006 during Finland's EU Presidency. Bilateral trade which in 2007 was valued at Euro 645.08 million has grown by over 20%. Two-way investments are growing with Finnish majors like Nokia, Elcoteq, Kone and Wartsila now well established in India. Indian investments in Finland are also making an impact in areas such as ICT and renewable energy. Finland has one of the highest investments in R&D as a percentage of its GDP among the OECD countries and is continually increasing. It is now renowned for its environment-friendly, innovative technological capabilities which would be beneficial for India's booming economic development.

6976. (26-3-2008) NEW DELHI : The Minister of Petroleum and Natural Gas, Shri Murli Deora has emphasized the need for India and Brazil to further enhance cooperation between the two countries specially in the oil and gas sector. During a meeting with Mr. Miguel Jorge, Brazilian Minister for Development, Industry and Foreign Trade, here today, Shri Deora said that the efforts are afoot in this direction as the two national oil companies of respective countries, ONGC(India) and Petrobras(Brazil) have entered into an arrangement for working together in exploration and production of hydrocarbons in India and Brazil. To a suggestion by Brazilian Minister to enhance ethanol blending Shri Deora informed that Government has already decided to endeavour blending ethanol with petrol at 10% against 5% being blended at present. The two Ministers expressed satisfaction at the efforts being made to take forward cooperation between the two leading developing countries which are emerging as major economic powers.

6977. (26-3-2008) NEW DELHI : Congress spokesman Smt. Jayanthi Natarajan said we welcome the order passed by the Hon'ble Supreme Court of India setting up a special investigation team to investigate afresh some of the important and extremely agonizing riots that took place in the aftermath of Godhra. The Indian National Congress has always stated that the investigations which were conducted by the state government were biased as well as mostly conducted with a view to covering up the acts of the main accused. The investigations by the state government were neither impartial nor effective. The order of the Supreme Court is a vindication of that stand and while welcoming the order we sincerely hope that the victims of the terrible riots will now be in a better position to get justice. Second, we would like to express our concern about the two and a half year old girl who is trapped in a bore well for the last 20 hours in a village near Agra. This is the fourth such incident which has occurred over the last year and we do believe that various state government and authorities should now consider ways and means and laws to ensure that such bore wells and other such hazard diggings should not be left unattended without any responsibility being taken for safety. To a question that Shri Pawar has come up with a suggestion that the UPA should collectively face the next elections, Smt. Jayanthi said whatever strategy is going to be adopted by the UPA will be decided among the leaders of the UPA and our Chairperson Smt. Sonia Gandhi. To a question that Congress Party's alliance partner NCP is planning to have an alliance with the BJP, Smt. Jayanthi said certainly this issue will be discussed within the UPA. However, we all know that this is an alliance at the national level and whatever alliances have been made will be addressed at the regional level. At the national level we are talking about the UPA which is being formed with the express process of giving this country a secular government. To a question as to who is the UPA's prime ministerial candidate and who is suitable in the NDA for the post, Smt. Jayanthi said when the election comes at that time we'll announce the same and as far as the NDA is concerned they are in a desperate hurry. As of now there is no vacancy for the post of Prime Minister as yet. They are always in a hurry because they don't have any progressive agenda and even within the NDA there is a long waiting list of would-be Prime Ministers. It would be in the greater interest of the country if they took up constructive issues in Parliament and outside rather than declaring prime ministerial candidates. To a question that it is surprising to say that there are no vacancies. You have a prime minister and despite that you are shying away from an incumbent prime minister, Smt. Jayanthi said I am not shying away from anything. We are not here to answer to an agenda because of a desperate opposition trying to make some news. We cannot answer that agenda. To a question that do you think the UPA is relevant even after completing five years, Smt. Jayanthi said I think the UPA has never been more relevant than at present because the UPA has conclusively demonstrated the success of coalition and alliance politics, of the spirit of give and take, which has characterized all the allies and the Congress Party in this government, where tremendous initiatives have been taken to fulfil the promises made in the Common Minimum Programme and very important steps taken to address the development needs of the aam admi. To a question on economic measures what is your Party doing on this front, Smt. Jayanthi said it is the same measure that any government takes such as check black-marketing, keep the prices under control. Every step the government is taking is for the benefit of the aam admi, to control the prices of essential commodities etc.

6978. (26-3-2008) NEW DELHI : Union Rural Development Minister Dr. Raghuvansh Prasad Singh has laid emphasis on the need of an appropriate land policy that ensures food security in a country like India. Inaugurating a seminar on land policy for Diversified and Inclusive Agricultural Growth here today Dr. Singh said the aspects of rehabilitation before land acquisition should not be ignored while going for the land acquisition in the name of developmental works across the country. Referring to the recently announced Rehabilitation and Resettlement policy, 2007 of the Ministry Dr. Singh said a number of incentives regarding proper and well thought rehabilitation of rural population have been introduced and even the landless persons will also be considered for getting the benefits from the package. On the impediments being experienced during the implementation of Rural Development schemes like the Indira Aawaas Yojana (IAY) and the Pradhan Mantri Gram Sadak Yojana (PMGSY) in the states and he said shortage of appropriate land is also one of the reason for it. Dr. Singh also advocated for the development of waste land for the purpose of land acquisition for Industrial purposes. He said the Department of Land Reforms has initated a National Land Resource Management Programme on a time bound basis under which the mapping of land will be done through the satellite and also the computerization of land record is being done for better performance. He assured all possible help in a making out an appropriate land acquisition policy for diversified and inclusive agricultural growth. The one day seminar was organized by the Agricultural Costs And Prices Committee, Ministry of Agriculture in collaboration with the Department of Land Reforms, Ministry of Rural Development. In addition to Dr. T. Haque Chairman, Agricultural Cost And Price Committee Land the Secretary Dr. P.K. Mishra, DAC also spoke on the occasion and highlighted the need of a well defined and meaningful policy for diversified and agricultural growth for the betterment of Indian Farmers.

6979. (26-3-2008) HYDERABAD: The Communist Party of India has demanded that the Centre amend the Special Economic Zones Act to remove the provisions declaring SEZ as a "foreign territory." It said all the laws of the land, including trade union rights, should be made applicable in the SEZs and the 'unreasonable tax exemptions' given to them should be withdrawn. The government should not acquire land for SEZs and it should, instead, ask the promoters to buy their own land from the market. The party said the government should provide a level playing field to all industries as giving concessions only to those in SEZs would be detrimental to industries elsewhere. This would ultimately lead to their shifting or closure. The 20th national congress of the CPI, in a resolution, expressed concern over the "reckless" manner in which the Centre was granting permission for SEZs.

6980. (26-3-2008) NEW DELHI : Following is the text of the speech of Finance Minister, Shri P. Chidambaram delivered at the Lee Kuan Yew School of Public

Policy in Singapore today: "It is an honour to be invited to speak at the Lee Kuan Yew School of Public Policy, Singapore. It would not be an exaggeration to say that Mr. Lee Kuan Yew is the founding father of modern Singapore. During his long tenure as Prime Minister, Mr. Lee Kuan Yew stood out as the symbol of a dynamic, progressive and pluralist city state. He was-and is-regarded as an unorthodox statesman. He is respected for his strong views and fearless expression of those views in world fora. Singapore, it is said, lives by its wits, and it is universally acknowledged that much of that wit and wisdom are owed to one person, Mr. Lee Kuan Yew. This School itself is a symbol of the global city that is Singapore in the making. As your Dean says in his welcome address on the web-site, "[w]hile [the] curricula.... are similar to those offered in other leading schools of public policy around the world, they are also outstanding for their emphasis on the public policy experiences of Asian countries and the critical challenges facing them." I am happy to note that the students of this School are drawn from all countries of the world and, especially, from Asia. Therefore, the matters that I speak on today may strike a chord in many of you and may remind you of your experience in your own country. The Indian experience over the last three decades has been one of sustained growth, with each decade being an improvement over the previous one. Between 1971-72 and 1980-81 the average GDP growth was 3.2 per cent a year. In the subsequent two decades, the growth rate was 5.4 per cent and 5.6 per cent a year, respectively. Since 2001-02, we have witnessed an average growth rate of 7.6 per cent a year until 2007-08. This experience is unique in many ways since it has been based on the principles of democracy and rule of law. This has allowed us to carry the people with us at every stage and, in spite of numerous challenges, we have not deviated from our reform agenda. The agenda is one of sustained growth in a market economy that takes care of its poor and disadvantaged. While markets ensure efficiency, a democratic governing system ensures that the reform process has a human face.

6981. (27-3-2008) NEW DELHI : The National Rural Employment Guarantee Act (NREGA) will become operational through out the country from the 1st of next month. Accordingly a series of events have been worked out by the Department of Rural Development in the Ministry of Rural Development. In order to publicize the NREGA on a wider scale the Union Minister for Rural Development Dr. Raghuvansh Prasad Singh has written to the Chief Ministers of all States/ Administrators of Union Territories to cooperate actively for the advocacy and promotional activities of programmes for disseminating information on NREGA at Gram Sabhas at village level and conventions at Block and District levels that involve public representatives as Local MPs, MLAs and representatives of PRIs during the month of April 2008. The minister has also requested them to ensure that NREGA workers accounts are opened in Post Offices and Banks so that the wage payment due to them is made through their accounts as this will ensure transparency in NREGA. Dr. Singh pointed has-out that opening account of wage earners in Post Offices and Banks is free of cost and no service charge is payable by the Department of Rural Development to either Banks or Post Offices. Dr. Singh has also urged the Chief Ministers and UT Administrators to review the status of the districts preparations in this regard. This includes : IEC activities specially convening Gram Sabhas to familiarize the local community about NREGA, Availability of a shelf of permissible projects in each Gram Panchayat proposed through people's participation, Identification and placement of key personnels for NREGA, specially Gram Rozgar Sahayaks for each Gram Panchayat, Technical and Computer Assistants, Data Entry Operators at Block level, Identification and deployment of dedicated Programme Officers at Block level, Training of all administrative and PRI functionaries, Setting up of Vigilance Monitoring Committees and training of its members, Opening of dedicated account for NREGA funds, Steps taken to equip Blocks with ICT infrastructures for MIS, Status of Completion SGRY works by March, 2008.

6982. (27-3-2008) NEW DELHI : The Union Urban Development Secretary Shri M. Ramachandran has been awarded the Degree of Doctor of Philosophy in Economics by the Lucknow University. His thesis was on Project Planning and Appraisal (with Special Reference to India). In his thesis he has suggested alternative approach to the process of project planning, starting from the stage of project identification to its completion and the need for accountability being ensured. Shri Ramachandran has done his MA in Economics from Maharaja's College, Ernakulam and M.Phil in Economic Planning from University of Glasgow. An IAS officer of 1972 batch, Shri Ramachandran was earlier Chief Secretary of Uttarakhand before coming to Government of India.

6983. (27-3-2008) NEW DELHI : Hampi, the seat of the great Pampapati or Virupaksha temple of Lord Siva, the patron-deity and family God of the Kings of Vijayanagar, stands on the southern bank of river Tungabhadra in the Bellary district and is about nine miles from the town of Hospet in Karnataka. It was the oldest and the most sacred temple of Vijayanagar. It has miraculously escaped destruction, which was the fate of Vijayanagar after the battle of Talikota in 1565 A.D. This great and ancient temple of Hampi originally had a small village around it. Long before the grand Vijayanagar Empire, it was a spot where there was nothing but nature in one of her wildest moods. On one side there were huge boulders and lofty hills scattered and on the other there were green trees and grass. River Tungabhadra flowed nearby.The majesty of huge tumbled boulders, the river, isolation, solitude and wild nature attracted a number of sages and ascetics to this spot. Sage Vidyaranya used the place for his meditation. Pampa is another name for the river Tungabhadra. Pampadevi is considered the daughter of Brahma and she performed penance on the Humakuta Hill. Visvesvara appeared before her and made her his consort. Deriving inspiration from the celebrated sage and philosopher, Madhava, Harihara and Bukka, two of the five sons of Sangama, laid the foundation of the city in 1336 A.D. and the kingdom of Vijayanagar was named after their Guru Vidyaranya. They made Pampapati or Virupaksha their patron deity and family god. On the northern bank of the river was the fort of Anegundi and Vijayanagar was on the southern bank.

6984. (27-3-2008) NEW DELHI : The Government has approved the appointment of Shri Raghu Menon as Chairman and Managing Director of the National Aviation Company of India Limited (NACIL), Ministry of Civil Aviation. According to an order dated 26th March, 2008, Shri Raghu Menon will be the CMD of NACIL on the superannuation of the present CMD, Shri V. Thulasidas which will be on 31st March, 2008. Shri Menon will continue as CMD till his superannuation from service, or until further orders, whichever is earlier and his appointment would be in the rank and pay of Secretary to the Government of India. Shri Menon, a Nagaland Cadre IAS officer of 1974 batch is presently Special Secretary and Financial Advisor, Ministry of Civil Aviation. In a separate order the Government has approved the appointment of Shri Vishwapati Trivedi, presently Joint Managing Director, NACIL, Ministry of Civil Aviation, as Additional Secretary and Financial Advisor, Ministry of Home Affairs.

6985. (27-3-2008) NEW DELHI : On the invitation of Shri Arjun Singh, Minister of Human Resource Development, H. E. Dr. Rawiya Bint Saud Al Busaidiya, Minister of Higher Education, Sultanate of Oman is on an official visit to India. She is being accompanied by Mr. Saud Mohammed Al-Timaml, Minister's Advisor for IC, Dr. Bakheet Ahmed Al-Mahri, Dean, University of Salalah, Mr. Hamad Bin Hamood Al Balushi, Director of the Dep. Of Foreign Scholarship and Mr. Yasser Al-Harthi, Official in the Minister's office. Dr. Bysauidiya called on Shri Arjun Singh today. Her delegation was accompanied by the Ambassador, Embassy of the Sultanate of Oman in New Delhi. The two Ministers had a very cordial meeting. The Omani Minister thanked Shri Arjun Singh for the invitation extended to her. She told the Hon'ble Minister for Human Resource Development that her visit was a very fruitful visit. During the last two days, she had visited a number of institutions like UGC, Delhi University, NCERT, NUEPA and JMI. She was impressed by the quality of academic facilities available in the Indian institutions. A MOU between the Indian Ministry of Human Resource Development and the Ministry of Higher Education, Sultanate of Oman was signed in December 2007. The MOU provides for cooperation between the two countries in the field of higher education through exchange visits of academic professionals in order to build understanding of each other's expertise and achievements. It also provides for organization of joint seminars, scientific programmes and training courses in areas of mutual benefit, joint research programmes, exchange of books, accreditation of Higher Education Institutions etc. Both Ministers expressed their keen desire to move forward and finalize some specific programmes under the framework of the MOU. Both sides agreed to finalize the Joint Working Group for this purpose very early. Some of the specific areas of mutual interest pertain to mutual recognition of educational qualifications and degrees, hosting of joint conferences in the areas of economic development, management, business and planning, joint supervision of Ph.D programme, exchange of faculty, twinning of institutions, programme on visiting fellow for short time etc. The Omani Minister informed that Oman already have a number of agreements with Indian institutions, particularly in the field of medicine, agriculture and marine science etc. They would like to further increase the number of such agreements with other Indian institutions. Areas of interest would be engineering, medicine science. Shri R. P. Agrawal, Secretary (HE), who was present in the meeting, apprised the Omani delegation that in the next Five Year Plan, Higher Education is to be given a lot of boost. Its budget will be increased 9 to 10 fold and a large number of Central Universities, IITs, IIMs and other colleges and polytechnics will be opened during the period. Although India may also face faculty crunch but we would definitely like to collaborate with Oman by way of providing Indian Academics for Omani institutions. The Omani delegation is scheduled to visit IIM, Ahmedabad and National Institute of Design in Ahmedabad on 28th March 2008.

6986. (27-3-2008) NEW DELHI : A Festival of Chinese Films will be held from March 28 to April 2, 2008 in Sirifort Auditorium II, New Delhi. Organised by the Directorate of Film Festivals, Government of India and Film Bureau, China State Administration of Radio, Film and Television, the Festival would showcase eight films from China. The Festival will be jointly inaugurated by Mr. Zhang Yan, China's ambassador to India, Secretary, Information and Broadcasting, Ms. Asha Swarup and Mr. Tong Gang, Director General, China State Administration of Radio, Film and Television (SARFT). Formal inaugural will be followed by the screening of film 'Gun of Mercy' directed by Xiao Feng. A nine-member Chinese delegation headed by Mr.Tong Gang, Director General, SARFT will be present in India during the Festival. Entry for the public is on passes available free and on 'first come first served' basis. However entry at the inauguration and opening film is by special invitation only. Chinese cinema industry: Since its very first motion picture, "Conquering the Jun Mountain (Ding Jun Shan)" made in 1905, the Chinese cinema has traveled a century long path of glory. Over the past century, the Chinese cinema has evolved from its very beginning to today's complete industry engaged in film production, theatrical distribution and exhibition and development of post-theatrical market such as DVD, internet, VOD, cable, merchandizing etc. China has more than 100 films studios and production companies of different sizes. The year 2007 saw a total production of 402 feature films and a considerable amount of science and educational films, documentary films and animation films, setting up the biggest record in history. By the end of 2007, China had 1,427 well-facilitated theatres in urban areas of the country, operating total of 3,527 screens, among which 493 were set up in 2007 alone. In addition, the

CCTV Movie Channel broadcasts 12 features films, both domestic and foreign, on daily basis, covering over 700 million TV viewers across the country. The Chinese cinema has witnessed increasing enhancement in international arena, particularly after worldwide release of Chinese hits like THE KNOT, THE ASSEMBLY AND KEKEXILI, among others, which are well received by the world audience. In 2007, 29 Chinese films received 49 accolades on 19 international occasions.

6987. (27-3-2008) NEW DELHI : An Environmental Project is normally sanctioned for a maximum of three years. The grant is payable in two installments each year on submission of Utilization Certificates, Expenditure Statement and Progress Reports. In the case of collaborative research carried out by a network of institutions, the Coordinating Institution is considered responsible for submission of the Utilization Certificate and Expenditure Statement and Progress Reports covering all the partners. The authorities of the institution(s) where the research activities are to be carried out receive the grants and are responsible for their disbursement, administration, and maintenance of accounts. In case any Investigator (including Lead or Principal Investigator) leaves the institute, responsibility for completion of the project is entrusted to another equally qualified Investigator by the Head of the Institution with approval of the Ministry, at no additional cost. All accounts in respect of the project are subject to audit by the institution auditors. On termination of the project, the duly audited accounts has to be submitted and the unspent balance, if any has to be refunded to the Ministry of Environment & Forests within six calendar months of completion of the project. Full and final payment is made after the acceptance of all the financial certificates, audit reports and final technical reports of the project. Ten (10) percent of the sanctioned amount is released only on completion of all closure formalities. During the course of implementation of the project, the Ministry of Environment & Forests deputes its staff or scientists from other institutions to visit the research institution(s) concerned to review progress. The selection, and appointment of Junior Research Fellows/Senior Research Fellows/Emeritus Scientists/Support Staff for the project is made by the Principal/Lead Investigator in terms of the procedures of the concerned Institutions for periods not exceeding the sanctioned duration of the project. The Qualification and experience should be followed as per the DST guidelines. Staff appointed for the research project is subject to the administrative control and service rules as applicable at the institute where they are appointed. In respect of particular research projects, at the time of sanction, the Ministry may prescribe requirements of prior approval by the Ministry before submitting for publication or conference presentation, papers or articles based on the Project. There is a provision to terminate the project also in case of unsatisfactory progress. In the event, after due enquiry, the Ministry concludes that the progress of a research Project is highly unsatisfactory and cannot be improved, it may terminate the Project. Upon such termination, full audited accounts and refund of all unspent balances will have to be made promptly to the Ministry.

6988. (27-3-2008) NEW DELHI : Maximum number of cases pertaining to cruelty to animals in the country have been reported from West Bengal. More than, 17,000 such cases were reported during the year 2006-07. West Bengal also tops in cruelty to animals during last 3 years *i.e.* 2004-05 to 2006-07. During this 3 years 40,000 animals were reported for facing cruelty. Delhi stands second followed by Uttar Pradesh in this cruelty. During last 3 years, 1389, 1572 and 1826 cases were reported respectively in Delhi. During the same period less than 4,000 cases were reported from Uttar Pradesh. 1541 cases were reported during 2004-05, 1296 cases during 2005-06 and 1127 cases were reported during 2006-07 in Uttar Pradesh. During the year 2006-07, 255 cases of animal cruelty were reported in Haryana, 79 in Kerala, 71 in Andhra Pradesh and 65 in Chhattisgarh. The number of persons convicted in this regard were highest in Uttar Pradesh followed by Delhi and West Bengal respectively. 4265 persons were convicted during 2004-05, 3338 were convicted during 2005-06 and 3037 were convicted during 2006-07 where as, 1389, 1570 and 1838 persons were convicted in Delhi during same respective period. The Government has made provisions to check such incidents. The Preventions of cruelty to animals (PCA) Act, 1960 was enacted by the Central Government to prevent infliction of unnecessary pain or suffering on animals. Prevention of Cruelty falls in the Concurrent List of the Constitution and hence the appropriate law enforcement machinery are the State Government/ Local Authorities. Animal welfare Board of India (AWBI), the statutory body under the Ministry of Environment & Forests addresses all the State Governments to enforce the provisions regarding cruelties to animals and to book the offenders suitably.

6989. (27-3-2008) NEW DELHI : There are 8 protected areas in the country for protection of Rhinoceros. Five areas National Parks and Three are Wildlife Sanctuaries. Out of this 5 protected areas are in Assam two in West Bengal and 1 in UP. The estimated population of Rhinoceros in Assam is more than 2000, 135 in West Bengal and 27 in UP. In the State of Assam, Kaziranga National Park has recorded 1855 Rhino, Manas National Park has 4, Orang National Park has 68, Pobitora Wildlife Sanctuary has 81, and Laokhowa Wildlife Sanctuary has recorded 1 Rhino. Except Manas National Park were the estimation was made during 2008, rest of the National Parks and Santuries had estimated the population during 2006. In West Bengal, Jaldapara Wildlife Sanctuary has recorded 108 and Gorumara National Park has recorded 27 Rhinoceros in the year 2006. Dudhwa National Park in Uttar Pradesh has recorded 27 Rhinoceros during 2008.

6990. (27-3-2008) NEW DELHI : RITES Ltd, a multi-disciplinary public sector enterprise has joined hands with Power Finance Corporation (PFC) by signing a Memorandum of Understanding (MOU) to have right fuel and cost effective transportation system for movement of the fuel within the country and import of the same. RITES has expertise and long experience in engineering design development & consultancy services in all facets of transport technology and infrastructure and has excellent knowledge and understanding of Indian and foreign market especially in railway, road, bridges, property development and building construction. At present, RITES is involved in the concessioning project in Tanzania and Mozambique where it is engaged in the rehabilitation, operation and maintenance of the railway network for 25 years. RITES has 51 per cent and 26 per cent stakes in these countries respectively. PFC is a Public Financial Institution and Non-Banking Financial Company engaged in providing fund and non-fund based support to various power utilities in power sector engaged in generation, transmission and distribution of power in India. Both the parties realize that the Indian economy has grown rapidly over the past decade with corresponding increase in the demand for energy and power. To meet the ever-increasing demand and to sustain existing growth, country needs to use the available resources and power conservatively. Coal is likely to be the main fuel for power generation as there is uncertainty as regard to availability of gas, its period and cost. In 11th and 12th plan coal and lignite based thermal projects have been identified for capacity addition. Keeping in view the availability of coal in the country, it is felt there will be a mismatch in demand and supply of coal and shortfall in the supply will have to be met through import of coal. Under the agreement, both the parties are desirous of combining their resources and expertise to facilitate import of coal from African countries and elsewhere, subject to the parties reaching a mutually satisfactory understanding to address the problem of power deficit and to fill the demand and supply gap in availability of coal for the thermal generation plants in India. PFC has identified funding of coal based thermal power projects as the mainstay for a long term sustainable growth of power sector and Indian economy and feels that there is a urgent need to supplement coal supplies from Indian mines that with imported coal on long term basis at competitive price. RITES, besides being a technical partner will identify the countries from where possibility of owning coal mining exists, excavation and transportation of coal is feasible for export of coal to India. RITES long overseas presence will be of immense help. Railways constitute the major system of coal transportation in India and coal is the largest single commodity transported by the Railways. RITES being a technical arm of Indian Railways will liaison with Railway authorities for carrying and expediting sectoral studies, development of suitable plans and ensure adequate rail network for coal movement, development of new rail links with Ports connectivity.

6991. (27-3-2008) NEW DELHI : The Indian Railways is expected to invest approximately 23.5 million US dollars for procurement of machines and approximately 140 million US dollars for modernisation of workshops over the next one year. This was stated by Shri R.K. Rao, Member Mechanical while inaugurating a two-day International Seminar on "Railway Workshop Modernisation & New technology in Machine Tools" organized by the Institute of Rolling Stock Engineers, COFMOW Chapter, here today. Shri Rao said that now the concept of 'workshop modernisation' itself has undergone a sea change The rapidly growing Indian economy is making huge demands on the infrastructure and logistics and the sprawling rail network of the Indian Railways has a definite edge in providing the most critical input to the economy namely transportation. To retain this edge improve further, the Indian Railways have a massive investment plant of Rs. 2,50,000 crore for the 11th Five Year Plan i.e Rs. 50,000 crore a year, Shri Rao said. A separate oerganisation by the name of COFMOW (the Central Organization for Modernization of Workshops) dedicated to modernizing age-old workshops, was set up with a World Bank loan in 1979. The initial task was to replace individual machines of pre-independence vintage on the condition basis. When this did not suffice, phased replacement of machines was resorted to an later machines were procured in batches as manufacturing lines for production of specific products with a predefined cycle. Indian Railways is one of the single biggest units under one umbrella in the world. It has more than 50 independent Mechanical Engineering Workshops and Production Units which undertake manufacturing, overhaul and repair activities for locomotives, coaches, wagons and other railway assets. Institute of Rolling Stock Engineers has been actively engaged in dissemination of Railway Engineering knowledge among its members, industry and users through a large pool of distinguished technical experts. It provides an opportunity to its member industries to gain from larger context and knowledge pool. During the two-day seminar, 30 papers will be presented by foreign as well as Indian Speakers who are leaders in their respective fields. Mr. Angelo Santanera from Italy, Mr. Rik Noppe from Belgium, Mr. Hofmann Matthias from Germany, Mr. Kumar Balan from Canada and Mr. Daniele Romanini from Italy are few of the distinguished speakers attending the seminar besides officers of Indian Railways who are responsible for production and maintenance of Railways rolling stock as well as machine tool maintenance in workshops and production units, RDSO, Railway Board and various PSUs. The Speakers would cover the areas concerning wheel machining automation, metal forming, metal cutting, metal finishing, rescue devices, measurement tools and role of simulators. The prominent foreign companies participating in the seminar are M/s Safop (Italy), M/s Fooke (Germany), M/s LVD Belgium (Italy), M/s Pama (Italy), M/s Niles (Germany), M/s Legris (France), M/s Jordi (Spain) and M/s Danobat (Spain).

6992. (27-3-2008) NEW DELHI : The Cabinet Committee on Economic Affairs today gave its approval of expenditure budget on Plan side of Rs.257.41 crore and phasing thereof, of the Ministry of Youth Affairs & Sports for development and upgradation/renovation of Competition Venue / Training Venues at Delhi University, Jamia Millia Islamia University and DPS, R K Puram.

6993. (27-3-2008) NEW DELHI : The Cabinet Committee on Economic Affairs today gave its approval for continuation of a dedicated Fund called the 'Social and Infrastructure Development Fund' beyond 2007-08 for funding the initiatives taken by the Government towards Social and Infrastructure development. The initiatives include upgradation of 1396 ITIs, Training of Farmers, Employment for Physically Challenged, Means cum-Merit Scholarships, Ground Water Recharge, Social Security through provision of death and disability insurance cover through LIC to rural landless households, and support to various institutes of Historical, Cultural, Economic and Agricultural significance, for improving infrastructure. The fund will be augmented as per requirement of the Government. In the current year 2007-08, an amount of Rs.6000 crore will be transferred to the 'Social and Infrastructure Development Fund'. As most of the schemes / programmes envisaged are capital in nature (funds being provided in the form of loans to create a corpus and earnings thereon deployed for funding the initiatives without depleting the corpus), the amount will be continued to be transferred to the Fund from the Capital section of the Consolidated Fund. However, owing to the nature of social sector expenditure, utilization of the Fund for incurring revenue expenditure will also be permitted in deserving cases.

6994. (27-3-2008) NEW DELHI : The Cabinet Committee on Economic Affairs today gave its approval for introducing a new Centrally Sponsored Scheme namely 'Multi-sectoral Development Programme' for minority concentration districts, with 100% central assistance, during the XIth Five Year Plan with an estimated expenditure of Rs.3780.00 crore. The programme aims at improving the socio-economic parameters and basic amenities in these districts for improving the quality of life of the people and reducing imbalances in line with priority attached to inclusive growth. Absolutely critical infrastructure linkages like connecting roads, basic health infrastructure, ICDS centres, skill development and marketing facilities required for improving living conditions and economic opportunities and catalyzing the growth process would also be eligible for inclusion in the plan. The focus on this programme will be on rural and semi-rural areas of the identified 90 minority concentration districts. Financial assistance would made available to these districts to address the 'development deficits' that were either not met fully by existing schemes / programmes or catered to by any scheme / programme of the State or Central Government. The programme will be implemented by the Panchayati raj institutions / line departments / agencies / Scheduled Area councils in accordance with the implementation mechanism in practice in the State/UT. A suitable monitoring system would be put in place. An independent in-depth evaluation would be made after two years to assess the need for any mid-term correction. The releases will be subject to a commitment form the State Government/ UT Administration that they will be constituting a State Level Committee / District Level Committee for implementation of the Prime Minister's New 15-Point Programme for the Welfare of Minorities, if not already done. State/UT would also notify a department in the State/UT with clear responsibility to deal with schemes for minority welfare. They will have to set up an IT enables cell in that department exclusive to look after the implementation, monitoring, reporting and evaluation of this programme.

6995. (27-3-2008) NEW DELHI : The Cabinet Committee on Economic Affairs today gave its approval for waiving the ceiling of Rs.1000 crore for equity investment by NTPC Ltd. to establish financial joint ventures and wholly owned subsidiaries in India or abroad for participating in the bidding called by State Utilities / Distribution licensees under case 2 of the bidding guidelines for setting up power projects (subject to the implementation of maximum 10 projects). The approved delegation will facilitate participation of NTPC in the bidding for the development of power projects initiated by utilities and result in greater competition and establishment of more public sector power projects.

6996. (27-3-2008) NEW DELHI : The Cabinet Committee on Economic Affairs today gave its approval for setting up a Joint Venture by M/s. Dailmer AG, Germany (DAG) to jointly incorporate a company, a Technology License Agreement and other agreements with Hero Group India with an investment of Rs.1650 crore constituting 60% of the equity capital for the purpose of designing, manufacturing and selling of commercial vehicles above 2.0T GVW for Indian domestic markets and overseas markets. The JV will also be sourcing components from India for Daimler's global requirements. The JV would also undertake research and development activity for new products and variants. FDI amounting to Rs.1650 crore (Approx.) will be received in the country.

6997. (27-3-2008) NEW DELHI : The Union Cabinet today gave its approval for authorizing the Reserve Bank of India to sign the proposed Currency Swap Agreement with the Bank of Japan to exchange an amount of US $ 3 billion against the respective domestic currency for mitigating short term Balance of Payment (BOP) problem. The actual draw down will be effected by RBI when the Government judges that it should be drawn down, after consulting RBI. It is an additional arrangement outside IMF to meet for short term liquidity in US $ during a Balance of Payment crisis. It is a cost effective tool of achieving the strategic objective of demonstrating regional cooperation.

6998. (27-3-2008) NEW DELHI : The Union Cabinet today gave its approval to increase the Block Grant for the seven IITs and IISc., Bangalore, from the year 2007-08 over and above the level approved by the Cabinet on 16.6.2005, by an ad hoc amount. Of the increased amount, Rs. 73.00 crores will be released during the year 2007-08. The balance increase of Rs. 72.5 crores due for 2007-08 will be released in 2008-09 along with the ad hoc Block Grant for financial year 2008-09. The Cabinet also gave its approval for undertaking of comprehensive exercise, ahead of time to revise the Block Grant scheme in a rational manner. The decision will help in restoring the financial health of IITs and IISc., Bangalore.

6999. (27-3-2008) NEW DELHI : The Union Cabinet today gave its approval for establishment of the North Eastern Institute of Ayurveda and Homoeopathy in Shillong (Meghalaya) as an autonomous organization under the Department of AYUSH at a cost of Rs. 67.51 crore. The decision will facilitate promotion of Ayurveda and Homoeopathy, the expansion of health care, improvement in the doctor-population ratio and R&D on bio-resources in the North East. BACKGROUND There are a total of 225 Ayurveda colleges and 181 Homoeopathy colleges in the country, out of which only one Ayurvedic College in Assam and three Homoeopathy colleges in Assam and Arunachal pradesh are in the North East. There are no teaching institutions in other States of the North East, even though there is considerable demand for Ayurveda and Homoeopathic systems in North Eastern States. Shillong is a central place in the north East where students and patients from the other North Eastern states can avail the facilities of Ayurveda and Homoeopathy in the proposed institute.

7000. (27-3-2008) NEW DELHI : Morocco will significantly enhance the supply of rock phosphate and phosphoric acid to India required for manufacture of DAP and other complex fertilizers. This indication was given in the meeting between the Moroccan Prime Minister, Mr. Abbas El Fassi with Mr. Ram Vilas Paswan, Minister of Chemicals, Fertilizers and Steel at Rabat. In the hour long meeting with the Moroccan Prime Minister, several issues including investment in Morocco by Indian companies in chemicals, fertilizers, steel, automobiles and cooperation in the field of mineral and oil exploration were discussed. Later, the delegation held a meeting with Mr. Mostafa Terrab, President and CEO of OCP, world's largest supplier of rock phosphate and phosphoric acid, at Casablanca. Mr. Terrab assured that as the leading supplier of rock phosphate and phosphoric acid, OCP would make all possible efforts to ship enhanced quantities of these raw materials/ intermediates required for phosphatic fertilizers with distinct and considerable price advantage to India vis-à-vis., the prevailing international price. India imports nearly 1.1 million tonnes of rock phosphate from Morocco, which is 22% of India's total import of rock phosphate. About 1.2 million tonnes of phosphoric acid is imported by India from Morocco, which is about 50% of India's total import. Besides, the possibilities of long term measures such as setting up of joint ventures in Morocco were also discussed. OCP offered two plots for Indian entities at Jorf Lasfer for setting up of phosphoric acid unit. India was also requested to participate in improving the mining of rock phosphate so as to increase its availability. OCP welcomed the participation of NMDC in this effort. Earlier in his meeting with Moroccan Minister of Energy, Mines, Water and Environment Ms. Amina Benkhadra at Rabat, Mr. Paswan extended the offer of providing services of National Mineral Development Corporation (NMDC), a PSU under the Ministry of Steel, for exploration of various minerals in Morocco. Morocco is reported to have reserves of gold lead, zinc, iron, silver and copper. It was decided that a Joint Committee comprising of representatives of ONHYM, the

Moroccan entity in mineral sector and representative of NMDC would work out the modalities and develop an action plan. The Moroccan Minister of Commerce and Industry will be meeting the delegation in Casablanca today for further talks on increasing cooperation in various industrial sectors. This meeting has been organized on the initiative of the Moroccan Prime Minister.

7001. (27-3-2008) NEW DELHI : The Appointments Committee of the Cabinet has approved the following appointments/extension: Shri Raghu Menon, IAS (NL:74) presently Special Secretary and Financial Adviser, Ministry of Civil Aviation as Chairman and Managing Director, National Aviation Company of India Limited, Ministry of Civil Aviation. Smt. Sushma Nath, IAS(MP:74), presently Secretary, Sixth Central Pay Commission, as Secretary Department of Expenditure, Ministry of Finance. Shri Vivek Mehrotra, IAS(HY:74), presently Special Secretary and Financial Adviser, Ministry of Home Affairs, as Secretary Department of Disinvestment, Ministry of Finance. Shri K.M. Acharya, IAS (MP: 74), presently Special Secretary, Department of Higher Education, Ministry of Human Resource Development, as Secretary Ministry of Social Justice and Empowerment. Smt. Sangita Gairola, IAS (RJ:77), presently in the cadre, as Additional Secretary, Ministry of Social Justice and Empowerment. Shri Viswapati Trivedi, IAS (MP:77), presently Joint Managing Director, National Aviation Company of India Limited, Ministry of Civil aviation, as Additional Secretary and Financial Adviser, Ministry of Home Affairs.

7002. (27-3-2008) NEW DELHI : The Government of India, Ministry of Health & Family Welfare, Department of Health has issued a draft notification proposing amendment to standards of rice bran oil under Prevention of Food Adulteration Rules, 1955. This notification has been published in Part II, section 3, sub-section (i) of the Gazette of India (Extraordinary) vide GSR No. 106(E) dated 25.2.2008. By this amendment, it is proposed to revise the unsaponifiable matter as well as lay down the limits of oryzanol content in the standards of rice bran oil. A time period of thirty days have been given for sending objections/suggestions. The notification is available on the website of Ministry of Health & Family Welfare *i.e.* http://www.mohfw.nic.in/pfa.htm. Objections/suggestions, if any on the draft rules, may be sent to the Secretary, Department of Health, Ministry of Health and Family Welfare, Government of India, Nirman Bhawan, New Delhi within the stipulated period.

7003. (27-3-2008) NEW DELHI : The Airports Authority of India (AAI) has began the process of legal due diligence for non-metro airports with the appointment of Legal Advisor for the process. The AAI has appointed M/s. M.V. Kini & Co., Mumbai as Legal Advisor for providing legal advisory services for the city side development of the four non-metro airports-Amritsar, Udaipur, Trichi and Vizag. The Legal Adviser will be advising the AAI on all legal matters associated with the successful conduct of the bidding process and execution of the Concession Agreement with the select bidder. The AAI is currently in the process of finalizing the other transaction documents for the projects.

7004. (27-3-2008) NEW DELHI : The Union Cabinet today gave its approval to increase the Block Grant for the seven IITs and IISc., Bangalore, from the year 2007-08 over and above the level approved by the Cabinet on 16.6.2005, by an ad hoc amount. Of the increased amount, Rs. 73.00 crores will be released during the year 2007-08. The balance increase of Rs. 72.5 crores due for 2007-08 will be released in 2008-09 along with the ad hoc Block Grant for financial year 2008-09. The Cabinet also gave its approval for undertaking of comprehensive exercise, ahead of time to revise the Block Grant scheme in a rational manner. The decision will help in restoring the financial health of IITs and IISc., Bangalore.

7005. (29-3-2008) ISLAMABAD: Pakistan People's Party chairman Asif Ali Zardari said on Friday that the incoming government intended to solve the Kashmir problem and "not just shadow-box" with it. "We have always said dialogue is a political tool that we have to use. We believe in dialogue under any condition and all conditions," Mr. Zardari said after a meeting with People's Democratic Party president Mehbooba Mufti at his home in the Pakistan capital. But emphasising that he wanted progress, Mr. Zardari said, "we do not want confidence-building measures, we want action." "If boys in Kashmir are to be given pens instead of guns, if they are given jobs, if they are allowed to meet their relatives in Pakistan, if we allow our Kashmiris to meet their Kashmiri brothers across the border, I think it will go a long way," Mr. Zardari said. The PPP co-chairman, who rarely accompanies his visitors out, emerged to escort Ms. Mufti to her car after their 30-minute meeting, and both jointly spoke to journalists waiting outside. His remarks appeared aimed at correcting an earlier impression he had given that India and Pakistan could "agree to disagree" on Kashmir while normalising relations between themselves, include opening out for more trade. That had provoked angry reactions from sections of Kashmiris who accused him of letting down the Kashmi cause, and concern among other Kashmiris who feared the peace process would now be put on the backburner. "We are totally involved with Kashmir, and we intend to solve the Kashmir problem and not just shadow-box on it," Mr. Zardari said. But intriguingly describing himself as a "junior partner" in the new ruling set-up, he said he had pledged to "my sister" that he would take the Kashmir policy to Parliament with a view to taking it forward Ms. Mufti, who is the Pakistan capital to attend a conference on regional stability, urged the new leadership to take forward the peace process and not put it on the "backburner" as the progress made in the last few years would be lost. She said there was peace on the border, and the roads had been opened across the Line of Control.

7006. (29-3-2008) NEW DELHI: Orissa, Madhya Pradesh, Gujarat and Punjab will each get an Indian Institute of Technology (IIT) while Tamil Nadu, Jammu and Kashmir, Jharkhand, Chhattisgarh, Uttarakhand and Haryana will each have an Indian Institute of Management (IIM). This was announced by Union Human Resource Development (HRD) Minister Arjun Singh on Friday, ending the uncertainty over the location. This has been a rather contentious issue ever since the government announced its intent to set up eight IITs and seven IIMs during the XI Plan period. While the Ministry earlier announced that four of the eight proposed IITs would be located in Andhra Pradesh, Rajasthan, Bihar and Himachal Pradesh, and one IIM was coming up in Shillong, the location of the remaining institutions was put on hold in view of the claims made by almost all State governments. Earlier, the PMO asked the HRD Ministry to put on hold decision on their location. Releasing the list, Mr. Singh said the Prime Minister had since approved the proposals. Also, the Institute of Technology at Banaras Hindu University will be converted into an IIT.

7007. (29-3-2008) CHENNAI: India's first centre dedicated to monitoring climate change and finding country-specific solutions was opened at Anna University by R.K. Pachauri, Chairman of the Intergovernmental Panel on Climate Change, on Friday. "Tamil Nadu has always been a few steps a head of the nation when it comes to innovation. The centre here in Chennai will serve the interests of the State as a whole and its people. I hope this will be one of many," Dr. Pachauri said. "The impact of climate change is serious. India is very vulnerable and Tamil Nadu is perhaps one of the more vulnerable States," he said. India, he said, needed to plan to adapt. This implied revamping drainage systems and rethinking hydroelectric power in the light of encroaching seas and changes in rainfall; preparing fisherfolk for changes in marine life as migration patterns changed; educating the people about the growth of vector-borne diseases and the regular cycle of heat waves, changing cropping patterns and agricultural practices and investing in research and development for crops suitable for the new conditions. "We have to meet the needs of the present generation without compromising on the ability of future generations to meet their needs," he stressed, adding that climate-friendly energy, such as solar power, offered India the chance to reach out to those for whom conventional energy has failed today. Minister for School Education Thangam Thenarasu said that the State government, which had earmarked Rs. 1 crore for the centre, was committed to the cause of understanding climate change. He announced that the government would be undertaking a concerted campaign to sensitise students to global warming by setting up eco-clubs in schools. The centre's new director A. Ramachandran said it would bring government agencies and universities together for integrated research to generate local data to understand the impact of climate change. Faculty members would be trained in the latest climate-modelling techniques in the U.S., Canada and Japan and the centre aimed to get the latest technologies such as carbon monitoring towers. A further Rs. 12 crore was expected from Central and State funds.

7008. (29-3-2008) NEW DELHI: In an alarming post-budget surge, the inflation rate soared to a 13-month high of 6.68 per cent in the week ended March 15 this year. The spurt in inflation, inching close to the peak of 6.73 per cent touched in February 2007, has been mainly due to a runaway increase in the prices of essential commodities such as staples, edible oils, vegetables and other food articles, coupled with higher costs of metals and fuel oils. With the point-to-point Wholesale Price Index-based inflation jumping from 5.92 per cent just a week ago and galloping towards the 7 per cent mark - much beyond the "comfort zone" of 5 per cent projected earlier by the Reserve Bank of India for 2007-08 - the government and the central bank's prime concern at the fag-end of the fiscal year would be to douse inflationary expectations and hold the price line. As an immediate move, before the official release of the WPI data on Friday, the government on Thursday night withdrew 40-50 items such as steel, cement and non-basmati rice, which hitherto enjoyed export benefits under the DEPB (duty entitlement pass book) scheme in its bid to discourage sales overseas and boost domestic supplies.

7009. (29-3-2008) RAMESWARAM: Vice-Admiral Raman Prem Suthan, Vice-Chief of Naval Staff-designate, on Wednesday gave a clean chit to INS Jalashwa, formerly USS Trenton, in which an accident occurred during an exercise in the Bay of Bengal last month. It was recently purchased from the U.S. Speaking to The Hindu after inspecting the naval detachment here, he said it was purely an accident. The Board of Enquiry, which investigated the incident, had submitted its report. The findings were being examined. Asked whether the accident was caused by technical faults, he said there was nothing wrong with the ship. There was a gas leak in the sewage treatment plant, resulting in the death of some personnel. The ship was back on track. Steps would be taken to prevent such accidents, he said.

7010. (29-3-2008) NEW DELHI: The Sashastra Seema Bal (SSB) and the Indo-Tibetan Border Police (ITBP) are set for an expansion with the induction of 33 battalions. The two paramilitary forces are guarding the country's borders along Nepal, Myanmar and China. The induction of 33,000 additional jawans will bring relief to those who, at times, spend close to one-third of their tenure in high altitudes and end up with severe ailments. The information on the status of the 20 battalions of the SSB and 13 battalions of the ITBP was given to Union Home Minister Shivraj Patil at a review meeting here on Thursday. Mr. Patil was told that 20 battalions for the SSB were approved in 2005 while the sanction for raising 20 battalions for the ITBP was granted in 2007. The SSB has trained its 20,000 men, and the ITBP 13,000 men and the remaining will be ready to join the force in 2008. The battalions were raised in a record time as it normally takes about two-and-half-years to prepare the jawans for induction. The Minister was told that besides strengthening patrol, additional manpower will bring relief to others in the two forces.

7011. (29-3-2008) KOLKATA: Trinamool Congress chief Mamata Banerjee said here on Friday that the Congress had become the 'A' team of the Communist Party of India (Marxist). Speaking at a rally of the employees of the Kolkata Corporation she said when her party was formed in 1998 "we had described the Congress as the CPI(M)'s 'B' team. But, after the recent Rajya Sabha elections, it was clear that the Congress has become its 'A' team." An Independent defeated the Trinamool nominee with the support of both the Left Front and the Congress in the elections to the Upper House held here on March 26. Ms. Banerjee ruled out having any truck with the Congress in the coming panchayat polls. "Election after election, we have been trying to forge a 'mahajot' [grand alliance] with the Congress against the CPI(M)-led Left Front. But our moves have been aborted as the Congress and the CPI(M) are engaged in a joint venture."

7012. (29-3-2008) NEW DELHI: Chief Ministers of nine States ruled by the Bharatiya Janata Party and its National Democratic Alliance partners will exchange notes here on Saturday on development-related issues and work out strategies to take on the United Progressive Alliance. At a similar meeting held a few months ago, it was decided that the Chief Ministers would prepare a report card to compare their achievements and juxtapose them with those of the Congress and its UPA allies. "Good governance is the issue," BJP spokesman Prakash Javadekar said when he was asked what the agenda was. Strategies for the Lok Sabha election would also be discussed. BJP president Rajnath Singh and other senior leaders would be present at the meeting at the residence of Leader of the Opposition L.K. Advani. Chief Ministers from the BJP-ruled Madhya Pradesh, Rajasthan, Chhattisgarh, Gujarat, Himachal Pradesh and Uttarakhand, and of Punjab, Orissa and Bihar are expected to attend. The BJP leadership has been projecting Gujarat as the "model State" for good governance but this stand has been resented by not only NDA Chief Ministers but also some BJP Chief Ministers themselves. One Janata Dal (United) leader said: "For us Nitish Kumar's government in Bihar, not Gujarat, is the role model."

7013. (28-3-2008) NEW DELHI : State Institute of Rural Development (SIRD), Karfecter, South Sikkim has undertaken a special project of floriculture under Swarnajayanti Gram Swarozgar Yojna taking into account the cluster approach. This means that instead of funding diverse activities each block will concentrate on select activities, to help the poor families sustain the particular activity for a longer period of time. SIRD has taken up floriculture to assist various Self Help Groups and families to earn a sustained income. With over 4,000 species of plants and shrubs, around 7,000 varieties of rare orchids and rhododendrons and mountain flowers of myriad hues and sizes, Sikkim is not just a paradise for nature lovers, but also a very important centre for floriculture. Some farmers are already exporting flowers abroad and are also supplying them in the domestic market. Making full use of this natural advantage. SIRD has undertaken Rs 695.44 lakhs project from 2006-07 till 2010-11. The aim of the project is to enable 2000 Below Poverty Line families to cross over the poverty line within a period of two-three years. This will include women, SC/ST and also the physically challenged. Two hundred new Self Help Groups have been targeted under the project till 2010-11. The project will also assist APL families and educated unemployed youth through schemes of National Horticulture Board or even State Programmes to become an example for BPL families. The special project sanctioned by the Centre will be for a period of five years. The project will mostly concentrate in South and West districts and some selected villages of North and East districts.

7014. (28-3-2008) NEW DELHI : The Annual Plan of Chhattisgarh for the year 2008-09 has been approved in a meeting between the Deputy Chairman, Planning Commission, Shri Montek Singh Ahluwalia and the Chief Minister of Chhattisgarh Dr. Raman Singh, here today. The Annual Plan size was agreed at Rs.9600 crores. This includes additional Central assistance of Rs.50 crores for establishing and strengthening of infrastructure for collection & marketing of minor forest produce. In his comments on the performance of the State, Deputy Chairman, Planning Commission, Mr. Ahluwalia said that the State had good growth rate and performance in terms of Panchayati Raj, Rural Development & Public Distribution System was satisfactory. He also complimented the State for performance during Tenth Plan and pointed out that both growth rate and per capita income were growing satisfactorily. However, efforts should continue to make growth more inclusive. Income supporting schemes specially in tribal areas should be encouraged. The State was asked to have more detailed district level planning to ensure that benefits of planning reach all sections of population. Focused attention was also needed to improve agricultural productivity and institutional delivery system also needs further strengthening. Efforts should also be made to further reduce T & D losses. Briefing the Commission on plan achievements and future strategy, Dr. Raman Singh said that the State has been listed among better fiscal performer by the Reserve Bank of India. Positive balance of current revenue has been maintained since inception. Broad objective of Plan for next year would include inclusive growth, achievement of millennium development goals and up-gradation of infrastructure. Substantial increase would be made in allocation for agriculture & allied sector along with increased emphasis on non-farm income. To further deepen the outreach of food security an outlay of Rs.772 crores would be provided. All villages and hamlets will have access to safe drinking water by March, 2009. Pipe water would be supplied to remaining 32 towns shortly.

7015. (28-3-2008) NEW DELHI : Shri Kamal Nath, Union Minister of Commerce and Industry, while calling on Mr. Goh Chok Tong, Senior Minister, Singapore has informed that there are more than 37 approved Indian joint ventures in Singapore and more than 30 wholly owned subsidiaries while several major Indian banks like State Bank of India, Bank of India, Indian Overseas Bank and Indian Bank and a number of private companies have branches in Singapore besides MMTC which has converted its representative office in Singapore into a wholly owned subsidiary. Senior officers from both the sides were also present during the meeting. As regards Foreign Direct Investment, Shri Kamal Nath informed that Singapore presently ranks 4th in terms of foreign direct investments inflows into India and first from ASEAN with a total investment of US$ 2694.81 million, which is 5.76% of the cumulative FDI inflow into India (in Rupees terms). The major investments approved have been in the areas of telecom, services sector, electrical equipments, fuels and transportation industries. He also expressed hope that both the sides would further expand bilateral trade and investment.

7016. (28-3-2008) NEW DELHI : Shri Kamal Nath, Union Minister of Commerce and Industry, during his address at the Mint Hindustan Times Luxury Conference, here today has stated that India today is no longer a mere testing ground for international luxury brands, but a lucrative market. Quoting from the report of Global Consulting firm A T Kearney, Shri Kamal Nath informed that the report recently placed India at the top of a list of emerging markets for global retailers in its 2007 Global Retail Development Index. "Indeed, if India was just a test market, such a high powered list of speakers would never have come for this conference! Many factors have contributed to this growth in demand for luxury goods. High salaries of employees in the corporate sector, emergence of new cities, a growing middle class, increasing number of working women, and rise of a new breed of self-employed entrepreneurs in a whole range of business sectors. Yes, we are proud of our new wealth. But let me also stress at this forum that India is a developing country with significant development challenges. The business of luxury cannot exist in a vacuum and must be seen from the overall context of equity and inclusiveness. I think it was Francis Bacon who once remarked: Money is like manure; it's not worth a thing unless it's spread around." he added. Smt Shobhna Bhartiya, Chairperson, Hindustan times Ltd and representatives from leading luxury brands were also present on the occasion. Explaining about the contribution to luxury Industry from an Indian Perspective, Shri Kamal Nath informed that 'Dharavi', which is supposed to be Asia's largest slum also doubles up as a giant manufacturing cluster. Over the years, many migrants have moved there and have set up one-room factories, which have become extremely successful businesses. Migrants from Gujarat have established a potters' colony, and tanners from Tamil Nadu have migrated to Dharavi and set up a flourishing leather tanning industry. Other artisans, like the embroidery workers from Uttar Pradesh, started the ready-made garments trade. The 15,000 odd one-room factories, at Dharavi manufacture products worth nearly 500 million dollars every year, a large proportion of which are exported. "My simple point of showcasing Dharavi is this: the skills of these artisans, and millions of others living in different pockets all over the country-can, and should be, effectively used by the global luxury players to develop their own low cost manufacturing bases. To be sure, quality could be an issue in the short term. But I am sure with the right environment and training, Indian artisans can work with European companies and develop world-class products for customers all over the world, he added. As regards FDI in luxury sector, Shri Kamal Nath stated that India is keen to encourage the entry of foreign investment in the luxury sector to offer more choices to the Indian consumer. But the Government of India would like to facilitate this entry, at a pace that does not put local manufacturers and unorganized retailers at a risk.

7017. (28-3-2008): MUMBAI: The Maharashtra Assembly, in an unprecedented step on Thursday, sentenced State Election Commissioner Nand Lal to two days of imprisonment for breach of privilege. Mr. Lal was arrested and sent to the Arthur Road jail here. The chairman of the privilege committee of the House, Chandrakant Chhajed, tabled his report in the House and stated that it was proved that Mr. Lal had committed the breach of the privilege of the House and moved that he be imprisoned for seven days. Chief Minister Vilasrao Deshmukh intervened saying that "seven days punishment was too much and it should be reduced to two days." The House accepted the amendment and passed the privilege motion against Mr. Lal. The State BJP president and an MLC, Nitin Gadkari, denounced the imprisonment of Mr. Lal and accused the State government of "indulging in politics of revenge that throttled democracy." Mr. Lal had issued an order on March 7, 2006, that only the State Election Commission had the powers to conduct elections of office bearers of civic bodies such as mayors, deputy mayors and chairmen. This had prompted a legislator, Janardan Chandurkar, to table a breach of privilege notice against Mr. Lal on March 27, 2006. His contention was that Mr. Lal's order was in contravention of the election law made by the legislature. The House had referred the matter to the privilege committee. Later, Mr. Chhajed told *The Hindu* that Mr. Lal had not responded to several summons of the privilege committee to appear before it.

7018. (28-3-2008) NEW DELHI : The government's hoax of loan waiver stands fully exposed now. The government's announcement of five year funding of loan waiver clearly depicts the political game plan of the Congress led UPA government. The government wants to usurp undeserved credit for Rs. 60,000 crore loan waiver whereas in reality it has provided only Rs. 10,000 crores and left burden on future government to foot the balance bill of Rs. 50,000 crores. This game plan is bound to get further exposed, after the detailed RBI guidelines are issued. The banks in a routine exercise provide for bad loans for all sectors including agriculture. Government wants to build upon these provisions and take credit for such write offs. Government must come clean how banks can issue "no dues certificate" to the farmers, without actually receiving any money from the government. The loan waiver announcement has already proved futile to ease the agrarian distress. Suicides continue unabated. 75 farmers from the Vidharbha region of Maharashtra have committed suicide during the last 15 days after the announcement of loan waiver. This has happened because the scheme has not covered the farmers in distress. Five acre ceiling is proving fatal and does not cover majority of dry land farmers. Further 70% farmers, who borrow from private moneylenders, are also not benefited. It is not the outstanding loans, which are waived but only overdue loans are covered, thus denying justice to the millions of honest farmers. It is already clear that 80% of the farmers do not get any benefit from the loan waiver scheme. The data collected by various state governments also testify to this fact. The present agriculture crisis is due to adhoc agricultural policies of UPA government. The recent decisions with regard to export and import policies on various food items weakens the basis of various technology missions launched to boost production of oilseed and other crops. The government decision not to increase sugarcane prices and continue with last years prices is yet another example of such adhocism. The government is consistently refusing to pay remunerative prices to the farmers. And it is dilly-dallying on recommendations of Commission of Agriculture Cost and Prices (CACP) about the MSP for this season. BJP believes that remunerative prices, agriculture loan at 4% of interest, Farm Income Guarantee Insurance Scheme, efficient market linkages, heavy public investment in irrigation and research, control on input cost and wide coverage of institutional credit along with storage facility can only address the agrarian crisis.

1719. (28-3-2008) BANGALORE: Passengers and crew members on board the Hyderabad-bound Kingfisher Airlines aircraft had a miraculous escape on Thursday night when the ATR 72-500 skidded on the runway at the HAL airport here. While the pilot said the aircraft hit a dog on the runway, airport sources said the aircraft was yet to gain velocity for take-off when the nose wheel broke and it skidded. At least four passengers were injured. The runway was closed for over three hours, causing flight delays and diversions. The incident occurred between 9.37 and 9.45 p.m. when the aircraft with 25 passengers and four crew members aboard was preparing to take off. Captain Mmopi was the main pilot. According to the commander, a black dog crossed the runway while the aircraft was on its take-off roll and because the runway was dimly lit, the crew did not notice the animal till it was too late to take evasive action. A Kingfisher release said: "The aircraft, having never left the ground, came to a halt on the runway and the crew performed an emergency evacuation of the passengers. Two guests stumbled and sustained sprain while all the others are safe. The injured were treated at a nearby hospital and discharged." The aircraft has been disabled and will have to be jacked up and towed off the runway. The Kingfisher team was on the spot and is expected to conduct a full investigation in conjunction with the DGCA and airport authorities. Top officials rushed to the spot to conduct a full investigation of the incident. Vijay Mallya, Chairman and CEO of Kingfisher Airlines, said: "I am happy that all guests on board our flight are safe. It is most unfortunate that the dog menace at airports in India still persists and that an incident occurred today in Bangalore. At Kingfisher Airlines, safety is paramount and I am glad that our crew handled this emergency successfully."

7020. (28-3-2008) NEW DELHI : Professor L.M. Patnaik today took over as the Vice Chancellor of the Defence Institute of Advanced Technology, Pune. Sixty-one year old Prof. Patnaik served as a Professor with the Department of Computer Science and Automation at the prestigious Indian Institute of Science, Bangalore since July 1986 before taking over the new assignment. A doctorate in Computer Systems and Architecture, Prof. Patnaik brings with him a rich experience of 37 years at the IIS, Bangalore in Parallel and Distributed Computing, Computer Architecture, CAD of VLSI Systems, Theoretical Computer Science, Real-Time Systems, Soft Computing and Computational Neuroscience. He has published over 600 papers in international journals and conference proceedings and has been intimately involved in a large number of government-sponsored research projects. Besides Prof. Patnaik is a co-author of ten books in the areas of VLSI System Design and Parallel Computing. He has also been the President of the Advanced Computing and Communications Society and the Computational Intelligence Society of India. Prof. Patnaik has won several awards and laurels including the Dr. Vikram Sarabhai Research Award in 1989, the Fourth Sir C V Raman Memorial Lecture Award in 2000, the Pandit Jawaharlal Nehru National Award for Engineering and Technology in 1999, the FICCI Award for Innovation in Material Science, Applied Research and Space Science for 2001-2002 and the Indian Science Congress Association's Srinivasa Ramanujan Birth Centenary Award for 2007-2008.

7021. (28-3-2008) NEW DELHI : The National Small Industries Corporation (NSIC) signed performance related Memorandum of Understanding (MoU) with Ministry of Micro, Small & Medium Enterprises (MSME) for the year 2008-09 here today. The MoU was signed by Shri Dinesh Rai, Secretary, Ministry of MSME and Shri H.P. Kumar, Chairman-cum Managing Director, NSIC. MoU 2008-09 envisages higher performance targets for NSIC to provide assistance to the micro & small enterprises in the year 2008-09.

7022. (28-3-2008) HYDERABAD: A.B. Bardhan was on Thursday re-elected general secretary of the Communist Party of India (CPI) for the fourth consecutive term at its 20th national Congress that concluded here on Thursday. Suravaram Sudhakar Reddy, MP, was elected deputy general secretary. Mr. Bardhan, 82, said he was keen on making way for others but party leaders insisted that he continue as general secretary at this critical juncture when new developments were unfolding. It was, therefore, decided to nominate a deputy general secretary who could share his burden. Inderjit Gupta, N. Giri Prasad and Mr. Bardhan himself earlier held this post which exists in the party constitution. Mr. Sudhakar Reddy (66), told reporters that the party would focus on its erstwhile strongholds such as Bihar and Jharkhand, besides working for a Left and democratic alternative to the Congress and the BJP. The party elected a nine-member secretariat including D. Raja, Gurudas Dasgupta, Nandagopal Bhattacharjee, C. K. Chandrappan, Shameem Faizee, Atul Kumar Anjan and Amarjeet Kaur. A 31-member national executive, including five new faces, was also elected. Among them is Annie Raja, wife of Mr. Raja. Addressing a public meeting later, Mr. Bardhan said the UPA government could proceed with the nuclear deal with the U.S. only if it was prepared for polls.

7023. (28-3-2008) NEW DELHI : Union Minister for Rural Development Dr. Raghuvansh Prasad Singh has urged all the Members of Parliament to launch the implementation of the National Rural Employment Guarantee Act (NREGA)on 1st April, 2008 or thereafter in few Gram Panchayats of their areas and to review the preparedness with the district officials to ensure that job cards are issued to every willing job-seeker, proper awareness generation is carried out and Bank/ P.O. accounts of wage seekers are opened. In a letter addressed to the MP's the minister said his ministry has notified the commencement of National Rural Employment Guarantee Act (NREGA) in all the remaining 274 districts of the country from 1.4.08. This brings the rural areas of the country in all the States and Union Territories within the ambit of National Rural Employment Guarantee Act. In the new districts, efforts have to be made to ensure that there is proper planning of projects for every Gram Panchayat so that work can be provided whenever any demand arises. For this purpose, the annual shelf of projects must be kept ready with administrative and technical sanction. Implementation of measures for transparency and public accountability such as proper maintenance and disclosure of public records including muster rolls, job cards, measurement books, case records, employment registers, etc. must be ensured. Social audit by the Gram Sabha of all the projects is a vital component of the Act that must be undertaken meticulously. Effective grievance redressal mechanism should be established and disposal of complaints should be ensured. Vigilance and Monitoring Committees must be properly constituted at the village and district levels and made effective. Constant verification of works and muster rolls should be undertaken to prevent malpractices in the execution of works. Referring to the success of Rural Development programmes the minister said till the end of February, 2008, his ministry has been able to invest Rs.13,101.5 crores in rural areas out of which Rs.8,892.45 crores have been spent on wages generating employment for 3.07 crore rural households. With this investment 121.64 crores persondays have been generated out of which 42.13% is accounted for by women, 27% by SC and 30% by ST groups. Altogether, 15.6 lakh projects have been taken up out of which 63.19% are water related which enhance land productivity. Dr. Singh said the NREG Act aims to enhance livelihood security in rural areas by providing 100 days of guaranteed wage employment in a financial year to every household whose adult members volunteer to do unskilled manual work. It provides a strong social safety net for the vulnerable groups by providing employment opportunity, particularly in moments when other employment alternatives may not be available to the rural households. It also strengthens the natural resource base of rural livelihood by promoting measures for water conservation, drought proofing, irrigation, land development, flood protection and rural connectivity. It also provides for irrigation facility, plantation, and horticulture and land development on the lands owned by households belonging to the SC/ST or on the lands of beneficiaries of land reforms, IAY and BPL families.

7024. (28-3-2008) NEW DELHI : Government of India have announced the issue of '8.40 per cent Oil Marketing Companies' Government of India Special Bonds, 2025' for Rs.9296.92 crore (nominal). The Special Bonds are being issued to four

Oil Marketing Companies as compensation towards estimated under-recoveries on account of sale of sensitive petroleum products during the current financial year (Rs.9076.41 crore) and settlement of contingent liabilities of Oil and Natural Gas Corporation Ltd. (Rs.197.37 crore) and Indian Oil Corporation Ltd. (Rs.23.14 crore) pertaining to the APM period. The Special Bonds are being issued at par to Indian Oil Corporation Ltd. (IOC) for Rs. 5121.62 crore, Bharat Petroleum Corporation Ltd. (BPCL) for Rs.2078.92 crore, Hindustan Petroleum Corporation Ltd. (HPCL) for Rs. 1899.01 crore and Oil and Natural Gas Corporation Ltd for Rs.197.37 crore on March 28, 2008 (Friday). The investment in the Special Bonds by the banks and Insurance Companies will not be reckoned as an eligible investment in Government securities for their statutory requirements. However, such investment by the insurance companies will be eligible to be reckoned as investment under "other Approved Securities" category as defined under Insurance Regulatory and Development Authority (Investment) Regulations, 2000. Further, the investment by the Provident Funds, Gratuity Funds, Superannuation Funds, etc. in the Special Bonds will be treated as an eligible investment under the administrative order of the Ministry of Finance. The Special bonds will be transferable and eligible for market ready forward transactions (Repo). The bonds, however, will not be an eligible underlying security for ready forward transactions (Repo/Reverse repo) with the Reserve Bank of India.

7025. (28-3-2008) NEW DELHI : The Ministry of New & Renewable Energy promoted deployment of 9 Solar Energy Plants during 2007-08 in 6 States of the Country. Out of this, Maharashtra tops the list with 3 Plants where as, Jammu & Kashmir got two such plants. Chhattisgarh, Haryana, Orissa and West Bengal each got one power plant during this period. The total capacity sanctioned for these plants is less than 2000 kWp. The capacity under implementation is more than 800 kWp. Out of different Plant Projects, all the 6 states have received one Solar Photovoltaic Power Plant Project. The state of West Bengal has been sanctioned highest capacity of 945.0 kWp followed by Chhattisgarh with 646.8 kWp. Besides these, Jammu & Kashmir and Maharashtra, each have been sanctioned Building Integrated Photovoltaic Power Plants (BIPV) with total sanctioned capacity of 18 kWp and one each SPV Power Pack of total sanctioned capacity of 8 kWp. The Ministry is promoting deployment of solar photovoltaic power packs/plants in different parts of the country under various programmes including remote village electrification programme by providing partial financial support. These projects are implemented through the state implementing agencies in their respective states. The total funds released to the state agencies are to the tune of Rs. 40 crores which includes funds for four ongoing projects also. These projects are likely to be completed during 2008-09. The projects for installation of solar photovoltaic power packs/plants are considered by the Ministry on the basis of proposals submitted by the States, as per provisions of the scheme, and availability of funds.

7026. (28-3-2008) NEW DELHI : Andhra Pradesh will raise Bio-diesel Plantations over 8,800 hectares spreading over 16 districts of state. The plants which are being raised are pongamia. The total cost for this plantation has been estimated at Rs.2341.49 lakh. The National Bank for Agriculture and Rural Development (NABARD) has sanctioned Rural Infrastructure Development Fund (RIDF) XIII Bio-diesel project for Andhra Pradesh. Out of the total outlay of bio-diesel project of Rs.2341.49 lakh, Rs.2224.46 lakh is loan component from NABARD and Rs.117.03 lakh is Government share. The Government of Andhra Pradesh is yet to grant Administrative Approval. However, Rs.20.00 crore has been released during the year 2007-08 under the previous RIDF bio-diesel project and an expenditure of Rs.13.28 crores has been incurred for raising bio-diesel plantations. The tree borne oilseeds have promising potential to supplement vegetables oil supply in the country. These oilseeds grow in poor soils under low rainfall conditions without competing with annual food crops thus filling gaps in ecological niche. Promotion and development of such crops also help societal needs of eco-conservation, expansion of rural industries, rural employment generation and also supplement the supply of alternate fuel to petro-diesel thus conserving the forex reserves.

7027. (28-3-2008) NEW DELHI : Shri M. Venkaiah Naidu, former President, BJP, while inaugurating the first National level Cooperative Cell Conveners and in-charges of the BJP at the Party Headquarters today, waged a scathing attack on the Congress and said that the UPA Government was the worst ever meek and weak Government which is anti-farmer, anti-poor, compromising on terrorism, pursuing vote bank politics. Shri Naidu called upon the party cadre to expose Congress betrayal. Shri Naidu said that the UPA has mismanaged agriculture with the result that there is a serious crisis in the agricultural sector, unprecedented food shortage, harmful food imports, frustration of farmers and the large scale farmers' suicides. He said that the loan waiver on the eve of elections without adequate budgetary support is an eye-wash, too little, too late, incomplete and divisive in nature. The loan waiver will boomerang on the Congress, Shri Naidu said. He said that there is a universal demand for total waiver for all categories without ceiling on land up to Rs.50,000, lowering interest rate to 4 per cent, migration of private loan to Banks. The UPA Government is silent on these demand because it has no commitment and concern for the farmers. He charged the Government for its callous attitude towards the common man and said the people are suffering because of the Government's wrong economic policies, unprecedented price rise, rising inflation, shortage of foodgrains, blackmarketing, which are causing hardship for the common people. Shri Naidu charged the UPA with total failure in tackling the terrorists' problem in the country and said the terrorists are having field day and the Government is unable to control their activities. Incidents after incidents are happening and the Government seems to be totally clueless and has proved to be the meek and weak Government since independence. The Prime Minister has no authority and the leadership of Congress, has no commitment to fight the terrorism. It has compromised with various terrorists and extremists' forces from time to time for short term political gains. Shri Naidu also criticized the UPA for its divisive vote bank politics. He called upon the party workers across the country to mount serious attack on this weak Government and expose their anti-farmer, anti-poor policies. After the budget the prices have gone up, the Government has remained a mute spectator. He called upon the workers to make anti price rise campaign a success from 7th to 14th April, a call given by the Central Party. Referring to Congress General Secretary Shri Rahul Gandhi's suggestion that there should be internal democracy within the political parties. Shri Naidu said that the congress leaders should fight for internal democracy in their own party, because congress thrives on nominations domination and follow the policy of selection and not the election. And Shri Naidu said that BJP is proud that it is the party, which holds regular elections every three years from village level to national level. Whereas Congress believes in dynasty and said that dynasty is not a substitute for democracy.

7028. (28-3-2008) NEW DELHI : Under alternative fuel for transportation systems, 10% Ethanol Blended Petrol (EBP) becomes mandatory from coming October. Earlier 5% blending of Ethanol with petrol was made mandatory by the Government since 9th October 2007 in the Country and 10% blending was made optional. During the last three years the Government has taken various steps to develop and promote use of alternative fuels like ethanol, bio-diesel and hydrogen for transport applications. The Ministry of Petroleum and Natural Gas (MoP&NG) has mandated the use of 5% Ethanol Blended Petrol (EBP), subject to commercial viability in the entire country with effect from 1st November 2006. Though North-Eastern States, Jammu & Kashmir, Andaman & Nicobar Islands and Lakshdweep have been exempted. As a result, release of 5% EBP has commenced at all locations in 15 States and 4 Union Territories. The modalities for implementation are being worked out by the Ministry of Petroleum & Natural Gas in consultation with stakeholders. A broad based programme for research & development, production and utilization of bio-diesel is under implementation by different Ministries. The Ministry of New and Renewable Energy (MNRE) has also prepared a Draft National Policy on Bio-fuels. Under its ongoing Research, Development and Demonstration Programmes, MNRE has supported field trials of different blends of bio-diesel in diesel cars, use of hydrogen as fuel in motorcycles and three-wheelers and introduction of hydrogen-compressed natural gas (CNG) blends in different vehicles. In addition, support is also being provided for development & promotion of battery operated vehicles.

7029. (28-3-2008) NEW DELHI : The two day International seminar on Workshop, Modernization and New Technologies in machine tools organized by Institute of Rolling Stock Engineers, COFMOW Chapter concluded successfully here today. The seminar was attended by 200 delegates from Indian Railways as well as leading International and Indian organizations. Twenty nine technical papers were presented by 11 overseas speakers and 18 Indian speakers. All the speakers shared the latest technical knowledge and advancement that are taking place in their respective fields, especially wheel machining automation, metal forming and metal cutting, compressed air solutions, simulators and welding technologies. The presentations made by M/s Safop (Italy), M/s. Fooke (Germany), M/s LVD (Belgium), M/s Kemppi (Finland), M/s Wheelabrator (Canada) and M/s Ingersoll (Rand) were highly appreciated by the delegates. The seminar has been immensely successful in achieving its objectives and the two days time has been gainfully utilized by all the participants in updating their knowledge and skill levels. The two-day seminar was inaugurated by Shri R.K. Rao, Member Mechanical, Railway Board here yesterday. Speaking on the occasion, Shri Rao said that the Indian Railways is expected to invest approximately 23.5 million US dollars for procurement of machines and approximately 140 million US dollars for modernization of workshops over the next one year. Shri Rao said that now the concept of 'workshop modernization' itself has undergone a sea change The rapidly growing Indian economy is making huge demands on the infrastructure and logistics and the sprawling rail network of the Indian Railways has a definite edge in providing the most critical input to the economy namely transportation. To retain this edge improve further, the Indian Railways have a massive investment plant of Rs. 2,50,000 crore for the 11th Five Year Plan *i.e.* Rs. 50,000 crore a year, Shri Rao said. A separate organization by the name of COFMOW (the Central Organization for Modernization of Workshops) dedicated to modernizing age-old workshops, was set up with a World Bank loan in 1979. The initial task was to replace individual machines of pre-independence vintage on the condition basis. When this did not suffice, phased replacement of machines was resorted to an later machines were procured in batches as manufacturing lines for production of specific products with a predefined cycle. Indian Railways is one of the single biggest units under one umbrella in the world. It has more than 50 independent Mechanical Engineering Workshops and Production Units which undertake manufacturing, overhaul and repair activities for locomotives, coaches, wagons and other railway assets. Institute of Rolling Stock Engineers has been actively engaged in dissemination of Railway Engineering knowledge among its members, industry and users through a large pool of distinguished technical experts. It provides an opportunity to its member industries to gain from larger context and knowledge pool.

7030. (28-3-2008) NEW DELHI : Government has approved Tea Quality Upgradation and Product Diversification Scheme for implementation by Tea Board during the XI Five Year Plan with an outlay of Rs. 230 crore. The scheme envisages payment of subsidy @ 25% of the actual cost of machinery for modernization of the processing factories by replacement of old & worn out machinery and for value addition by way of creating additional infrastructure for cleaning, blending, colour sorting, packaging etc. In the case of machinery for orthodox tea in 100% CTC factories and new factories set up by Self Help Groups the subsidy @ 40% would be provided. Besides subsidy @ 50% of the certification fee would be provided for ISO/HACCP and organic tea certification. The production of orthodox tea will have a subsidy @ Rs. 3/kg of annual production of leaf grade and Rs. 2/kg for dust grades and an additional incentive @ Rs. 2/kg of the incremental volume over the previous year. The scheme of "Export Development and Promotion of Spices" has been approved for implementation during XI plan period by the Spices Board with an outlay of Rs. 192.691 crore. Financial assistance would be provided for development of infrastructure for adoption of high tech in spice processing, technology and process upgradation, setting up of in-house labs and quality certification/accreditation. Financial assistance would also be provided for product development and research, spices processing in North Eastern Region, trade promotion, promotion of Indian spices abroad, infrastructure for common cleaning/grading/packing/storing & processing facilities (spices parks) and setting up of Sterilization Units. Spices Board would undertake market study abroad under the scheme. The Government has approved the scheme of "Development Support for Coffee" for implementation during the XI Five Year Plan by Coffee Board with an outlay of Rs. 310 crore. The scheme is aimed to provide support to coffee growers to improve farm productivity by way of replanting senile blocks; to support water augmentation, quality improvement of the product to augment growers realizations and pollution abatement; to support coffee development in North East Region and in non-traditional areas. During the XI plan the total plantation targeted for replantation is 40,000 hectares where subsidy will be provided @ 25%, 30% and 40% to the coffee growers having holdings of more than 10 hectares, 2-10 hectares and upto 2 hectares respectively. Out of Rs. 310 crore, Rs. 100 crore will be spent for replantation programme. Government has also approved the Rubber Plantation Development Scheme and Scheme for Rubber Development in North East Region for implementation during XI Five Year Plan for an outlay of Rs. 413.44 crore. The schemes envisages carrying out replantation/new planting in an area of 26750 hectares in North East Region. Besides, replantation would be carried out with subsidy in an area of 31750 hectares of which 30,000 hectares would be in traditional region and 1750 hectares in the non-traditional region. An area of 10000 hectares is proposed to be brought under new planting of which 7500 hectares will be in traditional region and 2500 hectares in non-traditional region. Necessary financial sanction has been issued for implementation of all these schemes from the year 2007-08 onwards.

7031. (28-3-2008) NEW DELHI : The Vice President of India Shri Mohd. Hamid Ansari released a commemorative postage stamp and the first day cover on noted Urdu poet Asrar-Ul-Haq 'Majaaz' at a function here today. He presented one set each of these to Mrs. Hamida Saleem, sister of Majaaz and to the Vice Chancellor of Aligarh Muslim University respectively. Addressing on the occasion the Vice President said that every youth of his age might have surely read and recited the lyrics of Majaaz and people in the every part of the world do recite his lyrics. He was a revolutionary poet and his writings have influence of Saaz and revolution.

He had an impact on an entire generation of people and his lyrics were full of romance and revolution. The Vice President lauded the effort of Department of Posts to honour Majaaz by bringing out a commemorative postage stamp as well as the first day cover on him. In his address, the Minister of State for Communication and IT Dr. Shakeel Ahmed said that it is the fundamental responsibility of Department of Posts to honour illustrious personalities of the country and very soon more such commemorative postage stamps will be released. Mrs. Hamida Saleem, sister of Majaaz in her speech threw light on some interesting aspects of Majaaz personality. Noted film lyricist Shri Javed Akhter, who is nephew of Majaaz, also shared his experiences. Smt. Gursharan Kaur, wife of the Prime Minister Dr. Manmohan Singh, Smt. Mohsina Kidwai, MP and former Union Minister, Smt. Shabana Azmi, former MP, Mr. I.M.G. Khan, Secretary (Posts), Mrs. K. Noorjeharn, Member (Operations & Marketing), Postal Services Board graced the occasion. A good gathering of eminent literary personalities, academicians, poets and other dignitaries is expected during the stamp release function.

7032. (28-3-2008) NEW DELHI : Prof. Saifuddin Soz, the Union Minister for Water Resources has expressed his satisfaction over the flow of Narmada river waters to the drought-prone districts of Barmer and Jalore in Rajasthan through the Narmada Canal project. Prof. Soz has congratulated the people of Rajasthan and expressed the hope that this will be of immense benefit to the people of the State. Sardar Sarovar Project, it may be mentioned, envisages construction of 458 km. long main canal in Gujarat to deliver 2500 cusec of water at the Gujarat and Rajasthan border near village Silu, Tehsil Sanchore, District Barmer (Rajasthan). There is a 74 km. main canal in the Jalore and Barmer districts in Rajasthan for utilizing allocated share of 0.5 million acre feet of Narmada water in Rajasthan. Prof. Soz said, the Union Ministry of Water Resources has been providing 90% assistance to the Government of Rajasthan for construction of the project. Similarly, the Government of India has also provided assistance under AIBP to the Government of Gujarat for the construction of main canal in Gujarat. The Central AIBP assistance provided to Gujarat and Rajasthan is Rs. 4887 crore and Rs.625 crore respectively for the Sardar Sarovar Project and the Canal System. Prof. Soz said that this was the highest allocation for any single project. Referring to the overall policy of the Union Government, Prof. Soz said that the assistance was also being provided to the Government of Rajasthan in project planning and in water management planning like the use of drip and sprinkler irrigation, etc. As a result of this, the command area of the project has increased from 75000 hectare to 2.46 lakh hectare to serve 233 villages besides providing drinking water to a population of about 3.7 lakh in 1107 villages and two towns along the irrigation canal. About the delay caused in the construction of the 4 major structures on the Narmada Main Canal, the Union Minister for Water Resources said that the problem was overcome by construction of a by-pass arrangement for ensuring early delivery of water to Rajasthan.

7033. (28-3-2008) NEW DELHI : SIMBEX is an acronym that stands for 'Singapore India Maritime Bilateral Exercises' and is an institutionalised and regular series of annual exercises conducted between the Indian Navy and the navy of the Republic of Singapore (RSN). The Indian Navy's operational interaction with the RSN, which commenced with modesty-pitched anti-submarine training exercises in 1994, has grown steadily and impressively over the past 14 years. 'SIMBEX 2008', currently being conducted on India's Eastern seaboard between the 16th and 30th of this month. For SIMBEX-2008, Singapore fielded one 'Endurance class' landing platform dock (RSS Persistence), one 'Formidable class' frigate (RSS Formidable), two 'Victory Class' guided-missile corvettes (RSS Vigilance and Valour), and one 'Fokker-50' maritime patrol aircraft. Indian participation in the exercise included one guided missile destroyer (INS Rajput), one guided-missile frigate (INS Gomati), two guided-missile corvettes (Kirch & Kuthar), two missile vessels (Vinash Vibhut), one fast attack craft (INS Trinkat), one submarine (INS VAGLI) shore-based fighter aircraft (IN Kiran & IAF MIG-27s) medium-range maritime patrol aircraft (Dornier) and shipborne helicopters. Bilateral interaction was progressed at sea as well as in harbour. Whilst the harbour phase focussed on sharing operational experiences through professional interaction, the sea phase concentrated upon the conduct of a plethora of exercises ranging from surface firings and anti aircraft engagements to anti submarine warfare exercises and serials involving the deployment and coordination of maritime patrol aircraft as well as shore based fighters. The Indian Navy lays great stress on enhancing and sustaining bilateral ties, as also on improving mutual understanding with regional navies, through exercises such as those of the SIMBEX series. These exercises not only provide immense training value to our sea going personnel but also help in fostering mutual trust and friendship between our respective nations, adding strength to our commitment and resolve to tackle common challenges with the maritime domain.

7034. (28-3-2008) NEW DELHI : Minister for Science & Technology and Earth Sciences, Shri Kapil Sibal, who is on a two-day bilateral visit to the Netherlands, met the President of the International Court of Justice (ICJ), Judge Rosalyn Higgins. The ICJ is the highest judicial organ of the United Nations with its seating the Hague. Judge Higgins emphasized the increasing importance of the Court in the resolution of disputes. She also appreciated India's contribution over the years. President of the ICJ lauded the support of the Govt. of India to the ICJ and recalled the great contributions made by Indian members of the Court. The Court is also presently grappling with the issues of applicability of international law in the enforcement of municipal laws, During the visit Shri Kapil Sibal will be signing a Memorandum of Understanding for cooperation in the field of Science, Technology and Innovation with the Dutch Minister of Economic Affairs H.E. Ms Maria van der Hoeven.

7035. (28-3-2008) NEW DELHI : The total approximate earnings of Indian Railways on originating basis during the period 10th March-20th March 2008 were Rs. 2300.09 crore compared to Rs. 1952.22 crore during the same period last year, registering an increase of 17.82 per cent. The total goods earnings have gone up from Rs. 1301.72 crore during 11th March-20th March 2007 to Rs. 1566.85 crore during 11th March-20th March 2008, showing an increase of 20.37 per cent. The total passenger revenue earnings during the period 11th to 20th March 2008 were Rs. 641.40 crore compared to Rs. 542.07 crore during the same period last year, reflecting an increase of 18.32 per cent. The total approximate number of passengers booked during the period 11th to 20th March 2008 were 186.97 million compared to 181.31 million during the same period last year, showing an increase of 3.49 per cent. In the suburban and non-suburban sectors, the number of passengers booked during 11-20 March 2008 were 103.88 million and 83.09 million compared to 104.66 million and 76.65 million during the same period last year, registering a decrease of 0.75 per cent and an increase of 8.40 per cent respectively.

7036. (28-3-2008) NEW DELHI : An amount of Rs. 600 crore has been tentatively allocated for Research, Design and Development in New and Renewable Energy Sector for the 11th Five Year Plan. During the last Five Year Plan period, Rs. 72.65 crore were spent for the same activities by the Ministry of New & Renewable Energy. The Ministry has financially sported about 600 RD&D Projects particularly in Slo9ar Energy Sector. The Ministry has launched some new schemes in addition to implementation of ongoing schemes to encourage large-scale use of solar energy in the country during the 11th Five Year Plan Period. The new schemes include 'Development of Solar Cities' and 'Demonstration Programme on MW size Grid Solar Power Generation'. In addition, Research and Development thrust areas for solar and other New and Renewable Energy Technologies for the 11th Five Year Plan period have also been identified and publicized through newspaper and website advertisements for further intensifying research and technology development in this area. Promotional measures taken by the Government and other associated agencies include publicity and awareness campaigns, amendment of building bye-laws for making the use of solar water heaters mandatory in certain categories of buildings, rebate in property tax/electricity tariff to the users of solar water heaters, etc. The Ministry of New and Renewable Energy supports Research, Design and Development (RD&D) activities in New and Renewable Energy including solar energy in the country. Comprehensive guidelines for supporting and accelerating pace of Research, Design and Development leading to eventual manufacture and deployment of various Renewable Energy Systems including solar energy have been put in place.

7037. (28-3-2008) NEW DELHI : The Minister for Shipping, Road Transport & Highways Thiru T.R. Baalu received from Shri S. Hajara, Chairman & Managing Director of the Shipping Corporation of India (SCI), a cheque for the Interim Dividend of 45% declared by the Company for the Financial Year 2007-08, amounting to Rs.101,78,65,035/- (Rs. 101.78 crore). This dividend amount reflects the earnings on the 80.12% shareholding of the Government of India in the SCI. As per the SCI's un-audited results for the quarter ending 31st December 2007, the Company has declared a net profit of Rs.565.21 crore for the first nine months of the financial year 2007-08. SCI is the first and only Indian Company to have earned a net annual profit of Rs.1000 crore and did it for the last three years in a row. The Shipping Corporation of India, a PSU under the administrative control of the Ministry of Shipping, Road Transport & Highways, is the largest shipping company in India, owning a fleet of 79 vessels of deadweight of 4.76 million tonnes, (comprising 39 tankers, 20 bulk carriers, 10 offshore vessels, 3 liner vessels, 3 chemical carriers, 2 LPG/ Ammonia carriers and 2 passenger carriers) which represent about 33% of India's tonnage. In addition, SCI also manages 50 vessels on behalf of ONGC and other Government departments. SCI has on order 28 ships of about 2.4 million deadweight worth over Rs.6,000 crores comprising of 2 VLCCs (which are currently the largest ships on order by any Indian shipping company) and several other vessels. The Company has an ambitious plan to order/ acquire 62 ships during the 11th Plan period. The SCI is also in the process of implementing an end-to-end integrated IT system covering its entire operations. The Company has also been awarded ISO 9001:2000 certification for implementing a company-wide quality management system.

7038. (28-3-2008) NEW DELHI : The 45th National Maritime Day Celebrations began here today with the inauguration of Merchant Navy Week by the Prime Minister Dr. Manmohan Singh. The Minister of Shipping, Road Transport & Highways Thiru T.R. Baalu pinned the first miniature merchant navy flag on the wearing apparel of the Prime Minister. On this occasion, the Secretary (Shipping), Shri A.P.V.N. Sarma also pinned the merchant navy flag on the wearing apparel of Thiru T.R. Baalu. Merchant Navy Week is celebrated throughout the country every year culminating into National Maritime Day on 5th April, in commemoration of the sailing of first Indian vessel SS Loyalty on its maiden voyage on 5th April 1919 from Mumbai to London. The principal objective of the Merchant Navy Week and National Maritime Day Celebrations is to create awareness amongst the countrymen about the Indian shipping industry and to underline its vital role in bolstering the country's economy. The activities of shipping industry and the requirements of seafarers are highlighted during the week long celebrations through different media which include special news-paper features, brochures/souvenirs, seminars, Radio/TV programmes, workshops, exhibitions, competitions etc. The theme for the 45th National Maritime Day is "MEETING MANNING NEEDS". On the occasion of inauguration of the Merchant Navy Week, the Prime Minister wished the seafarers and entire shipping fraternity a bright and successful future. Shri A.P.V.N. Sarma, Secretary (Shipping), Ms. Kiran Dhingra, Director General of Shipping, Shri S. Hajara, Chairman & Managing Director, Shipping Corporation of India and President, Indian National Shipowners' Association, Capt. Navin Passey, Chairman, FOSMA, Capt. S.S. Jairam, Chairman, MASSA and Shri Abdul

Gani Sarang, Secretary General, National Union of Seafarers of India also attended the inaugural function.

7039. (28-3-2008) NEW DELHI : The Ministry of Rural Development has granted Rs.63.93 crore to the State Government of Andhra Pradesh towards restoration of cuts imposed while releasing 2nd instalment of funds against the original allocation of Rs.281.78 crores under the Rajiv Gandhi National Drinking Water Mission of Centrally sponsored Accelerated Rural Water Supply Programme (ARWSP)-Normal Programme during the current financial year (2007-08). Up to 15 percent of funds released under this sanction may be utilised for Operation and Maintenance and up to 5 percent of funds will be spent for tackling sustainability measures. The release is being made for execution/completion of schemes to provide water facilities to rural habitations and schools. Priorities set in ARWSP guidelines and through other instructions issued from time to time has to be followed for coverage of rural habitations and schools.

7040. (28-3-2008) NEW DELHI : The Ministry of Environment & Forests has taken a number of steps for conservation & protection of medical plants. The United Nations Development Programme (UNDP) Project entitled 'National Programme on Promoting Conservation of Medical Plants & Traditional Knowledge for Enhancing Health & Livelihood Security' has been operationalised. It will be implemented in nine states, namely Karnataka, Kerala, Tamil Nadu, Maharashtra, Andhra Pradesh, Rajasthan, Orissa, west Bengal and Madhya Pradesh. The project is being coordinated by Foundation for Revitalization of Local Health Traditions (FRLHT), Bangalore. The Government is supporting a Centre of Excellence on 'Medical Plants & Traditional Knowledge' at FRLHT, Bangalore. The National Afforestation Programme (NAP) Scheme is under implementation which includes models such as 'Mixed Plantation of Trees having Minor Forest Produce Medical Values' that relates to promotion of medical plants through afforestation and regeneration.

7041. (30-3-2008) NEW DELHI : The Forms for Return of Income are assessment year specific. Central Board of Direct Taxes have prepared and notified following eight Return Forms for assessment year 2008-09. The changes made by the Finance Act 2007 have been incorporated. (i) ITR-1-For Individuals having salary and interest income and no other income. (ii) ITR-2-For Individuals and HUFs, having income from any source except from business or profession. (iii) ITR-3-For Individuals and HUFs being partners in firms and not having proprietory business or profession. (iv) ITR-4-For Individuals and HUFs having proprietory business or profession. (v) ITR-5-Combined Form For return of income and fringe benefits for Firms/AOP/BOI. (vi) ITR-6-Combined Form for return of income and fringe benefits for Companies. (vii) ITR-7-Combined Form for return of income and fringe benefits for Charitable / religious trusts, political parties and other non-profit organizations. (viii) ITR-8-Stand alone form for return of fringe benefits for persons who are not liable to file return of income but are liable to file return of fringe benefits The return of income has to be filed by using the applicable form without any annexure (except for Form ITR-7) so as to facilitate electronic filing.

7042. (31-3-2008) NEW DELHI : National Projects Construction Corporation (NPCC) a Public Sector Enterprise, signed a Memorandum of Understanding for 2008-09 with the Ministry of Water Resources here today. The MOU signed between Shri Umesh Narayan Panjiar, Secretary, Ministry of Water Resources & Shri Arbind Kumar, CMD NPCC sets ambitious targets for 2008-09 towards faster growth of this 50 years Pioneer Construction Company. Shri S. Manoharan, Addl. Secretary, MOWR and other senior officers of MOWR & NPCC were also present on this occasion.

7043. (31-3-2008) NEW DELHI : The government has released Rs.541 crore for the industrialisation in the North Eastern Region. To clear the backlog and speed up the industrialisation, an amount of Rs.766 crore have been released upto 31.3.2008, of which Rs.541 crore (approx.) have been released on 29.3.2008 for industrial units in the North Eastern Region. With the announcement of Transport Subsidy Scheme, the industrialization in these States/UTs did get an impetus but the pace was quite slow. Ever since the inception of the Scheme till 2004, only Rs.507.61 crore were released in 31 years for North Eastern Region. In order to promote industrialization in the remote, hilly and inaccessible areas, the Central Government introduced the Transport Subsidy Scheme (TSS) on 23.7.1971. This Scheme is presently applicable to fourteen States/Union Territories including eight North Eastern States. The Scheme provides for subsidy upto 90% of the cost incurred on transportation of raw material and finished goods, for a maximum period of 5 years.

7044. (31-3-2008) NEW DELHI : The Duty Entitlement Pass Book (DEPB) Scheme, one of the most transparent exporter-friendly Scheme, was valid for shipments upto 31-03-2008. The DEPB Scheme has been extended till further orders. This will facilitate shipments to be allowed under the Scheme by the field formations of Customs even beyond 31/03/2008. Further, the DEPB rates announced w.e.f. 1/4/2007 and subsequent amendments made therein, shall continue for all exports under DEPB Scheme even after 31/03/2008. Directorate General of Foreign Trade, Ministry of Commerce & Industry New Delhi, 31st March, 2008

7045. (31-3-2008) NEW DELHI : The Ministry of Rural Development has granted a total of Rs 90.06 crores to the State Governments of Karnataka, Jharkhand and Maharashtra under the Rajiv Gandhi National Drinking Water Mission (RGNDWM) of Centrally sponsored Accelerated Rural Water Supply Programme (ARWSP) during the current financial year (2007-08). Of the total allocation Karnataka State Government will get Rs.37.60 crore for 16 projects to tackle 91 water quality affected habitations. For this release of Rs.1728.27 lakhs *i.e.* 45 percent of Central share of R.3840.61 lakh as 1st instalment is considered out of total project cost of Rs.5120.80 lakh. Release of Rs.2031.73 lakh as 1st instalment is considered foe tackling 3072 iron affected rural habitation using iron removal. Terafil filteration at the total project cost of Rs.6,000.oo lakh with Central Government share of Rs.4,500 lakh. In case of Jharkhand State Government Rs.42.57 crore have been earmarked as 1st instalment *i.e.* 45 percent of Central share of Rs.9461.4825 lakh for tackling 3392 quality affected habitations (Fluoride-3339; Arsenic-53) and 222 Fluoride affected schools under Revised Sub Mission programme of Accelerated Rural Water Supply Programme (Quality) during the current financial year. The State Government of Maharashtra will get an allocation of Rs.9.8890 crore towards remaining part of 1st instalment *i.e.* 45 percent of Central share of Rs.11,485.40 lakh for tackling 292 water quality affected habitations. The projects will be completed within two years or completion time mentioned in the DPR/FR/Typical estimates. This included tendering process also. Sustainability of water source selected for all the projects will have to be ensured by the State Governments. The revised guidelines on Sub-Mission on water quality will be followed and quarterly progress reports will have to be sent regularly.

7046. (31-3-2008) NEW DELHI : The Prime Minister Dr. Manmohan Singh said here today that the international community should consider creating financial mechanisms that will promote environment friendly technologies, transfer of such technologies to developing countries and promote environmentally sustainable development to deal with the challenge of Global Warming and Climate Change. The Prime Minister expressed these views at a meeting to discuss a Strategy Paper on Climate Change prepared by Lord Nicholas Stern, I.G. Patel Professor at the London School of Economics. Dr. Stern endorsed the Prime Minister's proposals made at the G8 Summit at Heiligendamm, Germany, last year. He commended India's efforts to understand and address the challenge of Climate Change. The Government is presently awaiting the National Action Plan on Climate Change to be drawn up by the Prime Minister's Council on Climate Change. The meeting was attended by the Union Finance Minister, the Union Minister for Science & Technology, the Deputy Chairman, Planning Commission, Mr. Nandan Nilekani, Dr. Nitin Desai, Dr. Kirit Parekh and officials of the Prime Minister's Office and Ministry of Environment & Forests.

7047. (31-3-2008) NEW DELHI : During the bilateral meeting between Shri Kamal Nath, Union Minister of Commerce & Industry and the visiting Swedish Minister of Foreign Trade, Ms. Ewa Bjorling, here today, Shri Kamal Nath informed that India is seeking active cooperation in the field of higher education. He further mentioned that India and Sweden have identified complementarities in high-tech areas of IT, biotech, automotive industry and electronics, and that, it is necessary for the two countries to catalyze cooperation in the region by involving industry, academia and local universities. The meeting was attended by Shri Ajay Shankar, Secretary (Industrial Policy & Promotion); Shri G.K. Pillai,

Commerce Secretary; senior officials from the Ministry of Commerce and Industry, Directorate General of Foreign Trade; representatives from the apex chambers and business communities from both sides. Both sides discussed about the development of trade and economic relations. While expressing his appreciation for the Swedish government's desire for enhanced engagement with India, Shri Kamal Nath stated that: "Sweden's strong interest to deepen and diversify relations with India especially in the area of trade and economic development as also in frontier areas of high technology". Shri Kamal Nath expressed satisfaction that based on the recommendations of the High Level Trade Group, both sides have started negotiations for a Broad-based Trade and Investment Agreement and two rounds of fruitful negotiations have already been held between India and the EU. As regards Indo-Swedish Joint Commission, Shri Kamal Nath stated that he recognises the importance of early holding of 15th meeting of the Joint Commission in 2008. Underlining India's liberalized overseas investment norms, Shri Kamal Nath informed that more than 13 Indian IT companies have their offices in Sweden. Wipro, TCS, Infosys, L&T, etc. have bagged important projects in Sweden and some them have their development centres in Sweden and their cumulative exports are estimated at US $ 80 million. A few Indian pharma companies have also formed collaborative relations to establish joint R&D facilities in Sweden.

7048. (31-3-2008) NEW DELHI : The BJP said here that it is indeed a matter of very deep concern that India under the UPA is increasingly entering into an era of food insecurity. This coupled with sharp increase in price of food grains and other articles of daily use clearly shows that the common man (Aam Adami) is the biggest victim of the gross mismanagement of the food economy and criminal indifference towards the need to check prices. The nation would like to know as to why we have so much of mismanagement of the food economy when a "well-known" economist Dr. Manmohan Singh is at the helms as the Prime Minister for the last about four years. In fact prices have continued to rise in the last four years. The nation is suddenly entitled to know as to why a food economy of surplus which the NDA government has left has become an economy of scarcity during the UPA regime. It is too well-known to be recalled that during the NDA regime particularly between the years 2000-2003 had the highest record of buffer stock of food grains and the situation was so comfortable that food grains worth 7000 crores were even exported in the year 2003 as plenty was available in India at reasonable affordable prices. Now the situation is so alarming that the prices of essential food articles have shown an alarming rise even after the presentation of the so-called pro-people budget in March. Series of steps have been taken which remains unexplained but have damaged the moral of Indian farmers. It is now too well-known that sub standard wheat were imported at higher prices from outside where as the Indian farmers were paid less during the course procurement. When the price of pulses were rising enormously, in disregards of all directives exemptions were granted to unscrupulous exporters enjoying patronage, to export Indian pulses abroad and earn huge profit. The matter was raised by the BJP and this led to the institution of CBI inquiry. In fact the government has never been serious in the management of food economy. The record of UPA in the last four years constitutes the biggest betrayal of Aam Adami. In fact comments of experts including the planning commission indicate that today the countries per capita availability of food grains has fallen to the levels of 1970s. Increasing demand, stagnating and declining output in the face of lack of policy initiative and direction to solve the problem make a heady cocktail for disaster of great magnitude. This crisis which is only going to worsens is a national problem which demands national solutions which is holistic and systematic. Every issue is interrelated ranging from declining productivity, low minimum support price, the cycle of debt forcing suicide and any proper initiative for agriculture growth in tune with contemporary needs. As demanded by the BJP National President Shri Rajnath Singh, the government must come out with the policy statement addressing the long term and short measures to contain this serious crisis and take Parliament into confidence.

7049. (31-3-2008) NEW DELHI : A cheque of Rs. 8.92 crores (interim dividend for 79.5% equity held by Government of India) was presented to the Minister of Civil Aviation, Shri. Praful Patel by the CMD, Pawan Hans Helicopters Ltd. (PHHL), Shri. R.K. Tyagi, here today. The year 2007-08 has been a year of all-round progress and growth of PHHL, a company owned by Government of India. The operating profit increased from Rs. 2.78 crores in 2006-07 to Rs. 8.37 crores in 2007-08. While the net profit after tax rose from Rs. 9.25 crores to Rs. 25.10 crores, the number of helicopters deployed rose from 21 to 24 and the fleet serviceability increased from 66% to 74% in the same period. The revenue hours have also witnessed an increase from 19290 to 21582 hours. During the year 2007-08, 12 AS4 compliant helicopters were offered to ONGC. The updation work of these helicopters was taken up by the engineers and technicians of PHHL. These 12 helicopters also included country's first full time medical evacuation helicopter which have been offered in an offshore configuration. PHHL has already been identified as a nodal agency for creation of heliports at Delhi and Mumbai. Once these heliports are in place, both the metros will have a great boost in helipad activities. The constructions of a helipad at Fata and of a hangar at Gauchar in Uttranchal are in full swing. PHHL has recently concluded MOU with IAF with the aim of induction of experienced pilots of IAF while ensuring an exciting career to IAF pilots after their illustrious contribution to the country through the IAF. MOU on similar lines is also being worked out with the Indian Navy. PHHL is also developing a concept on hotline washing of the power lines so that the power tripping in Northern India is minimized during winter months. For this a MOU between PHHL and Power Grid Corporation is under finalisation. During the year PHHL continued providing helicopter services to remote locations like Lakshadweep, A&N Islands and the North-East states including Arunachal Pradesh, Meghalaya, Sikkim and Tripura. PHHL continued its services to Kedarnath and from the 3 April 2008, PHHL is starting services from Katra to Vaishnodevi.

7050. (31-3-2008) NEW DELHI : The following is the text of the address of the Vice President of India, Shri Mohd. Hamid Ansari at the '1st Foundation Day Lecture' at the Rajiv Gandhi Centre for Contemporary Studies at the University of Mumbai today: "I am happy to be back in Mumbai University. It is a privilege to be invited to deliver the Foundation Day Lecture at the Rajiv Gandhi Centre for Contemporary Studies. Rajiv Gandhi was a visionary who focused on the future of this great land of ours. He was also a realist who appreciated that a vision of the future must of necessity be anchored in the present and build upon it. A professor of theoretical physics said some time back that the future 'will resemble a fairy tale'. This would undoubtedly be true of scientific advancement. Decades earlier the astronomer Nikolai Kardashev went further, to explore the world beyond the year 2100 in terms of its energy sources; his bench marks were the sun, the galaxy and the universe itself as the sources of energy. These perceptions, and similar other prognosis of the future, pose a question: how would social developments synchronise with this degree of change? 'The owl of Minerva', wrote the philosopher Hegel, 'spreads its wings only with the falling of the dusk'. He meant that philosophy understands only in hindsight. Would the speed of change and the compression of time impact on this process? Anticipating the nature, direction and pace of change in societies involves a three fold exercise of visualizing a better future based on projected scientific advancement, developing the requisite technological and societal instrumentalities, and doing so in the light of cumulative human experience. I would like to proceed on this basis to develop a vision of the future, and India's place in it. An exercise in futurology pertaining to a society and its place in the association of societies needs, however, to go beyond production and distribution numbers and focus on changes in awareness and perceptions. For this reason, a longer time span is unavoidable.

7051. (31-3-2008) NEW DELHI : Can we think of a normal delivery in a hospital having modern amenities at a throw away price of around Rs. 1500/- ? Well, it is possible with Lifespring hospitals making it a reality. Many women lose their lives every year in India due to pregnancy related complication and an equal number suffer moderate to severe infection. Lack of proper maternity care and less than satisfactory health care services in rural areas further aggravate the situation. Hindustan Latex (HLL), a mini ratna enterprise under the Ministry of Health and Family Welfare is all geared to add another chapter to its excellent track record through a new chain of modern yet affordable hospitals named Lifespring. These hospitals are literally springing surprises in health care especially maternity and child health care to women and children of low income households of rural India. Lifespring plans to open 20-25 bed small chain of hospitals to provide affordable quality health care to rural poor. In the coming years, the service segment will be a key thrust area for HLL. The company is in the process of setting up 30 LifeSpring Hospitals in the states of Andhra Pradesh, Karnataka and Maharastra. With focus on providing services like antenatal care, post natal care, both normal and caesarean delivery, family planning services and medical termination of pregnancy. Pediatric care including immunisation and diagnostic services will also be available in these hospitals at very reasonable price. Since health care costs significantly contribute to poverty in rural India, the efforts of Lifespring hospitals to ensure quality health care at affordable price is indeed a path-breaking move. Apart from Hospitals, the major focus will primarily be in the area of high quality health care delivery at affordable rates. Similarly HLL has set up HINDLABS-the Diagnostic Center-a partnership venture with the CGHS (Central Government Health Scheme). This Center located at New Delhi provides quality diagnostic services to the CGHS beneficiaries. The same services will also be provided to patients outside the CGHS too at affordable rates. This center has two major facilities-A Clinical specimen testing lab to deliver Pathology, Hematology and Biochemistry tests equipped with-Automatic Cell counter for Hematology, Semi auto Biochemistry Analyser, Electrolyte Analyser, Elisa Reader and Plate Washer, Auxiliary equipments like Incubator, Hot air oven etc., and a Diagnostic Imaging facility, provided with-High Frequency X Ray to deliver low dose high clarity X ray imaging, Ultrasound Scanner and ECG machine.

7052. (31-3-2008) NEW DELHI : The Rashtriya Swasthya Bima Yojana which was formally launched on the 1st of October last year, is scheduled to be operationalised from tomorrow. The Scheme envisages to provide smart card based cashless health insurance cover upto Rs.30,000 to all the BPL families in the unorganized sector in the next five years under the Health Insurance Scheme. An estimated six crore BPL workers in all 600 districts in the country @ one lakh workers per district would be covered @ 120 district per year starting from this financial year. The Central Government has already issued Guidelines and a Draft Tender Document has been prepared and sent to all the States. The Draft Contract Agreement, to be signed between the Insurance Companies and respective State Governments, has also been finalized and circulated. Medical procedures and their costs have been standardized by a group of experts. The draft MOU between Centre and the States has also been finalized. On the IT front, Guidelines for Smart Card hardware and the operating software as also the software for issuing smart card have been finalized and released. Similarly, the specifications for smart card handling devices have been finalized with the assistance from the World Bank. For security against issuance of duplicate/fake RSBY smart cards, the NIC has developed a Key Management System (KMS). A certification system has been put in place for software to be used. Preparations are underway for a back-end data base management. All these tasks are highly technical in nature and time consuming but these are imperative for smart card operation. When fully operational, these would make the scheme paperless. Under the Scheme, total sum insured would be Rs. 30,000/- per family, per annum, on a family floater basis. It would operate through cashless transactions and would cover hospitalisation expenses, taking care of most of the illnesses with as least exclusions as possible. An initial allocation of Rs.250 crore has been made in the budget 2008-09. The Centre would contribute 75% of the annual premium whereas the States would be contributing the remaining 25%. The Scheme also envisages the setting up of a Technical Cell to be set up by the Central Government to assist the States in preparation of projects and monitor and evaluate the implementation of the project. The States would put in place an institution for implementing the Health Insurance Programme.

7053. (31-3-2008) NEW DELHI : The Union Minister of Shipping, Road Transport and Highways, Thiru T.R. Baalu, on the recommendation of the Chief Minister of Jammu and Kashmir, has approved a sum of Rs. 20.78 crore under the Central Road Fund (CRF) Scheme for construction of 16 km long village road (3.75 m wide) with Retaining wall from Kahara Jai Road up to Village Jaurn in Doda district in Jammu and Kashmir. This road will connect village Kahara in Bhalessa area with Jai in Bhaderwah passing through the villages of Gugara, Malanu, Bithola, Bagdair, Halaran, Jooda and Shamdalian before entering the picturesque meadows of Jai in Bhaderwah thus opening up avenues of development for people of all these villages.

7054. (31-3-2008) NEW DELHI : India's external debt outstanding at the end of December 2007 was US$ 201.4 billion (Rs.794,017 crore), reflecting a rise of US$ 10.3 billion over the quarter. As compared to the level of US$ 169.7 billion at end-March 2007, India's external debt at end-December 2007 increased by US$ 31.8 billion. Valuation change, due to the depreciation of US dollar vis-a-vis major international currencies and Indian Rupees, accounted for US$ 1.1 billion of the increase during the quarter and US$ 6.0 billion during April-December 2007. The increase in external debt was mainly brought about by commercial borrowing and short-term debt. Based on original maturity, long-term debt accounted for 82.6 per cent and short-term debt comprised 17.4 per cent. Long-term debt rose by US$ 6.3 billion to US$ 166.2 billion and short-term debt by US$ 4 billion to US$ 35.2 billion over the quarter. Amongst the components of long-term debt, commercial borrowing increased by US$ 4.9 billion (9.4 per cent) to US$ 57 billion. While NRI deposits declined by 1.5 per cent (US$ 0.6 billion) to US$ 43 billion, multilateral debt, bilateral debt and export credit increased marginally to reach US$ 37.9 billion, US$ 17.3 billion and US$ 8.9 billion, respectively, at end-December 2007. Rupee debt continued to remain around the level of US$ 2 billion. Under short-term debt, while trade related credits rose by around US$ 4 billion, FII debt investment in Government papers rose by US$ 262 million over the quarter. In the endeavour to improve the analytical content of the report, the external debt stock at end-December 2007 is provided in terms of residual maturity as well, for the first time in the quarterly debt data release. Based on residual maturity, long-term debt accounted for 64 per cent of total debt at end-December 2007. Short-term debt by residual maturity, consisting of principal repayments due during a one-year reference period under medium and long-term loans, and short-term debt with original maturity of one year or less, accounted for 36 per cent of the total external debt.

7055. (31-3-2008) NEW DELHI : The Prime Minister, Dr. Manmohan Singh addressed the 23rd Raising Day of SPG in New Delhi today. Following is the text of the Prime Minister's speech: "It is a great pleasure for me to be in your midst once again. I sincerely compliment you for your thorough professionalism, your competence and dedication to work. The SPG has completed yet another year of highly satisfying service, notwithstanding the difficult and trying conditions under which you have to work. On this happy occasion I, my wife and our family extend our warm felicitations to all officers of SPG and to their families. I am delighted to greet all the officers and personnel who have won medals and trophies in recognition of their meritorious and distinguished services and for their excellence in different professional fields. We are all aware of the tragic circumstances under which the SPG came into being. These very circumstances highlighted the necessity of setting up a dedicated and specialised Protection Unit. It was also around that time that the scourge of terrorism appeared. SPG was, therefore, set up as a committed, disciplined and highly trained outfit, comprising handpicked officers, assigned the exclusive responsibility of providing discreet, yet effective and foolproof security to the highest political office of the country. Today, after 23 years, SPG has developed and evolved into a formidable force, displaying a high degree of professionalism and the most outstanding level of commitment to its responsibilities. It is indeed a matter of pride that India has such a committed and well-trained force, a force that is second to none in the world, for the security of the highest political leadership.

7056. (31-3-2008) NEW DELHI : The Group of Ministers would be (reviewing) the price increases in rice, wheat and edible oil and other essential commodities. The Government is considering both fiscal regulatory and supply side measures to rein in inflation. The Government has cut duties on manufactured products and edible oils. Import duties on import of different varieties of palm oil have already been reduced. In addition the government is planning to cut import duty on soya oil. The Government has also raised the minimum export price for non-basmati rice from $ 650, per tonne to $ 1000 to.restrict rice exports. Domestic supply is to be boosted by withdrawing incentives on exports of at least 40 items, including steel, cement and non-¬basmati rice. The tax refund scheme-Duty Entitlement Pass Book has been withdrawn and is temporarily suspended. Total number of items on which DEPB benefits have been withdrawn would be about 40-50. Export incentives are not to be provided for steel and the government has withdrawn tax refund schemes for exports of steel and cement and for a range o: products, including ferro-chrome-and non-basmati rice. The Government had already taken a decision last year to ban future trading in some agricultural commodities including wheat. The Government should review its decision and consider banning some more items if necessary. The Government should take immediate steps to prevent smuggling and hoarding. PDS System will have to be properly streamlined and supplies ensured by even increasing foodgrains if necessary. Further steps are on the anvil including reduction in custom duties and excise duties on many commodities. Steel and Cement market is likely to stabilize within six months consequent on completion of construction for Olympics in Beijing. Government should further step up contingency plan to control price rise. Rampant expectation of price rise would encourage speculation and hoarding would further fuel inflation.

7057. (31-3-2008) NEW DELHI : The Ministry of New and Renewable Energy has announced a demonstration programme to support mega watt size grid interactive solar power generation projects, up to a maximum capacity of 50 MW, in the country. Any registered company, as project developer, would be eligible to set up solar power projects on build, own and operate basis. Proposal from each project developer with a maximum aggregate capacity of 5 MW, either through a single project or multiple projects of a minimum capacity of 1 MW each, would be considered. A maximum of 10 MW capacity solar power generation projects would be considered in a State. Preference would be given to the projects from the States where the State Electricity Regulatory Commissions (SERCs) have announced or are in the process of announcing tariff for solar power. For the projects approved and commissioned by 31st December, 2009, the Ministry will provide generation based incentive up to Rs.12 per kWh for solar photovoltaic power and Rs.10 per kWh for solar thermal power fed to the grid by the solar power project developers, after taking in to account the tariff provided by the SERC or the utility. The Ministry will also provide incentive to the concerned utility and the State Nodal Agency, which will be involved in implementation and monitoring of the projects in that State.

7058. (31-3-2008) NEW DELHI : A total of 33 grid interactive solar photovoltaic power plants have been installed in the country with financial support from the Government. These plants, with aggregate capacity of 2.12 Megawatt, are estimated to generate about 2.55 million units of electricity in a year. In addition, around 14.5 lakh decentralized off-grid solar photovoltaic systems aggregating to about 125 Megawatt capacity have been installed in the country, which is capable of generating about 150 million units in a year. Further, a collector area of about 2.15 million square meter has been installed for solar water heating applications. The amount of energy generation depends on the use pattern of the system and climate of the place. Typically, a solar water heating system with 2 square meter of collector area can generate energy equivalent to up to 1500 units of electricity when the system is used for about 300 days in a year. The Government has taken several measures to reduce the cost of solar energy systems, which include: (i) research and development to improve their performance and reduce the consumption of materials, (ii) subsidy on selected solar energy systems; (iii) interest subsidy to provide soft loan to users and the manufacturers; (iv) concessional or nil import duty on some of the raw materials, components and products; (v) excise duty exemption; and (vi) 80% accelerated depreciation in the first year etc. Many incentive have been given to private agencies for research and generation of solar energy. All academic, research institutions and industries, including the private institutions are engaged in research in solar energy. They are eligible to receive grant for undertaking R&D. In addition, expenditure on R&D by the private industries is eligible for deduction from profits under Income Tax Act. Under grid interactive solar power generation, private companies are eligible to get production based incentive for power fed to the grid from megawatt capacity solar power plants set up on build own and operate basis in the country. Proposal from any project developer with a maximum aggregate capacity of 5 MW, either through a single project or multiple projects of a minimum capacity of 1 MW each, are being considered under the programme. Preference is given to the projects from the States where the State Electricity Regulatory Commissions (SERCs) have announced or are in the process of announcing tariff for solar power. For projects approved and commissioned by 31st December, 2009, the Ministry will provide generation based incentive up to Rs.12 per kWh for solar photovoltaic power and Rs.10 per kWh for solar thermal power after taking in to account the tariff provided by the SERC or the utility.

7059. (31-3-2008) NEW DELHI : The first ever Squadron of IAF, No. 1 Squadron aka 'The Tigers' would be celebrating its platinum jubilee on 01 Apr 07 at Air Force Station Gwalior. The No. 1 Squadron is the first squadron of IAF and was raised on 01 Apr 1933. The earliest history of IAF is synonymous with growth and advancement of 1 Squadron. The Squadron was formed with Wapiti aircraft and is presently operating the state of the art Mirage 2000s. The Squadron has the distinction of taking part in 11 operations pre and post independence which includes major operations such as, 1937 – Operations in hostilities in NW frontier province; 1961 – Operation Vijay – Liberation of Goa; 1965 – Indo Pak conflict; 1971 – Indo Pak conflict; 1999 – Op Fafed Sagar. The Squadron is recipient of the prestigious President colour in 1968, which it got at hands of Dr Zakir Hussain. On the occasion of its 75th anniversary the Squadron will be put up a ceremonial parade and fly-past at its base, Air Force Station Gwalior. The Marshal of IAF Arjan Singh and The Chief of Air Staff, Air Chief Marshal Fali Major would be present on this occasion. Air Chief Marshal Fali Major would unveil and present a Wapiti aircraft model to the Squadron. A Special day cover would also be released by the Marshal of IAF.

7060. (31-3-2008) NEW DELHI : All India Consumer Price Index Number for Industrial Workers (CPI-IW) on base 2001=100 for the month of February, 2008 increased by 1 point and stood at 135 (one hundred and thirty five). During February, 2008, the index recorded an increase of 6 points in Labac Silchar centre, 5 points in Darjeeling centre, 3 points each in Giridih, Kodarma, Bokaro, Quilon and Amritsar centres, 2 points in 10 centres and 1 point in 29 centres. The index decreased by 2 points each in Salem and Rourkela centres and 1 point in 8 centres while in the remaining 22 centres the index remained stationary. The increase of 6 points in Labac Silcher centre is mainly on account of increase in the prices of Rice, Wheat Atta, Masur Dal, Mustard Oil, Goat Meat, Pan Leaf etc. The increase of 5 points in Darjeeling centre is mainly due to increase in the prices of Rice, Wheat Atta, Masur Dal, Mustard Oil, Pork etc. The decrease of 2 points in Salem centre is mainly due to decrease in the prices of Rice, Arhar Dal, Poultry, Eggs, Onion, Garlic, Vegetable & Fruit items, Flower/Garlands etc., in Rourkela centre this decrease of 2 points is the outcome of decrease in the prices of Wheat Atta, Vegetable & Fruit items etc.

7061. (31-3-2008) NEW DELHI : On 27th March 2008, Department of Animal Husbandry, Dairying and Fisheries has notified outbreak of Avian Influenza among poultry in Jalpaiguri district [Jalpaiguri Sadar Block (Village Sabeber Kamar, Sampukuri para)]. The containment operations are being undertaken. Central Rapid Response Team from MOHFW has been deputed to the district. • In the earlier notified area of English Bazar block of Malda district, active house-to-house surveillance within the 0-3 Km is on. In 0-3 Km area a population of 220820 have been covered. 14 cases of fever/URI have been detected out of which one had history of handling of dead/sick birds. He had complaint of cough without fever and has no lower respiratory tract infection. This case does not fall under suspect case as per case definition. He is being monitored. • In 3-10 Km area a population of 158220 has been covered. 44 cases of fever/URI have been detected and none had exposure history. • Animal husbandry workers involved in containment operations are under medical supervision and chemoprophylaxis. 346 volunteers/ health workers are under • Adequate stock of Oseltamivir, personal protective equipments are available with the State/district authorities. • There is no suspect case of human avian influenza.

7062. (31-3-2008) NEW DELHI : Department of Animal Husbandry, Dairying and Fisheries has notified outbreak of Avian Influenza among poultry in Jalpaiguri district [Jalpaiguri Sadar Block (Village Sabeber Kamar, Sampukuri para)] on 27th March, 2008. The containment operations are being undertaken. Central Rapid Response Team from MOHFW has been deputed to the district. In the affected area of Jalpaiguri district active house-to-house surveillance has started in 0-3 Km area. A population of 19555 has been covered. 10 cases of fever/URI have been identified in the community. None of them had exposure to infected poultry. In the identified hospital 14 cases with fever/ URI have reported of which one case with fever and URI is admitted but has history contact with infected poultry. • 137 animal health workers are under medical supervision and chemoprophylaxis. • In the earlier notified area of English Bazar block of Malda district, active house-to-house surveillance within the 0-3 Km is on. In 0-3 Km area a population of 217999 have been covered. 15 cases of fever/URI have been detected with no history of handling of dead/sick birds. • In 3-10 Km area a population of 34901 has been covered. 49 cases of fever/URI have been detected and none had exposure history. • 209 Animal husbandry workers involved in containment operations are under medical supervision and chemoprophylaxis. • Adequate stock of Oseltamivir, personal protective equipments are available with the State/district authorities. • There is no suspect case of human avian influenza.